Her mon mæg giet gesion hiora swæð

ANGLO-SAXON ENGLAND

2

Edited by

PETER CLEMOES

MARTIN BIDDLE

RENÉ DEROLEZ

STANLEY GREENFIELD

PETER HUNTER BLAIR

PAUL MEYVAERT

RAYMOND PAGE

JULIAN BROWN

HELMUT GNEUSS

LARS-GUNNAR HALLANDER

JOHN LEYERLE

BRUCE MITCHELL

FRED ROBINSON

CAMBRIDGE

At the University Press

1973

Published by the Syndics of the Cambridge University Press
Bentley House, 200 Euston Road, London NW1 2DB
American Branch: 32 East 57th Street, New York, NY10022

© Cambridge University Press 1973

ISBN: 0 521 20218 3

Printed in Great Britain
by W & J Mackay Limited, Chatham

DA
152.2
A75
v.2
(2)

Contents

Contents

*Abbreviations listed before the bibliography (pp. 303–4) are used throughout
the volume without other explanation*

Illustrations

ACKNOWLEDGEMENTS

By permission of the Trustees of the British Museum the design on the cover is taken from the obverse of a silver penny issued to celebrate King Alfred's occupation and fortification of London in 886

Permission to publish a photograph or photographs has been granted by the Cleveland Museum of Art (pl. I*a*), the Trustees of the British Museum (pls. I*b*, *c*, *d* and *e*, II*a*, *b* and *f* and IV*a*), the Trustees of the British Museum and the Moyse's Hall Museum, Bury St Edmunds (pl. III*g*), Bibliothèque Nationale, Paris (pl. II*c*), St Godehard's, Hildesheim (pl. II*d*), the Lambeth Palace Library, London (pl. II*e*), the Metropolitan Museum of Art, New York (pl. II*g*), the University of Glasgow (pl. III*a*), Kongelige Bibliotek, Copenhagen (pl. III*b*), the Pierpont Morgan Library, New York (pl. III*c*), Musée de Saint-Omer (pl. III*d*), Bibliothèque Royale, Brussels (pl. III*f*) and the Dean and Chapter of Westminster Abbey (pl. IV*b*)

Preface

This second volume, like its predecessor, seeks to foster cooperation between scholars in the various branches of Anglo-Saxon studies. Its aims are to promote those qualities of fundamental research that are of common concern to all – a power of original enquiry, an understanding of the primacy of evidence and of its opportunities and limits, skill in technical analysis and logic in reasoning – and to encourage a manner of presentation that will make plain an author's methods and results beyond the immediate circle of his fellow experts. We hope to show that contacts between the disciplines can lead to a better sense of proportion as well as to an enlarged field of vision.

Place-names, charters and coins are among the forms of historical evidence studied in this issue. Manuscripts – illustrated, liturgical and vernacular – are also examined. The topics treated range from the course of English settlement in the south-east to the power and influence wielded by one of the leading aristocratic families of southern England in the tenth century and to the possible presence of Jews in England in the eleventh. An important liturgical manuscript, the Bosworth Psalter, is more securely localized than ever before (at either Christ Church, Canterbury, or, most interestingly, Westminster Abbey), while the exemplars used for the Vercelli Book, one of our main codices of vernacular literature, and the area in which it is likely to have been written are greatly clarified. Several motifs in Old English prose and poetry are elucidated and the influence of Christian doctrine on the poetry is considered in an article reviewing the present state of knowledge and opinion and in a lively discussion about *Beowulf*. It is fitting too that in the year in which the thirteen hundredth anniversary of his birth is being observed there is a survey of Bede's achievements as an outstanding representative of early medieval culture and as a teacher who exerted a decisive influence on the civilization of the Middle Ages. The bibliography for 1971 continues the annual series inaugurated in volume 1, and, as mentioned in that volume, there will be an index to *Anglo-Saxon England* 1–5 in the fifth issue.

As before, I am grateful to my fellow editors, to the contributors – not forgetting the compilers of the bibliography – and to the Cambridge University Press for their ready cooperation. Mrs Janet Godden has again given invaluable help with preparing the typescript and checking the proofs.

PETER CLEMOES
for the editors

Material may be submitted to any of the editors, but it would be appreciated if the one most convenient regionally were chosen (Australasian contributions should be submitted to Bruce Mitchell) unless an article deals mainly with archaeology, palaeography, art, history or Viking studies, in which case the most suitable editor would be Martin Biddle (archaeology), Julian Brown (palaeography and art), Peter Hunter Blair (history) or Raymond Page (Viking studies). A potential contributor is asked to get in touch with the editor concerned as early as possible to obtain a copy of the style sheet and to have any necessary discussion. Articles must be in English.

The editors' addresses are

Mr M. Biddle, Winchester Research Unit, 13 Parchment Street, Winchester, Hampshire (England)

Professor T. J. Brown, Department of Palaeography, King's College, University of London, Strand, London WC2R 2LS (England)

Professor P. A. M. Clemoes, Emmanuel College, Cambridge CB2 3AP (England)

Professor R. Derolez, Rozier 44, 9000 Gent (Belgium)

Professor H. Gneuss, Englisches Seminar, Universität München, 8 München 40, Schellingstrasse 3 (Germany)

Professor S. B. Greenfield, Department of English, College of Liberal Arts, University of Oregon, Eugene, Oregon 97403 (USA)

Dr L.-G. Hallander, Lövångersgatan 16, 162 21 Vällingby (Sweden)

Mr P. Hunter Blair, Emmanuel College, Cambridge CB2 3AP (England)

Professor J. Leyerle, Centre for Medieval Studies, University of Toronto, Toronto 181 (Canada)

Mr P. Meyvaert, Mediaeval Academy of America, 1430 Massachusetts Avenue, Cambridge, Massachusetts 02138 (USA)

Dr B. Mitchell, St Edmund Hall, Oxford OX1 4AR (England)

Dr R. I. Page, Corpus Christi College, Cambridge CB2 1RH (England)

Professor F. C. Robinson, Department of English, Yale University, New Haven, Connecticut 06520 (USA)

Place-names from *hām*, distinguished from *hamm* names, in relation to the settlement of Kent, Surrey and Sussex

JOHN McN. DODGSON

The element OE *hām*, 'a village, a village community, an estate, a manor, a homestead',[1] is generally reckoned to belong to an early stratum of English place-names.[2] Within this stratum, and especially in the type in *-ingham* from OE *-ingahām*, it is associated with place-names from OE *-ingas* and *-inga-* (the genitive composition form).[3] The same common antiquity is noted on the

---

[1] *EPN* 1, 226; *DEPN*, pp. 213–14. The following abbreviations are used in this article and its appendices: Bach = A. Bach, *Deutsche Namenkunde* 11: *die deutschen Ortsnamen* (Heidelberg, 1953–4); *BCS* = *Cartularium Saxonicum*, ed. W. de G. Birch (London, 1885–93); *BNF* = *Beiträge zur Namenforschung* n.F.; *DB* = *Domesday Book*, ed. A. Farley and H. Ellis (London, 1783–1816); *DEPN* = E. Ekwall, *The Concise Oxford Dictionary of English Place-Names*, 4th ed. (Oxford, 1960); *EPN* = A. H. Smith, *English Place-Name Elements*, EPNS 25–6 (Cambridge, 1956); EPNS = English Place-Name Society; *JEPN* = *Jnl of the Eng. Place-Name Soc.*; *KPN* = J. K. Wallenberg, *Kentish Place-Names, a Topographical and Etymological Study of the Place-Name Material in Kentish Charters dated before the Conquest*, Uppsala Universitets Årsskrift 1931, Filosofi, Språkvetenskap och Historiska Vetenskaper 2 (1931); Margary = I. D. Margary, *Roman Roads in Britain*, 1 vol. rev. ed. (London, 1967): the numbers which Margary gives to Roman roads are used below, in both the text and maps; *NoB* = *Namn och Bygd*; *PN-ing*[(1)] and *PN-ing*[(2)] = E. Ekwall, *English Place-Names in -ing*, Skrifter utgivna av Kungl. Humanistiska Vetenskapssamfundet i Lund 6 (1923) and 2nd ed. (Lund, 1962); *PNK* = J. K. Wallenberg, *The Place-Names of Kent* (Uppsala, 1934); *PNSr* = J. E. B. Gover, A. Mawer and F. M. Stenton, with A. Bonner, *The Place-Names of Surrey*, EPNS 11 (Cambridge, 1934); *PNSx* = A. Mawer, F. M. Stenton and J. E. B. Gover, *The Place-Names of Sussex*, EPNS 6–7 (Cambridge, 1929 and 1930); Sandred = K. I. Sandred, *English Place-Names in -stead*, Acta Universitatis Upsaliensis, Studia Anglistica Upsaliensia 2 (1963); *Studies* (1931) = E. Ekwall, *Studies on English Place- and Personal Names*, Kungl. Humanistiska Vetenskapssamfundet i Lund, Årsberättelse 1930–1: 1 (Lund, 1931); *Studies* (1936) = E. Ekwall, *Studies on English Place-Names*, Kungl. Vitterhets-, Historie- och Antikvitetsakadamiens Handlingar 42:1 (Stockholm, 1936).

For help in the preparation of this article I am grateful to colleagues at University College London, and in the Survey of English Place-Names: Mr Kenneth Wass of the Department of Geography drew the maps; Professor Randolph Quirk obtained a grant for me from University College towards the cost of the preparation; Mr Alexander Rumble and Miss Joy Hubble verified the more difficult map-references from old editions of the Ordnance Survey maps; Mr Rumble corroborated the reading discussed below, p. 31, n.1; and Mrs Doris Lord made the typescript. To Professor Clemoes I am grateful for his lucid perception and patience as editor.

[2] *DEPN*, p. xv, (*b*), and *EPN* 1, 227, (2).

[3] *DEPN*, p. xv, (*b*); *PN-ing*[(1)], pp. xix, 122–8 and 152–8; *PN-ing*[(2)], pp. 117–73; and *EPN* 1, 227, (2) (iii).

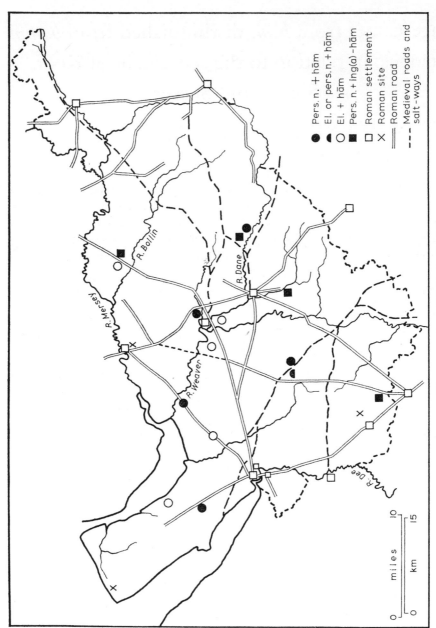

FIG. 1 Place-names from OE *hām* in Cheshire

Pers. n. + hām
El. or pers. n. + hām
El. + hām
Pers. n. + ing(a) - hām
Roman settlement
Roman site
Roman road
Medieval roads and salt-ways

R. Bollin
R. Dane
R. Mersey
R. Weaver
R. Dee

miles
km

continent between place-names from OHG -*heim* and those from OHG -*ing*.[1] In recent years an attempt has been made at a re-appraisal of the value of the place-name from OE -*ingas, -inga-*, including the numerous -*ingahām* type, as evidence of the progress of the English settlements,[2] while other recent work has seen the beginning of an examination of the place-names containing OE -*hām* and the compounds *wīc-hām, hām-tūn, hām-stede*[3] and *hām-st(e)all*: the distribution of the compound *wīc-hām* has been shown to be related very particularly to Roman roads and Roman archaeology,[4] and it has been recognized that in Cheshire (see fig. 1), place-names in -*ham* from -*hām* and in -*ingham* (<-*ing(a)hām*) are distributed in a pattern based on the run of the Roman roads.[5] This latter realization suggests a refinement upon Ekwall's observation[6] that the distribution of place-names from -*ingahām* is related to Roman roads, for it is likely that in the -*ingahām* structure it is the -*hām* element that is to be associated with the distribution along the Roman roads, and not the -*inga*- element which interested Ekwall. Further work in progress on place-names in -*ham* from -*hām*[7] provides yet more evidence of the existence in England of a relationship corresponding to that on the continent between OHG -*heim* place-names and settlement in Roman contexts.[8] The accompanying general illustration of south-east England (see figs. 2 and 3) is sufficient to show that in, say, Sussex and Hertfordshire the -*ham* and *hām-stede* names are often close to Roman roads and to areas developed in Roman times, whereas in some parts of the south-east these name-types and Anglo-Saxon pagan burial-sites appear to exclude each other. The -*ham* names of Hertfordshire, Middlesex and Essex still await detailed attention,[9] but it is expected that the problems of distribution and typology in these counties will be less difficult than they are in Sussex, Surrey and Kent. The distribution of names in -*ham* in Essex is selective and regional, an effect discernible even in P. H. Reaney's distribution-map of '*ham(m), hamm* and -*ingaham*' in Essex,[10] which lacks the

---

1 Bach, pt 2, §§463, 477–8 and 581–5.
2 A. H. Smith, 'Place-Names and the Anglo-Saxon Settlement', *Proc. of the Brit. Acad.* 42 (1956), 67–88; J. McN. Dodgson, 'The Significance of the Distribution of the English Place-Name in OE -*ingas, -inga-* in South-East England', *MA* 10 (1966), 1–29, and 'The English Arrival in Cheshire', *Trans. of the Hist. Soc. of Lancashire and Cheshire* 119 (1967), 1–37; and Sarah Kirk, 'A Distribution Pattern: -ingas in Kent', *JEPN* 4 (1972), 37–59.
3 For *hām-stede* see Sandred, pp. 65 and 88.
4 Margaret Gelling, 'English Place-Names Derived from the Compound *wīchām*', *MA* 11 (1967), 87–104.
5 Dodgson, 'The English Arrival in Cheshire', pp. 10 (fig. 2) and 15.
6 *PN-ing*⁽¹⁾, p. 163; cf. *PN-ing*⁽¹⁾, pp. 155ff.
7 Dr Barry Cox is expected to bring out in *JEPN* 5 (1973) the eagerly awaited results of a study of Midland place-names, in which the distribution of names from OE *hām* in an extensive tract of country is examined in detail. This will enable us to ascertain whether the Roman road pattern governs this distribution in the larger area as consistently as it does in Cheshire.
8 Bach, pt 2, §§477–8.   9 Work on these, and on the Chiltern region, is in hand.
10 EPNS 12 (Cambridge, 1935), end-pocket.

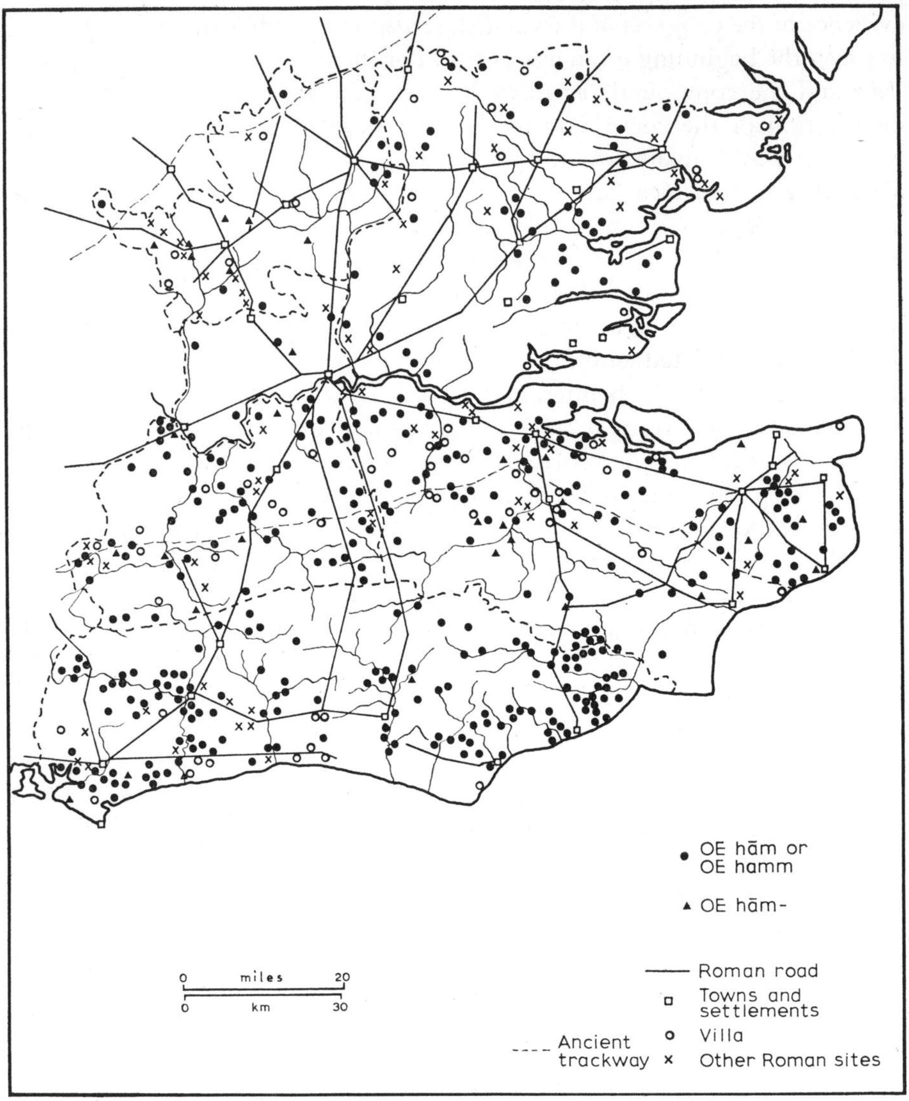
OE hām or
OE hamm
OE hām-
Roman road
Towns and
settlements
Villa
Other Roman sites
Ancient
trackway
0 miles 20
0 km 30

FIG. 2 Place-names in *-ham* and Roman sites in south-east England

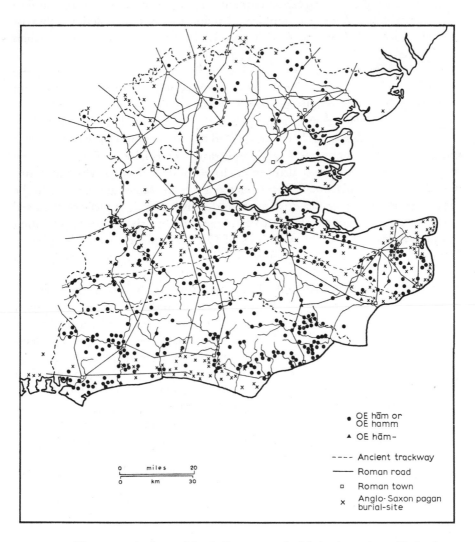

Legend:
- OE hām or OE hamm
- ▲ OE hām-
- ---- Ancient trackway
- —— Roman road
- □ Roman town
- × Anglo-Saxon pagan burial-site

miles 0 — 20
km 0 — 30

FIG. 3   Place-names in -*ham* and Anglo-Saxon pagan burial-sites in south-east England

5

Roman archaeological information which would have more readily explained the pattern. The purpose of this essay, then, is, as an experiment, to identify the place-names in *-ham* from *-hām*, and the place-names from the compounds of *hām,* in an area of early English settlement – Kent, Surrey and Sussex – and to discover whether their geographical distribution is controlled by that of Roman roads and Romano-British sites or by that of Anglo-Saxon pagan burial-sites.

The difficulty in the way of this exercise is the occurrence of the place-name formed from OE *-hamm,* which is open to confusion with the place-name from *-hām,* since both elements in unstressed final position in a compound place-name have a similar pronunciation [-(h)əm] which is likely to be spelt *-ham.* The element OE *hamm* has been considered to have meanings 'an enclosure, a meadow, a water-meadow'[1] and 'meadow, especially a flat, low-lying meadow on a stream', and also 'an enclosed plot, a close',[2] while in continental Germanic place-names the element OHG *hamm* appears with the meanings 'a pasture, or meadow, surrounded by a ditch', 'a piece of enclosed land, a meadow', 'a dead arm of a river', 'the bend of a river'.[3] But Dr Gelling has demonstrated[4] that the meanings of OE *hamm* which are discernible in English place-names are more specifically (1) 'land in a river-bend', (2) 'a promontory', (3) 'a river-meadow', (4) 'dry ground in a marsh', and (5) 'a cultivated plot in marginal land'. It is interesting to observe in this series of meanings the range and the contrast between natural features and man-made development, and between lowland, flat, waterside sites and those that are upland, 'dry' and high-relief. Confusion between the two types of place-name, those from OE *-hām* and those from OE *-hamm,* is likely to arise if a *hām,* village, type of settlement was sited in a *hamm* topography (say, in any of Dr Gelling's senses 1, 2 and 4), or a *hamm* (in sense 5) was created at a *hām,* or a *hamm* (in any of senses 1–4) came to be thought the most distinctive feature about the site of a *hām.* For any place in which all these topographical conditions cannot be definitely excluded there are grounds for deriving a name in *-ham* from either *-hām* or *-hamm.*

An elaborated form of Margaret Gelling's typology of *hamm* sites is used in this essay, the elaboration being the result of my observation of the sites. My classification comprises:

> *hamm* 1   'land in a river-bend'
> *hamm* 2a 'a promontory of dry land into
>   marsh or water'

[1] *EPN* I, 229, *s.v. hamm.*   [2] *DEPN,* p. 214, *s.v. ham(m).*
[3] *DEPN, ibid.,* and Bach, pt 1, §§296, 302, 314 and 375.
[4] Margaret Gelling, 'The Element *hamm* in English Place-Names: a Topographical Investigation', *NoB* 48 (1960), 140–62.

> hamm 2b   'a promontory into lower land,
>   even without marsh or water';
>   perhaps hence 'land on a hill-spur'
> hamm 3   'a river-meadow'
> hamm 4   'dry ground in a marsh'
> hamm 5a   'a cultivated plot in marginal land'
>   b   'an enclosed plot, a close'
> hamm 6   'a piece of valley-bottom land hemmed
>   in by higher ground'.

This set of meanings gives figurative extension to the basic sense of 'a surrounded, hemmed-in place'. Based on these values for *hamm*, an analysis of the place-names in *-ham* in Kent, Surrey and Sussex produces three categories: first, the names whose Old English or Middle English spellings (*-hamm*, *-homm*, *-ham(m)e*, *-hom(m)e*) show the geminated consonant of OE *hamm* or the dat. sg. *-e* inflexion which is regular for OE *hamm* but not for OE *hām*; second, the names which appear likely to be from OE *-hamm* on account of the site or status of the places to which they refer, although spelling is not indicative; and third, the names which do not fall into either of these categories.

By this process of distinction and elimination it is possible to isolate the few names in *-ham* which do not have the spellings of the *hamm* element and which do not refer to sites with *hamm* characteristics and to use these as representatives of the type from *-hām*. But, of course, the process is artificial and the distinctions made may well be too arbitrary. A few names written off as probably from *-hamm* will have been *-hām* names. In a number of instances there is uncertainty, both in fact and in opinion. My method has been first to isolate the names in *-ham* which demonstrate distinctive spellings from *-hamm*. These are listed in Appendix I. These names are useful in two ways. They show that the range of first elements combined with *-hamm* is very similar to the range of first elements which is found with *-hām*; and they mark the sites which may be used as topographical models to help the recognition of a *hamm* behind a non-committal *-ham* spelling in another name. My second step (very arbitrary, but nonetheless effective in prospecting a mass of material) has been to assume that any name which exhibits only *-ham* spellings and never *-hamm*, *-homm* etc., is from *-hām*, provided that (1) the place is an ancient manor or an ancient parish or is otherwise historically distinguished as an important centre of settlement, (2) it is on record before, say, 1300–50 as something more than a field-name or boundary-point and (3) the site does not have a topography which might be that of a *hamm*. These names are listed in Appendix II, along with those from the compounds of *hām*. My third stage has been to try to assess the relative probability of derivation from *-hamm* or derivation from *-hām* in each doubtful case. The supposition of a -*hamm* origin is to be preferred if a name refers to an unimportant and obscure hamlet, farm, piece of land or physical feature, even if the name is recorded early. Similarly it is to be preferred – since it seems improbable historically that a new place-name would be formed in -*hām* in late Old English – if a name in -*ham* is first recorded after, say, 1300, unless there are special considerations in favour of admitting the *possibility* of -*hām*, such as composition with an Old English monothematic personal name of an archaic type, or an ancient manorial status of the place, or a topography not describable as a *hamm*. Appendix III contains the names which I consider (1) more probably from -*hamm* than from -*hām* and (2) more probably from -*hām* than from -*hamm*. Correspondingly the distribution-maps (figs. 4–6) carry four kinds of symbol: one for the names whose spellings indicate that they are from -*hamm*, another for the names considered to be from -*hām*, a third for those names that are probably from -*hamm* but possibly from -*hām*, and a fourth for those names that are probably from -*hām* but possibly from -*hamm*. The choice between categories (1) and (2) in list III, and, more fundamentally, the choice between list II (so far as it concerns names in -*ham*) and list III, are a matter of judgement, both in field work and map-reading. It has to be emphasized that unless there are unequivocal OE and ME -*hamm*, -*homm* spellings, even the most obvious topographical evidence justifies only a statement of probability. The list of -*ham* names in Appendix II and lists III1 and III2 therefore depend on the exercise of a fallible expert judgement.

The names in the categories '*hamm*', '*hām*', 'probably *hamm*' and 'probably *hām*' are plotted in figs. 4–6 in relation to the Anglo-Saxon pagan burial-sites listed in Meaney[1] and in *Medieval Archaeology*, the Roman villas, potteries, buildings and settlements (but not the small or isolated finds) from the *Ordnance Survey Map of Roman Britain*,[2] and the principal Roman roads.[3] It will be observed that the place-name material available for Sussex is greater than that for Kent or that for Surrey. This may to some extent be due to differences in the degree of intensity of coverage attained by the various place-name surveys,[4] but it probably also reflects differences of terrain and dialect. New work on these three counties will probably alter the balance a little by revealing hitherto unknown minor names in -*hamm* or in -*ham* from -*hamm*, but it is unlikely that the information on major names – those of parishes and ancient manors – will be much altered.

The distribution-map for Kent (fig. 4) shows that names in -*ham* of whatever origin lie mostly north of the Weald – no farther south than the sands and

[1] Audrey L. Meaney, *Early Anglo-Saxon Burial Sites* (London, 1964).
[2] *Map of Roman Britain*, 3rd ed. (Ordnance Survey 1956).
[3] Taken from Margary.
[4] *KPN, PNK, PNSx, PNSr* and *DEPN*.

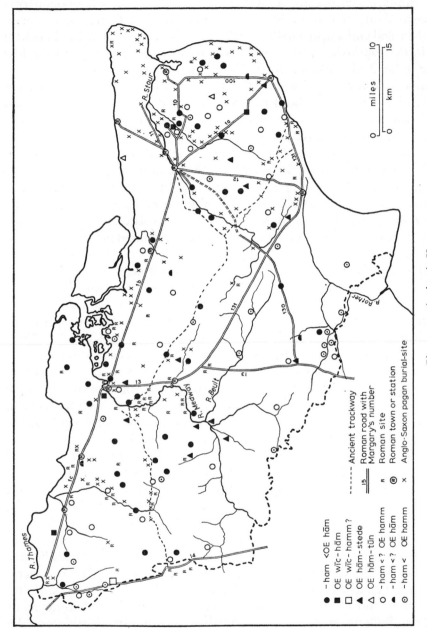

FIG. 4 Place-names in -*ham* in Kent

Legend:

- ham < OE hām
■ OE wīc - hām
□ OE wīc - hamm?
▲ OE hām - stede
△ OE hām - tūn
○ -ham < ? OE hamm
◐ -ham < ? OE hām
◒ -ham < OE hamm
⊙ Anglo-Saxon pagan burial-site

—— Ancient trackway
----- Roman road with
   ___
   15 Margary's number
R Roman site
⊛ Roman town or station
×

miles 10
km 15

sandstone ridges which extend along the north edge of the Weald parallel to the south-facing chalk scarp of the North Downs. The line of this boundary is represented in west Kent by the distribution of Westerham, Ightham, Wrotham and Offham, in middle Kent by that of Otham, Bearsted and Lenham and in the south-west part of east Kent by that of Mersham and the lost *Stanstede* (marked as a *hām-stede*) in Aldington.

Among the relatively few examples in the Weald, there is in the extreme south, on the north-east border of Sussex, a cluster of names from *-hamm* which mark a concentration of ripuarian and formerly estuarine sites along the Rother and Brede levels (cf. the Sussex map (fig. 6) at this sector). The names of uncertain origin at this end of the Weald are probably also from *-hamm*, e.g. Farningham (Cranbrook), Freezingham (Rolvenden) and Ethnam (Sandhurst). The two latter are obviously *hamm* sites by topography. Farningham in Cranbrook is not a reliable instance of any sort. *Langham* (now Halden Place in Rolvenden) may be thought ambiguous. Isolated to the west of this group there is Highams in Goudhurst, which, being plural in form, is likely to be a *hamm* name.

Hemsted in Benenden at the junction of the two Roman roads, Margary 13 and 130, is a *hām-stede*; the next instance to the east, *Langham* (i.e. Halden Place), may be a *-hām* name (see below, App. III1, p. 37); and further to the east along the Roman road Margary 130 there is the isolated example Great Engeham in Woodchurch (Little Engeham is half a mile due south of it). These three sites are obviously related to the line of the Roman road through the Weald. Further west there is a group of four *hām-stede* and two *-hām* names on the middle reaches of the Medway and its tributaries, south of the sandstone ridge. The more westerly of the two *-hām* names is Peckham – West Peckham, East Peckham being 3 miles further south-east on the north bank of the Medway. This group of names, East and West Peckham, Tutsham (West Farleigh) and the *hām-stede* names, Hamptons (West Peckham), Whetsted (Capel), Hampstead (Yalding) and Nettlestead, is distributed in relation to the river system and to the valleys in the sandstone ridge which the river has cut, and also to the Roman archaeology of the middle Medway region. To the north-east there are the Roman villa sites of East Barming and Teston; adjacent to West Peckham and Hamptons there is the Roman villa site in Plaxtol. The north edge of the area in which these *hām-stede* names lie was obviously developed in Roman times, but the *Map of Roman Britain* reveals no villas or settlements farther south than these. It looks as if these *hām-stede* and *-hām* names south-west of Maidstone, at the confluence of the Medway, Beult and Teise, indicate settlements in the north edge of the deep Weald along the river-line, extending southwards from the limit of the Romano-British development.

In the Kent of the Downs and their long north slope the distribution of names from *hām* is controlled by two factors: geographical features and Roman archaeology. In north-west Kent, Lewisham, East Wickham and Eltham are near to principal Roman roads. The Darenth valley, rich with Romano-British and Anglo-Saxon sites, shows Farningham and Shoreham. The lower Medway area contains Burham, Wouldham, the lost *Hamstede* in Halling, Wickam in Strood, Friningham, Chatham and Gillingham, of which the last four belong as much to the area of Watling Street and the Medway estuary as to the heavily settled river valley. In Hoo hundred, in a district with a number of Romano-British and Anglo-Saxon sites, there are Stoke, Higham and Dalham.

As a glance at the map will show, some of the -*hām* names are distributed along and parallel to Watling Street and Pilgrims' Way and others are along and parallel to the north-flowing rivers Darenth and Medway and their valleys. The north–south grain of the drainage valleys on the dip-slope of the North Downs is a factor in the situation of the three instances in the north of west Kent, Cudham, Fawkham and Meopham, which do not appear to conform to the road-and-river axis of distribution. Cudham is a 'pers. n.+*hām*'. The place is 2 miles north of Pilgrims' Way, 2¾ east of the Roman road Margary 14, 3 south-east of the Roman villa at Keston and 2 north-east of the Roman temple at Titsey. It is on a route, in part a ridgeway, which runs in a direct line from the crest of the North Downs escarpment to the Roman villa site at Keston. It is virtually surrounded by evidences of Roman development, even if it can hardly be said to be near to them. Perhaps more interesting is the fact that Cudham is on the east brink of, and near the head of, a long valley whose lower part is occupied by the Cray. Cudham stands at an altitude of 574 ft, steeply above a valley floor at 450 ft. It is a prominent site on the lip of the valley. The Cray valley is heavily marked in the *Map of Roman Britain* with occasional finds, which suggest that there was settlement up the valley as well as the station on Watling Street. Cudham probably marks an Anglo-Saxon extension, farther up this valley into the wooded clay-with-flints land, beyond the limits of the area of Romano-British development. Fawkham and Meopham are east of the Darenth valley. Fawkham ('pers. n.+*hām*') is on a valley floor at 300 ft under a brink at 450 ft, in a valley running down to the north from Brands Hatch (TQ/5764) and South Ash (TQ/5963) to Longfield (TQ/6069). It is 1½ miles west of the Roman site at Ash. Meopham, another example of the 'pers. n.+*hām*' type, 4 miles to the east, lies along a ridge running down from 650 ft to 350 ft over 4 miles: the village stands at 450 ft, as if on a ridgeway from Pilgrims' Way down towards Watling Street, and on the west brink of a valley whose bottom is here at 300 ft and which runs down north-eastward past Luddesdown and Cuxton to the Medway. Fawkham (4½ miles south of Watling Street, 1½ west of the Roman site at Ash (TQ/608650) and 2 east of the Darenth valley with its numerous Romano-British and Anglo-Saxon sites) and Meopham (2¼ miles east of the Roman site at Ash, 3 south of Watling Street, 4 south-east of the Roman site at Spring Head in Swanscombe and 2½ north of Pilgrims' Way) are at once near enough to and distant enough from the discovered Romano-British settlement pattern for interpretation as extensions into new ground made by English settlers opening up the higher recesses of the dip-slope *combes* and *denes* beyond the area developed in Romano-British times.

In east Kent we begin with a problem. Chartham, Chilham and Godmersham lie along the Great Stour. Chartham and Godmersham would be on a Roman road projected by I. D. Margary[1] as Margary 130, from Canterbury to Ashford. All three are certainly distributed along Pilgrims' Way and the river. Chartham appears to be on a Roman road. But the Roman road from Ashford to Canterbury, Margary 130, may have gone by Wye (TR/0546), Crundale parish church (TR/085487) and Sole Street (TR/0949), as 'the old street' of *on þa ealdan stræte* in *BCS* 378 on the boundary of Godmersham at TR/094493.

A 'street' on this alignment would affect our analysis of the position of Bodsham Green and Elmsted, marked on fig. 4 west of Stane Street, Margary 12, east of the suggested Wye–Crundale road to Canterbury and north of the Folkestone extension of Pilgrims' Way. This sets them in an area of Romano-British chance finds, but with no Romano-British settlements or villas and nearly no Anglo-Saxon pagan burial-sites. The three places are beside the same valley (a long inlet in the 400-ft contour) which runs down northward to Petham and then opens westward to Chartham. These places are, again, situated at the upper reaches of a valley. But here the Romano-British archaeology is a matter of roads at a mile or two distant and an area of sparse isolated finds. This pattern does not suggest an expansion out of an area broken in by Romano-British development. These are places in the farther secluded ends of a dip-slope valley reached by side paths off convenient but distant Roman roads.

This distant and guarded geographical relationship with the Roman road pattern appears to hold for the other east Kent names. The *hām-stede* next east, Palmstead (Upper Hardres), lies at 440 ft on the broad back of a ridge between valleys, of which the one on the east opens at Kingston on to the Dover–Canterbury Roman road and the one on the west runs down to Bridge, farther north on the same road. At the east end of the county the names Finglesham and Mongeham represent sites originally coastal.[2] The southerly of them is Great Mongeham. Little Mongeham, not marked on fig. 4, is a mile

---

[1] Margary, p. 47.   [2] See Sonia Chadwick Hawkes's map, *MA* 2 (1958), 4, fig. 2.

to the west-south-west of it. Doubtless there were spurs here from the Dover–Richborough Roman road, Margary 100. The only other *-hām* name referring to a place which does not lie along a Roman road is Alkham. Alkham, and Terlingham 4 miles south-west of it, on the Folkestone branch of Pilgrims' Way would be on a route leading from Pilgrims' Way north-eastward along a line of ridge and valley to Temple Ewell, where it led to the Dover–Canterbury Roman road and a further north-eastward track beyond it. Alkham is accessible from routes across the top and the bottom of the deep valley in which it lies. It is yet another 'valley' settlement, outside the range of the Romano-British distribution-pattern.

The distribution of names from *-hām* in Surrey (see fig. 5) falls into an over-all pattern, in that the majority are north of Pilgrims' Way. This is a model also followed by the *-hamm* names. In south-east Surrey there is a cluster of them, seven identified by spelling and one, Hathersham in Outwood, by conjecture. This is a district in which, as the name Outwood itself indicates, the settlement pattern was originally one of Weald *denns*, forest out-pastures which would be first the seasonal outposts and then the permanent colonies of home villages in the Downs: for example, Merstham had *denns* at Lake (TQ/2944).[1] This group of *-hamm* names and the two or three other Weald *-hamms* in the extreme south-west of the county are interesting as showing the use of *hamm* for wealden settlements. There may be need for an appraisal of the element *hamm* as one of the terms used to describe a wealden settlement, alongside OE *falod* and OE *denn*.[2] The questionable example Merstham, which may be a *hām*, and which is isolated on Pilgrims' Way half-way between two Roman roads, is in fact precisely situated at the intersection of Pilgrims' Way and the natural dry-valley gap-route through the North Downs. The north end of this emerges at Croydon and it is followed from Purley northwards by the Roman road Margary 150[3] which gives Streatham its name.

The *-hām* names in north-east Surrey, Hatcham, *Washingham* and Streatham, are on Roman road alignments, Margary 1, 150 and 15. The group in east Surrey, Sanderstead (the *hām-stede* in that group), Warlingham, Woldingham and Chelsham, lies between the Roman roads Margary 150 and 14, convenient for but removed from them, the sites dictated by the valley-and-spur topo-graphy of the dip-slope of the Downs. Sanderstead and Warlingham, in fact, appear to be on a ridgeway route leading diagonally but very directly from Margary 14 at the crest of the Chalk scarp, near Tatsfield, down to Margary 150, where it cuts into the Croydon–Streatham alignment. Chelsham is at a

---

[1] See *PNSr*, p. 293, *s.n. Greatlake Fm* and *Littlelake Fm*; and *JEPN* 3 (1971), 8 and 19.
[2] See H. C. Darby, 'Place-Names and the Geography of the Past', *Early English and Norse Studies Presented to Hugh Smith in Honour of his Sixtieth Birthday*, ed. A. Brown and P. Foote (London, 1963), pp. 6–18, esp. 14–18. [3] See above, p. 8, n. 3.

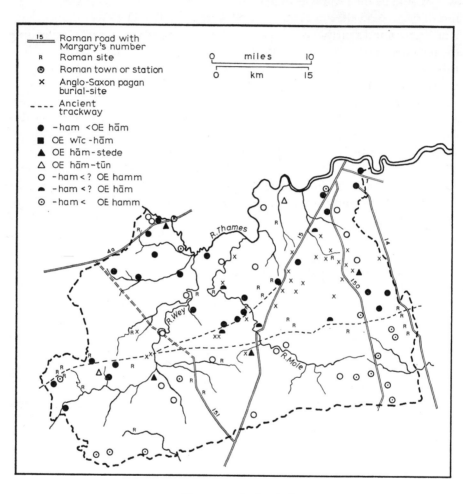

FIG. 5   Place-names in *-ham* in Surrey

particularly interesting place where an alternative zig-zag traverse of the valley south of Skid Hill has superseded the original one used by Roman road Margary 14. The original Roman zig-zag traverse is followed, as is the rest of this stretch of the road, by the Kent–Surrey boundary. This road appears to have formed the base-line for the original demarcation of the entire length of the boundary between Kent and Surrey. At Chelsham, the county boundary still follows in detail the original zig-zag although this section of the road has long ago fallen out of use. The new traverse through Chelsham evidently did not replace the old one until after the county boundary had been drawn along the old one. This raises a question whether Chelsham is deliberately sited upon the new traverse, i.e. was established by means of settlement on the road, or whether the new traverse diverted the old road through Chelsham because Chelsham was already there with its convenient accommodation-paths, a ready-made alternative route.

Next there is the run of names along Stane Street (Margary 15), Mitcham, Cheam, Epsom, Mickleham and Hampstead (Dorking). The first three lie along the tail of the dip-slope of the Downs, Mickleham is in the gap where the Mole passes through the Downs and Hampstead is in the vale between the chalk and the sandstone ridge. The group of names Effingham, Bookham, Fetcham and Pachesham lies between the Mole and Pilgrims' Way. The place-name Leatherhead, OE *lēoda-ride*, 'the people's road', indicates[1] that there was a major route crossing the Mole here. Presumably this was a route from Epsom to Guildford across the angle between Stane Street and Pilgrims' Way, and Fetcham, Bookham and Effingham would lie on it. They lie at a convenient spring-line on the dip-slope, parallel to the 200-ft contour.

Ockham and *Hundulsam* (Weybridge) are beside the Wey: they are not obviously related to the road pattern. Then there is a group, Chobham, Windlesham, Woodham (Chertsey) and Hersham (Chertsey), in the north-west of the county, in the low-lying country along the two streams called the Bourne which join the Thames near the Wey, and near to them are Egham, Rumshot (Egham) and Bakeham (Egham). These three are on the Roman road (Margary 4a) through Staines. Windlesham is in the angle between Roman road Margary 4a and the probable line of another Roman road, Margary 151. Hersham and Woodham, part of the group but not aligned on the roads, probably represent, with them, a process of settlement in the basin of the Wey, based on the Thames and the road alignments.

In west Surrey there is a group Tongham, Puttenham, Rodsell, Wreccles-ham and Frensham. A little to the east is Unstead (Shalford), a *hām-stede* name. Unstead and Frensham show an extension of the *hām* distribution into the

[1] *DEPN, s.n. Leatherhead.*

fringes of the Weald, but no farther than the vale under the Downs scarp (as in Kent, farther east). Wrecclesham, Tongham, Puttenham and Rodsell are sited in relation to Pilgrims' Way and the crest of the chalk Downs. Rodsell is not a regular -*hām* formation: it shows an occasional use of -*hām* as a suffix to a place-name.

In Surrey, the distribution patterns of the *hām* names, the Anglo-Saxon pagan burial-sites and the Romano-British archaeological sites are to some extent distinct and to some degree related. The *hām* names are distributed on the fringes of the area which contain the Romano-British sites and the Anglo-Saxon pagan burial-sites. The spatial relationship in east Surrey appears different from that in west Surrey mainly because of the greater number of archaeological sites in east Surrey.

In the map of Sussex (fig. 6) most noticeable are the names from -*hamm*. Their distribution is general. But it is very notable in river-side sites in the Weald, especially along the Rother and Arun in west Sussex, and along the former shores of the levels of the Rother, Brede and Tillingham in east Sussex, as well as on the edges of Pevensey Levels and of the Bulverhythe marshes east of Bexhill and west of St Leonards.

Names from *hām* do not occur north of the South Downs. Except for Hempstead[2] in Framfield, for the group in the Selsey peninsula and for the three names near Hailsham, the pattern of distribution is along the north and south edges of the Downs at the edge of the Weald, along the coast and along the Roman roads. A few names lie in the middle of the Downs, but these are places in the natural gap-routes through the hills. Upwaltham is in a significant valley leading one of the diversions of the Roman road Margary 15 over the brink of the Downs at Duncton. The Roman bath-house site at Duncton indicates the possibility that such a route may have existed in antiquity: moreover its position under the Downs (SU/960166) indicates the possibility of other Romano-British sites along the broad shelf between the bottom of the scarp and the valley of the Rother, the district in which Graffham is situated. The position of Graffham, Sussex, is the counterpart to that of Lenham, Kent, on a shelf of sandy soil under the Downs escarpment and related to a ridgeway which runs east and west along that hill-edge and intersects the Roman roads east and west of the site and traversing the country in a north to south direction.

The Rother marks the bottom of the scarp-foot vale and Selham here occupies a similar site to that of Westerham, Kent, between the chalk and the deep Weald. Patcham is in the dry-valley gap through the Downs behind Brighton and is probably sited with relevance to a southward extension of Roman road Margary 150. Muntham is beside the Findon valley gap through the Downs behind Worthing; close by is the site of a Romano-British settlement under Blackpatch Hill. The isolated instance, Hempstead[2] in Framfield, a *hām-stede*

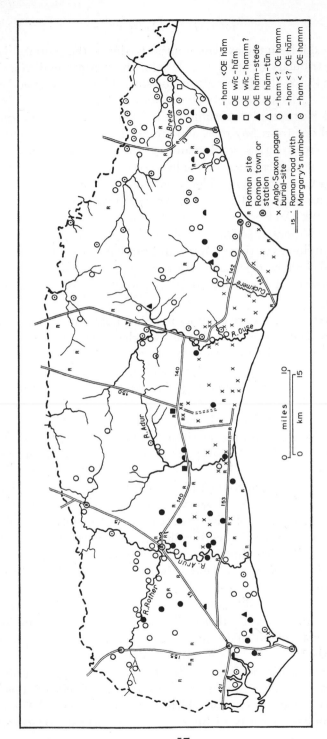

Key:

- ham <OE hām   ●
- OE wīc-hām   ■
- OE wīc-hamm?   □
- OE hām-stede   ▲
- OE hām-tūn   △
- -ham <? OE hamm   ○
- -ham <? OE hām   ◐
- -ham <   OE hamm   ◑
- -ham <   OE hamm   ⊙

R   Roman site
⊚   Roman town or station
×   Anglo-Saxon pagan burial-site
15   Roman road with Margary's number

FIG. 6   Place-names in -*ham* in Sussex

out in the Weald, is on the extreme southern edge of the central ridge of the Weald, on a tributary of the Ouse. It is at the western end of a ridgeway running from Uckfield to Etchingham, and since it is not far east of the Roman road Margary 14 its site is probably related to these route-lines. Hailsham, Magham and Hempstead[1] (Arlington) form a group of three names, two from *hām* and one from *hām-stede*, and are not in juxtaposition with either a known Roman road or a known Roman site. However, they occupy sites on the 100-ft ridge which extends across the head of Pevensey Levels and separates these from the Cuckmere. This ridge would offer a route northward from the easternmost massif of the Downs, and from Roman road Margary 142, towards the Weald. (An iron-mining industry in Roman times is reported from TQ/5616 in Chiddingly.) In fact, Hailsham and Magham may well have been tidal sites in Anglo-Saxon times – much like present-day Bosham in Chichester harbour – and could be regarded as former coastal sites, similar in type to the lowland coast sites of the group south and south-east of Chichester, in the Selsey region.

In these three south-eastern counties in general the names from *hām* lie outside the Weald. They occur in the districts which geography and soil-type have always rendered most inviting to settlement. To some extent, then, the *hām* names are bound to appear in the same districts as the Romano-British settlement features. However, within this general probability, there is a significant particular characteristic in their distribution. The names from *hām* are either *on* a Roman road or at a discreet distance from one. Also Pilgrims' Way is an important east–west axis for the distribution of Roman villa sites shown in the *Map of Roman Britain*. Figs. 4–6 give an impression that the *hām* names appear on Roman roads and near to them or in some sensible relationship with them : such a distribution-pattern could indicate that these names were given when districts which had developed in Roman times, and areas immediately outside these districts, were being colonized by the English. The relevance of a Roman background is clear in the Darenth valley in Kent where the *hām* names are close to Roman villa sites. In fact there is evidence here of continuous occupation of territory and use of land, whereas the habitations changed, the Roman *villa* being succeeded by the neighbouring *hām*.

Comparison of the distribution of the *hām* names with that of the Anglo-Saxon pagan burials indicates that while the two distributions are in general separate, they coincide in a fair number of instances: the overlap that is discernible is at the fringe of the pagan burial districts.

Yet there are districts outside the Weald which do not contain *hām* names. There is an area of west Sussex north of Chichester which contains no such names and no pagan burials but which does contain several Roman sites. Thanet in Kent has no *hām* name but contains a Roman site or so and quite a number of Anglo-Saxon pagan burial-sites. In the part of Sussex from Beachy Head westwards to Brighton there are no *hām* names in the Downs, and yet there are Romano-British archaeological features and a number of Anglo-Saxon pagan burial-sites. Conversely, in north-west Surrey and in a small district in mid-Kent south-west of Maidstone there is a distribution of -*hām* and *hām-stede* names which lie on or beyond the limits of the distribution of Roman sites and Anglo-Saxon pagan burials.

Comparison of the distribution-pattern of names from OE -*ingas*, -*inga*- with that of names from -*hām* can be focused most conveniently by a comparison of the figures accompanying this article with those in *Medieval Archaeology* 10 (1966), 10–11, of which especially the map of Surrey (p. 11, fig. 4) should be compared with the Surrey diagram of the present article (above, fig. 5). It will be seen most easily from these Surrey diagrams that the distribution of the -*hām* names is not clearly separated from that of the Anglo-Saxon pagan burial-sites as the distribution of the -*ingas*, -*inga*- place-names is.

If these various factors of comparison are brought together, the following hypotheses can be offered:

(*a*) since the *hām* names occur on the edges of the Romano-British settlement pattern, and in a distribution which extends out from that pattern, the users of this type of name recognized the Romano-British pattern and settled around it and beyond it;

(*b*) since the *hām* names occur in districts where there are *no* Anglo-Saxon pagan burial-sites, the type was in use after the pagan burial fashion had become obsolete; but, since the type also appears in districts where there *are* pagan burial-sites, some *hām* names were contemporary with the pagan burial custom;

(*c*) since names from '-*inga*-+element' occur in the Weald[1] whilst *hām* names or '-*inga*+hām' names rarely do, the *hām* type of name was not in use during the colonization of the Weald whereas the '-*inga*-+element' type still was; and furthermore, since this was so, the *hām* type was earlier than the '-*inga*-+element' type and the -*ingahām* type was a 'late' variety of the *hām* one.

The tenor of our evidence is therefore that in this part of England place-names in *hām* preceded the formation of the -*ingas*, -*inga*- names and persisted contemporaneously with them. The distribution of the *hām* type indicates that it came into use at the very beginning of a colonization phase during which the Anglo-Saxons moved beyond the immigration areas comprising the pagan burial districts of Thanet, the South Downs of Sussex and the dip-slope of the Downs in east Surrey and during which they began to take over the available

[1] *MA* 10 (1966), 8.

land within, on the edge of and beyond the districts that had been occupied and developed in Roman times. In the three south-eastern counties the *hām* names record a process which took place in the fifth and sixth centuries. In Cheshire they mark an English 'take-over' in the seventh century. There is a similarity of spacial and sequential model in the two areas, even though their chronology is different. For the purposes of extrapolation, it appears likely that the *hām* name can be taken as a clue to the order of colonization of a district in which it occurs. Of course, there remains, now, the problem of the names from *-hamm*, an element which, in its early range, may be contemporary with *hām*, but which lived on into modern times as a dialect substantive.

APPENDICES

The information is presented in the following order in most cases: a parish-name, or another place-name followed by the name of its parish in brackets; the National Grid reference; leading bibliographical references; the earliest form and date, and any useful variants (often without source-reference in order to save space); a statement on the structure of the name, i.e. whether the first element is an Old English monothematic personal name (pers. n.[1]), an Old English dithematic personal name (pers. n.[2]) or an Old English common element (el.); notes on the etymology of the name and/or the topography of the site. For the abbreviations used, see above, p. I, n.I.

APPENDIX I

PLACE-NAMES WHOSE OE OR ME SPELLINGS INDICATE DERIVATION FROM OE '-HAMM'

Kent

BAYHAM (Lamberhurst, also in Frant parish, Sussex): in Kent at TQ/644369, in Sussex TQ/649363; *DEPN, PNK* 201, *KPN* 342, *PNSx* 374; *Begeham* 1208, *Beghehamme* 1315. The sites lie in a valley bottom where three valleys meet, i.e. in a valley bottom broadened at a confluence, which indicates a *hamm* 3 or 6. The structure of the name may be an OE fem. pers. n. (*Bæge*)+*hamm*, but it is more likely another instance of OE *bēg-hamm* as in *Begeham*, Kent.[1]

BECKENHAM: TQ/374696; *DEPN, PNK* 8, *KPN* 212 and 357; pers. n.[1] The site of the old village is now obscured by building. It was on a tributary stream of Pool River and the parish occupied the ground between that and Ravensbourne, in the confluence of which lies Bellingham.

BELLINGHAM (Lewisham): TQ/374725; *DEPN, PNK* 6, *KPN* 300, *PN-ing*[2] 118, *MA* 10 (1966) 22; pers. n.[1]+*-inga-*. The site was in the confluence of Pool River and Ravensbourne but no detailed topography is now discernible.

---

[1] See below, App. III1, p. 34, *s.n. Baytree.*

BILHAM (Kingsnorth): TR/023391; *PNK* 416; el. There is no marked topography here, and this is not a waterside place. Probably a *hamm* 5.

COBHAM: TQ/670683; *DEPN, PNK* 110, *KPN* 244; pers. n.[1] The hall at Cobham (TQ/683699) is at the head of an inlet of the 300 ft contour under a promontory of the 350 ft contour containing the Cobham hill-fort. The village (TQ/670683) is on the end of a ridge on an isolated island contour of 350 ft. There is no clear topographical *hamm*.

ELHAM: TR/177437; *DEPN, PNK* 431, *KPN* 194; el. This lies in the valley of Nail Bourne where the valley bottom broadens opposite the opening of side valleys into the steep sides of the main valley. This would appear to give a topographical model for a *hamm* 6 with a *hamm* 3. However, if the first el. is OE *āl*, 'an eel', the term *āl-hamm* might refer to some sort of eel-pond, by an extension of usage parallel with the use of OE *geard*, 'enclosure, yard', in the term *fisc-geard*, 'fishpond, fish-trap'.

FORSHAM (Rolvenden): TQ/835293; *PNK* 351; el. The site is above the 50 ft contour on a quarter-mile bench in a rounded promontory overlooking half a mile of levels to Hexden Channel. It is the next promontory east from Kensham. The topography indicates a *hamm* 2a.

HARRIETSHAM: TQ/866527; *DEPN, PNK* 211, *KPN* 294; pers. n.[2] The site of the church is on a shelf of the 300 ft contour, in a broad level at the head of R. Len, and could be a *hamm* 2, 3 or 5.

HOMERSHAM (Smarden): not named in Ord. Surv. 1 in maps, but 2½ in and 6 in maps show it at TQ/871447; *PNK* 400; unidentified first el., perhaps OE *omore* (bird name; cf. ModE *yellow-hammer*). The site would have been low-lying meadowland near R. Sherway; a *hamm* 3.

KELSHAM (Headcorn): TQ/814443; *PNK* 215; pers. n.[1] The location is on the north bank of R. Beult; a *hamm* 3.

KENSHAM (Rolvenden): TQ/825297; *PNK* 353 and 460, *KPN* 120, *PN-ing*[2] 119, *BNF* 2 (1967) 380; pers. n.[1]+*inga*-. The hamlet lies below the 100 ft contour overlooking a promontory half a mile long and of 50 ft elevation between two streams which run into the Hexden channel. This is a *hamm* 2a.

LOSSENHAM or **LOSENHAM** (Newenden): TQ/839278; *DEPN s.n. Losenham, PNK* 342, *KPN* 34 and 359, *Studies* (1931) 27; pers. n.[1] Both Ekwall and Wallenberg derive this from -*hām*, but the -*hamm* spelling *Losnehamm*' 1242 is sufficient for the present exercise. The location is a promontory on the Hexden channel opposite Kensham and Forsham. This is a *hamm* 2a.

MAYTHAM (Rolvenden): TQ/848305 or 866285; *DEPN, PNK* 354, *KPN* 362; el. TQ/848305 is the site of Maytham Hall near Rolvenden, on a promontory of the 150 ft contour over the bench of the 100 ft contour on which lies Rolvenden Layne. But TQ/866285 is the site of Maytham on the Rother levels near the Isle of Oxney. This is a marshland site, with no meanders and no elevations, but it is obviously at an old low-tide fording-place of the former estuary of Newmill Channel; so it could mark a *hamm* 2 as well as a *hamm* 3 and a *hamm* 4.

MISLEHAM (Brookland): TQ/994264; *PNK* 477; *KPN* 171; unidentified first el. This is a level marshland site in Walland Marsh; a *hamm* 4.

MOTTINGHAM: TQ/423728; *DEPN, PNK* 7, *KPN* 210 (and 216 *s.n. Moaten-den*), *PN-ing*[1] 28, *PN-ing*[2] 120, *MA* 10 (1966) 22; pers. n.[1]+-*inga*-.

ODIAM or **ODGIAM** (Smarden): TQ/905435; *PN-ing*[2] 125, *KPN* 186; pers. n.[1] There is no remarkable topography.

OTTERHAM (Upchurch): TQ/834674; *PNK* 272; unidentified first el. The site is in a bay of the 50 ft contour overlooking a tidal marsh (Horsham Marsh) and Otterham Creek in the Medway estuary; a *hamm* 2, 3 or 4.

PETHAM: TR/130513; *DEPN, PNK* 546, *KPN* 288; el. The site is between the 200 ft and 250 ft contours, in a valley whose bottom is at 200 ft and whose brink is at 400 ft, and at a place where side valleys cause a broadening of the bottom land; another *hamm* 6 like Elham. There is another Petham in west Kent.

RUSHAM (Wingham): TR/253584; *PNK* 538; el. At an inlet of the 50 ft contour; probably a *hamm* 6.

WICKHAM, WEST: TQ/389648 (the location of Wickham Court); *DEPN, PNK* 29, *KPN* 212, *MA* 11 (1967) 90; OE *wīc*+*hamm*, although the analogy with *wīc-hām* names is remarkable, and is remarked by Dr Gelling in *MA* 11, in that Wickham Court is only about 300 yds off the Roman road Margary 14. Wickham Court and the parish church stand on a knoll or breast of the 300 ft contour over a 250 ft base, in the angle of two broad valleys.

WITTERSHAM: TQ/898269; *DEPN, PNK* 489, *KPN* 319; pers. n.[2] The site is at the end of a 200 ft contour ridge, on the 150 ft contour, which here forms a promontory overlooking the Rother levels. Ham Green in Wittersham (TQ/893263) is another *hamm* site, on a promontory of 50 ft elevation between streams and overlooking the marshland.

YALDHAM (Wrotham): TQ/586887; el. (*eald*) or pers. n.[1] (*Ealda*). The site is on the 400 ft contour and at the head of an inlet of the 350 ft contour where a water-course rises. The -*hamm* may refer to the promontory of the 450 ft contour just above and to west of the site, i.e. it may be a *hamm* 2b.

Surrey

BROADHAM (Oxted): TQ/387513; *PNSr* 334; el. No remarkable topography; a low-lying situation half a mile from a stream; a *hamm* 3 or 4.

CATERHAM: TQ/335554; *DEPN, PNSr* 311 (corrected by *EPN* 1 *s.v.* **cadeir*, cf. *JEPN* 1 (1969) 44); *Catheham* 1179, *Catenham* 1198, *Katherham* 1200, *Katrehamme* 1263. Both Ekwall and EPNS editors take the final el. to be -*hām* despite the -*hamm* spelling, because of their feeling that *hām* would be more appropriate than *hamm* in a compound with British **cadeir*, and hence in so important and ancient a monument of the contact between Saxon and Briton (before the Briton's names were over-looked). Furthermore the place is a parish – it has become important – and this suits the meaning of *hām* rather than that of *hamm*. It has to be remembered, however, that *hamm* may be as ancient a word as *hām*, and that, since Caterham is not even recorded until a century after Domesday Book, it may not have been an important centre in Anglo-Saxon times; and finally, it is not at all certain that the first el. is the PrWelsh word **cadeir*, 'a chair', as it is in Catterlen, Cumberland, and Chadderton, Lancashire.[1] The -*r*- in Caterham could well be the same intrusive -*r*- as is found in Tuesley (*PNSr* 200); and it is remarkable that it is to *r* that the second *n* of Sanderstead (*PNSr* 53) was dissimilated rather than to *l*. Caterham could well be explained as originally *Catenham* (as spelt in 1198) from OE **Cattanhamm*, with first el. an OE pers. n. *Catta,* or an OE fem. **catte,* derived from OE *catt,* 'a (wild-)cat'. Caterham should be seen as at least probably a place-name in -*ham* from OE -*hamm.* What is not clear is whether the *hamm* is cadastral or topographic. The site referred to may be the valley at TQ/341555 now occupied by the main street and the railway station, i.e. a *hamm* 6, or it may be the promontory at TQ/337555 up the hill from the town, i.e. a *hamm* 2.

CHARTHAM (Lingfield): TQ/380406; *PNSr* 328, *NoB* 48 (1960) 158; el. The first el. is OE *cert,* 'rough ground'; cf. Chartham, Kent. The site could be a *hamm* 2, 3 or 6.

CLAPHAM: TQ/292753; *DEPN, PNSr* 21, *Studies* (1936) 136, EPNS 14 liv; el. The topography is obscured by building.

CRABHAMS (Chiddingfold): *PNSr* 192. On record rather too late for the purpose of this exercise: the first form is *Crabbehammes* 1448, 'the crabtree paddocks'.

FARNHAM: SU/8447; *DEPN, PNSr* 169, *NoB* 48 (1960) 142 and 158; el. The first el. is OE *fearn,* 'bracken'. The *hamm* was probably an enclosure; cf. *fearn edisc* 824 *BCS* 378.

HALLAMS, THE (Wonersh): TQ/038453; *PNSr* 254, *NoB* 48 (1960) 158; *Hullehammes* 1418. Also rather too late for our purposes, but deserves mention as an instance of a *hamm* up a hill, or, rather, up *in* a hill. The site is on a spur of the 300 ft contour on a bench of 250 ft on the side of a valley with a stream in it. The *hamm* term could indicate enclosures, or, especially, enclosures within a topographical feature (here, a valley in the 250 ft contour with a sill three-quarters of a mile lower down).

IMBHAMS (Haslemere): SU/925337; *PNSr* 205; el. The first el. is OE *imbe,* 'swarm of bees', and since there is no distinctive topographical feature here, the *hamm* must have been some sort of enclosure in the forest – perhaps a garden for beehives.

LAGHAM (Godstone): TQ/363480; *PNSr* 318; *EPN* 11 *s.v. lagge*; el.+*hamm, homm.* The spelling *Lagholm* 1349 indicates OE *homm.* The first el. is OE *lagge,* 'a marsh'. The site in a *hamm* 2*a,* 4 or 5.

MILLFIELD (Great Bookham): *PNSr* 101; *le Mullehamme* 1331. A field-name rather than a place-name; a *hamm* 1 and a *hamm* 3.

MIXNAMS (Chertsey): *PNSr* 111, *NoB* 48 (1960) 142. From OE *mixten+hamm,* 'dung pounds', hardly a settlement-name; a *hamm* 5*b.*

PEPPERHAMS (Haslemere): SU/903333; *PNSr* 206; *Piperham c.* 1180, *Pyperhammes* 1453; unidentified first el.; a *hamm* 6 and a *hamm* 5.

PRINKHAM (Lingfield): *PNSr* 330; pers. n.[1] The name is that of the meadowland along Eden Brook (TQ/4244); a *hamm* 1.

STONE HALL (Oxted): *PNSr* 334, *NoB* 48 (1960) 158; from OE *stān* and *hamm*; a *hamm* 5*b.*

[1] See discussion *DEPN,* p. 93, *s.n. Chadderton.*

SUGHAM (Lingfield): TQ/382449; *PNSr* 331, *NoB* 48 (1960) 158; el. or pers. n.[1] The site is water-meadows beside a feeder of Eden Brook; a *hamm* 3.

TEDHAM (Horne): *PNSr* 322, *NoB* 48 (1960) 158; pers. n.[1] A *hamm* 5.

WICKHAMS COPSE (Shere cum Gomshall): *PNSr* 253; *Wykehammes* 1485. Recorded too late to be useful to the present exercise but deserves mention in case it should turn out to be analogous with West Wickham, Kent, as a variant of the *wīc-hām* type (important for association with Roman roads).

Sussex

ASHBURNHAM: TQ/6814; *DEPN, PNSx* 477. This is an instance of *-ham* from OE *-hamm* added in early Middle English, to a place-name in OE *burna* which itself is a river-name. The site of Ashburnham Place (TQ/688146) is on the 50 ft contour by Ash Bourne under the side of the ridge which ends to the south-west in the promontory occupied by Kitchenham. The place is a a broadened valley bottom where the 50 ft to 100 ft shelf is wider at the confluence of streams; a *hamm* 3 and a *hamm* 6.

BARHAM (Northiam): *PNSx* 522; el. This would be a *hamm* 5a or b.

BARKHAM (Fletching): TQ/438216; *DEPN, PNSx* 345; el. The site is in a nook of the 100 ft contour beside a shelf of 50 ft to 100 ft with a stream in it which joins R. Ouse at Sharpsbridge (37 ft). Perhaps a *hamm* could lie on a shelf in a hillside; cf. Blackham (below).

BAYHAM (Frant): see above, under *Kent*.

BEDDINGHAM: TQ/445079; *DEPN, PNSx* 357, *PN-ing*[2] 123, *NoB* 48 (1960) 159, *MA* 10 (1966) 24; pers. n.[1]+*-inga-*. The place is beside Glynde Reach, in low-lying land in the big opening off the east side of the R. Ouse levels south of Lewes. In olden days Beddingham would have been on the south shore of a tidal estuary creek, and on a tongue of land between Glynde Reach and a creek immediately south of Beddingham and north of Cobbe Place (TQ/445075). It would be a *hamm* 2a.

BINEHAM (Chailey): TQ/388199; *PNSx* 297; el. Bineham lies in a bulge of the 100 ft contour between two feeders of Longford Stream. The term *hamm* may refer to meadows by the stream near which Bineham stands, i.e. a *hamm* 3. It is not a pronounced topography.

BIVELHAM (Mayfield): TQ/631263; *PNSx* 382; pers. n.[1] The site is below the 150 ft contour in a tongue between R. Rother and a tributary joining from the north. Here also there is a marked widening of the Rother bottom-land as various feeders enter. It is a variety of *hamm* 2, a pointed promontory of two contours between two streams, with the river at 117 ft and the village at less than 150 ft, with a half-mile interval between the 150 ft and 250 ft contours.

BLACKHAM (Withyham): TQ/500378; *PNSx* 370, *NoB* 48 (1960) 159; el. The topography of Blackham is interesting. Blackham Court (TQ/500378) is beside a watercourse on a bench of the 150 ft contour. This bench is shaped like the palm and fingers of a hand: several inlets into the 200 ft contour open on to it. The site overlooks R. Medway. Blackham village (TQ/500395) is on a breast of the 200 ft contour a mile south-west of the confluence of Kent Water and R. Medway. This site is on a hill-spur (it is another 'two-contour' tongue) between Kent Water and R. Medway. If the *hamm* element in the place-name refers to the village site, this is a *hamm* 2, but if Blackham Court is the site referred to, the *hamm* must be either an enclosure at the place or the bench or shelf of ground between 150 ft and 200 ft; cf. Barkham (above).

BODIAM: TQ/782255; *DEPN*, *PNSx* 518, *PN-ing*[2] 125; pers. n.[1] (in gen. sg. or with -*ing* suffix). The Grid reference is that for the modern village and medieval castle. There is another village site and manor house and church at TQ/785260, which occupy a tongue of land on two contours, pointing east, between Kent Ditch and R. Rother. It is a *hamm* 2. The situation resembles that of Lossenham, Kent, 4 miles away.

BOSHAM: SU/803038; *DEPN*, *PNSx* 57 (which prefers OE -*hām*), *NoB* 48 (1960) 147; pers. n.[1] The site is on the end of a peninsula beside an arm of Chichester harbour, in a low-lying terrain and on a stream. This is a *hamm* 2 and possibly also a *hamm* 4 and a *hamm* 5.

BROOMHAM[1] (Catsfield): TQ/720137; *PNSx* 485; el. The place lies above the 150 ft contour overlooking a valley with a stream. The topography of Broomham[1] resembles that of Blackham Court, a *hamm* 5 or 2b.

BROOMHAM[2] (Laughton, Ripe): TQ/127523; *PNSx* 403; el. The site is in a bay of the 100 ft contour beside a stream; a *hamm* 3.

BUCKHAM (Isfield): TQ/449200 to 450204; *PNSx* 396, *NoB* 48 (1960) 159; el. The site is on the ridge of a promontory between rivers: it may be a *hamm* 2 or 5.

DALEHAM (Fletching): *PNSx* 346; el.

ERSHAM (Hailsham): TQ/5908; *PNSx* 436; pers. n.[2]

ETCHINGHAM: TQ/711261; *DEPN*, *PNSx* 455, *PN-ing*[2] 124, *MA* 10 (1966) 24; pers. n.[1] The site is at the end of a promontory of two contours between R. Rother to the north and R. Dudwell to the south. The village lies between the stream (at 50 ft) and the first contour (100 ft). It may be noticed that there is here a junction of river-flats into a broad bottom-land. The characteristics of the locality combine the *hamm* 5 promontory with a *hamm* 3 and a *hamm* 6.

FELPHAM: SZ/949998; *DEPN*, *PNSx* 140; el. The topography is not discernible and the district has been affected by coast erosion. The locality is flats by the sea, east of Aldingbourne Rife.

FILSHAM (Hollington): TQ/783095; *PNSx* 504; pers. n.[1] This site is on the 100 ft contour, at the top of a two-contour tongue between two streams, and it overlooks a great basin of river meadow which is also overlooked by Pebsham and Worsham; a *hamm* 2, a *hamm* 3 and a *hamm* 6.

FRANKHAM (Wadhurst): TQ/591315; *PNSx* 386; pers. n.[1] The second el. is identified as OE -*hamm* because of the ME spelling -*hame*, which is taken to stand for *hamme*, the dat. sg. inflected form of *hamm*. The site of Frankham is on a promontory of the 500 ft contour, the snout of a ridge, with denes to north and south, but no traditional *hamm*-like topography, unless it be a *hamm* 2b and comparable with the topography of 'the two *hamms*' near TQ/296566 and TQ/295572 in the bounds of Merstham, Surrey, in *BCS* 820.[1]

GLOTTENHAM (Mountfield): TQ/729222; *PNSx* 475, *PN-ing*[2] 124, *MA* 10 (1966) 24; pers. n.[1]+-*ing(a)*-. The site is on the 100 ft contour on a two-contour promontory between Glottenham Stream to the north and Darwell Stream to the south. The water is at about 48 ft–50 ft, and the site is on rather a steep slope; a *hamm* 2b.

HANKHAM or **HANDCOMBE** (Westham): TQ/620055; *PNSx* 447, *NoB* 48 (1960) 159; pers n.[1]. This place stands above the 50 ft contour on a sort of island on the west side of the Pevensey marshes. It is a *hamm* 4.

HIGHAM (now Winchelsea): TQ/9017; *DEPN, PNSx* 538, *NoB* 48 (1960) 147; el. This site is the peninsula between R. Brede and Dimsdale Sewer and Pett Level, and it is partly separated on the west side from Wickham (TQ/898165) by a stream running north into R. Brede. Whether or not the first el. is OE *ēg, īg*, 'island, water-meadow', or OE **īg (īw)*, 'yew tree', does not affect the formal identification of the second el. as -*hamm*, but it would be useful to know the first el. in order to determine whether the sense of the second is a *hamm* 1, 3 or 4 on the one hand or 2 on the other.

ICKLESHAM: TQ/880165; *DEPN, PNSx* 510, *NoB* 48 (1960) 159; *Ikelesham, Icoleshamme* 770 (*c.* 1300) *BCS* 208, *Yclesham, Icles-, Iklesham* 12, *Hykelingesham* 1288, *Ikeleshamme* 1379; pers. n.[1]+*hamm*, with an alternative form containing the gen. sg. of an -*ing* suffix derivative place-name **Hykeling*. The place-name is of a kind discussed in *BNF* 3 (1968) 141–56, esp. 149, *s.n. Muggleswick*. The site is a model for a *hamm* 2a and b or a *hamm* 3. The village lies under the 150 ft contour above a bay in the 100 ft and 50 ft lines, overlooking the Brede levels. It is a question whether the place-name refers to the levels and the village is named from a particular part of them, or the settlement was named from a feature in its vicinity but not *at* the village-site.[2] But Icklesham stands on a peninsula too, and it might appear from this example that a place could be called *hamm*, i.e. could be thought to be *at* a *hamm*, when it actually stood 50 ft or 100 ft higher than, and some distance away from, the marsh or meadow-land to which the name referred.

ILSHAM (extinct parish, lost place near Climping, west of Littlehampton): *PNSx* 139; pers. n.[1] No topographical observation can be made.

KITCHENHAM[1] (Ashburnham): TQ/681131; *PNSx* 478, *NoB* 48 (1960) 159; pers. n.[1] The site is at the end of the two-contour promontory at the end of the ridge under which Ashburnham lies. It is a *hamm* 2.

KITCHENHAM[2] (Peasmarsh): TQ/883250; *PNSx* 532; pers n.[1] Cf. prec. The site is a *hamm* 2 on a tongue of the 50 ft contour projecting into the Rother levels on the opposite side of R. Rother from Ham Green and Wittersham, Kent.

LEASAM HOUSE (Rye Foreign): TQ/909215; *DEPN, PNSx* 537; pers. n.[1]

---

1 In section (a)2 of the bounds as defined by A. R. Rumble, 'The Merstham (Surrey) Charter-Bounds, A.D. 947', *JEPN* 3 (1971), 6–31, at pp. 6 and 12–13.

2 For an example of this, cf. Tranmere, Cheshire, EPNS 47, 257–8, where a settlement inland is named after a sandbank offshore or on the coast.

The site is on the 100 ft contour of a broad promontory overlooking a tributary of the R. Tillingham; a *hamm* 2.

LIDHAM (Guestling): TQ/842168; *PNSx* 509, *NoB* 48 (1960) 159; pers. n.[1] This is another *hamm* 2 promontory site. The next promontory to the west is Doleham, the next to the east Snailham.

LONEHAM (Udimore): TQ/893192; *PNSx* 517; pers. n.[1] Probably a *hamm* 5*b*.

MALHAM (Wisborough): TQ/062287; *PNSx* 134; el. The site is at a broadening of the valley of R. Arun. Malham stands on a broad shelf of 50 ft to 100 ft elevation overlooking another between the water-line and 50 ft. It is a *hamm* 3, but may also be the sort of 'shelf' *hamm* observed at Barkham and Blackham; see above.

MERSHAM (Wartling): TQ/665118; *PNSx* 484; first el. unidentified. The location forbids identification of this place with *Mereshamm, Mæreshamm* 947 (13th) *BCS* 821 and 822; *PNSx* 484; el. *Mereshamm* adjoined Hankham (TQ/6205) and Glynleigh (TQ/6006) near Pevensey Levels. It would be a *hamm* 1, 2*a* or 3. Mersham belongs to App. III1; see below, p. 44.

METHERSHAM (Beckley): TQ/863268; *PNSx* 528, *NoB* 48 (1960) 159; *Maderesham* 1185, *Madreshamme* 1288; perhaps pers. n.[2] The first el. is said in *PNSx* to be OE **Mæðhere* for which is cited Madresfield, Worcestershire,[1] but for this place-name Ekwall[2] and Smith[3] propose OE *mæðere*, 'a mower'. The site is an 'island' of 50 ft contour out in the Rother levels: this is a *hamm* 4 and a *hamm* 2.

NORTHIAM: TQ/829245 site of parish church; *DEPN, PNSx* 522, *NoB* 48 (1960) 159. The place-name is *Higham* (OE *hēah*) with the affix OE *norð*, 'north'. The site would be a *hamm* 2*b* or 5*a*.

OCKHAM (Ewhurst): TQ/784249; *PNSx* 520, *NoB* 48 (1960) 159; el. The site is below the 50 ft contour under a rounded prominence which overlooks the upper level of R. Rother opposite Bodiam: a *hamm* 2.

PADGHAM (Ewhurst): TQ/804250; *PNSx* 520, *PN-ing*[2] 125, *NoB* 48 (1960) 159; pers. n.[1] The site is two miles east of Ockham. It is above the 50 ft contour at the end of a two-contour promontory with streams to south and east and R. Rother to north. It is a square and rounded promontory with a hollow in the end of it just below the site of Padgham; a *hamm* 2*b*.

PADIAM (Icklesham): TQ/908185, Padiam Sewer; *PNSx* 512; *Padyham* 1368, *Padihammesherst* etc., 1413. This may be a manorial place-name, i.e. named after someone with the surname from Padgham. However the name referred to low-lying land in the Brede levels, and so it could well be a *hamm* 1–4.

PAGHAM: SZ/883975; *DEPN, PNSx* 92; pers. n.[1] The location is in a peninsula between Pagham Rife (into Pagham Harbour) and the seaside: a flat, low-lying coastal and estuarine site, a *hamm* 2–5.

PELSHAM (Peasmarsh): TQ/877207; *PNSx* 532; pers. n.[1] The site is at the 150 ft contour at the head of a valley and on a 100 ft shelf; a *hamm* 2*b* or 5. It is near to Tillingham (TQ/887204) which stands on a 50 ft shelf, further east, where it forms a promontory; see below, App. III1, p. 46.

---

[1] See A. Mawer, F. M. Stenton and F. T. S. Houghton, *The Place-Names of Worcestershire*, EPNS 4 (Cambridge, 1927), 209.   [2] *DEPN, s.n.*   [3] *EPN* II, *s.v. mæðere*.

PUSLINGHAM[1] (lost, Eastbourne, TV/6199): *PNSx* 432, *PN-ing*[(2)] 124; pers. n.[(1)]+-*ing(a)*-.

RUTTINGHAM (Fletching): TQ/445247; *DEPN, PNSx* 347, *PN-ing*[(2)] 124, *MA* 10 (1966) 24; pers. n.[(1)]+-*ing(a)*-. The site is on a ridge on the parish boundary between Fletching and Maresfield; a *hamm* 2b or 5a.

SNAILHAM (Guestling): TQ/8517; *PNSx* 510, *NoB* 48 (1960) 159; el. Lower Snailham (TQ/852172) at 50 ft to 100 ft, is the original settlement, Upper Snailham (Icklesham, TQ/859170), at 150 ft, was *Grafhurst* 1296. Lower Snailham is on the south shore of Brede Level at 50 ft to 100 ft on a peninsula 1 mile long and half a mile wide pointing north-west, rising to 164 ft from a 12 ft water-level. This instance is a very prominent example of a promontory *hamm* 2.

STOCKINGHAM (lost, Laughton): *PNSx* 402, *PN-ing*[(2)] 125, *MA* 10 (1966) 24; el.+-*inga*-.

STONEHAM (South Malling): TQ/422119; *PNSx* 355, *NoB* 48 (1960) 159; el. The site is *opposite* a loop in R. Ouse: a *hamm* 1 and a *hamm* 3.

UCKHAM (lost, Battle): *PNSx* 499; pers. n.[(1)]

WELLINGHAM (Ringmer): TQ/435136 Upper Wellingham, TQ/430133 Wellingham House; *DEPN, PNSx* 357, *PN-ing*[(2)] 125, *MA* 10 (1966) 24, *NoB* 48 (1960) 158; el.+-*inga*-. The *hamm* refers to meander-loops of R. Ouse; a *hamm* 1.

WESTHAM: SZ/638045; *DEPN, PNSx* 446, *NoB* 48 (1960) 159; el. The site is at the south end of the low ridge on which Hankham lies. It is a 22 ft to 50 ft elevation outside the west gate of *Anderida* with old marsh- and tide-flats to north (Pevensey Haven), south and west (at Mountney Level). It has now no particular shape, but long ago it was probably either a peninsula or an isthmus, a *hamm* 2b or 4.

WILSON'S CROSS (Ashburnham): cf. Wilson's Fm TQ/672132; *PNSx* 479; *Wylesham* 1296, *Wyleshammes Crouche* 1379. *PNSx* 479 offers an OE pers. n. **Wil* for first el., but it may be a common noun, e.g. OE **wil*, 'trap, snare'.[2] Probably a *hamm* 5b.

WITHYHAM: TQ/494355; *DEPN, PNSx* 370, *NoB* 48 (1960) 159; el. The site is on a tongue, rising through two contours, at the junction between two streams which join to form a feeder of R. Medway; so the topography is both a promontory, a *hamm* 2b, and a broadening of a river valley bottom, a *hamm* 6.

WYNDHAM (Shermanbury): TQ/236194; *PNSx* 213; *Wyndeham* 1248, *Wynde-hamme* 1288. *PNSx* 213 suggests an unsatisfactory personal name for first el.; it is more likely OE (*ge*)*wind*[(2)], 'something winding, a winding stream or path or ascent', although there is no such element in the modern topography. The site is in low-lying land between two streams; a *hamm* 3.

---

1 Puslingham ought to have been in the list of ' ?-*inga*-' place-names in Sussex, *MA* 10 (1966), 24.
2 See *Studies* (1936), p. 156, and *EPN* II, 265, *s.v. wil*.

APPENDIX II

PLACE-NAMES FROM OE '-HĀM', 'WĪC-HĀM', 'HĀM-STEDE' AND 'HĀM-TŪN'

Kent

a. Place-names from OE -hām

i. With an OE personal name as first element (pers. n.[1] unless otherwise stated)

ADISHAM: TR/227543; *DEPN, PNK* 520, *KPN* 8.
BARHAM: TR/209501; *DEPN, PNK* 552, *KPN* 87 and 357.
BODSHAM GREEN (Elmsted): TR/109457; *PNK* 425, *KPN* 9.
CHILHAM: TR/067535; *DEPN, PNK* 372, *KPN* 29 30 and 332.
CUDHAM: TQ/445599; *DEPN, PNK* 23, *KPN* 361.
ELTHAM: TQ/426745; *DEPN, PNK* 2, *KPN* 361. *DEPN* proposes pers. n.[1] in gen. sg. and is preferable to the others.
FAWKHAM: TQ/585655; *DEPN, PNK* 41, *KPN* 245 and 358.
GODMERSHAM: TR/062509; *DEPN, PNK* 377, *KPN* 145; pers. n.[2]
IGHTHAM: TQ/595565; *DEPN, PNK* 153, *KPN* 362.
LENHAM: TQ/898522; *DEPN, PNK* 223, *KPN* 94 and 359.
LEWISHAM: TQ/383753; *DEPN, PNK* 6, *KPN* 209 and 359.
MEOPHAM: TQ/644660; *DEPN, PNK* 103, *KPN* 71 and 359.
MERSHAM: TR/053395; *DEPN, PNK* 417, *KPN* 199 and 359.
OFFHAM: TQ/657573; *DEPN, PNK* 149, *KPN* 254.
OTHAM: TQ/797535; *DEPN, PNK* 228, *KPN* 90, *EPNS* 7 437.
RODMERSHAM: TQ/925618; *DEPN, PNK* 263; pers. n.[2]
STOKE: TQ/823752; *PNK* 123, *KPN* 36; pers. n.[2]
TEYNHAM: TQ/965637; *DEPN, PNK* 278, *KPN* 83.
TUTSHAM (West Farleigh): TQ/705525; *PNK* 160.
WOULDHAM: TQ/713644; *DEPN, PNK* 152, *KPN* 123 and 360.
WROTHAM: TQ/612592; *DEPN, PNK* 155, *KPN* 71 and 360.

ii. With a significant word as first element (OE unless otherwise stated)

ALKHAM: TR/255424; *DEPN, PNK* 438, *KPN* 360; *ealh,* 'temple' (a heathen significance).
BURHAM: TQ/727623; *DEPN, PNK* 147, *KPN* 305; *burh,* 'fortified place'.
CHARTHAM: TR/107550; *DEPN, PNK* 369, *KPN* 46; *cert,* 'rough ground'.
CHATHAM: TQ/757677; *DEPN, PNK* 127, *KPN* 226; PrWelsh *cę̄d* from Brit *cēto-,* 'a wood', probably part of an old pre-English place-name to which OE *-hām* was added. This may be noted again in the place-name Faversham, Kent, and perhaps Caterham, Surrey.[1]
DALHAM (High Halstow): TQ/773754; *DEPN, PNK* 119, *KPN* 301; *dæl,* 'valley', or *dǣl* (Kt *dēl),* 'a share of land'. Topography does not suggest a valley.
DOWNHAM (lost, in Littlebourne TR/198598): *PNK* 523 and 520; *dūn,* 'hill'.

---

[1] See discussion above, p. 22.

FAVERSHAM: TR/010617; *DEPN, PNK* 286, *KPN* 117; **fæfer*, a loan-word from a Brit. form of Lat. *faber*, 'smith'.

FINGLESHAM (Northbourne): *DEPN, PNK* 570, *KPN* 169; *þengel, fengel*, 'prince'.

HIGHAM, HIGHAM UPSHIRE: TQ/713713; *DEPN, PNK* 116, *KPN* 51; *hēah*, 'high'.

HOUGHAM: TR/279399; *DEPN, PNK* 562, *KPN* 361; either a pers. n. **Huhha*, or *hōh*, 'a spur, a promontory'.

ICKHAM: TR/221581; *DEPN, PNK* 521, *KPN* 33; *gēoc*, 'a yoke'.

PECKHAM, EAST and **WEST**: TQ/665487 and 645525; *DEPN, PNK* 159 and 163, *KPN* 289; *pēac*, 'hill'.

SHOREHAM: TQ/518616; *DEPN, PNK* 66, *KPN* 144; *scora*, 'a steep bank, a cliff'.

THURNHAM or **THORNHAM**: TQ/805575; *DEPN, PNK* 233; *þorn*, 'thorn tree; a tract of thorn scrub'.

WALTHAM: TR/108485; *DEPN, PNK* 548; *weald*, 'forest'.

WESTERHAM: TQ/447540; *DEPN, PNK* 75, *KPN* 227; *wester*, adj., 'west, westerly'.

iii. With an OE *-ing* or *-ingas* formation as first element

ENGEHAM [-ndʒ-][1] (Woodchurch): TQ/942375; *PNK* 365, *PN-ing*[(2)] 118 and 171; pers. n.[(1)]+-*ing* (sg.).

FARNINGHAM: TQ/549669; *DEPN, PNK* 40, *KPN* 326, *PN-ing*[(2)] 118 and 119, *MA* 10 (1966) 22; uncertain base+-*inga*- (gen. pl.).

GILLINGHAM: TQ/782691; *DEPN, PNK* 128, *KPN* 303, *MA* 10 (1969) 22, *PN-ing*[(2)] 119; pers. n.[(1)]+-*inga*- (gen. pl.).

ISLINGHAM (Frindsbury): TQ/750690; *PNK* 115, *KPN* 47 and 48, *PN-ing*[(2)] 11 and 119, *MA* 10 (1966) 22; pers. n.[(1)]+-*inga*- (gen. pl.).

MONGEHAM, GREAT and **LITTLE** [-ndʒ-]: TR/350515 and 333509; *DEPN, PNK* 569, *KPN* 44, *PN-ing*[(2)] 120, *MA* 10 (1966) 22; pers. n.[(1)]+-*ing* (sg.).

RAINHAM: TQ/815659; *DEPN, PNK* 261, *KPN* 115, *PN-ing*[(2)] 120, *MA* 10 (1966) 22; pers. n.[(1)]+-*inga*- (gen. pl.).

TERLINGHAM (Hawkinge): TR/213391; *PNK* 451, *PN-ing*[(2)] 120, *MA* 10 (1966) 22; pers. n.[(1)]+-*inga*- (gen. pl.).

WINGHAM: TR/242575; *DEPN, PNK* 537, *KPN* 158; -*inga*-, gen. of a pl. folk-name in -*ingas*. The basis of the folk-name is in doubt; it is either a pers. n. **Wiga*, or *wīh, wēoh*, 'a shrine, an idol', as in Wing, Buckinghamshire[2] and Wye, Kent.[3]

b. Place-names from OE wīc-hām

WICHAM (Strood): TQ/722688; *PNK* 119, *MA* 11 (1967) 91.

[1] Apparently ignored *BNF* 2 (1967), 372.
[2] This is controversial. See *DEPN, s.n.*; EPNS 2, 86; 12, liii; and 14, lvi; *PNK*, p. 384; *PN-ing*[(1)], pp. 67–8; *PN-ing*[(2)], p. 47; and R. E. Zachrisson, *A Contribution to the Study of Anglo-Norman Influence on English Place-Names* (Lund, 1909), p. 89.
[3] *DEPN, s.n.*; *PNK*, p. 384; and *KPN*, p. 182.

WICKHAM, EAST (Bexley): TQ/468769; *DEPN, PNK* 15, *MA* 11 (1967) 90.

WICKHAM, WEST (TQ/389648): see above, App. I. It illustrates the similarity of form and context between place-names in *-hām* and place-names in *-hamm*.

WICKHAM BUSHES (Lydden): TR/246456; *PNK* 453, *KPN* 265, *MA* 11 (1967) 90.

WICKHAMBREUX: TR/221587; *DEPN, PNK* 527, *KPN* 277 and 357 n.1, *MA* 11 (1967) 91.

c. Place-names from OE hām-stede, *'a homestead, the site of a dwelling'*

BEARSTED: TQ/801555; *DEPN, PNK* 202, *KPN* 18, Sandred 89 and 210.

ELMSTEAD or **ELMSTED**: TR/116448; *DEPN, PNK* 425, *KPN* 118, Sandred 214.

HAM(E)STEDE (lost, near Buckland TR/3042 near Dover); Sandred 218 n. 1.[1]

HAMPSTEAD (Yalding): TQ/6950; *PNK* 170, *KPN* 110, Sandred 65 85 and 217.

HAMPTONS (West Peckham): TQ/625523; *PNK* 159, *KPN* 93 and 21, Sandred 231.

HEMSTED (Benenden): TQ/802338; *DEPN* (Hemsted near Cranbrook), *PNK* 348, *KPN* 341, Sandred 88 and 217.

HORSTED (Chatham): TQ/748648; *DEPN, PNK* 128, *KPN* 206, Sandred 218–19.

NETTLESTEAD: TQ/684520; *DEPN* (which, however, identifies the early forms with Nettlestead near Chelsham, Surrey), *PNK* 162, *KPN* 227 and 301, Sandred 221.

PALMSTEAD: TR/165480; *PNK* 543, *KPN* 41, Sandred 222–3.

STANSTEDE (Aldington): *PNK* 464, *KPN* 109, Sandred 226–7.

WHETSTEAD (Capel): TQ/656459; *PNK* 176, *KPN* 179, Sandred 227–8.

d. Place-names from OE hām-tūn, *'home farm, enclosure in which a homestead stands'*

HAMPTON (Herne): TR/158680; *PNK* 510.

KITTINGTON (Nonington): TR/275516; *PNK* 536.

Surrey

a. Place-names from OE -hām

i. With an OE personal name as first element (pers. n.[(1)] unless otherwise stated)

BAKEHAM (Egham): SU/997702; *PNSr* 120.

CHELSHAM: TQ/387583; *DEPN, PNSr* 313.

CHOBHAM: SU/973617; *DEPN, PNSr* 114.

EGHAM: TQ/013713; *DEPN, PNSr* 119.

---

[1] Here also should be noted the lost *Hamstede* near Halling (TQ/6864) which appears only in *hiuetinhamstedi* 765–91 (12th) *Textus Roffensis* (facsimile ed. P. H. Sawyer), EEMF 7 and 11 (Copenhagen 1957 and 1962) 11, 129r, presented as *hiuæinhamstedi* in *BCS* 260; see *KPN*, p. 75, and Sandred, p. 233. The first el. is OE *hīewet*, 'a hewing, a cutting, a place where trees are cut down'; see *EPN* 1, *s.v.* The form was mishandled by Birch. Kemble's reading, nearest to the MS form, is preferred by me, Professor Alistair Campbell and Mr Alexander Rumble on palaeographical grounds, whence speedily taken up by Dr Sandred as a corrigendum in *NoB* 59 (1971), 37–9.

EPSOM: TQ/208608; *DEPN, PNSr* 74.
FETCHAM: TQ/149555; *DEPN, PNSr* 76.
FRENSHAM: SU/837407; *DEPN, PNSr* 177.
HATCHAM (Deptford, Kent, and Camberwell, Surrey): TQ/3678; *DEPN, PNSr* 21, *PNK* 2.
HUNDULSAM (lost, approx. at Oatlands TQ/090650 in Weybridge): *PNSr* 98.
OCKHAM: TQ/066565; *DEPN, PNSr* 143.
PUTTENHAM: SU/93047; *DEPN, PNSr* 209.
WRECCLESHAM (Farnham): SU/826453; *DEPN, PNSr* 175; pers. n.[2] (*DEPN*).

ii. With a significant OE word as first element

BOOKHAM, GREAT and **LITTLE**: TQ/135546; *DEPN, PNSr* 99 and 101; *bōc*, 'beech'.
CHEAM: TQ/243639; *DEPN, PNSr* 43; **ceg*, 'stump'.
HERSHAM (Chertsey): TQ/002658; *PNSr* 109; *heals*, 'neck'.
PECKHAM (Camberwell): TQ/3476; *DEPN, PNSr* 20; *pēac*, 'hill'.
RODSELL (Puttenham): SU/920457; *PNSr* 210. OE *-hām* added to a place-name; *Redessolham, Reddesolham DB*, but *Radesole* 1274.
STREATHAM: TQ/300717; *DEPN, PNSr* 33; *strǣt*, 'paved (Roman) road'.
TONGHAM (Seale): SU/885485; *DEPN, PNSr* 182; *tang*, 'tongs, fork'.
WINDLESHAM: SU/928636; *DEPN, PNSr* 152. The explanation in *PNSr* 152 is now outmoded, as also perhaps is the *DEPN* explanation, by the derivation of Windsor, Berkshire, from **windels*, 'windless', which may be the word in Windlesham.
WOODHAM (Chertsey): TQ/035625; *DEPN, PNSr* 112; *wudu*, 'wood'.

iii. With an OE *-ing* or *-ingas* formation as first element

EFFINGHAM: TQ/117537; *DEPN, PNSr* 102, *PN-ing*[2] 122, *MA* 10 (1966) 25; pers. n.+*-inga-* (gen. pl.).
WARLINGHAM: TQ/355585; *DEPN, PNSr* 339, *PN-ing*[2] 122, *MA* 10 (1966) 25; pers. n.+*-inga-* (gen. pl.).
WASHINGHAM (lost, approx. Clapham Common TQ/285750 in Battersea): *PNSr* 15, *PN-ing*[2] 123, *MA* 10 (1966) 25.
WOLDINGHAM: TQ/371558; *DEPN, PNSr* 339, *PN-ing*[2] 123, *MA* 10 (1966) 25; an *-inga-* (gen. pl.) form on an unidentified base.

b. Place-names from OE hām-stede

HAMPSTEAD (Dorking): TQ/158486; *PNSr* 271, Sandred 245.
RUMSHOT (Egham): TQ/025709; *PNSr* 123, Sandred 248.
SANDERSTEAD: TQ/342614; *DEPN, PNSr* 53, Sandred 248. The explanation attempted in *PNSr* 53-4 is superseded by *DEPN* and Sandred 248-9. The latter neatly razors the problem of a difficult reading.
UNSTEAD (Shalford): SU/992452; *PNSr* 247, Sandred 249.

c. Place-names from OE hām-tūn

HAMPTON (Seale): SU/906465; *PNSr* 182.
ROEHAMPTON (Putney): TQ/225737; *PNSr* 28.

Sussex

a. Place-names from OE -hām

i. With an OE personal name (pers. n.[1]) as first element

BABSHAM (Bersted): SU/9201; *PNSx* 91.
CAKEHAM (West Wittering): SZ/785975; *DEPN, PNSx* 88.
COKEHAM (Sompting): TQ/1705; *PNSx* 201.
COOTHAM (Storrington): TQ/075145; *DEPN, PNSx* 162.
HAILSHAM: TQ/590095; *DEPN, PNSx* 435.
MAGHAM (Hailsham): TQ/608113; *PNSx* 437.
MUNDHAM, NORTH and **SOUTH**: SU/875022 and 877005; *DEPN, PNSx* 72.
MUNTHAM (Findon): TQ/111097; *PNSx* 198.
OFFHAM (South Stoke): TQ/025095; *DEPN, PNSx* 142.
PATCHAM: TQ/301090; *DEPN, PNSx* 293.
SIDLESHAM: SZ/852992; *DEPN, PNSx* 85, Sandred 258.
WEPHAM (Burpham): TQ/043083; *PNSx* 167.

ii. With a significant OE word as first element

BURPHAM: TR/040090; *DEPN, PNSx* 166; *burh*, 'fortified place'.
CLAPHAM: TQ/093063; *DEPN, PNSx* 195, *Studies* (1936) 137, EPNS 14 xlvi, corrections to pp. 22 and 146; **clopp(a)*, 'hill, hump'.
COLDWALTHAM: TQ/025165; *DEPN, PNSx* 126 and 77; *weald*, 'forest'.
GRAFFHAM: SU/927170; *DEPN, PNSx* 21; *grāf*, 'grove, copse'.
OREHAM (Henfield): TQ/223135; *PNSx* 218; *ora*, 'a river bank, a shore'.
PARHAM: TQ/060140; *DEPN, PNSx* 152; *peru*, 'pear-tree'.
SELHAM: SU/9320; *DEPN, PNSx* 28; **s(i)ele, *s(i)elet*, 'sallow, sallow copse' (*DEPN*).
SHOREHAM, OLD: TQ/208065; *DEPN, PNSx* 246 and 247; *scora*, 'steep hill-side, cliff'.
THAKEHAM: TQ/110173; *DEPN, PNSx* 180; *þæc*, 'thatch', or *þaca*, 'thatched roof'.
UPWALTHAM: SU/943137; *DEPN, PNSx* 77; *weald*, 'forest'. This is an apparent analogue of Coldwaltham (see above) and the common Waltham type of name, usually explained as from *-hām*. The site of this one is a valley bottom and could be a *hamm* 6.
WILTING (Hollington): TQ/772109; *PNSx* 504, *MA* 10 (1966) 23, *PN-ing*[2] 41. This place-name should be listed here in case the alternation *Wiltingham* DB but *Witinges* DB, *Wiltinges* (12th), is evidence of that occasional addition of *-hām* to a place-name which is seen in Rodsell, Surrey (above).

b. Place-names from OE wīc-hām

WICKHAM (Hurstpierpoint and Clayton): TQ/291167 and 296164; *PNSx* 275, *MA* 11 (1967) 92.
WICKHAM (Icklesham): TQ/898165; see below, App. III1, p. 47.
WYCKHAM (Steyning): TQ/190133; *PNSx* 237, *MA* 11 (1967) 92.

c. Place-names from OE hām-stede

BERSTED, NORTH and **SOUTH**: SU/9201 and 9300; *DEPN, PNSx* 90, Sandred 251.
BRACKLESHAM (East Wittering): SZ/805965; *PNSx* 87, Sandred 253. An example of a place-name first recorded as a *hām-stede* type but thereafter always as a *-hām* type, whereas in the case of Sidlesham, Sussex (SZ/8598), the earliest form and the majority of the rest are in *-hām*, but *hām-stede* forms intrude early. These names illustrate the near synonymity of *-hām* and *hām-stede* in place-names.
HEMPSTEAD[1] (Arlington): TQ/575102; *PNSx* 409 and 440, Sandred 255 and 256 (the latter cites *KPN* 110 n.1, an important identification).
HEMPSTEAD[2] (Framfield): TQ/487216; *PNSx* 393, Sandred 256.

d. Place-name from OE hām-tūn

LITTLEHAMPTON: TQ/030020; *DEPN, PNSx* 169.

APPENDIX III

PLACE-NAMES FROM EITHER OE '-HAMM' OR OE '-HĀM'

1. Place-names more likely to be from OE *-hamm* than from OE *-hām*

Kent

AYLESHAM (Nonington and Womenswold): TR/240521; *PNK* 534. First recorded in the fourteenth century. Wallenberg's attempt at an etymology is not to be relied on, because the forms *Elis-, Aylis-, Eyles-, Hayles-* at dates from 1367 to 1445 are not safe evidence of so old a personal name as OE *Ægel*. This place-name may be a manorial transference through a surname from Aylsham, Norfolk. However, the late record may be accidental, the first el. may be the OE pers. n., and the place-name may deserve consideration. We have then to note that the site, which was in former times divided between two parishes, is on a promontory of the 250 ft and 300 ft contours and could have been a topographical *hamm* 2b or an upland *hamm* 5a.

BAYTREE (Hoo All Hallows): TQ/8477 may or may not be the location of *Begeham* 1253, as supposed in *PNK* 122; *KPN* 342. *PNK* 122 proposes *bēg-hamm* from OE *bēg*, 'a berry', whence 'a berry-bearing tree'. That this was a common noun composition is indicated by the recurrence of the name at *Begeham* 1253 in Bircholt Hundred (*PNK* 423, *KPN* 342). An instance of the type may also occur at Bayham, Kent, and Sussex.[1]

---

[1] See above, App. I, p. 20.

BETTESHANGER: TR/312525; *DEPN, PNK* 578. Included only because of Wallenberg's identification of the place with *Bedesham* 1086 *DB* and *c.* 1100 *Domesday Monachorum* (*Victoria County History, Kent* III), which Ekwall does not adopt. *Bedesham DB* is formally identical with the *Bedesham* 1278 of Betsham (Southfleet), but Wallenberg obviously assumes that it is for Betteshanger, that it contains a mistake for *Bedles-* (gen. sg. of OE **gebytle* (Kt **betle*), 'house') and that the final el. shows a substitution of OE *hangra* for *-hamm* or *-hām*. The site is at a promontory (hence *hangra*) and could be a *hamm* 5b.

BOCKHAM (Bircholt), now called Brockham: TR/073408; *PNK* 423, *KPN* 339; pers. n.[1] The site is in a recess in the 250 ft contour which would have contained a piece of ground surrounded on three sides by somewhat higher ground; it may be, topographically, a kind of *hamm* 6.

BOLEHAM MARSH (lost, Shorne): *PNK* 117, *KPN* 54; *bulan ham* 774, *BCS* 213; OE *bula*. This was the name of a tract of Shorne Marshes (TQ/6974) near the boundary of Higham Upshire. It indicates a tract of Thames-side marsh and meadowland where cattle were bred and pastured, rather than a village or manor; hence a *hamm* 3 or 4, not a *hām*.

BROXHAM (Edenbridge): TQ/457483; *PNK* 73, *KPN* 213; OE *brocc*, 'badger', or the same as a pers. n. **Brocc*. The site is on a gentle, broad promontory between two streams. The place was a Weald *denn* belonging to Bromley, Kent. Both circumstances suggest a *hamm* 2 or 5 rather than a *hām*, and OE *brocceshamm*, 'badger's meadow', is probably the best suggestion.

CAULDHAM (Capel le Ferne): TR/245388; *PNK* 422; OE *cald*, 'cold'. Wallenberg notes the high altitude and the exposed position, which probably forbids him from offering *-hamm* – he proposes *-hām*. The village is under the summit of a 595 ft hill, between the 500 ft and 550 ft contours, at the head of a valley overlooking Capel le Ferne village. In view of the secondary status of the site and of the lateness of the record, the place-name ought to be considered as OE *cald-hamm*, 'cold paddock', an upland *hamm* 5.

CHIMHAMS (Farningham): TQ/567643; *PNK* 41, *EPN* I s.v. **cimb*; *Chimbeham* 1203; OE **cimb*, 'edge'. The first el. refers to the brink of a steep-sided valley. The position of the place is eccentric in relation to the parish of Farningham, the place is of secondary, hamlet, status and the site, at about 490 ft between two 500 ft contour lines, near the brink of the north-east slope of the Maplescombe valley, would suit an upland enclosure, a *hamm* 5. Chimhams would be a suitable place for an upland meadowing hamlet out on the backside of the parish.

COOKHAM (St Paul's Cray): TQ/486697; *PNK* 23; OE *cōc*, 'cook', or *cocc*, 'a hill, a heap', or *cocc*, 'a cock(bird)'. The name occurs elsewhere, which suggests a common feature, rather than the specialized relationship suggested by *cōc*, 'cook' (cf. below, next item). The site of this is at an upland hollow, a valley of the 150 ft contour, in the high ground on the outskirts of the parish (cf. above, preceding item), and the topography suggests a *hamm* 6 (a piece of ground surrounded by higher ground, a piece of valley bottom) and a *hamm* 5.

COOKHAM HILL (Rochester): TQ/739657; *PNK* 124. If not a manorial extension from a surname from elsewhere, this is another instance of *cocc*[1] or *cocc*[2] with *-hām* or *-hamm.* Cookham near Rochester and Cookham near St Paul's Cray would then both be upland *hamm* names in sense 5, denoting, originally, outlying enclosures in the upland and outer parts of their parent parishes, but it is impossible to tell whether it was hills, haycocks or woodcocks which distinguished them.

ETHNAM (Sandhurst): TQ/811270; *PNK* 344; ?*Echenham* 1313. More information is needed about the early form of this place-name before the first el. can be identified. The second el. is probably *-hamm,* for the site is a clear model of a two-contour promontory *hamm* 2a on the north shore of the upper level of R. Rother.

FARNINGHAM (Cranbrook): TQ/805355. See below, App. III2, p. 47.

FREEZINGHAM (Rolvenden): TQ/865303; *PNK* 352, *KPN* 89, *PN-ing*[2] 119, *MA* 10 (1966) 22, *BNF* 2 (1967) 373 and 3 (1968) 168; pers. n. with an *-inga-* (gen. pl.) formation. The final el. must be *-hamm* despite the ambiguous spellings, since the site is obviously at a *hamm* 2 and 3. The place stands on the 50 ft contour at the end of a promontory of that contour into the upper level, Newmill Channel, of R. Rother.

FROGHAM[1] (Nonington): TR/256504; *PNK* 535; OE *frogga,* 'frog'. The site is between the 200 ft and 250 ft contours on the west side of a valley running up from Nonington village into higher ground to the south-west. It would suit a *hamm* 5 and a *hamm* 6. Cf. below, next item.

FROGHAM[2] (lost, Ham, TR/3254); *PNK* 584. Obviously another frog-ridden meadow. This one, however, was not upland, but was probably in the marshy ground between Ham (itself a *hamm* name) and Worth.

GAYSHAM (Westerham): TQ/431554; *PNK* 75; pers. n.[1] The site is on a bench under the scarp of the North Downs, between the 450 ft and 500 ft contours. The altitude and the distance from watercourses deterred Wallenberg from proposing *-hamm,* but these circumstances do not prevent the occurrence of the el. in sense 5. This is a minor place, and late on record, more like a *hamm* than a *hām.*

HEAVERHAM (Kemsing): TQ/570587; *PNK* 57; OE *eofor,* 'boar' or 'wild boar' (see *EPN* 1, *s.v. eofor*). The topography is not suggestive. The lateness of record and the subordinate status of the place in its parish suggest that this was an upland enclosure of the *hamm* 5 type.

HIGHAM[1] (Hadlow): TQ/603487; *PNK* 178; OE *hēah,* 'high'. This is a late-recorded minor place-name; the site is on a promontory of the 150 ft contour into a broad shelf of the 100 ft level bounded to the west and south by a stream which joins R. Medway. Topographically this is not a clearly marked promontory *hamm,* but there are enough characteristics to suggest a *hamm* 2. However, *Higham* is a common place-name type – there are six in Kent alone – and the type requires more detailed investigation for that reason. It might then appear that the *-ham* in the *Higham* names is often, perhaps usually, a *hamm* in an upland and outback relationship to some centre of population such as a parish nucleus or a parent village; in effect, the two Cookhams and Heaverham (see above) are 'high *hamms*' in relation to their parish villages. What needs to be discovered, but cannot be until more material is available and more detailed field-work has been done, is whether the name *Higham* indicates that there was also in the vicinity a lower *hamm* from which the high one needed to be distinguished. Of course Higham Upshire, OE *heahhaam* is unequivocally -*hām*.

HIGHAM[2] (Littlebourne): TR/198598; *PNK* 524, *KPN* 51; OE *hēah*, 'high'. The site is just under the 100 ft contour on the narrow ridge between the Stodmarsh stream at Elbridge (TR/2059) and the Westbere marshes on R. Great Stour (TR/1960). It is on a ridge between streams and overlooking a riverside marsh. It is topographically suitable for description as a *hamm,* and it is high up in comparison with its surroundings.

HIGHAM[3]: see below, Higham, Great and Little.

HIGHAM[4]: see next item.

HIGHAM, GREAT and **LITTLE** (Milsted): TQ/922575; *PNK* 254; OE *hēah*, 'high'. These two places are about two miles south-east from Milstead. They occupy a promontory of the 350 ft contour at the north-west entrance of the valley, 250 ft, in which lie Doddington (TQ/9357) and Newnham (TQ/9557). Great and Little Higham appear to have been *hamms* in sense 2 or 5 and to have been outlying hill-enclosures in their parish. They might suggest for the place-name *Higham* the general sense 'upland close'. With this meaning may be taken HIGHAM[3] (Monks Horton, TR/1240, *PNK* 427), HIGHAM[4] (Patrixbourne, TR/1755; *PNK* 545, *KPN* 51) and HIGHAMS (Goudhurst, TQ/7237; *PNK* 309).

HIGHAMS: see preceding item.

HORSHAM (Upchurch): TQ/837675; *PNK* 272; *hors,* 'a horse'. The site is topographically suitable to be a *hamm,* being marshland beside R. Medway.

LANGHAM (lost, probably Halden Place in Rolvenden): TQ/850330; *PNK* 353, *KPN* 171; *Lanoham* 833, *BCS* 407; OE *lang,* 'long'. The distribution of Halden Place, Little Halden (TQ/853327) and Halden Lane Farm (TQ/845325) indicates that the place-name Halden extends over quite a mile of ground. It may be that Halden Place, on Halden Lane, marks the former site of a lost, long, straggling village along Halden Lane from TQ/845325 to TQ/850330. But alternatively *Langham* may be describing the long inlets of the 50 ft contour at the head of Newmill Channel (a tidal creek in Roman times) or the Halden names may mark the extent of upland back-closes of Rolvenden parish. 'Long *hamm*' is as likely as 'long *hām*', since *Langham, BCS* 407, is listed among a number of small holdings (*terriculis*) in the Weald and the Ebony marshlands.

LAYHAM'S (West Wickham): TQ/400625; *PNK* 29; *Leyham* 1289; OE *lǣge,* 'fallow'. The name recurs in Leigham, Surrey (see below). These places were minor hamlets in their parishes, which indicates secondary settlement at the location of some 'fallow enclosures'; a *hamm* 5.

LUDDENHAM: TQ/993632; *DEPN, PNK* 287, *KPN* 245; pers. n.[1] This is a village, an ancient manor and a parish: -*hām* would not be unexpected here. Yet the site is apt for the term *hamm,* being under a bay in the 50 ft contour on the edge of Luddenham Marshes; a *hamm* 3 or 4.

NEWNHAM: TQ/954576; *DEPN, PNK* 287; *Newenham* 1177. Also listed

below, App. III2, among the names in -*ham* which might possibly be derived from
-*hām*, on account of its parochial status. But its site lies in the hollow at the junction
of two valleys under moderate 50 ft slopes and the topography might suit a *hamm*
2*b* or 6. With this should be taken NEWNHAM (Wickhambreux, TR/2257; *PNK*
527; *Ne(u)wenham* 1240), which is likely to have been a new *hamm*. It is strange that
the place-name types *Newnham* and *Higham* in the three most south-eastern counties
should be so consistent in form. If it is significant of antiquity that the el. -*hām* is
usually compounded with the strong adj. *hēah* rather than the weak form *hēa* (thus
Higham rather than *Hen-*, *Hanham*), as stated in *EPN* II 227, *s.v.* *hām* (2) (iv), then it
should also be significant that place-names in -*ham* more frequently take the weak
form of the adj. *nīwe* than the strong one. There must be some reason for the consistent
occurrence of weak inflexion in *Newnham*, strong inflexion in *Higham*. It may be a
difference in age; the Newnhams may be all younger than the Highams. It may,
however, be a difference in syntax, in that the first el. of the *Higham* type may have
been a substantive use of the adj.

PEDHAM or **PETHAM COURT** (Eynsford and Swanley): TQ/528677;
PNK 39; *Petham* 1203, *Pettham* 1240; OE *pytt*, 'a pit, a hole'. Petham Court is in a
recess of the 250 ft contour overlooking a wide valley which runs up from Swanley
village: the name indicates an upland *hamm* 5 or 6. This name is identical with Petham
in east Kent (see above, App. I, p. 22): it means '*hamm* with a pit in it' or 'enclosure
at a deep hole or hollow'.

SEPHAM (Shoreham): TQ/510600; *PNK* 68; *Sepham* 1258. Still a mysterious
name, and for the time being Wallenberg's association of this name with *Sydenham*
and with the *Chippenham* type must be accepted. The second el. would then be -*hamm*,
the first el. unknown.

STANHAM (Dartford): TQ/530749; *PNK* 35; *Stonham* 1254; OE *stān*, 'stone,
rock'. A hamlet of Dartford parish, perhaps, as the first el. indicates, a quarry enclosure, a *hamm* where stone was obtained, but the site is a *hamm* 2*a* and 3.

STOCKHAM (Swingfield): TR/227443; *PNK* 455; *Stocham* 1275; OE *stocc*,
'tree stump'. This name indicates a place where timber has been cut down to make
clearings; a *hamm* 5*a* or *b*, of tree-stocks.

SYDENHAM (Lewisham): TQ/352717; *DEPN, PNK* 7, *KPN* 363; *Chipeham*
1206; pers. n.[1] The final el. is quite ambiguous; it could be -*hām* or -*hamm*. The
topography of Sydenham does not resolve the ambiguity of form. It shows that
Upper Sydenham (TQ/346717) is in a valley in the 200 ft and 300 ft contours under
the east side of the Penge hills and that Lower Sydenham (TQ/363715) is on a broad
shelf of the 100 ft and 150 ft contours below the valleys' entrance, which might be a
suitable location for upland enclosures belonging to, and on the outskirts of Lewisham parish. A preference for -*hamm* in this name is encouraged, however, by its
being apparently analogous with the *Chippenham* series of place-names (see *DEPN*,
s.n.) in which the Gloucestershire and Wiltshire examples both contain -*hamm*.
The first el. of this type of name is not identified.

TRAPHAM (Wingham): TR/231570; *PNK* 538; *Tropham* 1270, *Trepham* 1278.
An inexplicable first el. and an ambiguous second el. The site is at an inlet of the

50 ft contour at the head of a tributary of the Little Stour; a *hamm* 3, 5 or 6 is possible. See below, next item.

TWITHAM (Wingham): TR/260568; *PNK* 539; OE *$þwīt$, 'a clearing, a meadow', or *(ge)þwit*, 'cuttings, shavings'. Smith (*EPN* II, *s.v.*) prefers *(ge)þwit*. This is a difficult name formally and the site has no distinctive topographical features. However, this place, Trapham (see above, preceding item) and Rusham (see above, App. I, p. 22) are of secondary status as hamlets in Wingham parish and it is more likely that there would be three *hamms* in a parish than that so confined an area would contain three *hām* settlements.

WETHAM GREEN (Upchurch): TQ/845683; *PNK* 274; OE *wēt*, 'wet'. This place and Ham Green (TQ/847687) occupy a peninsula in the Medway estuary. Wetham Green is on the edge of Horsham Marsh (see above, under *Horsham*). It is in every respect like a *hamm* 2–4.

WINCHAM BRIDGE (Bexley): approx. TQ/456739; *PNK* 15; *Wyncheham* 1327. *EPN* II, *s.v. wince*, gives *-hām* as the second el. and *PNK* 15 proposes '*-hām*, or probably *-hamm*'. The first el. is OE *wince*, 'a winch', but whether referring to some engine or applied figuratively to some twisting or winding feature of the place cannot be perceived. In view of the obscurity of the site and the date of record, *-hamm* is the preferable second el.

Surrey

BALHAM (Streatham): TQ/287734; *DEPN, PNSr* 33; *Bælgenham* 957 (13th) *BCS* 994, *Belgeham* DB etc.; el. The place is first mentioned as a spot on the boundary of Battersea to and from which the boundary perambulations proceeded: this makes a *hamm* 5 rather more probable than a *hām*.

BENSHAM (Croydon): TQ/319675; *PNSr* 49; *Benchesham* 12th, *Bunchesham* c. 1300, *Benchelesham* 1200, *Bynchesham* 1328. For the first el. *PNSr* proposes the gen. sg. of the OE pers. n. *Bynic*, but it could be taken from a topographical use of OE *benc*, 'a bench', with, in one form, *hyll*, whence **Bences-, *Benc-hylles-*. The site, west of Thornton Heath railway station, would be a level, or a slight hollow by a stream, under the end of the bold spur of high ground at Grangewood. This site would be a *hamm* 3 or 5.

BROCKHAM GREEN (Betchworth): TQ/196495; *DEPN, PNSr* 282; OE *brōc*, 'marsh, stream', or *brocc*, 'badger'. The site is a *hamm* in the confluence of Tanners Brook and R. Mole, between the latter and a tributary of the former.

BURGHAM or **BURPHAM** (Worplesden): TQ/006530; *DEPN, PNSr* 162, *NoB* 48 (1960) 158; OE *burh*, 'fortified place'. The site is inside a circular meander of R. Wey: a *hamm* 1 or 2a.

CROHAM (Croydon), **CROHAMHURST** (Sanderstead): TQ/335635; *PNSr* 50; OE *crāwe*, 'a crow'. The locality occupies a likely site for a *hamm* 2b or 5 or 6: the old 'manor house' of Croham was at the north-west end of the present Croham Hurst wood. The *hamm* would have been either Croham Valley at TQ/335639 or the promontory, at Crohamhurst, of the 250 ft or 300 ft contours. The valley is the most likely site, where the last trace of the *hamm* may survive as a playing field.

GRAFHAM (Bromley): TQ/019415 to 022419; *PNSr* 228; OE *grāf*, 'grove, wood'. The site is a *hamm* 2*b*.

GRAPSOME, THE (lost, Hook, TQ/1864): *PNSr* 58; *Grapelingeham* 1179, *Grapeling(g)esham* 1189; first el. an OE pers. n. **Grǣpeling* or some other -*ing* formation, perhaps a common noun. Note that the -*ing* formation appears in gen. sg. inflexion. This place-name looks like the kind discussed *BFN* 3 (1968) 141ff. Both *PN-ing*[2] and *MA* 10 (1966) 1–29 ignore it. The second el. could be either -*hām* or -*hamm*; the name is listed here because the site is not discernible and the place was not an important one.

GREENHAMS (Mickleham): *PNSr* 82. A minor place-name, recorded too late for the purpose of this study. The pl. form indicates field-names.

HATHERSHAM (Nutfield): TQ/307447; *PNSr* 303; *Heddresham* 1196, *Hadresham* 1201. For the first el. *PNSr* proposes an OE pers. n. **Hæðhere*, of a type considered unlikely by Ekwall (*DEPN, s.n. Harrington*). It is likely that the first el. is OE **hǣddre*, 'heather'. There is no remarkable topographical feature here and the place is in a district of Wealden out-woods and *denns*, not major settlements, and so the name indicates a heathland enclosure, a *hamm* 5.

HERSHAM (Walton on Thames): TQ/115641; *DEPN, PNSr* 97, *NoB* 48 (1960) 158; pers. n. **Hæferic*. *NoB* 48 describes this as a *hamm* of R. Mole: it is within a mile of a big *hamm* 1, but it would appear most likely to be a *hamm* 3.

LANGHAM (Egham): TQ/007714; *PNSr* 126; OE *lang*, 'long'. The place is a minor settlement in the low-lying part of Egham parish; hence -*hamm* (3, 4 or 5*b*) rather than -*hām*.

LEIGHAM (Streatham): approx. TQ/309720; *PNSr* 34; OE **lǣge*, 'a fallow'; see above, p. 37, Layham's, Kent.

PETERSHAM: TQ/180730; *DEPN, PNSr* 64; pers. n.[2] The final el. may be -*hām*, but the place is part of the *hamm* (1 and 3) in which Ham parish lies (TQ/1772).

RUSHAM (Egham): TQ/002702; *PNSr* 124; OE *risc*, 'rush'. Like Langham, above, a minor settlement in Egham; the site is at a little hollow at the head of a watercourse and could be a *hamm* 3, 5 or 6.

SNOWDENHAM (Bramley): TQ/003442; *PNSr* 227; pers. n.[1] The site is beside a stream at the edge of a shelf where the contours widen out for the opening of a side-valley; a *hamm* 3 or 6.

TIPHAMS (Ockley): TQ/162390; *PNSr* 278 *s.n. Tipholm*; *Topeham* 1332; unidentified first el. The site is in a valley in a bay of the 250 ft contour, with two streams: it may be a *hamm* 5 or 2.

TYLLINGEHAM (lost, Shere cum Gomshall): approx. TQ/080480; *PNSr* 6 *s.n. Tillingbourne* 251 *s.n. Tenningshook* and 281, *MA* 10 (1966) 25. The Tillingbourne runs from TQ/120469 to SU/996480. It is called *aqua de Tyllingeham* 1279, which could be construed as an -*ingahām* name. But *Tyllingeham* 1279 could alternatively be 'the *hamm* of *Tyllinge*', whilst Tenningshook Wood (Shere, TQ/0748), which is *Tillingshokes* 1336, could be 'the spurs of land belonging to *Tilling*', indicating a lost place-name, a sg. -*ing* formation *Tilling(e)*. Since the form in -*ham* appears only once, and

40

then only as the identification of a stream, it seems more likely that it represents a *hamm* 3, 4 or 6 than a *hām*.

WALSHAM MEADOW (Pyrford): TQ/049576; *PNSr* 133; pers. n.[1] The site, meadows beside R. Wey, is a *hamm* 1 and 3.

WONHAM (Betchworth): TQ/220498; *PNSr* 284, *NoB* 48 (1960) 158; OE *wōh*, 'crooked, awry'. The site is in an angle between the north bank of R. Mole and a tributary brook: a *hamm* 1, 2 or 3.

Sussex

ALBURSHAM (lost, Waldron, TQ/5419): *PNSx* 405; pers. n.[2] The site is not known; there are no *-hamm* spellings, but this is not the parish-name. Waldron is the capital settlement, and is named in *DB*. The territory of this parish contains Brailsham (see below), Waldron (OE *weald-ærn*, 'house in the forest') and *Albursham*. This and Brailsham were probably two woodland or upland *hamms*; a *hamm* 5.

ALVERSHAM (lost, East Lavington, SU/9517): *PNSx* 110; pers. n.[2] The place is not recorded until 1229 and is a minor settlement in Woolavington; probably a woodland *hamm* 5.

AMBERSHAM, NORTH and **SOUTH**: SU/9222; *DEPN, PNSx* 97; pers. n.[1] The site of South Ambersham is SU/916207 in a *hamm* of R. Rother; a *hamm* 1.

ASHAM (Beddingham): TQ/440062; *PNSx* 358; pers. n.[1] **Assa* or OE *assa*, 'an ass'. The place is a minor settlement subordinate to Beddingham (itself a *hamm*; see above, App. I, p. 24) and lying in a coomb in the Downs; more likely a *hamm* 6 than a *hām*.

BARNHAM: SU/960040; *DEPN, PNSx* 137; pers. n.[1] The site would suit *-hamm*, being in low-lying country on a 20 ft to 30 ft knoll among marshes lying 3 ft to 6 ft above datum.

BARPHAM (Angmering): TQ/068089; *PNSx* 164; OE *beorh*, 'hill'. The topography of the site at Lower Barpham (TQ/071092) is that of a great dry valley in the South Downs, with floor at 200 ft to 250 ft and steep sides to 450 ft. This is a candidate for identification as a *hamm* 6. The two Barphams would represent upland outback hill-paddocks for Angmering.

BILLINGHAM (Udimore): TQ/864195; *PNSx* 517, *PN-ing*[2] 123; *Byllyngham* 1401. The site may be a *hamm* – it overlooks the flats of R. Tillingham. This name was not included in the *MA* 10 (1966) lists because it is too late on record, the first el. could be too many things, the *-ing* suffix could be in too many alternative modes and the final el. is too likely to be *-hamm*.

BIRDHAM: SU/823002; *DEPN, PNSx* 80; OE *bridd*, 'a young bird'. The place is in a low-lying level district. There is no distinctive topographical feature. Ekwall obviously decided in favour of *-hamm* to give the name some such sense as 'enclosure where birds feed', since a 'bird-*hām*' would be hard to imagine.

BITTLESHAM (Kirdford): SU/970282; *PNSx* 103. Recorded too late to be useful for the present exercise, this is the name of an insignificant minor place at a *hamm* 1 and a *hamm* 2b.

BLEATHAM (lost, Egdean): *PNSx* 101; OE *blēat*, adj., 'wretched, miserable, naked, bare'. This was probably an enclosure in the valley of the stream near Egdean (SU/9919); a *hamm* 3.

BRAILSHAM (Waldron): TQ/561196; *DEPN, PNSx* 406; *Breilesham* 1230, *Brailesham c.* 1250; OE **brægels*, 'burial-place' (*DEPN*). The site is near a *hamm* 1 but could also be a *hamm* 2 or 5, since it lies on a narrow ridge between two streams. The place is a subordinate settlement in Waldron parish, not recorded until 1230, whereas Waldron is a Domesday Book manor. This suggests a *hamm* rather than a *hām*. The first el. also suggests as the best sense for the name 'enclosure at a burial-place': a *hām* would be unlikely to be near a burial-place, even in the pre-conversion period.

BROADHAM (Singleton): SU/888146; *PNSx* 54; OE *brād*, 'broad'. The site is in a bay of the 350 ft to 400 ft contours north of Levin Down hill: the topography shows a broadening of the valley here; a *hamm* 5.

BROOMHAM (Guestling): TQ/852152; *PNSx* 509; OE *brōm*, 'gorse, broom'. To be taken with Broomham (*PNSx* 403) and Broomham (*PNSx* 485), both of which have -*hamm* spellings (see above, App. I, p. 25).

CALCETTO PRIORY (Lyminster, TQ/0204): at Church Farm, TQ/023047; *PNSx* 171; OE *pinn*, 'a peg', or pers. n.[1] *Pinna*. This is a minor place-name; probably a *hamm* 3.

CALEM WOOD (Mayfield): TQ/614260; *PNSx* 382; *Carleham* 1320. As is indicated by the unsatisfactory dismissal by *PNSx* of the possibility of a ME loan-word from OScand, the etymology of this name is not yet established. It is a minor place-name, which may well be a ME formation, and the site is in a side-valley overlooking R. Rother; probably therefore a *hamm* 5 or 6, not a *hām*.

CHALKHAM (South Malling): TQ/435115; *PNSx* 354, *MA* 10 (1966) 23, *PN-ing*[2] 123; an -*ing* formation on pers. n.[1] The site is between the river and the 50 ft contour on the east bank of R. Ouse, in a broad flat ground, which suggests a *hamm* 3.

CHESTHAM (Henfield): TQ/216179; *DEPN, PNSx* 216; *Chustham* 1305, *Chestham* 1313; might be OE *ciest*, 'coffin', or *ceast*, 'strife'. There is no marked topography – this would be a *hamm* 5.

CHIDHAM: SU/793039; *DEPN, PNSx* 59, *NoB* 48 (1960) 147; *Chedeham* 1193; OE *cēod(e)*, 'a bag', figuratively 'a hollow, a bay'.[1] *PNSx* seeks in vain an OE pers. n. and does not commit itself on the second el.; *NoB* 48 notes the site on a peninsula in Chichester Harbour and pronounces it a *hamm*. The whole peninsula is a *hamm* 2a.

CHILSHAM (Herstmonceux): TQ/635135; *PNSx* 480; pers. n.[2] The second el. is a *hamm* 2, the site being on a promontory, a spur between two valleys and brooks: the next such promontory to the south-east is Nunningham (see below). Also in Herstmonceux parish are Fareham, Pebsham and Clippenham (*PNSx* 481–2).

CLAVERHAM (Arlington): TQ/536090; *PNSx* 409; OE *clǣfre*, 'clover'. The site is low-lying beside a tributary of the Cuckmere River: a *hamm* 3. Sessingham (see below, App. III2, p. 50) is nearby.

---

[1] See *EPN* 1, *s.v. cēod(e)*, and E. Ekwall, *Studies* (1931), p. 70.

CLIPPENHAM (Herstmonceux): TQ/623155; *PNSx* 482; first el. unidentified. This is a minor place and the name is recorded too late (1578) to support -*hām*. The site, on a 100 ft ridge between two streams, could be a *hamm* 2b or 5.

COBHAM (lost, Rotherfield): *PNSx* 377. *PNSx* offers pers .n.[1] *Cobba*+*ham*(*m*). The name does not appear in the 6 in. OS maps of Rotherfield (TQ/5530), and so the site is not known.

COLEHAM (Fletching): TQ/406240; *PNSx* 346. *PNSx* offers pers. n.[1] +*hamm*. The site is a *hamm* 1 and a *hamm* 3 near R. Ouse.

CRAINHAM WOOD (Ewhurst): TQ/772238; *PNSx* 522; *Cran(e)ham* 1207; OE *cran*, 'a crane'. The site and the secondary status of the place suggest -*hamm* rather than -*hām*. OE **crana-hamm*, 'cranes' meadow', would give as good sense as **crana-hām*, 'cranes' village'. There are in the same parish the *hamm* names Ockham and Padgham (see above, App. I, p. 27) and Udiam (see below). The site is a *hamm* 3 at the opening of a side-valley on to the meadows of R. Rother, near Udiam.

CROWHAM (Westfield): TQ/817169; *PNSx* 505, *NoB* 48 (1960) 159. For the first el. *PNSx* proposes OE *croh*, 'saffron' (see *EPN* 1, s.v. *croh*[1]), but EPNS 14 li and 127 follows *Studies* (1936) 167, taking it to be an OE **crōh*, 'nook, corner', supposed by Ekwall (see *EPN* 1, s.v. **crōh*[2]), a word also found for Crowhurst (*PNSx* 502). *PNSx* proposes -*hamm* for the second el., and *NoB* 48 points it out as one of the *hamms* of R. Brede.

DEDISHAM (Slinfold): TQ/111327; *PNSx* 159; pers. n.[1] The site is a *hamm* 3 on R. Arun.

DOLEHAM (Westfield): TQ/832167; *PNSx* 505, *NoB* 48 (1960) 159; OE *dāl*, 'dole, allotment'. The site is a typical promontory *hamm* 2.

DURHAMFORD (Sedlescombe): TQ/772189; *PNSx* 525; *Deramford* 1296. A minor place, not near a major settlement, and hence more likely at a *hamm* than at a *hām*. *PNSx* explains the name as OE *ford*, 'ford', added to a place-name *deor-hamm*, 'animal paddock', perhaps more precisely a 'deer-fold'; a *hamm* 5b. Topographically the site would be a *hamm* 3 and a *hamm* 6.

ELKHAM (Petworth): SU/994256; *PNSx* 116; *Eclesham, Elkesham* 1242, *Ulkeham c.* 1280, *Elkeham* 1310; probably pers. n. The site is a *hamm* 2b.

ERRINGHAM, OLD (Old Shoreham): TQ/205077; *PNSx* 246-7, *PN-ing*[2] 124 and 165, *MA* 10 (1966) 23, *BNF* 2 (1967) 352 and 3 (1968) 171; an -*ing* formation on pers. n. The final el. is probably a *hamm* 1 and 3. Ekwall's caution (*PN-ing*[2] 124) about the site not suiting -*hamm* is the result of bad map-reading. Old Erringham is on the 100 ft contour, 80 ft or so above the river-banks. But it will be observed, both from the OS 1 in. map and on the ground, that before the motor-road and railway were built, there was a great loop, bight and meander of the river immediately south of Old Erringham Farm, and the ground here must have been a *hamm* 1.

FAREHAM (Herstmonceux): TQ/642142; *PNSx* 481; OE *fearn*, 'bracken'. The minor status of the place, the occurrence in the same parish of Chilsham and Clippenham (see above) and of Nunningham and Pebsham (see below), and the site on a promontory between two streams all suggest that this name refers to a *hamm* 2a rather than to a *hām*.

FINCHAM (Hartfield): TQ/463337; *PNSx* 367; OE *fin*, 'heap' or 'hill'. This would be a *hamm* 5.

FLANSHAM (Felpham): SU/960012; *DEPN*, *PNSx* 140. *DEPN* confesses defeat and *PNSx* flounders to no avail. The final el. is -*hamm* on account of the site, very low-lying and bounded by watercourses; a *hamm* 4, 'dry ground in a marsh'.

FLEXHAM PARK (Egdean): TQ/0022; *PNSx* 102; OE *fleax*, 'flax'. This is the name of the ground occupying the triangle between converging streams and valleys at TQ/005215; a *hamm* 2 or 3. A **fleax-hamm* might well be a water-side place in which flax was grown or processed.

FOXHAM (lost, Crowhurst TQ/7411): *PNSx* 502; *Fuccesham* (lit. *Fuccer*-) 772 (c. 1300) *BCS* 208; pers. n.[1] This was an outlier of the manor of Bexhill. It would be such a *hamm* as has been suggested for some of the Kentish specimens – a place upland and outlying from its parent settlement: a *hamm* 5a.

KELSHAM or **KILSHAM** (Petworth): SU/966196; *PNSx* 117; *Kelesham* (13th); pers. n.[1] The site is at the base of a meander loop of R. Rother, a typical *hamm* 1.

KINGSHAM and **KINGSHAM WOOD** (Chithurst): SU/836255; *PNSx* 33; *Kyngesham* 1285; OE *cyning*, 'king'. The wood is on Hammer Stream and overlooks a water-meadow *hamm* 3. The hamlet is low-lying, in the bend of a stream, a *hamm* 1.

KITCHINGHAM (*PNSx*) or **KETCHINGHAM** (1 in. OS New popular edn) (Etchingham): TQ/708279; *PNSx* 456; pers. n.[1]. The site is a narrow *hamm* 3 beside R. Limden, where a small side-valley opens on to the river. A quarter-mile upstream is another such site, Burgham (Etchingham). Etchingham itself is a *hamm* site and is so spelt.

LAMPHAM DROVE (Pevensey): TQ/655073; *PNSx* 445; OE *lamb* (gen. pl. *lamba*), 'lamb'. This would be a pasture for lambs in Pevensey Marshes; a *hamm* 3, a *hamm* 4 and a *hamm* 5b.

LANGHAM WOOD (Houghton): SU/995116; *PNSx* 129; OE *lang*, 'long'. An upland, woodland, minor name; probably a *hamm* 5b or 2b. Cf. Langham, Kent (above).

MARSHAM (Fairlight): TQ/878128; *PNSx* 508, first element OE *mersc*, 'marsh'. The second el. occurs in the plural, *Mersehams* 1340, indicating ME pl *hammes*. The situation of Marsham Farm is at an altitude of more than 100 ft. It stands on a steep-sided 70 ft promontory with streams a quarter of a mile north, east and south. The stream to the north is Marsham Sewer. The site is a good example of a *hamm* in the 'promontory' sense, a *hamm* 2.

MERSHAM (Wartling): TQ/665118; *PNSx* 484, and see above, App. I, p. 27; first el. unidentified – there is not sufficient reliable material. However, the site is a typical *hamm* 2a or b south-east of Nunningham Stream.

MICHELHAM (Arlington): TQ/558093; *PNSx* 409; OE *micel*, 'big'. The place is inside a bend in the Cuckmere River, a *hamm* 1. Cf. Mitcham and Mickleham, Surrey (above).

MIDDLEHAM (Ringmer): TQ/442119; *PNSx* 356; *Middleham* 1248, *Midlyngham* 1288; OE *middel*, 'middle', with an alternative -*ing* suffix derivative. The name is usually compared with Southerham (see below). The site is at a recess in the 150 ft contour. If the *hamm* were topographical, it would have to be the wide ground between the 100 ft and 50 ft contours below Middleham. Probably a *hamm* 5.

NEPSAMS (lost, Fairlight, TQ/8612): EPNS 7 v, addendum to p. 507; *Efflesham* 1296, *Neplesham* 1332 etc. First el. obscure. This was a minor name in Fairlight parish, like Marsham (see above). The pl. form suggests that the name eventually came to describe a group of *hamms* resulting from land-divisions in an original *hamm*.

NEWNHAM PARK (Buxted): TQ/492288; *PNSx* 391; OE *nīwe* (wk. dat. *nīwan*), 'new'. A secondary place in its parish; the name not recorded until 1266. The site is on a hill-spur on the 600 ft contour in Ashdown Forest; probably a *hamm* 2b and a *hamm* 5a. A new *hamm* is probable at such a date whereas a new *hām* is not. See above, p. 37, Newnham, Kent.

NUNNINGHAM (Herstmonceux): TQ/639132; *PNSx* 481, *PN-ing*[2] 124, *MA* 10 (1966) 23; *-ingas* folk-name. Ekwall thinks the final el. is *-hamm*. The site is on a promontory of the 50 ft contour between two brooks, next to and similar to Chilsham (see above).

NUTHAM BARN (Horsham): TQ/163254; *PNSx* 228; OE *hnutu*, 'nut-tree'. A place beside a stream on the edge of Horsham parish, probably a woodland *hamm* 5, but a *hamm* 3 and a *hamm* 4 are possible.

OTHAM (Hailsham): TQ/588058; *DEPN, PNSx* 437; pers. n.[1] Both *DEPN* and *PNSx* propose *-hām* as the second el. Otham occupies a low-lying site suggesting a *hamm* 4 or 5. Hailsham parish also contained Ersham (see above, App. I, p. 25), and, of the next adjacent settlements, Priesthaws (*PNSx* 448, *s.v. Priesthaus*) is at a *hamm* site (1, 2a and 4) and Shepham in Westham (*PNSx* 449) is at a *hamm* site and probably has a *-hamm* name (see below).

PALLINGHAM (Wisborough): TQ/044224; *DEPN, PNSx* 134, *PN-ing*[2] 124, *MA* 10 (1966) 23; *-ingas* folk-name. *PN-ing*[2] gives the wrong reason for preferring *-hamm*. The site is in a great meander loop of R. Arun; a *hamm* 1.

PEBSHAM (Bexhill): TQ/765089; *PNSx* 493; pers. n.[1] The site is a promontory of the 50 ft contour, between two watercourse valleys running into the river at Bulverhythe. This would be a *hamm* 2b. Worsham and Filsham are on similar sites.

PECKHAM (Framfield): TQ/494168; *PNSx* 393; OE *pēac*, 'hill'. Probably a *hamm* 5, a paddock on a hill. The place is above the top end of a side-valley opening on to the valley of a tributary of R. Ouse.

PICKHAM (Guestling): TQ/867149; *PNSx* 509; pers. n.[1] A secondary place in Guestling parish, like Snailham (see above, App. I, p. 28) and Broomham (see above); not recorded until 1220; the site is a promontory *hamm* 2.

PITSHAM (Cocking): SU/878194; *PNSx* 16; pers. n.[1] The second el. is probably a *hamm* 5.

RATHAM (Funtington): SU/812063; *DEPN, PNSx* 61; *Roteham* 1279. The first el. may be pers. n.[1] in gen. sg., but OE, *rōt*, adj., 'cheerful', might be suggested; the name would then indicate a cheerful plot. The place is on a stream at a broad inlet of the 50 ft contour; so a *hamm* 3 and a *hamm* 5 are likely.

SAKEHAM (Shermanbury): TQ/223190; *PNSx* 213; pers. n.[1] The site is a *hamm* 3 in the confluence between R. Adur and a tributary stream.

SALTHAM (North Mundham): SU/889013; *PNSx* 75; OE *salt*, 'salt'. The place is in low-lying ground, formerly marshy, between streams which were probably tidal in former days; a *hamm* 2a or 4. Close to Saltham is Crimsham (see below, App. III2, p. 49).

SESSINGHAM: see below, App. III2, p. 50.

SHEPHAM (Westham): TQ/597055; *PNSx* 449; OE *scēap*, 'sheep'. A late minor name for a sheep-pasture; the site is a *hamm* 2a and a *hamm* 4.

SHOPHAM BRIDGE (Sutton): SU/985185; *PNSx* 121; pers. n.[1] The site is obviously a *hamm* 3 on R. Rother.

SMALLHAM (West Grinstead): TQ/184230; *PNSx* 187; OE *smæl*, 'narrow'. A minor place-name in the parish, not recorded until 1327; the first el. also suggests *-hamm* rather than *-hām*.

SOUTHERHAM (South Malling): TQ/425094; *PNSx* 355; OE *sūðerra*, comp., 'more southerly', or perhaps *sūðer*, adj., 'south, southern'. This name is usually compared with Middleham (see above). The site is in a recess, a cleft, in the 50 ft and 100 ft contours under Mount Caburn, and opening onto the Brooks of R. Ouse. It exemplifies a *hamm* 6 and a *hamm* 3.

STEDHAM: SU/8622; *DEPN, PNSx* 29; *Steddanham* 960 *BCS* 1055, *Stedeham* 1086 *DB, Stodeham* 1187; OE *stēda*, 'steed', alternating with *stōd*, 'a stud'. Ekwall hazards also on OE pers. n. **Stedda*, hypochoristic form of *stēda*. The whole sense would be 'stallion's *hamm*', a *hamm* where a stallion would stand. The site is at the base of a meander loop in R. Rother: an obvious *hamm* 1.

STOPHAM: TQ/025185; *DEPN, PN-ing*[2] 50, *PNSx* 120; *Stopeham* 1086 *DB, Stopham* 1234; OE **stoppe*, 'hollow, pit', from *stoppa*, 'a pail' (*DEPN*), or pers. n.[1] **Stoppa* (presumably a nickname 'Bucket'; *PNSx*). Whichever is preferred, the site is at the base of a meander half-loop of R. Rother to west and south, at the confluence with R. Arun which is the east edge of the *hamm*: it is a *hamm* 1 and a *hamm* 3.

TILLINGHAM (Peasmarsh): TQ/889205; *PNSx* 532, *PN-ing*[2] 125, *MA* 10 (1966) 23; *-ingas* folk-name. The site is on the 50 ft contour on the side of a promontory rising to 100 ft projecting into the levels of R. Tillingham between that river and a tributary: a typical promontory *hamm* 2. Pelsham is on the next promontory.

TODHAM (Eastbourne): SU/904208; *PNSx* 18; *Tadeham* 1086 *DB, Tadham* 1274; pers. n.[1] (*PNSx*) or OE *tāde*, 'toad'. The site is a *hamm* 3 on R. Rother.

UDIAM (Ewhurst): TQ/771242; *PNSx* 520, *PN-ing*[2] 125, *BNF* 3 (1968) 171, *NoB* 48 (1960) 159; *Hudeham* 1180, *Hudi(h)am c.* 1207; perhaps an *-ing* formation on pers. n. The final el. is probably *-hamm*, since the place is on a round promontory of the 50 ft contour containing a height of 192 ft and lies between 50 ft and the river-bank (18 ft): a *hamm* 2 and a *hamm* 3.

WAKEHAM (Terwick): SU/819229; *PNSx* 43; pers. n.[1] The site overlooks the meadows beside R. Rother; a *hamm* 3.

WARNHAM: TQ/159335; *DEPN, PNSx* 238, *Studies* (1936) 68; *Werneham*

1166, *Warenham* 1219, *Wernham* 1256. The first el. is remarkably ambiguous, as *DEPN* and *Studies* (1936) make clear. In the latter Ekwall proposes the meaning 'low-lying meadow where stallions grazed', from **wrǣna*, 'a stallion', and *-hamm*.

WASHINGHAM (Greatham): TQ/049157; *PNSx* 151, *PN-ing*[(2)] 125, *MA* 10 (1966) 24; *-ingas* folk-name. The place lies in a bight of the valley of R. Ouse near Greatham, and the basis of the folk-name is OE **wæsse*,[1] 'a wet place, swamp, marsh'; a *hamm* 1, a *hamm* 3 and a *hamm* 4.

WENHAM (Rogate): SU/789236; *PNSx* 41; pers. n. The site overlooks the meadows of R. Rother; a *hamm* 3.

WICKHAM (Icklesham): TQ/898165; *PNSx* 512, *MA* 11 (1967) 92. Formally the name resembles OE *wīc-hām* (see above, App. II, p. 34), but in fact it is probably another instance of *wīc-hamm* like West Wickham, Kent (see above, App. I, p. 22). The site does not appear to follow the association with Roman roads discerned for other place-names in Wickham (< *wīc-hām*). This Wickham is over the 50 ft contour on the end of a promontory, separated from the peninsula on which Winchelsea (formerly *Higham*) lies, by an isthmus at 16 ft to 11 ft above sea-level. It overlooks an inlet of Brede Levels to the north and Pett Level and Dunsdale Sewer to the south. Wickham is therefore a promontory *hamm* site, a *hamm* 2.

WYTHIHAM (1327, lost, West Grinstead): *PNSx* 370 n.2; OE *wīþig*, 'a withy, willow'. A minor place-name rather than an ancient settlement-name. The first el. also suggests *hamm*, 'marshy enclosure where willows grow'; a *hamm* 1, 3, 4 or 5.

2. Place-names more likely to be from OE *-hām* than from OE *-hamm*

Kent

BETSHAM (Southfleet): TQ/605715; *PNK* 47; pers. n.[(1)] Neither spelling nor topography is decisive. Wallenberg, *PNK*, prefers *-hām* rather than *-hamm*, probably on account of the monothematic OE pers. n.

FARNINGHAM (Cranbrook): TQ/805355; *PNK* 320, *KPN* 327. Entered in this list without much assurance. This name has claims to be regarded as a *-hām* one only on account of its similarity to the *-ingahām* type. In fact, it may well be a manorial transference, through a surname from Farningham in north Kent.

FRININGHAM or **FRINNINGHAM** (Thornham or Thurnham): TQ/820589; *PNK* 235 and 40, *KPN* 326–7, *MA* 10 (1966) 22, *PN-ing*[(2)] 119. See discussions in these sources. This name might well belong in App. II, among place-names from OE *-hām*; it is placed here to allow for the uncertainty of form of the first el. and the uncertainty of the identification of its earliest record, which may leave it open to interpretation as a late-recorded minor name from *-hamm* rather than an early major name from *-hām*.

NEWNHAM: TQ/954576; *DEPN, PNK* 297; OE *nīwe*, 'new'. Since this is a parish-name, *-hām* might be preferred, as Ekwall and Wallenberg propose. But see above, App. III1, for discussion of Newnham as a *-ham < -hamm* place-name type.

---

[1] See *EPN* II, 237, *s.v. *wæsse*.

PINEHAM (Whitfield): TR/315455; *PNK* 566, *KPN* 305; OE *pinn,* 'a peg', or pers. n. **Pinna.* Formally the second el. could be *-hām* or *-hamm,* but the place was a manor in *DB* and this status requires us to prefer *-ham.*

Surrey

COBHAM: TQ/109599; *DEPN, PNSr* 87, *NoB* 48 (1960) 158. This is an ancient settlement and manor. Yet its site is a most obvious *hamm.* Despite the complete absence of *-hamm, -homm* spellings, and despite the importance of this place (a history purported to go back to the seventh century), the configuration of the river-bend in which stands Cobham Court (TQ/110595) and the opposite bend inside which lies Cobham Park, compels reservations about deriving this place-name from *-hām.*

DIRTHAM LANE (Effingham): TQ/105531; *PNSr* 102; OE *drit,* 'dirt'. The second el. could be *-hām* but the sense of the first el. and the location near the parish boundary would suit well with a *hamm* 5. However the place is named in *DB* and this status requires allowance to be made for *-hām* rather than *-hamm.*

MERSHAM: TQ/289534; *DEPN, PNSr* 300; first el. uncertain. For the second el. Ekwall supposes *-hamm, PNSr* supposes *-hām.* The site of Merstham, at the entrance to Gatton Bottoms, is a *hamm* 6. But this is an ancient manor and settlement – it had its own *denns* in the Weald – and so it has the status of a *hām.*

MICKLEHAM: TQ/170535; *DEPN, PNSr* 81, *NoB* 48 (1960) 158; OE *micel,* 'big'. *PNSr* 81 prefers *-hām* as final el. and compares Mitcham (*PNSr* 51). *DEPN* allows either *-hām* or *-hamm.* *NoB* 48 emphasizes the conspicuous *hamm* (1 and 3) at the place. Mickleham is an ancient manor and parish. To that degree it is a *hām*: but it stands on a *hamm,* and so the *-hām* el. is in question.

MITCHAM: TQ/269687; *DEPN, PNSr* 51, *NoB* 48 (1960) 158. There is much the same problem here as with Mickleham, save that at Mitcham the configuration of the site is less remarkable than it is at the other place. I am more ready to agree with *DEPN* upon OE *micel+hām* than with the ambiguity of *PNSr* 51.

PACHESHAM (Leatherhead): TQ/150580; *PNSr* 80; pers. n.[1] The place was a Domesday Book manor and its name contains an archaic OE pers. n. as first el., which suggests *-hām* for the second el., although the place is not a parish-centre and the site resembles a *hamm* 1, 2 or 3.

Sussex

APPLEDRAM: SU/840032; *DEPN, PNSx* 65; OE *apuldor,* 'apple-tree'. Both authorities admit *-hām* or *-hamm,* since the sense would be like that of the following name. But Appledram is the name of a parish and is on record from the eleventh century, which indicates the possibility of a *hām.*

APPLESAM (Coombes): TQ/195072; *PNSx* 224. This could well be emended with a new derivation, replacing the pers. n. invented *PNSx* 224 by OE *æppel,* 'an apple', in the sense 'apple-tree'.[1] In this place-name, as well as in the preceding one, *-hamm* would give good sense ('apple-tree enclosure' or 'orchard'), but so would *-hām* ('apple-tree village; homestead at an apple-tree'). Furthermore the place was

---

[1] See *EPN* I, *s.v. æppel.*

a manor in *DB,* which suggests *-hām* and leaves the name to this list rather than to App. III1.

BEDHAM (Fittleworth): TQ/017222; *PNSx* 126; pers. n.[1] An unimportant place in a secluded valley, but the first el. appears to be an old pers. n.[1] and the site is not definitely shaped like a *hamm.* Of course it might be a *hamm* 5 or 6, for it is in old woodland and the place stands on the steep brink and in the bowl of a 250 ft deep coomb.

BILSHAM (Yapton): SU/970020; *PNSx* 145; pers. n.[1] The spelling *Bilsom* 1732 is far too late to be relied upon as significant of *-hamm.* Bilsham (*DB*) is earlier on record than Yapton (12th) and it could well be the senior settlement site: but the site is a *hamm,* low-lying, beside the stream Ryebank Rife, opposite Flansham.

BOREHAM STREET (Wartling): TQ/665113; *DEPN, PNSx* 483. This is a common type of place-name, occurring also in Essex and Hertfordshire. The first el. is OE **bor,* 'a hill'. *PNSx* 483 proposes OE *bār,* 'a boar',+*hamm,* but *EPN* 1 42, *s.n. bor*[1], follows *Studies* (1936) 131 with OE **bor+hām.* Whether *PNSx* 483 proposes *-hamm* for semantic reasons ('boar-pen') or on account of the topography is not clear. The place is on a promontory between Nunningham Stream and Wallers Haven and could be a *hamm* 2.

BURGHAM (Etchingham): TQ/702279; *PNSx* 456; OE *burh,* 'fortified place'. Since Burgham was a *DB* manor, its name deserves consideration for inclusion in the *-hām* list, but the site is at one of the *hamms* of the little R. Limden, the next one north-west from Kitchingham, or Ketchingham, and this makes the final el. ambiguous.

CRIMSHAM (Pagham): SZ/897009; *PNSx* 94; pers. n.[1] This is not an important place so much as a place with a long purported history: it is a manor house (*hām*) at a site which is a *hamm* like the neighbouring Saltham (see above, App. III1, p. 46). The first el. need not be the pers. n. **Crymi* cited by *PNSx* 94; it could be (another invention) the el. OE **cryme,* 'a crumb of land', discerned in EPNS 45 171.

EARTHAM: SU/939093; *DEPN, PNSx* 70; OE *erþ,* 'ploughing, ploughed land'. As second el. *-hamm* would give good sense. The site is at a large bay in the 250 ft contour, and so *-hamm* may be topographically justified here. But Eartham is a parish and a name from *-hām* might be likely.

GREATHAM: TQ/045155; *DEPN, PNSx* 151; OE *grēot,* 'gravel'. It is an open question whether the place is named from a settlement or the settlement is named from the place. The site is a *hamm* 1 and a *hamm* 3, but Greatham is a parish and was a manor in *DB,* which indicates the possibility of *-hām.*

HARDHAM: TQ/039175; *DEPN, PNSx* 128, *BNF* 3 (1968) 170, *MA* 10 (1966) 24, *PN-ing*[2] 125; OE fem. pers. n.[2] in gen. sg. and with *-ing* formation. I am not as sure now as I was in *BNF* 3 that this is a place-name from *-hām* or that it is to be regarded as primarily an *-inga-* place-name. The *-ing* formation is only an alternative to the gen. pers. n. The problem in the present exercise is the ambiguity of the *-ham* spellings. Hardham *is* a parish, and its name formally resembles a numerous class of *-hām* compositions, but the site is a *hamm* 1, a great loop of R. Arun south of Pulborough.

HIGHAM (Northiam): TQ/820249; *PNSx* 523, *NoB* 48 (1960) 159; OE *hēah*, 'high'. This is a *DB* manor. The site is rather too uphill to be a *hamm* 1,2 or 3 on R. Rother, but it could well be a *hamm* 5.

HORSHAM: TQ/175305; *DEPN, PNSx* 225; OE *hors,* 'a horse'. As final el. *hamm* would give good sense, 'horse paddock, horse meadow'. The name may be compared with Stedham (SU/8622; *DEPN, PNSx* 29), which seems to be 'stallion's *hamm*'. Horsham is not at a particularly marked topography. It is an ambiguous *-hām/-hamm* form. However Horsham is a parish and the place is recorded early, and so *-hām* is strongly supported.

KINGSHAM (Donnington): SU/857037; *PNSx* 69; OE *cyning,* 'king'. The site may be a *hamm* and the place is of secondary status in Donnington parish; but this was a royal estate by name, so that *-hām* is possible.

RACKHAM: TQ/050135; *DEPN, PNSx* 156. In *DEPN* the first el., OE *hrēac,* 'rick, heap, stack', is taken to be *Hrēac,* a name for Rackham Hill, $+hām$. In *PNSx* the name is thought to be OE **hrēac-hamm*, perhaps 'a rick-yard'. The spelling *Racomb* 1724 is too late to be relied on, but the sense 'rick-*hamm*' is at least as likely as a hill-name 'Hayrick'. However Rackham is a parish, and so it is possible that the name contains *-hām*.

SESSINGHAM (Arlington): TQ/540083; *DEPN, PNSx* 410, *MA* 10 (1966) 23, *PN-ing*[2] 124; pers. n.[1]$+$*-inga-* (gen. pl.). There are no *-hamm* spellings and *DEPN* and *PN-ing*[2] cite *-inga-hām*. The site is on a brook at an inlet of the 50 ft contour in flat ground by Cuckmere River, not far from Claverham and Michelham, and it is probably a *hamm* like that at Erringham. However Sessingham was a manor in *DB* and *-hām* remains likely as final el. in the name.

TELHAM (lost, Battle): *PNSx* 499. This place is not on record until *Telleham* (12th), and the site is not known: there is clear doubt about the authenticity of the name Telham Court (TQ/756149, formerly Quarry Hill), and Telham Hill (TQ/759139) and Telham Place (TQ/765138) are not of ascertained antiquity. Telham Hill is a promontory site, a promontory of the 300 ft contour, and could be a promontory *hamm* 2. However, since the name cannot be clearly associated with *-hamm*, it is listed here as a possible *-hām* name.

WORSHAM (Bexhill): TQ/754091; *DEPN, PNSx* 494; pers. n.[1] Great Worsham and Worsham Manor (TQ/760095) are on a promontory site but do not necessarily form a promontory *hamm*. Great Worsham itself, however, *is* at a *hamm* site. But this is an ancient manor and *-hām* would not be unexpected in such a name.

The beginning of the year in England, c. 500–900

KENNETH HARRISON

Writing a little before the year 1000, Ælfric in a homily on the Feast of the Circumcision (1 January) had this to say about the beginning of the year:

We have often heard that men call this day 'the day of the year', as if this day were foremost in the year's circuit; but we find no explanation in Christian books, why this day is accounted the beginning of the year. The old Romans, in heathen days, began the year's circuit on this day; and the Hebrew people at the vernal equinox; the Greeks on the summer solstice; and the Egyptian nations began the reckoning of their year at harvest. Now our reckoning begins, according to the Roman institution, on this day, for no religious reason, but for the old custom. Some of our service books begin on the Lord's Advent; yet it is not on that account the beginning of the year.[1]

Byrhtferth's Manual, written not long afterwards, is a rather diffuse work, relying heavily on Bede; in discussing the month of January, Byrhtferth remarks that 'the first day, and the whole month, is hallowed by Christ's nativity',[2] and, while placing January at the forefront of the year, cannot be said to have untangled Ælfric's problem, which the historical resources of the time did not allow him to do. If we are better placed today, we must nevertheless find our way through four or five centuries during which the calendar was unsettled, when primitive reckonings by the moon and the arbitrary system of indictions were slowly absorbed into the Christian era. Without attempting to cover all the ground that an answer to Ælfric would require, a few points can be isolated and a few positions made clear, as far as the sources would seem to allow.

THE DIONYSIAC TABLES

Although the Easter tables of Dionysius are familiar to the medieval historian,

---

[1] *The Homilies of the Anglo-Saxon Church: the First Part containing the Sermones Catholici or Homilies of Ælfric,* ed. B. Thorpe (London, 1844–6) 1, 99. I am grateful to Professor Dorothy Whitelock for this reference and for much else, as will appear.

[2] *Byrhtferth's Manual,* ed. S. J. Crawford, Early English Text Society 177 (London, 1929), 63. *The Menologium,* of about the same date, after mentioning the Nativity goes on to say that January is the start of the year: *Anglo-Saxon Minor Poems,* ed. E. van K. Dobbie (New York, 1942), p. 49.

they are seldom mentioned in any context but that of annalistic writing or as the source of the Years of Grace in Bede's chronology. They were calculated in the first instance for the ninety-five-year term stretching from 532 to 626, divided into five cycles of nineteen years each; a second series from 627 to 721 was calculated by one Felix, called Gillitanus;[1] and they became authoritative in the west partly through the influence of Bede's *Historia Ecclesiastica*.[2] And, it is fair to add, on other merits: an earlier computation by Victorius of Aquitaine, besides being less accurate, did not include several features, such as indictions and the lunar cycle, by which Dionysius, or rather, his predecessor Cyril, created a 'ready reckoner' or conversion table, that went far beyond the needs of anyone seeking only the date of Easter. The nature of this ready reckoner will be clear from the extract from the first nineteen-year cycle, from 532 to 550 inclusive, shown in table 1.[3] Certain particulars are left out, since

TABLE I

Anni domini	Indictiones	Epactae	Lunae circulus	Dies dominicae festivitatis
DXXXII	X	NUL.	XVII	III id. Apr.
DXXXIII	XI	XI	XVIII	VI kal. Apr.
DXXXIIII	XII	XXII	XVIIII	XVI kal. Mai.
DXXXV	XIII	III	I	VI id. Apr.
DXXXVI	XIIII	XIIII	II	X kal. Apr.
....	....	....	....	....
DL	XIII	XVIII	XVI	VIII kal. Mai.

they are of no concern here; only the early years of the cycle, and the last year, are quoted for illustration. The four remaining decennovenal cycles, each drawn up separately, carried the information down to 626.

The column for epacts is of some importance, since the number of the epact denotes the age of the new moon, diminished by one day, on the first day of that year. Like many others, the nineteen-year cycle of Dionysius starts with *epacta nulla* on 1 January, and calculations of the date of Easter are based on the Julian calendar.[4] Ælfric would not have included Easter tables among his

[1] *Bedae Opera de Temporibus*, ed. C. W. Jones (Medieval Academy of America, Cambridge, Mass., 1943), p. 73.

[2] *Venerabilis Baedae Opera Historica*, ed. C. Plummer (Oxford 1896). Cited henceforth as *HE*, and notes as Plummer, *Opera Historica* II.

[3] B. Krusch, 'Studien zur christlich mittelalterlichen Chronologie', *Abhandlungen der Preussischen Akademie der Wissenschaften, Phil.-Hist. Klasse* 7, no. 8 (Berlin, 1938), 70; Migne, *Patrologia Latina* 67, cols. 493–8.

[4] Krusch, 'Studien', p. 60 and F. Ruhl, *Chronologie des Mittelalters und der Neuzeit* (Berlin, 1897), pp. 179–80. Only in the Alexandrian cycle did the pattern of epacts change in September. Dionysius had to face the problem of reconciling Alexandrian (luni-solar) epacts with the Roman (solar) calendar.

'Christian books', for they lack scriptural or patristic authority. Turning to the *lunae circulus*, we have here the cycle of which Meton (about 430 BC) was the originator in the Mediterranean world, based on the fact that nineteen solar (tropical) years equal 6,939·6 days and 235 lunar (synodical) months equal 6,939·7 days, so that every nineteen years the new moons occur again on the same solar days; and on this cycle all Easter calculations are based. By inserting embolismic, or intercalary, months into seven of the nineteen years a luni-solar calendar is created, not very accurate by modern standards but establishing a reliable sequence of years. And it is important to recognize that a luni-solar calendar can be checked by observation of the phases of the moon. That such a calendar was employed by the Anglo-Saxons in pre-Christian times we know from Bede, *De Temporum Ratione*, ch. xv.[1] Since the Dionysiac tables contain a column for *lunae circulus* as well as for *anni domini*, dates derived from a luni-solar reckoning could readily be transferred to the Christian reckoning; and the nature of several dislocations – as they appear to be – among the early annals of the *Anglo-Saxon Chronicle* can be interpreted as a break-down in the process of transfer.[2] In the same chapter of *De Temporum Ratione* Bede refers to the feast at midwinter, which the pagans took as the beginning of the year: 'incipiebant autem annum ab octauo kalendarum ianuariarum die, ubi nunc natalem domini celebramus'. Bede, therefore, did not make Christmas the start of his year, but 1 January, as his practice shows: thus in *De Temporum Ratione*, ch. xxii, he says 'Si ergo uis scire hoc uel illo die quota sit luna, computa dies a principio mensis ianuarii usque in diem de quo inquiris . . .' and again, for days of the week, 'computa dies a Kalendis ianuariis usque . . .'.[3] The opinion put forward by R. L. Poole that 'Bede in his theoretical work *De Temporum Ratione* states, as a matter which needs no explanation, that the year reckoned from the Incarnation began on Christmas Day' is not true;[4] Bede nowhere says so.[5] We can combine 'romani a bruma . . . inchoant [annum]' (*De Temporibus*, ch. ix) with '[dominum] in solstitio brumali VIII Kalendas ianuarias natum' (*De Temporum Ratione*, ch. xxx), but the former refers to Roman usage (from Numa, it was believed) before the Julian calendar was adopted.[6] To a contemporary of Bede there could be no doubt where the Year of Grace started; by Ælfric's time it had become 'the old custom'.

Computing is one matter, popular usage another. By about the end of the

[1] Jones, *Opera de Temporibus*, p. 211.
[2] K. Harrison, 'Early Wessex Annals in the Anglo-Saxon Chronicle', *EHR* 86 (1971), 527–33.
[3] Jones, *Opera de Temporibus*, p. 223.
[4] R. L. Poole, *Studies in Chronology and History* (Oxford, 1934), p. 8.
[5] A point already noticed by C. W. Jones, *Saints' Lives and Chronicles in Early England*, (Ithaca, N.Y., 1947), p. 210, n. 65.
[6] Jones, *Opera de Temporibus*, pp. 236 and 298. In his notes pp. 354–7, Jones would partly attribute the preservation of 1 January as New Year's Day to Bede and his followers.

fourth century, or a little earlier, the church had fixed its celebration of the Nativity on 25 December, 'in solstitio brumali', the time of the winter solstice. The octave of this feast lasted until 1 January, blurring the distinction of dates, and we shall find that for a considerable stretch of the eighth and ninth centuries a popular reckoning of the year from Christmas was to all intents and purposes universal. In Rome at least the kalends of January were distinguished by celebrations of a rather jolly character, which earned the disapproval of Boniface,[1] and as a festival the day would not commend itself to the church at large. By contrast, the ecclesiastical calendar, and the martyrologies that arose from it, began on 1 January, although, as Ælfric noted, the beginning of the ecclesiastical year was often fixed at Advent. In the long run nobody could escape from the Julian calendar; but the rough-and-ready Christmas reckoning is understandable, and Midwinter lingered as a name even after the Conquest.

The second column of table 1, containing the indictions, now calls for consideration. It is hardly necessary to explain that indictions run in fifteen-year cycles, starting with AD 312. What is called the Greek indiction, beginning the year on 1 September, is regularly found in papal documents from the time of Pelagius II (584);[2] Gregory the Great's letters to the Augustinian mission are dated by indiction alone, and when Archbishop Theodore arrived from Rome in 669 he, too, employed this indiction for his official acts. As a complication, in *De Temporum Ratione* (ch. XLVIII), written in 725, about six years before the *Historia*, we have the categorical assurance that 'incipiunt autem indictiones ab VIII kal. octobres ibidemque terminantur'. Did Bede take this statement from a computistical tract, now lost? He often followed the custom of his day by quoting written sources without acknowledgement, though scrupulous enough about the spoken word. Or did he believe that the indiction should be brought into line with the equinox? To these questions an altogether satisfactory answer has not yet been found;[3] asking them is only a signal to the effect that from 725 onwards we must take account not only of the indiction employed by the papal chancery, 1 September, but also of what seems to be – though we cannot be sure – Bede's invention of 24 September, the 'Bedan indiction', also known as 'Caesarean' from its employment under the Holy Roman Empire.

[1] Monumenta Germaniae Historica, Epistolae III, ed. E. Dümmler (Berlin, 1892), 301.
[2] P. Jaffé, *Regesta Pontificum Romanorum,* 2nd ed. (Leipzig, 1885), p. ix.
[3] Jones, *Opera de Temporibus,* p. 268. Dr N. Brooks has drawn my attention to a paper by J. Halkin, 'La Nouvelle Année au 23 Septembre', *AB* 90 (1972), 56, where it is stated that, from the fourth century until the middle of the fifth, the Byzantine year was sometimes reckoned from the birthday of the Emperor Augustus, 23 September, coinciding with the autumnal equinox. Yet the choice of 24, rather than 22 or 23, September is curious. In a calendar so adjusted that *epacta nulla* falls on 1 January, as in the first year of a Dionysiac nineteen-year cycle, there is another *epacta nulla* on 24 September, which may explain Bede's preference for this day; the equinox can vary from year to year, whereas the epact is fixed.

BEDE'S 'HISTORIA ECCLESIASTICA'

A puzzling item in the *Historia* was noticed some seventy years ago by Plummer.[1] Since we are told that King Oswiu died on 15 February 670 and the next king, Ecgfrith, on 20 May 685 in the fifteenth year of his reign, from this and other apparent contradictions Plummer concluded that Oswiu must have died in 671, and that Bede or his transcribers had made a mistake. Later scholars have hesitated between these figures; yet the puzzle was not manufactured by Bede but arises from the assumption that a king succeeds immediately after the death of the preceding ruler. Apart from the interregnum between James II and William and Mary, the sovereigns of England have indeed ascended the throne in this fashion since Plantagenet times. We are not bound to suppose, however, that such ideas are applicable to seventh-century Northumbria. Writing within a few years of the event, Eddius Stephanus records a two-month interregnum between the accession of King Osred and the death of his father, power meanwhile being seized by an interloper;[2] and although we need not decide that hitches of this kind always occurred, equally the occasion need not have been unique. Once the assumption is discarded, it seems evident that Ecgfrith's regnal years were counted from a day lying between 1 and 17 September 670 and that all the statements made by Bede are in harmony.[3] There still remains a more general problem: did Bede, when writing the *Historia,* adopt the indiction as the starting-point of his year? R. L. Poole, whose wide experience as a chronologer lent considerable force to his argument, wrote as follows:

The *Annus Domini* was a recent importation. It was not intended to provide an era for historical purposes; its object was merely to serve as a reference in Easter tables. Naturally therefore it was taken as running on the same lines as the Indiction; and as the Indiction began four months before what we call the current year, so was the Year of Grace reckoned.[4]

Although the opening sentence is undoubtedly true, the remainder is rather questionable; still, Poole's theory should be judged by his own criterion that 'the acceptance of this principle for the period with which we are concerned will, I believe, produce harmony among a number of dates which are regarded as discrepant'.

These dates largely centre round the reign of Ecgfrith, and Poole took his stand on the interpretation of a comet which Bede records in 678, though in

[1] Plummer, *Opera Historica* II, 211.
[2] *The Life of Bishop Wilfrid, by Eddius Stephanus,* ed. B. Colgrave (Cambridge, 1927) ch. LIX, p. 128. Bede, who was not writing a political history, does not mention the affair.
[3] K. Harrison, 'The Reign of King Ecgfrith of Northumbria', *Yorkshire Archaeol. Jnl* 44 (1972), 79.
[4] Poole, *Studies,* p 40.

fact it appeared to European eyes about mid-August 676 and was visible for some three months. Dismissing the possibility that Bede was wrong, Poole argued from manuscript evidence that the figure was originally written 677, and 'reckoning that year from the Indiction of 1 September, his [Bede's] date included almost the whole of the time during which the comet was visible'.[1] This interpretation was challenged by Wilhelm Levison, arguing again chiefly on textual grounds.[2] But there is another objection to Poole's reasoning. Bede and his contemporaries well knew that the duration of comets can vary; seven to eighty days are the limits given by Bede himself, and no ominous significance was read into the length of time as such.[3] What startled them, and still surprises us, is the sudden brilliant appearance of a hairy star in the skies: 'apparuit mense Augusto stella quae dicitur cometa . . .' (*HE* IV. 12), a sentence that comes next before the downfall of Bishop Wilfrid. A comet appearing in the middle of August was a portent then but not in September.[4] Bede made a mistake over the date, perhaps let down by his source; what matters to the chronologer is that Ecgfrith's eighth year was thought by Bede to include the month of August 678.[5]

Levison's other arguments were more broadly based, although, like Poole, he believed that Ecgfrith had succeeded immediately on Oswiu's death, and his chronology has not been generally accepted. And we are faced with still another problem. In Ecgfrith's third year a council took place at Hertford, presided over by Archbishop Theodore;[6] the acts are dated 'die XXo IIIIo mensis Septembris, indictione prima', that is, 24 September of the indictional year beginning 1 September 672.[7] Bede wrote 'Factum est autem haec synodus anno ab incarnatione Domini DCLXX tertio', and Levison proposed that Bede had made a small mistake: 'he simply forgot that the indictions did not change, with the years of Incarnation, on Christmas Day, but four months earlier'.[8] We can, however, exonerate Bede from a mistake of this kind by looking at the matter in another way, by supposing him faced with an entry in a Dionysiac table: (in the margin) 'concilium in loco Herutford die XXo IIIIo Sept.' and (in the adjacent columns of the table) 'AD DCLXXIII, Ind. I'.

---

[1] Poole, *Studies*, p. 43.

[2] *England and the Continent in the Eighth Century* (Oxford, 1946), p. 267.

[3] *De Natura Rerum,* PL 90, col. 244.

[4] According to *ASC* C, the comet of 1066 (Halley's) appeared on 24 April and 'swa scean ealle þa. vii. niht' – a spectacle of shortest duration, yet it had done its work and the Bayeux Tapestry makes it foreshadow the Battle of Hastings in October.

[5] Harrison, 'The Reign of King Ecgfrith', p. 79. [6] *HE* IV. 5.

[7] That Theodore used the Greek indiction is shown by the date 'sub die XV Kalendas Octobres, indictione VIIIa', 17 September 679, for the Council of Hatfield (*HE* IV.15) in Ecgfrith's tenth year. The comet was dated by Bede to August 678, in Ecgfrith's eighth year; hence he came to the throne between 1 and 17 September 670.

[8] Levison, *England and the Continent,* p. 267.

People accustomed to using these tables would find no problem here.[1] The indiction was the official reckoning, and any date falling between 1 September and 31 December 672 was properly described as AD 673, indiction I. As it turned out, the acts of the council were dated by the day of the month and the indiction only, and Bede filled in the Year of Grace quite correctly.[2] If he had written 672 he would have broken his own rule, in *De Temporum Ratione*, ch. XLIX, for finding the indiction, namely to the *annus domini* add three and divide by fifteen, the remainder being the indiction.[3] There was no need for the Year of Grace to be reckoned from the indiction; it had been fixed by its inventor to begin on 1 January, with the Julian calendar, and Bede would have acted strangely if at the moment of promoting AD as a historical era he had changed the start of the year without warning.[4]

Poole's arguments, therefore, are capable of another interpretation, and a consequence of those arguments needs to be mentioned very briefly, since it has called forth a series of emendations to the text. For example, Bede says that King Edwin was killed in battle on 12 October 633[5] and King Oswald nine years later on 5 August,[6] the year 642 being given in the Recapitulation,[7] and he goes to considerable trouble over explaining why Oswald was deemed to have reigned nine years.[8] Since Edwin died in October, however, by the requirements of Poole's theory the year should be changed to 632, and consequently Oswald died in 641, a date which now seems to be generally accepted.[9] Yet not only has the theory been applied in an inconsistent fashion – the month of August falls into the 'neutral' part of the year, unaffected by the indiction, and it is not clear why an event in October should be preferred *a priori* – but we must suppose Bede wrong; and wrong not about an event distant in time and place, but about the fate of a Northumbrian hero, the martyr-king whose death, translation and miracles occupy six chapters of the book[10] and whose fame had spread to Germany and Ireland in Bede's lifetime.[11] In addition, there is no manuscript evidence in favour of emending the date.

---

[1] It seems that the Dionysiac tables were formally introduced at the Synod of Whitby in 664 (Poole, *Studies,* p. 32), but how much earlier they came into use is not at the moment clear.

[2] Harrison, 'Reign of King Ecgfrith', p. 81.

[3] Jones, *Opera de Temporibus,* p. 269. In practice he could get the number from a Dionysiac table.

[4] Levison (*England and the Continent,* p. 277), in arguing that Bede began the year at Christmas, quotes a passage from *De Temporum Ratione,* ch. XLVII (Jones, *Opera de Temporibus,* p. 267), in which the occurrence of that festival at Rome is dated 'anno ab eius incarnatione iuxta Dionysium septingentesimo, indictione quarta decima'. Levison continues: 'The 14th Indiction began on 1 September 700; therefore Christmas 701, as mentioned, would have been Christmas of A.D. 700 if the number of the year had changed on the 1st of January.' It was indeed Christmas 700, because the year A.D. 701 is here qualified by the indiction.

[5] *HE* II. 20.   [6] *HE* III. 9.   [7] *HE* V. 24.   [8] *HE* III. 1 and 9.

[9] *Handbook of British Chronology,* ed. Sir F. Maurice Powicke and E. B. Fryde, 2nd ed. (Royal Historical Society, London, 1961), p. 11.   [10] *HE* III. 9–13 and IV. 14.

[11] *HE* III. 13. In contrast, Bede does not state the day or month of Wilfrid's death, and gives the year only by inference: for a discussion see my forthcoming article in the *Yorkshire Archaeol. Jnl,*

Again, Pope Honorius wrote a letter to Honorius of Canterbury dated 11 June, 7th indiction, i.e. 634,[1] in which he made arrangement, in case either occupant of the Canterbury and York sees should die, for the surviving bishop to consecrate a successor. With this letter came the *pallium*, sent to each bishop as a concession in view of the distance involved, 'pro qua etiam re singula uestrae dilectioni pallia pro eadem ordinatione celebranda direximus'. In a letter to King Edwin,[2] not dated but thought to have been written at the same time,[3] the pope writes 'duo pallia utrorum metropolitanarum, id est Honorio et Paulino, direximus'. It seems clear that in June 634 the pope was unaware of the death of Edwin and the flight of Paulinus to Kent. We do not know how quickly news could get to Rome at this time, or how soon after the battle it became possible to send a messenger. At a much later date, in 1051, Robert of Jumièges was appointed to the see of Canterbury; from the C and E versions of the *Chronicle* it can be shown that he set off before 25 March and returned on 27 June.[4] This period of about fourteen weeks for the double journey tallies with a calculation that in the twelfth century a normal traveller, on horseback, took about seven weeks for the single journey, in reasonable weather.[5] On the other hand Archbishop Theodore's journey occupied the year May 668–May 669, although in his case entertainment and fatigue took their toll; his party had reached northern France (Paris, Meaux, Sens) when the approach of winter forced them to stop.[6] If Edwin was killed in October 633, more especially if messengers were delayed in starting and travelled part of the way on foot, the news might well not have reached Rome in eight months; if his death was in October 632, it seems very unlikely indeed, whatever the circumstances, that the news should have taken twenty months.

It would seem that when confronted by the official acts of Theodore, Bede felt obliged to take notice of the indiction; left to his own devices he ignored it.[7] Throughout the *Historia* we discover the indiction only in official documents, with one exception[8] and that in a papal context. As a historian Bede

---

'The Deaths of King Aldfrith and of Bishop Wilfrid'. Some difficulties over the career of Archbishop Deusdedit seem to have been resolved by P. Grosjean, 'La Date du Colloque de Whitby', *AB* 78 (1960), 235–8. Bede's date for the consecration of Archbishop Willibrord is considered below, p. 69.

[1] *HE* II. 18.   [2] *HE* II. 17.   [3] Plummer, *Opera Historica* II, 110.

[4] *The Anglo-Saxon Chronicle: a Revised Translation*, ed. D. Whitelock, D. C. Douglas and S. I. Tucker, (London, 1961), p. 116. (This work is cited henceforth as Whitelock, *ASC*.) The C text is here starting the year at Lady Day; Easter was on 31 March; and by dating Robert's appointment to mid-Lent 1050, and his return to 1051, with the information from E that he went to Rome 'in the course of the same Lent', C tells us that he started before 25 March.

[5] R. L. Poole, 'The Early Correspondence of John of Salisbury', *Proc. of the Brit. Acad.* 11 (1924) 31–2; repr. *Studies*, pp. 263–4. I am grateful to Professor Whitelock for raising this point of time.

[6] *HE* IV. 1.

[7] Although in his formal letter, 5 November 734, to the bishop (later archbishop) of York, he employed the formal style of the indiction; see Plummer, *Opera Historica* I, 423 and II, 388.

[8] *HE* II. 4.

could not be expected to approve this arbitrary and ambiguous form of reckoning, and such was his influence in promoting the Christian era that we shall find the indiction soon losing the primacy, or virtual monopoly, it had once enjoyed.

ANNALS AND CHARTERS

After Bede, the Recapitulation with which he ended his work,[1] drawn up in annalistic form, received additions for some seventy years. The manuscript tradition of these Northumbrian annals in their Latin version, included in the *Historia Regum* ascribed to Simeon of Durham,[2] has been discussed by P. Hunter Blair,[3] and by C. Hart;[4] they were also drawn on, as is well known, by the D,E recension of the *Chronicle*.[5] In general there is good agreement over dates, although between 776 and 789 the *Chronicle* seems for the most part to be a year ahead, probably owing to an error of transcription in the archetype.[6] When adjustment is made, the balance of evidence would strongly suggest that the year began at Christmas throughout this series of annals, at all events decidedly not with the 'Bedan indiction' on 24 September. Independent light on Northumbrian practice is revealed by Alcuin's preference for beginning the year 'cum nato Christo et crescente luce', in opposition to those at the court of Charles the Great who argued for the indiction.[7] It is desirable to mention here, in passing, that the time-reckoning of the Northumbrian annals is on occasion remarkably precise, day and month being given for mundane events, and eclipses down to the hour. In other kingdoms, and at a later date, this degree of precision was not to be attained.

Next we consider the evidence to be derived from charters.[8] Mostly they originate from Mercian kings, and it will be convenient first to consider the extensive series preserved from the reign of King Cenwulf. As to regnal years, Offa had died in 796 on 26 July (Simeon) or 29 July (*ASC*); Ecgfrith his son reigned 141 days;[9] thus, if Cenwulf came to the throne immediately, his reign began 14–17 December 796, a date not in conflict with charter evidence, as we

---

[1] *HE* v. 24.   [2] *Simeonis Monachi Opera*, ed. T. Arnold, Rolls Series (1885).
[3] *Celt and Saxon: Studies in the Early British Border*, ed. N. K. Chadwick (Cambridge, 1963), p. 63.
[4] C. Hart, 'The Ramsey Computus', *EHR* 85 (1970), 29.   [5] Whitelock, *ASC* p. xiv.
[6] K. Harrison, 'The Beginning of the Year among Bede's Successors', *Yorkshire Archaeol. Jnl* 42 (1967), 193. The opening paragraphs of this paper are now obsolete.
[7] MGH, Epistolae IV, ed. E. Dümmler (Berlin, 1892), 231; Levison, *England and the Continent*, p. 277.
[8] Printed *Cartularium Saxonicum*, ed. W. de G. Birch (London, 1885–93), cited henceforth as *BCS*. This discussion would not have been possible without the help of Professor Whitelock, who supplied me with a select list of some eighty documents and, more important still, her comments on the reliability of the material and on a number of debatable points. I have also drawn on P. H. Sawyer, *Anglo-Saxon Charters: an Annotated List and Bibliography* (Royal Historical Society, London, 1968), and occasionally on M. Treiter, 'Die Urkundendatierung in angel-sächsischer Zeit', *Archiv für Urkundenforschung* 7 (1921), 53.
[9] Whitelock, *ASC* pp. 31 and 36.

shall presently see. The documents involving Cenwulf (and other kings) and Archbishop Wulfred of Canterbury are set out in table 2. *BCS* 322 (contemporary copy) is of 805, 13th indiction, 8 Cuthred of Kent, 26 July, 'die sabbati

TABLE 2

BCS number	Indiction	AD	Day	Regnal year	Wulfred's year
316	12	804	—	8 Cenwulf	—
321	13	805	—	9 Cenwulf	*electus*
322	13	805	26 July Saturday	8 Cuthred of Kent	*sedens in solio*
332	4	811	21 Apr.	15 Cenwulf	6
335	4	811	1 Aug.	15 Cenwulf	6 (?7)
341	5	812	—	16 Cenwulf	7
378	2	824	—	2 Beornwulf	19
379	2	824	30 Oct.	—	—
384	3	825	—	3 Beornwulf	20

quo transfiguratus est Christus'; and 26 July was a Saturday in 805. Haddan and Stubbs, supposing the feast to be on 6 August (a Wednesday in 805), as it is now, held that Wulfred had been consecrated on the previous Sunday, because the grant is made to him 'sedenti in archiepiscopatus solio'.[1] But the Transfiguration has been an unsteady feast, celebrated on a variety of days, and only settling down to 6 August in commemoration of the victory over the Turks at Belgrade in 1456. Anciently it fell on 26 July, as in the Martyrology of Oengus, or 27 July, as in Willibrord's Calendar, besides other days;[2] perhaps 26 July was the day of Wulfred's enthronement, as Haddan and Stubbs suggest, but, being a Saturday, can hardly represent the consecration, which presumably took place on one of the Sundays after the death of his predecessor Æthelheard, 12 May 805.[3] We turn next to *BCS* 321 (contemporary) which is signed by

[1] *Councils and Ecclesiastical Documents relating to Great Britain and Ireland,* ed. A. W. Haddan and W. Stubbs (Oxford, 1869–78) III, 559. As a parallel to this use of *solium,* Alcuin writes to Æthelred of Northumbria (790–5) 'non decet te in solio sedentem regni rusticis uiuere moribus' (MGH, Epistolae IV, 71).

[2] *The Martyrology of Oengus,* ed W. Stokes, Henry Bradshaw Society 29 (London, 1905), 72 and *The Calendar of St Willibrord,* ed. H. A. Wilson, HBS 55 (London, 1918), 35; on the whole question see F. G. Holweck, *Calendarium Liturgicum* (Philadelphia, 1925), pp. 230 and 258.

[3] Haddan and Stubbs, *Councils* III, 468. Professor Whitelock thinks that *sedenti in solio* could merely mean 'occupying the archiepiscopal see'. Dr N. Brooks takes it as evidence that Wulfred was not yet consecrated, and has kindly furnished me (9 June 72) with the following note, which corrects my earlier view that the consecration took place before 26 July 805:

'If one accepts *BCS* 322 as evidence that Wulfred was not consecrated by 26 July 805, then the other Wulfred charters fall into place. One can accept the evidence of *BCS* 335 that his consecration must have been after 1 August 805, and of *BCS* 378 that the Council of *Clofeshoh* of 824 was in his nineteenth year; *BCS* 379 shows this to have taken place at the end of October, and Wulfred's consecration is therefore pushed to October 805 or later. Thus there is no need to amend *BCS* 355, and no need to assume that there was one Council at *Clofeshoh* before 24 July and another in October [which I had previously thought]. In this context there is no significance in the fact that *BCS* 378

Wulfred as *electus*; according to the *Chronicle* he received the pallium in 804 (*recte* 806, since at this point *ASC* is two years behindhand). This charter is therefore in order, but *BCS* 316 is a late copy that seems to have been interfered with: 804, 12th indiction, 8 Cenwulf and witnessed by *Wlfredus archiepiscopus*. Thomas Elmham, in whose compilation the text is preserved, was a monk of St Augustine's, Canterbury, writing in the fifteenth century, and his material will have passed through the hands of transcribers who had access to copies of the *Chronicle* from the end of the eleventh century at latest.[1] From one copy, or some other source, they may well have derived the year 802 for the death of Æthelheard,[2] given as 803, *recte* 805, in extant versions of the *Chronicle*; nothing could be more natural than to substitute, in a document dated 804, the name of Wulfred for his predecessor. The years AD, indictions and regnal years of the remaining charters in table 2 offer no problem; Cenwulf was dead in 821, according to the *Chronicle*.

With these problems out of the way, the remaining Cenwulf charters which are of value for dating purposes can be collected into table 3.[3] In *BCS* 309,

TABLE 3

BCS number	Indiction	AD	Day	Regnal year of Cenwulf
293	7	799	—	3
296	7	—	17 July	3
308	11	803	6 Oct.	—
309	11	803	12 Oct. Thursday	7
310, 312	11	803	12 Oct.	—
326	15 (?1)	808	16 Apr. Easter Day	12
340	5	812	31 Oct.	—
348	7	814	25 Nov.	—
350	7	814	26 Dec.	18
353	7 (?8)	815	19 Mar.	19
357	9	816	—	20
358	9	816	27 July	20
359, 360	10	817	—	21

issued at a Council of *Clofeshoh*, Cenwulf's seventh year is correct for October 803, and 12 October was a Thursday in that year; although *BCS* 308 omits the regnal year it has seven witnesses in common, and like *BCS* 310 and 312 was issued at this same council. All are authentic texts, though, except for *BCS* 310

and 379 are in different formulas. *BCS* 378 is in favour of Canterbury, and drafted by the Canterbury scriptorium, *BCS* 379 in favour of Worcester and drafted by that scriptorium.'

This straightforward view has the advantage of avoiding emendation. The former charter, witnessed by Beonna (of Hereford) as *electus*, will have been drafted earlier than the latter, where he is *episcopus*. Perhaps *sedens in solio* can be taken in the sense of 'administering the see'.

[1] Whitelock, *ASC* pp. xii–xvii.
[2] *Historia Monasterii S. Augustini Cantuariensis,* ed. C. Hardwick, RS (1858), pp. 13 and 339.
[3] The forged *BCS* 338 and suspicious *BCS* 349, with no regnal year in any case, have been omitted.

and 312, known from late copies only. The 11th indiction expired, however, on
1 (or 24) September 803, and if we are to insist that these charters are using an
indictional year beginning in September then emendation of the *annus domini* is
required for them and for *BCS* 379 (table 2) as well. It is altogether more likely
that by this period the indiction was being copied mechanically from the
column next to the *annus domini* in a Dionysiac table (see table 1) without
thought for its real significance.[1] That the copying could be careless, initially or
at a later stage, is shown by *BCS* 326, because Easter Day did fall on 16 April in
808, for which the proper indiction is 1; and unless the regnal year and *annus
domini* are both wrong, then the indiction of *BCS* 353 should be 8. In *BCS* 350
(a late transcript but genuine) if the regnal year is right the *annus domini* will be
813 in modern reckoning though 814 by a year changing at Christmas, and the
indiction becomes correct also. As for *BCS* 340 and 348, in the absence of a
regnal year it does not seem possible to decide whether indiction or *annus
domini* is wrong, if Christmas dating is systematic throughout this reign; from
the consistent look of table 3, and the particular weight attaching to *BCS* 309
and its neighbours, we can hardly doubt that it was.

With these pointers from Mercia in the early ninth century we may now
work backwards through the eighth. *BCS* 236, from the Worcester cartulary, is
probably genuine: 780, 3rd indiction, *passio Sancti Mauricii*, i.e. 22 September.[2]
BCS 235 is a forgery, also dated to 22 September 780, 3rd indiction, adding 23
Offa; but if the date is sound – as opposed to the content of the charter – and
if the year began at Christmas, then it would seem that Offa came to the throne
after 22 September 757.[3] Information from the reign of his predecessor
Æthelbald is perhaps less meagre than would appear from table 4. Bede states
that Tatwine was consecrated to Canterbury in 731, in the fifteenth year of
Æthelbald, on Sunday 10 June.[4] *BCS* 152 is dated 2nd indiction, 17 Æthelbald,

---

[1] Expressed in another way, the charters in tables 2 and 3 dated in the critical period 25 September
to 24 December (or 30 December), that is, *BCS* 308, 309, 310, 312, 340, 348, 350 and 379, carry an
indictional number that is one too few if we assume that the people who drafted them were using
an indiction beginning in September and a Year of Grace beginning on 25 December (or 1 January).
Hence the ecclesiastical scriptoria began their indictional years and Years of Grace at the same time.
(It should be noted, as Dr Brooks reminds me, that *BCS* 310 and 312 are contemporary copies.)
On the evidence of *BCS* 350 the year began at Christmas, in agreement with other evidence from
Alcuin and the Northumbrian annals. Of Carolingian practice it has been said that 'fréquemment on
a fait concorder l'indiction avec l'année de l'Incarnation ou même avec l'année du règne' (A.
Giry, *Manuel de Diplomatique* (Paris, 1894), p. 728).

[2] In a paper by P. Chaplais, to which Professor Whitelock has drawn my attention, 'Some Early
Anglo-Saxon Diplomas on Single Sheets: Originals or Copies?' *Jnl of the Soc. of Archivists* 3
(1965–9), 325, it is stated that this charter shows use of the 'Bedan indiction' of 24 September.
This would be true only if we could be assured that the scribe did not take the indiction from the
column adjacent to the *annus domini* in a Dionysiac table, as indicated above.

[3] Unfortunately the reliable *BCS* 202–4, 223, 230 and 239 do not carry regnal years, and *BCS* 232,
256, 265, 267 and 269 are too muddled to be of use.

[4] *HE* v. 23 and 24.

TABLE 4

BCS number	Indiction	AD	Day	Regnal year of Æthelbald
(Bede and ASC)	—	731	10 June	15
152	2	—	*die indictionis*	17
149	15	—	29 Oct	22
150	—	—	29 Oct	22
154	4	736	—	—
162	10	742	—	27 (?26)
178	2	749	—	33

die indictionis, i.e. 1 or 24 September 733; and taken together these sources would indicate that Æthelbald came to the throne on or after 2 or 25 September 716, in which year King Ceolred died.[1] But BCS 149 and 150 raise a difficulty, since Bishop Wor (Ealdwine) of Lichfield is a signatory to both and he is stated by Simeon to have died in 737.[2] Birch's emendation of the regnal year to *XVII* then leaves the indiction still hanging in the air, since it should be *secunda* for October 733. No sense can be made of these figures; yet the chief interest of table 4 lies in the transition from dating by indiction alone to dating by indiction together with *annus domini*. It is true that BCS 162 and 178 are later copies, the former with suspicious features (and seemingly the wrong regnal year), so that the Year of Grace could have been added; yet when we consider that Bede's *Historia* was circulated in 731 (or 732) the use of this style seems reasonable enough in 742 or 749. Much better evidence comes from BCS 154, of 736, 4th indiction, a grant by Æthelbald preserved in a contemporary copy, which has had the benefit of a careful scrutiny by Sir Frank Stenton.[3] It contains the title *rex Britanniae*, perhaps an equivalent of *Bretwalda*, as Professor Whitelock suggests; yet Stenton's examination throws no doubt on this title or its context or – though the point is not explicitly made – on the year and style. Certainly we can say that not all documents carrying the indiction alone have been interpolated.[4] Abroad, the first official use of the Year of Grace appears in the preamble to the *Concilium Germanicum* of 21 April 742, without the indiction.[5] And Krusch has found an entry in Berlin Phillipps 128 to the effect that *Teudericus rex Francorum* died 737 years 'a nativitate autem Domini usque ad praesentem annum'.[6] At the same period, in England, the indiction begins to

[1] *HE* v. 24.
[2] Northumbrian annals in *Simeonis Monachi Opera* II, 32. Dates from this source are usually reliable.
[3] 'The Supremacy of the Mercian Kings', *EHR* 33 (1918), 439.
[4] Thus, apart from others, of the charters preserved in Elmham's *Historia*, ed. Hardwick, genuine or spurious, and ranging from 675 to 737, printed by Birch as BCS 35, 36, 42, 67, 73, 88, 90, 141, 149 and 150, all except BCS 42 are dated only by the indiction.
[5] MGH, Legum II, *Capitularia Regum Francorum,* ed. A. Boretius (Hanover, 1883), p. 84.
[6] B. Krusch in *Mélanges Chatelain* (Paris, 1910), p. 232. At the Council of Chelsea in 816 (Haddan and

take a lower place; after *BCS* 149 and 150, which seemingly cannot be later than 737 since they are witnessed by Bishop Wor, hardly any more charters are dated by indiction alone.[1]

The remaining material from Mercia starts after the death of King Cenwulf in 821; according to *BCS* 370 (contemporary copy) his successor Ceolwulf I was 'consecrated' in 822, 15th indiction, on 17 September, and although the true date could be 821 – reckoned as 822 from the Greek indiction on 1 September – a revival or survival of this reckoning seems to be unlikely when some other considerations are taken into account. In the first place, 17 September was an Ember Day (suitable for ordinations) in 822 but not in 821. Again, Cenwulf died at Basingwerk in Flintshire, apparently while engaged in trouble with the Welsh;[2] we have seen that the death of one monarch need not always be immediately followed by accession of the next; and the rite of 'consecration' could also be delayed.[3] If Mercian practice remained as in Cenwulf's reign, the year changed at Christmas and 17 September 822 is the right day. Next year Ceolwulf was expelled, according to the *Chronicle*; it has already been noticed that *BCS* 379 (see table 2) is signed by Beonna as *episcopus*, and may have been drafted later than *BCS* 378,[4] in Beornwulf's second year (and Wulfred's nineteenth, which ran approximately from June (or October) 823 to June (or October) 824); moreover Pope Eugenius II was elected on 24 May 824 and *BCS* 379 is signed by one Nothelm 'praeco a domino Eugenio Papa';[5] hence the date cannot be 30 October 823, and again the year changed at Christmas. A contrary impression is conveyed by *BCS* 400 (contemporary copy): 831, 9th indiction, 1 Wiglaf (who came back to rule in 830, according to the *Chronicle*), 'die V feria kal. Sept.', the first day of the month being a Thursday in 830 but a Friday in 831. Unless we are prepared to emend to *VI feria*, as Birch suggests, the year changed with the indiction, and it was not the 'Bedan indiction' of 24 September. Perhaps in agreement is *BCS* 432, of 841, 3rd indiction, 3 Beorhtwulf of Mercia, Christmas Day; the indiction is for 840, but this is not a contemporary copy, though genuine, and the doubtful *BCS* 433, purporting to be issued on the same day, has *indictione IIIIa*. To set against these charters, and in agreement with *BCS* 379, we have the authentic *BCS* 448, of 845 (indiction damaged), 'die dominica, VI Id. Novemb.', and 8 November was a Sunday in

---

Stubbs, *Councils* III, 593) the English bishops were encouraged to use AD because 'qualis annus Domini conputatur, aut a quali Archiepiscopo ... constitutum est illud iudicium. I owe this reference to Professor Whitelock.

[1] The exceptional *BCS* 296, of 799, has been included in table 3 only on this account, and not for its reliability, which has been discussed by Levison, *England and the Continent*, pp. 230 and 249, n. 3.

[2] F. M. Stenton, *Anglo-Saxon England*, 3rd ed. (Oxford, 1971), p. 230.

[3] A century later Edward the Elder died on 17 July 924, but Athelstan's 'coronation' did not take place until 4 September 925: Whitelock, *ASC*, p. 69.

[4] See above, p. 60, n. 3.

[5] A. J. Thorogood, 'The Anglo-Saxon Chronicle in the Reign of Ecgberht', *EHR* 48 (1933), 358.

845. From Wessex, the genuine *BCS* 419, of 838, 1st indiction, is dated 'III feria die uero XIII kl. Decembr.', and 19 November was a Tuesday in 838; again, *BCS* 449 (contemporary) has 845, 8th indiction, 'die II feria, XVI kl. Decembr.', and 16 November was a Monday in 845. Finally *BCS* 451, of 848, 10th indiction, 'secunda die natalis Domini', can mean 26 December on either reckoning. Thus the simple emendation of *BCS* 400 proposed by Birch receives support from a considerable body of evidence on either side of 830–1, from Wessex as well as Mercia.

Much of the remaining Wessex material survives in doubtful shape, as a result of interference at Winchester or elsewhere in the eleventh century: *BCS* 377, 410, 413, 447, 468 and 483 can be rejected because they are suspicious or unhelpful. Four other charters, *BCS* 389–93, are perhaps of greater importance for facts than figures, and although forged or interpolated are worth considering because of their value for the history of Egbert's reign.[1] The first part of *BCS* 389 states that it was written in 825, 3rd indiction, on 19 August; the second part has 'singrapha caraxatum est VII Kl. Ian.', i.e. 26 December; there is no mention of a change in the year, but *BCS* 390 adds the final date 826, 4th indiction, 24 Egbert and *ducatus XIIII* (a reading supported by *BCS* 393, whereas *BCS* 391 has *ducatus XIII*).[2] If Egbert came to the throne after 19 August 802 the regnal year is correct. Professor Whitelock suggests that *ducatus* may refer to his conquest of Cornwall, recorded by the *Chronicle* under 813 (*recte* 815). Now this Winchester source is undoubtedly right about another of Egbert's campaigns in 825, and hence that date cannot have been taken from any surviving versions of the *Chronicle*, which are two years behind at this point; the possibility arises that *ducatus XIIII* is also correct, in which case the conquest of Cornwall could be referred to 812 instead of 815. Last of all, *BCS* 510 is an Old English diploma, 864, 12th indiction (*tacencircole*), 26 December, evidently of 863 in modern reckoning whether the year started at Christmas or with the indiction.[3] Later material is scanty and not helpful.

Thus from the documents considered here we may provisionally adopt the following conclusions:

(a) *BCS* 154, of 736, appears to be the first charter of undoubted authenticity to carry the Year of Grace as well as the indiction. Although there is no *a priori* reason why charters should not have been dated by this style in earlier times – if we remember the Synod of Whitby in 664 – we do not yet have satisfactory evidence that they were.

[1] Whitelock, *ASC*, p. 40, n. 5.
[2] This date could be an argument in favour of a year beginning in September; but the change of indiction could also arise from thoughtless copying in accordance with the change of year at Christmas.
[3] Also printed *Anglo-Saxon Charters*, ed. A. J. Robertson (Cambridge, 1939), pp. 16–19.

(*b*) Since *BCS* 149 and 150 cannot well be later than 737, we seem here to be reaching the limit of dating by indiction alone; and, in spite of its being included as a formality in most of the dated charters, we should perhaps be on guard against assigning too much weight to it in later times (cf. *BCS* 326, table 3).

Admittedly these conclusions can only be tentative, since there is some difficulty in deciding whether correction, omission or addition of a dating clause could have taken place. And further, remembering that several kingdoms are involved, none of which had a 'chancery' in any recognizable sense, there may have been more variation in practice than we are inclined to admit. Turning to the more important question of when the year began, it does not seem possible, from lack of evidence until the death of Offa, to decide from charters alone between the indiction and Christmas. But the Northumbrian annals, taking the record from Bede's lifetime to 806, offer no convincing evidence that the year began in September; and in the last decade or two, when months and days are more freely sprinkled into the narrative, a Christmas dating is abundantly clear. Thereafter the Mercian and Wessex charters carry on in the same vein,[1] with increasingly strong evidence in favour of Christmas until *BCS* 449, of 845, from which time until the close of the ninth century no unambiguous charter information is available.

THE 'ANGLO-SAXON CHRONICLE'

This continuing and substantial agreement is fortified by annals in the *Chronicle* until at least as far as 823 (*recte* 825).[2] Nothing, then, prepares us for the undeniable fact that during the latter part of the ninth century, from 851 at latest, the *Chronicle's* year begins in the autumn.[3] Its compilers could have had two starting points to choose from, one precise and the other not:

(1) If a precise reckoning from the Greek indiction of 1 September were chosen we should have to postulate an antiquarian revival or a new and powerful influence, perhaps from as far afield as Rome. Alternatively, Bede's preference for 24 September, operating through a copy of *De Temporum Ratione*, may have been the deciding factor. Yet there is a serious objection to thinking of any precise date for the beginning of the year, namely, the imprecise nature

---

[1] It will be noticed that *BCS* 308–12 and 379, where the evidence for Christmas dating seems to be unequivocal, were issued at Councils of *Clofeshoh* and must surely represent official practice.

[2] Thorogood, 'The Anglo-Saxon Chronicle in the Reign of Ecgberht', pp. 355–7. And the annal for 827 (*recte* 829) opens with a lunar eclipse 'on middes wintres mæsse niht' – actually the early hours of Christmas Day.

[3] M. L. R. Beaven, 'The Beginning of the Year in the Alfredian Chronicle', *EHR* 33 (1918), 238 and Whitelock, *ASC* p. xxiv.

of the annals themselves. Proof of the autumn dating in this section of the *Chronicle* has been arrived at almost entirely through a study of outside sources – northern detail preserved by Simeon, Roger of Wendover and others, together with material from continental annals; thus the *Chronicle* compares unfavourably in this respect with the Annals of St Bertin, 830–82.[1] And the text itself is very meagre: after Easter (853); in the harvest season (877); after twelfth night, at Easter, the seventh week after Easter (878); an eclipse, but not even the month given (879); before Christmas (885); a comet, after Easter at the Rogation Days or before (891); the death of King Alfred, six days before All Saint's Day (900). The last item apart, woolly writing of this character does not suggest an urge to restore the indiction in either of its forms; the word *tacencircol* never occurs. King Alfred's remarks, often quoted, about the decay of learning in his time may sound overdrawn; yet his complaints are true both of Latinity and of writing in the native tongue,[2] and find an echo in chronology as well.

(2) A vague concept, such as that of 'the campaigning season'. During the first half of the ninth century it seems to have been only in summer that the Vikings were a menace, and then chiefly near the coast. Not until 850–1 did they winter for the first time in Thanet;[3] then in 855 they are found as far inland as the Wrekin (*BCS* 487), though they may only have started from Wales; and by 865–6 the great Danish army was wintering in East Anglia. Since these land forces often changed their quarters during the autumn, annalistic writing may have been adapted to this hard circumstance; and it has been suggested that for the period 892–6, where the narrative has a distinctive style, 'the writer of these annals is thinking rather of campaigning years than in calendar years'.[4] For the remaining annals of this period, until about a dozen years after Alfred's death, it may be preferable to think of 'autumn dating', rather than in precise measure. Yet the change of style from Christmas becomes less strange if we suppose that the *Chronicle* may not be an 'official' document, although King Alfred could well have encouraged its circulation. Sir Frank Stenton has argued, from internal evidence, that it was written for a person of rank in the south-western shires; in diocesan terms, Sherborne rather than

[1] A recent edition is that of F. Grat *et al.* (Société de l'Histoire de France, Paris, 1964).
[2] F. M. Stenton, *The Latin Charters of the Anglo-Saxon Period* (Oxford, 1955), pp. 39–43 and D. Whitelock, 'The Old English Bede', *Proc. of the Brit. Acad.* 48 (1962), 74–5. In this paper (p. 66) Professor Whitelock also observes that the translator has omitted some references to the indiction.
[3] So *ASC,* but other evidence suggests wintering in Kent some fifty years earlier; see N. Brooks, *England before the Conquest: Studies in Primary Sources presented to Dorothy Whitelock,* ed. Peter Clemoes and Kathleen Hughes (Cambridge, 1971), pp. 79–80. I am grateful to Mr Hunter Blair for drawing my attention to this point.
[4] Whitelock, *ASC* p. xxiv; for a more detailed discussion see Professor Whitelock's Appendix to the introduction to *Two of the Saxon Chronicles Parallel,* ed. C. Plummer on the basis of an ed. by J. Earle (repr. Oxford, 1952), pp. cxxxix f.

Winchester, for all that its tone is secular and not ecclesiastical.[1] If the character of the annals does not allow of any proof that the year began with an indiction – as against 'the autumn'– we have to consider the possibility that this style may have survived, or been revived, in another context.

The date of King Alfred's death was fixed by W. H. Stevenson to 26 October 899, the available evidence leading him to think that the year began on 25 March, and that the figure 900 given by version A of the *Chronicle* must be emended.[2] In a more extended study, establishing the date of Athelstan's death, M. L. R. Beaven held that the year began with the 'Bedan indiction', or at all events in the autumn;[3] it seems almost certain that this king died on 27 October 939, yet version A of the *Chronicle,* by now reverted to Christmas reckoning for other events, makes the entry under 940. Since these annals cannot be called contemporary, a suspicion arises that the compiler may have consulted a regnal list which began the year with an indiction,[4] not in itself an improbable circumstance in view of the conservatism that surrounds royalty in life or death. If such a list were on strict indictional principles the date would have read 'VI Kal. Nov. Indictione XIIIa', that is, the indiction for 940 which began on 1 or 24 September 939. A difficulty worth mentioning, however, is that the compiler of this annal could have followed a practice similar to one noticed earlier[5] and taken the *annus domini* from the column adjacent to the indiction in a Dionysiac table, or calculated it, yielding 'VI Kal. Nov. DCCCCXL'. And if the date in the regnal list had been written 'VI Kal. Nov. DCCCCXL, Indictione XIIIa', meaning 27 October 939 to people like Bede and his contemporaries, strictly brought up, these particulars could have been read as 940 in a later age, when to all appearances the indiction had lost a good deal of ground. There seems to be no difficulty over the death of King Eadred, which is recorded by the A version as 23 November 955; his successor Eadwig issues charters in 956,[6] and can hardly have been crowned later than January of that year.[7] May it not be that the Athelstan entry is due to a simple but understandable mistake?

If the evidence from annals and charters has been properly read, during the century between about 740 and 840 the 'Bedan indiction' could be a mirage,

---

[1] 'The South-Western Element in the Old English Chronicle', *Essays in Medieval History presented to T. F. Tout,* ed. A. G. Little and F. M. Powicke (Manchester, 1925), p. 15. Two bishops of Sherborne figure in a military capacity: Ealhstan fighting the Danes in 845 and his successor Heahmund killed in battle in 871.

[2] 'The Date of King Alfred's Death', *EHR* 13 (1898), 71.

[3] 'The Regnal Dates of Alfred, Edward the Elder and Athelstan', *EHR* 32 (1917), 517.

[4] Whitelock in Earle and Plummer, *Two Saxon Chronicles,* p. cxlii.

[5] Above, p. 62.

[6] Sawyer, *Anglo-Saxon Charters,* pp. 207 ff. Some at least are not suspicious.

[7] *Memorials of St Dunstan,* ed. W. Stubbs, RS (1874), p. lxxxviii. It has been calculated (Whitelock, *ASC* p. 5, n. 1), that Eadwig was probably crowned on 26 January, the third Sunday after Epiphany in 956 – not the second, as Stubbs has written, probably by a slip of the pen.

and the Greek had dropped to insignificance. Further study of material from the *Chronicle* will no doubt clear up the uncertainty between indiction and 'autumn'. Meanwhile it seems fair to conclude that although Bede did not invent the Christian era he presented it in a form so well adapted to the piety and comprehension of the Anglo-Saxon church that this era may have come into operation, as a prime reckoning, far more quickly than we have been accustomed to allow.

APPENDIX

THE CONSECRATION OF WILLIBRORD

Bede states that Archbishop Willibrord was consecrated (to Utrecht) by Pope Sergius at Rome, in the church of St Cecilia on her festival, 22 November 696;[1] in religion he took the name of Clement. Willibrord's Calendar contains in the left-hand margin of the table for November an entry, almost certainly in his own hand, stating that he was consecrated in AD 695 – an early example (728) of dating by the Incarnation; on the right-hand side an entry in a different hand, 'ordinatio domini nostri Clementis', begins on a level with 21 November, which was a Sunday in 695.[2] Neither 21 nor 22 November was a Sunday in 696. The discrepancy was brought forward by Poole in support of his theory that Bede began the year in September,[3] so that the figures mean 22 November 695 in our reckoning; and this date is of more than limited interest since it is an element in deciding when the *Historia* was written.[4] If there were only one discrepancy to account for, as between the years 695 and 696, Poole's argument would be powerful. But there is also a discrepancy over the day, in an account otherwise circumstantial: not only does Bede name the church, but adds that Willibrord left Rome for his diocese fourteen days after arriving in the city, and thus lends an air of enthusiasm and despatch to the proceedings. Bede's source may have been the priest Nothelm, who visited Rome to search the papal archives,[5] or perhaps Acca, bishop of Hexham, a friend of Willibrord.[6] On the other hand 21 November 695, a Sunday and the eve of St Cecilia, makes equally good sense and we appear to have it in the hand of the archbishop himself and one of his *familia*, unless the second entry was made after his death. Moreover, 21 November was a Sunday in 728, when Willibrord's note was made, and we can hardly doubt that it celebrates the thirty-third anniversary of his consecration, both day and year; if we inspect the days on which 21 November fell in adjacent years the significance of 728 becomes apparent.[7] Bede's information about the day must surely be at fault; in the matter of the year he put down 696, but, as in the case of the comet of 676, could

---

[1] *HE* v. 11. [2] Wilson, *Calendar of St Willibrord*, pp. 13 and 42 and pl. xi.
[3] Poole, *Studies*, p. 36.
[4] *The Moore Bede*, ed. P. Hunter Blair, EEMF 9 (Copenhagen, 1959), 30.
[5] *HE Praefatio*.   [6] *HE* iii. 13.
[7] 725 (Wednesday), 726 (Thursday), 727 (Friday), 729 (Monday), 730 (Tuesday) and 731 (Wednesday). Willibrord was about seventy at this time and could not know he would live for another decade.

have been given the wrong figure for that also. This date is not of such cast-iron character as to lend support to a theory; rather, it needs to be interpreted in the light of any theory that comes to hold the field. It is a good deal more likely, we may reflect, that Bede was misled over a ceremony in Rome than over the battle in Shropshire where King Oswald met his end.[1]

A little while later, on the continent, we come across a still more remarkable circumstance; no run-of-the-mill consecration but the martyrdom of Archbishop Boniface of Mainz and his fifty-three companions. The year is given as 754 by the tradition of Fulda, where he was buried, and as 755 by his biographer Willibald, representing the tradition of Mainz;[2] yet these two places are no further apart than, say, York and Jarrow. Boniface was killed on 5 June, in the 'neutral' part of the year, and so, as Plummer says of a similar trouble, 'the question of the Indiction mercifully does not come in'.[3]

[1] See above, p. 57.   [2] Levison, *England and the Continent,* p. 90, n. 2.
[3] Plummer, *Opera Historica* II, 61.

Bede and medieval civilization

GERALD BONNER

The mortal remains of the Venerable Bede rest today in the cathedral church of Christ and Blessed Mary the Virgin, Durham. They were brought there in the early eleventh century by one Ælfred Westou, priest and sacrist of Durham and an enthusiastic amateur of that characteristically medieval form of devotion expressed in the acquisition, by fair means or foul, of the relics of the saints to the greater glory of God. The removal of Bede's remains to Durham, involving as it did considerable preliminary planning and solitary nocturnal vigil before the final successful snatch, was one of his more brilliant coups, upon which he seems especially to have preened himself. The bones were first kept in the coffin of St Cuthbert, being subsequently removed to a reliquary near the saint's tomb. In 1370 they were placed in the Galilee Chapel, where they now lie under a plain table-tomb of blue marble, made in 1542 after the medieval shrine had been defaced. Bede himself would certainly have preferred that his body should have been left in its grave among his brethren at Jarrow, there to await the coming of Christ which he so ardently desired to see; but if a removal had to be made, we need not doubt that he would have been content to lie at Durham, near but not too near the shrine of St Cuthbert, the great saint and patron of the north, under a modest tombstone, so much more in keeping with his nature than the earlier and richer shrine, despoiled by the commissioners of Henry VIII.

Bede in his writings gives many accounts of miraculous happenings; but no cult of miracles was associated with his name. Rather, there was a spontaneous recognition of his quality, expressed in St Boniface's phrase: 'a candle of the church'. In him may be seen an outstanding example of that flowering of Christian culture in Northumbria produced by the encounter between the Irish tradition of Iona and Lindisfarne and the Latin order of Wearmouth and Jarrow in the seventh and eighth centuries. This flowering is an astonishing phenomenon, inviting exaggerated comparisons with Periclean Athens or the renaissance of the twelfth century in western Europe. But when all qualifications have been made and all proportions duly guarded, there remains an extraordinary cultural achievement, accomplished within a few generations from the time of the conversion to Christianity. Works of art like the Codex Amiatinus and the Lindisfarne Gospels and the Ruthwell and

71

Bewcastle crosses; vernacular poems like those of Cædmon and *The Dream of the Rood*; and Latin compositions like the anonymous lives of Gregory the Great and Cuthbert and Eddius Stephanus's biography of Wilfrid – all these are a testimony to a genius latent in the Northumbrians and brought into being by the inspiration of Christianity. To these must be added the work of Bede. Bede cannot, of course, be regarded simply as a Northumbrian, nor even as an English, figure. He is a European, writing in the international – or supranational – tradition of the Fathers of the Church; but even in this he may be said to exemplify Northumbrian tradition. After all, the uncial hand of the Codex Amiatinus and the inhabited vine-scroll ornamentation of the Ruthwell cross are themselves a reminder of continental associations.

The character of Bede – 'vir maxime doctus et minime superbus' as William of Malmesbury called him[1] – presents something of an historical anomaly. Our biographical information is scanty in the extreme, so that our knowledge of his personality has to be formed from his writings – and Bede is one of the least egotistical of authors. Yet in a strange fashion Bede reveals himself through his pages, disarming criticism and making his reader feel that he knows the writer as a man.[2] One may indeed believe that it is Bede himself, as well as his writings, who has attracted many of the scholars who have studied them. In Charles Plummer, one of the greatest of Bede's editors, whose personal life in no small measure resembled that of his author,[3] Sir Roger Mynors has noted 'qualities of heart as well as head',[4] and one may observe similar qualities in more recent students of Bede, like Max Ludwig Wolfram Laistner and Bertram Colgrave.

There is an historical cliché to the effect that St Augustine of Hippo resembles a man standing on the frontiers of two worlds: the ancient world that was passing away, and the medieval world that was coming into being. In a certain sense the same is true of Bede. In the circumstances of his life he was a man of the early Middle Ages, as surely as Augustine was a man of the later Roman Empire; but as a Christian teacher – and this would seem, from the circumstance of Bede's life and from his own words[5] to have been his own view of his vocation – he stood in an unbroken tradition, descending from the Fathers of the Church. Indeed, as everyone knows who attempts to work on the text of Bede's scriptural commentaries, he has so thoroughly assimilated

1 William of Malmesbury, *De Gestis Regum Anglorum,* ed. W. Stubbs, Rolls Series (1887–9) I, 1.
2 W. P. Ker, *The Dark Ages* (Edinburgh and London, 1923): 'The reputation of Bede seems always to have been exempt from the common rationalist criticism, and this although his books are full of the things a Voltairian student objects to' (pp. 141–2).
3 See the memoir by P. S. A[llen], 'Charles Plummer 1851–1927', *Proc. of the Brit. Acad.* 15 (1929), 463–76 (pub. sep. 1931): 'The keynote of his life was to take as little as possible for himself in order to have the more to give to others' (p. 466).
4 *Bede's Ecclesiastical History,* ed. B. Colgrave and R. A. B. Mynors (Oxford, 1969), p. lxxiii.
5 *HE* v. 24.

the patristic idiom and the patristic fashion of thought that it is often difficult to decide whether he is quoting from another author or expressing himself in his own words. There is no question here of conscious plagiarism, for Bede, more than most medieval authors, is anxious to acknowledge his indebtedness to others.[1] Rather, he regarded his commentaries as elementary text-books for those unable or unwilling to read more distinguished authors and his own contributions as little more than glosses on what had already been said authoritatively by those greater than he. A good example of this is provided by his treatment of the verse: '[Ishmael] shall be a wild man, his hand against all and the hands of all against him; and he shall pitch his tents over against all his brethren' (Genesis XVI.12). To explain this passage, Bede first quotes Jerome, without naming him: 'He declares that his seed will dwell in the wilderness – that is, the wandering Saracens with no fixed abode, who harry all the peoples dwelling on the borders of the desert and are assailed by them.'[2] Bede then adds his own observation: 'But these things are of the past. For now is *his hand against all and the hands of all against him* to such a degree that they oppress with their domination the whole of Africa throughout its length and hold the greatest part of Asia too, and some part of Europe, hateful and hostile to all.'[3] In this comment Bede makes no mention of the period of more than three centuries which had elapsed between Jerome's day and his own. He does not question the identification of the Saracens with the descendants of Ishmael, or with the Arab invaders of Syria, Egypt and Spain. He accepts the tradition and merely brings it up to date.[4]

Bede's sense of writing within the patristic tradition is exemplified in another way, in his detestation of heresy and schism. He denounces the 'Arian madness' which corrupted the whole world and even invaded Britain[5] and sees it prefigured in the Pale Horse of the Apocalypse;[6] declares that the precepts and promises of Holy Scripture overturn both the Adoptionism of the Photinians and the Dualism of the Manichees;[7] and warns his readers that Donatists and all others who separate themselves from the unity of the Catholic Church will have their place with the goats at the left hand of Christ on the Day of Judgement.[8] The menace of Pelagianism is recognized and its teaching

---

[1] See E. F. Sutcliffe, 'Quotations in the Venerable Bede's Commentary on St Mark', *Biblica* 7 (1926), 428–39 and M. L. W. Laistner, 'Source-Marks in Bede Manuscripts', *JTS* 34 (1933), 350–4.

[2] Hieronymus, *Hebraicae Questiones in Libro Geneseos* XVI. 12, ed. P. Antin, Corpus Christianorum Series Latina 72, 21, lines 1–4.

[3] Bede, *Libri Quatuor in Principium Genesis* IV (XVI. 12), ed. C. W. Jones, CCSL 118A, 201, lines 250–6.

[4] On this, see R. W. Southern, *Western Views of Islam in the Middle Ages* (Cambridge, Mass., 1962), pp. 16–18; but note the qualification by C. W. Jones, CCSL 118A, ix, n. 19.   [5] *HE* I. 8.

[6] Bede, *Explanatio Apocalypsis* VI. 7, ed. Migne, Patrologia Latina 93, col. 147 C and D.

[7] Bede, *In Cantica Canticorum Allegorica Expositio* VI (PL 91, col. 1205 A and B).

[8] *In Cant.* V (PL 91, col. 1183 B); cf. *In Primam Epistolam S. Iohannis* (PL 93, col. 90 A and B).

denounced.[1] Julian of Eclanum, the ablest of the Pelagian apologists, had written a commentary on the Songs of Songs which was apparently still extant in Bede's time and Bede, when writing his own commentary explaining the canticle as an allegory of Christ and his church, devoted the first book to a refutation of Julian's teaching.[2] This concern with doctrinal error of the past seems to the modern reader somewhat surprising. Pelagianism, it is true, is often said to be a heresy to which the English are prone and Pelagian writings were still in circulation in Bede's day; but none of Bede's contemporaries was likely ever to see a Manichee,[3] while Donatism had never had much appeal outside Roman Africa and by Bede's day was as dead as Arianism. But such considerations probably never entered Bede's mind. For him the faith of the Fathers was as his own and their enemies were to be regarded as his.

It is, therefore, difficult to exaggerate the extent of patristic influence on Bede and misleading to confine it to the Latin tradition or even to those among the Greek Fathers whose works we know to have existed in Latin translation. Two examples of occasions on which Bede draws on an unexpected Greek tradition are provided by his sermon on the Decollation of St John Baptist. In this, Bede remarks that we ought not to celebrate our birthdays with feasts or at any time indulge in carnal delights but rather anticipate the day of our death with tears, prayers, and frequent fastings.[4] This rather depressing exhortation appears at first sight to be no more than a typical expression of claustral asceticism, and when a patristic source is discovered it comes as no surprise to find that Bede's immediate inspiration appears to be St Jerome who, with characteristic erudition, points out that the only persons recorded in scripture as having celebrated their birthdays were Pharaoh, who hanged his butler, and Herod, who beheaded John the Baptist.[5] But behind Jerome, and the source upon which he drew, is Origen;[6] and Bede here stands in a tradition of thought going back to the great Alexandrian exegete of the third century. Whether Bede had actually read Origen's homily for himself is not clear. It was available in Latin translation, and we know that the Latin version of another of Origen's homilies in the same series was used by Bede in his commentary on Samuel.[7] More than this we cannot say.

---

[1] Bede, *In Ep. I Ioh.* (PL 93, cols. 88B, 98B and C and 100A).
[2] Bede, *In Cant.* I (PL 91, cols. 1065 C-77B).
[3] I assume the virtual extinction of Manichaeism in western Europe between the end of Roman rule and its reintroduction from the east in the eleventh century; see Steven Runciman, *The Medieval Manichee* (Cambridge, 1955), p. 118.
[4] Bede, *Homeliarum Evangelii Libri II* II. 23, ed. D. Hurst, CCSL 122, 351, lines 92–5.
[5] Hieronymus, *Commentariorum in Evangelium Matthei Libri Quatuor* II (XIV. 7) (PL 26, col. 97 B and C).
[6] Origen, *In Leviticum Homilia* VIII. 3, ed. W. A. Baehrens, Die Griechischen Christlichen Schriftsteller, Origenes Werke VI, 396, line 20–397, line 4.
[7] Bede, *In Primam Partem Samuhelis Libri IIII* I (I Reg. IV. 18; CCSL 119, 45, lines 1420–3), citing Origen, *In Lev. Hom.* II. 2–4 (GCS, Origenes Werke VI, 292, line 4–296, line 22).

The second example is even more interesting. In the same sermon Bede refers to Herod's fatal promise to the daughter of Herodias, remarking that if we perceive that the performance of an incautious oath will entail a greater crime than its violation we should not hesitate to perjure ourselves and so avoid committing the worse offence – a piece of advice which directly contradicted the ethical assumptions of Bede's society, in which oath-breaking was one of the most shameful crimes that a man could commit.[1] Now in this case, as in the preceding instance, Bede's obvious source of inspiration is Jerome who, however, merely says that he will not excuse Herod for keeping his oath, since if the girl had demanded the murder of his father or mother he would certainly have refused.[2] It is Origen, in his commentary on Matthew, who says that the guilt of oath-keeping which led to the killing of the prophet was greater than the guilt of oath-breaking would have been.[3] Had Bede read Origen on Matthew? No Latin translation survives and the problem arises: is it possible that Bede had actually read the original Greek? Dom Hurst appears to think that he may have done so, judging from the reference in his edition of Bede's sermons.[4] I am not fully convinced of either Bede's ability or the availability of a Greek manuscript. Perhaps we should assume a Latin translation which has perished, or some reference in a florilegium? The problem remains; but the essential point is that Bede was drawing on a tradition which looks back to the third-century school of Alexandria. Dom Leclercq has emphasized the importance of the influence of Origen in determining the character of biblical exegesis in the west during the Middle Ages.[5] These examples, in indicating Bede's utilization of the past, also reveal his anticipation of the future.

It is not necessary to labour the theme of Bede's devotion to the Fathers, in view of his declared desire to walk 'iuxta vestigia patrum'.[6] Nevertheless, it should be added that his attitude to patristic authority was in no way servile, and he was prepared to disregard patristic exegesis if it seemed to him unreasonable. Thus, in discussing why Cain's offering was rejected by God and Abel's accepted, he is concerned to defend the calling of the husbandman, and to see Cain's sin, not in his offering but in the mind in which he made the offering: 'Cain was not rejected on account of the humble nature of his offering, seeing that he offered to God from his habitual livelihood. It was rather on

---

[1] I am grateful to Mr Christopher Ball of Lincoln College, Oxford, for pointing this out to me.
[2] Hieron., *In Matt.* II (XIV. 7) (PL 26, col. 97 C).
[3] Origen, *Matthäuserklärung* x. 22, ed. E. Klostermann, GCS, Origenes Werke x, 30, lines 20–3).
[4] Bede, *Hom.* II. 23 (CCSL 122, 352, lines 108–15).
[5] *The West from the Fathers to the Reformation, The Cambridge History of the Bible* II, ed. G. W. H. Lampe (Cambridge, 1969), pp. 194–6.
[6] Bede, *Expositio Actuum Apostolorum*, ed. M. L. W. Laistner (Cambridge, Mass., 1939), p. 3, line 9; *In Regum Librum XXX Quaestiones, Prolog.* (CCSL 119, 293, line 23); and *In Cant.* VII (PL 91, col. 1223 A).

account of the impious mind of the man who offered that he was rejected together with his gifts by him who searches all hearts.'[1] The significance of this exegesis lies in the fact that it ignores the view of Ambrose, whose treatise *De Cain et Abel* Bede had used in composing his commentary, that Abel's sacrifice was preferred to Cain's because it consisted of living animals and not insensate vegetables.[2] Ambrose was, for Bede, a great authority. He had, indeed, for a time been deterred from writing his own commentary on Luke because of the existence of Ambrose's;[3] but when the need arose, he was prepared to maintain his own opinion.

Indeed, when full justice has been done to the influence of the Fathers upon Bede, it remains true that his life was lived in another world than theirs, and that his learning and culture, however profound, were not those of a man of the later Roman Empire but of the Middle Ages. Bede's very scholarship is of a different character from that of Ambrose, Jerome and Augustine and, more important, his outlook is different. One obvious distinction is, of course, that they were all Latin speakers by birth, while Bede was not. For him Latin could never have the flavour and nuances of a mother tongue. This may explain why his Latin verses have never aroused much enthusiasm, even in the kindest critics[4] – few men can hope to write poetry in a foreign tongue.[5] Nevertheless, as we shall see, there are reasons for not laying too much stress on the alien character of Bede's Latin. Rather, the essential difference between Bede's Latin culture and that of the Fathers is that Bede had no foundation of classical literature such as they enjoyed. M. L. W. Laistner in a brilliant paper drew attention to Bede's limitations, and demonstrated how many of his citations from the classical authors were probably at second-hand, in contrast to those from Christian poets.[6] Here is the great cultural change; and if we are to understand Bede, we must try to discover how it came about.

Some clue to the problem is provided by Dom Jean Leclercq in a beautiful and learned study of monastic culture in the west during the early Middle

---

[1] Bede, *In Gen.* IV (IV. 3–4; CCSL 118A, 74, lines 42–6 and 49–52).

[2] Ambrose, *De Cain et Abel,* IV, IV. 3–4 (PL 14, col. 337B).

[3] Acca, *Epistola ad Bedam, apud* Bede, *In Lucae Evangelium Expositio* (CCSL 120, 5, lines 5–18).

[4] Helen Waddell, *The Wandering Scholars,* 7th ed. (London, 1934): 'He is a greater critic than craftsman; there are cadences in his prose lovelier than anything in his poetry' (pp. 38–9); and F. J. E. Raby, *A History of Christian-Latin Poetry,* 2nd ed. (Oxford, 1953): 'His was not a poetic nature' (p. 146).

[5] A fact of which Bede was aware. See his remark on Cædmon's hymn: 'Neque enim possunt carmina, quamvis optime composita, ex alia in aliam linguam ad verbum sine detrimento sui decoris ac dignitatis transferri' (*HE* IV. 24).

[6] M. L. W. Laistner, 'Bede as a Classical and a Patristic Scholar', *TRHS* 4th ser. 16 (1933), 69–94, repr. *The Intellectual Heritage of the Early Middle Ages: Selected Essays by M. L. W. Laistner,* ed. Chester G. Starr (Ithaca, N.Y., 1957), pp. 93–116 (to which all references are made); see esp. pp. 95–9.

Ages[1] which, although concentrating upon the period from the Caroline reform to the rise of Scholasticism, also throws light on the earlier period from the lifetime of St Benedict onwards and makes several references to Bede. Reading this work one is constantly carried into the world of Wearmouth and Jarrow. First, Leclercq emphasizes the significance of the Benedictine tradition in early medieval western monasticism.[2] Here, at first sight, some difficulty appears to arise. Was Bede in fact a Benedictine? We have been warned not to give too much credence to the belief that Wearmouth and Jarrow were centres of Benedictine monasticism or that Bede, from his earliest profession, was a Benedictine monk. 'Although the influence of the Benedictine Rule may have been considerable, especially as the eighth century advanced, the composite or mixed rule was probably characteristic of much of Anglo-Saxon monasticism during Bede's lifetime'[3]– such is the judgement of one expert. For our purposes, however, the question is not whether the rule occupied 'a preponderant though not an exclusive position'[4] in Benedict Biscop's foundations, but rather to what degree Bede's mind and thought were shaped by it. It is generally agreed that there is only one direct citation from the Rule in Bede – that from ch. 7 in the commentary on Ezra and Nehemiah;[5] but Dom Justin McCann has identified two unmistakable citations in the *History of the Abbots*[6] and to these may be added the 'dura et aspera' of ch. 58, cited in the commentary on the First Epistle of John,[7] while the 'compunctione lacrimarum' of ch. 20 is quoted in Bede's sermon on St John the Evangelist and echoed in the *De Tabernaculo*.[8] There is, indeed, an opportunity for a

[1] J. Leclercq, *The Love of Learning and the Desire for God: a Study of Monastic Culture*, trans. C. Misrahi (New York, 1962).

[2] *Ibid.* pp. 19ff.

[3] Peter Hunter Blair, *The World of Bede* (London, 1970), pp. 197 and 199.

[4] Justin McCann, *Saint Benedict* (London, 1938), p. 233. Dom McCann notes that not only were abbatial elections governed by the Rule (Bede, *Historia Abbatum*, §§11 and 16, ed. C. Plummer, *Venerabilis Baedae Opera Historica* (Oxford, 1896) I, 375 and 381; and *Vita Ceolfridi auctore Anonymo*, §16, ed. Plummer, *Bede* I, 393) but also Bede, *Hist. Abbat.* contains unacknowledged borrowings from the Rule: 'vero regi militans' (§I (Plummer, *Bede*, p. 365) from *Benedicti Regula, Prolog.*, 3, ed. R. Hanslik, Corpus Scriptorum Ecclesiasticorum Latinorum 75, 2) and 'in pistrino, in orto, in coquina' (§8 (Plummer, *Bede*, p. 371) from *Reg.* XLVI. 1 (CSEL 75, 112–13)).

[5] Bede, *In Ezram et Neemiam Libri III* III (CCSL 119A, 350, line 466–351, line 473); *Reg.* VII. 6 and 7 (CSEL 75, 40–1).   [6] See above, n. 4.

[7] Bede, *In Ep. I Ioh.*: 'Quae enim natura dura sunt et aspera, spes coelestium praemiorum et amor Christi facit esse levia' (PL 93, col. 113 C); *Reg.* LVIII. 8: 'Praedicentur ei omnia dura et aspera, per quae itur ad deum' (CSEL 75, 134).

[8] Bede, *Hom.* I. 9: 'Contemplativa autem vita est cum longo quis bonae actionis exercitio edoctus diutinae orationis dulcedine instructus crebra lacrimarum conpunctione adsuefactus a cunctis mundi negotiis vacare et in sola dilectione oculum intendere didicerit' (CCSL 122, 64, lines 163–7), and *De Tabernaculo* III: 'Duobus namque modis lacrimarum et compunctionis status distinguitur' (CCSL 119 A, 137, lines 1700–2); *Reg.* XX. 3: 'Et non in multiloquio, sed in puritate cordis et conpunctione lacrimarum nos exaudiri sciamus' (CSEL 75, 75). It is, however, to be noted that this expression is to be found in Cassian, *Collationes*, IX. 28 (CSEL 13, 274, line 18), which was available in Bede's library, and cannot therefore constitute a decisive argument.

detailed study of the influence of the Rule on the thought of Bede by some competent scholar. For the present we need only observe that Bede was plainly within the Benedictine tradition in the broad sense of the term, and it is easy to imagine him thoroughly at home in the company of Benedictine scholars like Jean Mabillon and Bernard de Montfaucon. Now the attitude of the Rule to monastic scholarship, as interpreted by Dom Leclercq, is that while a knowledge of letters is regarded as being necessary and normally part of a monk's life, such knowledge forms no part of his vocation, his ideal, or of his monastery's ideal. For the monk the only values are those of eternal life, the only evil sin.[1] Any approach to Bede as a scholar must be conditioned by this view. His concern with the study of scripture – the aspect of his work which most impressed his contemporaries – was determined by pastoral rather than academic considerations. Bede is a literary artist by nature rather than by intention.

Reading Leclercq's study one is made aware how remarkably Bede's writings fit into the pattern of monastic culture as there described. Besides the bible and the Rule, those twin bases of early western monasticism, Leclercq points to St Gregory as the great doctor of monastic spirituality[2] – and we remember Bede's devotion to the greatest of popes. He speaks of the desire for celestial contemplation as being characteristic of the medieval religious life[3] – and we recall how often the theme of contemplation appears in Bede's writings. He tells of the importance of the Song of Songs as an influence on the theology of the medieval cloister[4] – and Bede's commentary comes to mind. He refers to the debt owed by medieval monasticism to Latin patristic tradition[5] – and we recall Bede's frequent quotation from Ambrose, Jerome and Augustine. He speaks of the importance of history as a monastic literary genre[6] – and one remembers that the *Ecclesiastical History* is, in a sense, Bede's crowning achievement. In all these details, and in many others, Bede is wholly within the monastic culture described by Dom Leclercq.

It is in the light of these considerations that we can discuss the problem of how, and why, Bede differs from his predecessors the Latin Fathers. It has been remarked above that his Latin differed from theirs in being an acquired tongue and one that was not, like theirs, formed by a profound study of the pagan classics. Nevertheless, there are two considerations which suggest that too much stress should not be laid on the alien character of Bede's Latinity. First, the position of Wearmouth and Jarrow in Northumbrian monasticism was peculiar, in that they represented a sophisticated and cosmopolitan community constantly in touch with the outside world in general, and with Rome and Italy in particular. In such a society the study and use of

[1] Leclercq, *Love of Learning*, p. 31.   [2] *Ibid.* pp. 33–43.   [3] *Ibid.* pp. 57–75.
[4] *Ibid.* pp. 90–3.   [5] *Ibid.* pp. 103–5.   [6] *Ibid.* pp. 156–60.

Latin was more than a mere liturgical, or even theological, exercise; and the presence of an Italian like John the Archchanter, brought to Northumbria to ensure the correct singing of the Roman chant, would require the use of Latin for the purpose of oral communication. The Latinity of Wearmouth and Jarrow was therefore influenced by the living tradition of the Roman church. But there is another, deeper reason why Bede's Latin should not be regarded as a foreign language, as we commonly use the term today. For a man like Bede, as for Alcuin, Anselm and Bernard of Clairvaux, Latin was not a foreign tongue at all; it was the tongue of the church. Dom Leclercq[1] refers to the question raised by Wolfram von den Steinen in his book *Notker der Dichter und seine geistige Welt* as to why Notker wrote his famous sequences in Latin and not in his German mother-tongue, to which von den Steinen replies that for Notker and for others like him – among whom he specifically mentions Bede – there was no choice. Their native language was inadequate to express their thoughts.[2] Latin was the language of the bible, the liturgy, and of Christian culture; and there was no other literary culture available to Bede in Northumbria.

Thus Bede learned Latin in order to be a monk and a priest. He learned it accurately enough from the standard grammars and, inevitably, read Vergil; but once he was trained it was to the study of the bible and the Fathers that he directed his attention. He had, of course, a number of stock quotations from classical authors at second hand, which he was prepared to employ for the purposes of literary embellishment or illustration;[3] but he had little inclination to add to this store and even less opportunity, in view of the resources available to him in the library of Wearmouth and Jarrow.

One of the most valuable of the many contributions made by the late Max Laistner to Bedan studies was the famous article on the library of the Venerable Bede.[4] Lacking as we do any contemporary catalogue of the library of Benedict Biscop's foundations, it is possible to estimate its resources only by reference to citations, either avowed or unacknowledged, in Bede's writings, and here Laistner's pioneering work is of fundamental importance. In the very nature of things it could not be definitive, and since its publication some additional works have been identified. For example, it would seem that we can add St Cyprian's *De Unitate Ecclesiae* and his fifty-sixth letter to Laistner's list, together with Jerome's Letter 22.[5] Furthermore, as we have seen, Bede may have

---

[1] *Ibid.* p. 57.

[2] Steinen, *Notker der Dichter und seine geistige Welt* (Berne, 1948) 1, 76–80, esp. 79–80.

[3] Ruby Davis, 'Bede's Early Reading', *Speculum* 8 (1933), 179–95 and Laistner, 'Bede as a Classical and a Patristic Scholar', pp. 93–8.

[4] 'The Library of the Venerable Bede', *Bede: his Life, Times and Writings*, ed. A. H. Hamilton Thompson (Oxford, 1935), pp. 237–66; repr. *Intellectual Heritage of the Early Middle Ages*, pp. 117–49.

[5] Bede, *Hom.* II. 22 (CCSL 122, 347, lines 205–9) citing Cyprian, *De Unitate*, 4 (on which see Maurice

had access to Origen's commentary on Matthew, either in the original Greek or in Latin translation. Further research will no doubt add more volumes to the total, though it is difficult to believe that Laistner's list will be enormously enlarged, so thoroughly did he do his work. It is, of course, impossible to be certain that any particular citation is necessarily given by Bede at first hand; but when due allowance has been made for intermediate sources, we are entitled to use Laistner's list with some confidence.

Now from this list it appears that the authors used by Bede are predominantly ecclesiastical, with the writings of the greater Latin Fathers being most abundant. Furthermore, the titles of the works identified lend support to Leclercq's view that monastic readers primarily looked in the Fathers for what would be most helpful in leading the monastic life.[1] Overwhelmingly, Bede's library consists of commentaries on scripture, patristic treatises, or secular works like Pliny's *Natural History*, which would be of value in biblical exegesis. The standard grammaraians are there of course – Donatus, Charisius, Diomedes, Pompeius and the rest – but their function is to train men to read the bible and the Fathers; and if Vergil is present – and no one could have kept him out – he is balanced and indeed overwhelmed by Christian poets like Ambrose, Prudentius, Paulinus, Sedulius and Arator. This is understandable; Benedict Biscop and Ceolfrith had not faced laborious and dangerous journeys to Rome to build up a classical institute. As a result, Bede's is a theological library, designed for a monastery inspired by the spirit of the Benedictine Rule rather than by the principles for study laid down by Cassiodorus for his monastery at Vivarium in the middle of the sixth century;[2] for Cassiodorus, although a sincere Christian, made far greater provision for the liberal arts in his programme of monastic studies than did St Benedict. In the second book of the *Institutes* Cassiodorus provides for a course of study which anticipates the later medieval *trivium* and *quadrivium*: first grammar, rhetoric, and dialectic; then arithmetic, music, geometry and astronomy. There is no hint in Bede of any such programme.[3] He knows Cassiodorus indeed; but he knows him as the former senator suddenly transformed into a teacher of the church and the

Bévenot, *The Tradition of Manuscripts* (Oxford, 1961), pp. 53 and 89, n. 7); and *In Apoc.* II. 9: 'sicut Beatus Cyprianus sub Deciana contigisse conquestus: "volentibus," inquit, "mori non permittebatur occidi"' (PL 93, col. 158 B) citing Cyprianus, *Epistulae*, LVI. 2; 'maxime cum cupientibus mori non permitteretur occidi' (CSEL 3(2), 649, line 20). I am indebted to Fr Bévenot for this reference.

[1] Leclercq, *Love of Learning*, p. 104. His remark that Augustine's 'polemics against the Manichaeans or the Neoplatonists had lost all timeliness for the medieval monks and therefore did not claim their attention' is only partly true of Wearmouth and Jarrow, since there were a number of Augustine's anti-Manichaean treatises in Bede's library. It is however significant that they were all concerned with scriptural exegesis and not with a direct attack on Manichaean doctrines.

[2] *Ibid.* pp. 28–31.

[3] See Pierre Riché, *Éducation et Culture dans l'Occident Barbare, 6e–8e Siècle,* Patristica Sorbonensia 4 (Paris, 1962), 434 ff.

author of a commentary on the psalms and not as an educational theorist.[1]

It may therefore be said that the cultural activities of Wearmouth and Jarrow were, in the last resort, determined by utilitarian motives; the highest utilitarianism, it is true – the salvation of souls – but utilitarian nevertheless. In the long run this utilitarianism was to have important cultural consequences, as is clearly seen by G. P. Fedotov, in his classic study *The Russian Religious Mind,* when he comes to discuss the problem of why there was no flowering of culture in medieval Russia as there was in France, Germany and England, finding the answer, rather unexpectedly, in the fact that in the ninth century the Slavs received the bible and the liturgy in Slavonic translations, to which were later added some works of theological and scientific content. As a result, there was no intellectual stimulus for the Slavs similar to that supplied in the west by the study of Latin, and the Slavonic bible and liturgy, priceless endowment as they undoubtedly were for Russia's spiritual life, were also an ambiguous gift, in that the Russian intellect was for a long time stunted by the absence of external occasions for exercise. On the other hand, says Fedotov:

The western barbarians, before they were able to think their own thoughts and to speak their own words – about 1100 AD – had been sitting for five or six centuries on the school bench, struggling with the foreign Latin language, learning by heart the Latin Bible and the Latin grammar with Virgil as the introduction to the Bible. Men of the dark ages had no independent interest in culture. They were interested only in the salvation of their souls. But Latin gave them the key to salvation. As the language of the Church, Latin was a sacred tongue and everything written in it became invested with a sacred halo. Hence the popularity of Ovid in medieval monasteries, and the Latin versifying of Irish saints, such as Columban, who in their severe asceticism and primitive rudeness of life did not yield to the anchorites of Egypt and Syria. For the Irish the *Trivium* and *Quadrivium* were the way to the Latin Bible.[2]

Fedotov's judgement agrees very well with the estimate which has just been attempted of the character of study at Wearmouth and Jarrow, and it may be remarked in passing that, in the light of what he says about the effect of a vernacular literature on medieval Russia, it may be counted fortunate that the development of an Old English literature went hand-in-hand with, and not to the exclusion of, the study of the universal Latin. Bede, we know, was familiar with the poems of his own English tongue, and enthusiastically praised the poetry of his fellow-countryman Cædmon, and it is certainly a matter for regret that no examples of his own vernacular writing survive;[3]

[1] Bede, *In Ez. et Neem.* II (CCSL 119A, 295, lines 283–5).
[2] Fedotov, *The Russian Religious Mind* (New York, 1960), p. 39. For a more reserved comment on Irish classical studies see Riché, *Education et Culture*, pp. 371–83.
[3] I can see no safe grounds for regarding the Death Song as Bede's own composition. Only a small and late group of the manuscripts of the *Epistola de Obitu Bedae* assigns the poem to Bede himself, and so the evidence for his authorship is at best weak. See Colgrave and Mynors, p. 580, n. 4.

but we may be thankful that his legacy to posterity was written in the international language of the medieval west.

The monastic and utilitarian character of the library available to Bede explains the character of his work. His great contribution to computistical studies – a contribution of such importance that as late as 1537 it was possible to publish his writings for their practical, and not for their historical, value[1] – was inspired by the practical issues of his day. This does not mean that Bede was lacking in scientific curiosity. A modern historian of science has said of the *De Temporum Ratione* that 'it contains the basic elements of natural science', pointing out that Bede, in his discussion of tides, was the first writer to enunciate the principle known as 'the establishment of a port';[2] but while computistical arithmetic, astronomy and cosmography engaged Bede's attention, he was not concerned with the more abstract discipline of geometry.[3]

Furthermore, the nature of Bede's education and the character of the literature available to him helps to shed some light on his attitude to the pagan classics. Notoriously, he is hostile, more hostile than his master, Gregory the Great. An often cited example is his comparison of those who leave the heights of the word of God to listen to worldly fables and the teachings of the demons to the men of Israel who went down to the Philistines unarmed to have their agricultural implements sharpened (I Samuel XIII.20), and another is his identification of the honey which Jonathan ate, in ignorance of his father's orders (I Samuel XIV.27), with pagan literature.[4] These are in marked contrast to Gregory, who considered both passages as furnishing a justification for secular studies.[5] It should however be observed that when Bede comes to expound the significance of the episode of Jonathan, the great warrior who climbed the rocky crag and smote the Philistine, he wishes to use it as an example of how a teacher of the church may be led astray by the enticements of pagan literature, citing the famous story of how St Jerome was scourged in a vision before the judgement seat of God for having been a Ciceronian rather than a Christian.[6] Bede's object, however, is less to condemn pagan literature

---

[1] The Cologne ed. of Noviomagus, 1537. See C. W. Jones, *Bedae Pseudepigrapha: Scientific Writings Falsely Attributed to Bede* (Ithaca, N.Y., 1939), pp. 1 and 7.

[2] A. C. Crombie, *Augustine to Galileo,* 2nd ed. (London, 1969) I, 41.

[3] Riché, *Éducation et Culture*, pp. 434–6.

[4] Bede, *In I Samuhelem* II (I *Reg.* XIII. 20 (CCSL 119, 112, lines 1853–9) and XIV. 27 (*ibid.* p. 120, lines 2169–96)).

[5] Gregory, *In Librum Primum Regum*, ed. P. Verbraken, CCSL 144, 470–2.

[6] Bede, *In I Samuhelem* II (I *Reg.* XIV. 27): 'Ionathan igitur qui prius scopulorum dentes et ictus devicerat ensium qui hostis audacia compressa suis victoriae salutisque praebuerat improvisa subito blandientis gastrimargiae culpa consternitur. Et nobiles saepe magistri ecclesiae magnorumque victores certaminum ardentiore quam decet oblectatione libros gentilium lectitantes culpam quam non praevidere contrahebant adeo ut quidam eorum se pro hoc ipso scribat in visione castigatum obiectumque sibi a domino inter verbera ferientia quod non christianus sed Ciceronianus potius esset habendus' (CCSL 119, 120, lines 2170-9); Hieronymus, *Epistulae,* XXII. 30, ed. I. Hilberg, CSEL 54, 189–91.

than to demonstrate that even great Christian saints continue to be tempted to small sins in order that they may be reminded that their virtues are a gift of God.[1] Pagan eloquence may legitimately be employed to support and sweeten authority;[2] and Bede is aware that neither Moses nor Daniel nor St Paul utterly eschewed pagan learnings or letters.[3] Bede's recognition that the reading of the pagan classics may be of value is clear, if grudging, and was in full accord with the teaching of the Fathers of the Church. Like them, however, he was in his heart doubtful about the reading of the pagan authors by a Christian; and his basic hesitation and suspicion could only be confirmed by the fact that he was unable to take the vision of Jerome other than seriously. Indeed, from the theological viewpoint it taught an unquestionable truth. The demands of Christ are absolute, and if a concern for Cicero leads a man to neglect them, then Cicero must be rejected as giving occasion for sin.

There is, however, one important difference between Bede and the Fathers. For them, the temptation offered by the pagan classics was a very real one. As children their minds had been formed by Vergil and Cicero, Plautus and Terence, and however hard they might try they could never entirely break the spell. Bede's education, on the other hand, had been a progress from the grammarians directly to the bible, without any intervening stage of concentrated literary study. Indeed, apart from Vergil and Pliny, his classical reading seems to have been slight, and his learning mostly from other men's quotations. In describing the dangers of the classics he was denouncing a peril to which he had never been exposed. And this held true, not only in respect of the danger of distraction from the heavenly to the temporal, but also in respect of a reversion to paganism. For the Fathers the classics were, in a very obvious fashion, a temptation to apostasy. For Bede and his age they could never be that. The classical deities might be demons, masquerading as gods; but fundamentally they were literary fictions, without any power to move to adoration. The paganism of Bede's world was German heathenism, not the literary paganism of classical antiquity. This fact may help to explain the revival of classical studies in the Carolingian period. They were no longer, in themselves, a danger to a man's soul.

We have, then, suggested a way in which Bede, although inspired by and thinking within the tradition of the Fathers, nevertheless inhabits another intellectual world from theirs, even within the confines of his monastery of Jarrow. The world of Bede is a monastic world, his culture a monastic culture, designed to bring men to heaven. Of course, the Fathers were equally

---

[1] *Ibid.*: 'Sed et auditorum fidelium non pauci magna virtutum gratia pollentes minoribus vitiis temptari non desinunt quod divina geri dispensatione non latet ut qui minora certamina per se superare nequeunt in magnis quae habent non sibi aliquid tribuere sed solo patri luminum gratias agere discant' (CCSL 119, 120, lines 2179–84).

[2] *Ibid.* (lines 2186–94).   [3] *Ibid.* (XIV. 28–9; CCSL 119, 121, lines 2209–16).

concerned to bring men to heaven, and many of them were monks; but the majority of them received their education not in the cloister but in the secular schools. Thus Bede's world, although not a narrow one, was narrower than theirs.

But Bede's world differs from that of the Fathers in another way which is more difficult to describe. Put briefly and misleadingly, it is a world in which Christianity has triumphed. Clearly, in the most literal sense of the words this statement is untrue, for the Fathers, after the legal suppression of paganism had begun in earnest at the end of the fourth century, were accustomed to think of themselves as living in Christian times, while the age of Bede was a harsh and barbarous one, as appears all too clearly in the atrocities of nominally Christian kings like Cædwalla of Wessex on the Isle of Wight or Egbert of Northumbria in Ireland;[1] while across the Channel, in the Low Countries and Germany, paganism flourished and the work of the English mission to the continent, begun in Bede's lifetime, was ultimately to be accomplished only by the ruthless extirpation of heathenism wherever the Frankish armies got the upper hand. Yet in spite of this, and in spite of the alarm for the future of Northumbria expressed at the end of the *Ecclesiastical History* and the *Letter to Egbert*, there is in Bede a note of optimism. The night of infidelity has been dispersed by the Sun of Righteousness,[2] and now Christ and his bride the church go forth to the vineyards: '*In the morning,* therefore, he says, *let us go forth to the vineyards,* as though he should say openly: Because the night of ancient unbelief has passed, because the light of the bright gospel already begins to appear, *let us,* I pray, *go forth to the vineyards,* that is, let us labour in establishing churches for God throughout the world.'[3]

It is in the spirit of this passage that we should, I think, understand St Boniface's famous reference to Bede as a candle of the church in the letter sent to Archbishop Egbert of York in 746–7, asking him to send copies of Bede's scriptural commentaries.[4] It is easy when we read it today to impose our own preconceptions upon it, and to think of Bede's life shining with a small but clear flame in a waste of great darkness, the early Middle Ages; but such a romantic image was surely far from Boniface's thought. Rather, our image

[1] Bede, *HE* iv. 16 [14] and 26 [24].
[2] Bede, *In Cant.* ii: 'Sicut enim tenebras noctis, sic etiam recte per austeritatem hiemis et imbrium, tempestas exprimitur infidelitatis, quae totum orbem usque ad tempus regebat Dominicae incarnationis. At ubi Sol iustitiae mundo illuxit, abscedente mox ac depulsa prisca brumalis infidelitatis perfidia, flores apparuerunt in terra, quia initia iam nascentis Ecclesiae in sanctorum fideli ac pia devotione claruerunt' (PL 91, col. 1110 C and D).
[3] *Ibid.* iv (col. 1202A).
[4] Boniface, *Ep.* 91, ed. M. Tangl, *Die Briefe des heiligen Bonifatius und Lullus,* Monumenta Germaniae Historica, Epistolae Selectae 1, 207, line 17; cf. *Ep.* 75 *ibid.* p. 158, lines 8–11) and 76: 'quem nuper in domo Dei apud vos vice candellae ecclesiasticae scientia scripturarum fulsisse audivimus' (*ibid.* p. 159, lines 13 and 14).

should be of some great basilica ablaze with brightness, with the great candles of the apostles and the saints and the lesser lights of humbler Christians, all afire with the love of God; and among them Bede, shining with a light hardly less than that of the apostles, a great candle in the house of God. What we somewhat condescendingly call the Dark Ages did not necessarily seem so dark to those who lived in them. Rather, they seemed the age of the triumph of Christ and his church.

Such an interpretation of the mood of the age will explain certain features of Bede's thought which are otherwise puzzling. Let us consider first the *Ecclesiastical History*. It has been observed of this work:

No single term will describe Bede's book. It includes a great deal of material quoted from papal and episcopal letters, *concilia*, epigraphic and verbal accounts; it ignores and thus condemns to oblivion, the greater part of the history of the period with which it deals, yet it repeats in detail the lives of monks who took no part in the public affairs of their day ... As an *ecclesiastical* history – and no event without ecclesiastical relevance is mentioned in the book – Bede's work is an adjunct to scriptural study, that study which he elsewhere described as his life's occupation.[1]

With all this we may agree, except the first sentence. The work is, as Bede says, an ecclesiastical history, composed in the tradition of Eusebius of Caesarea, whom Bede knew in the Latin version of Rufinus. Eusebius was aware, when he embarked upon his *History*, that he was in effect creating a new type of historiography, unknown to the pagan,[2] and the novelty of his enterprise is reflected by his lengthy citations from his authorities. Professor Momigliano, in an important article, has drawn attention to this particular feature of Christian history, destined to make a peculiar contribution to the technique of scientific historiography, though without actually abolishing the style of the classical historians. 'We have learnt', he says, 'to check our references from Eusebius ...'[3] – though we have contrived to secularize him by the use of footnotes. Bede, in the *Ecclesiastical History*, followed the Eusebian tradition. Where he differs from Eusebius is not in his method but in his ability to exploit his materials – Sir Frank Stenton's comment that 'in an age when little was attempted beyond the registration of fact, he had reached the conception of history'[4] is not likely to be applied to the Father of Church History. Yet so far as the philosophy which underlies their work is concerned, Eusebius and Bede are in agreement. Both saw ecclesiastical history as a

---

[1] W. F. Bolton, *A History of Anglo-Latin Literature* (Princeton, New Jersey, 1967) I, 171 and 172.
[2] Eusebius, *Ecclesiastica Historia*, 1.i.5 (GCS, Eusebius Werke II (1), 8, lines 17–21). On this see Arnaldo Momigliano, 'Pagan and Christian Historiography in the Forth Century A.D.', *The Conflict between Paganism and Christianity in the Fourth Century,* ed. A. Momigliano (Oxford, 1963), p. 90.
[3] *Ibid.* p. 99.   [4] Stenton, *Anglo-Saxon England,* 2nd ed. (Oxford, 1947), p. 187.

struggle between the new nation, the Christians, and the devil.[1] Both wrote
to record the victory of the church: Eusebius in the conversion of Constantine,
Bede in the conversion of the English. The difference between them – a
difference fraught with portentous consequences – is that while Eusebius took
for his field the Roman Empire, Bede confined his to a particular race within a
limited locality. In so doing he was, of course, only following a trail already
blazed by Gregory of Tours and Cassiodorus in his lost work on Gothic
history; but the very fact that he did is significant. Here, as in his biblical
commentaries, Bede stands in the tradition of the Fathers but points the way to
another age.

Let us consider another aspect of this idea of the triumph of Christianity.
Perhaps the most significant, and certainly the most distinctive, contrast
between the culture of Bede and that of the Fathers – and one which also
helps to explain his attitude to the pagan classics – is to be found in the fact
that he had at his disposal a corpus of Christian poetry, as distinct from the
literature of theological works composed according to the rules of literary
composition, which he shared with the Fathers. In this respect the two treatises *De Arte Metrica* and *De Schematibus et Tropis*, regarded by Bede as constitut-
ing a single treatise and dated by Laistner to 701 or 702,[2] are instructive. In
the *De Arte Metrica* not only are Bede's examples taken overwhelmingly from
Christian poets – this, after all, was determined by the resources of his library
– but when he lists the three types of poetry, dramatic, narrative, and mixed, he
gives examples both from pagan authors and from the Old Testament.
Vergil's ninth eclogue is matched by the Song of Songs; to the *Georgics* and the
De Rerum Natura of Lucretius are opposed Proverbs and Ecclesiastes; the
Odyssey and the *Aeneid* have the book of Job as their Christian equivalent.
Apud nos – 'our authors' – is Bede's theme.[3] The Christians have their own
literature and do not need the pagans any more. Similarly in the *De Schematibus
et Tropis* Bede observes that Holy Scripture surpasses all other writings, not
only by authority, because it is divine, or by utility, because it leads to eternal
life, 'sed et antiquitate et ipsa positione dicendi' – by age and style.[4] We
have come a long way from the days when Jerome found the language of the
prophets barbarous, or the young Augustine, excited to the pursuit of philosophy by reading the *Hortensius*, found himself repelled by the style of the
bible, so inferior to that of Cicero.[5] Some three centuries before Bede's lifetime

[1] Momigliano, 'Pagan and Christian Historiography', p. 90.
[2] Laistener, *A Hand-List of Bede Manuscripts* (Ithaca, N.Y., 1943), pp. 131–2.
[3] Bede, *De Arte Metrica*, 25, ed. H. Keil, *Grammatici Latini* VII (Leipzig, 1880), 259–60.
[4] Bede, *De Schematis et Tropis* (PL 90, col. 175 B).
[5] Hieron., *Ep.* XXII. 30: 'si . . . prophetam legere coepissem, sermo horrebat incultus' (CSEL 54, 189, lines 17–18); and Augustine, *Confessiones*, III. 9 (CSEL 33, 50, lines 4–14). Both these works were apparently available to Bede.

Augustine of Hippo had produced, in the *De Doctrina Christiana*, a theory of a Christian culture in which the scriptures would take the place of the pagan classics and secular studies would be pursued insofar as they provided material for the Christian exegete. At about the same time Prudentius, the first great Christian poet, and Paulinus of Nola were beginning to provide the church with a corpus of poetry in addition to the liturgical hymns which had already been composed by Hilary of Poitiers and Ambrose of Milan, and Prudentius and Paulinus would be supplemented by the works of Sedulius, Arator and Venantius Fortunatus, all known to Bede. The question whether these writers were, in respect of literary quality, the peers of the great pagan poets is for our purposes irrelevant. So far as Bede was concerned, both the resources of his library and his own writings represent the embodiment of the programme of study proposed by Augustine, even to the extent of his warning expressed – ironically enough in a phrase of Terence! – against any excessive pursuit of learning beyond the bounds of the church of Christ: 'Ne quid nimis!'[1] Thus Bede's attitude to the classics was not simply determined by the consideration that they might be harmful; rather they had, in a certain sense, become unnecessary, in view of the existence of a specifically Christian literature. This particular assumption of Bede was not shared by the scholars of the Caroline renaissance, who decided that Christian writings alone could not provide the norms of the Latinity which they desired. Few will doubt that they were right in their decision; but Bede's position, granting his premises, was unassailable, and most of us, it may be added, would be well content if we could emulate Bede's Latin style, formed as it was on the grammarians and the Fathers.

We have hitherto considered Bede as a writer who is a key figure in the transmission of patristic tradition and who also modifies that tradition and adapts it to the conditions of his own age. In this respect no one could have been better fitted to be one of the great teachers of the early Middle Ages, in which his influence was immense, as is demonstrated in the most obvious way by the great quantity of manuscripts of his writings which have survived.[2] A few examples of the range of his influence may be given, without any claim to be comprehensive. His *De Arte Metrica* was still in use at the cathedral school of Fulbert of Chartres in the eleventh century,[3] while the *De Temporum Ratione* (described by a leading modern authority as being still 'the best introduction to the ecclesiastical calendar')[4] was, as we have seen, published in the sixteenth century for practical, and not historical, reasons. Again, the

---

[1] Augustine, *De Doctrina Christiana*, II. XXXIX 58 (CSEL 80, 74, line 12). On all this, see H.-I. Marrou *Saint Augustin et la Fin de la Culture Antique*, 4th ed. (Paris, 1958) and esp. pt 3, ch. 3: 'La Formation de l'Intellectuel Chrétien'.

[2] For which see Laistner, *Hand-List*.

[3] See H. O. Taylor, *The Medieval Mind*, 4th ed. (London, 1925) I, 300.

[4] C. W. Jones, *Bedae Opera de Temporibus* (Cambridge, Mass., 1943), p. 4.

Ecclesiastical History enjoyed a popularity which was not confined to England[1] where, in the twelfth century, it was to be a source of inspiration to the historian William of Malmesbury.[2] Yet again, Bede's biblical commentaries, the part of his work which his contemporaries most highly valued, enjoyed a remarkable renaissance of popularity during the fifteenth century, if the number of manuscript copies which have survived is any indication.[3] We are not here concerned to give a description of the diffusion of Bede's writings[4] or to give a detailed account of his influence in any particular field. Rather, if we are to regard Bede as an outstanding representative of early medieval culture and a teacher who exercised a decisive influence on the development of the civilization of the Middle Ages, it would be well to conclude this paper by a consideration of what he did not contribute, to note his deficiencies as well as his achievements, and to establish what was lacking in the Christian culture of Northumbria, of which he was the outstanding representative, which later thinkers and scholars would have to supply.

In the *Ecclesiastical History* when he comes to describe the Council of Hatfield of 679, Bede gives part of its confession of faith, declaring its adhesion to the doctrine of the first five ecumenical councils and of the council 'which was held in the city of Rome in the time of the blessed Pope Martin, in the eighth indiction, in the ninth year of the reign of the most religious Emperor Constantine',[5] that is, the Lateran Synod of 649, convened by Pope Martin I under the influence of St Maximus the Confessor, who was probably present at it, to condemn the Monothelite heresy. Now Bede in his writings makes very little mention of Monothelitism, and none at all of St Maximus, one of the greatest of the later Greek theologians, who had lived in exile in the west, at Carthage from 632 onwards, and then at Rome from about 646 until about 655. It seems curious that Bede should know nothing about this great theologian and catholic Confessor, whose teaching was later to influence the thought of St Bernard,[6] but such is apparently the case. Now if one turns from the thought of Bede to that of Maximus, one enters another world,[7] the sophisticated world of Greek patristic theology in which all the resources of Greek philosophy and Christian experience were applied to the solution of the mystery of the union of the two natures, divine and human, in Christ. To this world, Bede is a stranger. This is not to say that he was intellectually inferior to Maximus – one cannot fairly compare the biblical scholar and historian with the dogmatic

---

[1] Laistner, *Hand-List,* p. 94.   [2] *De Gest. Reg. Angl.,* ed. Stubbs i, i and 59.

[3] Laistner, *Hand-List,* p. 7.

[4] For which, see Dorothy Whitelock, *After Bede,* Jarrow Lecture 1960.

[5] Bede, *HE* iv. 17 [15].

[6] See E. Gilson, *The Mystical Theology of St Bernard,* trans. A. H. C. Downes (London, 1940), pp. 25 ff.

[7] See the excellent study by Lars Thunberg, *Microcosm and Mediator: the Theological Anthropology of Maximus the Confessor* (Lund, 1965).

and philosophical theologian – but rather, that there was a department of Christian theology which was unfamiliar to Bede as it would not be, for example, to St Anselm at a later date.

How did this come about? Here again, an examination of Bede's library as established by Laistner is revealing, always allowing for the omissions and errors of such a reconstruction. If one looks at the titles of the works available to Bede, one is struck by the absence of books of philosophical theology or of a metaphysical content. Bede did not, apparently, have access to Augustine's early philosophical writings, the *Contra Academicos*, the *De Beata Vita* or the *De Ordine*, nor did he have the *De Trinitate*, perhaps the greatest of Augustine's theological works, nor any of the treatises of the fourth-century Latin Christian Platonist Marius Victorinus. Again, he did not have a copy of Chalcidius's commentary on part of the *Timaeus*, one of the very few Platonic sources available in the Latin west in the early Middle Ages, or of a work like that of Apuleius, *De Deo Socratis*. One can understand the absence of such works from a monastic library; but what is surprising is the lack of any work of Boethius, either the *Consolatio* – an omission so remarkable as to cause Laistner to remark upon it in his article on Bede's library[1] – or of the theological tractates and translations.

The implications of this deficiency in his library are clear: Bede was deprived, through no fault of his own, of precisely the sort of works needed by a Latin divine to whom the writings of the Greek Fathers were not available, if he aspired to be in any sense of the term a dogmatic theologian. To suggest that, had such works been available, Bede would have produced great works on dogmatic theology would be wholly unwarranted; and in any case such an achievement, however admirable and desirable in itself, would have been of less value to the church of his day in England or on the continent of Europe than what he actually achieved. The process by which the barbarian kingdoms, established after the ending of Roman rule in the west, were turned into the civilized states of the Middle Ages was a gradual one, requiring several centuries of diligent scholarship to prepare the way for the renaissance of the twelfth century. To that renaissance Bede contributed much; but there are some things – its philosophy and its humanism – in which he had no share. The cultural achievement of Northumbria was a limited one, the work of a small élite of monks and clerics and a few cultured laymen within a restricted field, and it was within that field that Bede made his great contribution to medieval civilization. Bede was, without question, a great intellect, a great teacher, and a great Christian; but it is important in any evaluation of his work to maintain a sense of proportion. Bede served later generations as a

[1] Laistner, 'The Library of the Venerable Bede', p. 264.

commentator, a grammarian, an historiographer and a computist. This is his achievement, and it is enough to establish his greatness.

Yet having said this, it does not seem enough; for a man's performance is, after all, dependent upon his opportunities, and when all reservations have been made it is astonishing that Bede, a 'grandchild of pagans' and a 'child of barbarians'[1] should have become a Doctor of the Church and provide, in Plummer's words, 'the very model of the saintly scholar-priest'.[2] In attempting to determine the place of Bede in medieval civilization, it would be well to remember the words of Fedotov previously quoted, that 'the western barbarians, before they were able to think their own thought and to speak their own words . . . had been sitting for five or six centuries on the school bench'. It is a measure of his greatness that for more than three of those centuries they sat under the instruction of the Venerable Bede.

[1] Leclercq, *Love of Learning,* p. 45.   [2] Plummer, *Bede* 1, lxxviii–lxxix.

An interim revision of episcopal dates for the province of Canterbury, 850–950: part II

MARY ANNE O'DONOVAN

For part I see *ASE* 1 (1972), 23-44. Information about the conventions and abbreviations used is given *ibid.* pp. 24–6.[1]

Lichfield

Tunberht

Last name in the Lichfield list in FW *Lists* and *GP* (as Tunfrith) before a gap of about fifty years until Ælfwine (Ælle); the other lists end with his predecessor Cyneferth, whose last signature appears in 843–5 (*BCS* 452; see part I, *Hereford, Deorlaf*). Tunberht signs first in *BCS* 448, an original charter dated 8 November 845. He is probably intended by the Hunberht of *BCS* 450, dated 25 December 845 (see *ASE* 1 (1972) 18, n. 1). He also appears in two dubious documents, *BCS* 453 and *BCS* 454. *BCS* 453 is dated 840, with corresponding indiction and regnal year, but its formulae are suspect (Sawyer 191) and its episcopal witnesses belong to some years later (in particular Alhhun of Worcester). *BCS* 454 is dated 844, with an indiction suitable for late 847 or for 848, the date preferred by Birch. Opinions of the authenticity of the charter are divided (Sawyer, 197): in his later work Stenton accepted its evidence (*A-S England*, p. 41), and it seems a very odd charter for a forger to concoct, as it records the monastery giving land to the king, in return for certain concessions. 847 would be relatively easy to misread as 844 (*VII* for *IIII*).

Tunberht last signs in *BCS* 492, probably an acceptable charter, dated 857 (Sawyer 208). FW *Lists* says that he was bishop in the time of Kings Alfred and Burgred, 871–4, but increasingly one suspects that this is a post-Conquest deduction, and unreliable.

The Viking period

There is a gap in the episcopal lists for this period, which is probably due to

---

[1] I am most grateful to Professor Dorothy Whitelock for considerably revising and improving part II of this article; she has generously contributed the results of much research of her own.

the upheavals caused by the Viking invasions. It is not clear what happened to Lichfield in the late ninth century. Lichfield itself is just north of Watling Street, the boundary settled between Alfred and Guthrum in 886–90 (see *EHD*, p. 380), but about half the diocese remained outside the Danish area, and must have needed episcopal administration in the period between Tunberht's disappearance and Ælfwine's appointment some time in Edward's reign.

The *Handbook*, following Searle, inserts the names of Eadberht, Wulfred and Wigmund into the gap. Various bishops appear in the Mercian charters of this period, and very probably two or three belong to Lichfield, but the problem is to decide which, since Lindsey also has a broken succession at this point and Leicester may have had unrecorded bishops in the gaps between Ceolred and Alhheard, and between Alhheard and Cenwulf (the last two being seated at Dorchester).

In translating and commenting upon a Mercian charter of 875 (*BCS* 540; *EHD*, pp. 491–2), Professor Whitelock has given the argument for assigning Eadberht, who appears here and earlier in 869 (*BCS* 524), to Lichfield; she points out that the sees of Worcester and Hereford are represented, and that, of the other Mercian sees, Lichfield is the most likely since Lindsey and Leicester were already under Danish control. However in 873–4 the Danes were in Repton, not far from Lichfield, and 874 saw a Danish-supported king on the Mercian throne. Lindsey was occupied by the Danes in the winter of 872–3, although they were moving through the area between East Anglia and Northumbria before then.

It might therefore be useful to discuss the problem of all three Mercian dioceses – Lindsey, Leicester and Lichfield – together at this point. Nor should London be forgotten (see below, *London, Deorwulf, Swithwulf* and *Heahstan*), for there is a gap of about thirty years (*c.* 867–97) during which no London bishop makes an appearance. It is not clear which court the bishops of London would attend. Though in the early ninth century London was definitely a Mercian see, much of its diocese was in Essex, which passed under West Saxon control in 825. Hence it is not surprising to find Deorwulf of London witnessing a charter of Æthelberht, king of Kent and Wessex (*BCS* 502, 860–3; see below, *London, Deorwulf*). But London itself, with those parts of its diocese in Middlesex and Hertfordshire, seems to have remained Mercian. It is possible therefore that a bishop at a Mercian court could belong to London, though no weight can be attached to the Crowland forgery, *BCS* 461, dated 851, in which Deorwulf's successor Swithwulf witnesses an alleged charter of Beorhtwulf of Mercia. However, there is no obvious break in the London episcopal succession, and as there are never too many bishops to be contained by the other Mercian sees, London is here omitted as an unnecessary complication. The East Anglian sees are likewise discounted. East Anglia after 827 was almost certainly an independent kingdom, and its bishops would not attend the Mercian court. Moreover East Anglia was the first area occupied by the Vikings, and had no ally among the other English kingdoms.

The chief difficulty lies in assigning the various bishops who appear in the Mercian charters to any one particular see when at least three sees have broken records during this period. Lichfield's gap has already been outlined. The last definite appearance of Ceolred of Leicester is in 869, and his successor Alhheard of Dorchester first appears in 888. Lindsey's last recorded bishop, Beorhtred, signs finally in 862 (*BCS* 535; see part I, *Canterbury, Ceolnoth*) before the Danes had taken over the area, and the see reappears united with Dorchester in the later tenth century.

The following bishops witness Mercian charters of this period: Wulfsige, Eadbald, Burgheard, Eadberht and Wulfred. None of them appears in the episcopal lists. Of the four earlier bishops, Wulfsige signs once in 862 (*BCS* 503 and *BCS* 535; versions of the same charter, Sawyer 209), and in 866 (*BCS* 513 and *BCS* 514; the latter seems to be a forgery, based on the former, Sawyer 212 and 211). There were two other bishops of the same name, in the late ninth and early tenth centuries, from London and Sherborne, but neither could be signing then. Eadbald also witnesses *BCS* 513 and *BCS* 514 (866). Burgheard signs *BCS* 524, dated 869, which Stenton treats as reliable (*Latin Charters of the Anglo-Saxon Period* (Oxford, 1955), pp. 64–5). Eadberht signs in 869 (*BCS* 524) and 875 (*BCS* 540 and *BCS* 541; the first is reliable, the second less so: Sawyer 215 and 216).

If one attempts to fit these bishops into vacant sees, Wulfsige must be assigned to Lichfield, since the other two are not vacant in 862. Eadbald must then go to Lindsey, since he and Wulfsige both sign the same charter in 866, and Ceolred occupied Leicester at least until 869. Burgheard and Eadberht would then fit into Lichfield and Lindsey, since Ceolred of Leicester is still in evidence in the charter of their first appearance. There is little indication as to which bishop belongs to which diocese, although one might argue for Eadberht's belonging to Lichfield on the grounds that he appears at a date when part of Lichfield was in English hands, whereas by 875 Lindsey was completely under Danish rule. On the other hand Burgheard and Eadberht both appear at the same time, and one must reckon with the likelihood that bishops may have attended the Mercian court as refugees, after they had lost possession of their sees.

The next floating bishop, Wulfred, signs between 883 (*BCS* 551) and 889 (*BCS* 561; see Sawyer 346). *BCS* 547, which he signs, is dated 880, but its indiction fits 887, which makes it unreliable evidence here. All the charters he attests (*BCS* 547, *BCS* 551, *BCS* 552, *BCS* 557 and *BCS* 561) are Mercian, and he probably belongs to Lichfield, since, if Lindsey was vacant after about 872, it is unlikely that a new bishop would be appointed for a diocese completely in Danish hands.

Three unassignable bishops, Wighelm, Wigmund and Wilferth, appear in charters issued by Edward the Elder and witnessed by bishops both from Wessex and from Mercia. The bishoprics vacant in the early tenth century are Lichfield, Dorchester and Selsey, Lindsey still being an unlikely appointment. It seems likely that Wighelm was a bishop of Selsey, and he is discussed below, under that see.

Wigmund appears in various charters with dates between 900 and 903, several of them from Winchester. He signs *BCS* 596, a suspicious grant to New Minster (Sawyer, 360), with date, regnal year and indiction all pointing to a date in the autumn of 900, and *BCS* 607 (Sawyer 361), which is the record from the Worcester cartulary of a grant dated 900 with the indiction 7, which would fit 904. The indiction may be a misreading of III or IV as VII. He witnesses *BCS* 603, which is acceptable; dated 903 with a corresponding indiction, it records the replacement of a destroyed charter, and survives in what is probably a tenth-century copy (Sawyer 367); also an acceptable charter *BCS* 605 (Sawyer 1443), the witness-list of which is preserved in a better form in the *Liber Vitae of New Minster and Hyde Abbey* (ed. W. de G. Birch (London, 1892), pp. 156–7), but this cannot be dated more closely than 899–908, from the appearance of King Edward and of Denewulf, bishop of Winchester.

Wilferth has a more tenuous existence. The suggestion has been made that this name arose from confusion with Wærferth, bishop of Worcester, but this is highly improbable, for both he and Wærferth attest *BCS* 603 (903); and in the witness-list to *BCS* 605 as preserved in the *Liber Vitae* of New Minster in the early eleventh century, his name Wilferth is unlikely to be intended for Wærferth; nor is *Wil-* a likely misreading of *Wær-*. Wilferth is intended by *Wiferth* in *BCS* 596 (900, see above), by *Wiserth* in *BCS* 597 and by *Wifhith* in *BCS* 598, both dated 901 and suspect (Sawyer 365 and 366); as *Wiferth*, he also attests *BCS* 602 (?903, spurious, Sawyer 370).

Wigmund and Wilferth could belong to Lichfield or to Leicester, now transferred to Dorchester; again there is little to influence the distribution. It seems unlikely that a bishop would be appointed for Lindsey at this date, and London was occupied.

The question still remains as to whether it is wise to make any assignation of bishops to particular sees in this period of confusion, for it ignores the possibility of *chorepiscopi*.

Ælfwine (Ælle)

In FW *Lists* and in a twelfth-century continuation of the episcopal list for Lichfield in BM Cotton Vespasian B. vi (see K. Sisam, 'Cynewulf and his

Poetry', *Studies in the History of Old English Literature* (Oxford, 1953), p. 6) both versions of the name are given; in *GP* the shortened form only. Ælfwine appears first in *BCS* 632, a charter dated 9 September 878, but probably belonging to 9 September 915 (see below, *Worcester, Æthelhun*). In fact, two bishops of this name sign it, but the first, spelt *Ælfwyn*, is probably for Æthelflæd's daughter, with a miscopied title (Stenton, *Abingdon*, p. 24). Ælfwine appears as *Ælle* or *Ella* in several charters, including *BCS* 641 (925) and *BCS* 707 (935). He last signs in 925, once as *Ella* (*BCS* 707), once as *Ælfwine* (J. 10 in *Early Charters of the Cathedral Church of St Paul, London*, ed. M. Gibbs, Camden 3rd ser. 58).

Wulfgar

In FW *Lists* and *GP* Ælle is followed by Alfgar, an error for Wulfgar. FW tends to replace *Wlf-* by *Alf-*. In the continuation to the list in BM Cotton Vespasian B. vi (see above, under *Ælfwine (Ælle)*), Wulfgar appears as *se gyldene*. He signs *BCS* 765 (960 for 941), *BCS* 771 (942), *BCS* 812 (witness-list 943–7, probably 946; see part I, *Dorchester, Æthelwald*) and *BCS* 815 (946).

Cynesige

In FW *Lists* and *GP*. His signatures appear regularly from 949 (e.g. *BCS* 876 and *BCS* 882). There is another bishop of this name who appears first in Athelstan's reign. He is referred to as bishop of Berkshire in *BCS* 687, a memorandum of a grant made during the archiepiscopates of Wulfhelm of Canterbury and Hrothweard of York (i.e. 926–31). Hrothweard however is not given the title of archbishop, and Stenton (*Abingdon*, pp. 34–6) suggests that this is because he had not yet received the pallium. He signs with full title in 928, which gives the closer limits 926–8 to the grant of *BCS* 687. In the Anglo-Saxon version (*BCS* 688) Cynesige is referred to as *Wynsige*, but in view of his other appearances the former seems preferable. This Cynesige signs from 931 to 934, possibly in 937 (*BCS* 716; see part I, *Cornwall, Conan*, in 942 (*BCS* 771) and in the witness-list attached to *BCS* 812 (943–7, probably 946; see part I, *Dorchester, Æthelwald*). The two Cynesiges may be identical, the bishop of Berkshire being translated to Lichfield when the latter see fell vacant.

Cynesige's last signatures appear in 963 (*BCS* 1112, *BCS* 1119 and *BCS* 1121), and his successor Wynsige signs two charters dated 964 (*BCS* 1134 and *BCS* 1135). *BCS* 1135 is dated late in the year, 28 December, which in modern reckoning would be 28 December 963. However the charter itself is at least interpolated (Sawyer 731), and so its evidence is not unconditionally acceptable.

Lindsey

Beorhtred

Appears as Eadwulf's successor in some of the episcopal lists (CCCC 183,

BM Cotton Tiberius B. v and FW *Lists*, in all under *Lindisfarorum*, and in *GP* under Dorchester). Eadwulf last signs in 836 (*BCS* 416), and Beorhtred first appears in 839 (*BCS* 421). His signatures continue until 862 (*BCS* 535, see part I, *Canterbury, Ceolnoth*). FW *Lists* says that his episcopate continued until the time of Alfred and Burgred (871–4), but this may well be only an assumption.

In the only two lists which continue after Beorhtred, BM Cotton Tiberius B. v and *GP*, the next name is that of Leofwine, who does not appear until the mid tenth century; *GP* attributes to him the combining of the two dioceses (Leicester and Dorchester) and FW *Lists*, which ends the Lindsey list with Beorhtred, puts Leofwine in its list headed *Nomina episcoporum Leogerensium*, after Ceolred, who last appears in 869 (see above, *Lichfield, the Viking period*), with the statement that Leofwine combined the diocese of Leicester and Lindsey and ruled in the time of King Edgar. For possible bishops of Lindsey during the later ninth century (see above, *Lichfield, the Viking period*). Leofwine first signs in 953 (*BCS* 899 and *BCS* 900), and appears to have been bishop of Lindsey alone for some years before Dorchester was added (see the discussion by Professor Whitelock referred to in part I, *Dorchester, Osketel*).

London

Ceolberht

In all the episcopal lists. He signs first in 824 (*BCS* 378), his predecessor having last appeared in 816. Ceolberht's latest signature occurs in *BCS* 448 (8 November 845).

Deorwulf

Follows in the lists of CCCC 140, CCCC 173, BM Stowe 944, FW *Lists* (mis-spelt *Ceorulfus*) and *GP* (mis-spelt *Cerulf*). His profession to Archbishop Ceolnoth survives (*BCS* 498). He appears in two charters. The first, *BCS* 502, has a date 790, altered from 860. It is issued in the name of Æthelberht, king of Wessex and Kent, i.e. after he became king of the whole kingdom in 860; its witness-list, which can be dated 858–862 or 863, looks genuine; (see below, *Rochester, Wærmund*). Deorwulf's second appearance is in *BCS* 1210, of which there is a rather better text in *Early Charters of the Cathedral Church of St Paul, London* (J. 4). It has been tampered with, the king's name being given as Edgar, and Archbishop Oda added to the list of witnesses, but it seems based on a genuine charter of Æthelred I of Wessex, and has date and indiction for 867. It is a grant of land in Essex to St Paul's at the request of Bishop Deorwulf and Ealdred *princeps*. On the relation of the bishops of London to the West Saxon kings see above, *Lichfield, the Viking period*.

Swithwulf

Follows Deorwulf in the lists cited above. Swithwulf signs once only, in a spurious Crowland charter (*BCS* 461), dated 851. The witness-list has no coherence and cannot belong to the given year. Its interest here is that it gives Swithwulf the title of bishop of London, thus distinguishing him from his near contemporary Swithwulf of Rochester, who appears in *BCS* 548 (880) and *BCS* 562 (889).

Heahstan

Follows Swithwulf in CCCC 140, FW *Lists* and *GP* (as *Etstan*). His name is omitted in CCCC 173, as well as in BM Cotton Tiberius B. v and *Textus Roffensis*, both of which jump from Deorwulf's predecessor, Ceolberht (the last name in BM Cotton Vespasian B. vi), to Theodred; in BM Stowe 944 Heahstan has been misplaced among the eighth-century bishops. He does not appear in the charters, but he received a copy of Alfred's translation of the *Cura Pastoralis* between 890 and 896 (cf. *EHD*, p. 817) and his death is recorded in *ASC*, *s.a.* 897 (B, C and D misname him *Ealhstan*). For a discussion of the London lists, see Page, *EpLists* (1965), pp. 91–2.

Wulfsige

Follows Heahstan in CCCC 140, FW *Lists* and *GP*. CCCC 173 and BM Stowe 944 (which omit Heahstan) have the reversed sequence Æthelweard, Wulfsige. Wulfsige's signatures appear from 900 (*BCS* 596; see above, *Lichfield, the Viking period*) to 909 (various Winchester charters, e.g. *BCS* 620, *BCS* 623 etc.), and in *BCS* 605 (899–908; see above, *Lichfield, the Viking period*). If the *Wulfricg* of the spurious charter *BCS* 568 (871–99) is intended for Wulfsige, most probably the bishop of Sherborne is meant, since this is a local West Saxon charter, with only one episcopal witness. The Bishop Wulfsige of *BCS* 667 (930 for *c*. 949, see part I, *Crediton, Æthelgar*) is Wulfsige II of Sherborne.

Æthelweard and Leofstan (possibly Heahstan or Ealhstan)

These bishops appear only in episcopal lists, Æthelweard in CCCC 140, CCCC 173, BM Stowe 944, FW *Lists* and *GP*, Leofstan in the same, except that CCCC 173 and Stowe 944 call him *Leofusta* and FW *Lists* and *GP* have *Ealhstan*. Since the next bishop, Theodred, appears in 926, Æthelweard and Leofstan fall within the period of Edward's reign from which no royal charters survive. This being so, there is no way of confirming their existence, or of resolving the confusion over Leofstan's name (see Page, *EpLists* (1965), pp. 91–2).

Theodred

Appears in most of the episcopal lists, and calls himself bishop of the people of London in his will; in this he appears also in charge of Suffolk, with a centre at Hoxne, if not of the whole diocese of East Anglia (see *Anglo-Saxon Wills,* ed. D. Whitelock (Cambridge, 1930), no. 1). His first signatures occur in 926 (*BCS* 658 and *BCS* 659). He also appears in the witness-list of *BCS* 635, a charter dated 921; the witness-list however belongs to the years 931–4. He signs frequently until 951, when he appears in *BCS* 890 and *BCS* 892. He also witnesses *BCS* 910, which has the date 956, with an indiction for 955. The witness-list is very curtailed, and it is probably safe to assume that it has been tampered with, since his successor appears in 953. FW *Lists* and *GP* have Wulfstan as following Theodred, and then Beorhthelm, whereas all other lists which reach this date (CCCC 140, CCCC 173, BM Stowe 944, BM Cotton Tiberius B. v and *Textus Roffensis*) omit Wulfstan. No Bishop Wulfstan appears in the charters at this time, but Beorhthelm attests *BCS* 899 and *BCS* 900 (both 953 and acceptable). This can only be the bishop of London, as neither of his namesakes at Winchester and Wells can appear so early. There is then only a space of two years into which Wulfstan could be fitted.

Ramsbury

Athelstan

Named as the first bishop of Ramsbury in the episcopal lists and in the Plegmund narrative (e.g. *Crawford Charters* VII; Robinson, *Saxon Bishops,* pp. 7–24), the division of the West Saxon sees being placed in 909 or 910 (see below, *Winchester, Frithestan*). Athelstan does not appear elsewhere, his successor signing almost immediately after the 909–24 gap in the charter evidence.

Oda

Follows Athelstan in the lists. Called Oda 'se goda'. He appears first in *BCS* 660, dated 927 (Sawyer 398). The witness-list is not in its original state, since the bishops witnessing are given their sees, which is a later practice, and moreover Oda is miscalled bishop of Sherborne. Likewise Bishop Ælfheah is assigned to Winchester, but if 927 is correct this must be the less important Ælfheah of Wells. Robinson (*St Oswald,* pp. 43–4) does not like the charter, and certainly it has been tampered with, but need not be completely discarded. Oda's next signature is in *BCS* 663 (Sawyer 400) a charter dated 16 April 928, with corresponding dating apparatus, which is fairly acceptable, although it has one or two dubious features (e.g. the use of *singrapham*). The *Vita Odonis* (*AngSac* II, 80) says that Oda was appointed bishop by King Athelstan; if this is reliable it would, combined with *BCS* 660, limit his succession to September

924–7. The Life is however post-Conquest (see Robinson, *St Oswald*, pp. 45–51), and this detail does not appear in the pre-Conquest sources.

Oda signs frequently from 928 until his translation to Canterbury in 941 (see part I, *Canterbury, Wulfhelm* and *Oda*).

Ælfric

Follows Oda in the episcopal lists, though omitted by FW *Lists* and *GP*. It is not certain whether Oda relinquished Ramsbury immediately when he was translated to Canterbury. Throughout Ælfric's episcopate his signatures are indistinguishable from those of his namesake at Hereford, except when both attest *BCS* 885 in 949. One Bishop Ælfric continues to sign up to 951 (*BCS* 890 and *BCS* 892, both acceptable). There is no clear indication which it is, although perhaps it is more likely to be the bishop of Hereford, since Oswulf, the next bishop of Ramsbury, also signs in 951, before the autumnal indictional change (*BCS* 891). Oswulf also appears in *BCS* 887, which has the date 950 and corresponding indiction, but the witness-list is not a possible one for this date (Sawyer 553).

Rochester

Tatnoth

Follows Beornmod in the lists in CCCC 140, CCCC 173, BM Stowe 944 and *Textus Roffensis*. Tatnoth appears as bishop elect in 844 (*BCS* 445 and *BCS* 446), and as bishop in 845 (*BCS* 448 and *BCS* 449). His episcopate is limited only by the appearance of his successor.

Badenoth

Follows Tatnoth in the lists in CCCC 140 and *Textus Roffensis*. He does not appear in the charters of this period, but a Bishop Badenoth witnesses a Rochester charter of 765 (*BCS* 196). The witness-list is suspect as it has Jænberht signing as archbishop a year too early (*Councils* III, 403), and it is this section of the charter which contains Badenoth. It is an extremely rare name, and so the Rochester scribe responsible for copying or concocting this part may have drawn on the episcopal list.

(Wærmund)

The *Handbook* includes at this point a Bishop Wærmund, who does not occur in the episcopal lists, on the evidence of *BCS* 502. This charter is dated 790 (altered from 860) and is a grant of King Æthelberht of Wessex and Kent (860–5) to Bishop Wærmund of Rochester. The text of the charter looks more fitting to the eighth century, and the proem is identical with that of *BCS* 257, a grant by Offa to an earlier Wærmund of Rochester. The witness-list of *BCS*

502 belongs to 858–862 or 863, the *terminus ante quem* being given by the presence of Swithhun of Winchester, who died on 2 July in 862 or 863; Wærmund is not in the list of signatures. It is a suspect charter, and a second Bishop Wærmund of Rochester may never have existed. He appears nowhere else.

Cuthwulf

Follows Badenoth in the same lists. Otherwise he appears only as the beneficiary of *BCS* 518 (868). The Cuthwulf who signs from 839 to 857 is the bishop of Hereford; as all the charters he signs are Mercian there is no chance of confusion.

Swithwulf

Follows Cuthwulf in the same lists. He witnesses a grant to himself and St Andrew's church (Rochester) in 880 (*BCS* 548). The charter does not survive in a good copy, as the king is called Æthelwulf instead of Alfred (not a slip likely to be made by a forger); moreover the witness-list suits the date, but lacks a regnal signature. Swithwulf also appears as the donor and a witness in *BCS* 562 (889), a reputable charter. He was the recipient of a copy of the *Cura Pastoralis* (890–6; see *EHD*, p. 817), and his death is recorded in *ASC* during the years 893–5 or 894–6 (see part I, *Dorchester, Alhheard*).

The episcopal list in *Textus Roffensis* has Burgric as Swithwulf's successor, though he does not appear in CCCC 140. He appears in the shorter lists, between Beornmod and Ælfstan in BM Cotton Tiberius B. v, BM Stowe 944, FW *Lists* and *GP*, and between Tatnoth and Ælfstan in CCCC 173; this does not help here. A bishop of this name appears in Athelstan's reign (see below), but there is no sign of a Burgric at this earlier date. It seems likely that Burgric's name was originally lacking from the exemplar of the list in the *Textus Roffensis,* as it is from CCCC 140, and was later wrongly inserted into the former list after comparison with one of the other lists which contain his name. Accordingly he is omitted at this point.

Ceolmund

In the lists of CCCC 140 and *Textus Roffensis*. He signs from 900 (*BCS* 596; see above, *Lichfield, the Viking period*) to 909 (various bad Winchester charters (e.g. *BCS* 620 and *BCS* 623), including some fairly reputable charters: *BCS* 607 (900?, see above, *Lichfield, the Viking period*), *BCS* 603 (903) and *BCS* 605 (899–908).

Cyneferth

Follows Ceolmund in the same lists. He signs first in 926 (*BCS* 658 and *BCS*

659), and appears fairly often up to and including his last appearance on 26 January 933 (*BCS* 695 and *BCS* 696).

Burgric

This is probably the proper place for a bishop of Rochester of this name, for several lists (see above) place one immediately before Ælfstan. The Bishop Burgric who appears in charters of this period fits neatly in the gap between better accredited bishops of Rochester, and in one (albeit spurious) witness-list he is assigned to Rochester (*BCS* 719, dated 937). At first sight his signatures seem to start before Cyneferth's have ended, for he appears in *BCS* 670 and *BCS* 671, both dated 931. Both however belong to 934 or 937 × 939 (see part I, *Crediton, Æthelgar*). Likewise he signs *BCS* 682, which Birch dates 931, although the charter lacks any dating clause; the witness-list is limited to the years 935–937 or 938 by the signatures of Ælfheah of Winchester and Ælfheah of Wells (see below, under the respective dioceses). Burgric also signs *BCS* 699, dated 933 perhaps for 936 (see below, *Winchester, Ælfheah*). He signs *BCS* 701, a Worcester charter dated 7 June 930, with corresponding regnal year, but with indiction, epact and concurrent for 934. This charter was probably modelled on *BCS* 703, from York, which Burgric signs and which has the same dating clause, with 930 in error for 934; it too is dated 7 June, but was issued at Nottingham, while *BCS* 701 was issued at London. *BCS* 703 is the more reliable. Burgric also witnesses *BCS* 702, dated 28 May 934, which places his accession between January 933 and May 934. He continues to sign until 946 (*BCS* 813).

After Burgric, the next name in the Rochester list is Ælfstan. He cannot be distinguished from Ælfstan of London until they both sign *BCS* 1134, in 964, with the names of their sees. It is usually assumed that the Ælfstan who signs from 961 (*BCS* 1066) is the bishop of London, which is probable enough. It has been suggested that a Bishop Beorhtsige, who appears in 949 (*BCS* 880), 951 (*BCS* 892) and 955 (*BCS* 909 and *BCS* 911), may belong to Rochester. This is possible, but he could be a suffragan somewhere.

Selsey

Guthheard

Follows Cenred in the episcopal lists. He signs first in 845 (*BCS* 448), his predecessor having last appeared in 839 (*BCS* 421). Guthheard only appears once more, in the witness-list of *BCS* 502 (860–July 862 or 863; see above, *Rochester, Wærmund*).

(Wighelm)

After Guthheard, the next bishop in the fuller lists (BM Stowe 944 and CCCC 173) is Beornheah, who emerges in Athelstan's reign – an apparent

gap of about sixty years. Among the unassignable bishops in the charters of
Edward the Elder (see above, *Lichfield, the Viking period*) is one called Wighelm,
who is sometimes assigned to Selsey. This is probable, because of his witnessing, as the sole episcopal witness, the first part of *BCS* 640 (Sawyer 1206)
concerning a land-transaction in Sussex, when the second part of the document
records that the original piece of land was sold to a later bishop of Selsey,
Wulfhun. The charter cannot be safely dated except to Edward's reign.
E. E. Barker ('Sussex Anglo-Saxon Charters', *Sussex Archaeol. Collections* 87
(1948), 138–9), would narrow the date to 899–905, by identifying one of the
witnesses, Eadwald, with a king's thegn killed in the Kentish forces at the battle
recorded *ASC* 905 BCD (true date probably late in 902). But Eadwald was not
an uncommon name; another man bearing it was killed in the same encounter.
Wighelm signs also *BCS* 596, which is a suspicious New Minster charter
dated late in 900, *BCS* 603, which is an acceptable text of 903, and *BCS* 605
(early in Edward's reign), on all of which see above, *Lichfield, the Viking period*.
He signs also *BCS* 611 (Sawyer 1286), with date and indiction for 904, and
several spurious Winchester charters of 909 (*BCS* 620, *BCS* 623, *BCS* 624 and
BCS 625; *BCS* 627, *BCS* 628 and *BCS* 629).

Beornheah

Follows Guthheard in the lists in BM Stowe 944 and CCCC 173. He appears
first in 925 (*BCS* 641), although he is one of the seven bishops mentioned in the
Plegmund narrative as consecrated on the same day (see below, *Winchester, Frithestan*). It may be that his consecration (with that of Cenwulf of Dorchester)
was added to the original story to make it yet more impressive, and really
belongs to a later year. If it did take place in 909, Wighelm, if a bishop of
Selsey, would appear to have died soon after signing the charters of 909.
Beornheah last appears as the beneficiary of *BCS* 669 in April 930.

Wulfhun

Follows Beornheah in the same lists. He signs in June 931 (*BCS* 675, a reputable charter, though the epact and concurrent have been miscopied) and in
November of the same year (*BCS* 677). His signatures continue until 940 (*BCS*
753 and *BCS* 758).

Alfred

Follows Wulfhun in the same lists, and is included in most of the shorter
lists. At the beginning of his episcopate he is indistinguishable from his
namesake at Sherborne, whose successor does not appear until 943. Alfred's
signatures continue into 953 (*BCS* 898, *BCS* 899 and *BCS* 900). He was probably
succeeded by a Beorhthelm, not in the lists; in a forthcoming article, Professor

Whitelock suggests that a bishop of this name in *BCS* 930 (956) and *BCS* 997 (957) belonged to Selsey, and was probably the *electus* of *BCS* 986 (956); he may have been translated to Winchester in 958.

Sherborne

Ealhstan

Follows Wigberht in all the episcopal lists. The date of his consecration is uncertain. The *ASC* entry, *s.a.* 867, which records his death says that he had held the bishopric for fifty years, that is from 817–18, but *BCS* 377 has his signature as bishop elect in 924 for 824, with indiction and regnal year corresponding to the latter date. The witness-list is not above suspicion, as the bishops of Sherborne and Winchester are given their diocesan titles, which is not common diplomatic practice until the later tenth century; moreover Ealhstan is misnamed *Alfstan*. The entry in *ASC* must have been made within twenty-five years of Ealhstan's death, and Asser (ch. 28) also mentions the length of his episcopate, but the round figure may be inexact and the charter evidence cannot be ignored. The date must remain uncertain.

Heahmund

Follows Ealhstan in all the full lists except FW *Lists*. He is probably intended by the *Eadmund* of *BCS* 1210 (867; see above, *London, Deorwulf*), and signs *BCS* 518 and *BCS* 520 in 868. He appears as bishop elect in *BCS* 519, a single-sheet charter dated 888, which is generally accepted as an original or early copy. Excluding Heahmund, the signatures of King Æthelred and Archbishop Ceolnoth limit the date to 865–70, and it has therefore been postulated that the charter scribe miscopied 888 for 868 (see Sawyer 1204). The date is not clearly written: the scribe has written the V overlapping the third X, and it may be intended as 878. With such evidence of carelessness it might therefore be a mistake to assume that the original date was 868: 867 would fit both the witnesses and Heahmund's appearance as bishop in 867 (*BCS* 1210). But as neither charter is without fault it would perhaps be safer again to leave the question open.

ASC records Heahmund's death at the Battle of *Meretun*, *s.a.* 871.

Æthelheah

Follows Heahmund in all the full lists (in FW *Lists* he follows Ealhstan). He appears in three, perhaps four, charters. *BCS* 543 is a Winchester lease, which looks reputable. It has no date, but the presence of King Alfred and Bishop Ealhferth of Winchester gives the limits 871–7. *BCS* 531 is another undated charter with the same limits from the same witnesses, but the text is a very poor one, and other factors point to a date later in the reign. *BCS* 549 is not much better. It is misdated 979 where 879 was probably intended; Professor Finberg (*ECW* 416) has shown how the indiction might have been miscopied. *ECW* 415 (*BCS* 545) has the signature of a bishop *Ewellial*, which might be Æthelheah in garbled form. The charter has the impossible date 851 and looks spurious.

The only indications of the termination of Æthelheah's episcopate are his successor's appearance, and perhaps Æthelheah's non-appearance in King Alfred's will. It has been suggested (*EHD*, p. 494) that the reference to the 'bishop of Sherborne' with no name given means that the see was vacant at the time, or that the occupant looked as if he would not outlive the king. The will is dated by ecclesiastical witnesses to 873–88, and the appearance of Ealdorman Æthelred as a beneficiary probably indicates a date after Ceolwulf had lost control of Mercia and before Æthelred married Alfred's daughter, since this would almost certainly have been mentioned. Ceolwulf is last mentioned in 877 (*ASC*), and the marriage took place before the end of 889 and perhaps in 887 (Stenton, *A-S England*, p. 260).

Wulfsige

Follows Æthelheah in all the full lists (in FW *Lists* and *GP* he is called *Alfsige*). Wulfsige signs first in 889 (*BCS* 561). He also signs *BCS* 567, which is a very suspect charter dated 892 (Sawyer 348), and, if *Wlfricg* is meant for Wulfsige, *BCS* 568, which is dated only by King Alfred's and the bishop's own appearance. Wulfsige received a copy of the *Cura Pastoralis* in 890–6 (*EHD*, p. 817). A Wulfsige signs from 900 to 909, who is almost certainly the bishop of London, as Asser, the next bishop of Sherborne, appears in the charter of 900. Asser was already a West Saxon bishop before he was appointed to Sherborne (see part I, *Cornwall, Asser*), but he does not appear in the charters earlier, perhaps because he was only a suffragan. There is no reason to suppose he was not bishop of Sherborne by 900. It is sometimes suggested that Wulfsige was transferred to London, but there is no direct evidence for this, only the coincidence in dates.

Asser

Appears in all the episcopal lists. He signs perhaps from 900 (*BCS* 596; see above, *Lichfield, the Viking period*), certainly from 903 (*BCS* 600 and *BCS* 601), to 904 (*BCS* 611 and *BCS* 613). His death is recorded *ASC* 909 A (910 CD) and *Annales Cambriae, s.a.* 908.

Æthelweard

In all the full lists. In *GP* Sigehelm appears between Asser and Æthelweard, because William of Malmesbury accepted the belief of the monks of

Sherborne that the Sigehelm who carried Alfred's alms to India in 883 (*ASC*) was the bishop of Sherborne of this name who follows Æthelbald in the lists (*GP*, p.177). Æthelweard does not appear elsewhere. The Æthelweard *episcopus* who signs *BCS* 627 (909) is a mistake for Æthelweard ætheling. In *GP* and CCCC 183 the division of the see of Sherborne is placed after his name, although he does not occur in the Plegmund narrative (see below, *Winchester, Frithestan*). He may have died soon after election, soon enough for a successor to be appointed to take part in the mass consecration by Plegmund.

Wærstan

Follows Æthelweard in the full lists, and is named as the bishop consecrated for Sherborne in the Plegmund narrative. He does not appear in the charters. An addition to annal 918 in the C manuscript (Oxford, Corpus Christi College 157) of FW *Chron* records his death in 918. This may be unreliable, though an addition in the same manuscript *s.a.* 943 seems correct for a change-over at the see, though it has the names wrong. A story which reached William of Malmesbury (*GP*, p. 177) that he was killed at the Battle of *Brunanburh* (937) is impossible.

Æthelbald

Follows Wærstan in all the full lists. He does not appear elsewhere, except that the addition to manuscript C of FW *Chron* wrongly says he died in 943, and was succeeded by Alfred.

Sigehelm

In all the full lists. He signs from 925 (*BCS* 641) to 932 (*BCS* 689, *BCS* 690 and *BCS* 692). The *Siglem* of *BCS* 597 (901) is probably meant for Wighelm of Selsey (see *ECW* 35).

Alfred

In all the full lists. His signatures are difficult to disentangle from those of a Bishop Alfred who appears in charters from *c*. 915 to at least 934, and later from those of Alfred of Selsey, whose predecessor last signs in 940. A Bishop Alfred signs *BCS* 632, a Mercian charter dated 878, probably for 915 (see below, *Worcester, Æthelhun*). An *Elured* signs *BCS* 697 (933), who could be the bishop of Sherborne or the other, probably Mercian, Alfred, but this charter is a Chertsey forgery (Sawyer 420). In 934 (*BCS* 702, *BCS* 703 and *BCS* 705) two Alfreds sign, and one must be the bishop of Sherborne. One Bishop Alfred signs the spurious *BCS* 738 (843 for ?934), *BCS* 707 (935) and *BCS* 716 (937; see part I, *Cornwall, Conan*). In *BCS* 744 (939) a Bishop Alfred received a grant of land in Dorset and regranted it to a woman called Beorhtwynn; he is likely to be the bishop of Sherborne rather than the possibly Mercian Alfred. One Alfred continues to sign frequently from 940 on. The next bishop of Sherborne, Wulfsige, appears in 943. It would seem as if the Alfred who signs from 940 is the bishop of Selsey, for his position in the witness-lists does not alter significantly at any time. William of Malmesbury's story of the death of a bishop of Sherborne at *Brunanburh* (see above, under *Wærstan*) could not be true of Alfred if the interpretation of *BCS* 744 is correct.

Wulfsige

In all the full lists (FW *Lists* and FW *Chron, s.a.* 958, wrongly call him *Alfsi*). He signs from 943 (*BCS* 783, *BCS* 784 and *BCS* 788) to 957 (*BCS* 998, *BCS* 999 and *BCS* 1004), and once in 958 (*BCS* 1032). The next name in the lists is Ælfwold, but the oldest Life of St Dunstan (*Memorials*, p. 38) says that the successor to Archbishop Ælfsige of Canterbury in 958 or 959 was a certain Beorhthelm, *Dorsætensium prævisorem*. From this source FW *Chron, s.a.* 958, takes its statement that *Alsius Dorsetensium episcopus* was succeeded by Beorhthelm, and under 959 it mentions his appointment to Canterbury; but in the C manuscript *Dorsetensium episcopus* had been altered to *Sumorsetensium episcopus* in a hand which may be that of the author himself. Since there was certainly a bishop of Wells of this name at the time, the alteration may be correct; the author of the Life of St Dunstan may have put Beorhthelm at Sherborne in error. It is also possible that Beorhthelm of Wells may have held Sherborne in plurality for a short time, from 958. If we reject these explanations, we must assume a different Beorhthelm, appointed to Sherborne in 958, translated to Canterbury, and sent back to Sherborne to make room for Dunstan at Canterbury in 959 or early in 960. The signatures of Ælfwold of Sherborne are difficult to distinguish from those of Ælfwold of Crediton, who signs from 952–3 to 973; both, however, appear in 964 (*BCS* 1134 and *BCS* 1143). There are two bishops of this name also in *BCS* 1079 (961), but the title of the second is probably a mistake for abbot; he appears at the bottom of the list of bishops, preceded by Bishop Æthelwold, who was only an abbot until 963, while in *BCS* 1120 (963) both Æthelwold and Ælfwold appear as abbots. Ælfwold may have become bishop of Sherborne in 963 or 964. If we reject as an error the assigning of Beorhthelm to Sherborne, Wulfsige may have held the see until 964; otherwise he was succeeded by Beorhthelm in 958.

Wells

Athelm

Named as the first bishop of Wells in the episcopal lists and in the Plegmund narrative (see below, *Winchester, Frithestan*). He was translated to Canterbury after Plegmund's death in 923 and before Athelstan's coronation in September 925 (see part I, *Canterbury, Plegmund* and *Athelm*).

Wulfhelm

Follows Athelm in the lists. He signs once as bishop in 925 (*BCS* 641), before following Athelm to Canterbury after the latter's death in January 926 (see part I, *Canterbury, Wulfhelm*).

Ælfheah

Follows Wulfhelm in the lists. He probably signs first in 927 (*BCS* 660; see above, *Ramsbury, Oda*), then in 928 (*BCS* 663), and then on into the 930s. After 934 an Ælfheah appears at Winchester, and both sign in 935 (*BCS* 707), and in 937 (*BCS* 714); for *BCS* 699 and *BCS* 705 see below, *Winchester, Ælfheah*. The two Ælfheahs are distinguishable; the bishop of Wells is usually found somewhere in the middle of the episcopal witnesses, whereas Ælfheah of Winchester is found almost invariably at or near the head of the list. Ælfheah of Wells does not appear after 937.

Wulfhelm

Follows Ælfheah in the lists. His signatures can be confused with those of another Wulfhelm who appears in charters of 931 (*BCS* 675), 934 (*BCS* 702 and *BCS* 703) and 937 (*BCS* 716; two Wulfhelms attest here) and who cannot be assigned to any known see (see part I, *Hereford, Wulfhelm*). If one can accept the testimony of *BCS* 716 (see part I, *Cornwall, Conan*), with two Wulfhelms, one of whom must belong to Wells, this dates the change-over to 937. Otherwise, since only one Wulfhelm then signs until two appear in the witness-list attached to *BCS* 812, belonging to 943–7, probably before late 946 (see Whitelock, *Æthelgifu*, p. 43), it could have occurred later, though it is most likely that it is Wulfhelm of Wells who signs from 938 to 956. He makes two appearances in 956 (*BCS* 923 and *BCS* 969). The next bishop of Wells, Beorhthelm, first appears in 956, when he signs several charters in company with his namesake of London. It is sometimes stated that Beorhthelm of Wells is the king's kinsman to whom, as bishop elect, Eadwig made a grant in 956 (*BCS* 986), but it is possible that this was a bishop of Selsey, perhaps to be identified with the Beorhthelm who became bishop of Winchester in 958, who certainly was a kinsman of the king (see above, *Selsey, Alfred*).

Winchester

Helmstan

Follows Eadhun in all episcopal lists. Eadhun last signs in 838 and Helmstan first appears in 839 (*BCS* 421). Helmstan made his profession to

Archbishop Ceolnoth (*BCS* 424). He appears in *ECW* 567, dated 26 December 841 (in modern reckoning 840) and in *ECW* 566 (cf. *ibid.* pp. 206–9), dated 844, a dubious document, although the witness-list looks possible for the date.

Swithhun

Follows Helmstan in all the lists. His ordination is given as 29 or 30 October (*Councils* III, 634). These were Sundays in 853 and 852 respectively. He made his profession to Archbishop Ceolnoth (*BCS* 463). His first signatures are in 854. Several of the charters of this date (e.g. *BCS* 470) belong to the decimation group and their testimony is of doubtful value; but he also witnesses *BCS* 481, a Malmesbury charter of this year which seems independent of this group. It has a seemingly reputable witness-list, including an ealdorman Sigeric who does not occur elsewhere, and the indiction matches the date. The charter may have a genuine base. Otherwise, Swithhun's earliest reliable signature is in 856 (*BCS* 491). He leases land to King Æthelbald in 858 (*BCS* 495), and attests *BCS* 499 and *BCS* 500, both in 860, *BCS* 504 (862) and *BCS* 508 (863). These last two charters have been suspected because the king's name is Æthelred, who did not succeed until 865, but Professor Darlington suggests that he may have been sub-king of the western area in his brother's lifetime. Swithhun is said to have held the episcopate for ten years (*Councils* III, 634). His Life by Goscelin (*Acta Sanctorum*, July 1 (2nd ed., Paris and Rome, 1867), 290–2) dates his death to 862, as does FW *Chron*, dating it as Thursday 2 July, which is correct for 862, but may be the author's own calculation. *ADL* records it *s.a.* 861, *GP s.a.* 863. 861 is too early, but one cannot pronounce firmly between 862 and 863. 2 July is the date given already in a ninth-century calendar (*English Kalendars before A.D.* 1100, ed. F. Wormald 1, Henry Bradshaw Society 72 (1934): Oxford, Bodleian Library, Digby 63).

Ealhferth

Follows Swithhun in all the lists except CCCC 183. He signs once in 867 (*BCS* 1210; see above, *London, Deorwulf*), three times in 868 and once in 869 (*BCS* 525). He also appears in three charters of Alfred's reign, two of which, *BCS* 531 and *BCS* 543, are given a closer dating only by his signature (871–7; see above, *Sherborne, Æthelheah*). The third, *ECW* 415, has an impossible date and is not acceptable.

Tunberht

Follows Ealhferth in all the lists except FW *Lists*, CCCC 183 and BM Cotton Tiberius B. v, where he is omitted. In *GP* he is mis-spelt *Dunbeorht*. He signs once as bishop in 877 (*BCS* 544), in a grant to the refectory at Winchester, which is not entirely above suspicion. An Abbot Tunberht, presumably of

Winchester, appears in *BCS* 531 and *BCS* 543, the former a suspicious Shaftesbury grant, the latter a Winchester document, and it seems likely that it is he who was promoted to the episcopacy. Tunberht's death (with his name as *Dumbert*) is recorded in FW *Chron, s.a.* 879, after an entry about the Viking army corresponding to that under the same year in *ASC*; both chronicles mention an eclipse, probably that of 20 October 878. But as there is no reason to believe that FW *Chron* took its episcopal accessions and obits from the same source as the events in its annals, the fact that the latter are or may be misdated need not cause us to assume that its dates of episcopal succession share the same error.

Denewulf

Appears in all the lists. His accession is dated 879 by FW *Chron*. He appears in *BCS* 549, dated 979 probably in error for 879 (see above, *Sherborne, Æthelheah*). His signatures then occur from *c*. 901 to 904, and his death is recorded in *ASC* 908 A and 909 CDF. FW *Chron* has 909, but its dates for the previous and following years are a year late in comparison with *ASC* A and with the Mercian Register. Denewulf appears as the beneficiary of *BCS* 622, a lease which Birch dates 909, though there is no date in the document. The witness-list however includes Frithestan, Denewulf's successor, and there are evidences of miscopying (see *Anglo-Saxon Charters*, ed. A. J. Robertson (Cambridge, 1939), pp. 296–8).

Frithestan

Appears in all lists. His succession is recorded in *ASC* 909 A (910 C, D and FW *Chron*). According to the Plegmund narrative (see *Crawford Charters* VII and Robinson, *Saxon Bishops,* pp. 7–24) three new sees were created for Wessex, namely Crediton, Ramsbury and Wells, and Plegmund consecrated seven bishops in one day, one for each of these sees, as well as Wærstan of Sherborne, Frithestan of Winchester, Beornheah of Selsey and Cenwulf of Dorchester. Robinson assigns the division of the two West Saxon sees into five to 909, putting together the date of Frithestan's accession and of Asser's death, the account of the division in the episcopal lists, especially the near contemporary CCCC 183 (*c*. 935), and the Plegmund narrative. Certainly the year 909 would be a good time for the division, with both Winchester and Sherborne vacant, though the story of the seven bishops consecrated in one day may well have been improved upon in the telling. CCCC 183 places the division of Winchester *tempore Frithestani* and says after Æthelweard (Assers' successor at Sherborne) 'deinde in tres parrochias diuisa est'. Yet it is possible that Frithestan was consecrated before the division. *ASC* definitely places Asser's death after Frithestan's accession, and then Æthelweard had to be

elected to Sherborne, to die, and to be replaced by Wærstan in time for Wærstan to be the bishop consecrated at the mass consecration. Moreover the
various Winchester charters of 909, some of which mention the division
(*BCS* 620, *BCS* 625, *BCS* 628 and *BCS* 629), are witnessed by Bishop Frithestan,
by the bishops of London and Rochester, and by Wighelm, who may be
Beornheah's predecessor at Selsey. Admittedly the charters are all very dubious
as they stand, but it is odd that, apart from Frithestan, none of the new bishops
appears. If Frithestan's consecration belongs to 909, and the other bishops
were consecrated soon after, perhaps by 910, it would be simple for Frithestan's name to be added to the Plegmund narrative later, to complete the
pattern. This argument is put forward as a tentative alternative to Robinson's
reconstruction, and the dates in the lists have been left as *c*. 909.

Frithestan otherwise appears in charters in 928 (*BCS* 663), 929 (*BCS* 665 and
BCS 666) and 931 (*BCS* 674). This is infrequent for the major bishopric of
Wessex, and it may well be due to whatever infirmity led to his resignation.
ASC A, written during these years at Winchester, records that Byrnstan
succeeded in 931 (see below), and that Frithestan died in 932. FW *Chron*,
perhaps merely enlarging on this, has *s.a.* 932: 'Frithestan, bishop of Winchester, a man of the most exalted piety, continued to reside at Winchester,
after the holy man Byrnstan had been ordained his successor in the bishopric',
and Frithestan's death is recorded in the following year (see below).

Byrnstan

Follows Frithestan in all the lists except CCCC 183, where he is omitted.
His ordination day is given in *ASC* A as 29 May, which effectively fixes the
year as 931, in which 29 May was Whit Sunday. The evidence offered by *ASC*
A for Byrnstan's episcopate is contradictory, although it should be our best
authority. The difficulty lies in the dating. Up to and including 920 (*s.a.* 924,
corrected from 923) A is out of joint in its dating. Then a new scribe begins a
fresh page with an annal recording Edward's death and Athelstan's succession
s.a. 925, a date which is the result of a correction. Then follow several blank
annals and Byrnstan's accession *s.a.* 931, which has been altered from 932.
The alteration, back-dating events by a year, continues to 941, originally 942.
The alteration of 932 to 931 was a correction, as is shown by the Whitsun
ordination, but the case for 934 to 933 is less clear. This annal contains Byrnstan's death and Athelstan's expedition to Scotland, which latter is placed in
934 by the other versions of *ASC* and by the charter evidence (see Stenton,
A-S England, p. 342). Ælfheah's accession to Winchester is the next annal, 935
corrected to 934, and the next entry is the Battle of *Brunanburh* recorded under
938, corrected to 937 (which then agrees with the other chronicles). Thus the
original dating of A was out at 932, correct at 934 and out again at 938. It must

be on this dating that the scribe of the 932 annal calculated the length of Byrnstan's episcopate as two-and-a-half rather than three-and-a-half years, although the latter looks correct when one examines the charter evidence.

Byrnstan signs several reputable charters in 931, 932 and 933. He signs high in the list in *BCS* 702, a charter issued at Winchester on 28 May 934. His name is included also at the bottom of the episcopal witnesses of *BCS* 703, issued at Nottingham on 7 June 934, on the expedition to Scotland. This appearance looks rather like a copyist's afterthought: it seems unlikely that the bishop, who was to die in a few months' time (at Winchester, if William of Malmesbury is to be believed), would go so far north on a military expedition. Byrnstan's death-day is given by *ASC* A as All Saints' Day, 1 November, and almost certainly belongs to 934.

Frithestan's death cannot safely be assigned to 932, since a year has been lost in *ASC* between 931 and 934, and it is impossible to say whether this was 932 or 933. One might argue that since the 931 annal took up two lines it is 932 that has been lost, and Frithestan therefore died in 933, but it is a tenuous argument.

Ælfheah

Appears in all the lists. *ASC* A records his succession for the year following that of Byrnstan's death (*s.a.* 934, originally 935), as does FW *Chron, s.a.* 935. There are however three charters in which Ælfheah appears before 935, with no possibility of confusion with his namesake at Wells. *BCS* 694 is a grant of privileges to the bishopric of Crediton, dated 933 with the corresponding indiction and witnessed by Ælfheah of Winchester. It exists in single-sheet form, written in a later tenth-century hand (Sawyer 421). The text is in a style very typical of Athelstan's charters. However either the date or the witness-list is wrong, for Byrnstan was still alive in 934. *BCS* 699 is also dated 933, with no indiction, and is signed by both Ælfheahs. The charter is oddly but not impossibly worded, and the date might well have been miscopied from 936 (*III* from *VI*). *BCS* 705, with its Anglo-Saxon version *BCS* 706, is less easy to assess. It was issued at Frome, and dated 16 December 934, with the indiction for 934, although strictly it should have been changed after September. Athelstan had returned to Wessex from his Scottish expedition of the autumn by then (he was at Buckingham on 12 September, according to *BCS* 704), and it is possible that Byrnstan's successor had been appointed and consecrated within six weeks of his death. But there is the evidence of *BCS* 707 to be considered, dated 935, although the indiction is a year behind. It is a reputable charter, and includes the following witness: 'Ego Ælfheah Wintoniensis aecclesiae provisor in electione sua confirmavi'. If this means, as I understand it, that Ælfheah was bishop elect but not yet consecrated in 935, this would accord with the *ASC* entry and would discredit the evidence of *BCS* 705 on this point.

Ælfheah signs up to and including 951, and his death is recorded in *ASC* 951 A on 12 March.

Worcester

Alhhun

There is some uncertainty about his name. He is called *Alhuuine* or *Alhwinus* in the lists in CCCC 140, FW *Lists* and *GP*, where he follows Heahberht. *BCS* 448, considered an original, has *Alhhun*, which is the form in FW *Chron* and in most charters; *BCS* 488, a cartulary copy, has *Alhhuno* in the text and *Alhwine* in the witness-list. *BCS* 490, on the other hand, a lost Somers charter, calls him *Alhwine*, and Wanley in his *Catalogue* (G. Hickes, *Linguarum Veterum Septentrionalium Thesaurus* II (Oxford, 1705), 302) says it was a cyrograph with the bottom half of the letters *CYROGRAPHUM ALHWINI EP.* 7 *ÆÐEL-WULFI DuCis* in the upper margin.

His predecessor Heahberht last signs in *BCS* 443 (843–4) and in *BCS* 450, a rather suspect charter dated 25 December 845 (in modern reckoning 844). Alhhun first appears in *BCS* 448, dated 8 November 845, and in *BCS* 452, dated 843–5 (or December, 844–5, if *BCS* 450 is reliable evidence – the date of *BCS* 452 depends on Alhhun's appearance). He also signs *BCS* 453, dated 840 with corresponding indiction and regnal year, but the text is suspect, and the evidence of *BCS* 443 is to be preferred. He witnesses *BCS* 454, dated 844 probably for 847 or 848 (see above, *Lichfield, Tunberht*). FW *Chron* gives Alhhun's succession *s.a.* 848, but this is strongly contradicted by the charter evidence. Alhhun signs until 869 (*BCS* 524).

Wærferth

Follows Alhhun in the lists mentioned above. Wærferth first appears in 872 in *BCS* 533, issuing a reputable lease (Sawyer 1278) whose reference to tribute paid to the Vikings at London accords with the entry in *ASC*. FW *Chron* records his accession, followed by the Viking occupation of London, which reinforces the sequence of events. However, it adds that Wærferth was ordained bishop at Pentecost, on the seventh of the Ides of June, which was Pentecost in 873. If one accepts the evidence of *BCS* 533, either Florence had a record of a consecration at Pentecost (or guessed that this was the occasion) and calculated it for 873 by mistake, or had the date VI Ides of June, a Sunday in 872, and misread it and connected it with the date of Pentecost in 873.

Wærferth continues to appear until 904 (*BCS* 608 and *BCS* 609), perhaps until 907 (*BCS* 616, a suspicious document; Sawyer 1282). His death is recorded in FW *Chron, s.a.* 915, which may be the true date, though the other events in this annal probably took place in 914.

Æthelhun

His succession to Wærferth is recorded in FW *Chron, s.a.* 915 (see above). His name follows Wærferth's in CCCC 140 and in FW *Lists* (except that Dublin, Trinity College 502, E5, 23 has the sequence Wærferth, Wilferth, Æthelhun). Æthelhun signs once, in *BCS* 632, a Mercian charter which is dated 878, but which from internal evidence (the reference to *Weardburg* and the witness of Abbot Egbert, who died in 916) should belong to 915. Æthelhun's death and the succession of Wilferth are recorded in FW *Chron, s.a.* 922. The other events in this annal may perhaps belong to 921.

Wilferth

In FW *Lists* as above, but omitted in CCCC 140. FW *Chron* records his succession in 922 (see above). He appears as the donor of land to the *familia* at Worcester in 922 (*BCS* 636). He signs twice in 925 (*BCS* 641, miswritten *Wlbred*, and *BCS* 642), and once in 928 (*BCS* 663). The wording of the last charter is not above suspicion, but both the dating clause and the witness-list are full and coherent. His death and Cenwald's succession are entered in FW *Chron, s.a.* 929.

Cenwald

Appears in both episcopal lists mentioned above. His accession is given as 929 in FW *Chron* (see above). He travelled round the continent in 929 (Stenton, *A-S England*, p. 444) and he appears in charters from 930 (*Crawford Charters* IV and *BCS* 669). Unless one accepts FW *Chron*, one can date his succession in 928, the last appearance of his predecessor, or in 929.

Cenwald signs frequently until 957, under which year his death is recorded in FW *Chron*. He signs also once in 958 (*BCS* 1042) in company with Dunstan, his successor at Worcester, who signs as bishop. This charter was issued by Edgar, as king of the Mercians, and concerns the Oxfordshire, not the Hampshire, Wootton. The appearance of Dunstan as bishop in Cenwald's lifetime may give support to the account in the earliest Life of St Dunstan (*Memorials*, pp. 36–7) which says that Dunstan, when recalled from exile by Edgar, was at first consecrated bishop without a see, and later became bishop of Worcester. It is possible, therefore, that Cenwald lived until 958.

Athelstan 'Half King' and his family

CYRIL HART

Anglo-Saxon genealogy is full of pitfalls, and it is not to be wondered that no one has followed the pioneer work of W. G. Searle in reconstructing the pedigrees of some of the noble houses. Much of the source material is suspect, or too vaguely worded for precise conclusions as to family relationships. The whole topic bristles with difficulties, yet its importance is fundamental; for this as for other periods, detailed examination of family ties and estates supplies essential background information for anyone seeking to uncover the interests and pressures which helped to formulate national policy.[1]

Most of the ninth- and tenth-century ealdormen were scions of cadet branches of the royal house, but unlike their continental counterparts none of them, not even the noblest and the most powerful, succeeded in establishing

[1] The following abbreviations are used in this article: *Athelney = Two Cartularies of the Benedictine Abbeys of Muchelney and Athelney*, ed. E. H. Bates, Somerset Record Society 14 (1899); *BCS = Cartularium Saxonicum*, ed. W. de Gray Birch (London, 1885–93); *Cart Rams = Cartularium Monasterii de Rameseia*, ed. W. H. Hart and P. A. Lyons, Rolls Series (1884–93); *Chron Abingd = Chronicon Monasterii de Abingdon*, ed. J. Stevenson, RS (1858); *Chron Rams = Chronicon Abbatiae Rameseiensis*, ed. W. Dunn Macray, RS (1886); *Crawford Charters = The Crawford Collection of Early Charters and Documents*, ed. A. S. Napier and W. H. Stevenson (Oxford, 1895); *CW =* C. Hart, 'The Codex Wintoniensis and the King's Haligdom', *Agricultural Hist. Rev.* 18 (1970), Supplement, pp. 7–38; *DB = Domesday Book*, ed. A. Farley and H. Ellis (London, 1783–1816); *ECDC =* H. P. R. Finberg, *The Early Charters of Devon and Cornwall*, 2nd ed. (Leicester, 1963); *ECEE =* C. Hart, *The Early Charters of Eastern England* (Leicester, 1966); *ECStP = Early Charters of the Cathedral Church of St Paul, London*, ed. M. Gibbs, Royal Historical Society, Camden 3rd ser. 58 (London, 1939); *ECW =* H. P. R. Finberg, *The Early Charters of Wessex* (Leicester, 1964); *ECWM =* H. P. R. Finberg, *The Early Charters of the West Midlands* (Leicester, 1961); *EHD = English Historical Documents* 1, ed. D. Whitelock (London, 1955); Harmer, *SelEHD = Select English Historical Documents of the Ninth and Tenth Centuries*, ed. F. E. Harmer (Cambridge, 1914); Kemble = *Codex Diplomaticus Ævi Saxonici*, ed. J. M. Kemble (London, 1839–48); *LE = Liber Eliensis*, ed. E. O. Blake, RHS, Camden 3rd ser. 92 (London, 1962); *LH = Liber Monasterii de Hyda*, ed. E. Edwards, RS (1866); *Lincs DB = The Lincolnshire Domesday and the Lindsey Survey*, ed. C. W. Foster and Thomas Longley, Lincoln Record Society 19 (Lincoln, 1924); *Memorials = Memorials of St Dunstan*, ed. W. Stubbs, RS (1874); *New Monasticon =* W. Dugdale, *Monasticon Anglicanum*, ed. J. Caley, H. Ellis and B. Bandinel (London, 1817–30); Robertson, *Charters = Anglo-Saxon Charters*, ed. A. J. Robertson, 2nd ed. (Cambridge, 1956); *St O =* 'The Anonymous Life of St Oswald', *The Historians of the Church of York and its Archbishops*, ed. J. Raine, RS (1879–94) I, 399–475; TRE = the time of King Edward the Confessor. Charters are quoted by the numbers assigned to them in their respective editions. The mark ' × ' between two dates indicates that the event in question took place anywhere between these dates inclusively; the mark '—' between two dates indicates that they come from a single source – usually a charter – which cannot be dated more closely.

dynasties of any permanence. Athelstan 'Half King' at the height of his power governed in virtual autonomy a province the size of Normandy, and owned in addition extensive estates outside his ealdordom; as the most influential adviser of a teen-age monarch he became for a while virtually the regent of all England, and subsequently he fostered one of the æthelings; nevertheless his family was completely bereft of influence before the end of the century, in sharp contradistinction to those of the dynastic rulers of Flanders, Normandy and Aquitaine.

Athelstan was probably the second of four sons of Æthelfrith, one of the three sub-ealdormen of Mercia in the closing years of the ninth century. These ealdormen were each allotted an area to govern under Ealdorman Æthelred of Mercia and his wife Æthelflæd, the sister of King Edward the Elder of Wessex. Æthelflæd's uncle Æthelwulf, who was the senior of the three, was responsible for the western territories, and possibly also for central Mercia.[1] The sphere of influence of Alhhelm, the junior ealdorman, seems to have been limited to the Mercian lands bordering on the northern Danelaw.[2] Ealdorman Æthelfrith, with whom we are chiefly concerned, appears first to have controlled the southern and eastern territories of Mercia.[3] After the turn of the century, when his colleagues Æthelwulf and Ælhhelm disappear from the scene, he may have taken over their ealdordoms also, for there are no records of any other successors. Indeed, when one recalls that Ealdorman Æthelred himself was incapacitated by illness from at least 902 onwards,[4] it seems very likely that Æthelfrith became the principal lieutenant of Æthelflæd, Lady of the Mercians, in her campaign against the Danes. As far as one can tell, he was the only active ealdorman in Mercia at this period.

[1] He was a descendant of King Cenwulf of Mercia and the brother of King Alfred's wife Ealhswith, and is named in or witnesses (sometimes as Æthulf) the following charters of the period 866 × 897: *BCS* 513, 522, 552, 557 and 575; *ECWM* 267; Harmer, *SelEHD* xiv; and *ECStP* p. 2, n. 2 (a forgery utilizing a genuine witness list of the year 867). Two of these show that his ealdordom included the territory of the Hwicce. He died in 901 (*ASC* 902 A).

[2] He witnesses the following charters of the period 884 × 896: *BCS* 537, 552 and 557; and Harmer, *SelEHD* xiv. Probably he is to be identified with the Alchelm who received land in Derbyshire from Æthelflæd, Lady of the Mercians, in 900 (*BCS* 583).

[3] His wife was the lady named Æthelgyth to whom a large estate at Princes Risborough, Buckinghamshire, had been left by her father Æthulf or Æthelwulf (*BCS* 603; it is unsafe to identify him with the Ealdorman Æthulf referred to above, n. 1). It is likely that the Mercian witenagemot which met at Princes Risborough in 884 (*BCS* 552) was being entertained by Æthelfrith, who was certainly in possession of the estate in 903. Ealdorman Æthelfrith figures in or witnesses the following charters of the period 883 × 904: *BCS* 552, 557, 595, 603 and 606–8; and Harmer, *SelEHD* xii and xiv. He also witnesses the doubtful *BCS* 632, dated Monday 9 September 916. He may be the thegn who witnesses *ECStP* p. 2, n. 2 (an authentic list dated 867) and *BCS* 522. His own charters were destroyed by fire (*BCS* 603 and 606 and *ECStP* p. 4, all constructed from the same formula. Of these, the two first are independent texts. The St Paul's charter is incomplete; it may be a copy of one of these, or a third independent text utilizing the same diplomatic.)

[4] F. T. Wainwright, 'Æthelflæd, Lady of the Mercians', *The Anglo-Saxons: Studies in some Aspects of their History and Culture presented to Bruce Dickins,* ed. Peter Clemoes (London, 1959), pp. 53–69, esp. 56.

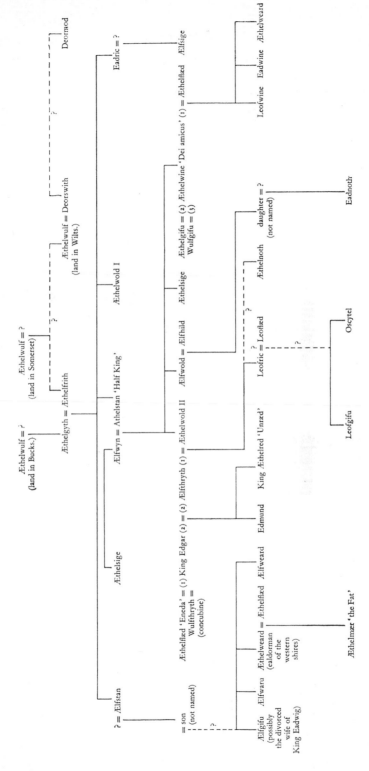

Genealogical table

In spite of these widespread Mercian responsibilities, Ealdorman Æthelfrith is more likely to have descended from the West Saxon than from the Mercian royal house. His estates lay principally in Somerset and Devon, and he is the only Mercian ealdorman known to have witnessed charters of King Edward the Elder; as we shall see, his children's interests were predominantly in Wessex. His appointment to a Mercian ealdordom must have antedated by some years Æthelflæd's marriage to Ealdorman Æthelred, and affords our earliest evidence (if we accept Æthelfrith's West Saxon antecedents) of King Alfred's control of Mercian affairs, brought about doubtless by pressures arising from the Danish settlement. It looks rather as if King Alfred seized the opportunity to appoint a West Saxon to fill the vacuum created when some members of the original Mercian nobility transferred their allegiance to the Danes.[1]

Ealdorman Æthelfrith appears to have survived until at least 916.[2] Two years later, the West Saxon royal house took over direct control of Mercia, and under the new régime all of Æthelfrith's four sons became ealdormen in the second quarter of the century.

Ælfstan, the eldest, was appointed to this rank in or before 930, and may in fact have succeeded to his father's ealdordom.[3] He died before he could achieve much seniority. Royal diplomas of the period 930 × 934 are unique in the precision of their dating clauses; the day and place of ratification are always recorded, and we are able therefore to trace Ælfstan in 934 riding in the king's company northwards as far as Nottingham, where he witnessed a charter on 7 June.[4] As Ælfstan then ceases to witness, it appears likely that he died during the campaign in Scotland that summer.[5]

The next son of Æthelfrith was Athelstan 'Half King', the principal subject of this essay, but we will pass on for a moment to review the careers of his younger brothers, Æthelwold and Eadric, who appear in the charters as thegns from 931 onwards. They witness high up on the lists from the outset, and as was the custom with brothers, their names often appear adjacent to

[1] On this, see *The Anglo-Saxon Chronicle: a Revised Translation*, ed. D. Whitelock, D. C. Douglas and S. I. Tucker (London, 1961), p. 60, n. 4; *Crawford Charters* p. 85; and E. V. Gordon, *The Battle of Maldon*, 2nd ed. (London, 1949), p. 16.

[2] *BCS* 632.

[3] He witnesses the following charters: *BCS* 620 (see *ECW* pp. 244–6), 623–5, 627, 632, 669, 1343, 674–7, 689, 692, 703, 696 and 635 (a charter of King Athelstan dated 11 January 933, which has been amended by the substitution of King Edward's name). Some of these charters contain spurious elements, but the witness-lists are mostly reliable. Ælfstan's son received an estate in Hampshire (Harmer, *SelEHD* xx), and may have been the father of Æthelweard, ealdorman of the western shires. [4] *BCS* 703.

[5] From similar evidence it seems likely that the West Saxon ealdorman Osferth, who was closely related to the royal house, perished during the same campaign. In addition, the following Scandinavian earls stop witnessing Athelstan's charters after 7 June 934: Regenwold, Thurferth, Haddr and Inwer. It seems likely that these too, or some of them, were killed in the fighting.

each other in the witness-lists, with Æthelwold normally taking the senior place.[1] Eadric was more often at court in the early years. After 934 however Æthelwold's seniority becomes more apparent, and his name is separated from Eadric's by those of several other thegns.

Æthelwold (whom we shall designate as Æthelwold I, to distinguish him from his nephew and namesake) was created ealdorman in 940, during the first few months of the reign of King Edmund. His jurisdiction lay in Kent and in the adjacent shires.[2] Just before his appointment, he received from King Edmund an estate at Chelworth, in Crudwell, Wiltshire, which he gave to Glastonbury during his lifetime; it must have been one of the earliest endowments of that monastery during Dunstan's abbacy.[3] Æthelwold I died in 946 and his will survives; it disposes of land 'acquired from the king' in Hampshire, Wiltshire, Berkshire, Surrey and Sussex.[4] There is no reference to any patrimony. Almost certainly he died a bachelor, for there is no provision for the soul of a wife or for any offspring. He directed that his *læn* lands should be disposed of for his soul; the booklands forming the remainder of his property were divided between his brothers and their descendants, with the exception of twelve hides at *Wilig* which he left to the Old Minster at Winchester for his burial fee.[5]

[1] *BCS* 674, 677, 689, 702–3 and 706 are all witnessed by the two brothers in adjacent places in the lists. Other charters witnessed by Æthelwold as thegn are *BCS* 707, 714, 721, 730, 734, 742, 753, 758 and 762. Eadric witnesses as thegn, in addition to the group referred to above, the following charters: *BCS* 669, 1343, 675, 692, 635 (dated 933), 695–6, 705, 707 and 714, *ECW* 436 and *BCS* 730, 734, 742, 748, 753, 758, 762–3, 765, 767 and 770.

[2] It is probable that he succeeded one Ælfwold, who witnessed as ealdorman the following charters dated 926 × 938: *BCS* 658–9, 663–6, 669, 1343, 675–7, 689, 691–2, 635 (dated 933), 695–6, 702, 703 (= 1344), 705, 714 and 716–18, *Athelney* 97 and *BCS* 729–31. Æthelwold I witnesses the following charters as ealdorman: *BCS* 748, 758, 762–4, 767, 769–70, 772, 774–5, 777–8, 780, 782–4, 791–2, 795–6, 798, 801–2, 808 and 813–14.

[3] This may be deduced from an entry in the Glastonbury landbook, recording King Edmund's gift of Chelworth to someone named Æthelwold who was presumably a thegn, since he was not given the title of ealdorman (*ECW* 257). The thegn Æthelwold who witnesses charters of the period 931 × 940 is almost certainly the brother of the 'Half King', since, after the appointment of Æthelwold I as ealdorman in 940, no thegn of this name witnesses until 956. That Æthelwold I gave Chelworth to Glastonbury during his lifetime may be surmised from the absence of any reference to the estate in his will, together with the fact that the text of King Edmund's charter was preserved in the Glastonbury landbook.

[4] Harmer, *SelEHD* xx.

[5] This estate has been identified with the ten hides at Codford and Stockton in the Wylye valley which belonged to Winchester Cathedral at the time of Domesday (*ECW* p. 88 and *CW* p. 13). Its interest for us lies in the fact that the same estate had been granted by King Edward the Elder to someone named Æthelwulf in 901 (*BCS* 595 and *EHD* p. 499). An Old English endorsement to this grant records that the land was settled by Æthelwulf on one Deorswith, presumably as part of a marriage agreement between them; Deorswith's relative (perhaps brother) named Deormod, who figures in the endorsement, was King Alfred's *cellerarius* and the most powerful royal official at court at this period (*BCS* 567). The descent of Wylye to Æthelwold I suggests that Æthelwulf was his ancestor, and in the genealogical table I have placed him provisionally as Ealdorman Æthelfrith's brother. Whatever the precise kinship, it is clear that Deormod was related by marriage

From 942 onwards, Æthelwold I's brother Eadric held the adjacent ealdordom in central Wessex, having succeeded a *dux* called Ælfhere.[1] King Edmund granted him estates in Wiltshire and Dorset which descended to the nunnery at Shaftesbury, presumably by gift of Eadric or his descendants;[2] later, King Eadred gave him land in Sussex with which he endowed Abingdon,[3] and further land on the Berkshire Downs which became another of the earliest endowments of Glastonbury.[4] It is interesting that Eadric had already received lands in these last two places, by the will of his brother Æthelwold I; whether King Eadred's charters were mere confirmation of Æthelwold's bequest, or whether they recorded the grant of additional estates at these places, we do not know. Eadric survived his brother Æthelwold I by three years; his will has not come down to us. He was succeeded as ealdorman of mid-Wessex by Æthelsige.[5]

This account of the brothers of the 'Half King' suggests an answer to the first question occurring to anyone examining his career. Why was he appointed to rule East Anglia, rather than his father's ealdordom of south-east Mercia, or the portion of Wessex from which the family sprang? The reason may be simply that these ealdordoms did not fall vacant at the appropriate time. The East Anglian ealdordom, we may safely assume, was created by Edward the Elder soon after his reconquest of the eastern Danelaw, and it is a reasonable

to the family of the 'Half King'. He witnesses as thegn the following Wessex charters, usually as the first of the thegns subscribing: *BCS* 549 (879); 568 (881–8); 550, 567 (as *cellerarius*) (892); 590, 594 and 596, Harmer, *SelEHD* xvi (900); and *BCS* 588, 595, 597–8 (901); 601 (903); 604, 611–13 (904); 620 (inaccurately given as 'Deormund'; see *ECW* 244–6), 623–5 and 627–8 (909). In 892–9 King Alfred granted him five hides at Appleford, Berkshire in exchange for land at Horn Down in East Hendred, Berkshire (*BCS* 581). Appleford descended to Abingdon, possibly via the family of the 'Half King'.

1 Ælfhere witnesses as ealdorman the following charters dated 939 × 941: *BCS* 734, 741–3, 748, 753, 762 and 764–5. Eadric witnesses as ealdorman the following charters: *BCS* 775, 777, 784, 787, 789, 814–15, 818, 874, 820–2, 824, 830, 832, (834), 864–6, 868–71, 875 and 883. J. Armitage Robinson assigned to this Eadric a group of Mercian charters of the period 878 × 925 (*The Times of St Dunstan* (Oxford, 1923), pp. 39 and 42–50), but this supposes that he was active as an ealdorman until he was at least ninety, a phenomenal age for the period. It seems probable from the witness-lists that the Eadric of some of these early charters was the thegn who ceases to sign in 932.

2 *BCS* 769 and 981, charters from the Shaftesbury cartulary relating to lands at Beechingstoke, Wiltshire, and Mapperton, Dorset, which (as *DB* shows) were Shaftesbury property TRE.

3 *BCS* 834, relating to Washington in Sussex. *Chron Abingd* 1, 141 states that Eadric gave this estate to Abingdon. According to a later charter, also preserved at Abingdon, it came into the hands of King Edgar, who gave it to Bishop Æthelwold, who had been abbot there (*BCS* 1125). He exchanged it for estates which he used to endow his foundations at Thorney and Peterborough (Robertson, *Charters* xxxvii; and *ECEE* pp. 162 and 179).

4 *BCS* 828, relating to Ashbury (see M. Gelling, *Berkshire Archaeol. Jnl,* 63 (1967–8), 5–13); Eadric gave it to Glastonbury during Dunstan's abbacy (Oxford, Bodleian Library, Wood 1, 245). Presumably the 'Ælfsige mine breðer suna' who was left land at *Carcel* by Æthelwold I (Harmer, *SelEHD* xx) was a son of Eadric. *Carcel* has been located tentatively at Silchester, Hampshire.

5 Æthelsige witnesses as ealdorman charters dated 951 × 958 (no charters survive for 950). Early attestations include *BCS* 891, 887 and 905; late ones include *BCS* 1022, 1027–8 and 1033–4.

conjecture that Athelstan 'Half King' was appointed to succeed in this office the Ealdorman Alfred who witnesses in 930 and 931.[1]

Athelstan first witnesses as ealdorman a charter dated 30 August 932, and from then until his retirement in 956 he ruled with outstanding ability what was without a doubt the largest and wealthiest province of the English crown. From evidence drawn mainly from the second half of the century we can tell that at the smallest estimate his ealdordom included, besides East Anglia proper (Norfolk and Suffolk), the whole of Cambridgeshire and Huntingdonshire, plus the fenland territory that was later known as the Holland division of Lincolnshire,[2] together with the eight hundreds of Oundle, comprising the north-east quarter of Northamptonshire, part of which was to become the Soke of Peterborough. But close examination of the lists of ealdormen witnessing the charters of King Athelstan and his successors forces one to the conclusion that the 'Half King' governed an area far greater than this; it appears in fact to have embraced the whole of the eastern Danelaw from the Thames to the Welland, bounded to the south-east by Watling Street and on the north-west by the territory of the Five Boroughs. Indeed, if I have judged correctly, the ealdordom of Athelstan 'Half King' comprised all those parts of the Danelaw upon which a system of hidation was imposed by Edward the Elder to replace for taxation purposes the Danish carucation; with the possible exception of Holland, its northern limits were marked by the line of cleavage between the hidated shires and those which remained carucated to the time of Domesday and later.[3]

It is a measure of Athelstan's achievement that the eastern Danelaw remained in subjection to the West Saxon royal line, its inhabitants loyal and quiescent, throughout the period of his rule. We hear of no revolts,[4] no collaboration with the Danes of northern England in subversive movements, no encouragement of Viking raiders along the eastern coastline. He brought the administration of East Anglia into line with the system operating in Wessex, English Mercia and the south-east. In matters of local interest, the Danes were allowed a considerable measure of autonomy, but in national affairs such as the raising of the geld and the provision of military service, the area was no less effectively governed than the rest of the territories subject to the English crown. While Athelstan kept his ealdordom under such control, Kings Edmund and Eadred

---

[1] Alfred witnesses as ealdorman *BCS* 669, 674 and 677.   [2] See below, Appendix I.

[3] The viewpoint here put forward in detail, based on charter evidence, is in complete harmony with that of Chadwick, elaborated by Eric John, derived largely from a law of King Edgar, IV Edgar 15. See H. M. Chadwick, *Anglo-Saxon Institutions* (Cambridge, 1905), p. 178, n. 1, and E. John, *Orbis Britanniae* (Leicester, 1966), pp. 221–2.

[4] The incident recorded in *ASC* 952 D, in which King Eadred ravaged Thetford in retaliation for the assassination by its citizens of Abbot Eadhelm of St Augustine's Canterbury, is perhaps an exception. The circumstances of this affair are quite obscure, but there is nothing to suggest anything in the nature of a revolt by the Danes.

were enabled to recover during the years 942 × 946 first the northern Danelaw, then Northumbria, and finally to conquer Strathclyde. One cannot doubt that Athelstan should be credited with a major share in the planning and execution of these highly successful campaigns.

The 'Half King' was a constant and powerful friend of the English church, both nationally and within his own ealdordom of East Anglia, where the conversion of the Danes was zealously consolidated and a diocesan framework reconstituted.[1] His wife Ælfwyn, whom he must have married soon after receiving his ealdordom, appears to have come from a Huntingdonshire family whose estates were destined to form the nucleus of the large endowment of Ramsey Abbey.[2] It is probable that the household of the 'Half King' was centred somewhere in this neighbourhood, in thickly wooded territory on the edge of the fens.

Athelstan was aided in the administration of his ealdordom by a number of subordinate Danish earls and English ealdormen. They are referred to in two Abingdon charters dated 956 which he witnessed *cum cæteris suffraganeis*,[3] and their position must have been rather similar to that of the sub-ealdormen under Æthelred of Mercia at the end of the ninth century. We know the names and spheres of influence of some of these men. Earl Thurferth, who surrendered his army of Northampton to Edward the Elder in 917, continued to govern Northamptonshire under the suzerainty of the East Anglian ealdordom until 934.[4] Earl Scule, who witnesses charters from 931 to 949, is referred to in the *Liber Eliensis*.[5] Professor Whitelock has suggested that his area of jurisdiction comprised the six hundreds attached to Sudbourne in Suffolk.[6] The name of another Scandinavian earl, Haddr, appears next to that of Scule so consistently in charters of the period 931 to 934, that one cannot doubt that he too came from East Anglia, but we have no means of locating him more precisely.[7] Earl Halfdene, who witnesses from 934 to 958, appears together with Earl Scule as a co-signatory to a will dated 943 disposing of lands in Hertfordshire

---

[1] D. Whitelock, 'The Conversion of the Eastern Danelaw', *SBVS* 12 (1937–45), 159–76.

[2] *Chron Rams* pp. 52–4. Ælfwyn is said to have had *inclyta genealogica* (*ibid.* p. 11). Her brother Æthelsige witnessed a Ramsey deed in 975–92 (*ibid.* p. 75), and acted as surety when estates in Huntingdonshire were sold to Peterborough Abbey in 971–3 (Robertson, *Charters* p. 75; cf. *ECEE* p. 163). Ælfwyn died on 8 July 983. As with several other Ramsey benefactors, the date of her death can be reconstructed from lists in *Cart Rams* III, 165–6, and *New Monasticon* II, 566, on the reliability of which see C. Hart, 'Eadnoth, First Abbot of Ramsey and the Foundation of Chatteris and St Ives', *Proc. of the Cambridge Ant. Soc.* 56–7 (1964), 61–7, esp. 62.

[3] *BCS* 924 and 949. In the former of these, the bishop of Winchester witnesses 'cum cæteris coepiscopis'. Similar phrases recur in *BCS* 751 (940) and 890 (951), in which the archbishop of Canterbury witnesses 'cum suffraganeis præsulibus', and 'cum ceteris suffraganeis'. See also *BCS* 658–9 (926), referring in parenthesis to 'dux Æþelredo cum ceteris comitibus'.

[4] He witnesses *BCS* 1343, 677, 689 and 1344.

[5] *LE* p. 111. He witnesses *BCS* 674–5, 677, 689, 702, 1344, 716–18, 812, 820 and 882–3.

[6] *LE* p. xiv.

[7] He witnesses *BCS* 674–5, 677, 689, and 1344.

and Bedfordshire, and it is possible that his earldom lay in this region.[1] Earl Hereric, who is known to us only from the *Liber Eliensis*, was a contemporary of Ealdorman Athelstan who owned land, and perhaps held jurisdiction, in Cambridgeshire.[2]

An ealdorman named Uhtred, who witnesses from 931 to 946, should probably be assigned to Essex.[3] He was succeeded by Ælfgar, ealdorman of Essex from 946 to 951, but there is then a gap in the succession to the East Saxon ealdordom until Byrhtferth commences to witness in 955. There is good reason to suppose that Essex was to some extent subordinate to Athelstan 'Half King' throughout this period.[4]

Two years before Ælfgar succeeded to the East Saxon ealdordom, his daughter Æthelflæd became the wife of King Edmund; we can only speculate to what extent this union may be regarded as an example of the influence of the 'Half King' in national affairs. Edmund was a youth of eighteen upon his accession, and within a few months we find Æthelwold I, brother of the 'Half King', appointed to an ealdordom embracing Kent, Surrey, Sussex and possibly Berkshire. When two years later the third surviving brother Eadric became Ealdorman of Wessex, the three between them controlled over half of King Edmund's kingdom. In charters from 943 onwards, Athelstan 'Half King' habitually witnesses first and his brother Æthelwold I second among the *duces*; Eadric signs in the third to sixth place until his brother Æthelwold's death in 946, after which he is second only to the 'Half King'. The three Mercian ealdormen (not related to each other) witness in more lowly positions, and the only other ealdordom south of the Humber was that of the western shires (Dorset, Somerset and the Dumnonian peninsula), whose ealdorman Wulfgar witnesses only three of the thirteen diplomas surviving for the years 944 to 946. The power wielded by the 'Half King' and his brothers throughout King Edmund's reign can be compared only with that of Godwine's family a century later.

Nor was this all. By his first wife Ælfgifu, King Edmund had two sons, Eadwig and Edgar, and a fundamentally important but rarely quoted passage in the *Ramsey Chronicle* reveals that after Ælfgifu's death in 944, the infant ætheling Edgar did not remain with his step-mother Æthelflæd, Edmund's

---

[1] He witnesses *BCS* 702, 1344, 716–18, 812 (the will) and 1044.
[2] *LE* pp. 87–8.
[3] He is to be distinguished from a second Uhtred, who witnesses from 930 to 934 as ealdorman, probably of north-west Mercia.
[4] Ealdorman Ælfgar's family estates were disposed to either side of the Essex–Suffolk border. Later in the century, the jurisdiction of Ealdorman Byrhtnoth of Essex is shown by *LE* to have extended to Cambridgeshire and Huntingdonshire, which were clearly part of the East Anglian ealdordom; Byrhtnoth also held lands in Suffolk, Cambridgeshire and Northamptonshire. Professor Chadwick thought that Byrhtnoth's ealdordom was subordinate to that of Æthelwine of East Anglia (*Anglo-Saxon Institutions*, p. 177, n. 1), an opinion shared by Eric John (*Orbis Britanniae*, p. 222).

second wife, but was fostered instead by Ælfwyn, the wife of the 'Half King'.[1] Of the four sons of the 'Half King', Æthelwine the youngest was perhaps three or four years older than Edgar, and so they would have been brought up together. Reared in such a household, Edgar became steeped in the ideals underlying the great movement for monastic reform of which his foster brother Æthelwine was to become the principal lay patron in England. One cannot doubt that in their childhood both Edgar and Æthelwine came under the influence of Abbot Dunstan of Glastonbury, who was a close friend of Ealdorman Athelstan and his brothers as early as 946.[2] Edgar's later education took place under Abbot Æthelwold of Abingdon,[3] of which house Athelstan 'Half King' was one of the earliest benefactors.[4] Athelstan's fostering of the ætheling Edgar was therefore profoundly significant. Edgar became the most Christian monarch of the Anglo-Saxon era, and the repercussions of his upbringing were to shape the course of English history throughout the next century.

For the whole of his brief reign, the young King Edmund remained strongly under the influence of his mother Eadgifu and the 'Half King', who between them must have decided much of the national policy. Nor was the position much changed when Edmund's brother Eadred succeeded in 946. Eadred's adult years were clouded by chronic illness,[5] and the responsibilities of the 'Half King' continued unabated. Athelstan's brother Eadric died in 949, and for the rest of King Eadred's reign his royal diplomas are usually witnessed by four ealdormen only, with the 'Half King' continuing to head the list. After the disappearance from the witness-lists of the ealdorman of south-east Mercia in 949,[6] and Ealdorman Ealhhelm of central Mercia at the end of 951,[7] the 'Half King' appears to have taken over control of these two territories, in addition to his existing commitments. Here, as in East Anglia, Athelstan must have had suffragans, but they cannot be identified as witnesses to royal diplomas.

The strength of Athelstan's position is further reflected in the ownership by himself and his family of considerable estates outside the limits of his own

[1] *Chron Rams* pp. 11 and 53.
[2] *Memorials* pp. 44–5. It will be shown that Athelstan possessed substantial estates in Somerset, which he must have visited from time to time; later they all descended to Glastonbury. The early benefactions to Glastonbury of his brothers Æthelwold I and Eadric have been mentioned already. In my forthcoming *Early Charters of Northern England and the North Midlands* I put forward the thesis that the 'Half King' had control over the issue of royal diplomas for Mercia and the Danelaw in the period 942 to 955, and that they were produced by a Glastonbury scribe under the supervision of his friend Dunstan.
[3] John, *Orbis Britanniae*, pp. 159–60.   [4] Robertson, *Charters* XXII.
[5] *Memorials* pp. 46–8.
[6] The south-east Mercian ealdordom was held by a second ealdorman named Athelstan, who witnessed from 940 to 949. There is no evidence that he was related to the family of the 'Half King'.
[7] Ealdorman Ealhhelm of central Mercia witnessed from 940 to 951.

ealdordom. I have described already the holdings of his brothers in Wessex, the Thames valley, and in the south-east, some of which reverted to Athelstan upon their death. We cannot know the full extent of Athelstan's own possessions, for eventually he became a monk, and as such would not have made a will. One assumes that he inherited from his father and his elder brother lands in south-east Mercia and adjacent areas acquired during their tenure of that ealdordom, but the only record we have of a property that may have come from this source concerns the forty hides in the Vale of the White Horse with which he endowed the minster at Abingdon before he himself achieved power in East Anglia.[1] Much later, he added to this a further ten hides at Appleton nearby, which he had received from King Edmund.[2]

We know nothing of Athelstan's landed possessions within his East Anglian ealdordom, but they must have been substantial. His father's own estates were located in the western shires, and much of this ancestral land came into Athelstan's hands, including a large holding somewhere in Devon which he exchanged after his move to East Anglia for forty hides at Hatfield in Hertfordshire; subsequently, when he retired to Glastonbury, he left this Hertfordshire estate to his sons.[3] Two other Devonshire estates, at Uplyme[4] and at Brampford Speke,[5] granted to Athelstan in later years, were used by him to endow the abbey of Glastonbury, which also received from the 'Half King' a chain of villages in the delectable country to the north of the Mendips in Somerset. Of these, twenty hides at Wrington and Burrington came to him from his father Æthelfrith,[6] and ten hides at Clutton from one Æthelwulf, who may have been his paternal grandfather;[7] to these were added five hides at

---

[1] Robertson, *Charters* XXII concerning Uffington, Berkshire, dated perhaps 927–8.

[2] *BCS* 777 dated 942. There is no direct evidence that Athelstan left this estate to Abingdon, but such a descent may be inferred from its proximity to Uffington, and from the fact that Athelstan's landbook was preserved at Abingdon, being entered in the abbey's cartulary.

[3] *LE* pp. 79–80.

[4] *BCS* 728 dated 938; six hides at Uplyme, Devon. In *Proc. of the Dorset Nat. Hist. and Archaeol. Soc.* 86 (1965), 160–1, I wrongly placed this estate at Lyme Regis, Dorset, but a recently discovered sixteenth-century perambulation of Uplyme has so many boundary marks in common with those of Athelstan's charter that the location at Uplyme is now fully established. The charter is preserved in the Glastonbury cartulary, and the gift of the estate by Athelstan is recorded in the abbey's list of benefactors. See further, H. S. A. Fox, 'The Boundary of Uplyme', *Trans. of the Devon Assoc.* 102 (1970), 35–47.

[5] *BCS* 799 dated 944. The gift of this estate to Glastonbury by Athelstan is recorded in lists of Glastonbury benefactors; see *ECDC* pp. 11–12.

[6] *BCS* 606 dated 904. J. Armitage Robinson, *The Times of St Dunstan*, p. 46.

[7] *ECW* 406. Æthelwulf had received this estate from King Æthelwulf of Wessex 839 × 858. He is not to be identified with Æthelwulf the father of Æthelgyth, mother of the 'Half King', for this second Æthelwulf was a Mercian; nor could he have been the Æthelwulf who obtained Wylye in 901 (*EHD* p. 499), although he may have been the latter's father (see above, p. 119, n. 5). Some slight support for my suggestion that the Æthelwulf who held Clutton was the paternal grandfather of the 'Half King' derives from the very strong alliterative tradition followed in naming members of the family. Æthelweard, killed at *Assandun* in 1016, was the son of Æthelwine, son

Forscote near Radstock by King Athelstan,[1] and a further twenty hides at
Mells by King Edmund.[2] This large group of estates formed a major part of
Glastonbury's early endowment; Uplyme, Wrington and Mells remained for
nearly six centuries in the abbey's possession, until the Dissolution.

In addition to these widespread properties, Athelstan 'Half King' received
from his brother Æthelwold I a substantial holding at Broadwater in Sussex,
and another at *Niwantun* (possibly Newton St Loe, six miles from the family
estate at Clutton in Somerset), but their descent cannot be traced.[3] Altogether
we have record of no less than 200 hides at some time or other in the personal
possession of the 'Half King', and it is probable that he held as much again
for which no written evidence survives. A truly regal endowment, unmatched,
as far as one can tell, by any lay person in the tenth century other than the kings
of England themselves.

The death of King Eadred on 23 November 955 led to a profound change
in the circumstances, if not the fortunes, of the 'Half King' and his family.
Eadwig the new monarch, a youth of fifteen who appears to have been brought
up in Wessex,[4] commenced his reign inauspiciously by a major confrontation
with the monastic party, headed by Dunstan, during his coronation banquet.
Dunstan was banished and Queen Eadgifu's estates confiscated. Significant
changes followed in the composition of the witan, affecting in particular the
lay and ecclesiastical establishment north of the Thames. Cynesige, bishop of
Lichfield, a relative and supporter of Dunstan and a regular attendant upon
King Eadred, appeared only rarely before the new king's presence.[5] By the
end of 955 an ealdorman (yet another Athelstan) had been appointed to
hold jurisdiction in south-east Mercia,[6] and a month or two later Eadwig

of Athelstan, son of Æthelfrith, who died *c.* 916. If Æthelwulf was not the paternal grandfather
of the 'Half King', he was doubtless some other close paternal ancestor. Moreover, it is likely
that he had royal connections, for his descendant Æthelwine is described in the *Vita Oswaldi* as
being 'progenitus ex regali prosapia', and in the *Ramsey Chronicle* as being 'ab atavis regibus
præclara ingenuæ successionis linea transfusus' (*Chron Rams* p. 11).

1 *ECW* 431, a lost charter dated 924–39, details of which are preserved in lists of benefactors to
Glastonbury.
2 *BCS* 776 dated 942, a Glastonbury charter. Athelstan's gift is recorded in lists of benefactors to
Glastonbury; cf. *ECW* 445.
3 Harmer, *SelEHD* xx.
4 If *BCS* 949 means what it says, Eadwig's *adoptivus parens*, i.e. foster-father, was one Ælric, otherwise
unknown, to whom Eadwig gave an estate in Berkshire. Moreover *BCS* 810, a charter of King
Eadwig dated 956 that survives only in a heavily modified version, confirms to a thegn called
Æthelgeard 'quod michi a puerili juventute exibere studuit' the possession of estates in Berkshire
(on this charter, see *CW* p. 17, n. 3, where it is referred to as no. 78 in the *Codex Wintoniensis* series).
If Eadwig was brought up in Berkshire, one might hazard the suggestion that his later education,
like that of his brother Edgar, took place under Abbot Æthelwold at Abingdon.
5 Cynesige witnesses the large majority of the surviving charters of King Eadred, but of the fifty-
odd charters of King Eadwig issued in 956 with witness-lists that have survived, Cynesige witnesses only three (*BCS* 924, 949 and 921).
6 It is necessary to distinguish carefully between the three ealdormen named Athelstan who witness

created his kinsman Ælfhere ealdorman of central Mercia.[1]

The 'Half King', who had probably been administering both these territories in addition to his East Anglian responsibilities, could hardly have enjoyed the new situation. Having alienated the sympathies of his elder statesmen, the young king was pursuing a wild and irresponsible policy of packing his council with new men whose loyalty had been purchased by large scale handouts of the West Saxon royal demesne.[2] With his old friends of the monastic party in disgrace, the 'Half King' was left in a dangerously isolated position, and turned to his immediate family for support. Of his four sons only Æthelwold II (the number serves to distinguish him from his uncle and namesake who died in 946), then in his early twenties, was old enough to shoulder responsibility and buttress the family influence in affairs of state. Athelstan brought him to court, married him off to the daughter of the thegn with the most powerful interests in the western shires, and persuaded King Eadwig to endow him with estates near the ancient family holdings in Somerset.[3] It may well be that initially Æthelwold II was being groomed for a West Saxon

charters in the mid-tenth century. Athelstan 'Half King' of East Anglia commences to witness as ealdorman in 932. In 940 and 941 he usually appears as third, in 942 as second, and from 943 until midsummer 956 as first of the ealdormen subscribing. A second ealdorman named Athelstan commences to witness towards the end of 940 (*BCS* 757). By 944 he takes third place in the witness-lists, a position he retains until his last signature early in 949 (*BCS* 875). He always appears below the 'Half King' in the witness-lists, and it is very probable that his ealdordom lay in south-east Mercia. From early in 949 to the end of 955, only one ealdorman named Athelstan witnesses; this is the 'Half King' (*BCS* 883, 879, 880, 894, 892, 891, 895, 899, 900, 908, 903, 905 and 887, in chronological order). A third ealdorman named Athelstan commences to witness at the beginning of King Eadwig's reign, usually in third position until the retirement of the 'Half King'. In *BCS* 917, dated 23 November–31 December 955, the first charter he witnesses, he is given the nickname *Rota* (?'the Red') to differentiate him from the 'Half King'. After the retirement of the 'Half King', Athelstan 'Rota' jumps to first place among the ealdormen witnessing King Eadwig's charters; this group comprises, in chronological order, *BCS* 965, 978, 956, 948, 1009, 930 and 927 (all issued in the autumn of 956), 1029 (with an authentic witness-list dated Christmas 956), 988, 997, 999, 1001, 1003 and 994 (all dated 957). After King Edgar's revolt in the summer of 957, Ealdorman Athelstan 'Rota' ceases to subscribe to King Eadwig's charters, but in 958 he commences to witness those issued by Edgar as King of Mercia. Until Edgar's accession to the whole kingdom of England in 959, Athelstan 'Rota' usually witnesses in second place among the ealdormen; thereafter until 965 he witnesses in third place. In 966 he witnesses fourth, and from 967 to 970 his position varies between fourth and first. The last surviving charter witnessed by Athelstan 'Rota' is *BCS* 1268. He married Æthelflæd of Damerham, the daughter of Ealdorman Ælfgar of Essex and the widow of King Edmund; her sister Ælfflæd married Ealdorman Byrhtnoth of Essex.

1 Ealdorman Ælfhere of central Mercia commences to witness on 12 February 956 (*BCS* 919 and 1002). By 957 he is the third of six ealdormen habitually witnessing King Eadwig's charters. He then left court with Edgar, and from 958 until his death in 983 is always first among the ealdormen witnessing the charters of King Edgar and his son King Æthelred 'Unræd'.

2 John, *Orbis Britanniae*, pp. 190–1. The biographer of St Dunstan describes Eadwig as 'losing the shrewd and wise who disapproved of his folly, and eagerly annexing ignorant men of his own kin' (*Memorials* p. 35).

3 This statement rests on charter evidence, interpreted as follows. Charters issued during the reign of Eadred are not witnessed by any thegn named Æthelwold. Charters issued by King Eadwig during 956 can be divided into two groups, according to whether or not they are witnessed by an

appointment, and that the influence of the 'Half King' suffered a sufficiently large set-back in the early months of Eadwig's reign for such a project to be abandoned. At all events, by the summer of 956 Athelstan 'Half King' had decided to retire from worldly affairs, and as a preliminary step Æthelwold II was appointed to be his understudy in the East Anglian ealdordom; possibly his early responsibilities lay in Essex, for Ealdorman Byrhtferth of Essex ceased to witness on the eve of Æthelwold's appointment. For two or three months in the late summer and early autumn, Athelstan continued to witness first and Æthelwold II last of the six ealdormen currently subscribing to King Eadwig's diplomas,[1] and then the 'Half King' left court to become a monk at Glastonbury, where until recently his friend Dunstan had been abbot. Æthelwold II succeeded to full control of his father's ealdordom, with a new ealdorman, Byrhtnoth, to serve under him in Essex; a year later, when an understudy with eventual succession was appointed to Æthelsige's ealdordom of the West Saxons, it was not Æthelwold II, but Ælfhere's brother Ælfheah who received the post.[2]

Although Eadwig's policy had secured him some degree of support in Wessex, he failed utterly to establish his position north of the Thames, and in the summer of 957 his brother Edgar, a boy of fourteen, broke away and with

ealdorman named Æthelwold. Charters of the first group, without Ealdorman Æthelwold's signature, are often witnessed by a thegn named Æthelwold (as is *BCS* 917, dated 23 November–31 December 955), but no charter in the second group is witnessed by a thegn of this name. So many charters were issued in this year, that the division cannot be due to mere coincidence; the only reasonable conclusion is that the thegn Æthelwold witnessing many of the first group of charters is identical with the Ealdorman Æthelwold who witnesses the second group. No charter of King Eadwig dated later than 956 is witnessed by a thegn named Æthelwold. It cannot be doubted that the thegn Æthelwold who witnesses Eadwig's earlier charters (before being made ealdorman) was the recipient from King Eadwig of fifteen hides at Bleadon, Somerset (*BCS* 959), and four hides at *Wudetune* (? North Wooton near Shepton Mallet, Somerset) (*BCS* 969), and land at Sharpham, Somerset (*ECW* 482), all in 956. These properties lie near other lands belonging to the family of the 'Half King'. It seems likely that the thegn Æthelwold who received Camerton, Somerset, from King Eadred (*ECW* 463) was the same man. In 961 King Edgar issued a diploma granting to his faithful minister Æthelwold a small estate of one hide at Evesty in Somerset (*BCS* 1074; cf. H. P. R. Finberg, *West Country Historical Studies* (Devon, 1969), p. 37, n. 2). The recipient, who does not witness Edgar's charters, has not been identified; he was not Ealdorman Æthelwold II, but he may have been related to the family of the 'Half King'.

We have it on the authority both of Byrhtferth's *Vita Oswaldi* and of Florence of Worcester that Æthelwold's ealdordom was in East Anglia. The *Vita* establishes also that he was the son of the 'Half King' and that he was the first husband of Ælfthryth, who was to become Edgar's queen. *ASC* D shows that Ælfthryth was the daughter of Ordgar, who became ealdorman of the western shires in 964. The *Vita Oswaldi* wrongly names her father Ordmær.

1 The following charters were witnessed by both Athelstan 'Half King' and his son Æthelwold II, among the *duces*: *BCS* 934, 974, 983, 982, 945, 946, 925 and 957. These were all witnessed in addition by Athelstan 'Rota'.

2 *BCS* 1004, dated 957, is witnessed by the *duces* Æthelsige and Ælfheah. *BCS* 1005, issued in the same year (King Eadwig's name was later erased and replaced by that of King Edgar in the introductory rubric), grants land to the *dux* Ælfheah, and the cartulary text is witnessed by the *dux* Ælfsige (in error for Æthelsige). Æthelsige continues witnessing King Eadwig's charters as ealdorman to the end of 958 (*BCS* 1002, 1027–8 and 1033–4).

the support of local bishops and ealdormen set himself up as king of Mercia, Northumbria and East Anglia. Naturally Æthelwold II was one of the ealdormen who transferred his allegiance. In charters of the year 958 issued by Edgar as king of the Mercians, Æthelwold II usually witnesses fourth of the five ealdormen subscribing. According to a late but often reliable source, he was entrusted by Edgar with the overlordship of York and southern Northumbria.[1] There are no grounds known to me for rejecting this assertion. His youth precluded Æthelwold II from achieving the dominance of the king's council that had for so long been enjoyed by his father, but the family fortunes were greatly improved on Edgar's accession because Edgar at once brought his three remaining foster brothers, Ælfwold, Æthelsige and Æthelwine, into his court. Their influence may be gathered from the earliest diploma known to have been issued in Edgar's name, in which they appear as third, first and fourth respectively in the list of subscribing thegns.[2]

Before attempting biographies of these young men, we might deal with the marriages of King Edgar, for they were linked closely with the affairs of the family of the 'Half King'. Precocious in an age favourable to precocity,[3] Edgar was married twice by the age of twenty-one and in between he had a concubine. We are indebted to Florence of Worcester for details of his first wife, by whom was born Edward the Martyr. Her name was Æthelflæd 'Eneda', and she was the daughter of one Ordmær, whom Florence calls an ealdorman. Strangely, no ealdorman or thegn of this name witnesses surviving royal diplomas of the tenth century. Florence, one feels, made a mistake about Ordmær's rank.[4] According to a statement in the *Liber Eliensis*, Athelstan 'Half King' exchanged land in Devonshire, which he had inherited from his

[1] Gaimar, *Lestorie des Engles*, ed. T. D. Hardy and C. T. Martin, RS (1888–9), 3843–8.

[2] *BCS* 1023, a charter from a late Wells register relating to land in Worcestershire, in which the name of Edgar the donor has been replaced by that of King Eadred by the copyist, who was doubtless responsible for deleting the dating clause. This otherwise unexceptional charter is to be dated after 9 May 957, when Eadwig still retained control of the territory north of the Thames (*BCS* 999), and before 2 June 958 when Oda, archbishop of Canterbury, one of the witnesses, died.

[3] My impression after a general review of tenth-century royal diplomas is that young noblemen at court often began to witness royal diplomas as thegns at about the age of seventeen or eighteen. While still in their early twenties they were sometimes raised to positions of rank and responsibility, either within the royal household or as ealdormen. Most of the ealdormen died in or before their forties; very few, such as Byrhtnoth of Maldon and Æthelwine of East Anglia, survived into their fifties or perhaps their early sixties, and none as far as I can discover reached the age of seventy. Ecclesiastics and noblewomen often survived longer. The precocity of the period is further illustrated by listing the ages of the tenth-century kings of England at the dates of their accession to the throne. Edward the Elder was at least thirty, and Athelstan at least twenty-six, but Edmund was only eighteen, Eadred perhaps twenty-four, Eadwig fifteen, Edgar fourteen (Mercia) and sixteen (all England), Edward the Martyr thirteen, and Æthelred 'Unræd' a child of ten. The opportunities for the ealdormen and bishops to direct national policy will be self-evident.

[4] Probably Florence was following Byrhtferth's *Vita Oswaldi*, where Ordmær is incorrectly named as the father of Edgar's wife Ælfthryth (his second wife if we assume Wulfthryth to have been his concubine).

father, for forty hides at Hatfield in Hertfordshire, belonging to a *vir potens* named Ordmær and his wife Ealde.[1] We are unable to date the transaction more closely than between 932 (when Athelstan obtained his ealdordom, within which Hatfield lay) and 956 (when he retired). But if Ordmær had a daughter, it is entirely reasonable to suppose that she might have become acquainted with Athelstan's foster son, the ætheling Edgar. Moreover, the 'Half King' gave Hatfield to his sons when he became a monk, but it was removed from their possession by Edgar after he became king; Edgar claimed that the estate had been left to him by Ordmær and his wife after their deaths. It was not until Edgar himself died that his foster brothers were able to recover the property. We are tempted to suggest that the Ordmær who exchanged Hatfield with Athelstan and the Ordmær who was the father of Queen Æthelflæd were one and the same man, and that Edgar's interest in the estate arose from his marriage to Æthelflæd. By this transaction with Athelstan, Ordmær secured a large estate in Devon, an ancestral property of the family of the 'Half King', the exact location of which unfortunately eludes us. The name Ordmær alliterates suggestively with those of the house of Ordgar, whose family produced an ealdorman of the western shires and two high reeves of Devon, and founded Tavistock Abbey.[2] In 964 Edgar took for his second queen Ælfthryth, the daughter of Ealdorman Ordgar and the widow of none other than Æthelwold II, ealdorman of East Anglia and Edgar's foster brother.[3] It will be recalled that Æthelwold had married Ælfthryth in 956.[4] They had a son Leofric before Æthelwold's death in 962; from the genealogical table it will be seen that he was the half brother of King Æthelred 'Unræd'. There are good reasons for identifying him with the Leofric who together with his wife Leoflæd founded St Neot's Priory in Huntingdonshire between 979 and 984.[5] This Leofric had a brother Æthelnoth, who, if this

[1] *LE* p. 79.
[2] H. P. R. Finberg, 'The House of Ordgar and the Foundation of Tavistock Abbey', *EHR* 58 (1943), 190–201; 'Childe's Tomb', *Lucerna* (London, 1964), pp. 186–203.
[3] Florence of Worcester, *s.a.* 964; *ASC* 965 D. The date is securely established as 964 by *BCS* 1143, a grant by King Edgar to his queen Ælfthryth, in the fifth year of his reign.
[4] See above, p. 127, n. 3.
[5] For the early history of St Neots Priory, see *LE* pp. 102–4, *ECEE* pp. 28–9 and M. Chibnall *Proc. of the Cambridge Ant. Soc.* 59 (1966), 67–70. Leofric the founder endowed it with two hides at Eynesbury and six at Waresley (both in Huntingdonshire), and nine at Gamlingay in Cambridgeshire. At one time his father also held three hides at Wangford, Suffolk, and an estate at Abington, Cambridgeshire (*LE* p. 104). Leofric's family lands were therefore very substantial; moreover they were concentrated within the area in which the 'Half King' and his sons held most of their East Anglian landed property. Furthermore Ealdorman Æthelwine is found later to be in possession of the Wangford and Abington estates (*LE* pp. 103–4). Admittedly the three hides at Wangford were purchased by Æthelwine from the abbey of Ely, but it appears highly likely that he had some personal interest in the estate; presumably he was already in possession of another three hides there before his purchase from Ely, for he gave six hides altogether at Wangford to Ramsey Abbey (*ECEE* p. 241). We know from a reliable source that Æthelwine was the patron and protector both of St Neots Priory and of Crowland Abbey in 991 (*Chron Rams* p. 96); by the end of the

equation is correct, must have been another son of Ealdorman Æthelwold II.[1] A Ramsey record shows Leofric witnessing a land transaction there on 14 June 987, after which we lose sight of him.[2]

Returning to Æthelwold II's brothers, we shall find it convenient to deal with them in order of seniority, as they are listed in the *Ramsey Chronicle*.[3] Ælfwold is a common name, and at first sight it appears hazardous to attempt to identify Æthelwold II's brother Ælfwold in the charters. It is well known however that brothers commonly appear in adjacent places in the witness-lists, so that we can differentiate between our Ælfwold, who witnesses with Æthelsige and Æthelwine, and another Ælfwold who usually appears together with a thegn named Ælfric. Moreover, we would not expect a son of the 'Half King' to witness King Eadwig's charters after the revolt of Edgar; on the other hand it is likely that he would subscribe to diplomas concerning Mercia and the Danelaw. Using these criteria, we find Ælfwold of East Anglia witnessing King Edgar's charters as a thegn from 958 to 972.[4]

It is possible that he is the Ælfwold who received four hides at Withiel Florey in Somerset from King Eadwig in 956, before the retirement of the 'Half King' to Glastonbury;[5] he may also have received from King Eadwig an estate at *Peasucmere* (unlocated, but probably in Somerset),[6] and it is quite certain that he is the Ælfwold to whom King Edgar granted fifteen hides at Aspley Guise in Bedfordshire and ten hides at Kington in Warwickshire. The two landbooks recording these grants were issued on the same occasion in 969, and they have identical formulas and witness-lists.[7] Both were preserved at Worcester, and it is likely that Bishop Oswald of Worcester prevailed upon

century, Leofgifu and Oscytel, who were probably the children of Leofric and Leoflæd, appear to have controlled both houses. (*The Ecclesiastical History of Orderic Vitalis*, ed. M. Chibnall (Oxford, 1969) II, 341–2). The lay founder of a monastic establishment at this period was almost by definition the member of a noble house, and the evidence outlined above suggests to me the strong probability that Leofric the founder of St Neots and Leofric the son of Ealdorman Æthelwold II were in fact one and the same man.

[1] *LE* p. 104.

[2] *Chron Rams* p. 61. I have preferred the evidence of the B version of the *Ramsey Chronicle*, which names Leofric's father as Æthelwold and elsewhere as Æthelward, to that of the A version, which calls him the son of the better known Æthelwine, founder of Ramsey. On the few occasions upon which the two versions disagree on fundamentals, B is usually the superior. William of Malmesbury has an apocryphal story mentioning an unnamed son of Æthelwold, whom he claims to be illegitimate (*Gesta Regum* ch. 157).

[3] *Chron Rams* p. 12.

[4] Charters thought to be witnessed by Ælfwold, son of the 'Half King': *BCS* 1023, 1042–4, 1052 (958); 1072, 1076, 1079 (961); 1092 (962); 1112–13 (963); 1134, 1143 (964); 1176, 1189 (966); 1200, 1209 (967); 1221 (968); 1268 (970); and 1282 (972). Charters witnessed by other thegns named Ælfwold: *BCS* 917 (955); 919, 932, 943, 948, 961, 966, 981–2, 986, 1002, 1029 (956); 999, 1003 (957); 1030, 1045–6, 1051 (959); 1120–1 and 1124–5 (963); and Kemble 663 (988). Charters witnessed by thegns named Ælfwold who cannot be identified with certainty: *BCS* 1066–7, 1080, 1319 (961); 1043 (962); 1198 (967); 1230 (969); and 1295 (973); and Kemble 1276 (975–8); 611 (977); and 621 (979).

[5] *BCS* 960.   [6] *ECW* 648.   [7] *BCS* 1229 and 1234.

King Edgar to grant these estates to Ælfwold in compensation for the loss of Huntingdonshire properties, the reversion of which was given by Ælfwold for the endowment of Ramsey Abbey, founded by Oswald and Ælfwold's brother Æthelwine II during that year.[1] The original diploma for Aspley survives, and bears a unique endorsement in which King Edgar calls Ælfwold his *leofan, getreowan þegne*.[2] The companion charter for Kington also survived in the original at Worcester until 1642, but unhappily it was lost soon afterwards.

Ælfwold had other dealings with Ramsey Abbey, recorded in the chronicle of the house.[3] His wife Ælfhild, who survived him, was also a benefactress of the abbey, and their daughter's son Eadnoth became a novice there.[4] Ælfwold's prominent place in the monastic reform movement will be considered when we come to deal with the career of his brother Æthelwine. He died on 14 April 990, and was buried at Ramsey.

Æthelsige, the third son of the 'Half King', witnesses along with his brothers Ælfwold and Æthelwine from 958 onwards, but usually in a higher position in the lists. He also appears far more frequently than the others; by the beginning of 962 his place has become more clearly defined, and he regularly witnesses third of all the thegns subscribing.[5] Few surviving charters of the first five years of Edgar's reign were issued without Æthelsige's subscription, and it is apparent that he was a high official at court. He became in fact Edgar's *camerarius* or chamberlain, and in 963 he was addressed by this title in a diploma of King Edgar granting him ten hides at Sparsholt, one at Balking, and a mill at Drayton, all in Berkshire.[6] We have no knowledge of the precise duties of his office (they may not have been all that clearly defined), but he must have been an intimate of the king, one of a very small group regularly present at his most confidential councils and a keeper of his secrets. Soon after the Berkshire charter was issued, Æthelsige appears to have resigned his position and he ceased to be in constant attendance upon the king; for the next five years he witnesses charters only when visiting court with his brother Ælfwold, and after 968 he does not subscribe at all.[7] It is apparent from entries in the

[1] *BCS* 1061 and 1310–11; *ECEE* 26 and 28.
[2] C. Hart, 'Contemporary Endorsements to the Royal Landbooks', *Agricultural Hist. Rev.* 18 (1970), Supplement, pp. 20–4, esp. 23.
[3] *Chron Rams* pp. 60–3 and 78–9; *ECEE* pp. 42 and 234.
[4] Ælfhild's will survives: *BCS* 1061. It cannot be dated very closely.
[5] During this period Æthelsige witnesses *BCS* 1023*, 1040, 1042*–4* (958); 1035, 1051 (959); 1053–5, 1058 (960); 1066–7*, 1080, 1319, 1071*–72*, 1074–7* 1079* (961); 1083, 1085, 1094 (962); 1118, 1099, 1100, 1114, 1101, 1116–17, 1119–20 and 1123–5 (963). That the thegn Æthelsige witnessing this group of charters was the son of the 'Half King' is established by the fact that in those charters marked with an asterisk in the above list his name appears in the lists next to those of his brothers Ælfwold and Æthelwine. The thegns named Æthelsige witnessing a few of these charters much lower on the lists are clearly other persons.   [6] *BCS* 1121.
[7] Æthelsige witnesses the following charters of this period in an adjacent position to his brother

Liber Eliensis however that he remained an active participant in his brother Æthelwine's administration of East Anglia. He also maintained a connection with the family foundation at Ramsey, and witnessed a deed there on 14 June 987.[1] He died on 13 October in the same year. We have no knowledge of any issue.

According to the *Ramsey Chronicle* the fourth and youngest son of Athelstan 'Half King' was named Æthelwine.[2] For five years from 958 he witnessed as thegn, but immediately upon the death of his brother Æthelwold II in 962 he succeeded to the East Anglian ealdordom.[3] We do not know why his two elder brothers were passed over when the appointment was made; perhaps King Edgar knew Æthelwine best because they were nearest to each other in age, and were educated together.

Some indication of Æthelwine's influence in national affairs may be gained from his position among the ealdormen in the witness-lists of royal diplomas. In the early years of his ealdordom, Æthelwine was rated fourth in precedence, those above him being the two brothers Ælfhere of central Mercia and Ælfheah of Wessex, and Athelstan 'Rota' of south-east Mercia, in that order. Byrhtnoth of Essex always witnesses below him.[4] In 964 King Edgar appointed his father-in-law Ordgar as ealdorman of the western shires and gave him third position in the hierarchy; Athelstan 'Rota', Æthelwine and Byrhtnoth all dropped a place.[5] In 970 Ælfheah, Ordgar and Athelstan 'Rota' all ceased to witness, and for the next four years the only ealdormen subscribing to King Edgar's charters were Ælfhere, Æthelwine, Byrhtnoth and Oslac of Northumbria, in that order.[6] It is not clear who was responsible for England south

Ælfwold: *BCS* 1134, 1143 (964); 1176, 1189 (966); 1200, 1209 (967); and 1221–6 (968). He also witnesses an unpublished Burton charter, William Salt Library 84/2/41, a contemporary text dated 968, as *pedisequus*, in fourth position after three *disciferi*.

[1] *Chron Rams* p. 61.   [2] *Ibid.* p. 12.

[3] Æthelwine witnesses as thegn *BCS* 1023, 1042 (958); 1055 (960); 1066–7, 1080, 1319, 1071–2, 1075–7, 1079 (961); 1082, 1092, 1085 and 1095 (962). It is most satisfactory to find that no thegn named Æthelwine witnesses later charters of King Edgar, and that for the year 962 those charters not witnessed by Æthelwine as thegn are witnessed by him as ealdorman. The identity of the thegn Æthelwine witnessing from 958 to 962 is thus established beyond all reasonable doubt.

[4] The following charters are included in this group: *BCS* 1083, 1093–4, 1096 (962); 1118, 1101, 1114, 1099, 1100, 1116–7, 1119, 1120, 1124, 1121, 1125, 1112–13, 1123 (963); 1134 and 1142–3 (964).

[5] Æthelwine witnesses the following charters in this group: *BCS* 1164, 1169, 1171–2 (965); 1176, 1189–92 (966); 1197, 1199, 1200, 1209 (967); 1213, 1221–7, 1216–17 and 1220, *ECW* 108 (968); and *BCS* 1230, 1234 (969); 1257 and 1266 (970).

[6] This group of charters comprises: *BCS* 1268, 1260, 1302 (970); 1270 (971); 1282, 1286–7, 1309 (972); 1301, 1303–5, 1307 (974); 1312–13 and 1316 (975). It is highly likely that King Edgar's fourth and last surviving law code is to be assigned to this period. The received view, elaborated by Liebermann and followed by Robertson, would date it 962 or 963 because of the plague referred to in the preamble, which is identified with the visitation recorded in *ASC* 962 A. Epidemics were however common and recurrent, and the safest way to date this code is from cap 15 which entrusts its distribution to the ealdormen Ælfhere and Æthelwine. Charter evidence quoted above shows them to have been dominant in the period 970 to 975, and no other dates are nearly as plausible.

of the Thames during this period, but Ælfhere is the most likely candidate.

Æthelweard, ealdorman of the western shires, first appears in 975 as witness to the last surviving charter of Edgar's reign,[1] and Eadwine, ealdorman of Sussex (including probably Kent and Surrey), in 977 in one of the rare diplomas that have come down to us from the reign of Edward the Martyr.[2] Eadwine vanishes from the lists in 982, and Ælfmær, ealdorman of Wessex, died in the same year.[3] Ealdorman Ælfhere died in 983, and from then until 990 the order of precedence is Æthelwine, Byrhtnoth and Æthelweard.[4] Ælfric Cild, who succeeded to his brother-in-law Ælfhere's ealdordom, witnessed for only a year before his banishment; afterwards, from 984 to 990, Mercia is unrepresented in the witness-lists.[5] The only other ealdormen witnessing in the early years of Æthelred's reign are Thored of Northumbria (occasionally, from 979),[6] and Ælfric of Wessex (regularly, from 982). From the end of 984 to 990 therefore, the only ealdordoms represented in the lists are those of East Anglia, Essex, the western shires, Wessex and Northumbria, in that order.

To summarize, Æthelwine witnesses fourth from 962 to 965, then fifth to 970, then second to 983, and finally he heads the list of ealdormen until 990. From 970 to 975 England south of the Thames is not represented in the lists, and from 985 to 990 Mercia is not represented. There is no evidence that the overall administration of these territories was in the hands of ealdormen who did not witness royal diplomas; the more one studies the charters against the background of national politics of the period, the less likely does such a solution appear. By far the most probable explanation is that Ælfhere of Mercia managed in addition the West Saxon ealdordom of his late brother Ælfheah from 970 to 975, and that Æthelwine took charge of Mercia as well as East Anglia from 985 to 990, as indeed his father the 'Half King' appears to have

---

[1] *BCS* 1316. In addition to the ealdormen mentioned in the text, Æthelmær of Wessex witnesses Kemble 611 (977); 621 (979); 624, 626 (980); 629 (981); 632 and 1289 (982). Ealdorman Leofwine, otherwise unknown (unless he be the son of Ealdorman Æthelwine, but this is altogether conjectural), witnesses *EHD* pp. 522–3 (977). Ealdorman Ælfsige, also otherwise unknown, witnesses Kemble 1316 (975).

[2] Kemble 611.

[3] Eadwine witnesses Kemble 621 (979); 624, 626 (980); 629 (981); 632, 1278 and 633 and *LH* p. 217 (982). His death is recorded *ASC* 982. Robertson, *Charters* LIX shows that he was a member of the anti-monastic party. Æthelmær, whose death is also recorded in *ASC*, does not appear as a witness to surviving charters. The date of his appointment is unknown.

[4] Æthelwine witnesses as second ealdorman in precedence the following charters: Kemble 621 (979); 624, 626 (980); 629 (981); 632, 1278 and 633 (as third), *LH* p. 217 (982); and Kemble 636 and 639 (983). He witnesses as first of the ealdormen the following charters: *LH* p. 288, Kemble 1279–80 (983); 1281–2, 641 (984); 648, 650, 652, 1283 (985); 654–5 (986); and 657–8, *LH* p. 231 (as third) (987); Kemble 663–5, *LH* p. 238 (988); *EHD* p. 533 (989); and Kemble 673 and 712–13 (990).

[5] Ælfric Cild witnesses as ealdorman *LH* p. 228 and Kemble 1279–80 (983); and 1281–2 (984).

[6] Thored witnesses as ealdorman: Kemble 621 (979); 633 (mis-spelt Godwine) (982); 636 and 639, *LH* p. 228, Kemble 1279–80 (983); 1282 (984); 648, 650, 1283 (985); and 663 (988); and *EHD* p. 533 (989).

done before him in the period 951 to 956. As with the 'Half King', both Ælfhere and Æthelwine may have had suffragans who did not witness royal diplomas.

The evidence thus laboriously garnered from the charters dovetails remarkably with what the narrative sources have to tell us of the period of Æthelwine's ealdordom. We find Ælfhere of Mercia dominant in the closing years of Edgar's reign, throughout the brief reign of Edward the Martyr and in the early years of King Æthelred 'Unræd'. His anti-monastic inclinations were held in check during Edgar's lifetime, but afterwards only Æthelwine and Byrhtnoth and their supporters were left to oppose him.[1] There followed a long power-struggle that ended with Ælfhere's death in 983 and his brother-in-law's banishment two years later. Æthelwine and Byrhtnoth, aided no doubt by Ealdorman Æthelweard in the west country, now had at least six clear years for restoration of the great monastic endowments upon which rested the whole structure of the reform movement erected by Bishops Dunstan, Oswald and Æthelwold. In the fenlands they had the powerful support of Æthelwine's brother Ælfwold, who did not scruple to put to death the chief despoiler of the estates of Peterborough Abbey, a crime for which Ælfwold received full absolution from Bishop Æthelwold, whom he sought at Winchester barefoot as a penitent.[2] In Mercia, the reconstruction of the *status quo ante* in houses such as Winchcombe and Worcester is much easier to understand if we postulate that Æthelwine had direct control of the Mercian ealdordom during this period.

It may seem strange to talk of such a reconstruction during a reign as troubled as that of Æthelred 'Unræd', but if we scrutinize the course of events as recorded in the *Anglo-Saxon Chronicle* we shall find that the stability of the kingdom remained virtually intact until the deaths of Byrhtnoth and Æthelwine in 991 and 992 respectively. Until then, the Vikings could mount raids that penetrated only short distances and for short periods from the seaboard; thereafter, they were able to cross the country with impunity. Danegeld was not raised to buy them off until after Byrhtnoth had died at Maldon, and Æthelwine, already a sick man, was preparing at Ramsey for his end.[3]

Within his own ealdordom as in national affairs, Æthelwine exercised his great power no less effectively than his father had before him. In the pages of the *Liber Eliensis*, and to a lesser extent the *Ramsey Chronicle*, we are permitted

---

[1] D. J. V. Fisher, 'The Anti-Monastic Reaction in the Reign of Edward the Martyr', *Cambridge Hist. Jnl* 10 (1952), 254–70.

[2] *St O* p. 446; *LE* pp. xii–xiii. Ælfwold's action in restoring these Peterborough properties could hardly have been undertaken before the banishment in 985 of Ælfric Cild, who had challenged Bishop Æthelwold's right to some of the Thorney endowments after King Edgar's death; *ECEE* p. 163.

[3] *Chron Rams* p. 101. Æthelwine suffered from *podagrae pedum* (*ibid.* p. 183). This is usually translated as 'gout', but the ability of medieval physicians to diagnose gout accurately is questionable.

to watch him go about his duties; no other ealdorman of the tenth century or earlier has had his activities recorded in such detail for posterity. We find him presiding over meetings of the whole shire, of groups of hundreds and even of a single hundred. Sometimes he sits with a royal reeve, but only once (in spite of what we are led to expect from the laws) with the diocesan bishop; when Bishop Æthelwold of Winchester is present, his interests are restricted to matters concerning the endowment of his foundations at Ely, Peterborough and Thorney. The sites of such meetings are of absorbing interest because of their antiquity; they were always held out-of-doors. One of the Ely hundreds gathered under Æthelwine's presidency in the cemetery at the north gate of the monastery, a holy sanctuary from the time of the seventh-century foundation. At Cambridge, representatives of the citizens and the adjacent hundreds were called by Æthelwine to attend a moot within the Roman fortifications on Castle Hill. Most notably, Æthelwine held a land plea at Wandlebury, the Iron Age fortress in the Gogmagog Hills not far from Cambridge.[1]

Æthelwine, we are told, had his hall and kept his court at Upwood near Ramsey, a site that would clearly repay surveying with a view to excavation if and when the opportunity occurs. He held also, on lease from Ely, the five-and-a-half hundreds of Wicklow, together with Sudbourn, Stoke and Woodbridge, all in Suffolk. He owned land at Wangford, Suffolk, and at Abington, Cambridgeshire; at Kelling, Norfolk, and at Gedney, Lutton and Tydd in Holland. Together with his brothers Ælfwold and Æthelsige, he laid claim to a large estate at Hatfield, Hertfordshire. Ælfwold the Fat at Chippenham, Cambridgeshire, acknowledged Æthelwine's brother Ælfwold as his lord; Æthelwine's son Leofwine claimed land at Oakley and Weekley, Northamptonshire, and tenanted further estates at Thurning and Barnwell in the same county. All of this is in addition to the large estates in Huntingdonshire, Cambridgeshire, Norfolk and Suffolk, with which Æthelwine, his three wives, Æthelflæd, Æthelgifu and Wulfgifu, his brother Ælfwold and his sister-in-law Ælfhild endowed his foundation at Ramsey.

The family properties in the west country had, however, passed into the hands of others. The 'Half King' had exchanged some of them for the Hatfield estate, and the remainder he gave as a handsome endowment on accepting the tonsure at Glastonbury. Lands in Somerset held by his two sons, Æthelwold II and Ælfwold, were forfeited when they defected to join Edgar in Mercia in 957. Nevertheless, Ealdorman Æthelwine kept in close contact with Glastonbury, where his father had been buried. It was while attending another funeral there, nearly twelve years after his father's retirement, that Æthelwine was

---

[1] Pleas were held at this great heathen sanctuary in 990–2, in 1049 and in 1133–5; on one occasion it was chosen as a meeting-place for representatives of nine counties (*ECEE* pp. 42 and 51).

persuaded by Bishop Oswald of Worcester to found a major abbey on his property in the East Anglian fenlands.[1]

It is not generally appreciated that the monastery of Ramsey which resulted from this conversation, with Oswald as its spiritual director and Æthelwine as its lay founder and patron, was the first of the great fenland abbeys to be created, the prototype of a remarkable group of institutions which were to transform the history of eastern England over the succeeding six centuries; scattered parcels of their widespread endowments of a millenium ago still set the pattern of land holding in the fens to this day. Some time before his attendance at the Glastonbury funeral, Æthelwine had erected at Ramsey a tiny wooden chapel and installed three monks there. After the funeral, having visited and approved the site, Oswald sent twelve more monks from his foundation at Westbury on Trym. Under their leader Eadnoth, they built a larger wooden chapel with conventual outbuildings, whereupon Oswald appointed Germanus to be their prior on 28 August 968. The foundations of Bishop Æthelwold of Winchester at Ely (970), Peterborough (probably 971)[2] and Thorney (973) were but a development of Oswald's initiative; unlike Ramsey, they lacked individual lay patrons of great power, and their endowments had to be built up piecemeal by Æthelwold. Æthelwine helped to organize the legal side of Æthelwold's land transactions, but he and his family were not called upon to provide from their own personal resources a nucleus of estates for any of Æthelwold's foundations, with the single exception of Crowland.

It will be shown in Appendix I to this paper that Holland formed part of the East Anglian ealdordom, and that much if not all of this fenland territory was in the personal possession of the ealdorman. The surviving records of Crowland make poor materials for history, but it cannot be doubted that Ealdorman Æthelwine provided the land for the foundation endowment of this house, and the Ramsey claim that he was in a special sense Crowland's patron and protector is no more than the simple truth. We are unable to supply with any precision a date for its foundation, but study of Æthelwold's land transactions shows that the Thorney endowments must have antedated those of Crowland, so that our outside limits are 974×984.

Æthelwine's three sons, Leofwine, Eadwine and Æthelweard, had insignificant careers that do not merit our attention beyond noting that the *Ramsey*

[1] *St O* pp. 427 and 430–3. St Oswald must have sounded Æthelwine's intentions some time before the Glastonbury funeral, for by this time he had already inspected and rejected three sites within Æthelwine's ealdordom, Benfleet in Essex, Ely in Cambridgeshire and St Albans in Hertforshire.

[2] The claim in *ASC* E that Peterborough was refounded in 963 is unsupported elsewhere and is probably untrue; it was preceded in point of time by Ely (*Vita Æthelwoldi* ch. 17), and the earliest acceptable evidence for the existence of Peterborough Abbey is *BCS* 1270, dated 971. Eric John (*Orbis Britanniae*, p. 264) has shown that the English Benedictine revival had not extended beyond Abingdon, Glastonbury, Winchester and Worcester by Easter 964.

Chronicle contains a few entries about them. It is just possible that Leofwine became an ealdorman for a short period before he died, and we know that Æthelweard perished at *Assandun* in 1016. The fortunes of other and more famous collaterals, members of the house of Ealdorman Æthelweard of the western shires, have received the able attention of other writers;[1] I have suggested in the genealogical table their possible relationship with the family of the 'Half King'.

A brief consideration of the unique nicknames given in their lifetimes to the two principal holders of the East Anglian ealdordom forms a fitting conclusion to this review. Byrhtferth of Ramsey, writing between 995 and 1005, says that Athelstan was called 'Half King' 'quia tantæ potestatis extitit, ut regnum et imperium cum rege temere sua ratione dicitur'; his son Æthelwold II, successor to the ealdordom, is said by the same author to have secured from the king 'principatum Orientalis regni', and after his marriage he took his bride Ælfthryth 'ad suum regnum'.[2] These phrases need not be taken too seriously, for Byrhtferth was given to hyperbole. Nevertheless, Athelstan's nickname reflects the power he wielded; he and his family shaped the course of national history for the greater part of the tenth century. The direction upon which they set the country's affairs gave rise to the second nickname by which the family is remembered. 'Dei amicus', the title given to Æthelwine by Florence of Worcester, is unlikely to have been Florence's invention. Perhaps he was translating (or mistranslating) a vernacular by-name. But, whatever the precise form of the original epithet, the reference can only be to Æthelwine's leadership of the cause of the newly founded monasteries of Edgar's reign. The family interest in the Benedictine reform movement started very early in the century – perhaps even before its introduction to England. The first endowment of Abingdon by the 'Half King' coincided with the reform of Fleury, which occurred at a time when Dunstan and Æthelwold were not yet priested. A glance at the genealogical table will show the astonishing power, range and consistency of the family's support for monasticism throughout the century.

APPENDIX I

HOLLAND AND THE EAST ANGLIAN EALDORDOM

It has long been recognized that the mid-tenth-century administrative unit known as the Five Boroughs of Nottingham, Leicester, Derby, Lincoln and Stamford was formed from the districts occupied and settled by five Danish armies in the last quarter

---

[1] *The Chronicle of Æthelweard,* ed. A. Campbell (London, 1962), pp. xii–xvi and references there cited.
[2] *St O* p. 428.

of the ninth century, and that the shires of Nottingham, Leicester and Derby that came into being some time during the tenth century preserve in their boundaries the limits of settlement of the individual Danish armies centred on each of these fortified towns. In a recent study of the origins of Lincolnshire, Alan Rogers repeats a question that has often been posed before: why did two out of the five boroughs fail to adopt this pattern?[1] Why was it that the territory of the ancient kingdom of Lindsey, which formed the settlement area of the Danish army of Lincoln,[2] became in later centuries not a county in its own right, but merely one of the three divisions of the huge conglomeration known as Lincolnshire? More important still, what became of 'Stamfordshire', if indeed such a unit ever existed?

It is my conviction that the problem is capable of solution along the following lines: the territory of 'Stamfordshire' comprised what still survives at the time of writing as the county of Rutland, together with the Parts of Kesteven in Lincolnshire. We know that a large portion of what is now Rutland had become part of the dowry of the queens of England by the third quarter of the tenth century,[3] and there is really no reason why one should not assume the arrangement to have been initiated immediately after King Edmund's redemption of the Five Boroughs in 942. The integrity of 'Stamfordshire' had in any case been broached as early as 918 or thereabouts, when Edward the Elder took away from it the two hundreds of *Hwicceslea* to complete his newly created county of Northampton.[4] It was not until the middle of the twelfth century that *Hwicceslea* was reunited with its neighbouring wapentakes north of the Welland to form the county of Rutland as we know it today.[5]

Either the two components of 'Stamfordshire' were already in existence as separate units of administration before the area had been settled by the Danes, or they were created soon after that settlement, for the name 'Kesteven' derives from an administrative unit that had its meeting-place in the forest which formed its dominant feature. The wood of *Ceostefne* or Kesteven is first referred to by Æthelweard, who was utilizing an annal for the year 894 from a lost manuscript of the *Anglo-Saxon Chronicle*.[6] The Ramsey chronicler, drawing from a contemporary record of the reconsecration of his abbey church in 991, now unhappily also lost to us, tells us that the great men of East Anglia, and of 'Cantebruge scira, Hertford scira, Bedeford scira, Huntedune scira, Hampton scira' (i.e. Northamptonshire) and 'de Ketstevena' attended the ceremony.[7] There is every reason to accept the account as authentic; the inclusion of Kesteven would complete the list of provinces in which Ramsey Abbey held estates. The omission of the word *scira* after Kesteven is noteworthy; nevertheless one cannot doubt that it was at that time regarded as a separate unit of administration. We do not hear of Kesteven again until *DB Chetsteven*, but this last

1 Alan Rogers, *A History of Lincolnshire* (Henley-on-Thames, 1970), ch. 6, 'The County and its Origins'.
2 F. M. Stenton, 'Lindsey and its Kings', *Preparatory to Anglo-Saxon England*, ed. D. M. Stenton (Oxford, 1970), pp. 127–35, esp. 133–4.
3 Gaimar, *Lestorie des Engles* 4138.
4 C. Hart, *The Hidation of Northamptonshire* (Leicester, 1970), p. 13.
5 *Hwicceslea* was still part of Northamptonshire at the time of the Northamptonshire Survey, which was compiled *c.* 1130.
6 *The Chronicle of Æthelweard*, ed. Campbell, pp. xxviii–xxx and 51.   7 *Chron Rams* p. 93.

form agrees so admirably with the spelling of the B recension of the *Ramsey Chronicle* that we are constrained to accept Ekwall's derivation from Brit *ceto-*, Welsh *coed*, 'wood', plus OScand *stefna*, 'a meeting' i.e. 'an administrative district with a common meeting-place'.[1]

Acceptance of this hypothesis concerning the fate of 'Stamfordshire' still leaves only partially solved the problem of the origin of Lincolnshire, for we have yet to take into account the Parts of Holland, which form the third component of the modern county. In 1954 H. E. Hallam pointed out 'there are few documentary sources for the history of the ninth, tenth and eleventh centuries in Holland'.[2] Since he wrote, an edition has appeared of a hitherto unpublished recension of the foundation charter of Thorney Abbey, composed between 973 and 975. A notable passage claims that estates in *Holande* named *Giddanig, Hludantune, Angarhala* and *Tid* were bought from a *dux* named *æðelwine* by Bishop Æthelwold of Winchester for twenty silver pounds plus 200 gold mancuses, plus in addition fifteen fertile hides in *Grantandene* (Great and Little Gransden in Huntingdonshire and Cambridgeshire). The king is said to have sold to Æthelwold the soke over these territories ('reatus emendatione quam Dani *socne* usitato nominant vocabulo'), together with his consent to the transaction for a further 100 gold mancuses.[3]

A commentary on some aspects of this highly important entry appears elsewhere;[4] what concerns us here is that the estates comprised the double hundred (of twenty-four carucates) of Gedney, Lutton and Tydd St Mary in the wapentake of Elloe in the Parts of Holland, and that the *æðelwine dux* who sold them to Bishop Æthelwold was none other than Æthelwine 'Dei amicus', ealdorman of East Anglia and son of the 'Half King'.

Evidently Æthelwold did not use them for the endowment of Thorney after all, for the passage referring to his purchase of these estates is deleted from the second recension of the abbey's foundation charter, drawn up in the period 975 × 984, and in *DB* we find that they had been in the possession of Ælfgar, earl of East Anglia during Harold's exile in 1051 and 1052, and again from 1053 to 1057.[5] Assuming that these properties had descended along with the East Anglian ealdordom, we are tempted to search Domesday for further evidence of Ælfgar's interests in the area. To our surprise we discover that of the eighty-four carucates at which the whole wapentake of Elloe was assessed in the time of the Confessor, no less than seventy-two were in Ælfgar's personal possession, either as demesne or as sokeland.[6]

These estates were inherited by Ralf the Staller, a Breton living at Norwich who held high office at court during the latter years of the Confessor's reign and who was appointed Earl of East Anglia by the Conqueror as soon as he gained control of the region.[7] Ralf the Staller died about 1069, leaving his son Ralf de Gael an extensive lordship in Brittany as well as the East Anglian earldom with its possessions in

[1] E. Ekwall, *The Oxford Dictionary of English Place-Names,* 3rd ed. (Oxford, 1947), p. 261.
[2] H. E. Hallam, *The New Lands of Elloe* (Leicester, 1954), p. 6.
[3] *ECEE* pp. 168 and 170–1.   [4] *Ibid.* pp. 180–1.
[5] *Lincs DB* 1/28–31, 14/97 and 57/51.   [6] See my forthcoming *Carucation of Lincolnshire.*
[7] Robertson, *Charters* pp. 464–5; Frank Barlow, *Edward the Confessor* (London, 1970), pp. 164–5 and 190–1; and D. C. Douglas, *William the Conqueror* (London, 1964), pp. 231–4.

Holland. When Ralf de Gael revolted in 1075 and fled to his Brittany lordship, his earldom of East Anglia came into the hands of the Conqueror. Within the wapentake of Elloe, the double hundred of Gedney, Lutton and Tydd was kept as a royal estate, together with sokeland at Holbeach and the manor of Fleet, comprising forty carucates in all. The remaining thirty-two carucates at Pinchbeck, Spalding, Weston and Moulton were given to Ivo Taillebois, the Lincolnshire sheriff.[1]

When we turn to the two remaining wapentakes of Holland, we find from *DB* that by virtue of his East Anglian earldom, Ralf the Staller had held (either in demesne or as sokeland) eighty-four out of the total of 120 carucates forming the wapentake of Kirton, and at least forty-eight of the eighty-four carucates comprising the wapentake of Skirbeck. After Ralf de Gael's defection these were all granted by the Conqueror to Alan the Red, Count of Brittany, together with the remaining lands of the earldom in Norfolk and Suffolk.[2]

It is likely that the double hundred of Butterwick and Freiston in Skirbeck wapentake, comprising twenty-four carucates, was also initially part of the East Anglian earldom. Some time during the Confessor's reign – perhaps in September 1052 when Harold was restored in the tenure of the earldom and his sister Queen Edith was given back possession of her dowry – Butterwick and Freiston were given to Wulfweard the White, who held them in all probability of Queen Edith; she acquired extensive estates in what is now Lincolnshire, in addition to her dower lands in Rutland.[3] When Wulfweard died in 1084 or later this property was granted to Guy de Craon, who also inherited twenty-seven carucates divided between the three wapentakes of Holland that had been in the possession of Athelstan of Frampton, the only other landowner of significance in the area.

The table on p. 142 summarizes the situation. If one adds to the holdings of Earls Ralf and Ælfgar the two hundreds in the possession of Wulfweard and the estates of Crowland Abbey in the wapentakes of Elloe and Kirton (bearing in mind that Ealdorman Æthelwine had been the protector of Crowland and a probable contributor to its endowment), one finds that at the time of the Norman Conquest over eighty per cent of all the properties in Holland were or had been in the direct possession of the East Anglian earldom. Even if one declines to throw in the estates of Wulfweard and Crowland, the percentage drops only to seventy. We have to weigh this information against the fact that a substantial property in Holland was in the hands of the East Anglian ealdordom as early as 974, and then ask ourselves if an explanation of this overwhelming dominance can be found.

The answer, I would submit, lies in the history of the ealdordom as outlined in the above paper. It is a reasonable assumption, in the light of all the evidence, that when

---

[1] *Lincs DB*8 4/96-99.

[2] Sir Frank Stenton, *The First Century of English Feudalism,* 2nd ed. (Oxford, 1961), p. 26, talks of 'the Breton colony founded by Earl Alan of Richmond', but it must be remembered that Alan's fief in Lincolnshire was formed chiefly from the lands of Ralf the Staller and his son Ralf de Gael, and that there was probably a large Breton settlement in these territories before Alan took them over. Indeed, this may have been the very reason for the Conqueror handing over the fief to Alan of Brittany.

[3] *Lincs DB* 57/38-39. Robertson, *Charters* pp. 462-3.

Edward the Elder created the ealdordom of East Anglia, Holland was an integral component, and so it remained until the dissolution of the earldom by the Conqueror in 1075. It is at least arguable that the territory settled by the great army of Guthrum included Holland within its bounds; one might go further, and postulate that Holland formed part of the Middle Anglian lands absorbed into the East Anglian kingdom before the Danish invasion and settlement.

Land ownership in Holland from 1066 to 1086

c = carucates   b = bovates   8b = 1 c

	Elloe		Kirton		Skirbeck	
Wapentakes of Holland						
Domesday antecessors	c	b	c	b	c	b
Earl Ælfgar of East Anglia	72	3	0	0	0	0
Ralf the Staller, earl of East Anglia	0	0	83	6½	48	6
Athelstan of Frampton, son of Guthrum	9	0	7	3	11	0
Wulfweard the White	0	0	0	0	24	0
Crowland Abbey	3	0	4	5	0	0
Other small landowners	0	0	26	3⅔	0	2
Domesday tenants-in-chief	c	b	c	b	c	b
King	40	0	0	0	0	0
Count Alan of Brittany	0	0	90	6½	48	6
Ivo Taillebois	32	3	0	0	0	0
Guy de Craon	9	0	10	3⅔	35	2
Crowland Abbey	3	0	4	5	0	0
Other small landowners	0	0	16	3	0	0
Totals	84	3	122	2	84	0

If this supposition is correct, the fact that the East Anglian ealdormen and earls of the tenth and eleventh centuries held in their own hands the great majority of the individual estates in Holland, in addition to exercising a general lordship over the territory, also calls for comment. Holland was of course a much smaller unit then than it is today; places like Spalding and Holbeach were right on the seaboard of the Wash. Professor Hallam's valuable study of early reclamation of the fenland within the wapentake of Elloe led him to the conclusion that a series of sea-banks were constructed throughout the ninth, tenth and eleventh centuries.[1] Such substantial earthworks could only be undertaken by the concerted efforts of the whole of the inhabitants; the concentration of land tenure within the hands of a single powerful magnate must have facilitated greatly the process of reclamation.

One final point must be made. Sufficient evidence has now been accumulated to enable a date to be put forward with some degree of confidence for the formation of the county of Lincoln from its component parts of Lindsey, Kesteven and Holland. Freeman pointed out long ago that Earl Leofric's foundation of Stow St Mary and his grandson Eadwine's defence of Lindsey in 1066 show that Lindsey formed part of the Mercian earldom until the Norman Conquest.[2] What happened subsequently

[1] *New Lands of Elloe*, pp. 15–18.
[2] E. A. Freeman, *The History of the Norman Conquest of England*, 3rd ed. (Oxford, 1877) II, 576.

to the governance of Lindsey may still remain in doubt, but the present study has established that Holland remained a possession of the earls of East Anglia right up to the revolt of Ralf de Gael in 1075. One cannot conceive of a united Lincolnshire before this date, with its individual components under the jurisdiction of different magnates. The creation of Lincolnshire is best regarded therefore as one of the consequences flowing from the Conqueror's dismemberment of the East Anglian earldom after Ralf's defection. The amalgamation of Holland's administration with those of Kesteven and Lindsey must have been a complicated transaction. By the time of Domesday, the process was complete. Such a radical change in local government, involving the creation of a new English shire, is unique in the annals of the Norman monarchy; it must be left to others to ask the reason why.

APPENDIX II

THE DESCENT OF THE EAST ANGLIAN EALDORDOM

It will be apparent that if, as is claimed above in Appendix I, Holland descended with the ealdordom (later the earldom) of East Anglia from the time of its reconquest by Edward the Elder in 918 to the creation of Lincolnshire some time between 1075 and 1086, there cannot have been any substantial break in the continuity of tenure in this period. A list of the descent is given below. The longest gap in the succession (apart from the period 918 to 930 for which no documentary sources survive) lies between the banishment of Earl Thorkel in 1021 and the appointment of Harold in 1044 × 1045, and I think it very probable that this should be filled by the name of Osgot Clapa, one of King Cnut's Stallers, who is known to have had strong connections with East Anglia.

930 to 931	Alfred
932 to summer 956	Athelstan 'Half King'
Summer 956 to 962	Æthelwold, son of Athelstan
962 to 24 April 992	Æthelwine 'Dei amicus', brother of Æthelwold
993 to 1002	Leofsige (with Essex)
c. 1004 to 18 October 1016	Ulfcetel 'Snilling' (not given the rank of earl)
1017 to 11 November 1021	Thorkel the Tall
?c. 1026 to 1044 × 1045	Osgot Clapa, the Staller (not given the rank of earl)
1044 × 1045 to 24 September 1051	Harold Godwineson
24 September 1051 to September 1052	Ælfgar Leofricson
September 1052 to April 1053	Harold
April 1053 to autumn 1057	Ælfgar
Autumn 1057 to 14 October 1066	Gyrth, brother of Harold
March 1067 to c. 1069	Ralf the Staller

c. 1069 to 1075	Ralf de Gael
1075 to *c.* 1093	Alan the Red, Count of Brittany, founder of the honour of Richmond (holding the lands of the old East Anglian earldom without inheriting the title)

Some Irish evidence for the date of the *Crux* coins of Æthelred II

MICHAEL DOLLEY

In *Anglo-Saxon Coins*[1] G. Van der Meer has set out in a convenient and readily accessible form the sequence of six sexennial issues (and minor transitional types) which I had worked out during the preceding decade for the coinage of Æthelred II. For the *Crux* issue (Brooke 3; *BMC* iii.a; Hild. C – cf. North 770; Seaby 667)[2] the period of issue which I had proposed is from the autumn of 991 to the autumn of 997. I wish now to examine the bearing that some new evidence has on the dating of this issue, but before doing so I need to clarify a controversial feature of the identification of types that is the basis of my chronology for the reign. The six substantive issues which I had distinguished after studying a large number of hoards preserved intact in Sweden are *First Hand, Second Hand, Crux, Long Cross, Helmet* and *Last Small Cross,* but others, notably Mr C. E. Blunt,[3] Mr J. D. Brand[4] and, more seriously, Dr Bertil Petersson,[5] have sought to establish that *Second Hand* is no more than a late variant of a single *Hand* issue. Each of them has his particular argument to be answered, but first of all there is the relative scarcity of *Hand* coins generally that has to be explained, for Hildebrand has described a total of only 483 *First* and *Second Hand* coins combined, including only 192 of the latter, as against 790 *Crux* and 940 *Long Cross* pieces.[6] To my mind there is a quite simple historical reason. *Hand* coins according to my chronology are ascribed to the 980s: their relative paucity in Viking hoards is surely to be accounted for by the fact that really massive Danish attacks upon England did not begin until the

---

[1] Ed. [R. H.] M. Dolley (London, 1961), p. 186.
[2] The following abbreviations are used: *BMC* = *A Catalogue of the Coins in the British Museum. Anglo-Saxon Series* (London, 1887–93); Brooke = G. C. Brooke, *English Coins,* 3rd ed. (London, 1950); Hild. = B. E. Hildebrand, *Anglosachsiska Mynt i Svenska Kongliga Myntkabinettet funna i Sveriges Jord,* 2nd ed. (Stockholm, 1881); North = J. J. North, *English Hammered Coinage* 1 (London, 1963); SCBI = Sylloge of Coins of the Brit. Isles (London, 1958); *SCMB* = *Seaby's Coin and Medal Bull.*; Seaby = P. Seaby, *Seaby's Standard Catalogue: British Coins – England and the United Kingdom,* 11th ed. (London, 1972); SHM Inv. = manuscript accession registers (with supporting documentation) in the Katalog room of the (Statens) Historiska Museum, Stockholm; *SNC* = *Spink's Numismatic Circular*; Thompson = J. D. A. Thompson, *Inventory of British Coin Hoards A.D. 600–1500* (London, 1956).
[3] *NC* 6th ser. 19 (1959), *Proceedings,* p. iv.   [4] *SNC* 75 (1967), 63–5 and 94–5.
[5] H. B. A. Petersson, *Anglo-Saxon Currency* (Lund, 1969), *passim.*   [6] Hild., pp. 169–71.

990s, while it was not until 991 that Danegeld as such began to be paid.[1]

Mr Blunt has claimed that typologically the distinction between *First* and *Second Hand* is so small that the one issue could not have been effectively demonetized in favour of the other. To this it can be objected that, at the end of the reign of Edgar, there had been achieved, apparently with 100% success, a demonetization of coins (Brooke 5; *BMC* viii; Hild. C.1) with a reverse type identical to that of the issue which replaced them, while in both cases the obverse type is a profile portrait of the king. Mr Brand's arguments, on the other hand, are almost entirely metrological and necessarily involve the parallel demotion of *Helmet* to the status of a mere variety of *Long Cross*. They have been severely, but justly, criticized by Mr C. S. S. Lyon,[2] and so need not detain us here. It should perhaps be noted, though, that, since Mr Brand has used precisely the same arguments concerning both *Helmet* and *Second Hand*, the restoration of *Helmet* to the status of a substantive, i.e. sexennial, type would have as its necessary corollary the vindication of *Second Hand*. Dr Petersson's arguments, finally, are much more solidly marshalled. Again his main emphasis is on metrology, but interestingly he accepts that the substantive issues of the reign should each have the same period of currency. Reducing the number of substantive types to five, he argues that change of type occurred every seven years. For the *Crux* type, as against my dating of 991–7, he proposes 989–96, though he does not exclude the possibility of 988–95. Unlike some critics, too, he recognizes the need to be constructive. For instance it is little use to place *Crux* somewhat later than I do, as Dr Brita Malmer has hinted,[3] unless one is prepared to spell out exactly how the *Hand* coins are to be distributed over the years immediately preceding.

Where Dr Petersson and I find ourselves completely in accord, of course, is in our premise that all issues were of the same length. To some though, notably to Professor P. Grierson,[4] it seems improbable that the reform at the end of the reign of Edgar worked smoothly until the anarchy of the last years of Æthelred II. These critics would prefer to suppose that originally change of type was not at regular intervals, and that it is no more than a coincidence that towards the end of the reign the changes of type from *Long Cross* to *Helmet* and from *Helmet* to *Last Small Cross* appear to fit in so neatly with a sexennial cycle calculated from the autumn of 973.[5] Probably the ablest of the exponents of this line of argument is Mr Lyon,[6] and he has not avoided the problems by ignoring the consequences of his reasoning for the chronology of the earlier

[1] *ASC, s.a.*
[2] *BNJ* 35 (1966), 37; H. R. Mossop, *The Lincoln Mint* (Newcastle-upon-Tyne, 1971), pp. 11–19.
[3] B. Malmer, *Nordiska Mynt Före År 1000* (Bonn and Lund, 1966), pp. 238–9.
[4] *NC* 7th ser. 6 (1966), *Proceedings,* pp. viii–xiv.
[5] *BNJ* 35 (1966), 34–7, and works there cited.
[6] *BNJ* 39 (1970), 199–200.

part of the reign. In particular he is now on record as having suggested that *Long Cross* may have been in currency as early as 994.[1]

What has been too long ignored is the evidence from Ireland. At the end of the tenth century the Dubliners began to put out a coinage of their own, the types for the first two decades and more being those of contemporary pennies from England.[2] The earliest of these coins are of *Crux* type, and there is a lack of continuity between them and later coins of Dublin that suggests an interruption accompanied by a complete change of mint-personnel as regards both the engraving of the dies and the actual production of coin. This particular problem, however, is one that need not detain us, and it is sufficient to note that the *Crux* coins of Dublin constitute a well-defined entity.[3] There are eighty-six specimens known to me in the public collections of Europe, and perhaps another dozen in private hands. The great majority can be shown to derive from one major hoard discovered at Clondalkin on the outskirts of Dublin around the year 1830.[4] Two more of the coins occurred in a find of 1912 near Dungarvan in Co. Waterford, and one has recently come to light in archaeological excavations at Armagh.[5] Others may derive from a shadowy Irish find of *c.* 1840.[6] In none of these cases were there found non-Irish coins critical for the date of the *Crux* coins in question. A discovery made *c.* 1830 at Inchkenneth in the Hebrides suggests, however, that the Dublin coinage had begun before rather than after the millennium,[7] and the same is true of two Swedish and one Icelandic hoard-provenances.[8] Two further Swedish finds were concealed too late in the eleventh century to be material.[9] On the hoard-evidence, then, one is already inclining to the view that the *Crux* coins of Dublin belong a little, say two or three years, before the end of the tenth century, and an analysis of the extant specimens leads to the further suggestion that the issue

---

[1] 'If their return to Scandinavia occasioned the influx of these coins, the *Long Cross* issue would have begun in 994, against Dolley's date of 997 and Petersson's of 996' (*ibid.* p. 200). Note, though, that consideration is not given to the fact that the earliest coins of Olaf Tryggvason and of Olof Skötkonung are of *Crux* and not *Long Cross* type; see below, p. 153.

[2] [R.H.] M. Dolley, *The Hiberno-Norse Coins in the British Museum,* SCBI (1966). In preparation is an SCBI fascicule embracing the 440 Hiberno-Norse coins in the Royal Coin Cabinet at Stockholm – more than 370 of them from the two decades *c.* 1000–*c.* 1020 where the representation in the British Museum trays amounts to no more than forty-one.

[3] For a corpus of the specimens in public collections see my forthcoming contribution to the *Festschrift* in honour of Dr Olof von Feilitzen.

[4] Dolley, *Hiberno-Norse Coins,* p. 55.   [5] *Ibid.* p. 57.

[6] J. Lindsay, *A View of the Coinage of Scotland* (Cork, 1845), pp. 1–3.

[7] Dolley, *Hiberno-Norse Coins,* p. 58.

[8] The Swedish are the 1807 Myrungs hoard from Gotland (SHM Inv. 394) and the 1924 Igelösa hoard from Skåne (SHM Inv. 17532), and the Icelandic is the 1930 hoard from Gaulverjabaer (*Nordisk Numismatisk Årsskrift* 1948, 52, no. 90). In all three finds the latest English coins present are of *Long Cross* type and occur in substantial numbers.

[9] The finds are the 1913 hoard from Sandtorp in Central Sweden (SHM Inv. 14935) believed to have been concealed *c.* 1030, and the 1942 hoard from Halsarve on Gotland for which an early-twelfth-century date is not impossible (SHM Inv. 23040).

was a very compact one with striking occupying weeks rather than months. It is also clear that, since two or three of the pieces (e.g. SCBI B/M HN 17) imitate the late variety of English *Crux* penny for which the name *Small Crux* has been proposed (Brooke —; *BMC* —; Hild. C.a – cf. North p. 113; Seaby 667A), the Dublin *Crux* coins as a whole were not earlier than the last months of the *Crux* emission in England. If my original chronology be correct, this entails a *terminus post quem* for the *Crux* coinage of Dublin little, if any, before 997, while if it is Dr Petersson's that is preferred any date before 995 is likewise precluded. That the Dublin coins have occurred only in the one find in any quantity may be thought, of course, yet another indication that the emission was one of relatively short duration. Had the coins been in issue over a period of years one might have expected a succession of finds where they preponderate.

The great majority of the *Crux* imitations emanating from Dublin have obverse legends composed of four distinct elements. These may be normalized with some confidence:

SITI RX DIFLIN MEox.

Since the 1830s numismatists have seen in the prototheme the name Sihtric, which has been consistently identified as that of the famous Sihtric Silkbeard, Brian Bóromha's adversary at the battle of Clontarf in 1014. The deuterotheme undoubtedly is to be read R*ex*, while the third and fourth elements together are almost certainly a contraction for *Diflinme(nnorum)*, 'of the Dubliners'. Thus the sense of the legend as a whole is 'Sihtric, King of the Dubliners'. That DIFLIN, which also occurs as a mint-signature on the reverse of many of the coins, is Dublin (MIr *duibh linn*, 'black pool') cannot well be doubted, and so the attribution of these coins to Dublin seems incontrovertible. Sihtric Silkbeard, too, actually was king at Dublin for part, though not all, of the period when the *Crux* type is thought by me to have been current in England. Where numismatists have erred, though, is in accepting 989 as the year of his accession. The chronology of the years following the murder of Glún Iairn in 989 has still to be worked out in detail, but elsewhere[1] I am showing that much the greater probability is that Sihtric did not immediately succeed Glún Iairn, and that he was a grandson, and not a son, of Anlaf Quaran Sihtricsson who survived the bloodbaths of *Brunanburh* in 937 and of Tara in 980 before dying in belated penance at Iona in 981. What historians have been pointing out for years, too, is that Sihtric figures in none of the Irish sources before 993, and a whole generation ago Curtis was making a convincing case for his not becoming undisputed king of Dublin until 994.[2] In other words, what we know

---

[1] In a forthcoming paper in the *Jnl of the R. Soc. of Antiquaries of Ireland*.

[2] E. Curtis, *A History of Ireland*, 6th ed. (London, 1950), p. 27. In his *History of Medieval Ireland*,

of Sihtric's career fits in admirably with the evidence that some of his earliest coins imitate the late, *Small Crux*, variant of the *Crux* type which is unlikely to have been current in England on any telling before 995, and which I would date to the first half of 997.

Support for this interpretation comes from a discovery made by Mr W. A. Seaby in 1970.[1] One of Sihtric's *Crux* imitations is from a reverse die used originally with an English obverse by a moneyer named Sigeric at Watchet in Somerset; two examples of the Sihtric striking are in the National Museum of Ireland, a third is in the Ulster Museum and a fourth is at Copenhagen, while at least five examples of the original striking in combination with an Æthelred obverse are in the trays of the British Museum, the Taunton Museum, the Royal Coin Cabinet at Stockholm and the University Museum at Lund.[2] Two points deserve to be noticed: firstly all extant Æthelred coins of Watchet in this type seem to be from a single pair of dies, and secondly the reverse die as used at Dublin was markedly rusty. This second observation implies that the die had not been used for some time before its re-use at Dublin, while the first suggests that only one pair of dies had been supplied to the Watchet mint. Almost by definition they would have been sent down at the inception of the *Crux* type, so that Mr Lyon's percipient remark that the obverse exhibits 'early' features should occasion no surprise. Sigeric, after all, had been striking at Watchet in both the *Hand* issues, and one suspects that he may have been appointed the sole moneyer of the mint at the time of Edgar's great monetary reform.[3] What is intriguing is that Sigeric's *Crux* coins of Watchet are his last. The *Long Cross* coins of this place were all struck by a certain Hunewine, and Sigeric vanishes from the numismatic scene. That there are no *Crux* coins of Watchet by Hunewine and no *Long Cross* coins of the mint by Sigeric, argues that the appointment of Hunewine broadly coincided with the inception of the *Long Cross* issue. This seems even more clearly the case when we note that a Hunewine who may be presumed to be the same individual – the name is a rare one – was still striking at Exeter and Ilchester (Somerset) at the very end of the *Crux* issue: he is known there for the very rare *Intermediate Small Cross/ Crux* mules (Brooke —; *BMC* iii; Hild. C.b – cf. North 771; Seaby —), which were incontrovertibly associated with the last few months, if not indeed weeks, of the *Crux* emission. But we can refine on the time of Hunewine's appointment even more narrowly. The recorded weights and the forms of the obverse legends of Hunewine's earliest coins at the Bristol Channel mint suggest that he began striking there a few weeks at least after the *Long Cross* issue had

---

2nd ed. (London, 1938), p. 7, 1000 is given as the date of Sihtric's accession, but the pendulum had swung too far in the other direction.

[1] *SCMB* 1971, 90–1.

[2] The present location of a sixth English striking (R. C. Lockett coin sale, Glendining, 6–9 June 1955, lot 686c) is unknown to me.　　　[3] *SCMB* 1972, 176–8.

begun: still to be recorded are Watchet *Long Cross* coins which both were certainly struck to the initial 27 grain weight-standard and bear the reading ANGLORX, criteria which in combination are appropriate to the original issue of *Long Cross* coins from west country mints generally.[1] The suggestion is, then, that something happened at Watchet not long before the introduction of the *Long Cross* type which explains the removal of Sigeric's rusty reverse die of *Crux* type to Dublin, an absence of striking at the beginning of the *Long Cross* issue just when the mint could be expected to have been more than usually productive,[2] and the transfer to the mint, by way of Ilchester apparently, of an established moneyer from the nearest major centre of coin-production.

In the *Anglo-Saxon Chronicle* Watchet figures on only three occasions. The first mention is *s.a.* 914 when a Viking force from Brittany raided up the Bristol Channel and came ashore to the east of the town. It is, of course, irrelevant to our present purpose, though it is curious that survivors of the luckless raiders ended up in Ireland. The second and third references both fall in the first half of the reign of Æthelred II. The first of these is *s.a.* 988 – or 987 according to MSS E and F – when 'Watchet was ravaged'. The sack appears to have come early in the year, but according to my reckoning that the *Crux* issue began in the autumn of 991 this is at least three (or four) years too early for the abstraction of Sigeric's *Crux*-type reverse die. Similarly, on Dr Petersson's preferred reckoning that the issue began in 989 the sack is still too early by at least a year, while by his alternative computation that 988 saw the start of the emission it would be feasible only if one could accept that his septennial cycle began in January. In any case, in 988 Glún Iairn's murder was still in the unpredictable future, and the accession of Sihtric lay five or even six years ahead. And if Sigeric really had given up striking after losing his die early in 988, why, after the mint had stood idle for years, was Hunewine appointed not at the very inception of the *Long Cross* issue but at least a month or so afterwards? We can safely conclude from all this that the sacking of 988 (or 987) was not the event in question.

---

[1] *SNC* 69 (1961), 240–1. One apparently unique Watchet coin (*BMC* Æthelred 338) does have the fuller rendering of the ethnic as ANGLORX but weighs no more than 24·7 grains; Hild. Ethelred 3882–4 weigh 21·6, 23·3 and 27·9 grains respectively and have no fuller form of the ethnic than ANGLO followed by a mark of contraction – a die also used in the case of SCBI *Copenhagen* 11, no. 1274 where the weight is 26·8 grains; two coins in the List hoard (J. Kersten and P. La Baume, *Vorgeschichte der nordfriesischen Inseln* (Neumünster, 1958), nos. 583–4) bear an obverse legend which ends ANGLO and weigh no more than 20·3 and 22·1 grains respectively; an eighth coin in the possession of Messrs A. H. Baldwin & Sons Ltd also reads ANGLO and weighs only 21·6 grains.

[2] The English hoard-evidence for this period suggests strongly that demonetization of an old issue was achieved very early in the currency of its successor, and it is reasonable to conclude that the bulk of the coins of a particular type would have been struck within a matter of months after its introduction.

Some Irish evidence for the date of the 'Crux' coins of Æthelred II

The third mention of Watchet is *s.a.* 997: 'In this year the Viking army went round Devon into the mouth of the Severn and ravaged there, both in Cornwall, in Wales, and in Devon. And they landed at Watchet and did much damage there, burning and slaying; and after that they turned back round Land's End to the southern side . . .'[1] On my reckoning, for the first nine months of 997 the main *Crux* type was still very much legal tender, while along with Sigeric's obsolescent and rusted reverse die there would be lying around for the raiders to carry off plenty of examples of the recently introduced *Small Crux* coinage which was soon to be the subject of imitation in Dublin.[2] By the same calculation, Hunewine would still be striking his *Intermediate Small Cross/Crux* mules at Exeter and Ilchester,[3] and, most important of all, Sihtric Silkbeard by this time was securely, if only recently, established in Dublin and in a position to ensure that his name appeared on the new coinage.

According to Dr Petersson's reckoning, however, any *Crux* die lying around in 997 and gathered up by the raiders and passed to the Dubliners was one year, perhaps two, out of date, and consequently we have to make the unlikely supposition that in Dublin a frankly imitative coinage began with copies of coins no longer current – nor indeed available – in England. This is in contrast with the solid evidence[4] that by the millennium at the very latest the Dublin mint was busily turning out coins copying the current English *Long Cross* type. This evidence also disposes of the hypothesis that the *Long Cross* type was introduced in England as late as the opening years of the eleventh century.[5] Any chronology, in fact, that does not allow the Hiberno-Norse *Crux* imitations to fall naturally into place at the end of the period of currency of their English prototypes contradicts the evidence of the hoards. There is only one hoard – Clondalkin, from the hinterland of Viking Dublin – where *Crux* coins of Sihtric are not accompanied by *Long Cross* prototypes and/or imitations, and, as a die-study of the Dublin *Crux* coins has proceeded, it has become increasingly obvious that the size of the issue was minimal. Indeed, were it not for the lucky chance of the Clondalkin hoard, it must be doubtful if there would be known today as many as a dozen of the pieces in question. Of their *Long Cross* successors from Dublin on the other hand the tally runs into hundreds – there are 230 with more than thirty recorded hoard-provenances in the Royal Coin Cabinet at Stockholm alone – and it is significant that they should be relatively common in those Scandinavian hoards where *Long Cross* itself is the latest English type. In the Igelösa hoard from Skåne, for

---

[1] The translation is that of Professor Whitelock (*The Anglo-Saxon Chronicle,* trans. D. Whitelock with D. C. Douglas and S. I. Tucker (London, 1961)) except that I have substituted 'Viking' for 'Danish'– *se here* does not have to be specified in the original.

[2] Dolley, *Hiberno-Norse Coins,* pl. i, 17 is a case in point, but there are other coins in the National Museum of Ireland where the *Small Crux* prototype is just as obvious.

[3] E.g. Hild. Ethelred 546.   [4] See below, p. 152, n. 1.   [5] See above, p. 146, n. 3.

example, there are at least nine Hiberno-Norse coins of *Long Cross* type, and in the List hoard from Sylt no fewer than twenty-six.[1] Against this background it seems undeniable that the emission of the *Crux* coins of Sihtric not only was brief but also came at the very end of the *Crux* issue in England.

To sum up. I suggest that the historical evidence and the numismatic evidence make a true match only in terms of the sack of Watchet in 997 and of my ordering of the issues of Æthelred II on a sexennial basis. The first coinage of Dublin after Sihtric became king, probably in 994, was an imitative one, and one of the varieties copied, *Small Crux*, belongs, as all agree, late within the *Crux* issue; used, and also copied, at Dublin was a rusted reverse die which earlier had struck all the extant *Crux* coins of Watchet; and the moneyer at Watchet to whom it had been issued was replaced by another who began striking there a few weeks after the *Long Cross* issue began: all this evidence, some of it new, receives a full and sufficient explanation only if we relate the sack of Watchet recorded in the *Anglo-Saxon Chronicle s.a.* 997 and my postulated change of coin-type from *Crux* to *Long Cross* in the autumn of 997.

Nearly twenty years ago I suggested that *Long Cross* must have been superseded by *Helmet* just about the time that Wilton was burned down in 1003,[2] and more recently Mr Lyon has demonstrated just how well the sack of Oxford at Christmas 1009 accords with my further supposition that *Helmet* in its turn had given place to *Last Small Cross* in the autumn of that year.[3] If the *Long Cross* and *Helmet* types each lasted six years, there seems no reason why the *Crux* type should have been current for any other period. In other words, the *Crux* type, superseded in the autumn of 997, ought to have been introduced towards the end of 991. Certainly it cannot have begun much later, if only because the relative paucity of all *Hand* coins in Scandinavian hoards makes it clear that *Crux* coins were used to pay the first major Danegeld which was collected at the end of 991.[4] In theory, of course, *Crux* might have begun even earlier, but then critics of the sexennial cycle would have to answer Dr Petersson's arguments, as well as mine, that each substantive type was of the same duration until the complete breakdown of public order at the close of Æthelred's reign. Moreover, the number and the topographical pattern of extant coins of the *Benediction Hand* variety (Brooke —; *BMC* ii.f; Hild. B.3 – cf. North 769; Seaby 666), intermediate between *Second Hand* and *Crux*, suggest that they still had not been effectively demonetized when collection of the fatal tribute began.

Once it is conceded that the *Crux* type was in issue from 991 to 997, there are

[1] SHM Inv. 17532 – two of the coins are in Stockholm and seven in the University Museum at Lund: Kersten and La Baume, *Vorgeschichte*, pp. 473–4. Both hoards embrace all significant varieties of the Dublin penny of *Long Cross* type.
[2] *Nordisk Numismatisk Unions Medlemsblad* 1954, 152–6.
[3] *BNJ* 35 (1966), 34–7.   [4] *ASC, s.a.*

exactly thirteen years to be occupied by the coins of Æthelred which are demonstrably earlier. The most natural division is to allow one year for the winding up of the *Small Cross* issue, initiated by Edgar and continued unchanged under Edward the Martyr, and twelve years for all coins of the *Hand* type. Twelve years are, of course, exactly twice six, and it cannot well be coincidence that there are two main divisions of the *Hand* type, and that beside the hoards where *First Hand*, but not *Second*, occurs,[1] there are early *Crux* hoards where the only *Hand* coins are of the *Second Hand* and *Benediction* varieties.[2] But I am anxious not to anticipate another paper which will discuss not only the date of Edgar's reform of the coinage but also a range of arguments in support of the view that the *Hand* type falls naturally into two substantive issues. Here I wish only to observe that for *Crux* to have its hey-day *c.* 995 accords well with the evidence of Viking imitation generally. Sihtric was not the only Scandinavian monarch to begin a 'national' coinage with copies of English coins of *Crux* type. The mid-990s saw precisely the same phenomenon in Denmark, Norway and Sweden. Although Sven Tveskjaeg had been undisputed ruler of Denmark since 985, Olaf Tryggvason of Norway seems to have been in no position to strike coins before his return from England after his baptism at Easter 995, and the many points of resemblance between the exceptionally rare coins of Sven and those of Olaf make it more than likely that they were put out, if not on one and the same occasion, at least by a single moneyer who passed from the one court to the other.[3] As for Olof Skötkonung of Sweden, the date of his accession falls most probably in or around the year 994.[4] In other words there are extremely good reasons why the historian should resist any attempt to abridge the issue of *Hand*-type coins that involves moving back the dates of the *Crux* and *Long Cross* types. No arrangement of the Anglo-Saxon prototypes is plausible that postulates the inauguration of the derivative coinages on the basis of the obsolete – be it at Trondheim(?), Sigtuna or Dublin! It is especially relevant that the *Long Cross* issue can be

---

[1] E.g. the 1914 Pemberton's Parlour hoard from Chester (Thompson 85, but the estimate of concealment *c.* 985 is demonstrably too late: *NC* 4th ser. 20 (1920), 141–65) and the neglected but critical 1835 hoard from Vaalse in Denmark (SCBI *Copenhagen* 1, 27; Æthelred coins listed *ibid.* 11, xiv), but it is only with the publication of the Swedish material that the picture will begin to emerge in all its clarity.

[2] E.g. the 1886 Isleworth hoard (Thompson 203, but the estimate of concealment *c.* 980 is demonstrably too early: *NC* 3rd ser. 6 (1886), 161–3) and the 1942 Lymose hoard from Denmark (SCBI *Copenhagen* 1, 29; Æthelred coins listed *ibid.* 11, xii).

[3] Pp. 229–40 of B. Malmer, 'A Contribution to the Numismatic History of Norway during the Eleventh Century', *Commentationes de Nummis Saeculorum IX–XI in Suecia Repertis,* ed. N. L. Rasmusson and L. O. Lagerqvist, 1 (Stockholm, 1961) are unquestionably the best and fullest treatment of the Norwegian and Danish coins in question.

[4] B. Malmer, *Olof Skötkonungs Mynt och Andra Ethelred-Imitationer* (Stockholm, 1965) neatly if legitimately side-steps the problem of an absolute chronology, but 'ca 995–1022' are the dates for Olof's reign which appear in L. O. Lagerqvist, *Svenska Mynt under Vikingatid och Medeltid* (Stockholm, 1970) and may be taken as reflecting the best and most recent Swedish historical thinking.

shown to have been imitated at Dublin and at Sigtuna, where alone the
tradition of minting took root with striking continuing without break into
the succeeding century, as soon as the first of the new coins began to arrive in
those places, and equally it is clear that the striking of *Crux* imitations was
immediately discontinued.[1] The reason for this popularity of the *Long Cross*
type is not hard to find: the initial issue was composed of coins consistently
heavier than anything turned out by the English mints since Edgar's reform,
and if subsequent issues within the type failed quite to maintain the standard,
it still is true that the mean weight of *Long Cross* pennies from the emission as
a whole works out at a figure well above the average for the later Anglo-
Saxon series generally.

[1] In this connection I am particularly grateful to my old friend Förste antikvarie Lars O. Lagerqvist
for going through with me in 1972 the relevant sections of his 1961 *licentiatavhandling* entitled
'Studier i Äldre Nordisk Mynthistoria' – a piece of research which it is hoped may still appear in
printed form.

The round, cap-shaped hats depicted on Jews in BM Cotton Claudius B. iv

RUTH MELLINKOFF

Individualized portraiture is rarely found in early medieval art. Personalities or groups were more often identified by context or inscription or some significant motif. To those who knew the biblical stories and legends, individuals portrayed in scenes such as Abraham's sacrifice of Isaac, or Moses and the brazen serpent, or the Last Supper, could be easily identified. Iconographical motifs not only served to identify particular prophets, apostles, saints and others, but also often established the character of certain groups. In the latter case, costume played an important part, and especially the head-dress. In western medieval European art a king can be recognized by his crown, a monk by his tonsure, a bishop by his mitre, a divine being by its nimbus and so on. While there were variations and some exceptions, nevertheless head-dress and costume were useful devices for ordinary labelling.

Within these conventions, how did the Jews fare? An iconography for Jews *per se* did not exist in early Christian and Byzantine art, nor (as far as the evidence thus far shows) did it in Carolingian, Ottonian or later Byzantine art.[1] There was no representation of a 'Jewish' costume, nor any specific 'Jewish' iconographical motif. Jews of the Old Testament and the New are identifiable from the context of the story or legend depicted.[2] An iconography for Jews seems only to have appeared later. It has been suggested that pictorial characterization of Jews with distinctive motifs began with the First Crusade, that is, about 1096.[3] The motif most generally noted is the pointed hat, often referred to as the *Judenhut*. It became the most typical and outstanding feature

---

[1] Portrayals of contemporary medieval Jews in a secular context are extremely rare in early medieval art. An unusual example, however, of medieval portraiture can be seen in a caricature of a group of English Jews at the head of a roll of the Issue of the Exchequer of 1233; see *Exchequer of Receipt*, Jews' Roll, n. 87: Hilary Term, 17 Hen. III, in the Public Record Office, London. See Cecil Roth, *Essays and Portraits in Anglo-Jewish History* (Philadelphia, 1962), pp. 22–3, for a description of the members of the Norwich community.

[2] As, e.g., the Israelites in the Carolingian bible of San Paolo fuori le Mura. For a reproduction of one of the folios see Hanns Swarzenski, *Monuments of Romanesque Art,* 2nd ed. (Chicago, 1967), pl. 58, fig. 1.

[3] Bernhard Blumenkranz, *Le Juif Médiéval au Miroir de l'Art Chrétien* (Paris, 1966), p. 19. He concludes: 'Nous avons pu constater une différence profonde entre le haut et le bas moyen âge; la coupure se place en 1096, l'année de la première croisade' (p. 135).

of Jewish costume as mirrored in medieval art long before it ultimately took a place among the official infamous badges Jews were required to wear during the Middle Ages. The Fourth Lateran Council called by Innocent III in 1215, establishing the requirement (canon 68) that Jews and Saracens be distinguished from Christians by a difference in their clothes,[1] was interpreted in different ways in various countries.[2] By 1267 the pointed Jewish hat was made obligatory for Jews in provincial church councils at Breslau[3] and Vienna,[4] where it was referred to as *cornutum pileum*.

The shape of the *Judenhut* varied considerably, but all varieties can be classified as pointed: some of the hats were conical; some were pointed, terminating in a knob; some were spiked; and some were distinctively funnel-shaped (see pl. I*a*).[5] The many variations can be observed repeatedly in the profuse representation in twelfth-, thirteenth- and fourteenth-century manuscripts.[6] The origin of this hat is still uncertain. Guido Kisch has argued that the older form of it (one that he believes was conical and low, without a brim or with a narrow one) goes back at least to the eleventh century and that later three different types evolved.[7] He suggests, however, that Jews were distinguished at least as early as the ninth century by their particular head-covering and by their beards. His argument is based wholly on textual allusions, of 'dress according to Jewish custom'.[8] Pictorial evidence is lacking. In a recent history of Jewish costume its author has singled out some miniatures in the Flemish Stavelot Bible (BM Add. 28106–7), of 1097,[9] as those containing the

[1] For a translation of canon 68 (with Latin on a parallel page), see Solomon Grayzel, *The Church and the Jews in the XIIIth Century,* rev. ed. (New York, 1966), pp. 308–9.

[2] For some literature on this subject see Ulysse Robert, *Les Signes d'Infamie au Moyen Âge* (Paris, 1891); Israel Abrahams, *Jewish Life in the Middle Ages* (London, 1932), pp. 320–3; Grayzel, *Church and Jews,* pp. 67–70; Joseph Reider, 'Jews in Medieval Art', *Essays in Antisemitism,* ed. Koppel S. Pinson (New York, 1942), pp. 51–2; and Guido Kisch, *The Jews in Medieval Germany* (Chicago, 1949), pp. 295–9, and 'The Yellow Badge in History', *Historia Judaica* 19 (1957), 91–101. (Raphael Straus, 'The Jewish Hat as an Aspect of Social History', *Jewish Social Stud.* 4 (1942), 59–72, is unfortunately too full of errors to be useful.)

[3] Julius Aronius, *Regesten zur Geschichte der Juden* (Berlin, 1902), no. 724, p. 302.

[4] See Ioannes Dominicus Mansi, *Sacrorum Conciliorum Nova et Amplissima Collectio* [facs. copy of orig. ed. of 1758–98] (Paris, 1903) XXIII, cols. 1174 and 1175.

[5] This is a depiction of Joseph in the Nativity; the leaf is dated *c.* 1170–80.

[6] For abundant and varied examples, see the illustrations in Blumenkranz, *Le Juif Médiéval;* see also the full-page diagram of Jewish head-dress (from the thirteenth century) in *The Jewish Encyclopedia* (New York–London, 1916) VI, under *head-dress;* see also the illustrations in Alexandre comte de Laborde, *La Bible Moralisée Illustrée* (Paris, 1911–27); and the many examples in Hanns Swarzenski, *Die lateinischen illuminierten Handschriften des XIII. Jahrhunderts* (Berlin, 1936). Two different types can be observed on two panels of the bronze doors from San Zeno; see Albert Boeckler, *Die Bronzetür von San Zeno, Die frühmittelalterlichen Bronzetüren* III (Marburg, 1931), pls. 18–24 for one variation and 60, 66, 68–9 and 70–1 for the other.

[7] Kisch, 'The Yellow Badge', p. 95.   [8] *Ibid.* pp. 92–3 and 95.

[9] Alfred Rubens, *A History of Jewish Costume* (London, 1967), p. 106. For comments and references about the Stavelot Bible see Swarzenski, *Monuments,* pp. 30, 55, 58, 65, 67 and 72 and pls. 97, 98, 110, 150, 162 and 184; Carl Nordenfalk, *Romanesque Painting* (Lausanne and Paris, 1958), pp.

earliest illustrations of the pointed Jewish hat, as for example, the hat on Joel, 218r (see pl. II*a*).[1]

If this is as early an artistic representation of the pointed *Judenhut* as can be traced, there is earlier artistic evidence of quite another kind of head-covering for Jews, namely, a round, cap-shaped hat. The earliest representations of this type of hat I have thus far located occur in an English vernacular manuscript, the Old English prose version of the Pentateuch and Joshua, BM Cotton Claudius B. iv,[2] dated 1025–50. These rounded hats depicted on Jews (here the Israelites of the Old Testament) have not to my knowledge previously been noted. The interest and concern with the more prevalent pointed hat have perhaps caused this evidence of another hat tradition to be overlooked. It is on 107v that this motif appears first, in an illustration of the investiture of Aaron. Aaron is depicted twice on this page wearing a type of round, cap-shaped hat – in the upper right corner with Moses (see pl. I*b*)[3] and again in the lower left corner (see pl. I*c*). It is, however, only on 121r (see pl. I*d*) and on subsequent folios, as for example 139v (see pl. I*e*),[4] that illustrations of rounded hats for other Israelites occur. The slight variations in the design of the hats are due most likely to the individual bent of the several artists who worked on the manuscript.[5]

That Israelites are portrayed earlier in the manuscript without any head-gear suggests the possibility that the artists believed, or were instructed, that the Jews were required to wear these hats only some time *after* the reception of the Law. But, if so, it is difficult to determine exactly what the artists had in mind, for the only biblical law as to costume for the people was the law of the

166, 180, 181 and 190–2; K. H. Usener, 'Les Débuts du Style Roman dans l'Art Mosan', *L'Art Mosan*, ed. Pierre Francastel (Paris, 1953), pp. 104–9; and E. de Moreau, *Histoire de l'Église en Belgique* (Brussels, 1945) II, 335.

[1] The other hat types for Old Testament figures in this bible will be discussed later.

[2] See references for this manuscript in my *The Horned Moses in Medieval Art and Thought* (London, Berkeley and Los Angeles, 1970), p. 145, n. 1; at the time of writing, publication of a facsimile of the manuscript is awaited: *The Old English Illustrated Hexateuch*, ed. C. R. Dodwell and Peter Clemoes, EEMF 18.

[3] Moses is not portrayed wearing the round hat; rather he is shown wearing a horned headdress: see Mellinkoff, *The Horned Moses*, for a detailed study of this motif.

[4] The round hats are especially clear on 121r, 121v, 123v, 124v, 125r, 126r, 127v and 128r. On some later folios (136v, 137r, 138v, 139v, 140v, 141r and 141v) the hats have been rather bizarrely painted so that the crowns look like curly hair (see pl. I*e*). These folios, however, seem to have been executed in the same style as that of some earlier ones (e.g. 2r, 3r, 4v and 7v) where the curly hair is also found. While the round hat convention is not wholly adhered to, it is lacking mostly on some of the later, unfinished illustrations. I should, however, mention that two round hats are introduced earlier, on 76v, where they seem to have no significance, especially in relationship to the abundant and consistent sequence from 121r on.

[5] C. R. Dodwell believes, however, that all the illustrations were executed by a single artist; see his introduction to the facsimile. While the innovative iconographical programme surely seems to be the work of one person, I am presently unconvinced that the execution of the pictures themselves was achieved by only one artist.

Fringes (Numbers XV.38 and Deuteronomy XXII.12).[1] It should be emphasized that these hats were designed exclusively for the Israelites. No other individuals or groups wear these distinctive hats. For example, Egyptians are hatless unless in military garb, when they are shown wearing a kind of conical helmet; Pharaoh, of course, is portrayed with a crown. The rounded, cap-shaped, narrow-brimmed hats[2] thus represent what seems so far to be the earliest pictorial evidence of a specific iconographical motif for the portrayal of Jews.

That this motif is a head-covering focuses attention on another interesting problem. Great controversy has raged over whether or not Jews wore a head-covering during the ancient and early medieval periods, and whether the practice of covering the head was based on religious law or on religious custom. A difference of opinion on this subject has formed part of the basic conflict between Orthodox and Reform Judaism of the nineteenth and twentieth centuries.[3] It has been argued that until the thirteenth century there

[1] The fact that the hats first occur in the portrayal of Aaron at his consecration (Leviticus VIII.12; see above, p. 157, and pls. I*b* and *c*) invites us to ask what connection, if any, the artist responsible for this drawing thought these hats had with the mitre with which Aaron was invested at this ceremony. Mitres are referred to in Exodus XXXIX.26 (Vulg. *Et mitras cum coronulis suis ex bysso*) and Leviticus VIII.9 (Vulg. *Cidari quoque texit caput: et super eam, contra frontem, posuit laminam auream consecratam in sanctificatione*). Exodus XXXIX.26 is not rendered in the Old English text; but at Leviticus VIII.9 (*The Old English Version of the Heptateuch* etc., ed. S. J. Crawford, Early English Text Society o.s. 160 (repr. 1969 with the text of two additional manuscripts transcribed by N. R. Ker), 292) the Old English reads '7 band his heafod mid claðe 7 mid gehalgodan gyldenbende' ('and bound his head with cloth [i.e. a turban?] and with a consecrated golden ?band'). Mr Dodwell, in his introduction to the facsimile (see above, p. 157, n. 2), shows that the Old English text not infrequently influenced the illustrations, but here it does not explain the artist's treatment. Neither the translator nor the artist could have had any knowledge of what the Jewish High Priest's mitre was actually like, nor was the Christian bishop's mitre a clearly defined tradition in the eleventh century (see Mellinkoff, *The Horned Moses*, pp. 94 ff.); translator and artist each seems to have provided his version of Aaron's head-covering as he thought best.

As already pointed out (above, p. 157), the first examples of rounded hats for Israelites other than Aaron are on 121r (see pl. I*d*), where Aaron offers incense after the sedition and the deaths of the sinners (Numbers XVI.41–9). Why the artists (or their supervisor) chose this particular moment to introduce the motif for the Israelites in general is difficult to ascertain. It is on 122r that the giving of the priesthood to Aaron, his sons and the Levites is depicted (Numbers XVIII). Is it possible that the artists were thinking of this later event when they introduced the motif for the Israelites on 121r?

[2] This type should not be confused with the brimless skull-cap that can be found in later manuscript illuminations. See e.g., a fourteenth-century miniature reproduced by Blumenkranz, *Le Juif Médiéval*, p. 23, fig. 9. Blumenkranz says that this was 'le couvre-chef habituel dans la maison' (p. 23).

[3] The whole question of head-covering as representing a specifically Jewish tradition is of some interest here. The more modern Orthodox Jewish practice of covering the head at prayer or study or during secular occupations is not one that appears to be based on any law in the bible or Talmud; see Herman Hailperin, *Rashi and the Christian Scholars* (Pittsburgh, 1963), pp. 19–20: 'The custom, for example, of covering the head at prayer (nigh universal today) very likely became a distinctive observance which also witnessed the forced differentiation of Jews from Christians . . . We know that the custom of covering the head at prayer arose in Babylonia, and even there it was considered a pious custom and not a fixed law. We also know that as late as in Gaonic times the Palestinian Jews prayed without covering their heads.' See also Abrahams, *Jewish Life*, pp. 300–3.

was no distinctive dress for Jews[1] and, indeed, that before the thirteenth century the appearance of the Jews was enough like that of the general populace to induce Innocent III to promote the already mentioned canon 68 of the Fourth Lateran Council. There is evidence that the custom of covering the head was not common among the Jews of northern France.[2] On the other hand, Moses Maimonides, the twelfth-century Sephardic philosopher, thought it unbecoming for a scholar to study, teach or worship with uncovered head.[3] While the custom of covering the head ultimately became as binding a force as law (or more so), exactly when, where and how this custom became established is still uncertain.[4]

Another question that naturally arises is where the artists derived their model or concept of this type of hat for the Israelites. There is still some controversy around the question of whether or not there were any Jews living in England before the Norman Conquest. While it is believed that there were Jews in Roman Britain,[5] the present consensus is that if such a community existed it was subsequently eliminated by the invasions of Anglo-Saxons, and that settlement really began after the Conquest.[6] Another view, however, has been expressed suggesting that there were at least some settlements of Jews in England in the tenth century.[7] If there were no Jewish settlements in England before the Conquest, there is the possibility that Jewish merchants from northern France, Flanders, Spain or elsewhere, were observed wearing such hats on trips to England.[8] The existence of a permanent settlement of Jews in Rouen in the eleventh century – so close to England – is certain; and

---

[1] Abrahams, *Jewish Life*, pp. 302 and 309; and see Cecil Roth, *A History of the Jews in England*, 3rd ed. (Oxford, 1964), p. 95.

[2] L. Rabinowitz, *The Social Life of the Jews of Northern France in the XII–XIV Centuries* (London, 1938), p. 62: 'There is no question but that in their attire the Jews of Northern France during the period under review were completely undistinguishable from the Christians among whom they lived.' See also Abrahams, *Jewish Life*, p. 301 and n. 4.

[3] *Ibid.* p. 301 and n. 3.

[4] *Ibid.* pp. 300–2.

[5] See Shimon Applebaum, 'Were There Jews in Roman Britain?', *Trans. of the Jewish Hist. Soc.* 17 (1953), 189–205; see also, Roth, *History of the Jews in England*, pp. 1–2.

[6] For the view that there were no Jewish settlements in England before the Conquest, see Joseph Jacobs, *The Jews of Angevin England* (London, 1893), pp. 3–4; H. G. Richardson, *The English Jewry under Angevin Kings* (London, 1960), p. 1; and Roth, *History of the Jews in England*, pp. 2–4 and add. notes on p. 271.

[7] Bernhard Blumenkranz, 'Altercatio Aecclesie contra Synagogam, Texte Inédit du Xe Siècle', *Revue du Moyen Âge Latin* 10 (1954), 31–5.

[8] Roth, *History of the Jews in England*, p. 2, says that during the Saxon period the Jewish traders, so important in the Mediterranean area and on the European continent, may have extended their activities to England, but that evidence is scarce. It has been suggested that slave-traders were commonly Jews and that Ireland and Gaul were the main routes; see Jacobs, *The Jews of Angevin England*, p. 3: 'Altogether, therefore, I am inclined to refer the ecclesiastical ordinances to passing intercourse with Gallo-Jewish slave-dealers, and not to any permanent Jewish population of England before the Conquest.' See also, Frederick Pollock and Frederic William Maitland, *The History of English Law Before the Time of Edward I*, 2nd ed. (Cambridge, 1968) 1, 35, n. 2.

the Jewish community in London after the Conquest appears to have been formed from the community at Rouen.[1] If, however, all Jews during this period went bare-headed, then one must assume that the idea of the round hats depicted in Claudius B. iv was stimulated by folk-lore or legend. One should keep in mind, however, that the illustrations in this manuscript significantly reflect many aspects of contemporary eleventh-century English life.[2] They have, as a matter of fact, served as a source for British social historians of eleventh-century English costume, furniture, architecture and other native customs.[3] Furthermore, they contain original and novel iconography,[4] sometimes generated by the contemporizing of the biblical episodes. The possibility that the rounded, cap-shaped hats did in fact reflect some kind of a customary practice is strengthened by the fact that these examples are not the only ones. There is evidence of this type of hat in later artistic documents, and this evidence must now be reviewed.

The later examples are basically of two variations: one is quite similar to the type in Claudius B. iv but is sometimes depicted with a wider brim; the other is a rounded type but with a knob at the top. This latter variation does not seem to have evolved from the former, and, as will be seen, the two types occasionally occur in the same manuscript. Perhaps they represented variations of actual practice, but the present incomplete state of the evidence makes it uncertain. The greatest number of examples of the rounded Jewish hat occur in twelfth-century English art; however, as will be shown, similar hats can be noted in Flemish sources and a few scattered examples occur elsewhere.

The earliest examples subsequent to those in Claudius B. iv that I have so far observed occur in the Flemish Stavelot Bible, of 1097, mentioned already in the discussion of the pointed Jewish hat.[5] Old Testament figures are not

1 See Richardson, *The English Jewry*, pp. 1–5 and 23–5; and David C. Douglas, *William the Conqueror* (Berkeley and Los Angeles, 1966), pp. 313–14.
2 Dodwell's introduction to the facsimile (see above, p. 157, n. 2) includes an extensive analysis of the social elements in the pictures; he stresses the fact that they do not reflect the ways of a Mediterranean and early Christian way of life but rather the modes and fashions of northern Europe of the eleventh century.
3 E.g. George Taylor Files, *The Anglo-Saxon House, its Construction, Decoration and Furniture*, Inaugural Dissertation (Leipzig, 1893); J. O. Westwood, *Paleographica Sacra* (London, n.d.), pp. 144–5; and Thomas Wright, *A History of Domestic Manners and Sentiments in England during the Middle Ages* (London, 1862).
4 On the basic originality of the illustrations, see Dodwell's introduction to the facsimile. See also Francis Wormald, 'Late Anglo-Saxon Art: some Questions and Suggestions', *Studies in Western Art: Acts of the XX International Congress of the History of Art*, ed. M. Meiss (Princeton, 1963) i, 20; Otto Pächt, *The Rise of Pictorial Narrative in Twelfth-Century England* (Oxford, 1962), pp. 6–8, stressing the originality of the Anglo-Saxon artists even when working from older models; Mellinkoff, *The Horned Moses*, pp. 13–27; Meyer Schapiro, 'Cain's Jaw-Bone that did the First Murder', *Art Bull.* 24 (1942), 206; George Henderson, 'Cain's Jaw-Bone', *Jnl of the Warburg and Courtauld Insts.* 24 (1961), 108–14; and see Otto Pächt, 'A Cycle of English Frescoes in Spain', *Burlington Mag.* 103 (1961), 169.
5 See above, p. 156.

consistently depicted with a unique hat in this bible. There are several types and among them are rounded hats. Amos (219r) wears no hat; Obadiah (221r), Nahum (223v) and Zechariah (226r) wear pointed hats similar to Joel's (218r; see pl. II*a*); Job (4v) is represented with a square hat; and the rounded, cap-shaped hats are found on Micah (222r), Habakkuk (224r), Zephaniah (224v) and Haggai (225v; see pl. II*b*). The relations between England and Flanders before the Conquest – religious, political and artistic – were considerable,[1] and could explain the appearance of this motif in both areas; but they do not conclusively demonstrate its origin. Do the rounded hats in the Flemish bible represent traditions in this part of Europe that antedated those depicted in Claudius B. iv? Or, vice versa, was an earlier English custom transmitted to northern France–Flanders? These questions are easier to pose than to answer, for, whereas the evidence that there were no Jews (or just a few) living in England before the Conquest argues for a customary tradition originating in Flanders or northern France, the evidence already mentioned, that the custom of covering the head was not common among Jews in northern France during this time confounds the whole problem.

An unexpected early occurrence of a strikingly unusual hat motif in the Second Bible of Limoges (Bibl. Nat. lat. 8, 1), dated about 1100,[2] needs to be pointed out next. The hat in question (red in colour) is worn by Moses (52r; see pl. II*c*).[3] It is difficult to decide whether this is more akin to the rounded type of hat or to the pointed one. The relationships of this motif and of the other unusual ones in this bible to those of other manuscripts elsewhere in Europe are yet to be explained. What is certain is that its representation, however one classifies it, represents an unusual and isolated example for this early period in the Midi.

It is in the St Albans Psalter[4] of *c.* 1123 that the first English examples of the rounded Jewish hat subsequent to those in Claudius B. iv are found. It is of interest to note that here (as often elsewhere) only New Testament figures thought of in a special Jewish context are portrayed wearing it. For example, Joseph wears a rounded hat with a knob in the Nativity (see pl. II*d*) as well as in the Flight into Egypt.[5] And in the Descent from the Cross two figures,

---

[1] See Philip Grierson, 'The Relations between England and Flanders before the Norman Conquest', *TRHS* 4th ser. 23 (1941), 71–112; and C. R. Dodwell, *Painting in Europe, 800 to 1200* (Harmondsworth, 1971), p. 79.

[2] For extensive comments on this manuscript see D. Gaborit-Chopin, *La Décoration des Manuscrits à Saint-Martial de Limoges et en Limousin du IXe au XIIe Siècle*, Mémoires et Documents Publiés par la Société de l'École des Chartes, 17 (Paris–Geneva, 1969), 86–99; and see Jean Porcher, *French Miniatures from Illuminated Manuscripts* (London, 1960), p. 33.

[3] Moses is not portrayed with a hat elsewhere in the Limoges Bible; on 41r he is depicted with a halo.

[4] For a complete study of this psalter see Otto Pächt, C. R. Dodwell and Francis Wormald, *The St Albans Psalter* (London, 1960). [5] *Ibid.* pl. 20b.

probably Joseph of Arimathea and Nicodemus, are represented with rounded hats – one with a knob and one without.[1] Although the apostles were Jews they are not depicted wearing hats, rounded or pointed. Distinctions of this kind among the Jews of the New Testament will be noted later in the York Psalter.

The Great Lambeth Bible of c. 1140–60 (London, Lambeth Palace Library, 3)[2] contains Old Testament figures wearing various types of round hats, but with wider brims: some are plain round, others have knobs similar to those in the St Albans Psalter and some have a knob that is larger, longer and somewhat funnel-like in its design. A full-page illustration to the Book of Genesis (6r) shows us Abraham and Jacob wearing round hats with knobs;[3] an illustration to Numbers (66v) contains round hats for Israelites, with and without knobs, as well as some where the knob seems to have been expanded into a funnel.[4] This same mixture of types can be observed in the preface to the Book of Ruth (130r; see pl. IIe). Another example of the strange funnel-shaped knob is on 258r, a portrayal of scenes from Ezekiel.[5] Whether or not this latter type of hat bears any relationship to the funnel-shaped pointed Jewish hat discussed earlier is difficult to determine.

The English Psalter of Henry of Blois (BM Cotton Nero C. iv), of the mid twelfth century,[6] also provides evidence of a rounded hat tradition. Here the hats have small knobs. In the Presentation in the Temple (15r) the Jewish High Priest wears a rounded, knobbed hat;[7] and Joseph of the New Testament is similarly portrayed on the upper portion of 16r (see pl. IIf). One of the most fascinating examples occurs in the scene of the angel locking the damned in hell (39r). Here among the unfortunate victims are individuals who can be recognized and classified by means of their head-gear. In the hell's mouth one can identify two kings by their crowns – one in the centre of the mouth, upside down, and one similarly disposed at the bottom of the scene. A queen has also paid the price of sin; she can be identified by her crown and long flowing hair. The church is also well represented on this momentous occasion by three 'delegates', each identifiable by his tonsure. A man shown wearing a round hat with a knob is also present; the hat was surely meant to identify him as a Jew. These motifs are even more striking when seen in colour. The

1 Ibid. pl. 29b.
2 See C. R. Dodwell, The Canterbury School of Illumination 1066–1200 (Cambridge, 1954) as well as his, The Great Lambeth Bible (London, 1959).
3 Dodwell, Lambeth Bible, pl. i.   4 Ibid. pl. ii.   5 Ibid. pl. v.
6 See Margaret Rickert, Painting in Britain: the Middle Ages (Baltimore, 1954), pp. 93ff; Francis Wormald, 'The Development of English Illumination in the Twelfth Century', JBAA 3rd ser. 8 (1943), 41–2, and 'The Survival of Anglo-Saxon Illumination after the Norman Conquest', Proc. of the Brit. Acad. 30 (1944), 140–1; and T. S. R. Boase, English Art, 1100–1216 (Oxford, 1953), pp. 172–4.
7 See Wormald, 'The Survival of Anglo-Saxon Illumination', pl. 6.

crowns are emphasized by their gold colour; the round Jewish hat is rendered prominent by its red brim and red knob.[1]

Another interesting twelfth-century example, this time of the plain rounded hat, can be observed on a beautiful English ivory sculpture of the Flight into Egypt (see pl. II *g*).[2] This same type, but with a wider brim, can be seen as well on the English Malmesbury ciborium of *c.* 1175. One of the men who harasses Christ wears this hat in the scene of Christ bearing the cross, as does an Israelite in the foreground of the representation of Moses and the brazen serpent.[3]

Further examples of the round hat can be observed in two English psalters of the last part of the twelfth century. The plain rounded type appears in the York Psalter (Glasgow, University Library, Hunterian U.3.2) of *c.* 1170; the rounded type with a knob is in Copenhagen, Kongelige Bibliotek, Thott 143 of about the same period.[4] On the York Psalter, 17v, two scenes are portrayed: the angel announces the death of the Virgin and the Virgin tells the apostles of her approaching death. The artist has introduced a group of Jews behind St Peter; they are easily identified by their rounded hats.[5] As mentioned earlier, only certain New Testament Jews are given hats. The apostles, although they were Jews, are hatless. In the portrayal of the death of the Virgin (18r) the same iconography is repeated: the Jews are shown wearing rounded hats; the apostles are hatless (see pl. III*a*). Both of these folios are part of a group representing the apocryphal story of the death and Assumption of the Virgin. It is of interest to observe how close in design the hats in this psalter are to those in Claudius B. iv (cf. pls. I*d* and III*a*). The other psalter, Thott 143,[6] contains examples of rounded hats, both with and without knobs: Joseph wears the knobbed type in the Nativity (9v; see pl. III*b*) and again in the Flight into Egypt (12r);[7] in the Presentation in the Temple (12v) he wears a round, somewhat flattened, cap-shaped hat without a knob.[8]

Although England appears to furnish the most abundant examples of the rounded Jewish hat, the motif occurs, as already mentioned, in the Flemish Stavelot Bible. It can be observed in later Mosan (Flemish) art too. On the

---

[1] See Nordenfalk, *Romanesque Painting*, p. 157, for a colour reproduction.
[2] See Willibald Sauerländer in an exhibition review of 'The Year 1200', *Art Bull.* 53 (1971), 512, who states that there is general agreement on its English origin and says that he doubts that it could have been carved after 1160–70; Swarzenski, *Monuments,* p. 63, also describes it as English and dates it *c.* 1150.
[3] In the Pierpont Morgan Library, New York; see Swarzenski, *Monuments*, pl. 197, fig. 453.
[4] Regarding links between these two psalters, see T. S. R. Boase, *The York Psalter* (New York, 1962), pp. 5–7. See also O. Elfrida Saunders's description of the style of the York Psalter, *English Illumination* (Florence, 1928) I, 39, and fig. 44 ('Raising of Lazarus'), where more of the round hats can be seen.
[5] See Boase, *The York Psalter,* pl. 4.
[6] See *Greek and Latin Illuminated Manuscripts X–XIII Centuries in Danish Collections* (Copenhagen, 1921), pp. 32–42; see also Boase, *English Art*, pp. 243–4.
[7] *Ibid.* pl. 12.   [8] *Ibid.*

wings of a triptych, of *c.* 1150, from Stavelot[1] (now in the Pierpont Morgan Library), the story of Constantine's mother, Helena, finding the True Cross, is told on six enamel medallions. The Jews can be identified by their rounded hats (see pl. III*c*).[2] Especially striking is the representation on the magnificent foot of the cross of St Bertin of *c.* 1180,[3] now in the Musée de Saint-Omer. In the scene of Moses striking the rock the Israelites are represented by two figures wearing plain round hats.[4] Similarly a Jew marking the T on a house with the blood of the Passover lamb is round-hatted (see pl. III*d*), as are other figures standing nearby.

After the twelfth century there appear to be only scattered examples. The tradition can, however, be observed as far east as Poland, for in a miniature in a twelfth- or thirteenth-century manuscript, reportedly in a church at Krushvitz, Poland, Jews are portrayed wearing rounded hats (see pl. III*e*).[5] It has been suggested that this scene is a portrayal of Jews witnessing John's head being brought before Herod.[6] The famed Psalter of Ingeborg (Chantilly, Musée Condé lat. 1695)[7] provides examples in the early thirteenth century. Jesse wears a hat of the knobbed type, as does Aaron, in the Tree of Jesse (14v),[8] and Moses is portrayed wearing a rounded hat under a shawl or hood in the scene of Moses and the burning bush (12v).[9] As late as the fifteenth century a remnant of the tradition can be seen in a *Speculum Humanae Salvationis* (Brussels, Bibliothèque Royale, 9345). Here one finds Moses, in a detail in the upper right part of 123r (see pl. III*f*),[10] portrayed with three motifs as head adornment: he wears the rounded Jewish hat, thus identifying him as a Jew; a halo is drawn behind his head, thereby indicating his divine nature (for he was present at the Transfiguration of Christ); and his famous horns, so much a part of his iconography in medieval western European art, are also depicted, appearing to push their way through the rounded crown of the hat. This manuscript was

1 See Suzanne Collon-Gevaert, *Histoire des Arts du Métal en Belgique* (Brussels, 1951), pp. 168–73; see also André Grabar, 'Orfevrerie Mosane-Orfevrerie Byzantine', *L'Art Mosan*, ed. Francastel, p. 123.
2 Note that two of the hats in the background appear to be somewhat pointed.
3 Swarzenski, *Monuments*, p. 71, says that this was perhaps commissioned under Abbot Simon II (1177–86); see also Collon-Gevaert, *Histoire*, pp. 162–4. Four portrait busts of prophets in medallions wearing the round hats can be seen on 7v of Cambridge, Fitzwilliam Museum 241, a Flemish gospel book of the late twelfth century; see Francis Wormald and Phyllis M. Giles, *Illuminated Manuscripts in the Fitzwilliam Museum* (Cambridge, 1966), p. 10.
4 Swarzenski, *Monuments*, pl. 179, fig. 399. Rounded hats of this type are also present on an enamelled cross from the Meuse, attributed to Godfroid de Claire, now in the British Museum.
5 The photograph is after Ignacy Schiper, *Kultur Geschichte* (Warsaw, 1926), top fig. opp. p. 224.
6 *Ibid.* p. 216.
7 For a study of this psalter see Florens Deuchler, *Der Ingeborgpsalter* (Berlin, 1967); see also Jacques Meurgey, *Les Principaux Manuscrits à Peintures du Musée Condé* (Paris, 1930), pp. 15–19.
8 Deuchler, *Der Ingeborgpsalter*, pl. x.
9 *Ibid.* pl. viii.
10 I am indebted to Henry A. Kelly for calling this to my attention.

probably executed at the Benedictine abbey of Saint-Laurent at Liège.[1] If so, this would tie it to the earlier Flemish tradition, a late reminder of an almost forgotten, round, cap-shaped hat tradition for Jews.

It is interesting to find that during the twelfth century Jews were also portrayed with the more typical pointed hats in both Flanders and England. On a triptych from Liège of *c.* 1170 Jews wear the pointed hats.[2] Furthermore, distinctively conical hats on Jews can be seen on the twelfth-century English cross now in the Metropolitan Museum.[3] This evidence suggests that more than one hat tradition existed in England and Europe and that, furthermore, they may have occasionally overlapped. There is no reason to believe that there were rigidly separate Jewish hat traditions. The wearing of one kind of hat or another of varying design may reflect loose local customs. There is sufficient evidence, however, to attest the existence of a rounded Jewish hat tradition different from that of the more prevalent pointed *Judenhut* – at least within the conventions of art.

To summarize: the area for the rounded hat tradition seems to be centred in England and Flanders with most of the examples concentrated in the eleventh and twelfth centuries and most abundantly in England. Later the evidence dwindles, with only a few scattered examples; from the thirteenth century the pointed Jewish hat becomes the most commonly utilized motif for identifying Jews in medieval art, in England as well as in other northern European countries. The most significant aspect of the round hat tradition is its remarkably early appearance in Claudius B. iv, a manuscript whose illustrations strikingly reflect the architecture, furniture, customs and costume of early-eleventh-century England. I suggest that once again this manuscript is to be credited with an iconographic innovation, originality and novelty, in this case inspired by the contemporization of a biblical concept. The artists have portrayed the biblical Israelites with a round, cap-shaped hat that they may have observed on eleventh-century Jews.[4] These illustrations, therefore, not only represent artistic examples of a special iconographic motif for Jews earlier than any previously noted but also focus attention on two unresolved questions: in what way, if any, do these hats reflect an early Jewish practice of covering the head, and what weight, if any, do they add to the argument that there were some Jews living in England before the Conquest?

[1] Martin Wittek of the Bibliothèque Royale has given this as the place of execution and dates the manuscript *c.* 1428.
[2] See Swarzenski, *Monuments,* pl. 187, for a reproduction of the Liège triptych.
[3] For photos and bibliography see *The Year 1200: a Centennial Exhibition at the Metropolitan Museum of Art,* catalogue, ed. Konrad Hoffmann (New York, 1970), pp. 52–6.
[4] This is of course to be contrasted with the kind of innovation introduced by literal representation of the text itself, as in the case of the horned Moses.

c

a

b

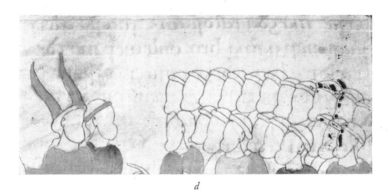

d

e

I*a* Single leaf from a gospel book, Cleveland Museum of Art, detail
b–e BM Cotton Claudius B. iv, details (*b* 107v, *c* 107v, *d* 121r, *e* 139v

a

b

c

d

e

f

g

II*a–b*   BM Add. 28106, details   (*a* 218r, *b* 225v)
    c   Bibl. Nat. lat. 8, 1, 52r, detail
    d   Hildesheim, St Albans Psalter, p. 21, detail
    e   London, Lambeth Palace Library, 3, 130r, detail
    f   BM Cotton Nero C. iv, 16r, detail
    g   English ivory, New York, Metropolitan Museum of Art, detail

b

a

c

d

e

f

III*a* Glasgow, University Library, Hunterian, U.3.2, 18r, detail
   b Copenhagen, Kongelige Bibliotek, Thott 143, 9v, detail
   c Stavelot Triptych, New York, Pierpont Morgan Library, detail
   d Foot of the cross of St Bertin, Musée de Saint-Omer, detail
   e MS at Krushvitz, Poland, detail
   f Brussels, Bibl. Royale, 9345, 123r, detail

g

III*g* Silver ring, Moyse's Hall Museum, Bury St Edmunds (twice actual size)

ı ꝺextꝛam tuam & ꝺeuoꝛauıt e
ſa ıuſtıtıa tua pupulū tuū hunc quı
ıs es ın uırtute tua· & ın pꝼectıone
t gentes & ıꝛae ſunt· ꝺoloꝛıſ co
ctoſ phılıſtaım·
anauꝛunt ꝺuceſ eꝺom· & pꝛıncı
o pꝛehenꝺıt eoꝛ tꝛmoꝛ·

us paꝛtıculam· ꝺecīm uıꝺelıcet
ıo meo mıhı oppıꝺo fıꝺelı quıab
uoaſſımo pꝑpetua laꝛgıtuꝛ ſum
ıs fılııſ uoacompoꝛ habeat & poſt uıtae
auctīn pꝛeꝺıctū puꝛ omnı chꝛıſthe ꝛꝑuıtu
ꝛeſtauꝛatıone·Sıquıſ ıgıtuꝛ hanc nꝛam
ıo ſcae ꝺī eccleꝛıaſ ꝺeſtıtuıꝛ baꝛıathıꝛ
tuıꝛ· ſınon ſatıꝛ factıone ꝺıſthꝺauꝛıt·
ꝛatuꝛ

IVa BM Add. 37517, 97v, detail
  b London, Westminster Abbey, W.A.M. x, detail

A rediscovered medieval inscribed ring

ELISABETH OKASHA

The silver ring illustrated in pl. III*g* has had a somewhat chequered history over the past years. From some time before 1911, when it was first published, until 1930 the ring was preserved in the Moyse's Hall Museum, Bury St Edmunds, Suffolk. In 1930 it was on display at the exhibition of English medieval art at the Victoria and Albert Museum in London. It subsequently disappeared from public view. In 1969 the Hon. Robert Erskine presented it to the Moyse's Hall Museum where it remains, acquisition number K. 132.[1]

The British Museum Research Laboratory has carried out a qualitative spectrographic examination of the ring, which indicates that it is an alloy of silver containing copper, gold, lead and traces of tin, bismuth and silicon. The laboratory report notes that this is a typical composition for an Anglo-Saxon silver object. The rim of the inside of the hoop is now encrusted with a black material which also appears in some of the lettering inside the hoop. The laboratory identifies this as silver chloride, formed by natural corrosion, with the black colour probably due to the exposure of the silver chloride to light, or to traces of silver sulphide.

The ring measures *c*. 2·2 cm in diameter, *c*. 0·5 cm in breadth and *c*. 0·15 cm in thickness. It contains two texts, text i on the inside of the hoop and text ii on the outside. There is now no sign of framing lines in either. The only decoration is an engraved symbol resembling a crown between the beginning and the end of text ii. The letters of the texts are *c*. 0·3 cm tall and there is some seriffing.

The script of text i is capitals with some lower-case letters (H and B), and one ligature (A/R). These features are perfectly consistent with an Anglo-Saxon date. The 'shallow' forms of C and E typical of post-Conquest inscriptions do, however, occur in both texts, but there is too little evidence to make it certain that we have here post-Conquest scripts.

Text i is clearly legible:

[1] I am most grateful to Mr A. R. Edwardson, Curator of the Moyse's Hall Museum, Bury St Edmunds, for his cooperation and help in allowing me to study the ring and for his permission to publish it. I should like to record my thanks to the staff of the British Museum Research Laboratory for examining, cleaning and photographing the ring. My grateful thanks are also due to Mr M. Dolley, Mr C. C. Oman, Dr R. I. Page, Mrs L. E. Webster and Professor D. M. Wilson for their help in various ways concerning this ring.

IOHNSE BEVERIYA/RCEB //[1]

There is a space following *iohnse* and one may also have been intended before it. Although the I of *beveriy* is clear, the possibility of its being intended for L with a short horizontal stroke (cf. the forms of C and E) cannot be ruled out. The S of *iohnse* has the lower loop joined to the stem; it is just possible that this is not S but miniscule D. The text probably reads: *iohnse beveriy arceb*, 'John of *Beveriy*, archbishop', though a reading *iohn de* is conceivable. *Beveriy* has been identified as Beverley, East Riding of Yorkshire, although this form of the name is not recorded. The most similar early spellings are the eleventh-century *Beuerlic, Beverlic* and *Beureli, Bevreli*;[2] forms with final *-y* do not appear before the twelfth century. All recorded forms of the name contain *-l-*, which, as noted above, is an easy emendation from *-i-*. The name Beverley is not found in use before the eleventh century; the earlier name, used by Bede, is *Inderauuda*.[3]

Text ii is highly deteriorated:

$$(A . E . STA .) R(. . .)G(. . .)N //$$

The first lost letter could be D or Ð, the second I, the third N or H, after which there may have been a space. The first letter lost after R could have been a word-division symbol and the last lost letter could have been A. The text reads: *(a.e.sta.) r(. . .)g(. . .)n* and cannot be meaningfully reconstructed or interpreted without reference to earlier readings. The meanings of both texts are discussed more fully after an account of these readings.

The ring has been previously published three times, by Smith,[4] in the 1930 Exhibition Catalogue of the Victoria and Albert Museum,[5] and by Oman.[6] Smith did not illustrate the ring but described it as containing 'a legend purporting to connect it with King Athelstan'. Nor was the ring illustrated in the Exhibition Catalogue. The texts were transliterated there, without translation, as:

IOHNSE BEVERIV A/RCEB
AÐEISTAN . R . A/N . GIVAN

Oman's illustration, which is a photograph not a line-drawing, shows part of

---

[1] The text is transliterated according to the following system: legible letters are shown in capitals, with // indicating the end of the text. '*A*' indicates a letter damaged but legible; '(*A*)' a damaged letter where the restoration is fairly certain; '(. . .)' three letters lost, the dots indicating the number; 'A/B' ligatured letters.

[2] See A. H. Smith, *The Place-Names of the East Riding of Yorkshire and York,* English Place-Name Society 14 (Cambridge, 1937), 192–4.

[3] *Ibid.* pp. 12 and 92.

[4] R. A. Smith, 'Anglo-Saxon Remains', Victoria History of the Counties of England, *Suffolk* (London, 1911) I, 349.

[5] Victoria and Albert Museum, *Exhibition of English Medieval Art* (London, 1930), no. 56, p. 12.

[6] C. C. Oman, 'Anglo-Saxon Finger-Rings', *Apollo* 14 (1931), 107 and fig.

text ii: the crown with the letters FAN to the left, A Đ and possibly E to the right. This photograph makes it clear that text ii was considerably more legible then than it is today. He read the texts as:

IOHNSE BEVERLY ARCEB
ATHELSTAN . R . AN . GIFAN

quoting Professor Max Förster's translations, 'John of Beverly Archbishop' and 'Athelstan King of the English Giver'. In correspondence with Oman, Förster considered these texts in greater detail. I am most grateful to Mr Oman for permission to refer to this correspondence. Förster there read text i as:

IOHNSE BEVERLS ÆRCEB

He took *iohnse* either as having a dative singular inflexion, or possibly as containing *iohn* with *se*, OE 'the'. He explained *Beverls* (or *Beverly*) as an abbreviation of the Latin *Beverlaiensis*, or of the Old English form of the name.[1] *Ærceb* he took as an abbreviation of OE *aercebiscop*. He read text ii as:

AĐELSTAN . R . ↑G . GIFAN

interpreting 'R .' as *rex* or *regis*, '↑G .' as *Anglorum*, and *gifan* as *gifen*, 'given', or as an oblique case of *gifa*, 'giver'. He thus translated the texts as 'Aðelstan, rex Anglorum, [has] given [this ring] to Johannes Beverlaiensis the Archbishop'.

We cannot now be certain exactly what these texts were intended to mean. Text i is best translated as 'John of *Beveriy*, archbishop'. *Iohnse* is a conceivable medieval spelling of *Johannes* and need not be (*pace* Förster) construed as dative singular or be split into two words. A reading *iohn de* makes good sense but is not entirely justifiable from the text. *Beveriy* seems likely to be an unrecorded, or perhaps inaccurate, spelling of *beverly* = Beverley; as noted above, only a small emendation is required actually to give this reading. The link the ring seems to make between someone called John, the title of archbishop and the place-name Beverley suggests that this is a reference to St John of Beverley, bishop of Hexham and then of York, whose death is recorded in 721 and whose body was buried in Beverley where he had previously retired.[2] Bishops of York are described as 'archbishop' from early times, although the first one to receive a pallium was Egbert in 735.

Text ii seems likely to have contained the words *aðelstan* and *gifan*, which fit the remaining traces of lettering. All earlier commentators are agreed on the former, two out of three on the latter, and in addition parts of both words are

---

[1] But cf. Smith, *Place-Names of the East Riding*, p. 193, who quotes the Latin adjectival forms *Beverlicensis* and *Bev-, Beuerlacensis*.
[2] *ASC* 721 DE.

clearly shown on Oman's photograph. Förster's suggestion that *gifan* is a form of the preterite participle (*giefen, gifen,* 'given') is possible, though it could equally be part of the construction 'was given' as of Förster's 'has given'. An oblique form of *gifa,* 'giver', is also possible. It is tempting to identify *aðelstan* with King Athelstan of Wessex, who attests charters as *rex Anglorum,* although he does not use this title on coins.[1] Indeed coin usage suggests a date after King Edgar for this title.[2] Although possible abbreviations for the title, neither Förster's 'R . ↑G .' nor Oman's 'R . AN .' is recorded.

With these texts, the ring could have been a gift presented at the shrine of St John at Beverley. King Athelstan of Wessex is recorded as making offerings there in 934.[3] However, as Oman pointed out, a ring of such trifling value is not very likely to have been a royal gift to an important shrine.[4] Oman thinks that the ring is more likely to have been a pilgrim's trophy bought at the shrine of St John, or alternatively a reward handed out at the shrine by King Athelstan to one of his followers.[5] Royal ring giving is of course well attested in Anglo-Saxon England. Either of these ideas seems quite possible; the former does not, of course, necessitate a pre-Conquest date for the ring.

As mentioned above, the ring was first published in 1911 when it was in the Moyse's Hall Museum. Unfortunately, however, the museum has no acquisition records dating from as early as this. Its provenance and history before 1911 are therefore unknown. It is conceivable that this ring is the one which was found in the coffin of St John of Beverley at the translation associated with his canonization in 1037. Leland records: 'Annulus cum fragmentis libri evangeliorum inventus in sarcophago S. Joannis.'[6] All subsequent accounts of this find derive from Leland, or possibly from his source, or from later versions dependent on these. The Beverley ring is now lost, unless it is indeed identical with the Moyse's Hall Museum ring, a supposition for which there seems to be no supporting evidence beyond that of the ring's text. The gospel book referred to cannot now be identified either.

From 1911 the view has been current that the Moyse's Hall Museum ring

---

[1] *Cartularium Saxonicum,* ed. W. de G. Birch (London, 1885–93) II, nos. 663, 664 and 708; P. H. Sawyer, *Anglo-Saxon Charters* (London, 1968), nos. 400, 399 and 429.

[2] Michael Dolley, in a personal communication.

[3] These offerings are mentioned in various sources, for example in a fourteenth-century document printed in *Chronicles of the Picts, Chronicles of the Scots, and Other Early Memorials of Scottish History,* ed. W. F. Skene (Edinburgh, 1867), pp. 221–4; and also in twelfth-century anonymous accounts of the miracles of St John of Beverley, printed in *The Historians of the Church of York and its Archbishops,* ed. James Raine, Rolls Series (1879–94) I, 264 and 297–8.

[4] Oman, 'Anglo-Saxon Finger-Rings', p. 107.

[5] C. C. Oman, in a personal communication, and in the correspondence with Förster referred to above.

[6] J. Leland, *De Rebus Britannicis Collectanea,* ed. T. Hearne, rev. ed. (London, 1770) IV, 102. Leland's reference for the section in which this occurs is: 'Ex libr: incerti autoris de vita S. Joannis archiepiscopi Ebor: sive de antiquitate Beverlacensi . . .'

is a forgery.[1] The word 'forgery' can of course cover a wide range of dates. Spectrographic analysis shows that there is no reason to doubt that the ring is medieval. There is not enough decoration on the ring to provide more accurate dating evidence. The crown is too simplified to help in dating, though I know of nothing similar to it from the Anglo-Saxon or early medieval periods. The subject matter of the texts certainly suggests a connection with St John of Beverley; the ring could have been a gift presented to his shrine or a trophy brought from it. King Athelstan of Wessex may also be referred to, although this identification is not certain either. Such texts could have been inscribed at any time in the Middle Ages and need not necessarily be contemporary with either of the people mentioned. Nor need the texts be contemporary either with each other or with the manufacture of the ring, though they do not give the impression of being modern workmanship. But if genuine they provide only a little evidence for dating: the spelling -*y* of *beveriy* and the 'shallow' letter forms favour a post-Conquest date over a pre-Conquest one. This is further supported by the reference to John as 'archbishop' and probably by the use of the place-name Beverley. In conclusion, the ring cannot be dated more closely than to the medieval period, while the texts are likely to have been inscribed in the early post-Conquest period. In this case, the term 'forgery' does not seem to be especially appropriate.

[1] Cf. Smith, VCH *Suffolk* 1, 349: 'the inscription does not inspire confidence'.

the question of B's origin has not yet been satisfactorily solved. This article attempts to set firm, partly new, limits to the possibilities.[1]

It will be best to start with the calendar. As has been mentioned already, it is somewhat later than the main part of the manuscript, and contains the feast of St Dunstan (who died on 19 May 988) but not that of St Ælfheah (who died on 19 April 1012). On these grounds Wormald dated it 988–1012. Bishop, however, had regarded any time up to Ælfheah's translation to Canterbury in 1023 as possible.[2] In fact the time-span should probably be narrower than Wormald's. For 17 March B contains an entry later erased but still legible: *Natale sancti Eadwardi regis.* Since we know that in 1008 the witan decreed 18 March as the day on which the feast of Edward the Martyr was to be observed throughout England,[3] and as this date is given in all later calendars, it seems likely that the entry in B was made earlier than this decree and that therefore 1008 is the *terminus ante quem* of B's calendar.[4]

In his study, which has not been superseded in sixty-five years, Bishop showed that the calendar goes back ultimately to a Glastonbury exemplar.[5] Compared with the Glastonbury calendar in Oxford, Bodleian Library, Bodley 579 ('The Leofric Missal'), however, it has been clearly modernized and specially adapted for use in Canterbury: the feasts of six former archbishops (Laurentius, Dunstan, Deusdedit, Honorius, Nothelm and Justus) and of Adrian, abbot of St Augustine's, have been added; and all except Nothelm's are distinguished as major feasts. Is then B's calendar from Christ Church or St Augustine's? The usual method of comparing all entries with later calendars cannot be applied in this case. The first calendar which is positively from Christ Church, BM Arundel 155, of the early eleventh century,

Cotton Vitellius C. xii, lists obits of several Ælmers but none on 26 March. There is an Ælfmær, abbot of St Augustine's and later bishop of Sherborne, who according to W. Stubbs (*Registrum Sacrum Anglicanum,* 2nd ed. (Oxford, 1897), p. 33) died on 18 September (1023). But the obit in Vitellius C. xii on 6 April, 'Obitus Aelmerus episcopus *qui fuit abbas huius loci*' (the italicized words are inserted by a later hand), shows that Stubbs, who relied on an entry in the *Liber Vitae* of Hyde (*Liber Vitae: Register and Martyrology of New Minster and Hyde Abbey, Winchester,* ed. W. de G. Birch (London, 1892), p. 272) is wrong here.
1 I am obliged to Professor H. W. G. Gneuss and especially to Professor P. A. M. Clemoes, who read an earlier draft of this paper and whose suggestions have contributed greatly to its improvement.
2 Wormald, HBS 72 (1934), 57; *The Bosworth Psalter,* p. 27.
3 *Die Gesetze der Angelsachsen,* ed. F. Liebermann (Halle, 1903–16) 1, 240 (V, 16. Atr.).
4 The erasure obviously cannot be dated. However, two possibilities might be considered. First, if the erasure was effected in 1008 or shortly thereafter, why was the new date not entered? A better context for the erasure might be the period of the apparent decline of Edward's cult in Canterbury after the Conquest (see below, p. 176). Bishop (*The Bosworth Psalter,* pp. 65 and 82) thinks that the Edward entry is a slightly later addition and that it was made on 17 March because 18 March was already occupied by another entry. The body of the calendar would nonetheless have originated before 1008: otherwise we should expect Edward on 18 March by the main hand.
5 This becomes apparent from a look at the format of Wormald's printed texts, HBS 72 (1934), nos. 4 and 5.

is not native to Canterbury but depends on Winchester, and the same is true of the representatives of St Augustine's.[1] Another possibility presents itself: in B the major feasts, i.e. those with proper masses, are distinguished by the letters *S* or *F* prefixed to the entries. The feasts of saints so marked in B offer a possible comparison with the saints who have proper masses in the St Augustine's missal, Cambridge, Corpus Christi College 270, of the late eleventh century. This missal, moreover, has the advantage of being older than the earliest calendars native to the abbey, which are thirteenth-century.[2] There are, in fact, about eighty agreements between the major saints' feasts in B and the *sanctorale* of CCCC 270. But these are of no significance as nearly all these feasts are distinguished in the same way in the Glastonbury calendar of the Leofric Missal, and all go back to the Gregorian sacramentary.[3] Then there are certain differences. In the first place twenty-two feasts with a proper mass in CCCC 270 are completely absent from B. Unfortunately this is of no help either, for two of these feasts were certainly introduced during the eleventh century[4] and the same possibility can be probably excluded only in the case of 7 May, St Liudhard.[5] In the second place CCCC 270 has no mass for thirteen feasts which in B are prefixed with *S* or *F*, among them English saints such as Edward the Martyr, Guthlac, Eadburg and King Oswald.[6] But again caution is needed. These feasts may have become lower in grading at St Augustine's during the eleventh century. Certainly this happened in the course of time at Christ Church, for already in the calendar of the early-eleventh-century Arundel 155 most of these feasts (except Edward and Oswald) have only a simple grading; several of them do not appear at all in the thirteenth-century calendar of BM Cotton Tiberius B. iii.[7] Consequently a comparison with CCCC 270 does not provide firm evidence for or against a St Augustine's origin for B's calendar.

This appears to leave only Bishop's approach.[8] B lacks a feast that is characteristic of, indeed peculiar to, St Augustine's, namely that of Bishop Liudhard on 7 May; he had accompanied Queen Bertha, wife of King Æthelberht, to Kent and was specially revered in the abbey, apparently because of his supposed

---

1 *The Bosworth Psalter*, pp. 30, 34 and 35.
2 *The Missal of St Augustine's Abbey, Canterbury*, ed. Martin Rule (Cambridge, 1896).
3 *The Bosworth Psalter*, pp. 15–16.
4 18 June Transl. s. Mildrethae and 13 September Transl. s. Augustini sociorumque.
5 See below, p. 177, n. 2.
6 17 March Natale s. Eadwardi regis, 11 April s. Cuthlaci anachoritae, 1 June s. Nicomedis m., 15 June s. Eadburge v., 23 June s. Æðeldryðe v., 21 July s. Praxedis v., 5 August s. Oswaldi regis et m., 24 August s. Patricii sen. in glæstonia, 31 August s. Aidani episc., 16 September ss. Lucie et Geminiani, 24 September Conceptio Johannis bapt., 25 September s. Ceolfriþi abb. in glæstonia and 31 October Passio s. Quintini m.
7 Edward, Guthlac, Nicomedes, Lucia et Geminianus and Conceptio Johannis bapt. were not originally in Tiberius; Edward was added in the fifteenth century. Eadburg and the three special Glastonbury feasts in B, Patrick, Aidan and Ceolfrith, are neither in Arundel nor in Tiberius.
8 For the following see *The Bosworth Psalter*, pp. 35–7.

merits in preparing the Augustinian mission.[1] In CCCC 270, as we have seen, his feast has a proper mass, and all later St Augustine's calendars and the twelfth-century martyrology BM Cotton Vitellius C. xii also contain it. The fourteenth-century calendar in Cambridge, St John's College 262, even promotes him to the rank of archbishop. In the calendars of Christ Church and other monasteries his name is never found. That his cult should have grown up in the century between B and the missal is improbable.[2] On the other hand, B contains an addition to the original Glastonbury calendar, St Salvius on 26 June, who reappears in all later Christ Church calendars, its martyrologies (BM Arundel 68, BM Royal 7. E. vi and London, Lambeth Palace Library, 20) and the benedictional BM Harley 2892, while in Arundel 155 his feast is added to the basically Winchester calendar. This saint is not met with, however, either in CCCC 270 or in the calendars and martyrology (Vitellius C. xii) from St Augustine's. Outside Canterbury we find St Salvius only in four English calendars.[3] Canterbury Cathedral owned relics of St Salvius of Valenciennes.[4]

These two features in themselves are surely enough to prove a Christ Church origin for B's calendar. But another piece of evidence which confirms this seems, strangely enough, to have escaped attention. The abbey of St Augustine's and to a lesser extent Christ Church were, as appears from their calendars and martyrologies, very particular about the epithets they bestowed on St Augustine, the missionary to England (26 May). Although Christ Church was the seat of the archbishop the abbey claimed greater prestige and importance because Augustine and his first nine successors were buried there.[5] This claim to have been instrumental in the Christianization of England is clearly expressed in the saint's epithet *anglorum apostolus*, which appears regularly in all the St Augustine's manuscripts that I have consulted.[6] That Augustine was considered by the abbey to have the standing of an apostle is equally

---

[1] See the St Augustine's martyrology, Vitellius C. xii, 128r: 'In cantia monasterio apostolorum PETRI et PAULI *depositio sancti letardi silvanectensis* episcopi et confessoris. qui cum filia regis francorum nomine Berhta in has partes directus est. ut eius sanctitatis exemplo christianę religionis cultum pagano adhuc regi coniuncta non mutaret' (the italicized words are in a later hand over an erasure). See also Bede, *Historia Ecclesiastica* I. 25.

[2] Liudhard was buried in St Augustine's. If the calendar in B was really from the abbey, we should expect him to have at least a simple feast, as has Nothelm.

[3] Salisbury, Cathedral Library, 150 (West Country, c. 969–78); BM Cotton Nero A. ii (Wessex, eleventh-century); Oxford, Bodleian Library, Hatton 113 (Evesham?, of the latter half of the eleventh century); and Rome, Vatican Library, Reg. lat. 12 (Bury, c. 1050).

[4] *Inventories of Christ Church, Canterbury*, ed. J. W. Legg and W. H. St John Hope (London, 1902), p. 80.

[5] See *The Canterbury Psalter*, facs. with introd. by M. R. James (London, 1935), p. 2.

[6] Calendars (26 May and Ordinatio s. Augustini on 16 November): Cambridge, Gonville and Caius College 238; Canterbury, Cathedral Library E. 19; BM Cotton Vespasian A. ii; and Cambridge, St John's College 262. Then the missal CCCC 270, the book of devotions Cambridge, University Library, Ff. 6. 16 and Joscelin, *Historia Translationis Sancti Augustini*, ed. Migne, Patrologia Latina 155, cols. 13–14.

apparent from the following entry in Vitellius C. xii, 130v: 'In britannia civitate dorobernię. natale *santissimi ac beatissimi patroni nostri*[1] A U G U S T I N I anglorum apostoli. Qui a beato papa Gregorio anglię destinatus cum evangelicis adiutoribus. regem Athelbertum cum gente sua convertit. et propter innumera miracula assumptus ad ęthera. sepultus est in monasterio apostolorum P E T R I et Pauli. in porticu aquilonali. unde apostolicis signis illustrissimus. ubique succurrit poscentibus.' Similarly two stanzas of hymns for St Augustine in Cambridge, St John's College 262, 74r and v, read:

Orbis quadri per climata
congaudeat ecclesia
exulta per apostolos
virosque apostolicos.

Augustine par angelis
consors datus apostolis
coequalis martyribus
non impar confessoribus.

The Christ Church monks, by contrast, saw in St Augustine not so much the apostle of the English as, understandably, their first archbishop. As a result we find the majority of entries in Christ Church manuscripts calling him *archiepiscopus*,[2] *anglorum archiepiscopus*[3] or *primus Cantuariensis archiepiscopus*,[4] although the monks in the cathedral do not seem to have been as rigid as their rivals in the abbey since several Christ Church calendars call him, in the St Augustine's manner, *anglorum apostolus*.[5] Apparently this term was less distressing to a monk of the cathedral than *archiepiscopus* was to one of the abbey. So consistently inflexible was the community of St Augustine's in this respect from the eleventh century to the fifteenth that we can confidently assume that the tradition goes much further back, certainly to the tenth century and possibly to the eighth when the custom of burying the archbishops in St Augustine's was discontinued by Cuthbert (758).[6] Against this background the entry in B's calendar for 26 May, *S A N C T I A U G U S T I N I A R C H I E P I S C O P I A N G L O R U M P R I M I* is clear proof that the calendar has a Christ Church and not a St Augustine's origin.[7]

---

[1] The italicized words are in a later hand over an erasure.

[2] Arundel 155; Cambridge, Trinity College 987; Paris, BN lat. 770; BM Egerton 2867 and other calendars; and the martyrologies BM Arundel 68 and London, Lambeth Palace Library, 20.

[3] *Decreta Lanfranci: the Monastic Constitutions of Lanfranc,* ed. and trans. D. Knowles (London, 1951), p. 59. [4] London, Lambeth Palace Library, 159, 224v.

[5] Oxford, Bodleian Library, Add. C. 260; BM Cotton Tiberius B. iii; Canterbury, Cathedral Library, Register K; BM Add. 6160; Oxford, Bodleian Library, Auct. D. 2. 2; and London, Lambeth Palace Library, 558.

[6] See Thomas of Elmham, *Historia Monasterii S. Augustini Cantuariensis,* ed. Ch. Hardwick, Rolls Series (1858), pp. 317–18.

[7] That the above-mentioned early archbishops, all buried in St Augustine's, are mostly omitted in later calendars of the cathedral, is no proof to the contrary. It is quite conceivable that for the adaptation of the Glastonbury calendar to the use in Canterbury, recourse was also had to the monastic tradition of St Augustine's. The early archbishops were an old cause for controversy in Canterbury (see M. R. James, *The Canterbury Psalter,* p. 2). But as monastic life in Christ Church had died out long before Dunstan's coming the abbey must have exercised some temporary influence in the age of reform.

But if this Christ Church origin is certain, why did Wormald attribute the calendar to St Augustine's? Bishop had made a mistake – which, however, does not invalidate his arguments – in dating Arundel 155 as late-eleventh-century.[1] In fact, for palaeographical reasons the manuscript must be much earlier, *c.* 1010–20.[2] Realizing this, Wormald inferred that if Arundel represented the pre-Conquest calendar of Christ Church then B could not.[3] However, I submit that this is too simple a conclusion. It is reasonable to assume that B's calendar derives from one brought from Glastonbury by Archbishop Dunstan, former abbot of that monastery, or by one of his assistants, and that this Glastonbury type of calendar remained in use throughout Dunstan's reign. How long it continued to be used after his death is uncertain, but some of B's feasts indicate that by its time there had been some Winchester influence: 2 July, *Sanctorum Processi et Martiniani. et sancti Swiðhuni* (bishop of Winchester); 8 July, *Sancti Grimboldi monachi* (abbot in Winchester); and 15 July, *Sancti Deusdedit archiepiscopi. et translatio Swiðhuni*. Possibly this influence was felt under Dunstan's successor, Æthelgar, who originally had been abbot of the New Minster, Winchester;[4] at any rate it seems hardly likely that he would have introduced a completely new calendar in the mere fifteen months that he was in office. Nor is his successor, Sigeric, likely to have done so, for he had been a monk of Glastonbury before his appointment to the bishopric of Ramsbury; probably B remained in use during his time. It is one of the next two archbishops who is likely to have made the change to a new calendar on a Winchester basis. The first of them, Ælfric (995–1005), may have been a monk of Glastonbury but later he was certainly either a monk or even abbot of Abingdon, the mother house of Winchester; a reforming bishop, he drove the last secular clergy from Christ Church, as we shall see. His successor was Ælfheah (1005–12), formerly bishop of Winchester. Attribution of the change to his archiepiscopate is favoured by an indication that Arundel 155 is an early example of the new calendar: on 19 May the entry *ET SANCTI DUNSTANI EPISCOPI* follows the old sacramentary feast of St Potentiana, just as it must have done when it was first added, whereas in all later calendars from Canterbury Dunstan comes first.[5] The situation can thus be summed up as follows: B's calendar is a Christ Church product; under either Archbishop

1 *The Bosworth Psalter,* pp. 30–2. Bishop once comes very near the correct date: 'We may therefore conjecturally assign it to a date nearly coincident with that event [Ælfheah's martyrdom], say 1030' (p. 42).
2 Personal communication from T. A. M. Bishop; see also his *English Caroline Minuscule* (Oxford, 1971), fig. 24.
3 Personal communication.
4 For Dunstan's successors see R. R. Darlington, 'Ecclesiastical Reform in the Late Old English Period', *EHR* 51 (1936), 389–90.
5 Bishop (*The Bosworth Psalter,* pp. 32 and 88–9) thinks that the Dunstan entry in Arundel is indeed by a different though contemporary hand.

Ælfric or Archbishop Ælfheah the type of calendar it represents was replaced by a new one exemplified by Arundel 155.

The next step must be to consider the implications of this conclusion for the origin of the manuscript as a whole. A calendar was sometimes bound to a manuscript of a different origin,[1] and indeed for a long time B's calendar was thought to have belonged originally to another manuscript because its two leaves (fols. 2 and 3) are today smaller than the rest of the leaves. Ker, however, noticed that the pricks made for ruling the seventy-eight horizontal lines on each of these two folios appear also on the flyleaf (fol. 1) and the first two leaves of the psalter (fols. 4 and 5). This means, as he rightly saw, that the calendar leaves, originally pricked for twenty-five lines like the flyleaf and the psalter, had already been bound in their present position in B before being pricked again for seventy-eight lines for the writing of the calendar.[2] A close examination shows in addition that the pricks for the vertical ruling of the calendar leaves can also be found in the upper and lower margins of fols. 1, 4 and 5, while on the calendar leaves themselves only the upper ones have been preserved. This proves that the calendar leaves, the flyleaf and the leaves of the psalter were all originally the same size and that the lower margin of the calendar leaves was excised later, perhaps because it contained a mark of ownership.[3] One might also add that the flyleaf and the calendar leaves are of the same soft parchment. It is certain therefore that the calendar was copied directly into B.

Although it is now a fair assumption that the body of the manuscript, of slightly earlier date, had a common origin with the calendar, this is as yet by no means proved; the psalter might have left its place of origin soon after it was written. Consequently we must now see what internal evidence B's original contents provide. Our first hint comes from its division of the psalms. In most psalters of the Anglo-Saxon period the division into nocturns of sixes is marked only irregularly. B, however, and Arundel 155 (definitely written at Christ Church, as has been said already) are distinguished by regular divisions and 'this agreement in an unusual marking favours the attribution of [the Bosworth Psalter] to Christ Church'.[4] The text of the hymns and of the monastic canticles provides more pointers. As Gneuss has shown,[5] the hymnal is of the 'Canterbury Group' type, which in addition to B consists of Durham, Cathedral Library, B. III. 32, of the first half of the eleventh century, and BM Cotton Vespasian D. xii, of the middle of the eleventh century. Both these manuscripts (referred to as D and V respectively)

---

[1] E.g. Eton College 78 and Oxford, Bodleian Library, Ashmole 1525. The bodies of these manuscripts were written in Christ Church, but the calendars originated in St Augustine's.
[2] Ker, *Catalogue*, pp. 161–2.   [3] *Ibid.* p. 162.
[4] Sisam, *The Salisbury Psalter*, p. 4, n. 1.   [5] *Hymnar*, pp. 71–4.

are probably from Christ Church, the first very probably.[1] Although the textual relationships of this group are complicated because of frequent contamination with other manuscripts, the variants in B and D agree very often (less often with V) against other English hymnals of the period.[2] The evidence of the monastic canticles points in the same direction. Here the variants of B, D and BM Cotton Julius A. vi (mid-eleventh-century, probably from Christ Church)[3] stand as a group against those of V (which in this case features a 'Winchester' text imported to Canterbury)[4] and Cambridge, Corpus Christi College 391 (written *c.* 1065 at Worcester). But although the textual affinity between B and the fairly safely located D is very close, this is no proof of B's origin in Christ Church. Despite their rivalries, exchange of books between the abbey and the cathedral must have taken place,[5] and there is indeed a fourteenth-century St Augustine's manuscript (Cambridge, St John's College 262) whose text of the monastic canticles is even closer to D than is B. Thus, although in favour of Christ Church, the internal evidence of the original contents cannot prove more than a Canterbury origin for B.

The script of these contents – in my opinion the decisive evidence – remains to be discussed. But before it is considered, there should perhaps be raised the general question of whether this main body of B, with its Benedictine character, could have been written at Christ Church at all during the last quarter of the tenth century, since the *Anglo-Saxon Chronicle* records that Archbishop Ælfric drove out the secular clergy and installed monks in the cathedral after he returned from Rome in 997: 'He ða eft to Cantwarebiri gecyrde. 7 þa clericas ut of þam mynstre adraf. 7 þar binnan munecas sette. eal swa se papa him bebeod.'[6] Miss Margaret Deanesly has denied that there were any Benedictine monks at Christ Church before this event,[7] but Professor David Knowles believes that monks had been gradually introduced there by Archbishop

---

[1] Detailed description *ibid.* pp. 85–90 and 98–101.   [2] *Ibid.* pp. 127–9.

[3] Description and localization *ibid.* pp. 91–7. Gneuss thinks it quite likely that Julius A. vi was written at Canterbury. That D and this manuscript have their origin in the same place is fairly certain from their close textual affinity, in the Latin text as well as in the Anglo-Saxon gloss, and by the peculiar arrangement of these canticles, which differs from all other English and continental manuscripts.

[4] This probably derived from a manuscript from one of the monasteries founded by Bishop Æthelwold.

[5] There is one occasion on which a number of manuscripts may have been transferred from Christ Church to St Augustine's: *ASC* 1089 F records that after a revolution in St Augustine's the monks were driven out and replaced by twenty-four from Christ Church under the sub-prior Antonius (*Two of the Saxon Chronicles Parallel,* ed. C. Plummer (Oxford, 1892–9) I, 292). Although the account, written by a Christ Church monk, is probably biased and exaggerated, there may very well have been a certain influx of monks from the cathedral who brought books with them.

[6] Plummer, *Chronicles* I, 131.

[7] 'The Familia at Christ Church, Canterbury, 597–832', *Essays in Medieval History Presented to Thomas Frederic Tout,* ed. A. G. Little and F. M. Powicke (Manchester, 1925), pp. 1–13 and *The Pre-Conquest Church in England,* 2nd ed. (London, 1963), pp. 313–14.

Dunstan.[1] Given this more probable view the *Chronicle* entry must be interpreted as meaning that in 997 not the whole community but only the secular clergy still living among the monks were driven out. We may conclude therefore that from a historical point of view there is nothing impossible in a Christ Church origin for B before 997.

We must now turn to the script of B's psalter and other original contents. I am grateful to Mr T. A. M. Bishop for drawing my attention to a tenth-century charter preserved in Westminster Abbey, W.A.M. x, the Sunbury Charter (henceforth cited as SC).[2] In this document, written in Latin with Anglo-Saxon bounds, King Edgar grants to his kinsman Ælfheah land at Sunbury, Middlesex: 'decem videlicet cassatos loco qui celebri æt SVNNAN-BYRIG nuncupatur'. The date given is 962; but the extant charter, SC itself, is a copy produced somewhat later.[3] After carefully comparing SC with a microfilm of B, I am confident that both the psalter and the charter were written by the same scribe. Mr Bishop is of the same opinion. All the forms of the Anglo-Saxon minuscule in the two agree completely (see pls. IV*a* and *b*).[4] Characteristic features are the distinctive contrast of broad strokes and fine strokes; the somewhat square appearance; **a** formed like a **u** with the tops joined by a fine transverse stroke; **c** consisting of two strokes; tall **e** in ligature with a following **n, m**, insular **r**, insular **s** and **t**; the middle stroke of **e** curving down to the right when not in ligature; use of round, low and long **s**; the slightly exaggerated final stroke of **a** and **r** and the bow of **t** every now and then at the end of the line. In SC there is a tendency to develop a little blob at the end of the bow of free-standing **t**. This is found also towards the beginning of B; towards the end of B the blob becomes even more distinct. The abbreviation for -(*b*)*us* and the tail of **e** *caudata* also agree.

In the second half of the tenth century secular charters, both originals and

---

[1] *The Monastic Order in Britain*, 2nd ed. (Cambridge, 1966), pp. 696–7. Most important is the account in the *Vita Dunstani Auctore B* that Dunstan in a dream heard a new anthem: 'et conscriptam cuidam monacho tam recentem didicisse praecepit: et facto mane universos sibi subjectos, tam monachos quam etiam clericos, fecit hanc discendo personare' (*Memorials of Saint Dunstan*, ed. W. Stubbs, RS (1874), pp. 41–2).

[2] P. H. Sawyer, *Anglo-Saxon Charters* (London, 1968), no. 702; ptd and trans., with a facs., Ordnance Survey, *Facsimiles of Anglo-Saxon Manuscripts* (Southampton, 1878–84) II, Westminster Abbey 6; and ptd *Cartularium Saxonicum*, ed. W. de G. Birch (London, 1885–93), no. 1085 and *A Hand-Book to the Land-Charters, and Other Saxonic Documents,* ed. John Earle (Oxford, 1888), pp. 292–4. For the boundaries see W. H. Tapp, *The Sunbury Charter* (Sunbury-on-Thames, 1951).

[3] There is a group of five surviving Anglo-Saxon charters which were composed by one man whom R. Drögereit calls 'Eadgar A' ('Gab es eine angelsächsische Königskanzlei?', *Archiv für Urkundenforschung* 13 (1935), 335–436); of these, four were written by the same scribe (Drögereit equates scribe and author). The fifth, SC, is by a different hand. Further evidence is provided by the faulty date in the extant copy of SC (862 for 962, subsequently corrected).

[4] Drögereit ('Königskanzlei', p. 355, n. 4) considers it probable that the rustic capitals were copied from the original charter of 962.

copies, were often written in monastic centres,[1] and in the case of SC we can be confident that this is what happened. To understand this document we need to have in mind the complex history of the estate of Sunbury and for this up to 968 we have to turn to another document in the Muniments Room in Westminster Abbey (W.A.M. viii), bearing the endorsement *Sunnanburge talu* (henceforth cited as ST).[2] The script of ST points to the late tenth century. Written anonymously like all other Anglo-Saxon documents of its kind,[3] it tells how a certain Athelstan forfeited the Sunbury estate at law under King Eadred and lost it completely in the reign of King Edgar. Then it relates how, around the end of the 950s, the estate was bought by a certain Ecgferth, who made it over to Archbishop Dunstan in trust for his widow and child. But, ST continues, because of the circumstances of Ecgferth's death – possibly he committed suicide[4] – Sunbury and his other estate, Send, were confiscated by the crown and given by King Edgar to the ealdorman Ælfheah. This must have been in 962, when the original of SC was issued. The king accepted Dunstan's offer to pay Ecgferth's wergild, ST tells us, and granted the dead man a burial in consecrated ground; but he refused to give Sunbury back to Dunstan as by this time it was Ælfheah's legal possession. Finally, ST records, 'six years later', that is in 968, Dunstan bought Sunbury from Ælfheah for 200 mancuses. For the history of the estate after 968 our sources are two Latin charters at Westminster Abbey,[5] in which privileges are granted to the abbey and earlier gifts of land confirmed; in both documents Sunbury is named among Dunstan's donations to Westminster Abbey. These charters are definitely later forgeries by the Westminster monks,[6] but despite this it can be assumed that some of the details concerning the land-property of the abbey have a genuine basis,[7] and consultation of *Domesday Book* shows that most of the estates mentioned in the two charters were indeed owned by Westminster Abbey in the eleventh century, among them Sunbury: 'Manerium. SVNE-BERIE tenet abbas Sancti Petri. pro vii hidis . . . Hoc Manerium fuit et est in dominio æcclesiæ Sancti PETRI. Westmonasterij'.[8] Finally, from Matthew

---

[1] See *ibid.* pp. 416–17, and Pierre Chaplais, 'The Anglo-Saxon Chancery: from the Diploma to the Writ', *Jnl of the Soc. of Archivists* 3 (1965–9), 162–5.

[2] Sawyer 1447. For the best edition see *Anglo-Saxon Charters,* ed. A. J. Robertson (Cambridge, 1939), pp. 90–3 and 336–9; also *Facsimiles of Anglo-Saxon Manuscripts* II, Westminster Abbey 7; J. M. Kemble, *ArchJ* 14 (1857), 58–61; *BCS* 1063; Earle, pp. 201–3; and Tapp, *The Sunbury Charter,* p. 12 (like Earle, he reprints the mistakes in Kemble's text).

[3] See F. M. Stenton, *The Latin Charters of the Anglo-Saxon Period* (Oxford, 1955), pp. 43–4.

[4] See Kemble, *ArchJ* 14 (1857), 59, and Robertson, *Charters,* p. 338.

[5] Sawyer 894 and 1293.

[6] G. Hickes already recognized that Sawyer 1293 is spurious; see *Dissertatio Epistolaris* (Oxford, 1703), pp. 66, 68, 71 and 82.

[7] See *Anglo-Saxon Writs,* ed. F. E. Harmer (Manchester, 1952), pp. 338–9.

[8] *Domesday Book,* ed. A. Farley and H. Ellis (London, 1783–1816), 128b. The other estates are Hampstead (128a), Shepperton, Hanwell, Cowley, Hendon (Middlesex) (128b) and Parham

Paris we learn that in 1222, after arbitration, the estate came into the possession of the bishop of London.[1]

Since the two forged charters seem to hold good concerning the Sunbury estate, we should look at them more closely. One[2] purports to be by 'Dunstan, bishop of London', 959; it is very elaborate in its phraseology and grants extensive privileges to the abbey, while the other, called 'Telligraphus Æthelredi Regis' and dated 998, is far more moderate in this respect. The accounts of how the different estates came to Westminster are rather similar in wording and suggest a common source. The 'Æthelred' charter seems to be the earlier of the two forgeries: for one thing it is less blatantly spurious than the 'Dunstan' one and grants a less elaborate system of privileges, and for another it frequently gives details which the 'Dunstan' charter lacks and which, as complications of Westminster's right of possession, no forger would be likely to introduce. In the case of the Sunbury estate the simplified account in the 'Dunstan' charter reads: 'Item .x. cassatos emi ab Ælfego duce. ducentis mancusis auri. in loco qui Sunnabyri dicitur. et dedi prefato cenobio', whereas the fuller 'Æthelred' version is as follows: 'Item Sanctus Dunstanus emebat x. cassatos ab Ælfheago duce ducentis auri, in loco qui Sunnanburig dicitur, et accommodavit eos, insita ei largitate, cuidam viduæ diebus suis, Æðelflæd nomine, et post ejus finem redeat rus illud ad Westminster.'[3] We can be confident that the particulars which are in the 'Æthelred' text but not in the 'Dunstan' one were already in the documents which the 'Æthelred' forger had before him and are trustworthy, all the more so since they accord so well with the information in ST. In particular we need have no doubt about who the widow Æthelflæd was. Although ST does not name her, she must have been Ecgferth's widow, to whom, ST tells us, Dunstan had taken over an obligation when he accepted Sunbury in the first place: no one else could be expected to be given the usufruct of the estate when Dunstan eventually bought it back. Thus

(Sussex) (17a). Brickendon, Hertfordshire, was granted to Westminster Abbey in a will still extant (*Anglo-Saxon Wills,* ed. D. Whitelock (Cambridge, 1930), no. 13), but seems to have changed hands before 1086 (*DB* 136b, 139b and 140b). Ewell, Kent, is named in *Domesday Book* (11a) as the property of the bishop of Bayeux; *Bleccenham, Lothereslege, Codenhlaw* and *Paddington* are not mentioned there; for the first three of these and the difficult *Sillinctune* see *The Crawford Collection of Early Charters and Documents,* ed. A. S. Napier and W. H. Stevenson (Oxford, 1895), pp. 96–8.

The early history of Westminster Abbey is still obscure, not the least reason for this being the activity of its monks, who enjoy a dubious fame as forgers of documents. Their claim, repeated in several spurious charters, that Dunstan refounded the abbey was accepted by William of Malmesbury, Ralph of Devizes, John Flete and others (see the introduction to *John Flete's History of Westminster Abbey,* ed. J. A. Robinson (Cambridge, 1909)) but has been taken with a grain of salt in more recent times. Yet the combined evidence of SC, ST, Sawyer 894 and 1293 and *Domesday Book* suggests that Dunstan can indeed be regarded as the refounder of the abbey; see also Harmer, *Writs,* pp. 286–9.

[1] Matthew Paris, *Chronica Majora,* ed. H. R. Luard, RS (1872–83), III, 75. There are no indications that the abbey possessed Sunbury unlawfully.   [2] Sawyer 1293.

[3] This widow appears also, in another connection, in the 'Dunstan' charter; see below, p. 185, n. 1.

we can be secure in the belief that in 968 Sunbury passed to Ecgferth's widow and that it became the full property of Westminster Abbey only after her death.[1]

We are now able to see the nature of ST and SC in a clearer perspective. The original of ST, with its explicit assurance that nobody else had any claim to the estate ('unbecwedene 7 unforbodene wið ælcne mann to þære dægtide'), was designed to prove that Dunstan had acquired Sunbury from its rightful owner in 968 and that he possessed it legally; the original of SC, passed from Ælfheah to Dunstan as part of the transaction (or a copy of that original), was an essential supporting document. By the time of Æthelflæd's death, at the latest, a copy of each of these two documents was needed for Westminster Abbey. This need could have been supplied in any of three ways: original documents could have been transferred from Christ Church to Westminster; or copies, made at Christ Church, could have been sent; or documents at Christ Church could have been loaned to Westminster for fresh copies to be made there. At all events it is clear that SC, a copy of the original of 962, was written either at Christ Church or at Westminster and that St Augustine's does not come into question at all. Christ Church seems the more probable of the alternatives, for the cathedral would be more likely to produce copies in its scriptorium, with the large-scale resources that it must have had, than either to part with originals or to pass the job of copying on to someone else.[2]

When we consider what follows from these findings for the original contents of B, written as they were by the scribe who wrote SC, we can infer first of all that it would be too much of a coincidence if, after writing B at St Augustine's, the scribe moved to Christ Church or to Westminster Abbey and B went either

---

[1] Apparently Dunstan had bought another estate, Shepperton, Middlesex, from Æthelflæd. See the two entries in Sawyer 1293 and 894, immediately following the Sunbury notice: 'Et illam possessionem in Scepertune emi ab Ealfleda vidua. LX. bizanteis nummis. et dedi loco praescripto' and 'Et illa possessio in Scepertune redeat ad jus Sancti Petri in praefato monasterio post dies Æthelflædi'. Shepperton was owned by Westminster Abbey in 1086 (*DB* 128b). None of the many Æthelflæds recorded in W. G. Searle's *Onomasticon Anglo-Saxonicum* (Cambridge, 1897) can be identified with Ecgferth's widow.

[2] It is noteworthy, however, that of all the specimens in *Facsimiles of Anglo-Saxon Manuscripts* and *Facsimiles of Ancient Charters in the British Museum* (London 1873-8) two charters connected with Westminster Abbey are in a script closest to B's and SC's: BM Stowe Charters 32 (by three hands; the first can be neglected here) and 33 (Sawyer 1451 and 1450). These charters were probably not written at Canterbury: although they have to be dated very early (after 978 and 986 respectively) and seem to be fairly trustworthy in their contents, their extant forms cannot be regarded as entirely genuine and this points to a Westminster origin. Their scripts differ very slightly from B's and SC's and are nearer to the main hand of the Sherborne Pontifical (Paris, BN lat. 943), but the general similarity between all five of them is striking. Moreover the Sherborne Pontifical appears later in the possession of Bishop Wulsin (or Wulfsige) of Sherborne (992–1001), who according to the Westminster monks was made abbot of their community by Dunstan (see William of Malmesbury, *De Gestis Pontificum Anglorum*, ed. N. E. S. A. Hamilton, RS (1870), p. 178; Harmer, *Writs*, no. 86 and p. 320; and J. A. Robinson, *The Saxon Bishops of Wells*, British Academy Supplemental Papers 4 (1918), 67–8). This book bears the marks of a Canterbury origin in its style of ornamentation according to Talbot Rice (*English Art*, p. 197; for a different opinion see Ker, *Catalogue*, p. 438).

to Christ Church itself or to a place where a specifically Christ Church calendar was available to be copied into it: as in the case of SC we can eliminate St Augustine's as a place at which the main body of B could have been written. Next we can infer that, since St Augustine's is ruled out, the Canterbury affiliations of B's original contents[1] were with Christ Church, and from this we can conclude that the main body of B was written either at Christ Church itself or at a place at which this collection of Christ Church material and, a little later, the specifically Christ Church type of calendar were both available. We cannot say for sure that Westminster, the alternative suggested by SC, was not such a place; indeed we should expect that along with Dunstan's munificence towards the abbey there went some monastic influence by Christ Church. Westminster may well have received its first liturgical books from Christ Church and its first scribes may have been taught in Canterbury. Furthermore, although it seems doubtful whether the abbey would have simply taken over the Christ Church calendar,[2] we cannot distinguish between an original and a modified B-type Christ Church calendar from before the Conquest and so cannot tell whether the one in B incorporates any alterations made at Westminster. For instance, the inclusion of Bishop Aldhelm of Sherborne (25 May, in the original hand) could have had such an origin: there is no reference to Aldhelm in any other calendar or missal from Christ Church (or St Augustine's) or in B's ultimate original, the Leofric Missal; if Aldhelm is not merely an example of Winchester influence,[3] he might have been added by the Westminster monks, whose abbot Wulsin became bishop of Sherborne in 992. Or again, the unusual epithet for Westminster's patron, St Peter, on 29 June (*PASSIO SANCTI PETRI PRINCIPIS APOSTOLORUM*, whereas the Leofric Missal has *PASSIO APOSTOLORUM PETRI ET [PAULI]*) might be similarly explained. But still, as long as there is no real proof in favour of Westminster it seems safer to assume that the main body and calendar of B were written more probably at Christ Church. There is the same balance of probability in this case as in that of SC. And, incidentally, the same is true of ST also, for we might expect a Westminster copyist of that document to have brought the record up to date by adding at the end of it a reference to Dunstan's donation to the abbey.

It remains to ask when SC is likely to have been written, for this has implications for the dating of B. It could have been as early as 968, when the transaction between Ealdorman Ælfheah and Dunstan was carried out and the whole affair concerning Ecgferth's widow and Westminster Abbey was settled; or it could have been as late as Æthelflæd's death, when the estate

---

[1] See above, pp. 180–1.   [2] But see below, p. 187, n. 2.
[3] See above, p. 179. Along with several others from south-west England two pre-Conquest calendars from New Minster, Winchester, contain the feast of Aldhelm: BM Cotton Titus D.xxvii and Cambridge, Trinity College R.15.32.

actually passed into the abbey's possession, but we do not know when Æthelflæd died: the 'Telligraphus', purporting to be of 998, still speaks of the transfer of the estate to Westminster as in the future (*redeat*), but the compiler may have taken over the wording of a document composed in 968 and now lost.

We have now assembled evidence from the script of B's main contents and from the nature of those contents that the manuscript was originally produced in Christ Church, Canterbury, or possibly Westminster Abbey. The calendar, as we have seen, gives us no reason to suppose that B had moved by the time that this addition was made between 988 and 1008. None of the material which was added around or slightly later than the turn of the century provides any evidence for the subsequent history of the book;[1] nor is there a pressmark or other mark of ownership to tell us where it was during the rest of the Middle Ages. Its first owner known to us by name was Archbishop Cranmer (2r, *Thomas Cantuarien.*). There is, however, an interesting addition to the calendar which might give a clue: a thirteenth-century entry for 20 May (the only one of its period) reads *Sancti Æþelberhti martiris*. Now King Æthelberht of East Anglia (who died in 794) occurs infrequently in post-Conquest calendars and indeed his name is not found in any calendar known to be from Canterbury or in the oldest one from Westminster Abbey (BM Royal 2. A. xxii, *c.* 1200);[2] but his feast appears in two later Westminster calendars (Westminster Abbey Library, the Litlington Missal, of 1383–4, and Oxford, Bodleian Library, Rawlinson liturg. g. 10, of the second half of the fifteenth century), and not surprisingly so, for an important relic of Æthelberht's head was kept in a shrine in Westminster Abbey and, no doubt, that was why Osbert de Clare, prior of Westminster, wrote a Life of the saint.[3] On the other hand, if the Æthelberht entry might be evidence for thirteenth-century Westminster ownership, corroboration is unfortunately lacking in medieval book-lists from the abbey.[4] We have to be content with the possibility only.

---

[1] The Old English gloss to the psalter is closely related to those in Oxford, Bodleian Library, Junius 27 and BM Royal 2.B.v; see Sisam, *The Salisbury Psalter*, p. 56. But the Winchester origin of these two manuscripts (almost certain for the former, only possible for the latter) does not justify Wildhagen's speculation ('Studien zum *Psalterium Romanum*', p. 459) that B was moved from its original place and its gloss added by an elderly lady in Nunnaminster (Winchester).

[2] Interestingly enough this calendar, according to E. Bishop (*The Bosworth Psalter*, p. 125) is 'practically in its entirety' an adoption from Christ Church, Canterbury.

[3] See F. Wormald, *English Benedictine Kalendars after A.D. 1100* ii, HBS 81 (1946), 59–60. Of Wormald's post-Conquest calendars only those of Evesham, Gloucester and Muchelney have Æthelberht.

[4] Among the ninety-four books bequeathed to Westminster Abbey by Archbishop Simon Langham (1376) there is only a *psalterium glosatum* (see J. A. Robinson and M. R. James, *The Manuscripts of Westminster Abbey* (Cambridge, 1909), pp. 4–7), and the list of service-books in an inventory of the vestry (1388) (ed. J. Wickham Legg, *Archaeologia* 52 (1890), 233–5) is no help. Gasquet thought he had found B in a thirteenth-century list of Christ Church, Canterbury, books: 'Item psalterium cum ympnario' (*The Bosworth Psalter*, p. 4; and M. R. James, *The Ancient Libraries of Canterbury and Dover* (Cambridge, 1903), p. 140 (no. 1776)). But this description is much too indefinite.

The compilation of the Vercelli Book

D. G. SCRAGG

The Vercelli Book, as is well known, is a codex of the late tenth century containing a selection of religious prose and verse in Old English. Of the manuscript's twenty-nine items (some of which are defective owing to loss of leaves), six are alliterative poems and the rest prose homilies. There seems little doubt that one scribe (henceforth referred to as V) was responsible for writing the whole of the codex, even though the size of the writing changes considerably at various points, particularly towards the end of the volume where the lineation also changes.[1] As the earliest of the four extant poetic codices and the earliest surviving collection of homilies in the vernacular, the book is potentially a most important source of knowledge of tenth-century English; most linguistic studies which range over Old English as a whole have included some reference to it. Yet the language of the manuscript is a relatively neglected subject of study, the place of its composition has not been established and the circumstances of its compilation have not been fully explained.[2] This

---

[1] A full description of the manuscript is to be found in N. R. Ker, *Catalogue of Manuscripts containing Anglo-Saxon* (Oxford, 1957); cf. also the facsimile of the manuscript, *Il Codice Vercellese* (Rome, 1913), with an introduction in Italian by Max Förster (the facsimile foliated to reproduce the manuscript). The publication of a new facsimile in EEMF, with an introduction by Celia Sisam, is awaited.

The most convenient edition of the poetry in the Vercelli Book is *The Vercelli Book*, ed. George Philip Krapp, The Anglo-Saxon Poetic Records 2 (New York, 1932), from which the titles used in this paper are taken. Not all of the prose has yet appeared in a modern edition, and references to it are therefore to folio and line of the manuscript. Max Förster's definitive edition of the homilies was interrupted by the second world war, and only the first eight, together with the opening of the ninth, were published (*Die Vercelli-Homilien*, Bibliothek der angelsächsischen Prosa 12 (Hamburg, 1932; rptd without homily IX Darmstadt, 1964)). Another volume, set up in type but not printed, was lost during the war, and Förster handed the project and his materials over to Rudolph Willard of Austin, Texas, before his death in 1955. On the assumption that Willard will not now publish, a new edition is in course of preparation by Paul Szarmach of the State University of New York, Binghamton. Meanwhile, homilies IX, XV and XXII are available in Max Förster, 'Der Vercelli-Codex CXVII nebst Abdruck einiger altenglischer Homilien der Handschrift', *Festschrift für Lorenz Morsbach*, ed. F. Holthausen and H. Spies, Studien zur englischen Philologie 50 (Halle, 1913), 20–179; and homily XI is available in Rudolph Willard, '*Vercelli Homily XI* and its Sources', *Speculum* 24 (1949), 76–87; homily XIII in R. P. Wülker, 'Über das Vercellibuch', *Anglia* 5 (1882), 451–65; and homily XXIII in Paul Gonser, *Das angelsächsische Prosa-leben des hl. Guthlac* (Heidelberg, 1909; rptd Amsterdam, 1966).

[2] On the language of the manuscript see below, p. 195, n. 2. With regard to the book's origin the most recent commentator, P. O. E. Gradon in *Cynewulf's Elene* (London, 1958), pp. 3–5, discounts the earlier view of Förster that it was written in Worcester and, by implication, Vleeskruyer's

189

paper seeks to learn more of the book's origin in two ways: firstly, by examining its make-up in an attempt to determine the number and the nature of the sources that V used, and, secondly, by considering the distribution of distinctive linguistic forms in the manuscript in order to find out more about the nature of V's exemplars and about his background and training as displayed in his attitude to the language of his exemplars.

It is difficult to discern any principle of arrangement in the items of the collection. No attempt is made to follow the order of the church year, and the poems are distributed amongst the homilies in a way that is difficult to understand. Amongst the prose items there is considerable overlap, there being two Christmas homilies (v and vi, not consecutive but divided by two poems) and a number of Rogation pieces (xi, xii and xiii in a series for the three days of the festival, x independent of those three, and xix and xx, again intended to be read consecutively but independent of the other Rogation items). The fact that the second half of homily xxi is a version of homily ii suggests that the compiler of the collection was working so haphazardly that he inadvertently repeated material. Nevertheless some of the items have a deliberate relationship (e.g. the three Rogation homilies xi–xiii, and homilies viii and ix for the first and second Sundays after Epiphany), and there is evidence that the compiler drew upon at least one existing sequence of homilies in that homilies vii–x are numbered *ii–v*.[1]

It cannot be assumed that the items of the collection were copied in the order in which they now stand. The present order of quires was probably the final decision of V, whatever the order in which items and quires were written, for the quire signatures are contemporary, almost certainly in V's hand. But the end of a quire coincides with the end of an item twice in the volume, at fol. 24 (quire 3, homily iv) and at fol. 120 (quire 17, homily xxii), in each case a blank half page now remaining. The last leaf and the concluding signature of quire 3 are missing, and since there would not be room for a complete item on a single leaf, it is to be presumed that the lost leaf was blank except for the signature. Thus homily v, which begins at the head of quire 4, was not originally intended to follow homily iv; the writing of quire 4 had already begun (or was complete) when the two quires were placed together, otherwise the final blank leaf of quire 3 would have been utilized. There is no proof of the relative order of copying of the two quires,[2] and homily v may well have been planned as the

suggestion that it is a Mercian compilation (*The Life of St Chad* (Amsterdam, 1953), p. 58). She concludes: 'further research . . . might usefully start from the hypothesis that it is a Winchester or Canterbury book (perhaps with Glastonbury antecedents)'.

1 See discussion below, p. 193.

2 Quire 4 is unique in the manuscript in having twenty-nine lines to a page. Throughout the volume lineation varies according to gathering, but there is a basic division between quires 1–14 (excluding 4) with twenty-four lines (increased to twenty-five in quires 2 and 7) and quires 15–19 with from

opening item of a collection; it is a Nativity homily, and as such would be a suitable opening item for a collection following the order of the church year. (The homily survives in two other collections, Cambridge, Corpus Christi College 198, and Oxford, Bodleian Library, Bodley 340, in each case as the opening item.)

Quire 17 is not a full quire but consists of two single leaves (fols. 119 and 120); at least one more leaf must have been present when the manuscript was assembled, for the concluding signature of the quire is missing. The likelihood is that quire 17 has lost a number of leaves,[1] probably blank but perhaps containing another item. In either case, the two items now juxtaposed in the Vercelli Book, homily XXII which concludes on the two surviving leaves of quire 17, and the poem *Elene* which begins on the opening leaf of quire 18, are unlikely to have been consecutive in a source used by V. If, as seems probable, the lost leaf or leaves were blank, then the hiatus is similar to that between quires 3 and 4.[2]

Three blocks of quires have now been defined: A, quires 1–3, containing homilies I–IV; B, quires 4–17, containing homily V, *Andreas*, *Fates of the Apostles*, homilies VI–XVIII, *Soul and Body I*, *Homiletic Fragment I*, *Dream of the Rood* and homilies XIX–XXII; and C, quires 18 and 19, containing *Elene* and homily XXIII. The divisions between the blocks mark points at which the copying of items was not consecutive, and it is likely that at each of these points V turned to a different source. Differences within block B point to the use by a compiler of further sources for that block, though it cannot be shown definitely that material from some or all of them had not been combined already in a source used by V.

thirty-one to thirty-three lines. Differences in the size of script consequent upon lineation changes led Richard P. Wülker (*Grundriss zur Geschichte der angelsächsischen Litteratur* (Leipzig, 1885), p. 239) to postulate a second scribe for quires 15–19, and even to suggest the possibility of a third for quire 4. The major change in lineation after quire 14 is acceptable as a basic change of policy on the scribe's part, but the change to twenty-nine lines in quire 4 and then back to twenty-four/twenty-five subsequently shows a curious inconsistency. If, however, quire 4 was ruled (and perhaps partly written) before quires 1–3, the number of radical changes in lineation is reduced to the minimum of three.

[1] Eleven quires in the codex consist (or consisted before the loss of odd leaves) of four sheets of parchment folded to make eight leaves. Three more have an extra leaf inserted, making nine leaves, one has only three bifolia (six leaves), two have three bifolia and a single leaf (seven leaves), and one has five bifolia (ten leaves). It is thus unlikely that quire 17 when constituted had less than six leaves. It is clear that the two single leaves do not belong to an adjoining quire but are the remains of a separate one, because the Vercelli Book is unusual in having two signatures to each quire, a numeral at the head of the first page and a letter at the foot of the last. Quire 17's opening numeral remains, though its conclusion is lost.

[2] As with quires 3 and 4, there is no proof of the relative order of writing of quires 17 and 18, but two features make it probable that they were consecutive: the increase in number of lines per page which occurred in quire 15 is maintained throughout the rest of the book, and a sequence of four pen trials made by V, which take the form of the abbreviation *xb* (cf. Kenneth Sisam, *Studies in the History of Old English Literature* (Oxford, 1953), pp. 109–10), begins in quire 17 and continues in quire 18.

Sections A and C are each homogeneous palaeographically. The three quires of A are of similar length,[1] with twenty-four or twenty-five lines to a page, and the four homilies they contain are more or less uniform in presentation (e.g. each begins at the head of a page, each opens with an initial capital spread over two lines (except for homily I, the opening of which is obscured), and each has a letter or letters in square capitals following the initial, in homily II the capitals continuing for the full length of the first line). Section C has two quires of uniform length (eight leaves, except that the last leaf of the final quire, probably blank except for the signature, has been lost). The first item of C, *Elene*, is divided into numbered fitts, each separated by a blank line, and each opening with a large capital. Similarly, the only other item of C, homily XXIII, is separated from *Elene* by a blank line, and it too opens with a large capital.

Section B, however, contains a number of marked subdivisions. The section opens with homily V which, unlike the homilies of section A, is headed by a minuscule title in English and Latin (*To middan wintra. Ostende nobis domine*); the first word of the homily proper is capitalized, with the initial covering two lines. A half page is left blank at the end of the homily. The next item, *Andreas*, has sectional divisions separated by a single blank line, each section beginning with a capitalized word, the initial letter of which is larger than the rest. Two of the initials are slightly ornamented (on 47v and 51r) and that on 49r is a fine zoomorphic H. *Fates of the Apostles* is the first item in the codex which does not begin at the head of a page; instead, it is divided from *Andreas* in the same way that sectional divisions of the longer poem are separated. The first word of *Fates of the Apostles* lacks its initial (*H*) but in the space left for it and in the margin alongside, the faint outline of a zoomorphic design similar to that on 49r may be seen.[2] The manuscript presentation has been put forward as an argument in favour of the theory that the poem with its runic acrostic is an epilogue to *Andreas*,[3] but such a view is not supported by comparison with *Elene*, at the end of the Vercelli Book, where homily XXIII which follows it is presented like a section of the poem. Nevertheless there may be justification for seeing *Andreas* and *Fates of the Apostles* as having a longer manuscript history in common with each other than either has with neighbouring items in the Vercelli collection.

It has already been observed that homilies VII–X are connected by the

1 Quires 1 and 2 have four bifolia plus one leaf and quire 3 has three bifolia plus one leaf.
2 The ascender with a 'knucklebone' at the top and bulbous decoration half-way down is the most obvious, though itself faint. Also visible is the rounding of the bow. The lines are thin, but very black, a slight surrounding dusting of the parchment possibly suggesting a form of crayon- or pencil-work rather than ink. The marks appear not to have been noted previously and cannot be seen in Förster's facsimile. Together with the 'practice' initial on 109v (and another on 112r which is more likely to be the work of a later copyist), they offer interesting material for the study of manuscript illumination.
3 Cf. Ker, *Catalogue*, p. 461.

numerals *ii–v*. Superficial resemblances in the presentation of these items add to the impression that they form a collection which antedates the Vercelli one: each homily ends part way down a page and is followed after a break of one or two lines by new material; each has its introductory numeral on the blank line between it and the preceding item. Homily vi, preceding this group, begins at the top of a page, and has two lines of Latin title in minuscule; then, after a single-line break, the homily opens like those of the following group, with the first word capitalized and the initial letter of it larger. Thus this homily might be number i of the series. Ker's *Catalogue* mentions a numeral *i* attached to this homily. Miss Gradon has suggested that it is perhaps visible at the foot of the preceding page (54r), after the blank space left at the end of *Fates of the Apostles*,[1] but this is not so, as what can be seen in the Förster facsimile at this point is a reagent stain which shows through from the foot of 54v.[2] No numeral *i* exists, though this, it should be added, does not preclude homily vi from being the first of the numbered series. At the end of the group vii–x the numeral *vi* appears immediately after the close of homily x. The item which is so numbered might be expected to begin on the following line if the pattern of homilies vii–x were to be followed, but instead the rest of the page (about two-thirds of the whole) is left blank, homily xi, the next item, starting at the top of the next page (71v). Since no further numeral occurs in the codex, it is possible that homily xi on the new page represents the beginning of material taken from a fresh source, and is not the homily referred to by the numeral *vi*, especially as homily xi is clearly closely related to those that follow it, which are without numerals. The explanation for the homily numbered *vi* (whether it is the present xi or not) not being copied when the numeral was written may lie in the fact that homily x ends half way down the recto of the last sheet of a gathering: perhaps the scribe reached the end of the homily and wrote *vi*, fully intending to copy another homily immediately, without a break, as he had done with the preceding items, but broke off to prepare a new gathering, and, when returning to writing, began at the top of a fresh page either because the material was no longer what he would have copied as *vi* or because he had forgotten his earlier plan.[3]

---

[1] *Ibid.*; Gradon, *Cynewulf's Elene*, p. 5, n. 3.

[2] A number of pages in the manuscript are marked by discoloured areas which coincide with parts of the text which its first known modern transcriber, a German scholar called Maier, found difficult to read. It is normally assumed that reagent was applied by Maier to bring up faded passages, e.g. fol. 1, probably exposed before the present nineteenth-century binding was added, but it should be noted that reagent has sometimes been applied to words which had been scratched out, either by V or by a near-contemporary reader, e.g. at 65r15.

[3] Professor Clemoes, to whom I am grateful for a most helpful commentary on the first draft of this paper, has suggested to me that the numbers *ii–vi* may refer to the homilies *above* them. This solves the difficulty of the missing homily *vi* and also explains the absence of a number *i* at the beginning of the sequence, but leaves the odd circumstance that the scribe copied a sequence beginning with a homily numbered *ii*.

Homilies XI–XIII are related by their similarly worded minuscule rubrics: *Spel to forman, ðam ðorum* and *þriddan gangdæge*. Each homily ends part way down a page and is followed without a break by new material. Each, too, has its opening word in capitals with the initial letter over two lines. Homily XIV seems to be related to them, as it is the only other homily in the codex with a rubric, this time *Larspel to swylcere tide swa man wile*, which is written partly on the half line left at the end of the preceding homily, the only indications that it is the start of a fresh item being in the colour of the ink (not visible in the facsimile) and in the rather wider spacing of the letters in the rubric as compared with those in black ink. Again the opening word of the homily is in square capitals with the initial letter over two lines. In all four homilies the opening word or letter of the homily is in red also, and *a e n* of *amen* at the end of homily XIII are shaded in red. No colouring appears anywhere else in the manuscript.

Homilies XV–XVIII all follow on from each other and from the preceding item (homily XIV) without any space left in the manuscript, even to the extent, in homily XVIII's case, of the new piece beginning on the last line of a page. But the headings to these four are quite different from those to all other items in the collection, and yet are sufficiently uniform in themselves for the assumption to be made that they form another group from a single source: all four have Latin headings in square capitals and each opens with a capitalized abbreviation ($\overline{\text{M}}$) extending over two lines. The abbreviation is in itself distinctive, standing as it does for *Men þa leofestan*, a formula which elsewhere in the manuscript is either written in full or abbreviated with more indication of the whole phrase (e.g. *men þa ł, m̄ þa leofestan*).[1] Homily XVIII is followed by three short poems, *Soul and Body I*, *Homiletic Fragment I* and *Dream of the Rood*. A lost leaf after fol. 103 contained the end of the first poem and the beginning of the second, so that it is not possible to associate the three on grounds of manuscript presentation. *Dream of the Rood* begins on the last leaf of quire 14 and continues in quire 15; it is with the latter quire that the considerable increase in lines per page noted above[2] occurs.

Homilies XIX–XXI form a distinct group. The first and last have zoomorphic initial letters, while XX has a space for an ornate initial capital although no letter is omitted from the text. Partly filling the blank space are two early attempts at the opening letter (a large square *M*) and also one of the second letter (*E*); all three have been somewhat sketchily erased. At the foot of the

---

[1] The abbreviation *m̄* for the whole phrase also occurs frequently (ten times) within these four homilies. It is interesting to note the repetition of two opening formulae following the *M*-abbreviation in these items. Homilies XV and XVII have variations on one theme: 'Sægð us on þyssum bocum hu . . .' (XV) and 'Sægeð us 7 myngaþ þis halige godspelle be . . .' (XVII); while XVI and XVIII have another: 'Sceolon we nú hwylcumhwegu wordum secgan be . . .' (XVI) and 'Magon we nu hwylcumhwego wordum asecgan be . . .' (XVIII).

[2] P. 190, n. 2.

page (not visible in the facsimile) is a faint outline of a zoomorphic initial. The hesitation expressed in the erasures, the space ultimately left for an initial decoration, and the apparent practice outline of a zoomorphic design below suggest that the scribe felt bound to reproduce some decorative work but was in some way defeated by it.[1] Had a zoomorphic device been completed for homily xx, all three items would have had identical openings, being otherwise similar now (e.g. in having the opening word or phrase completed in large square capitals extending over two lines). Homily xxii, which is without any initial decoration, cannot be definitely associated with the group xix–xxi. It does not begin with the formula *Men þa leofestan* as they do, and the writing at its opening consists of finer strokes and slightly smaller letters than does that at the end of homily xxi (though this may be due merely to the scribe's use of a newly sharpened pen). It does, however, begin on the half page left blank at the completion of homily xxi.

The following are tentative groupings of the items in the codex, perhaps reflecting separate sources for the material. It is emphasized that these represent a useful working hypothesis rather than a definitive statement. The groups are separated on the basis of the evidence so far presented, dubious divisions being indicated by the use of lower case letters.

Group A   Homilies i–iv

Group B   ia   Homily v
           ib   *Andreas* and *Fates of the Apostles*
           2a   Homilies vi–x
           2b   Homilies xi–xiv
           3   Homilies xv–xviii
           4a   *Soul and Body I, Homiletic Fragment I* and *Dream of the Rood*
           4b   Homilies xix–xxi
           4c   Homily xxii

Group C   *Elene* and homily xxiii

The point has now been reached at which it is possible to consider the language of the codex. There is insufficient scope within the bounds of this paper to consider the language of individual items in the collection in detail; this has already been done for some of them,[2] and publication of more thorough

---

[1] Cf. the discussion on the decorated initial to *Fates of the Apostles* above, p. 192 and n. 2.

[2] Cf. for the poetry, Gradon, *Cynewulf's Elene; Andreas and the Fates of the Apostles,* ed. Kenneth R. Brooks (Oxford, 1961); *The Dream of the Rood,* ed. Michael Swanton (Manchester, 1970); Sisam, *Studies,* pp. 119–39; and Jane Weightman, *The Language and Dialect of the Later Old English Poetry* (Liverpool, 1907). On the prose, apart from the scattered comments of Förster, there are brief but accurate observations by Vleeskruyer, *St Chad,* valuable pointers by Hans Schabram, *Superbia* (Munich, 1965), pp. 77–87, and a circumscribed study of the unpublished homilies by Paul W.

investigations may profitably await the appearance of a complete edition of the prose. But relevant to the question of the compilation of the manuscript is the linguistic conformity, relatively speaking, which exists within some of the groups defined above. Furthermore, V's language (and perhaps the manuscript's origin) may to some extent be detected from an analysis of these separate groups. It can easily be seen that no scribe interested in the normalization of language has ever copied the whole of the Vercelli Book material; for the most part, V copied mechanically, and in doing so preserved invaluable linguistic material from his exemplars. But no professional copyist could avoid imposing his own forms on words of very frequent occurrence in a task as lengthy as the compilation of this codex. Clearly the dative article form *þam* is V's preferred spelling, for no variant occurs;[1] yet it cannot be assumed from this that no variant occurred in the exemplars. The imposition of a scribe's form is appreciable when the form is invariable, but it may occur when more than one spelling is regular also. V wrote the pronoun *heo* fifty-five times in the course of the manuscript, and *hio* sixty-nine times; it is not now possible to say which of these he preferred, if indeed he had a preference, but it is possible that in many of the instances he changed an exemplar *heo* to *hio* or vice versa without being aware that he had done so. It is even possible that he changed his practice at some point during the copying, since he changed other mechanical things like the number of lines to a page more than once, on one occasion radically.[2] Such self-evident observations are iterated to emphasize that the task of isolating V's forms from those of his exemplars is not easy, and that the conclusions which follow are necessarily tentative. They rely on an accumulation of relatively minor points, with disproportionate weight attached to a few forms and with very great danger of being misled by a scribe's mechanical error.

The value of the linguistic evidence and some of its attendant problems may be illustrated by considering first, in isolation, the occurrence of a single linguistic feature throughout the codex: the distribution of examples of the digraph *io*. The two sequences *io* and *eo* occur in Old English in words with Common Germanic (CG) *eu* and *iu*, and also in those with CG *e* and *i* in certain contexts (i.e. when subject to breaking or back mutation). The pattern observed in Old English texts is as follows: in Northumbrian *eo* is in general the reflex of CG *e* and *eu*, and *io* that of CG *i* and *iu*; Mercian (the Vespasian Psalter) shows a preference for *eo* for CG *e* and *i*, but confuses *eo* and *io* for

---

Peterson, 'Dialect Grouping in the Unpublished Vercelli Homilies', *Studies in Philology* 50 (1953), 559–65.

1 It is assumed that *ðam* is not a variant *spelling*. *ð* and *þ* are allographs of one grapheme, with a partial complementary distribution in the codex (*þ* is preferred in initial positions), just as long, low and round *s* are part of the grapheme < s > (and again one of them, the long form, is preferred initially).

2 See above, p. 190, n. 2.

CG *eu* and *iu* (in Rushworth[1] the spread of *eo* is even more pronounced); in West Saxon *eo* is generally preferred, though *io* occasionally appears in early West Saxon (especially in the *Cura Pastoralis*) for CG *i* and *iu*; in Kentish *io* is almost universal for CG *eu* and *iu* but both digraphs appear for CG *e* and *i*.[1] Although theoretically *io* is a useful guide to a manuscript's origin, in practice it has rarely proved so; for example, Dr Sisam's masterly study of the compilation of the *Beowulf* codex (from which the present paper has benefited greatly) failed to explain the distribution of *io* instances.[2] In the Vercelli Book the phenomenon has proved no less puzzling: as Sisam observed, 'most of the pieces have some *io* forms, but they cluster or thin out in a way that is hard to explain'.[3] But in table 1, showing the distribution and etymology of all the *io* words in the codex, a certain patterning may yet be discerned. The distribution of forms argues against them being in the main the introduction of V. The items after homily xv, with the exception of homily xxii and *Elene*, have few examples, yet since there are frequent instances in these two items, it cannot be assumed that V changed his practice after homily xv. The inevitable conclusion is that he was in some way influenced by the distribution of *eo* and *io* in his exemplars, a conclusion which may be tested against the separate exemplars defined in the groups stipulated above. Certainly there are significant differences in the distribution of forms in the various groups. For example, the greatest number of instances of *io* as the reflex of CG *e* and *eu* occurs in group B2, whereas groups B3 and B4b are completely free of them. Group B4b, in fact, has only one instance of *io*, and in group B3 they are scarce except in the first item of the group.

Table 2, which shows the comparative distribution of *eo* and *io* in some common words (all with CG *iu*), may make the situation clearer. Particularly noticeable are the complete absence of *eo* in group B2a and its scarcity in B2b. Furthermore the comparatively large number of instances of *io* for CG *iu* shown by table 1 to occur in homily xv, the first item of group B3, is seen to be confined to the four words of table 2, and is balanced by an equal number of instances of *eo* in the same words. If group B3's other linguistic evidence is reliable, its contents were derived by V from a Mercian source.[4] Yet in Mercian texts *io* forms ought to be rare, or at least not as frequent as they are in homily xv. Is it justifiable to see *io* in this homily as V's introduction? The twenty-six instances of *io* in the homily occur only in common words: parts of *bion, sio, diofol* and three examples of the possessive adjective *hiora*. With the exception of the last, these are words which occur very frequently with *io* in group B2, which V copied immediately before homily xv, and even in the case of *hiora*, a form almost never used in group B2 where *hira* and *hyra* are

---

[1] Cf. A. Campbell, *Old English Grammar* (Oxford, 1957), §§ 293–7, for further details.
[2] *Studies*, pp. 65–96 (esp. p. 93).   [3] *Ibid.* pp. 104–5.   [4] Cf. below, p. 202.

Table 1. *Distribution of the digraph* io *in the* Vercelli Book

Groups…	A				B1a	B1b	B2a					B2b				B3				B4a Poems			B4b			B4c	C	Total
Items…	I	II	III	IV	V	Andr.Fates	VI	VII	VIII	IX	X	XI	XII	XIII	XIV	XV	XVI	XVII	XVIII	1	2	3	XIX	XX	XXI	XXII	Elene XXIII	Total
io as a reflex of																												
CG ǎ	—	—	—	3	—	2	1	8	8	8	15	9	8	5	5	—	—	—	—	—	2	—	—	—	—	1	2	77
CG eu	—	1	2	—	1	—	—	5	4	6	—	1	1	—	—	—	—	—	—	—	—	—	—	—	—	—	3	24
CG ī	4	3	1	4	3	3	5	—	1	3	6	1	1	1	—	3	—	—	—	—	—	—	—	—	—	—	2	40
CG ĭ	1	—	—	—	—	—	—	1	—	—	3	—	—	—	3	—	—	—	—	—	—	—	—	—	—	—	1	9
CG iu	12	17	44	52	24	7	10	22	11	27	30	13	11	—	22	23	2	1	4	1	1	—	1	—	—	25	33	393
CG iu+i[j]	—	—	—	—	—	—	—	—	—	—	—	2	1	—	—	—	—	1	—	—	—	—	—	—	—	—	1	5
CG jǔ	—	—	—	—	—	1	—	—	1	—	3	—	—	—	1	—	—	—	1	—	—	—	—	—	—	1	1	9

Poems 1, 2 and 3 are respectively *Soul and Body I*, *Homiletic Fragment I* and *Dream of the Rood*

Also with io are *giomrunga*, 'lamentation', homily x/68r11 (CG g+ǣ+nasal), and three words of obscure etymology: *diogol*, 'secret', 1/2v2o (CG au+i[j] and suffix substitution -ol for -il?); *gebiordor*, 'birth', x/65v2o (CG e? perhaps an ablaut variant of CG -burþi-, OE gebyrde), and *sionesse*, 'incitement', xxii/11931 (CG sc+ŭ or ŭ)

Table 2. *Distribution of* eo *and* io *in four common words in the* Vercelli Book: beon, *'be'*; seo, *'the'*; heo, *'she'*; *and* deofol, *'devil'*

Groups…	A				B1a	B1b	B2a					B2b				B3				B4a Poems			B4b			B4c	C	Total
Items…	I	II	III	IV	V	Andr.Fates	VI	VII	VIII	IX	X	XI	XII	XIII	XIV	XV	XVI	XVII	XVIII	1	2	3	XIX	XX	XXI	XXII	Elene XXIII	Total
eo:																												
parts of beon	4	6	4	11	—	4	—	—	—	1	3	—	—	—	—	14	7	7	4	4	2	—	1	7	19	11	3	112
seo	1	2	2	—	—	6	—	—	—	1	2	—	—	—	—	2	8	1	—	—	—	—	3	16	12	3	11	70
beo	—	—	1	1	—	—	—	—	—	—	—	—	—	1	—	2	4	10	—	—	—	—	—	20	—	4	12	55
deofol	—	—	3	2	—	7	—	—	—	—	—	2	4	—	—	5	—	1	7	1	1	—	8	8	9	2	5	65
io:																												
parts of bion	6	3	7	32	11	1	6	6	—	10	13	9	4	—	6	17	1	3	—	—	—	—	—	—	—	6	1	142
sio	5	3	17	8	7	4	4	9	9	9	13	1	2	—	12	2	8	1	1	—	—	—	—	—	—	10	14	119
bio	—	1	15	4	6	—	4	5	—	2	4	1	1	1	—	2	4	10	—	—	—	—	20	—	—	7	18	69
diofol	—	9	5	8	—	2	2	—	3	—	—	2	4	—	4	4	—	—	3	—	—	—	—	—	—	2	—	56

beo and bio appear in *Elene* for 'they' as well as for 'she'; the numbers are inclusive

usual, there is the parallel of the pronoun *hio*. After homily xiv, instances of the digraph *io* in the codex reduce gradually until they disappear entirely in homilies xx and xxi. It is, then, reasonable to see all instances after homily xiv as having been introduced by V, who slowly forgot the digraph he became so accustomed to in the copying of group B2 and reproduced only the *eo* spelling of his exemplars for the material from homily xv to homily xxi. In homily xxii and *Elene, io* reappears in considerable numbers, presumably because once again *io* was used in the exemplars.

In group B4b there occurs a single instance of *io* in *bion*, 'bees' (107v26, homily xix), a form that baffled Sisam when he tried to determine the compilation history of the Vercelli Book.[1] But the form is explicable as long as it is recognized that V frequently copied mechanically and unintelligently, to the extent that he showed no grasp of the contextual meaning of words copied.[2] It is proposed that the fairly large number of *io* instances in homily xv were introduced by V, i.e. he changed his exemplar *beon, seo, deofol* and *heora* to *bion, sio, diofol* and *hiora* almost as often as he retained the exemplar spelling.[3] Subsequently, in homilies xvi–xviii, *io* occurs only eight times: *sio* twice, *diofol* three times, *giogoðhade* once, and once each *bioð* and *bion*, 'be'. In the poems which follow homily xviii, *siofa(n)* appears twice and there are two instances of *bioð*. Hence in more than twenty-two folios from the end of homily xv to the beginning of homily xix, V wrote *io* only twelve times. Some of the instances, particularly *giogoðhade* and *siofa*, may be exemplar spellings, but it is not likely that *io* was used regularly in the exemplars (i.e. more often than it appears here) because V was not interested in removing it, as may be seen by other parts of the codex, copied both earlier and later. It is very probable that at least nine instances of *io* here were introduced by V himself into words with which he was especially familiar, and that he further introduced *io* into *bion*, 'bees', of homily xix under the impression that this again was the common substantive verb.

The distribution of words with *io* has shown that some of the groups isolated by examination of the foliation and manuscript presentation have a measure of internal linguistic consistency. It may now be seen how far such consistency is maintained.

The four homilies of group A have nothing in common linguistically which they do not share with the rest of the codex, except such negative evidence as the fact that all four have frequent *io* spellings as well as many words with *eo*. There is slight evidence of a division between homilies i and ii on the one hand and iii and iv on the other; for example, in present tense verb inflexions the

---

[1] *Studies,* pp. 104–5.   [2] Cf. *hio dæleð* 62v7 written for *he todæleð.*
[3] Only *almost* as often, for though he wrote equal numbers of *eo* and *io* spellings in the first three words, he wrote *heora* ten times and *hiora* only three times.

former have mainly unsyncopated second and third person endings (e.g. *bebeodeð, cymeð, forgifeð* and *frinest*) while the latter have mainly syncopated ones (e.g. *cwyð, cymð, gifð* and *stent*).[1] Equally slight are occasional rare spelling variants which occur in both I and II (*scile* and *sin* for *scyle* and *syn*).[2]

Present tense verb inflexions mark off the first item of group B1, homily v, from the concluding items of A: homily v has no example of syncope other than *gefehð* (invariably contracted in Old English), unsyncopated forms appearing fourteen times (e.g. *cymeð, eteð, gifeð* and *læreð*). Again, no linguistic feature clearly links the items of group B1 (homily v, *Andreas* and *Fates of the Apostles*), though it should be noted that a slight emphasis on *o* rather than *a* before a nasal which distinguishes the homily (*gelomp, mon, monige* and *wommum*) also appears in the poems (*bona, con(n), geblond, gong, mon, wong* and *wonn*).[3]

The regular use of *io* in the homilies of group B2 has already been shown to mark these items off from those of preceding and succeeding groups, but it has also been shown in the distribution of *io* and *eo* in the four common words of table 2 that there are slight differences between homilies VI–X (classified B2a) and homilies XI–XIV (B2b). Consequently it will be best to examine the two groups separately. The first point to note about group B2a is that, despite the occurrence of distinct and significant linguistic features, there is not total consistency of language within the group. For example, though *io* for CG *e* and *eu* occurs very frequently, and the use of it in parts of *bion, sio, hio* and *diofol* is invariable, the preposition *in* appears frequently in only two of the items (homily VIII: *in* fifteen times, *on* fifteen times; homily X: *in* twenty-four times, *on* thirty-seven times) but rarely elsewhere (never in VI, three times in VII and twice in IX). It seems likely that V in the main reflected his exemplar with regard to *in/on* throughout the composition of the Vercelli Book,[4] and we have seen that the use of *io* in group B2a is probably also taken from the exemplar. This leads to the conclusion that whoever introduced the frequent examples of *io* in this group was less interested in regularizing either *in* or *on*, and a similar selective normalization is apparent in other linguistic forms. The sequence -*fn*- never appears in the group, giving way to the variant -*mn*- (*emne* and

---

[1] On the value of such verb inflexions for the study of dialect origins, cf. Sisam, *Studies,* pp. 123–6.

[2] Cf. Karl Brunner, *Altenglische Grammatik nach der angelsächsischen Grammatik von Eduard Sievers,* 3rd ed. (Tübingen, 1965), § 31, n. 2, and § 427.1.

[3] Except in common forms like *þone* and *þonne, o* for CG *a* before a nasal occurs only sporadically in the codex. A high proportion of the occasional forms in the prose appears in homily v, but the use is perhaps not regular enough for a definite conclusion on it as an exemplar spelling. Instances in *Andreas* and *Fates of the Apostles* are also slightly above average, though the spelling is not unusual in poetry.

[4] Cf. for example the complete exclusion of *in* from homilies XIX–XXI, which is consistent with late West Saxon practice and confirms the late West Saxon exemplar of the three homilies as postulated below, pp. 203–5.

stemne) in the twelve instances that occur (all in homilies VIII–X). The consistency with which -*mn*- is maintained in these homilies is remarkable when it is
compared with an equally consistent use of -*fn*- in other parts of the codex,
e.g. homilies I and IV which each have it seven times; the appearance of only
one or the other of the spellings within individual homilies suggests a faithful
reflection of the exemplars. The spelling -*mn*- is West Saxon according to the
grammars, being the dominant form in early and late West Saxon;[1] all the
early non-West Saxon texts preserve -*fn*-, and this is the spelling which
predominates in late manuscripts with non-West Saxon associations (the
Blickling Homilies and the Old English Bede). The only major non-West
Saxon text with -*mn*- is Rushworth[(1)], where it is probably due to West Saxon
influence. Luick states that -*mn*- is Kentish as well as West Saxon and indicates
its appearance in Middle Kentish (*Ayenbite* and William of Shoreham)[2] but all
commentators are agreed that it is non-Anglian. It is odd to find, then, that
the homilies of group B2a have clear evidence of Anglian origin. All have
a number of Anglian lexical items (e.g. *fylnes, gefeon, mitteðe, nænig, semninga,
unmanig, wea* and *ymbsellan*) and most of the present tense verb forms are
expanded (*cnawest, helpeð, siteð* etc.). It would appear that the exemplar of
group B2a was a collection of Anglian homilies assembled in the south-east
(where else could *io* have been regularized for CG *e* and *eu*?) by a scribe who
was not interested in excluding Anglian words or inflexions, but who did
introduce his own spellings (*io* and -*mn*-). Putting a date on this collection is
not easy; a south-eastern scribe working before *c.* 975 (the date of the Vercelli
Book) would not unnaturally be sufficiently free from late West Saxon
influence for the Anglian features mentioned to be perfectly acceptable to him.
On the other hand, he does seem to have been influenced by late West Saxon
in some respects: *y* appears for earlier *i*+*e* (present subjunctive of 'be' is
sy(n) eighteen times and *hy*, 'they', occurs eleven times), *y* appears for *i* in
unstressed positions (e.g. the suffix -*lyc* seven times) and *þænne* for *þonne* occurs
eleven times.[3] None of these features is general to the codex and they cannot
be attributed to V; they are exemplar spellings. Thus the homilies of group
B2a were drawn from a south-eastern homiliary (or a south-eastern copy of an
Anglian homiliary) written no earlier than the third quarter of the tenth
century.

The relationship of group B2a to group B2b is difficult to assess. The

---

[1] Sievers-Brunner, § 193.2 and Campbell, § 484. The position is confirmed by an examination of the
Ælfric material in *Homilies of Ælfric*, ed. John C. Pope, Early English Text Society 259–60 (London,
1967–8), where the ten instances of -*fn*- (against a great many of -*mn*-) are confined to four manuscripts associated with the south-east which have other occasional non-West Saxon forms (CCCC
162 and 303; BM Cotton Vitellius C. v; and Oxford, Bodleian Library, Bodley 343).

[2] Karl Luick, *Historische Grammatik der englischen Sprache* (Leipzig, 1914–40; rptd Stuttgart and
Oxford, 1964), §681 and n. 1.   [3] Cf. Sievers-Brunner, §§ 41 and 22, n. 2; and Campbell, §380.

homilies of B2b are linked to each other by their rubrics, and their lack of enumeration might be considered enough to distinguish them from those of B2a. But there are some linguistic links: *io* is almost as common in B2b as in B2a, for CG *e* and *eu* as well as for CG *iu*, and *sy(n)* appears three times and *þænne* four times. The reduced number of examples might be explained by the more limited sample available (group B2a covers seventeen folios, group B2b only nine) were there not contradictory evidence too: -*fn*- appears once in homily XI,[1] and *eo* reappears very occasionally in *beon, seo* and *deofol* in the last two items (cf. table 2). Finally, a practice which associates the two groups is the infrequency with which accent marks appear. In the codex as a whole, accents appear at fairly regular intervals (approximately one every ten lines in prose, rather more frequently in poetry) but in the 800 extant lines of group B2a only six accents occur, and they are hardly more frequent in the 400 lines of group B2b (ten instances).[2] Thus there are linguistic and presentational affinities between groups B2a and B2b, but conflicting evidence makes it unsafe to assume positively that they are from the same exemplar.

The items of group B3 have many more features in common than have the pieces in most other groups. For example, *g* is always preserved before *d* in the homilies of this group (in -*hygd*- and -*sægd*-), the four items have a preponderance of *cwom* forms against normal late West Saxon *com*,[3] weak class II verbs have the past suffix -*ad*- frequently (twenty-seven times), the possessive adjective *heora* is almost confined to this group[4] and the round *s* is used more frequently than in preceding groups.[5] All four homilies have frequent instances of the preposition *in* and many non-West Saxon lexical items (e.g. *nænig, fylnes, gefeon* and *semninga*). There are numerous examples of non-West Saxon spellings and accidental forms (e.g. smoothing in *gefehta*, non-West Saxon front mutation in *cerdest, eð, leg, legeleohte* and *hersum*, the Mercian past form *slepte*, and *sege* and *segon* as past forms of *seon*). Spelling, accidence and vocabulary concur in identifying all four homilies as of Anglian, probably Mercian, origin, and the relative infrequency of late West Saxon features indicates late transmission into the West Saxon scribal tradition.[6] The

---

[1] But -*mn*- appears once in each of homilies XIII and XIV.

[2] Full details of the accents and their use in the codex may be found in D. G. Scragg, 'Accent Marks in the Old English Vercelli Book', *Neuphilologische Mitteilungen* 72 (1971), 699–710. Evidence is presented there to show that V took his accents from his exemplars.

[3] Sixteen *cwom* forms but only four *com*. Cf. Sisam, *Studies*, p. 103.

[4] Of forty-four instances of *heora* in the codex, thirty-three appear in the homilies of group B3. The variant spelling *hiora* also appears in B3 three times, but is more frequently found elsewhere (especially in group A). The usual spelling of the word throughout, however, is *hira* or *hyra*, occasionally *hiera*.

[5] As against the long and low forms. This may not be dialectally significant, but perhaps shows V influenced by the script of his source.

[6] The dialectally significant linguistic forms referred to throughout this paper are, in the main, those generally agreed, and only limited references to the grammars are given. In the case of spell-

likelihood is that V derived group B3 from a Mercian homiliary.

The three sub-divisions of group B4 – the three short poems of 4a, the three homilies of 4b, and homily xxii in 4c – are linked by their sharing of a number of late West Saxon features, e.g. loss of *g* in *sarie* and *werie* (*Soul and Body* and homily xxi), *y* for earlier *i* in *synt* (*Soul and Body* and all four homilies) and the verb form *miht*(-) (*Dream of the Rood* and all four homilies). But the poems and homily xxii have other features which mark them off from the three homilies of B4b, notably their use of *io* and of some Anglian spellings (e.g. *bledum* and *wergas* in *Dream of the Rood* and *seted* and *uneðnessa* in homily xxii). The items of B4b, homilies xix–xxi, are intimately linked linguistically. Of the very many features common to them, but not found throughout the codex, the following are the most noticeable: the use of *y* for historical *i* in words with weak sentence stress (*ys* sixty times, *byð* twenty-eight times, *hyt* eight times and *hym* three times) and occasionally in unstressed syllables (*ælmys-*, *æryst*, *apostolys* and *hwilwendys*), the almost universal use of southern verb forms (present second and third persons singular inflexions with syncope and assimilation and stem vowels showing mutation, e.g. *cymð*, *bitt* ('pray'), *swylt* and *wiðstent*, and weak past participles with syncope and assimilation in stems ending in a dental, e.g. *gelæd* and *gemet*), weak class II verbs with the past suffix *-ud-*, *lufu* declined as a strong noun, the neuter accusative plural of *eall* inflected *eallu*, *eallo* and *ealle,* a high proportion of examples of *sceolon* against *sculon*, the element *-sæd-*, 'said', without *g*, and no examples of the preposition *in* which is frequent elsewhere in the codex. Many of the spellings and accidental forms cited are not only West Saxon features but those which appear only in the late Old English period,[1] and the vocabulary too contains many items especially frequent in late West Saxon religious prose: *forðsið*, *geleaflest*, *leohtbrædnes*, *leorningcniht*, *mannsliht*, *murcnung* and *ymbscrydan*. But against all this evidence must be set occasional suggestions of non-West Saxon origin for the material: the use of distinctly Anglian vocabulary, especially in homily xxi (*hleoðrian*, *morðor*, *sigor* and *wea*), and a few expanded verb forms (e.g. xix: *bebringeð* and *togecyrreð*; xx: *adwæscit*, *gecigeð* and *gedrefeð*; and xxi: *cymeð*, *demeð*, *ætyweð* and *behylfeð*). It is possible that the explanation for these forms is that all three homilies in group B4b are composite and utilize earlier English material. The second half of homily xxi (about eighty lines of text) is taken

---

ings and accidence quoted here, cf. Campbell, §§ 222, 220, 747 and 743. On dialect vocabulary, the studies by Jordan, Menner, Rauh, Scherer, Vleeskruyer and Sisam listed by Campbell, p. 367, have been cautiously relied upon, together with Schabram, *Superbia*. The work of Meissner (references in Campbell) is less reliable; some of the Ælfric 'coinings' he lists, for example, can be paralleled in the Vercelli Book.

1 That the spellings and accidence are late West Saxon, cf. the following (references are in the order of the features cited): Sievers-Brunner, §22, n. 2; Sisam, *Studies*, pp. 123–6; Campbell, §751.3; Sievers-Brunner, §413, n. 2; Vleeskruyer, *St Chad*, p. 133; Sievers-Brunner, §§ 293, n. 3, 92.2*a* and 214.3; and Campbell, §767, n. 1.

almost verbatim from an earlier independent homily which survives complete in a number of versions, one of them being Vercelli homily II. A few sentences of homily xx are drawn from a homily represented in the Vercelli collection by item III, while the opening sentence of xx is a slightly expanded version of that to homily XI. The composite nature of homily XIX has not been shown, for no study of its sources has yet been published, but transitions in the text suggest that it was compiled on the pattern of the two succeeding items.[1] It may be that all three homilies were compiled by the same person, for though the nature of the composition of xx and that of xxI seem rather different (earlier material in xx being rather better incorporated into the plan of the whole than is the case in xxI), the spelling and parts of the accidence in both are made to conform with standard late West Saxon. Compare the following pairs of sentences:

a { III: hio geicð þas andweardan god . . . 7 hio gemanigfealdaþ geara fyrstas (15v24)
{ xx: heo geycð þa 7weardan . . . 7 heo gemænigfylt gear (110r31)

b { II: in þam dæge þa synfullan heofiaþ 7 wepaþ, forþan hie ær noldon hira synna betan; ac hie sarige aswæmaþ (9v12)
{ xxI: on þam dæge þa synfullan heofað 7 wepað, forðan þe hie ær noldan hyra synna betan; ac hie þonne sceolon sarie aswæman (115r12).

In the codex as a whole, copying errors are fairly frequent, and some passages are so corrupt that no sense is discernible,[2] the likelihood being in many cases that the text had become corrupt during the course of a lengthy transmission. In the homilies of group B4b, however, there are very few places in which a copyist has blurred the meaning of a passage, the occasional error being so slight that it is perfectly acceptable to see it as the work of V.[3] The late West Saxon features of the group can hardly have been introduced by V since he shows no preference for such forms elsewhere; they appear to be indicative of the exemplar language, and suggest that the group is drawn from a recent exemplar, for only a copy made close in time to the writing of the Vercelli Book could show so much late West Saxon influence. Lack of serious error suggests a short transmission, and it is reasonable to assume that V was able to draw on good copy (perhaps even an authorial copy) of a series of homilies compiled in the second half of the tenth century from earlier vernacular material by a writer thoroughly at home in the standardized language then becoming current throughout southern England. The fact that the compiler of these homilies was able to draw on much of the material available to V (the

[1] Cf. the rather awkward introduction of *ðas gangdagas* in 107v5.
[2] For example, on 14r a contemporary copyist marked a short section for omission because no sense could be discerned. The excision marks appear suprascript in lines 23 and 24.
[3] In homily xx, for example, there are only six errors. Two are dittographic: *weg ge gelædde* 110v12 and *heafod leah leahtras* 110v15; two are minor omissions: of *bið* at 111r8, and of *is* at 111v8; in 111r9 *eallum forhæfdnes* was written for *eall unforhæfdnes*, and in the same line *idelne plegan* occurs as a nominative phrase.

use of parts of the homilies which V made his II, III and XI has been mentioned) suggests the possibility, probably incapable of proof, that he was working in the same criptorium as V.

In conclusion it must be observed that there is no proof that B4a, b and c were all taken from one exemplar by V, and certain features, e.g. the frequent occurrence of *io* in B4c, suggest that whoever imposed late West Saxon order on B4b did *not* copy B4c. But neither can it be shown definitely that the three groups are from separate sources, and they must remain, as yet, sub-divisions of one unit.

The evidence from group C is similarly inconclusive. Both the Cynewulfian *Elene* and homily XXIII, which consists of extracts from two books of the Old English translation of Felix of Crowland's *Life of St Guthlac*, have a few linguistic forms which are reminiscent of the items of group B4 (e.g. in *Elene io* is as common as in homily XXII, and in homily XXIII *miht* and *-ud-* as the past suffix of weak verbs class II associate the item with group B4b), but the two single leaves on which homily XXII is concluded suggest, as has been shown, a copying break between groups B4 and C. The two items of C have little in common with each other linguistically except that they are both of Mercian origin,[1] but they both tell lives of saints, and a common exemplar for them is not improbable.

Three exemplars have now been definitely established for the Vercelli Book material, a south-eastern homiliary of the second half of the tenth century (group B2a), a Mercian homiliary of unknown date (group B3) and a late West Saxon collection (group B4b). At least two other exemplars were used for the material in groups A and B1, and others may have been used for that in B2b, B4a, B4c and C. Attention must now turn from the exemplars to the scribe V. The first thing which can be said with some assurance is that the collection was not planned in its entirety before execution began, and the explanation for the confused order of items, with overlaps in content, is that a number of different exemplars were used for the material. Thus the Christmas homily which begins group B2 is preceded by a Christmas homily in B1, and group B2a concludes with a Rogation homily and is followed by three pieces for the same season in B2b and yet more in B4. The second interesting feature of the codex is the extraordinary variety of linguistic forms which occurs: V has preserved good late West Saxon in B4b alongside Mercian forms in B3 and Kentish ones in B2. In part this may be due to the date at which the codex was written; such homilies of the collection as reappear in eleventh-century

---

[1] The Mercian element of Cynewulf's language is now recognized; cf. Gradon, *Cynewulf's Elene*. The Life of St Guthlac, an east Mercian saint, was probably translated in that area; Mercian linguistic forms are frequent in the homily, e.g. the lexical items *hleoðrian, stræl* and *unmanig,* and the spelling of *caldan* and *leglican.*

manuscripts have the majority of the non-West Saxon forms removed. But it is also likely that the Vercelli Book was not written within the West Saxon area; the profusion of instances of *io*, *in* and expanded verb forms does not accord with what is known of, for instance, Winchester practice in the late tenth century,[1] and it seems sensible to begin the search for the scriptorium in which the codex was written outside the heartland of Wessex.

The search may begin, indeed, with the south-east. If the exemplar of group B2a was made in the south-east not long before this section was incorporated in the Vercelli Book, as was suggested above, it is reasonable to assume that the exemplar had remained there. It is also reasonable to expect a scribe to be able to obtain late West Saxon material of recent composition there (or anywhere in the south by that date), and the long association of Kent with the Mercian kingdom could well have facilitated access to a Mercian homiliary. If V were south-eastern trained, he would be very likely to accept non-West Saxon and West Saxon forms alike – the introduction of non-West Saxon forms into Ælfrician material by south-eastern scribes is exemplified throughout the eleventh century[2] – and the introduction of *io* by V into parts of the collection is best explained as the result of his south-eastern training or environment. Attention should also be focused on a scattering of south-eastern spellings found throughout the manuscript, e.g. *e* for *y* in *geðeldelice* 5v17, *wedewum* 18v2, *gerene* 88r20, *sendon* ('are') 88v15, *onherien* ('emulate') 101r11 and *scele* 119r6; and *y* for *e* in *gehyrnes* ('praise') 71r4, *acynned* ('bear') 86v13, *acynde* 91r6, *gefylde* ('feel') 97v24, *gescyndan* ('corrupt') 118v16, *gescyndendra* 120r27 and *brymela* 135r14. Many of these may result from a confusion of sense on the part of a copying scribe, but taken in conjunction with other evidence they may be seen as south-eastern forms. So too might other features which appear sporadically, e.g. the instability of initial *g*. Two marginal items noted by Sisam, while not offering proof in themselves of south-eastern origin, add to the weight of evidence: the use of the *xƀ* sign common in Canterbury manuscripts and the interpolated word *sclean* with a south-eastern spelling.[3] Finally, minute examination of a corrupt sentence at the end of homily III gives indisputable proof of south-eastern scribal interference which is possibly that of V. The sentence now reads: Þas þing us gedafenað gefellan mid fæder 7 mid suna 7 mid þam þam halga gaste a in ecnesse þurh ealra worulda woruld aa butan ende.' Joan Turville-Petre's study of this homily and its sources points out

---

[1] The controlled conditions in Winchester are admirably demonstrated by Pamela Gradon, 'Studies in Late West Saxon Labialization and Delabialization', *English and Medieval Studies presented to J. R. R. Tolkien*, ed. Norman Davis and C. L. Wrenn (London, 1962), pp. 63–76.

[2] Cf. Pope, *Homilies of Ælfric, passim.*

[3] Cf. Sisam, *Studies*, pp. 109–10 and 113, n. 2. Sisam thought that the word *sclean* was not in the hand of the main scribe, but it is not clear if he thought so only because the spelling *scl-* for *sl-* does not occur elsewhere in the manuscript. If the word was written later, it would indicate that the Vercelli Book remained in the south-east rather than that it was written there.

that part of the incomprehensibility here is the result of scribal omission of two phrases: *Cristes fultume þe mid* before *fæder*, and *leofað and rixað* after *gaste*.[1] Two linguistic points are significant: Kentish *e* for *y* in *gefellan*, 'fulfil', and the use of *in* rather than *on*, the only instance of *in* in this homily (*on* occurs twenty-eight times). Though *in* is a widespread feature of Anglian dialects, Professor Pope has suggested that it is also likely to be substituted for *on* in the south-east.[2] Although we can never be sure that the lacunae are due to V's carelessness rather than to that of an earlier scribe, and although *gefellan* and *in* might also be forms which occurred in the exemplar, it would be unreasonable to assume that V could have *copied* the dittography which produced *þam þam* and that he would have *reproduced* the omission of final *n* in *halga*. Hence some of the corruption of this sentence was introduced by V, and it is more than possible that the lacunae and the Kentish spellings are his too. It is not too wild a guess to see him leaving close scrutiny of his exemplar at this point, tired and bored at the end of a long copying task and believing that he knew the formulae of the traditional concluding sentence sufficiently well. The result is a hopelessly confused text, but also the recording of two forms which are indicative of V's own language.

Many later manuscripts containing parallel texts of homilies in the Vercelli Book have connections with the south-east, particularly those which overlap with the Vercelli Book in items which V appears to have drawn from more than one exemplar. CCCC 162,[3] for example, has four items paralleling those in the Vercelli collection, two in Vercelli group A and two in group B4b. Similarly CCCC 198[4] has four items paralleling ones in Vercelli A, B1 and B2, CCCC 303[5] has three items paralleling ones in Vercelli A and B4b, and Bodley 340[6] has five items paralleling ones in Vercelli A, B1 and B2. None of these manuscripts takes its text from the Vercelli Book, either directly or indirectly. The fact that scribes other than V could draw on the same range of material in the south-east is further proof that a library containing copies of all the homilies involved (I, III, V, VIII, IX, XIX and XX) existed in the Kentish area. At least one of the exemplars V used was south-eastern (group B2a), much of the material he drew upon was available for copying in the same area in the eleventh century and V himself seems to have introduced a number of south-eastern forms. The conclusion that the Vercelli Book is a Kentish compilation seems inescapable.

[1] Joan Turville-Petre, 'Translations of a Lost Penitential Homily', *Traditio* 19 (1963), 51–78.

[2] *Homilies of Ælfric*, p. 23, n. 3.

[3] On Canterbury connections cf. Ker, *Catalogue*, p. 56, and Pope, *Homilies of Ælfric*, pp. 23–4.

[4] CCCC 198 has Worcester connections, especially in the glosses by the 'tremulous hand', but there is reasonable indication that it originated in the south-east, or at least had 'a south-eastern book . . . in its pedigree' (Sisam, *Studies*, p. 155, n. 4); cf. also Pope, *Homilies of Ælfric*, p. 22.

[5] CCCC 303 was written at Rochester; cf. Ker, *Catalogue*, p. 105.

[6] Bodley 340 was written at Canterbury or Rochester; cf. Sisam, *Studies* pp. 150–3.

Portents and events at Christ's birth: comments on Vercelli v and vi and the Old English Martyrology

J. E. CROSS

Many curious traditions are gathered by medieval man to magnify the birth of Christ. Homilies and tracts transmitted the stories of the anonymous apocrypha but this present investigation uncovers well-known names and a different tradition. For the theme in Vercelli homilies v and vi Rudolph Willard[1] blazed the trail when he drew attention to *De Divinis Officiis Liber* (wrongly attributed to Alcuin)[2] and also to a sequence in Rome, Vatican Library, Reg. Cat. 49, which is now named *Catéchèses Celtiques*.[3] The historical information in both these Latin texts, however, clearly derives from Orosius's *Historiarum adversum Paganos Libri VII*.[4]

VERCELLI V

Comparison of Vercelli v with Orosius and *Cat. Celt.* suggests that the Old English homilist either drew variously on the words recorded in these two texts with others, or drew on some intermediary which was closer to Orosius than was *Cat. Celt.* and which had further information. For three of the four items in Vercelli v, Orosius and *Cat. Celt.* between them have very nearly all the Old English information, at times with parallel phraseology which can assist editors of the Vercelli text.

1. Þæt wæs sum þara wundra, þa se casere com to Rome [mid si]gefæste gefean *ond*

---

[1] In a review, (*Speculum* 9 (1934), 229–30) of *Die Vercelli-Homilien,* ed. M. Förster, Bibliothek der angelsächsischen Prosa 12 (1932). All references to the Vercelli homilies are to Förster's edition (rptd Darmstadt, 1964).

[2] As Willard notes. This text (Migne, Patrologia Latina 101, cols. 1174–5) may now be left out of the discussion since it has nothing distinctive in common with Vercelli v which is not in Orosius or in *Cat. Celt.*, and Vercelli v has material which is not found in the pseudo-Alcuin text.

[3] So named, discussed and edited by André Wilmart in *Studi e Testi* 59 (Vatican City, 1933), 29–112 (henceforth cited as *Cat. Celt.*). The manuscript is dated as tenth-century with 'a preference for the first half'; at the earliest it was copied at the end of the preceding century (p. 29). It has 'insular' features (p. 29) but is very tentatively placed in Brittany (p. 31). Our text is printed on pp. 98–105.

[4] *Pauli Orosii Historiarum adversum Paganos Libri VII,* ed. C. Zangemeister, Corpus Scriptorum Ecclesiasticorum Latinorum 5 (1882), my references being to book, chapter and paragraph.

mid blisse; ða æt þære ð[riddan] tide þæs dæges, þæt wæs æt underne, þa wæs [man]num on heofonu*m* gesine gyldnes hringes onlic[nes] ymbutan þa sunnan *ond* on þa*m* hringe wæs getacnod, þæt on his rice acenned wolde bion se æðeling s[e] is rihtlice nemned soðfæstnesse suna.[1] Þæt is þon*ne* [u]re Hælend Crist, þæt he mid his fægernesse gewlitgode þa sunnan, þe us[2] nu dæghwamlice lyhteð *ond* hie gesceop *ond* mid his mihte ealne middangeard receð *ond* styreð (Vercelli v, lines 67–77);

'Nam, dum urbem circa horam tertiam ingreditur, circulus aurei coloris circa solem apparuit. Quod sig[nificat] quia in eius tempore nasceretur is cuius potestas et pulcritudo et sapientia circumdaret omnem potestatem et omnem pulcritudinem et omnem sapientiam (*Cat. Celt.*, p. 99, lines 19–22);

Nam cum primum . . . urbem ingrederetur, hora circiter tertia repente liquido ac puro sereno circulus ad speciem caelestis arcus orbem solis ambiit, quasi eum unum ac potissimum in hoc mundo solumque clarissimum in orbe monstraret, cuius tempore uenturus esset, qui ipsum solem solus mundumque totum et fecisset et regeret (Orosius, vi.xx.5).

Orosius appears to be the source for the portent and its signification, but on one point of detail Vercelli v agrees with *Cat. Celt.* against Orosius: where Orosius speaks of the ring around the sun 'in the appearance of a rainbow', the other two note that it was 'a golden ring'. Relevantly the Old English Orosius also describes the portent as a golden ring: 'mon geseah ymbe þa sunnan swelce an gylden hring'.[3] Miss Bately has warned us that certain manuscripts of the Latin Orosius are closer to the Old English version than those used for Zangemeister's edition,[4] and so the possibility must remain that the detail of 'the golden ring' might have been in some Orosian manuscript, extant or lost.[5] If so, Vercelli v is closer to Orosius than to *Cat. Celt.*, especially

---

1 There is strong literary evidence that MS *soðfæstnesse sunu* is an error for *soðfæstnesse suna,* where *suna* may be a simplified or abbreviated form of *sunna,* 'sun', to correspond with a scriptural phrase, *sol iustitiae* (Malachi iv.2), which was used as a name for Christ and is a necessarily appropriate name in this general context. For detailed argument see J. E. Cross, 'The Literate Anglo-Saxon – On Sources and Disseminations', *Proc. of the Brit. Acad.* 58 (1972), 6–7.

2 MS *up.*

3 *King Alfred's Orosius*, ed. H. Sweet, Early English Text Society o.s. 79 (London, 1883), 248.

4 Janet M. Bately, 'King Alfred and the Latin Manuscripts of Orosius's History', *Classica et Mediaevalia* 22 (1961), 69–105.

5 Miss Bately has generously informed me that the 'golden ring' is not in extant manuscripts which are most closely related to the Old English version. Following Professor Whitelock's hint, she now suggests that a *circulus aureus* could have been derived from a misreading of a *circulus aereus* which is a feature of Octavian's entry in pseudo-Jerome's commentary on Luke (PL 30, col. 587); see now *England Before the Conquest: Studies in Primary Sources Presented to Dorothy Whitelock,* ed. Peter Clemoes and Kathleen Hughes (Cambridge, 1971), p. 249 and n. 5. This may well be the relevant stage for the Old English Orosius, but it may now be possible to trace the origin of the *aereus* and to offer a speculation for the Vercelli homily's 'golden ring'. A certain Julius Obsequens culled a *Prodigiorum Liber* (see below, p. 216) from Livy (a source for the Latin Orosius on this portent) and spoke of *sol . . . caeli orbe modico inclusus* (§68), 'the sun . . . enclosed in a small

since the signification in Vercelli recalls Orosius and is quite different from
that in *Cat. Celt.*

2. Þæt gelomp swa ilce se casere on his rice forgeaf ealle scylda Romwara folce.
Þa wæs on þan getacnod, þæt on his rice wolde cuman on middangeard, seðe
mancynne forgifan wolde ealle hira synna *ond* uncysta þurh rihtne geleafan *ond*
þurh soðe hreowe (Vercelli v, lines 78–82);

Et in eius tempore omnia debita regis dimittebantur ab eo. Quod significat quia
in eius tempore saluator nasceretur qui peccata omnibus per babtismum et
penitentiam indulgeret (*Cat. Celt.*, p. 99, lines 30–2);

ouansque urbem ingressus omnia superiora populi Romani debita donanda . . .
censuisset (Orosius, vi.xx.6).

The 'insular' Latin text is very close to Vercelli v for the description of the
event, which however derives from Orosius, but *Cat. Celt.* is echoed in
Vercelli for the signification, although this too had been suggested by Orosius's phrase: *debita peccatorum* (vi.xx.7).

3. Ond on þæs caseres dagum wæron genydde to rihtu*m* þeowdome *ond* to rihtre
hyrnesse ealle þa esnas, þe fra*m* hira hlaford ær gewiton *ond* him hyran noldon;
ond swa-hwylce-swa ne woldon hlafordas habban, ða wæron þurh raðe deaðe
gewitnode, *ond* on þam wæs þa getacnoð þæt þurh Cristes [lare] man-cynn
sceolde bion underþeoded anes Godes hyrnesse *ond* an Godes willan wyrcean,
ond swa þa-þe ne willað rihtu*m* geleafan onfon, þa bioð geniðrade in helle-
tintegro (Vercelli v, lines 82–90);

In eius quoque tempore serui dominos fugientes ad legitimum seruitium redire
coacti sunt, et qui dominos non recipiebant in cruces coegit. Sic et nunc in
Christi doctrina humanum genus ad unius dei cultum redigitur, et quotquot non
receperint eum in inferni cruciatum tradentur (*Cat. Celt.*, pp. 99, lines 46–9);

Caesar . . . triginta milia seruorum dominis restituit, sex milia, quorum domini
non exstabant, in crucem egit (Orosius, vi.xviii.33); restituendosque per Caes-
arem omnes seruos, qui tamen cognoscerent dominum suum, ceterosque, qui
sine domino inuenirentur, morti supplicioque dedendos (Orosius, vi.xx.7).

The form of words in *Cat. Celt.* is clearly an intermediary for Vercelli v here.

circle of sky'. This statement (from Livy?, but not in the extant books of Livy) appears to have
been abbreviated by pseudo-Jerome to *circulus aereus*, 'aerial circle'. Pseudo-Jerome (now dated
seventh- to eighth-century, with possible origin in Ireland, by B. Bischoff, *Sacris Erudiri* 6, (1954),
236–7), or at least its form of words, is a source for *Cat. Celt.*, since the signification of the portent
(as presented in this paper) is exactly as in pseudo-Jerome. For this portent and its signification
Cat. Celt. echoes the Orosian words in part and pseudo-Jerome in part and adapts *circulus aereus*
to *circulus aurei coloris*. These words found in *Cat. Celt.*, perhaps from an earlier exemplar, could be
the source for Vercelli v.

Both the event and the signification are presented in similar terms in the 'insular' Latin and Old English, whereas Orosius merely describes the event.

4. *Ond* in Agustes dagum wearð swa 'mycel sybb geworden on middangearde, þæt men wæpn ne wægon, forþamþe he in sybbe wel gesette middangeardes rice; *ond* mid wisdomes cræfte sio sibb wæs geseted geond ealne middangeard *ond* he eac sende his cempa wide geond manega mægða, þætte yfle men ne dorston nan wyht to teonan don for hyra egsan. In þære myclan sybbe wæs getacnod þære soðan sybbe cyme in middangeard; þæt wæs ure Hælend Crist þe us gesybbode wið englu*m* *ond* us geþingode wið God-fæder *ond* us to sybbe gelaðode *ond* he swa cwæð; *Beati pacifici, quo*niam *filii Dei uocabuntur* [Matthew v. 9], 'Eadige bioð þa sybsuman men, forþanþe hie bioð Godes bearn genemnde' (Vercelli v, lines 90–101).

Orosius mentions the *pax Augusti* a few times, linking it with the peace of Christ at iii.viii.5 and vi.xx.8,[1] and *Cat. Celt.* refers to the peace under three sub-headings: *portae Iani clausae fuerunt, arma in manibus non fiebant* and *bella cessauerunt.*[2] Neither, however, is verbally close to Vercelli v nor does either cite the Vercelli testimony of Matthew v.9. But the signification of the birth of Christ during a reign which brought universal peace was commonly noted,[3] and I suspect here that the Vercelli homilist (or his exemplar) followed normal practice for exegetical pieces by abstracting phrases or passages from varied authoritative predecessors. He certainly does this for the rest of the homily. Max Förster has already indicated that Gregory's *Homilia VIII in Evangelia* was used for five sections,[4] and even one which does not appear close could well derive from Gregory. Where Gregory says on the enrolment of the world (Luke ii.1)[5] 'Quid est, quod nascituro Domino mundus describitur, nisi hoc, quod aperte monstratur, quia ille veniebat in carne, qui electos suos adscriberet in æternitate', Vercelli v differs in adding a scriptural testimony of Luke x.20: 'On þan wæs getacnod, þæt he com on menniscu*m* lichoman se wolde his þara gecorenra naman awriten in ecre gemynde eadges lifes, swa he him gehet *ond* swa cwæð: *Gaudete et exultate, quia nomina uestra scripta sunt in celis*' (lines 117–21). But the testimony does not demand a new source. It is a continual delight to a reader of vernacular homilies to see how a scriptural echo in a Latin source is identified and sometimes presented as a direct quotation. Or again, since Gregory's homily viii (on the Nativity) does not give all the information needed for a verse-by-verse commentary on Luke ii.1–14, another small

---

[1] The *pax Augusti* is also referred to at i.i.6. [2] *Cat. Celt.*, pp. 99–100.
[3] See Bede, *In Lucae Evangelium Expositio,* ed. D. Hurst, Corpus Christianorum Series Latina 120 (1960), 45 on Luke ii.1; Bede, 'Homilia in Nativitate Domini', *Bedae Opera Homiletica,* ed. D. Hurst, CCSL 122 (1955), 37; and Ælfric, 'Sermo de Natale Domini', *The Homilies of the Anglo-Saxon Church: The First Part Containing the Sermones Catholici or Homilies of Ælfric,* ed. B. Thorpe (London, 1844–6) I, 32.
[4] Nn. 61, 73, 100, 109 and 123 to Förster's edition of the Vercelli homilies.
[5] Quoted by Förster, *ibid.* 61, from PL 76, where Gregory's *Homilia in Evangelia* are printed.

source is *Homilia V in Evangelia*, the Old English homily echoing two separate sentences of Gregory's explanation of 'good will' (Luke 11.14): '*Þæt* is se goda willa, þæt man oðrum þæs[1] unne, þe he wille, þæt him gelimpe *ond* þæt he on oðres gesyntum blissie *ond* gefeo, swa him on sylfum wille. Hæbben we forþam godne willan on ure heortan, forþanþe we ne bioð æfre idele godra weorca for Godes eagum, gif usse heortan bioð gefyllede mid godum[2] willan' (lines 200–6); cf. 'Voluntas autem bona est . . . sic de prosperitate proximi sicut de nostro profectu gratulari . . .' (§3)[3] and 'Ante Dei namque oculos numquam est vacua manus a munere, si fuerit arca cordis repleta bona volun-tate' (*ibid.*).

Other statements in Vercelli v have contact with Latin ideas and words as presented in *Cat. Celt.*, notably the interpretation of Cyrinus as Peter together with the testimony of Matthew xvi.16 (lines 125–30),[4] and the signification of the *binn* as God's altar (lines 158–60),[5] although this latter interpretation is found elsewhere.[6] It could well be that 'Primogenitus idest in babtismo et in resur[rectione] ac ascentione, siue primo[genitus] est totius creaturae' (*Cat. Celt.*, p. 101) suggested 'Ac he is frumbearn nemned forþan he is fruma eallra gesceafta and he ealle gesceop. Nænig ær him of helle astah, ne ænig ær him of deaðe aras' (lines 150–2). The interpretation of the 'edictum a Cæsare Augusto' (Luke 11.1) is slightly different from that in *Cat. Celt.*, 'Agustus totius mundi rex censum unicuique imperans deus pater intelligitur, qui est rex totius mundi, et qui misit censores, idest profætas et apostolos et doctores, ut totus mundus censum fidei redderet ei' (*Cat. Celt.*, p. 101), since Vercelli v regards the command of Augustus as that of Christ not of *deus pater*: 'swa wæs eft æfter þam Cristes bebod gastlice læded geond ealne middangeard þurh his þa halgan apostolas *ond* þa godan lareowas . . . geond ealne middangeard to eorðan gemærum' (lines 53–7). But Vercelli v could be a rewriting here on the basis of *Cat. Celt.* and Bede's commentary on Luke 11.1,[7] which says that the command is Christ's and also cites Mark xvi.15 as does Vercelli v (lines 58–60).

All the indications suggest that Vercelli v (or its exemplar) is a commentary conflated and reworded from various sources, and that, while the statement about the *pax Augusti* may be created from Orosius or an intermediary, the signification could be from such a source as Bede's homily on the Nativity

---

1 Omitting MS *ne*, as Förster suggests in n. 116.

2 Emending MS *godes* to *godum*, as Förster suggests in n. 119.

3 This sentence is quoted by *Cat. Celt.*, p. 103, but the Vercelli homilist or his exemplar clearly knew his Gregory, since the next sentence is presented earlier in Gregory's §3.

4 'Cirinus heres interpre[tatur], meliusque per Petrum sig[nificatur] qui est haeres Christi . . . a quo quasi praeside prima professio nominis Christi manifestari incepit cum diceret: Tu est Christus Filius Dei vivi [Matthew xvi. 16]' (*Cat. Celt.*, p. 100).

5 'hoc significat altare de quo pascuntur penitentes et innocentes pabulo corporis et sanguinis Christi' (*Cat. Celt.*, p. 101).

6 Pseudo-Jerome, PL 30, col. 587.   7 Ed. Hurst, pp. 45–6.

which cites Ephesians II.14, 'Ipse est pax nostra qui fecit utraque unum', and comments 'id est qui de angelis et hominibus unam Dei domum pius mediator et reconciliator instituit',[1] to include the ideas of Christ as 'þære soðan sybbe . . . þe us gesybbode wið englum' etc. (lines 96–7).

Vercelli VI is quite a different piece. The second part (lines 61–93) of this hundred-line address presents events of Christ's childhood from the apocryphal *Pseudo-Matthaei Evangelium*[2] and the first part (lines 1–60) narrates 'miracula que facta fuerant ante ad[uen]tum Salvatoris',[3] which need discussion here. All except one[4] of the four *miracula* could however have derived ultimately from Orosius, but the echoes are muffled and clearly differentiate Vercelli V and Vercelli VI in line of descent. Items one, three and four all appear to illustrate a similar dim recall. The fourth (lines 38–44) narrates that Augustus went to Bethlehem (not Rome) and saw, at the third hour of the day, the sun with a golden ring (as in the 'insular' tradition of Orosius),[5] but this has become threefold. The third item has similar contact with, but also difference from Orosius: 'unmanegum nihtum, ær Christ geboren wæs, onsprungon þry willas *ond* of þara anra gehwylcum ele fleow fram ærmergen oð æfen; and manna gehwylcum wæs forgifen, þæt he moste niman, swa he sylf wolde, þara-þe þær-to cwomon'[6] (lines 30–3). Orosius says: 'His diebus [when Octavian entered Rome] trans Tiberim e taberna meritoria fons olei terra exundauit ac per totum diem largissimo riuo fluxit' (VI.xviii.34, repeated at VI.xx.7).[7] We mark the similar flow of oil 'through the whole day' but that the one *fons* has become *þry willas,* just as the one ring around the sun has become threefold. Similar exaggeration causes the first item (lines 21–5) which refers to the universal peace, to be presented as a miracle (of man physically prevented from fighting) rather than an event. The tradition is in Orosius, as in others,[8] but the specification in Vercelli VI could be an elaboration on a form of words such as that in *Cat. Celt.*: 'in eius tempore arma in manibus non fiebant'.[9] In Vercelli VI Augustus eventually makes a speech

---

[1] Ed. Hurst, p. 37.   [2] See Förster's edition of the Vercelli homilies, pp. 134–6.

[3] Abstracted from the title of the address (*ibid.* p. 131).

[4] 'Swylce þæt eac ge-eode, þæt-te siofon nihtum, ær Crist geboren wære, þæt sio sunne æt midre nihte ongan scinan swaswa on sumera, þonne hio hattost *ond* beorhtost scinð; þæt tacnode, þæt he þas eorðlican sunnan nihtes scinende him to gisle beforan sende' (*ibid.* p. 132, lines 25–9).

[5] See above, p. 210 and n. 5.   [6] As MS; Förster's *cwonom* is an error.

[7] This was first recorded in Jerome's version of the *Chronicle of Eusebius*; see *Eusebii Pamphili Chronici Canones, Latine vertit, adauxit, ad sua tempora produxit S. Eusebius Hieronymus,* ed. J. K. Fotheringham (London, 1923): 'E taberna meritoria trans Tiberim oleum terra erupit fluxitque toto die sine intermissione, significans Christi gratiam ex gentibus' (p. 240).

[8] See above, p. 212, n. 3.   [9] *Cat. Celt.*, p. 100.

which is in no Latin text within my knowledge, but one more recall of Oro-sius (VI.xx.6) occurs in the Old English homilist's final command (lines 59–60) on the cancellation of debt.

I suspect (from experience in reading homily and commentary, no more) that the Anglo-Saxon or his exemplar wrote the introduction very freely from memory as prelude to his rendering of the *Pseudo-Matthaei Evangelium*.

THE OLD ENGLISH MARTYROLOGY

The description of the portents in the Old English Martyrology reveals a compiler who was either misled or had no regard for chronology or for authoritative tradition. For these are just portents, originally unconnected with any tradition about the birth of Christ, whether Orosian, apocryphal or exegetical. The passage is translated (and later quoted) from Cockayne's text[1] and is itemized for easier discussion of the ideas:

In this year (*i*) men saw three suns and (*ii*) at another time three moons; and (*iii*) the Romans saw a fiery ball (*cleawen*) fall from heaven and (*iv*) at another time a golden ball; and in this year (*v*) ears of wheat were seen growing on trees; and (*vi*) in a certain province (*mægð*)[2] when they broke their bread at meat[3] blood flowed from the loaf as it does from a man's body when he is wounded; and in this year (*vii*) many saw milk rain from heaven and (*viii*) a lamb speak in human manner in Egypt; and (*ix*) an ox spoke to the ploughman in Rome and it said: 'Why do you goad me? Good wheat will grow this year, but you will not exist then nor will eat of it.'

All except one of the portents here are noted in authors who are earlier than the exemplar of the Martyrology and the exception (*viii*) is paralleled in a text of the 'insular' area, although this text is of a later date. It is obviously difficult to indicate immediate sources, but the majority of the items (*i–vii*) certainly belong to the tradition exemplified in Livy, the Roman historian, who re-corded portents as facts which had been reported for the priests to divine. As is known, many books of Livy's history are lost, but some evidence exists for some of the content of the lost books in summaries, fragments and, most

---

[1] The passage for the birth of Christ is within a section of the Martyrology extant only in the margins of Cambridge, Corpus Christi College 41, pp. 122–32, 'printed inaccurately' by G. Herzfeld (*An Old English Martyrology*, EETS o.s. 116 (London, 1900)), according to N. R. Ker, *Catalogue of Manuscripts Containing Anglo-Saxon* (Oxford, 1957), p. 44. Often Herzfeld's inaccuracy is merely in the spelling of words, which is unimportant in a discussion of ideas, but a comparison of his text with that of T. O. Cockayne (*The Shrine* (London, 1864–70), p. 30) shows that two phrases containing important ideas are omitted from Herzfeld's text: *æt mete* in *vi* and *spæc on Rome* in *ix*. It has therefore seemed simpler to translate Cockayne's text and, below, to quote from it.

[2] In view of the general sources presented below I prefer to regard *mægð* as *provincia* as illustrated in J. Bosworth and T. N. Toller, *An Anglo-Saxon Dictionary* (Oxford, 1898), *s.v. mægð* IVc.

[3] Regarding 'at meat' as the fossilized modern English phrase meaning 'at a meal, at meals'.

importantly here, a *Prodigiorum Liber* gathered from Livy by Julius Obsequens.[1] Also later writers such as Orosius derived factual material from Livy. Thus by comparing descriptions and dates of portents in Orosius *and* Obsequens we may identify many which were obviously recorded in Livy's lost books, and by comparing certain dated portents in Orosius *or* Obsequens with those in other writers such as Pliny and Plutarch we may be certain that some more were generally known and were possibly in Livy also.

It is probable however that neither Orosius nor Obsequens was an intermediary and immediate source for the Martyrology. Some of the items are recorded in Orosius (certainly *ii, iv, v, vi* and *vii*), but it is unlikely that the compiler of the Martyrology would read Orosius and would omit those portents (taken up in Vercelli v) which were positively linked by the historian with the time of Augustus/Christ. Obsequens also has a full list of portents for the year when Octavian Augustus entered Rome, none of which was used in the Martyrology. The Martyrology also has information from the tradition of Livy (see below, the comment on (*vi*) the bloody loaves) which is not in Obsequens.

But five (*i, v, vi, viii* and *ix*) of the nine items in the Martyrology, including two (*viii* and *ix*) which at present seem rare, occur in a Latin poem, *Versus Sancti Patricii Episcopi de Mirabilibus Hibernie*, under a sub-heading, *Incipit de Signis et Prodigiis*. This poem is now assigned to Patrick, bishop of Dublin (1074–84), a man who had strong ties with the monastic school at Worcester under St Wulfstan.[2] The overlap of items between the 'insular' Latin poem and the Martyrology, together with the fact that some other items in Patrick's list are from the same *kind* of tradition[3] as that already mentioned, makes me suspect that both the Martyrology and the poem drew on collection(s) of portents already made. In my experience such men as the martyrologist and this poet normally would not go to the trouble of making their own collection from chronicles and histories,[4] and the correspondence in detail with earlier Latin texts which is indicated in some of the items below suggests that both writers had books open in front of them. This (these) would be something like Obsequens's collection but with additions. And it (they) could have been

---

[1] Obsequen's book is ed. and trans. A. C. Schlesinger, *Livy* (Loeb Classical Library (London, 1919–59)) XIV, 237–319.

[2] *The Writings of Bishop Patrick 1074–1084*, ed. A. Gwynn, Scriptores Latini Hiberniae 1 (Dublin, 1955), 56 ff.; on Patrick's contact with Worcester, see p. 6. Our section of the text is on p. 56.

[3] See J. E. Cross, '"De Signis et Prodigiis" in *Versus Sancti Patricii Episcopi de Mirabilibus Hibernie*', *Proc. of the R. Irish Acad.* 71 (1971), sect. C, 247–54.

[4] The possibility must remain for Patrick, although not I think for the dated group in the Martyrology, that the bishop collected his portents from annals. Dr Kathleen Hughes suggested this in a review of Professor Gwynn's edition (*MÆ* 26 (1957), 122–7). The parallels which she notes are not similar enough in detail to be Patrick's actual intermediary, but the general proposition, if extended to include Latin chronicles, is suggested by the identified sources below, most of which are recorded in the historical tradition which was available for annalists.

made either in England or in Ireland, since Patrick's ties were with both countries and the Old English Martyrology had contact with demonstrably Irish texts.[1]

Ultimate sources and/or parallels for the items in the Martyrology are as follows, but these are grouped where relevant, since a distinctive item may also help to identify an item which if it were alone would be commonplace, and a grouping may be distinctive where individually the items would be commonplace.

(*i*) '*men gesawon iii sunnan* ond (*ii*) *oþre siðe iii monan*'

Pliny (*Nat. Hist.* II.99) notes that the portent of three suns has appeared four times, and that three moons have appeared (II.100). Obsequens records the sight of three suns in §§ 32, 43, 68 and 70. Jerome's version of the *Chronicle of Eusebius* says: 'Romae tres simul exorti soles paulatim in eundem orbem coierunt'.[2] Bishop Patrick reports: 'tres simul in celo uisi sunt currere soles'. Orosius records the appearance of three moons (IV.xiii.12). The prudent may thus wish to regard these portents as commonplace. But only Obsequens §32 (from a lost book of Livy) has the collocation: 'In Gallia tres soles et tres lunae visae.' The three suns in Patrick's poem are followed immediately by the portent of fire pouring from the ground: 'terribilem quedam tellus effuderat ignem', and this grouping is found in Obsequens §43: 'In Piceno tres soles visi. In agro Vulsinensi flamma e terra orta caelumque visa contingere.' Jerome's statement, of course, is about a somewhat different phenomenon, recorded for the year in which Octavian entered Rome, and a similar statement in Obsequens §68 suggests that it was described in a lost book of Livy: 'soles tres fulserunt . . . et postea in unum circulum sole redactis multis mensibus languida lux fuit'.[3]

(*iii*) '*Romanan gesawon firen cleawen feallan of heofnum* ond (*iv*) *oþre siþe gilden cleowen*' and (*vi*) '*on sumere mæigðe þonne hi hira hlaf bræcon æt mete þonne fleow þæt blod of þam hlafe swa of mannes lichaman deð þonne he gewundod bið*'

No. *vi* is a distinctive item. Both Orosius (v.xviii.4 and 5) and Obsequens

---

[1] Herzfeld (*An Old English Martyrology*, p. xxxiii and nn.) demonstrates that Adamnán's *De Locis Sanctis* is a source and J. E. Cross ('The Days of Creation in the *Old English Martyrology*', *Anglia* 90 (1972), 132–8) shows that the passages on creation derive from pseudo-Isidore, *De Ordine Creaturarum Liber*, which in turn draws on *De Mirabilibus Sacrae Scripturae* written by Augustinus Hibernicus in 655.

[2] Ed. Fotheringham, p. 239.

[3] This particular portent turns up appropriately in the Chester play on the Nativity (*The Chester Plays*, ed. H. Deimling, EETS e.s. 62 (London, 1892, rptd 1926), 129):

> that day was seene verament
> 3 sonnes in the firmament,
> and wonderly together went,
> and turned into one.

(§54) record it and so it derives from a lost book of Livy. But Obsequens is not an intermediary for the Martyrology since he abbreviates and omits the placing of the event 'æt mete' and the comparison with the bodily wounds: 'Arretii frangentibus panes cruor e mediis fluxit', both comments being in Orosius: 'apud Arretinos cum panes per conuiuia frangerentur, cruor e mediis panibus quasi ex uulneribus corporum fluxit'. Bishop Patrick also has the portent in slightly changed and abbreviated form: 'Panibus incisis sanguis quoque fluxit abunde / coram conuiuis, quos signum terruit illud.' No. *iv* the 'golden ball', is also rare and happened in the same year as the 'bleeding loaves'. Again both Orosius and Obsequens record it and thus indicate an origin in Livy: 'In Spoletino colore aureo globus ignis ad terram devolutus' (Obsequens, §54); and 'conplures præterea in itinere uidere Romani globum coloris aurei caelo ad terram deuolui' (Orosius, v.xviii.6). The Martyrology again has more information than Obsequens has, since 'Romans' saw it, as in Orosius. No. *iii*, the portent of the fiery ball falling from heaven is a commonplace if it is a meteor (cf. Obsequens, §§ 11 and 45), but within the year of the other two portents, both Orosius and Obsequens describe a 'globus ignis' immediately after statements that many portents appeared in the city of Rome: 'nam sub ortu solis globus ignis a regione septentrionis cum maximo caeli fragore emicuit' (Orosius, v.xviii.3 and 4); and 'sub ortu solis globus ignis a septemtrionali regione cum ingenti sono caeli emicuit' (Obsequens, §54). Livy thus appears to be the ultimate source for all three portents.

(*v*) '*þi geare man geseah hwætes eare weaxen on treowum*'

Neither Orosius nor Obsequens specifically states that 'ears of corn' grew on trees. But Obsequens twice records 'fruges in arboribus natae' once without place (§30), but once at Bononia (§26) to identify this event with the same in Orosius, v.vi.3: 'in Bononiensi agro fruges in arboribus enatae sunt'. *Fruges* (fruits of the field) could obviously be specified as 'ears of corn' and this tradition also reached Bishop Patrick: 'spicas turba hominum iam uidit in arbore natas'.

(*vii*) '*þi geare manig seah meoloc rinan of heofnum*'

This is a commonplace happening which is always recorded in Obsequens with the curt phrase: 'lacte pluit' (§§ 14, 28, 30 (with oil), 35, 36, 40, 41, 43 and 50). Orosius records the portent once (iv.v.1) for a year which is too early for Obsequens's collection: 'lac uisum est manare de coelo'. This is translated in the Old English Orosius as 'rinan meolc of heofonum',[1] but our portent must remain a commonplace.

---

[1] Ed. Sweet, p. 162.

(viii) '*lamb spæcan on mennisc gecinde mid Egiptum*'

Patrick has this portent: 'agnus in Egipto mire fuit ore locutus', but I have not seen an earlier reference. The extant books of Livy record no 'speaking lambs' and the placing 'in Egypt' could preclude Livy. Yet the common details in the two 'insular' texts suggest that an earlier parallel/source will be found.

(ix) '*oxa spæc on Rome to þam ergendum* ond *he cwæð: to hwon sticast þu me; god hwæte geweaxeð to geare ac ne bist ðu þonne ne his ne abitest*'

Patrick has this portent: 'Bos loquitur Rome stimulanti uoce prophete: / "Copia farris erit uobis hominesque peribunt".' An earlier Hiberno-Latin text, the eighth-century *Liber de Numeris*, has this ox in a group with four other speaking animals, Eve's serpent, Balaam's ass, the centaur who spoke to Paul the Hermit in Jerome's *Vita* ch. VIII and a blackbird (*merulus*) who sang ps. XXIX.9 to an unnamed man of God. It reads: 'Bos vero cedenti se dixit: / "Non grana sed homines in Roma deficiant".'[1] All these statements, I suggest, derive in some way from Jerome's version of the Chronicle of Eusebius for the year of Julius Caesar's death in 44 BC: 'inter cetera portenta quae toto orbe facta sunt, bos in suburbano Romae ad arantem locutus est: frustra se urgeri, non enim frumenta sed homines breui defuturos'.[2] All the ideas in Jerome's statement are present in the Martyrology or in Patrick or in the *Liber de Numeris* and most are in all of them: the ox spoke (J, M, P and LN) to the ploughman (J and M) in Rome (J, M, P and LN) when goaded (J, M and P)[3] and prophesied (P, but this is assumed in J, M and LN), saying 'why do you goad me (M, cf. J 'frustra se urgeri'), there will be plenty of wheat (M, P and LN, but J as a negative) but men will die' (J, P and LN, and in M in the singular).

Jerome's hand in the transmission of this curious anecdote is strengthened by his recording of one more portent found in Patrick's poem. Bishop Patrick's 'ecce, lapis cecidit de celo magnus in amnem', which seems so vague, is, rather certainly, a misunderstanding of a famous event in antiquity caused by the brief record in Jerome: 'lapis in Aegis fluuios de caelo ruit'.[4] The placing of the event in Jerome identifies this as the fall of meteoric stone which

---

[1] R. E. McNally has already noted the similarity between the examples in the *Liber de Numeris* and in Patrick's poem in 'Der Irische *Liber de Numeris*' (unpub. thesis, Munich, 1957); on *Quinque animalia*, see pp. 97–8.

[2] Ed. Fotheringham, p. 239. It is possible that Jerome derived this event from a lost book of Livy, although Obsequens does not record it.

[3] Professor Gwynn offers two translations of *stimulanti uoce prophete*, both, however, taking *stimulo* in a figurative sense; the source now suggests that this translation is permissible: 'An ox speaks in Rome in the voice of a prophet to the one goading him (*stimulanti*)'.

[4] Ed. Fotheringham, p. 192.

Anaxagoras, the Greek philosopher, had predicted to prove his theory that the sun was made of burning stone.[1] The stone fell, according to Diogenes Laertius,[2] at Aegospotami, but Jerome[3] turned the second element of the place-name, Greek *potami*, into Latin *fluuios*, whence *amnis* ('river') of Patrick's poem.

[1] As Augustine has it in *De Civitate Dei,* xviii.xli: 'unde miror quur Anaxagoras reus factus sit, quia solem dixit esse lapidem ardentem'.

[2] *Diogenes Laertius, Lives of Eminent Philosophers,* ed. and trans. R. D. Hicks (Loeb Classical Library, London, 1925) I, 138 (bk II.10).

[3] Pliny, *Nat. Hist.* II, 149 refers to the event, but, although he also translates the second element of the place-name, he clearly presents *Aegospotami* as a place: *ad* (not *in,* as in Jerome) *Ægos flumen,* and avoids the splash.

An Old English penitential motif

M. R. GODDEN

Recent work on the two major Old English homilists, Ælfric and Wulfstan, has not been lacking, with new editions of their homilies and continued study of their sources and style. The anonymous homilies have received rather less attention, and this has meant that one important Old English homiletic type, the penitential homily, has been largely neglected. These 'exhortations to repentance, illustrated by devotional commonplaces' as the penitential homilies have been called,[1] are fairly rare in the work of Ælfric,[2] the most popular of the Old English homilists, but are common in the Vercelli collection and other anonymous collections like the Blickling Manuscript. They have been neglected, presumably, both because they are anonymous and because they are often composed of standard motifs and topics, unlike Ælfric's sophisticated syntheses of patristic sources and Wulfstan's use of contemporary detail. But we have recently come to accept that the process of selecting and adapting standard formulas and themes which lies behind Old English poetry can be of considerable interest, and the similar process involved in the composition of these penitential homilies seems also deserving of study.

In recent years Joan Turville-Petre has provided two extremely valuable studies of these homilies, and J. E. Cross has produced important work on several themes in the homilies, notably the *ubi sunt* theme.[3] The main concern of both scholars has been 'to trace those Latin works which transmitted devotional commonplaces and formulated their expression in vernacular literature'[4] and to show how the Latin sources have been adapted. It needs pointing out, however, that some of these commonplaces may have originated and been developed in the vernacular literature itself, and that even when a commonplace does have its origin in Latin works a study of its circulation,

---

[1] J. Turville-Petre, 'Translations of a Lost Penitential Homily', *Traditio* 19 (1963), 51.
[2] The best example is homily VII in the Second Series of *Catholic Homilies* (see *The Homilies of the Anglo-Saxon Church: the First Part, containing the Sermones Catholici, or Homilies of Ælfric*, ed. B. Thorpe (London, 1844–6)).
[3] J. Turville-Petre, 'Translations of a Lost Penitential Homily', and 'Sources of the Vernacular Homily in England, Norway and Iceland', *Arkiv för Nordisk Filologi* 75 (1960); and J. E. Cross, 'Ubi Sunt Passages in Old English: Sources and Relationships', *Årsbok Vetenskaps-Societeten i Lund* (1956), and 'The Dry Bones Speak – a Theme in some Old English Homilies', *JEGP* 56 (1957).
[4] J. Turville-Petre, 'Translations of a Lost Penitential Homily', p. 52.

development and use within the vernacular literature may be more rewarding than a study of its ultimate origins. The extent to which Old English homilists drew constructively on each other's work has not been properly recognized. Those homilies which show significant use of expressions and passages from other vernacular works are given the warning labels 'unecht' or 'a catena from various sources' or 'scissors and paste methods' and we tend to neglect them. But both Ælfric and Wulfstan frequently drew on their own earlier work, and Wulfstan often adapted passages and homilies by Ælfric, while Ælfric adapted a passage from the Old English Bede.[1] The use of Old English sources is as valid and can be as interesting as the use of Latin sources. And the penitential homilies in particular often borrow not merely ideas but previously formulated expressions of ideas, sometimes just a sentence and sometimes a whole passage. These expressions are adapted to suit the context and the interests of the individual homilist, but the sense of a traditional or established way of expressing a particular idea in the vernacular is respected and valued.

In this paper I want to look at one particular motif which is rare in Latin works but has a wide circulation in Old English, mainly in penitential homilies. To describe it as a motif is not very accurate since there is a standard form of expression involved as well as a particular idea or set of ideas, but no better term offers itself. The motif runs: it is better to be shamed for one's sins before one man (the confessor) in this life than to be shamed before God and before all angels and before all men and before all devils at the Last Judgement. It occurs in some fifteen Old English works, which can be roughly grouped according to the precise form that the motif takes. A group of seven express the motif in the form of a comparison ('shame now is better than shame later') and all refer to the hosts of angels, men and devils in the same words. A second group of six use a relative clause instead of a comparison ('he who is not shamed now must be shamed later') and refer to the three hosts in several different ways. And the remaining two express the motif in the form of a comparison, like the first group, but do not mention the three hosts. A survey

[1] Wulfstan's use of his own earlier work and of Ælfric is well documented in *The Homilies of Wulfstan*, ed. D. Bethurum (Oxford, 1957). For the major examples of passages which Ælfric drew from his own earlier work see P. A. M. Clemoes, 'The Chronology of Ælfric's Works', *The Anglo-Saxons: Studies in some Aspects of their History and Culture presented to Bruce Dickins,* ed. P. Clemoes (London, 1959), pp. 246–7. Ælfric's use of the Old English translation of Bede was pointed out by Professor Whitelock in her lecture on 'The Old English Bede', *Proc. of the Brit. Acad.* 48 (1962), 79, n. 10. Ælfric also reproduces a sentence from King Alfred's translation of the *Pastoral Care* (this has not, as far as I know, been noticed before): cf. Thorpe, *Catholic Homilies* II, 432, lines 31–4 with *King Alfred's West-Saxon Version of Gregory's Pastoral Care,* ed. H. Sweet, Early English Text Society o.s. 45 and 50 (London, 1871–2), I, 39, lines 16–18. The sentence comes originally from the Old Testament but the Old English is not a close rendering of the Latin and the identity of the two Old English versions cannot be coincidental.

of these examples of the motif will indicate the different forms that the motif takes and the kind of context in which it is set.[1]

The first example in this group occurs in an Old English *Ordo Confessionis* which has traditionally been associated with the Old English pseudo-Egbert *Confessional* and *Penitential*.[2] The *Ordo* occurs together with the *Confessional* and the *Penitential* in two mid-eleventh-century manuscripts, Cambridge, Corpus Christi College 190 and Oxford, Bodleian Library, Junius 121, and on its own in another manuscript of the same period, BM Cotton Tiberius A. iii. R. Spindler, in his edition of the *Confessional*, has argued that the *Ordo* was composed in the second half of the tenth century by the author of the *Penitential* and intended from the start to accompany the *Penitential*.[3] The first part of the *Ordo* describes the procedure for confession: the confessor, with the penitent kneeling before him, questions him on the faith, bids him refrain from various sins and practise various virtues, and concludes with an exhortation to confess everything and with a warning of the dangers of neglecting this advice – a warning expressed in the form of the motif. The various editions of the *Ordo* give a version of the motif based on the Cambridge and Bodleian manuscripts; thus Spindler's reads: 'betere is þe þæt þe sceamige nu her beforan me anum yrmincge þonne eft beforan gode on þam mycelan dome, þær heofonwaru and eorðwaru and helwaru beoð ealle gesomnode'.[4] But the Tiberius manuscript has a version which more closely parallels the form that the motif has in other works; it reads: 'betere þe is þæt ðe scamige nu beforan me anum. þonne eft on domes dæge beforan gode. and beforan eallum heofenwaran. and eorðwaran. and eac helwaran'.[5]

Several short pieces which are very similar to the pseudo-Egbert *Ordo*, all being designed as addresses to be spoken by the confessor to the penitent, also contain the motif, and in a similar form. The first of these pieces occurs in Cotton Tiberius A. iii, separated by forty-three leaves from the same manuscript's copy of the pseudo-Egbert *Ordo*; it was printed by H. Logeman in 1889 but without any discussion of content or sources.[6] It is almost entirely made

---

[1] The study which follows has benefited considerably from the advice of Professor P. A. M. Clemoes.

[2] It has been printed by B. Thorpe in his *Ancient Laws and Institutes of England* (London, 1840) II, 130–6; by R. Spindler in his *Das altenglische Bussbuch (sog. Confessionale Pseudo-Egberti)* (Leipzig, 1934), pp. 170–5; and most recently by J. Raith in the reprint of his *Die altenglische Version des Halitgar'schen Bussbuches (sog. Poenitentiale Pseudo-Ecgberti)*, Bibliothek der angelsächsischen Prosa 13 (1933, repr. Darmstadt, 1964), pp. xli–xlvi. The title *Ordo Confessionis* is Raith's.

[3] Spindler, *Confessionale Pseudo-Egberti*, pp. 160 and 165–8.

[4] *Ibid.* p. 171.   [5] Tiberius A. iii, 96v.

[6] H. Logeman, 'Anglo-Saxonica Minora', *Anglia* 12 (1889), 513–15.

up of passages which occur elsewhere in Old English. There is the motif at the beginning, as part of an exhortation to confession; a passage on penitence based on the Rule of Bishop Chrodegang, with some similarity in wording to the Old English version of this Rule;[1] then a passage on fasting in Lent extracted from a penitential homily by Ælfric;[2] and finally a passage on the procedure for confession drawn from the next chapter of the Rule of Chrodegang, again with resemblances to the Old English version. The motif itself reads: 'micle betere is þam men þæt him scamige her on life beforan anan men. his synna þonne him scyle eft gescamian on godes dome æt foran heofenwaran. and eorðwaran. and helwaran'.[3] This is very similar to the version in the pseudo-Egbert *Ordo* (the Tiberius text), the main differences being that both the confessor and the penitent are here referred to in the third person and that God is not included among the witnesses to the sinner's shame. But there is nothing else to show that the compiler of this address knew the *Ordo*, and if he had known it one would have expected him to borrow more than just the motif from there, since he was clearly quite willing to borrow from vernacular sources and the *Ordo* closely parallels his own work in content. The very next piece in the manuscript, a form of confession, does draw indirectly on the *Ordo*, as Spindler has shown,[4] but the same derivation cannot be assumed for this example of the motif.

Two more of these addresses for use by a confessor occur in an eleventh-century pontifical, BM Cotton Tiberius C. i. They have been printed and discussed by N. R. Ker.[5] Like the pseudo-Egbert *Ordo* and the Logeman piece, they give injunctions against various sins and exhort the penitent to confession, fasting and repentance. The first (Ker's text II) is addressed to an individual and begins with some instruction in the faith which resembles the questioning in the pseudo-Egbert *Ordo* but is in some respects closer to the Latin texts cited as sources for this part of the *Ordo* by Spindler.[6] The motif itself occurs towards the end of the address, following on from an exhortation to the penitent to confess to a priest and do penance if he has failed to observe the preceding injunction to be chaste during the week after Easter. This particular injunction has no parallel in the pseudo-Egbert *Ordo* or its Latin

[1] The equivalent passage is ch. 29 in *The Old English Version of the Enlarged Rule of Chrodegang*, ed. A. S. Napier, EETS o.s. 150 (London, 1916), and ch. 31 in the Latin version printed in Migne, Patrologia Latina 89.

[2] Thorpe, *Catholic Homilies* II, 98, lines 23–31 and 100, lines 9–11 and 19–22. For the corresponding passage in the address see Logeman, 'Anglo-Saxonica Minora', p. 513, line 30–p. 514, line 7 and p. 514, lines 16–21.

[3] Logeman, *ibid.* p. 513.   [4] Spindler, *Confessionale Pseudo-Egberti*, pp. 132–5.

[5] N. R. Ker, 'Three Old English Texts in a Salisbury Pontifical, Cotton Tiberius C. i', *The Anglo-Saxons*, ed. Clemoes, pp. 262–79.

[6] These texts are part of a pseudo-Bede penitential (printed by F. W. H. Wasserschleben, *Die Bussordnungen der abendländischen Kirche* (Halle, 1851), pp. 252–6) and part of the Rule of Chrodegang (ch. 32 in the PL edition).

sources, but the wording of the motif itself is very similar to that of the Tiberius text of the *Ordo*. It reads: 'betere þe is þæt þe sceamige her beforan anum menn þonne beforan ealre heofonware and eorðware. and helware'.[1] The main difference is that God is omitted from the witnesses to the sinner's shame, as in the Logeman piece. The second piece in Tiberius C. i (Ker's text III) is addressed to a congregation. Its list of sins to be avoided and its injunction to love God and practise charity agree very closely in wording with the similar passages in the pseudo-Egbert *Ordo*,[2] but it also includes several injunctions that are not in the *Ordo*. Its version of the motif is similar to the preceding examples but has been rewritten and expanded in such a way as to lose the basic contrast between shame before one man and shame before all beings: 'betere us is micele þæt we her on life ure synna geanddettan. and hi gebetan be ures scriftes tæcinge. þænne se deofol hy brede us forð on domes dæg. and us hearde þonne gesceamie beforan hefonwarum. and helwarum. and eorð-warum. and beforan gode þe ealra mæst is'.[3] The idea that any sins which are not confessed will be laid to the sinner's charge by the devil at the Last Judge-ment goes back at least as far as Alcuin and is extremely common in Old English homilies.[4] For the placing of God after the three hosts there is no parallel in other examples of the motif, but both the Logeman piece and the other piece in Tiberius C. i omit God altogether, and it may be that this piece belongs to the same textual tradition and has had God added again at the end. No other example lists the host of devils before the host of men, and this is probably just a scribal slip.

The last of these addresses for use by a confessor occurs in a margin in an eleventh-century manuscript made up mainly of Latin prayers, BM Cotton Galba A. xiv.[5] The manuscript has been badly burnt and very little of the address remains legible, but the wording of the motif appears to be identical with that of the Tiberius copy of the pseudo-Egbert *Ordo*. From the little else that sur-vives it seems that the address as a whole did not correspond throughout with the *Ordo*.

There are also two homilies which include the motif in a form like that already illustrated. The first is homily XXIX in A. S. Napier's collection of Old English homilies attributed to Wulfstan[6] (this particular homily is not by Wulfstan). The homily urges men to repentance because judgement is at hand, describes the Last Judgement, gives an account of the death of a sinner

---

[1] Ker, 'Three OE Texts', p. 276, lines 38–9.
[2] Cf. Ker, 'Three OE Texts', p. 278, lines 4–10 with Spindler, *Confessionale Pseudo-Egberti*, lines 15–19 and Ker p. 279, lines 2–5 with Spindler lines 22–6.
[3] Ker, *ibid.* p. 279, lines 9–13.　　　　[4] See below, p. 226.
[5] I was led to this text by the admirable index and the description of this manuscript in N. R. Ker's *Catalogue of Manuscripts containing Anglo-Saxon* (Oxford, 1957).
[6] *Wulfstan: Sammlung der ihm zugeschriebenen Homilien*, ed. A. Napier (Berlin, 1883), pp. 134–43.

and of the soul being fetched from the body by devils, and ends by urging men to save themselves from a similar fate by repenting. Almost the whole of the homily is paralleled in the same or very similar wording in other Old English works. The first part on repentance (up to p. 135, line 25) also appears as a set of directions to a confessor, in slightly different wording, in a collection of Old English penitential material in Oxford, Bodleian Library, Laud Misc. 482, and partly also in Napier's homily LVI. There then follows the motif, forming a neat transition from the theme of repentance to the topic of the Last Judgement. The description of the Last Judgement which follows closely parallels part of the Old English poem *Be domes dæge*. The account of the death of a sinner occurs in very similar wording as part of the introduction to an Old English penitential collection in CCCC 201. And in the final section there is a passage from a penitential homily by Ælfric and another which is very similar to the end of Blickling homily v.[1] The homily itself occurs in only one copy, a mid-eleventh-century manuscript from Worcester. The motif reads: 'selre us is mycele and ðearflicre, þæt we ure gyltas andetton anum men her on life, þonne we sceolon eft on þam dome þrowjan sceame beforan gode on his dome and beforan eallum heofonwarum and eorðwarum and helwarum'.[2] Karl Jost suggested that this sentence was based on the pseudo-Egbert *Ordo*,[3] and in its main points it does agree with the Tiberius text of the *Ordo*. But it agrees equally well with other versions of the motif in this group, such as the one in the Logeman piece, and in its opening words it particularly resembles Ker's text III from Tiberius C. i, where the motif begins: 'betere us is micele þæt we her on life ure synna geandettan'.

The other homily is the third of the *Lambeth Homilies* printed by Richard Morris from London, Lambeth Palace Library, 487.[4] This manuscript dates from about the year 1200, but Celia Sisam has shown that, while some of the homilies it contains are probably post-Conquest compositions, others are pre-Conquest works in later dress. She describes the third homily as one of those that 'certainly go back to Old English'.[5] In its main outlines the homily resembles the penitential homilies preserved in Old English manuscripts, dealing with confession, repentance, restitution and penance, though it lacks any eschatological material. It includes several ideas that are popular in the Old English homilies: the point that the devil cannot charge a man at the Last Judgement with sins that he has confessed in this life appears in Napier,

---

[1] All these parallels were noted by K. Jost, *Wulfstanstudien* (Berne, 1950), pp. 203–7, with the exception of the text in Laud Misc. 482, whose resemblance to part of Napier XXIX was pointed out by N. R. Ker, *Catalogue*, p. 421.

[2] Napier, *Wulfstan*, p. 136, lines 1–5.   [3] Jost, *Wulfstanstudien*, pp. 204–5.

[4] *Old English Homilies of the Twelfth and Thirteenth Centuries*, ed. R. Morris, EETS o.s. 34 (London, 1868) (*Lambeth Homilies*).

[5] C. Sisam, 'The Scribal Tradition of the Lambeth Homilies', *RES* n.s. 2 (1951), 110, n. 4. Her reasons with regard to this particular item are not clear to me.

homily XXIX, in Ker's text III from Tiberius C. i and in an unpublished homily in Cambridge, University Library, Ii.4.6;[1] the comparison of the whole age of this world to a twinkling of an eye also occurs, in similar wording, in Vercelli IV and thence in Napier XXX;[2] and the comparison of the man who gives alms from the proceeds of extortion with a man who kills a child and takes its head as a present to the father appears in similar wording in a pentential homily by Ælfric.[3] But in manner and details of content the Lambeth homily is rather different from the Old English penitential homilies, more intimate and specific. The motif appears as part of an exhortation not to hide any sins from the confessor, and reads: 'betere eow is þet eow sceamie biforen þam preoste ane. þenne on domesdei biforen criste. and biforen al hevene wara. and biforen al eorðe wara. and biforen al helle wara. and þa hwepere þine saule feren scal in to eche pine'.[4] The only significant differences here from the version in the pseudo-Egbert *Ordo* are the use of the specific term *preost* and the use of *crist* instead of *God*.

GROUP B

The first example of the motif in this group occurs in a work entitled *In Quadragesima De Penitentia*. This appears among a group of pieces at the end of Ælfric's *Catholic Homilies* in Cambridge, University Library, Gg.3.28 (*c.* 1000) and was printed from that manuscript by Benjamin Thorpe in his edition of the *Catholic Homilies*.[5] It is an admonition to confession and penance followed by a longish summary of the fundamentals of belief. As with many of the other texts discussed in this paper, it includes passages that are also found in other Old English works, in this case homilies of Ælfric: the admonition to confession and penance occurs also in homily XII in Alfric's *Lives of Saints*, and part of the homily on the Catholic faith from the First Series of *Catholic Homilies* is adapted here for the discussion of the doctrine of the Trinity.[6] Most scholars view the *De Penitentia* as entirely the work of Ælfric, but Karl Jost has suggested that it is a compilation of Ælfrician material made by someone other than Ælfric.[7] At first reading it does appear a rather random collection of topics with no single theme or purpose, but the reason for this particular

[1] See Morris, *Lambeth Homilies,* pp. 27-9; Napier, *Wulfstan,* p. 135, lines 25-32; Ker, 'Three OE Texts', p. 279, lines 9-13; and ULC Ii.4.6, 228v 11-15.
[2] See Morris, *Lambeth Homilies,* p. 33; *Die Vercelli-Homilien,* ed. M. Förster, Bibliothek der angelsächsischen Prosa 12 (1932), homily IV, lines 21-4; and Napier, *Wulfstan,* p. 148, lines 11-14.
[3] See Morris, *Lambeth Homilies,* p. 39 and Thorpe, *Catholic Homilies* II, 102, lines 11-13.
[4] Morris, *Lambeth Homilies,* p. 35, line 34-p. 37, line 2.
[5] Thorpe, *Catholic Homilies* II, 602-8.
[6] See Jost, *Wulfstanstudien,* p. 205, n. 1.
[7] See K. Sisam, *Studies in the History of Old English Literature* (Oxford, 1953), p. 166; Clemoes, 'The Chronology of Ælfric's Works', p. 218; and John C. Pope, *Homilies of Ælfric: a Supplementary Collection,* EETS 259-60 (London, 1967-8), I, 144, where the *De Penitentia* is listed as part of the Ælfric canon; and Jost, *ibid.*

collocation is evident once one recognizes its affinity to the standard procedure for confession. The first part serves the same function as the exhortation to confession which occurs in works like the pseudo-Egbert *Ordo*, while the second part replaces the standard questioning on belief in the Trinity and in the general resurrection and on the penitent's willingness to forgive others their sins with more detailed discussion of precisely these points. (Ker's text II from Tiberius C. i similarly substitutes a series of statements of faith for the question-and-answer passage in other addresses.) I see no reason to doubt Ælfric's authorship of the *De Penitentia*, which was presumably designed as an address for use by confessors during Lent.[1] The motif occurs in the first part of the work as part of the exhortation to confession, and reads:

Ne sceamige nánum men þæt he ánum láreowe his gyltas cyðe, for ðan se ðe nele his synna on ðissere worulde andettan mid soðre behreowsunge, him sceal sceamian ætforan Gode Ælmihtigum, and ætforan his engla werodum, and ætforan eallum mannum, and ætforan eallum deoflum, æt ðam micclum dóme, þær we ealle gegaderode beoð. Þar beoð cuðe ure ealra dæda eallum þam werodum, and se ðe nu ne mæg his gyltas for sceame ánum men geandettan, him sceal sceamian ðonne ætforan heofenwarum, and eorðwarum, and helwarum, and seo scamu him bið endeleas. (Thorpe, *Catholic Homilies* II, 602, line 31–604, line 6).

The motif is expressed twice over in different words. The second form is closer to the examples already discussed in its use of the terms 'heofenwarum and eorðwarum and helwarum', whereas the first sentence defines the three hosts more closely as angels, men and devils, but both have a defining relative clause instead of a comparison and both make a more specific reference to confessing sins than do the examples of the motif in group A.

This particular version of the motif occurs again in three different contexts. The first is only slightly different: among the early-eleventh-century additions to a collection of homilies in CCCC 198 is to be found the *De Penitentia* with the last part of Blickling homily x included at the end.[2] Ælfric himself is very unlikely to have been responsible for this addition, but it does provide an interesting example of the kind of composition and adaptation which is common in the Old English homiletic corpus, especially in penitential homilies. The additional passage[3] is highly relevant to the motif and to the *De Penitentia* as a whole, for it summons men to repentance and reminds them that life is transitory by describing an imaginary visit to the grave.

The second new context for this version of the motif is homily XII in Ælfric's

---

[1] Professor Clemoes ('The Chronology of Ælfric's Works', p. 222, n. 4) takes the view that the *De Penitentia* was an extract from an otherwise unknown letter by Ælfric.

[2] Again I am indebted to N. R. Ker's *Catalogue* for this reference (p. 81).

[3] *The Blickling Homilies,* ed. R. Morris, EETS o.s. 58, 63 and 73 (London, 1874–80), 111, line 15–115, line 25.

Lives of Saints,[1] which incorporates the whole of the admonition to confession and penance that forms the first part of the *De Penitentia*. Professor Clemoes takes the view that Ælfric transferred this admonition from the *De Penitentia* to the homily,[2] and this seems very probable. The homily is concerned with the need for repentance, confession and fasting, and intersperses the exhortation with exempla describing the fates of those who neglect the observance of Lent or do not make a true confession. The motif, like the rest of the extract from *De Penitentia*, is taken over with little change of wording.

The third new use to which this version of the motif is put is in London, Lambeth Palace Library, 489 (an Exeter manuscript dated by Ker to the third quarter of the eleventh century). Here Ælfric's homily on the *Pater Noster* from the First Series of *Catholic Homilies* appears with some passages omitted and new ones interpolated from a number of other sources, as Ker has shown,[3] and one of these interpolations is the motif. Among the other additional passages there is one (to the effect that at death our friends fall away and all depends on God) which was extremely popular among Old English homilists, occurring in homilies XXIV, XXX and LVIII in Napier's collection and in an unpublished homily in ULC Ii.4.6;[4] and a passage on the need to know the *Pater Noster* and the Creed which is also used in a homily by Wulfstan and in Napier LVIII.[5] The general direction of the changes is away from instruction and explanation and towards the exhortation to repentance and reminders of the Last Judgement which are characteristic of the Old English penitential homily, and the addition of the motif fits well into this pattern. Generally it may be said that the compiler has used various penitential commonplaces to create a new penitential homily out of Ælfric's original work of instruction and explanation. The motif is made to follow on from Ælfric's point that men pray for forgiveness in this life since there is no forgiveness in the next, and the wording is almost exactly the same as in the *De Penitentia*[6] except for the opening words, which read: 'Ði ne sceamige nanum cristenum menn þæt he andette his synna and bete swa his scrift him tæce',[7] where the *De Penitentia* reads: 'Ne sceamige nanum men þæt he anum lareowe his gyltas cyðe'.

Apart from these four uses of Ælfric's version of the motif, there are two other homilies that contain versions of the motif bearing some resemblance to

---

1 *Ælfric's Lives of Saints*, ed. W. W. Skeat, EETS o.s. 76, 82, 94 and 114 (London, 1881–1900).
2 Clemoes, 'The Chronology of Ælfric's Works', p. 221, n. 2.
3 *Catalogue*, p. 344.
4 See Napier, *Wulfstan*, p. 122, lines 4–9, p. 151, lines 9–14 and p. 306, lines 8–13, and ULC Ii.4.6, 230r13–20.
5 Bethurum, *Homilies of Wulfstan*, no. VIIIc, lines 148–53, and Napier, *Wulfstan*, p. 302, lines 3–8.
6 As Professor Clemoes points out ('The Chronology of Ælfric's Works', p. 221, n. 2), one small variation connects the Lambeth text more closely with the *Lives of Saints* homily than with the *De Penitentia*.
7 Lambeth 489, 35v25–36r2.

Ælfric's version. The first of these is homily XLVI in Napier's collection. This is a fairly typical penitential homily surviving in two copies, of which the earlier belongs to the middle of the eleventh century. It exhorts men to decent behaviour in church, almsgiving, confession and repentance, and urges them to think on the last Judgement, enlivening this exhortation with exempla, drawn from the *Visio Pauli*, describing the death of first a sinner and then a virtuous man, and with a dialogue between a man's sins and his soul. Once again, several passages reappear in other Old English penitential works.[1] The motif is rather ineptly placed between two injunctions to give alms, though its reference to the Last Judgement is picked up a little later; the homilist seems to be running through his devotional commonplaces somewhat thoughtlessly. The motif reads: 'We eow sæcgað to soðan, þæt, se ðe nele her his synna nu andettan his scrifte and betan, swa he him tæcð, hine sceal on domes dæg gesceamjan beforan gode and eallum his halgum and eac eallum deoflum . . .'[2] This resembles Ælfric's version in its use of the relative clause instead of a comparison, in its use of *andettan*, and in its use of more concrete terms instead of *heofenwaran*, *eorðwaran* and *helwaran*, though here the angels and mankind have been replaced by *halgum*, presumably meaning the righteous souls that are not judged and perhaps the angels too. And in the first part there is a further slight similarity of wording to Ælfric's version as it was adapted in the homily in Lambeth 489. But Napier XLVI has no other material in common with any of the four works that use Ælfric's version.

The other homily that contains a form of the motif bearing some resemblance to Ælfric's is an interpolated version of Ælfric's homily for the sixteenth Sunday after Pentecost (from the Second Series of *Catholic Homilies*). This occurs as one of several items which were added in the middle of the eleventh century to an earlier manuscript of Ælfric's First Series of *Catholic Homilies* (BM Cotton Vitellius C. v). The motif occurs in the interpolated section, which has been printed by Professor Pope as item XXVII in his edition of homilies by Ælfric.[3] The interpolation is made up mainly of three exempla describing the deaths of a sinner, a virtuous man and another sinner, but there is some penitential exhortation before and after the exempla (the motif occurs in the passage following the exempla). Professor Pope argues that the exempla (translated from the *Vitae Patrum*) are by Ælfric but that the flanking passages are not, and he suggests that the whole interpolation was extracted from some

---

[1] Thus Napier XLVI, p. 241, line 13–p. 242, line 1 also occurs as Napier XXX, p. 151, lines 14–27; Napier XLVI, p. 232, line 24–p. 233, line 1 and p. 239, lines 8–12 also occurs as Napier LVIII, p. 302, line 28–p. 303, line 12; and the dialogue between a man's sins and his soul also occurs alongside the *Institutes of Polity* in Junius 121.

[2] Napier, *Wulfstan*, p. 238, lines 10–13.

[3] Pope drew attention (*Homilies of Ælfric*, pp. 772–4) not only to this example of the motif but also to the ones in Napier XXIX, Napier XLVI and the *De Penitentia*.

lost anonymous homily, in which Ælfric's exempla had previously been combined with other material, and then added to Ælfric's homily for the sixteenth Sunday after Pentecost.[1] Like so many of the penitential works with which this paper is concerned, this interpolation is made up largely of passages that also occur or occurred in other Old English homilies. Apart from the motif, which is of course in many other works, there are the exempla, which were presumably originally issued by Ælfric as part of another homily, and passages of exhortation which, as Pope has shown, also occur in a homily by Wulfstan, and to these can be added the last sentence of the interpolation which occurs in a slightly different form in Napier's homily xxx.[2] The motif itself is given twice, in consecutive sentences:

betere is manna gehwylcum þæt him her on worulde (befor)an anum menn for his gyltum sceamige, þonne him sceamige (eft on) domesdæg beforan gode sylfum, and beforan eallum his englum, (and be)foran eallum heofonlicum werede, and beforan eallum eorðlicum were(de), and beforan eallum deoflum. Hit his eall soð þæt we gyt secgan wyllað: (Ðam) þe nele her nu his synna andettan his scrifte, and betan swa he him tæcð, him sceal on domesdæg sceamian beforan gode sylfum, and eallum his halgum and eallum deoflum. (Pope, *Homilies of Ælfric*, xxvii, lines 109–17)

The second of these sentences is clearly very closely related to the passage in Napier xlvi (the two or three lines that follow the motif in both works are also almost identical). The first sentence has the motif in a quite different form. It was described by Pope as an adaptation of the version of the motif in Ælfric's *De Penitentia*, but its affinity is rather with the examples in group A, all of which express the motif in the form of a comparison as this one does. In fact its closest resemblance is to the version in Vercelli homily viii, which has not been included within either group since it resembles group A in expressing the motif in the form of a comparison but does not have the reference to 'heofonwaran and eorðwaran and helwaran' which characterizes that group.

OTHERS

Vercelli viii's version of the motif reads: 'selre is, þæt man beforan anum men his gylta scamige þonne eft on domes-dæge beforan Gode sylfum and beforan his englum and beforan eallum þam heofen-cundan weorode'.[3] The

---

[1] Pope, *ibid.* p. 772.

[2] Cf. 'Ealle þa synna þe we her wyrceað, ealle hi beoð eft on us sylfum gesewene and geopenode, buton hi ær her on worulde gebette beon' (Pope xxvii, lines 121–3) and 'ðær þonne beoð on us sylfum gesyne and opene ealle þa gyltas, þe we æfre gefremedon and gedydon on þisum life ongean godes willan, buton hi beon ær her on worulde gebette gode to willan and us sylfum to þearfe' (Napier, *Wulfstan*, p. 149, lines 23–7).

[3] Vercelli viii, lines 12–15. Here and in other quotations from the Vercelli homilies I have silently incorporated minor corrections to the text proposed by the editor.

main similarity to Pope xxvii is the mention of both the angels and the heavenly *werod*, a tautology which appears in no other version, but there are other similarities of wording. There is of course the difference that the Vercelli homily refers only to the angels and not to the hosts of men and devils, but there is reason for thinking that the other two hosts were present in the source and were omitted by the author or scribe of the Vercelli homily.[1] Vercelli viii is mainly a description of the Last Judgement, with a long speech by the Judge, and the motif is used near the beginning to establish a relationship between the listener in the present and the Judgement in the future. The sources would appear to be mainly Latin: nothing in the homily apart from the motif reappears in similar form in other Old English works, and Professor Willard has shown that the long speech by the Judge is a condensation of a homily by Caesarius of Arles and that the opening passage may be based on the first homily of Gregory the Great[2] (though Gregory provides no parallel for the motif). But if these were the direct sources for the homily they have been very freely rewritten, and it may be that there were lost vernacular sources intervening.

My last example of the motif is rather different from all the others but seems to be related to them. It occurs in the Old English poem known as *Christ III* in the Exeter Book. *Christ III* is not a penitential work but a dramatic account of the events of Doomsday. Beginning at line 1262 the poet describes the miseries of the damned at the Last Judgement, and great emphasis is laid on their shame at having their sins revealed to all beings – God, the host of angels, all men and the devil.[3] The sins are dramatically viewed as stains on the souls of the damned, made visible through their bodies which have become as transparent as glass. After a few lines describing the envy that the damned feel for the righteous the poet returns to the subject of their shame before the assembled hosts, and this is the crucial passage (my italics):

> *þær hi ascamode,*   scondum gedreahte,
> swiciað on swiman;   synbyrþenne,
> firenweorc berað,   *on þæt þa folc seoð.*
> *Wære him þonne betre*   *þæt hy bealo-dæde,*
> *ælces unryhtes,*   *ær gescomeden*
> *fore anum men*   eargra weorca,
> godes bodan sægdon   þæt hi to gyrne wiston
> firendæda on him.   (1298–1305a).

The point of view is different, with the poet looking back from the Last Judgement to life in this world, instead of forward to the Last Judgement;

[1] See below, p. 237.   [2] R. Willard, 'Vercelli Homily viii and the *Christ*', PMLA 42 (1927).
[3] 1272–81. I quote from *The Exeter Book*, ed. G. P. Krapp and E. V. K. Dobbie, The Anglo-Saxon Poetic Records 3 (New York, 1936).

the reference to the shame of the damned before the assembled hosts is diffused over the whole fifty-line description instead of being crystallized in a few words following the reference to confession, as in the other versions of the motif; and instead of God and the three hosts the poem has merely *þa folc*. But the basic point of the motif, that it is better to confess now and be shamed before one man than to be shamed before everyone at the Last Judgement, is certainly there. E. B. Irving has shown that the source for this part of the poem was a sermon by Caesarius of Arles,[1] but, as Irving points out, this has no reference to confession. It seems likely that the emphasis in the Latin source on the sinner's shame at the Last Judgement reminded the poet of the Old English motif.

This survey shows that the motif had a considerable circulation. It occurs in addresses to be spoken by a confessor, in homilies by Ælfric and others, and in a poem. The manuscripts in which it appears range in date from about 975 (the Vercelli Book and the Exeter Book) to about 1200 (the Lambeth homilies), with many of them clustering around the middle of the eleventh century. The geographical spread of the manuscripts is also extensive: Cotton Tiberius A. iii, containing the pseudo-Egbert *Ordo Confessionis* and the address printed by Logeman, comes from Canterbury; Junius 121, containing another copy of the *Ordo*, and Hatton 113, containing Napier XXIX, were both written at Worcester; Cotton Galba A. iv, containing a fragmentary address for a confessor which uses the motif, probably comes from Winchester; the two confessional texts in Cotton Tiberius C. i were copied down at Sherborne; and Lambeth 489, with its composite homily using Ælfric's version of the motif, comes from Exeter.[2] The other manuscripts cannot be placed but no doubt some of them came from still other centres. When and where these texts were actually composed is less certain, though it is known that Ælfric's *De Penitentia* and his *Lives of Saints* XII were composed at Cerne Abbas in the last decade of the tenth century.[3] The address printed by Logeman, Napier XXIX, the homily in CCCC 198, the Lambeth 489 homily and Pope XXVII cannot have been composed before the eleventh century, since they all draw on the work of Ælfric (and the Lambeth 489 homily and Pope XXVII draw also on Wulfstan).

Some notion of the way in which this motif and others were used and transmitted by Old English writers can be gained by considering some of the motifs and topics which tend to appear with this one. In several works the motif is followed immediately by another, rather more common, one to the effect that all will be revealed at the Last Judgement and each man must then give

[1] E. B. Irving, 'Latin Prose Sources for Old English Verse', JEGP 56 (1957), 588–95.
[2] For the provenance of all these manuscripts, see Ker, *Catalogue*.
[3] See Clemoes, 'The Chronology of Ælfric's Works'.

account for what he has done in this life, good or evil. It is of course based on II Corinthians v.10: 'Omnes enim nos manifestari oportet ante tribunal Christi, ut referat unusquisque propria corporis, prout gessit, sive bonum, sive malum.' In the Junius manuscript of the pseudo-Egbert *Ordo* this motif is in a form close to the scriptural text (it does not appear at all in the other two manuscripts of the Ordo),[1] in Ælfric's *De Penitentia* and in Pope xxvii the emphasis is on the fact that all will be revealed,[2] and in Vercelli viii, Napier xxix and the address printed by Logeman there is a modified form with the notion of man's inability to hide anything from God at the Last Judgement.[3] *Christ III* too has a trace of this last idea.[4] Another, minor, motif that sometimes precedes the main one is the exhortation that the penitent should omit no sin in his confession, however great or small. This occurs in Vercelli viii, Napier xxix and Lambeth homily iii.[5] There are also particular topics or scenes which occur more than once. One such topic is the death of a sinner or a righteous man seen in a vision, with devils or angels coming to fetch the soul from the body. Three such visions are described in Pope xxvii; the descriptions, based on the *Vitae Patrum*, are by Ælfric but were almost certainly not composed to go with the motif – the two elements were combined by a later compiler. Napier xlvi contains accounts of two similar visions, based on the *Visio Pauli*. And Napier xxix includes a description of yet another such vision, probably drawn from a penitential address which occurs in CCCC 201 but going back ultimately to a Latin account of the vision of Macarius.[6] Another such topic is the visit to the grave of a relative or friend, which occurs in two homilies that use the motif, Lambeth homily iii and the homily in CCCC 198.

Such similarities of content might be explained by assuming that in each case the homilies concerned had a common source from which they derived both the main motif and the other motifs and topics which they have in common, or that one homily borrowed all these elements from another. Thus one might suppose that Lambeth homily iii and the CCCC 198 homily had a common source which contained both the main motif and the visit to the grave. But this does not fit the evidence. The versions of the main motif in Lambeth homily iii and CCCC 198 belong to two different groups and are not at all closely related. Conversely, Napier xlvi's version of the motif is very closely related to the one in Pope xxvii but its visions of the death of a sinner and the death of a righteous man are quite unrelated to the rather similar visions in the

---

[1] See Spindler, *Confessionale Pseudo-Egberti*, p. 172, n. to line 31.
[2] Thorpe, *Catholic Homilies* ii, 604, lines 2–3; and Pope, *Homilies of Ælfric*, no. xxvii, lines 121–3.
[3] Vercelli viii, lines 17–20; Napier, *Wulfstan*, p. 136, lines 5–8; and Logeman, 'Anglo-Saxonica Minora', p. 513, lines 14–16.
[4] 1310–11a.
[5] Vercelli viii, lines 10–11; Napier, *Wulfstan*, p. 135, lines 7–14; and Morris, *Lambeth Homilies*, p. 35, lines 30–1.
[6] See above, pp. 230 and 226.

Pope homily, going back ultimately to a different Latin source. Napier xxix's visions go back to yet another Latin source and in any case its version of the motif does not belong to the group to which Napier xlvi and Pope xxvii belong. Similarly, Napier xxix and *Lives of Saints* xii have in common not only the motif but another short passage as well: Napier xxix almost certainly derived this passage from the *Lives of Saints* homily but it cannot have taken its version of the main motif from there. Such similarities in the selection of motifs, topics and other passages are thus not generally due to textual relationships but reflect the common interests of authors working independently from the inherited stock of penitential literature. (The similarities of content between Vercelli viii and *Christ III* may be another example of this.) Where there *is* evidence that one work borrowed the main motif from another there is rarely evidence that any other material has been borrowed from the same source. For instance, the Lambeth 489 homily almost certainly took its version of the main motif directly or indirectly from Ælfric's *Lives of Saints* xii,[1] but it drew on eight other Old English homilies as well and so far as the *Lives of Saints* homily is concerned took nothing but the motif. The authors of these penitential works relied heavily on existing work in the vernacular, as I have tried to show, but they worked in a very independent fashion, selecting individual motifs, topics and passages from various sources and combining them in different ways.

This necessarily complicates the problem of establishing the transmission of the motif with which I am primarily concerned here, but some points can be made. The only attempt to ascertain the origins of the motif has been by Spindler, the editor of the pseudo-Egbert *Confessional*, who suggested as a source for the version of the motif in the pseudo-Egbert *Ordo Confessionis* a sentence from the Rule of Chrodegang which reads: 'Nimis enim improbus est qui ante oculos Dei peccat et homini confiteri erubescit.'[2] There is in fact a much closer parallel than this in a letter by Alcuin: 'Melius est habere unum hominem testem peccatorum suorum in salutem animae suae, quam spectare accusationem diabolicae fraudis ante Judicem omnium saeculorum et ante angelorum choros, et totius humani generis multitudinem'.[3] The letter, written to the monks of Ireland, survives in a ninth-century manuscript which was written on the continent but was in England at least by the end of the tenth century.[4] A still closer parallel has been pointed out to me by Dr Audrey Meaney of Macquarie University. It occurs in a homily attributed to another Englishman, St Boniface, and reads: 'Et melius est uni homini confiteri

---

[1] See above, p. 229.　　　　　　[2] Spindler, *Confessionale Pseudo-Egberti*, p. 147.
[3] PL 100, col. 502. The letter is also edited as no. 280 in E. Dümmler, *Epistolae Karolini Ævi* ii, Monumenta Germaniae Historica, Epistolae 4.
[4] The manuscript is BM Harley 208. For the provenance, see Ker, *Catalogue*, p. 304.

peccata, quam in illo tremendo judicio coram tribus familiis, coeli terraeque, et inferorum, publicari, et confundi pro peccatis, non ad emendationem, sed ad poenam perpetuam.'[1] There can be little doubt that this, or something closely related to it, was the ultimate source for the motif as it appears in Old English works. The only qualification needed is that most of the Old English examples mention God as a witness of the sinner's shame, before the three hosts, and Alcuin has this feature but the Boniface sentence does not; but this may be coincidental.

It has been customary to assume that all the examples of the motif hitherto identified in Old English stem from the one in the pseudo-Egbert *Ordo*.[2] This was a reasonable assumption so long as it was believed that the Rule of Chrodegang was the Latin source of the motif, as of other parts of the *Ordo*. But since it is now clear that this was not the case,[3] there is no reason to suppose that the *Ordo* version has any special status and that it was not merely derived from a source which it shared with the other Old English examples.

The examples of the motif in group A all have the same expression for the three hosts present at the Last Judgement – 'heofonwaru and eorðwaru and helwaru' – and are likely to go back to a single source which contained this expression. Textual similarities suggest some possible relationships within this group[4] but there is nothing very definite. The version in the pseudo-Egbert *Ordo* could be the earliest, since Spindler dates this work to the second half of the tenth century[5] and none of the others can be dated earlier than the eleventh century – the address printed by Logeman and Napier XXIX are certainly eleventh-century.[6] But there is nothing to show that the version in the *Ordo* was the source for the others in group A: none of the texts involved shows any signs of drawing other material from the *Ordo* (although many of them deal with similar subjects) except for Ker's text III from Tiberius C. i, and the wording of the motif in this text is very different from the *Ordo*'s.[7]

The examples of the motif in group B are characterized by their use of a relative clause instead of the original comparison, and presumably they all go back to some writer who made this substitution. There are reasons for thinking that this writer was Ælfric. Of the six texts in group B, the *De*

---

[1] Sermo IV § 6 (PL 89, col. 851D). The authenticity of the fifteen sermons attributed to Boniface is in doubt. Objections have been raised by, amongst others, J. A. Giles (*Sancti Bonifacii Opera Omnia* (London, 1844) II, 268) and H. Hahn ('Die angeblichen Predigten des Bonifaz', *Forschungen zur deutschen Geschichte* 24 (1884)). Both scholars consider the sermons to be more characteristic of a period slightly later than the time of Boniface.

[2] See Spindler's discussion of the *Ordo* in the introduction to his edition; Jost, *Wulfstanstudien*, pp. 204–5; and Pope, *Homilies of Ælfric*, p. 774 and n. 2.

[3] The version of the motif in the Tiberius manuscript of the *Ordo*, which Spindler printed as a variant, is closer to the Boniface sentence than is the version in Spindler's main text, based on the Cambridge and Oxford manuscripts.

[4] See above, p. 225.
[5] Spindler, *Confessionale Pseudo-Egberti*, p. 160.
[6] See above, p. 233.
[7] See above, p. 225.

Penitentia and *Lives of Saints* XII are of course by Ælfric; the composite homily in CCCC 198 clearly derives from the *De Penitentia*; the composite homily in Lambeth 489 derives its example of the motif from *Lives of Saints* XII; Pope XXVII draws heavily on Ælfric for other material; and Napier XLVI's example of the motif is identical with Pope XXVII's and must have the same origin. The use of a relative clause in the form 'se þe . . . se' is characteristic of Ælfric's writing, and he seems to have known a version of the motif in the original form of a comparison, since in what is probably his earliest use of the motif, in the *De Penitentia*, he uses the expression 'heofenwarum and eorðwarum and helwarum', which otherwise occurs only in group A versions. Possibly, then, all the examples in group B stem from Ælfric's rewriting of one of the group A examples, or of something very like them.

Vercelli VIII's version of the motif must be taken in conjunction with the first of the two examples in Pope XXVII, to which it is clearly related.[1] Vercelli VIII mentions only one of the three hosts, the angels, whereas Pope XXVII gives all three: it seems likely that their common source had all three hosts and that the second and third were subsequently omitted by Vercelli VIII, since the Boniface sentence has all three. The Vercelli Book also leaves out one of the three hosts (the devils) when they are referred to again in the context of the Last Judgement in homily X, and here a reference to 'heregas þreo' remains as evidence that the third host was certainly included originally.[2] The reasons for leaving out the second and third hosts in Vercelli VIII can probably be guessed: the reference to all the devils would not have been in accordance with orthodox Latin representations of the Last Judgement;[3] the reference to all mankind would have contradicted the point made a little later in the homily that some men would not be brought to the Last Judgement;[4] and by referring only to God and the angels the homilist or reviser would have brought his version of the motif more into line with Matthew XVI.27, which he quotes a few lines later. Pope XXVII, though later than the Vercelli homily, must thus derive its text of the motif not from Vercelli VIII itself but from some source lying behind Vercelli VIII which mentioned all three hosts. This may have been merely another version of the Vercelli homily that was in this respect closer to the original, for variant texts of other Vercelli homilies, preserving a different manuscript tradition, were circulating in the first half of the eleventh century and the variant text of Vercelli I at least often shows substantial differences in detail and wording from the text in the Vercelli Book.[5] This version of the

---

[1] See above, pp. 231–2.

[2] See *Il Codice Vercellese,* ed. M. Förster (Rome, 1913), 66v20. Another version of this homily, Napier XLIX, has the devils as well as the other two hosts at this point; see below, p. 238.

[3] See below, p. 238.   [4] Vercelli VIII, lines 44–7.

[5] The variant version of Vercelli I occurs in CCCC 162, CCCC 198 and CCCC 303, and Oxford, Bodeleian Library, Bodley 340. See the variant readings reported by Förster in his edition.

motif on which both Vercelli VIII and Pope XXVII drew seems to have been related to the group A versions rather than to go back independently to the Boniface homily or some similar Latin text, for it resembles the group A versions in including God as a witness of the sinner's shame (as the Boniface homily does not), in using the expression 'beforan anum men . . . sceamige' where the Boniface homily has 'uni homini confiteri peccata', and in rendering 'publicari et confundi' by the one word 'sceamige'.

The relationship of *Christ III*'s version of the motif to the others is less clear, for its resemblance is more in content than in form of expression. Yet it has the expression 'gescomeden fore anum men', which corresponds with the 'sceamige beforan anum men' of the versions in group A, Vercelli VIII and Pope XXVII rather than with the 'uni homini confiteri peccata' of Boniface or the 'habere unum testem peccatorum suorum' of Alcuin. This suggests that *Christ III*'s version does not go back independently to the Boniface homily but shares an intermediate source with the other versions. The connection between *Christ III* and Vercelli VIII noted by Willard may be significant.

One particularly interesting fact that emerges is the peculiarly Anglo-Saxon character of the motif. Not only did it circulate widely in Old English writings but the only two Latin works in which I have been able to find it were written by Anglo-Saxons – Alcuin and Boniface.[1] Moreover an important element of the motif, the notion of three hosts present at the Last Judgement, is itself characteristic of Anglo-Saxon writers: the usual representation of the Last Judgement in continental works (as in Alcuin's letter) has the angels and all mankind present, and sometimes the devil as prosecutor, but not the whole host of devils, whereas the concept of the three hosts, as in Boniface's homily, is very common in Old English writings generally. Its clearest expression is in Napier's homily XLIX (which survives in the Vercelli Book, the Blickling Book and several other manuscripts): 'gearelice witan þas heregas þreo, þa ðe mid syndon (an is se heofonlica ðreat, se ðe mid færeð and þe þenað; oðer is þæt eorðlice mægn, þe þu her samnast, and to dome cumen is; þridde is þæt helcunde wered, þe hider com, to ðam þæt heo woldan þine domas gehyran, and hu ðu þam forworhtum scrifan woldest)'.[2] The Latin source for this part of the homily contains no reference to the three hosts. Another, less explicit, mention of the three hosts comes in the fourth Vercelli homily: 'we stælan sculon on domes-dæge beforan ealles middangeardes deman and beforan eallum menniscum cynne; and ealle hellemægen þis gestal gehyrað. and eal engla werod and heah-engla beoð þy mete beforan Gode . . . and eall hel-warena mægen cymþ to þam dome, þæt hie þæt gestal gehyren and hu he þam

---

[1] Assuming that the 'Boniface' sermons are authentic; see above, p. 236, n. 1. If, as Hahn argues, they are Carolingian in origin, the use of the motif may reflect the influence of Alcuin.
[2] Napier, *Wulfstan,* p. 254, lines 11–17.

forwyrhtum deman wille'.[1] (These last two lines bear a close resemblance to the last part of the previous quotation, and hence the two examples of the concept may not be completely independent.) There is also a reference to the three hosts at the Last Judgement in Blickling homily VII: 'se ilca Scyppend gesittan wile on his domsetle: him biþ beforan andweard eal engla cynn & manna cynn, & eac swylce werigra gasta'.[2] Another reference appears in the Old English poem *Lord's Prayer II*:

> Ne magon we hit na dyrnan,   for ðam þe hit drihten wat,
> and þar gewitnesse beoð   wuldormicele,
> heofonwaru and eorðwaru,   helwaru þridde.[3]

And Wulfstan too refers to the three hosts: 'ðærto gesamnod wyrð eall heofonwaru and eall eorðwaru and eall hellwaru, and sceall þonne manna gehwylc gescad agyldan . . . þurh Godes mihte bið eal astyred ge heofonwered ge eorðwered ge hellwered'.[4]

The motif discussed in this article is one of many elements which recur in Old English homiletic and penitential literature, used in different ways by different authors. Its particular interest lies in the light that a study of it throws on modes of composition and the relations between texts; in its use of a set form of words, slightly modified each time but generally adhered to, over a wide range of texts; in its primarily Anglo-Saxon character; and in its neat formulation of a relationship between the two concerns that are central to the Old English penitential genre – exhortation to repentance and warning of future judgement.

[1] Vercelli IV, lines 107–14.   [2] Morris, *Blickling Homilies*, p. 83, lines 8–10.
[3] *The Anglo-Saxon Minor Poems*, ed. E. V. K. Dobbie, ASPR 6 (New York, 1942), lines 93–5. Similarities between parts of this poem and the motif as it appears in Napier XXIX have been noted by L. Whitbread ('"Wulfstan" Homilies XXIX, XXX and Some Related Texts', *Anglia* 81 (1963)), who suggests that the poem was a source for the motif. The evidence adduced does not seem to me to substantiate this view; the sermon by Boniface affords a much closer parallel to the motif than the poem does.
[4] Bethurum, *Homilies of Wulfstan*, no. VII, lines 107–9 and 115–16.

The cross as Christ's weapon: the influence of heroic literary tradition on *The Dream of the Rood*

MICHAEL D. CHERNISS

In spite of all that is known of the religious, cultural and literary background of *The Dream of the Rood* in general, the genesis of its form, and especially of its most immediately striking and unique feature, the device of the speaking cross, has so far resisted attempts at explanation and remains something of a mystery. Albert S. Cook long ago called attention to similarities between the mode of portrayal of the cross and the medieval traditions of epigram, epigraph and riddle, while not going so far as to suggest that these traditions had a direct influence on the poet.[1] Now it is true, of course, that our earliest text of the poem is the series of inscriptions on the Ruthwell Cross, but these inscriptions are strikingly different from all others from the Anglo-Saxon period through which inanimate objects are personified and speak. The inscription on Alfred's Jewel, 'Ælfred mec heht gewyrcean', for instance, and those, some of them in the first person, in Latin and English, on the blades, hilts and scabbards of various swords and knives[2] are generally quite brief – limited to a simple statement of the object's name, its maker's name or that of its owner – are seldom metrical and, most important, are not couched in the kind of heroic diction used in the poem. While it is quite possible that the poet sensed an analogy between such inscriptions and his personification of the cross, what these inscriptions manifestly lack is the literary quality intrinsic to his personification – whether on the Ruthwell Cross or in the Vercelli Book. Only a *literary* explanation can account for this.

In 1940 Margaret Schlauch attempted to demonstrate that the source of literary influence was classical and medieval Latin poetic tradition.[3] Pointing out that discourse by inanimate objects was a fairly common device in Latin verse and observing that formal Latin rhetoric treated prosopopoeia as one

---

[1] *The Dream of the Rood*, ed. Albert S. Cook (Oxford, 1905), pp. xliii–lii. More recently W. F. Bolton, 'Tatwine's *De Cruce Christi* and *The Dream of the Rood*', *ASNSL* 200 (1963), 344–6, has demonstrated some rather striking correspondences between Tatwine's Latin riddle and the Old English poem, but he admits that there is no proof of the direct influence of either poem upon the other.

[2] See Hilda Ellis Davidson, *The Sword in Anglo-Saxon England* (Oxford, 1962), pp. 42–50, 77–82 and 96–103.

[3] Margaret Schlauch, '*The Dream of the Rood* as Prosopopoeia', *Essays and Studies in Honour of Carleton Brown*, ed. P. W. Long (New York, 1940), pp. 23–34.

of its topics, she concluded that *The Dream of the Rood* owed its form, if not to the direct influence of Latin poems employing the device of prosopopoeia, at least to the Anglo-Saxon poet's familiarity with the study of rhetoric in the medieval schools. Her view has been widely accepted. But since she found no particular source for the portrayal of the cross and, indeed, the poems which she cited as formal analogues, like *De Nuce*, are scarcely like *The Dream of the Rood* at all in tone or seriousness of purpose, it seems likely that the influence of Latin rhetoric, however vital, was only at the level of technique.

The other potential source of literary influence is, of course, vernacular heroic poetry. That the cross speaks like an Anglo-Saxon retainer in the service of a secular lord is the accepted view of the poem's style in relation to this tradition.[1] Since, within the ancient cult of Christ as king, early Germanic poetry portrays him as the warrior chief,[2] it certainly follows that if an Anglo-Saxon poet chose to represent the cross as a human follower of Christ, he would portray it as an Anglo-Saxon retainer. None of this, however, accounts for the poet's striking portrayal of the cross as at once inanimate object and heroic retainer. The cross is not personified as fully human, for, even as it speaks, we remain aware of its non-human nature. In this paper I should like to consider as a background to this portrayal the element of personification present in the conception of weapons and trappings of war traditional to heroic literature. There is, I think, a specific analogy between the poet's treatment of the cross and this quasi-humanizing tradition. It seems to me that the idea of the warrior-Christ coalesced in the poet's mind with certain habits of thought and diction inherent in this tradition.

In a warrior-society like that depicted in Old English heroic poetry, where a man depends upon his weapons for his survival, it is probably inevitable that a close personal relationship should exist between a warrior and his weapons and war-gear. For example, Beowulf's remark that 'Nu sceall billes ecg, / hond ond heard sweord ymb hord wigan' (2508b–9)[3] implies an alliance between a man and his weapon as they unite in a common cause. The convention of personification is extremely useful to the poet as a means of expressing this relationship; in *Beowulf* weapons and war-gear often appear to have lives and thoughts of their own. When Beowulf prepares to dive into the haunted mere, for instance, the poet briefly describes his 'warrior's garments' in such terms. The corslet should 'sund cunnian' (1444b); it 'beorgan cuþe' (1445b) the

---

1 See especially Robert E. Diamond, 'Heroic Diction in *The Dream of the Rood*', *Studies in Honor of John Wilcox*, ed. A. Dayle Wallace and Woodburn O. Ross (Detroit, 1958), pp. 3–7.

2 See especially Rosemary Woolf, 'Doctrinal Influences on *The Dream of the Rood*', *MÆ* 27 (1958), 144–5. For a recent discussion of Cynewulf's portrayal of Christ in the Ascension as a Germanic chief, see Peter Clemoes, 'Cynewulf's Image of the Ascension', *England Before the Conquest: Studies in Primary Sources presented to Dorothy Whitelock*, ed. Peter Clemoes and Kathleen Hughes (Cambridge, 1971), pp. 293–304, esp. 294–6.

3 References are to *Beowulf and the Fight at Finnsburg*, ed. Fr. Klaeber, 3rd ed. (Boston, 1950).

body of its wearer. The bright helmet 'hafelan werede' (1448b) when it '... meregrundas mengan scolde, / secan sundgebland' (1449–50a). The sword's name is Hrunting; it has never failed any man in battle and this is not the first time 'þæt hit ellenweorc æfnan scolde' (1464). Beowulf speaks of Hrunting as if it were to be his companion in the coming battle: 'ic me mid Hruntinge / dom gewyrce' (1490b–1a). When Grendel's mother attacks, Hrunting '... agol / grædig guðleoð' (1521b–2a) upon her head, but it fails the prince at his need and for the first time its glory is diminished:

> ... se beadoleoma   bitan nolde,
> aldre sceþðan,   ac seo ecg geswac
> ðeodne æt þearfe;   ðolode ær fela
> hondgemota,   helm oft gescær,
> fæges fyrdhrægl;   ða wæs forma sið
> deorum madme,   þæt his dom alæg. (1523–8)

Nevertheless, when Beowulf returns the sword to Unferth, he praises it as a strong friend in battle and does not blame it for its failure: '... he þone guðwine godne tealde, / wigcræftigne, nales wordum log / meces ecge' (1810–12a).

Examples of the personification of weapons are fairly frequent in *Beowulf* and Neil D. Isaacs has discussed them exhaustively.[1] Such personification in Old English is not confined to *Beowulf*, however. In the first *Waldere* fragment, for instance, we hear of Waldere's sword, Mimming, which will fail no man who can wield it and will help Waldere against Guthhere (I, 2b–4a and 24–6a).[2] Mimming is a famous sword; it is 'Welande[s] worc' (I, 2), and a part of its history is given in the second *Waldere* fragment (II, 4–10). Waldere's byrnie (II, 18–24) is also personified; should an attack come, 'Ne bið fah wið me' (II, 22b). In *Finnsburh* defensive weapons seem themselves to respond to the enemy attack: 'scyld scefte oncwyð' (7a).[3]

In the early heroic literatures of western Europe famous swords always have proper names – Excaliber, Durendal, Gram, Tyrfing, Skofnung – and these names alone suggest that the habit of personification was widespread, even when the particular context furnishes no further information concerning a weapon's deeds or inner nature. Hilda Ellis Davidson, in her able study of Anglo-Saxon swords, observes that it is 'hard to determine how far the naming of swords was a literary convention only, and how far it existed as a practice among Anglo-Saxons and Vikings of an earlier period', though she finds some

---

[1] 'The Convention of Personification in *Beowulf*', *Old English Poetry: Fifteen Essays*, ed. Robert P. Creed (Providence, 1967), pp. 215–48.
[2] References are to *The Anglo-Saxon Minor Poems*, ed. E. V. K. Dobbie (New York, 1942), pp. 4–6.
[3] References are to *The Anglo-Saxon Minor Poems*, pp. 3–4.

archaeological evidence for the 'imaginative personification of the weapon at an early date'.[1] As a literary convention, however, there can be no question of its pervasiveness, which suggests that it is something more than a merely rhetorical device. Isaacs relates it to a habit of mind shared by Anglo-Saxon singer and audience:

This convention is accepted because it seems to have been understood by singer and audience that each thing in nature from man to stone and each thing created by man as well has a living, moving spirit of its own. Somewhere along the line there must have been a personification in the merely rhetorical sense, but this step was a mechanical, almost automatic operation within the framework of an already-established convention, not the framework upon which the convention was built.[2]

In *Beowulf*, *Waldere* and *Finnsburh* the poets conceive of some weapons, at least, as quasi-sentient beings with distinctive attributes and habits, and their personification follows from this conception.

Generally speaking, the weapons and armour that are personified in Old English heroic verse appear as warriors, as thanes of the lords whom they serve. Nægling fails to bite for Beowulf 'þonne his ðiodcyning þearfe hæfde' (2579), just as Hrunting fails 'ðeodne æt þearfe' (1525a). It is in terms of the lord–thane relationship that a poet can most forcefully express the closeness of the personal bond between a warrior and his weapons. Beowulf praises Hrunting by observing that 'þæt wæpen duge' (1660b); Isaacs has pointed out that *dugan* in *Beowulf* describes primarily persons, except when it is involved in personifications,[3] and its relationship to the noun *duguð* 'the collective body of tested warriors', is obvious. Even after Hrunting proves useless to Beowulf, he still considers it a good 'guðwine' (1810a), as we have seen. Anglo-Saxon warriors earn glory (*dom*) through praiseworthy deeds (*lofdædum*),[4] and Hrunting has similarly won 'dom' which fails for the first time against Grendel's mother (1527b–8). Failure in battle is ordinarily disgraceful for a warrior, which explains why Waldere speaks of his trustworthy byrnie as being 'ealles unscende' (II, 20a).

Swords are the weapons most frequently and fully depicted in Anglo-Saxon heroic literature. Their quasi-personalization combines the human attributes of the warrior-thane with the non-human ones of the sword itself. The ringing of the blade when it strikes is the 'singing' of swords like Hrunting (*Beowulf* 1521b–2a). A blade's efficiency depends upon its hardness and durability, as seems to be assumed even when this is not explicitly mentioned: this actual hardness and the seasoning of the veteran warrior are blended when a dangerous sword in *Beowulf* is described as 'scurheard' (1033a) and when

---

[1] *The Sword*, p. 102.   [2] Isaacs, 'Personification', p. 216.   [3] *Ibid.* p. 221.
[4] See, e.g., *Beowulf* 949–55 and *Widsith* 140–3.

Hrunting is said to be 'ahyrded heaþoswate' (1460a). Swords sometimes possess extra-natural properties. Their beauty consists in their brightness; they shine as if the light were their own. Hrunting is 'se beadoleoma' (*Beowulf* 1523a), another sword 'hildeleoma' (1143b); when the battle begins in the *Finnsburh* fragment, 'Swurdleoma stod, / swylce eal Finnsburuh fyrenu wære' (35b–6). Often swords are given supernatural or legendary associations; the one in Grendel's mother's cave, like those of Wiglaf and Eofor, is the work of giants.[1] Hand in hand with such mysterious origins go the various curses, taboos or peculiarities of behaviour attributed to a sword such as the one in the cave.

Reliable swords and battle-gear are commonly described by Old English poets as 'treasures', primarily because of their usefulness to their possessors. Hrothgar gives Beowulf a 'mære maðþumsweord' (1023a); Scyld goes forth on the sea with a great deal of 'madma', 'frætwa', with 'hildewæpnum ond heaðowædum, / billum ond byrnum' (36b–42); Waldere's Mimming is 'maðma cyst' (1, 24b). I have discussed elsewhere the function of treasure in the heroic world of *Beowulf* as the material manifestation of the moral virtue and worth of its possessor,[2] and since fine swords are ordinarily 'treasures', their possession denotes worthiness in the warriors who have them. Thus, because of the gold-adorned sword that Beowulf gives him, the Danish shore guard is 'on meodu-bence maþme þy weorþra / yrfelafe' (1902–3a); he augments his personal honour as he adds to his store of treasure. The heroic custom of a Germanic lord's giving rings, weapons and other valuables to his retainers represents his acknowledgement of the honour and glory that they have earned (or are expected to earn) in his service; Heremod was a bad lord because he failed to offer these physical symbols to his followers: 'nallas beagas geaf / Denum æfter dome' (1719b–20a).

Not only are weapons and war-gear often treasures; personified as loyal retainers they are entitled themselves to receive treasure as the symbol of their service. This takes the form of the gold and gems with which they are adorned. Anglo-Saxon warriors do not wear uniforms bedecked with medals and campaign ribbons; their valour and heroism can be seen only in their material treasures. In like manner, the durability of a good sword or helmet, its loyal service, must be reflected in its fine adornments. To decorate an object is, in heroic convention, to 'honour' it, to make its inherent worth apparent. Beowulf is 'wæpnum geweorðad' (250a), as is his troop of followers 'wæpnum gewurþad' (331a), while Hrothgar gives warriors 'hordweorþunge' for their deeds (951–3a); and by the same token Beowulf's helmet is 'since geweorðad'

---

[1] *Beowulf* 1558a, 1562b, 1679a, 2616a and 2979a.
[2] 'The Progress of the Hoard in *Beowulf*', *PQ* 47 (1968), 473–9. See also Ernst Leisi, 'Gold und Manneswert im *Beowulf*', *Anglia* 71 (1953), 259–73.

(1450b), the saddle given him by Hrothgar is 'since gewurþad' (1938b) and Waldere's byrnie 'golde geweorðod' (11, 19b).

The Old English Riddle 20 offers the most fully developed description we have of a sword as a heroic retainer.[1] Here a personified sword speaks, enumerating many of its essential qualities in a manner which should make its identity readily apparent. Emphasis falls upon its appearance, the service it performs and its lord's appreciation of this service. It is a fine weapon: '. . . wunderlicu wiht, on gewin sceapen, / frean minum leof, fægre gegyrwed' (1–2). Its 'byrnie', probably the blade,[2] is 'bleofag', and the hilt is equally brilliant (3b–4a). It wears all of the treasures with which fine swords are customarily adorned: 'wir' (4a and 32a), a 'wælgim' (4a), 'sinc' (6b and 10a), 'gold' (8a), 'seolfor' (10a), 'hringas' (23b), 'bearngestreon' (27a) and 'hæleþa gestreon' (31b). More than any human retainer it is completely subject to the will of its lord, who directs it to battle (5–6a); and again its non-human nature is implied when it is said often to kill 'gæstberend' (8b–9a). Because it injures people, it is hated and condemned by their friends (15b–17a),[3] but if it obeys its lord ('gif ic frean hyre'), it will partake of the treasures of men (24b–7a). Its lord, in his function as ring-giver (23b), gives it the treasure it bears (3–4 and 9b–10a), and praises its deeds in the mead-hall (10b–12). The statements that it has no avenging kinsman, may not increase its race and may not marry (17b–23 and 27b–31) are the sort of enigmatic remarks, inappropriate to a typical human warrior, which resolve themselves when this 'warrior' is properly identified as a sword.[4] Finally, the sword angers a 'wife', either because it could take her man from her as he goes to battle or, more plausibly, because she begrudges it its gold and gems (32–5a). The sword cares nothing for such feminine 'battle', however (35b).

In this riddle the convention of personification has become to some degree an end in itself, apart from any role which the personified weapon might play in a narrative context. Basic aspects of a sword are presented and seem meant to be appreciated by an audience familiar with swords as they appear in heroic

---

[1] All references to the Riddles are to the text of *The Exeter Book,* ed. G. P. Krapp and E. V. K. Dobbie (New York, 1936), pp. 180–210 and 229–43. It should be noted here that, while most commentators have accepted 'sword' as the subject of this riddle, the alternative solution 'hawk' has been argued, most recently by Laurence K. Shook, 'Old English Riddle no. 20: *Heoruswealwe*', *Franciplegius: Medieval and Linguistic Studies in Honor of Francis Peabody Magoun, Jr.,* ed. Jess B. Bessinger, Jr, and Robert P. Creed (New York, 1965), pp. 194–204.

[2] Davidson, *The Sword,* p. 153. I owe to Mrs Davidson's discussion of this riddle the interpretation of some of its more puzzling details.

[3] I suggest that the difficulty of interpreting lines 15b–17a may be resolved by repunctuating the text as follows: 'Oft ic oþrum scod, / frecne æt his freonde fah eom ic wide, / wæpnum awyrged.' Read 'I have often injured another [and so] I am savagely outlawed far and wide by his friend, condemned among weapons.'

[4] Mrs Davidson plausibly explains lines 22–3 as meaning that if it 'leaves' its lord and returns to the foundry to be melted down, then, and only then, can it produce 'offspring'.

poetry. Whatever intellectual pleasure this little poem could have afforded as a riddle must have grown directly out of the audience's perception of the speaker as a familiar object presented in a manner familiar but at the same time, because divorced from its more usual surroundings, misleading. The accepted convention of personification has been extended from third-person description of quasi-sentient objects to an object's first-person description of itself, but the habit of mind responsible for the convention remains precisely the same. Beyond this, because it presents mostly recognizable, familiar aspects of its subject, the riddle tells us what aspects of a sword the Anglo-Saxons would single out for attention. And the same can be said for the various other Old English riddles dealing with weapons and war-gear.

The speaker in Riddle 5, a shield, dwells upon the 'wounds' which it has suffered and its continuing endurance of these wounds. It distinguishes itself from human warriors only in that it expects no aid in battle and cannot be healed by any physician. The horn of Riddle 14 presents itself as a 'wæpen-wiga' (1a) and gives a full account of its functions as a battle-horn and a drinking-horn. Like the sword of Riddle 20, it refers frequently to the treasures which adorn it (2b, 3a, 7b, 9a, 11b and 15a). Riddle 53, about a battering-ram, holds particular interest here because of its structural similarity to the speech of the cross in *The Dream of the Rood*. This object lived a pleasant life as a tree in a forest, but one day it was 'deope gedolgod' (6a), 'dumb in bendum, / wriþen ofer wunda' (6b–7a) and 'wonnum hyrstum / foran gefrætwed' (7b–8a). Now it fights in battles and plunders the hoard in the company of warriors (8b–11a), leading them into dangerous places (11b–13). The subject of Riddle 55, probably a sword-rack, while not in itself a weapon, is identified through its association with weapons.[1] It resides on the floor of the hall, bearing four kinds of wood (of which it is made) and gold and silver (with which the swords are decorated) as well. It awaits those treasures which are its lord's weapons ('. . . oft wæpen abæd / his mondryhtne, maðm in healle, / goldhilted sweord'; 12b–14a). The helmet of Riddle 61 is 'frætwed' (8a) and resides in a chest until a woman fetches it for her lord. If his 'ellen dohte' (7), he places it upon his head (5–9a). Riddle 71 is fragmentary, but enough remains to identify the speaker as a sword or dagger. It speaks of its place of origin, a field[2] – like that of the battering-ram – and of the transformation of the raw material into an artifact by 'fire and file'. Like the sword of Riddle 20, it is 'wire geweorþad' (5a) and it speaks of its 'lord' (9b) and of the injuries it causes ring-adorned

---

[1] Frederick Tupper, Jr, *The Riddles of the Exeter Book* (Boston, 1910), pp. 188–90, solves this riddle as 'cross', but for a cross to be spoken of as 'rode tacn' (5–7a) would destroy the enigmatic quality desired in a riddle.

[2] Davidson, *The Sword*, p. 155, takes the 'field' to be the anvil on which the blade is forged, but this reading seems forced.

warriors (5b–8a).[1] Most commentators accept the solution 'lance' or 'spear' for Riddle 73. It speaks of its early life in a forest – again like that of the battering-ram – and its subsequent transformation into a weapon. It now serves a 'frean' (8a), 'gif his ellen deag' (9b). The damaged latter portion of the riddle is largely unintelligible, but the words 'dome' and 'mæ[r]þa fremman' (10a and 11b) appear to refer to its duties in battle, and a few later lines clearly refer to its appearance. Riddle 80 may be solved either as 'horn'[2] or 'sword'.[3] In any event, it is a piece of war-gear, '. . . æþelinges eaxlgestealla' (1), 'fyrdrinces gefara' (2a), 'cyninges geselda' (3a) and 'frean minum leof' (2b).

Riddle 30 is worth considering here, although its speaker is not a weapon but most probably a tree.[4] Its importance for us lies in its similarity in structure to Riddles 53 and 73 and its similarity in structure and content to the speech of the cross in *The Dream of the Rood*. The object first describes itself growing in a forest (1–4), like the battering-ram and the lance (or spear). It then rather abruptly begins to describe its transformed condition as a cross which is worshipped by men and women for its ability 'ycan upcyme eadignesse' (9). The structure is thus typical of those riddles which begin with the object as raw material and move to its transformed state as an artifact for human use. If the solution 'tree-cross' is correct, this riddle not only exemplifies the mental habit of relating an object to its materials, but also offers a specific analogy with *The Dream of the Rood*, for in both poems the cross speaks of its origin as a tree and of its new life as an object of worship.

Although they probably owe their original inspiration to the Anglo-Latin riddle tradition, and although Tupper, whose attitude toward suggested resemblances to Latin enigmas was scarcely congenial, had to acknowledge some Latin influence upon many of the Old English riddles,[5] the weapon-riddles appear typically Anglo-Saxon and heroic in their approach to their subject matter. Tupper certainly overstates his case in minimizing the importance of direct Latin influence on the Old English riddles, but nevertheless his general comments upon the 'closeness to life' of the entire *Exeter Book* collection seem to me for the most part just for the weapon-riddles:

The English poems smack far less of abstractions and of classical and biblical lore than the problems of Aldhelm; nor are they eked out with liberal borrowings from Isidore's *Entymologies*, like those of Eusebius . . . All these riddles, whether the subject be animate or inanimate, have at least one common characteristic, their human

---

[1] Davidson, *The Sword*, p. 155, takes the gold-adorned weeper of lines 5b–6 to be a woman, but there is no indication of the sex of this figure in the text.
[2] Tupper, *Riddles*, pp. 217–18.   [3] Davidson, *The Sword*, pp. 155–6.
[4] See Krapp and Dobbie, *The Exeter Book*, pp. 337–8, for a brief summary of the proposed solutions and for further references.
[5] See the notes to the individual riddles in his edition.

interest . . . The riddler may neglect place and form and color of his subject, but he constantly stresses its uses to mankind. Indeed, men are in the background of every riddle-picture; and the subject is usually viewed in its relation to them. The most significant expression of this relation is found in the motif of Comitatus, or personal service of an underling to his lord and master, that forms the dominant idea in many of our poems.[1]

I do not wish to suggest that the poet who composed *The Dream of the Rood* was directly influenced by the Old English riddles, or that his poem and the riddles shared a particular literary influence in the form of a common source. Quite apart from the possibility of direct relationships, what is important is that these poems share certain elements which appear to have been common in Old English heroic tradition. The riddles portray those aspects of their subjects that would have been most readily apparent to their poets and audiences, and by employing the heroic diction and the convention of personification they reveal fully certain tendencies inherent in the portrayal of the same subjects in narrative contexts. The tendencies which they reveal reappear in *The Dream of the Rood*, not, I suggest, because the poet necessarily knew the riddles, but because his habits of thought and expression had been shaped by the same poetic tradition as that which shaped the habits of the riddle poets. Given his formulation of Christ as heroic warrior, the poet of *The Dream of the Rood*, I believe, would have found it easy, indeed logical, to conceive of the cross – the only inanimate object which faces Christ's enemies with him – as the 'weapon' of heroic literary tradition. It would have seemed natural to him to envisage the close personal relationship between Christ and his cross as essentially the same as the intimate bond between a hero and his weapons in heroic poetry.

For one thing, I think certain obvious similarities in appearance between the cross and the favourite weapon of the Anglo-Saxon nobleman, the sword, would have presented themselves to the imagination of the poet. The basic shapes of the sword and cross are, of course, the same, and this essential similarity, however much it might be obscured by various kinds of artistic stylization in the plastic representation of crosses or by variation in the proportions of the vertical and horizontal cross-members, or by decorative embellishments of swords such as large pommels on hilts, could never be obliterated. Perhaps more immediately striking is the similar manner in which many splendid Germanic swords and equally splendid crosses are decorated: gold or silver on both is fashioned into intricate patterns, which are inlaid with enamel-work or semi-precious gems, principally garnets. The gold and

[1] *Ibid.* pp. lxxxvi and lxxxviii. Davidson, *The Sword,* pp. 156–7, comes to similar conclusions concerning the spirit of the Old English sword-riddles in comparison to the bookish products of Tatwine and Aldhelm. She finds the Latin riddles 'products of the study, not of men who were familiar with the sword as a weapon'. A reading of Riddle 35, translated from Aldhelm's *Lorica*, likewise gives one an impression of intellectuality quite unlike the heroic weapon-riddles.

gems which decorate the cross in *The Dream of the Rood* (6b–9a and 14b–17)[1] could equally well decorate a fine Germanic sword.

In function, as well as appearance, swords and crosses might well seem to an Anglo-Saxon to be related. Just as the cross is the symbol of the kingly power of Christ, the 'wealdendes treow' (17b), so the hilt of the temporal ruler's sword appears to have been the symbol of his kingly power.[2] The custom of swearing oaths upon one's own sword or upon one's King's, reflected in the word 'aðsweord' in *Beowulf* (2064a), is traditional in heroic culture,[3] and may owe its persistence through the centuries at least partially to Christian associations of the hilt with the cross. Further, the function of the cross, like that of any venerable weapon, is that it assists, and is in fact indispensable to, the defeat of its lord's enemies; as our poem makes clear, it is the 'sigebeam' (13a and 127a) of the 'sigora wealdend' (67a).

More particularly, several attributes of the cross in *The Dream of the Rood* parallel those ascribed to weapons in Old English poetry. I have already drawn attention to the correspondence, noticed by Cook,[4] between the cross's description of its origin in a forest and subsequent transformation into an artifact (28–33a), and Riddles 53 ('Battering-Ram'), 71 ('Sword' or 'Dagger') and 73 ('Lance' or 'Spear'), as well as 30 ('Tree-Cross'). The cross is 'wudu selesta' (27b) just as a sword may be 'iren(n)a cyst' (*Beowulf* 673a, 802b and 1697a). The brightness of the cross, 'leohte bewunden, / beama beorhtost' (5b–6a), recalls that of virtually every good sword and helmet in Old English, and its appearance, 'hwilum... / beswyled mid swates gange, hwilum mid since gegyrwed' (22b–3), is analogous to the two states of a sword, bloodstained in use and bejewelled when honoured as a possession.

Above all, it is the use of the same kind of personification – partly human, partly inanimate, partly supernatural – that reveals the basic affinity of the cross to the weapons of heroic tradition. The cross calls attention to its 'wounds' (46–7a and 62b), as does the shield in Riddle 5. Standing firm (42b–3 and 45b) while being soaked in Christ's blood (48b–9a), the cross recalls the swords hardened in the blood of battle in *Beowulf*.[5] The metaphorical use of *swat* for 'blood' (20a and 23a) is shared with *Beowulf*, where it appears to be a traditional metaphor for blood shed in battle, often with specific reference to the blood drawn by swords (1286a, 1460a, 1569a, 1606a, 1668a and 2966b); in *The Dream of the Rood* this 'sweat' signifies 'earmra ærgewin' (18–20a). The cross is Christ's 'bana' (66a), just as weapons causing death in *Beowulf* are 'banan' (2203b and 2506b). Like the sword of Riddle 20, it is en-

---

1 References are to *The Vercelli Book*, ed. G. P. Krapp (New York, 1932), pp. 61–5.
2 Davidson, *The Sword*, pp. 76–7 and 213.
3 *Ibid.* p. 185. Francis B. Gummere, *Founders of England*, with supplementary notes by Francis P. Magoun, Jr (New York, 1930), p. 249; first published as *Germanic Origins* (1892).
4 *The Dream of the Rood*, pp. xlvii–li.   5 See above, p. 245.

tirely subject to its lord's will and is an instrument, indeed an embodiment, of that will, as a weapon is but as a human retainer can never fully be. Like a loyal retainer it has the instinct to protect its lord, and, like a weapon, it has the ability to do so, but its first duty is that of obedience: 'Ealle ic mihte / feondas gefyllan, hwæðre ic fæste stod' (37b–8). The valour of this 'retainer' consists in its endurance of severe torment with and for its lord. Because of this service of suffering which it has given to Christ, and because of the spiritual service which it continues to perform for mankind, the cross is now honoured throughout the world (80b–2a). The outward manifestation of this service, of the inner virtue of the cross, is the treasure with which, like a worthy retainer or a worthy sword, it is adorned. Christ 'geweorðode' the cross by choosing it from the trees of the forest (90–1a); the cross served him loyally, and is now honoured by the gems that cover it: 'gimmas hæfdon / bewrigen weorðlice wealdendes treow' (16b–17). Moreover, quite apart from the gems and precious metals which adorn it, the cross itself is 'beacna selest' (118b), the token of salvation (117–21) to be honoured ('weorþian') by all (126b–9a), just as a fine sword may be a 'treasure', by virtue of its intrinsic value as an object useful to human beings. This intrinsic value of the cross, which the poet treats in the latter portion of the cross's speech and in the closing meditation of the dreamer (78–156), is supernatural, like that of a supernaturally created and endowed weapon. Indeed the poet never loses sight of the basically non-human nature of his speaking cross. Even though he presents it as a retainer, it is only briefly a part of the comitatus on Calvary. The personification is never permitted completely to take on its human identity. Throughout, the cross remains an object at once inanimate, human and supernatural and it is as such that it stands in the closest possible relationship to Christ the 'geong hæleð' (39a). If we infer that the poet regarded this object as analogous to the weapons of heroes in literary tradition we can account for some of its most striking features, as we have seen, and elucidate some of the interplay of the poem's powerful images. For instance, if 'sigebeam' (13a) carries implications of a victorious weapon (cf. 'sigewæpnum', *Beowulf* 804a), added point is given to the metaphorical stains and wounds of sin suffered by the dreamer (13b–14a).

Thus it appears likely that the portrayal of the cross in *The Dream of the Rood* had its genesis in the poet's mental fusion of the two traditions which were his legacy as a Christian and an Anglo-Saxon. Roman Christianity advocated such fusions whenever they were practicable; it attempted, usually with great success, to assimilate whatever it could of the culture of its pagan converts to its own teachings and customs. The poet who composed our poem united aspects of the Germanic heroic and Christian traditions by drawing upon the resources of his own imagination. He drew, I suggest, upon the heroic convention of the personification of weapons for his portrayal of the cross of

Christ: in his mind these habits of thought and diction, which he had absorbed along with his native poetic tradition, coalesced with the idea of the crucifixion, and, perhaps in a direct relationship with Old English riddles, perhaps in conjunction with the Latin rhetorical figure of prosopopoeia, or perhaps under the influence of both of these, produced his central poetic conceit, the speaking cross. In this synthesis he achieved much more than a merely rhetorical success.[1] Christianity enabled him to transcend secular heroic ideals and heroic literary tradition enabled him to illuminate Christian ideals. In *The Dream of the Rood* the mystery of the resurrection, the victory of Christ over his enemies through his death at their hands, finds its Germanic heroic correlative in the paradox of a weapon-retainer which by becoming the instrument of its lord's death becomes the instrument of his victory.

[1] Cf. Peter Clemoes, *Rhythm and Cosmic Order in Old English Christian Literature* (Cambridge, 1970), pp. 7–11, esp. 11.

The thematic significance of *enta geweorc* and related imagery in *The Wanderer*

P. J. FRANKIS

Our uncertainty about the full implications for poet and audience of particular words and phrases is a serious obstacle to our understanding of Old English poetry. With regard to the final section of *The Wanderer* (73–115) some advances in our knowledge and understanding have already been made, notably by Professor J. E. Cross in his studies of the Latin antecedents of two passages:[1] he shows that lines 80–4 use the motif of the Fates of Men, with the Old English *sum . . . sum . . .* structure translating the Latin *alius . . . alius . . .*, and that lines 92–6 are based on the *ubi sunt* topos of the transience of life. This information gives us a better grasp of the impact these lines may have had on an informed Anglo-Saxon audience and helps us to evaluate the poem; but many details still remain unclear. The present study is concerned with the context of these two passages (73–105), and in particular with the puzzling image of 'the work of giants' that has been destroyed by God (85–7).

The dominant themes in this part of the poem are the desolation of the world (73–4, 85 and 110), the loss of pleasure (79a, 86 and the *ubi sunt* passage, 92–6) and death (78b, 79b, 91, 99–100 and the *sum . . . sum . . .* passage, 80–4). With these themes are associated recurrent images of ruined buildings and walls (76b, 78a and 98), wind and storm (76a, 101b and 105), cold and its concomitants (77, 102–3a and 104b–5) and darkness (89, 96 and 103b–4a). In all this there is an obvious coherence, and in general it seems to meet Keats's requirement that 'poetry should surprise by a fine excess, and not by singularity'; the imagery of lines 85–7, however, is unexpected and perplexing, and is not likely today to 'strike the reader as a wording of his own highest thoughts':

> Yþde swa þisne eardgeard   ælda scyppend
> oþþæt burgwara   breahtma lease
> eald enta geweorc   idlu stodon.[2]

---

[1] J. E. Cross, 'On *The Wanderer*, lines 80–4', *Vetenskaps-Societetens i Lund Årsbok* (1958–9), 77–110 and 'Ubi Sunt Passages in Old English', *ibid.* (1956), 25–44. An earlier draft of the present study was read to a research seminar at the University of Newcastle upon Tyne in December 1970, and it profited from the discussion on that occasion; at a later stage Professor Clemoes was most generous in suggesting further improvements.

[2] 'Thus the creator of men laid waste this place until, deprived of the revelries of their inhabitants,

The connotations of the image of the work of giants become clearer when the other occurrences of the phrase *enta geweorc* in Old English poetry are examined; in *The Wanderer*, however, there is a small difficulty that may be mentioned first, namely, the precise meaning of *eardgeard*, literally something like 'native enclosure', hence presumably 'the place where one belongs'. In this passage it may refer specifically to the ruined buildings described in lines 75ff. (and could then be translated 'city', as recent editors of the poem suggest), or by analogy with *middangeard* it may mean 'world', either specifically in the sense of 'earth', or more generally referring to the whole physical and cultural milieu of the ruins and their builders, the 'world' of the ancients. The one other extant occurrence of *eardgeard* (*Christ* 55a) shows an identical ambiguity, since there it refers to the New Jerusalem and could equally well mean 'city' (i.e. Jerusalem) or 'world' (in the sense of 'other world', the heavenly world as opposed to the earthly, the natural home of the saints). I prefer to take *eardgeard* in *The Wanderer* 85a as referring to the ruins of 75ff., either directly as 'city' or (more probably) obliquely as 'the world of these buildings'.

The phrase *enta geweorc*, sometimes varied as *eald enta geweorc* (as here) or as *enta ærgeweorc*, occurs eight times altogether in extant Old English poetry. Three of the instances are in *Beowulf* (1679a, 2717b and 2774a) and the others (besides *The Wanderer* 87a) are in *The Ruin* (2b), *Andreas* (1235a and 1495a) and the *Cotton Maxims* (2a). In *Beowulf* 1679a it is applied to a sword that is also referred to in 1681a as *wundorsmiþa geweorc*. In 2717b it refers to the dragon's lair (probably an ancient burial-mound):

> Ða se æðeling giong
> þæt he bi wealle,   wishycgende,
> gesæt on sesse;   seah on enta geweorc,
> hu ða stanbogan   stapulum fæste
> ece eorðreced   innan healde.[1]

And in 2774a it refers to the dragon's treasure, the *hord* of 2773b. In the first and third of these cases the *entas* seem to be creatures similar in function to the dwarfs of Norse myth as workers in metal and makers of treasures (i.e. *wundorsmiþas*), but in the second they are the builders of ancient stone monuments, and their work is referred to in the words *stanbogan*, *stapulum* and *eorðreced*, and presumably *wealle*.

The phrase is likewise applied to ancient stone structures in *The Ruin*, *Andreas* and *Maxims*, but does not refer to metal-work or treasure outside

the old works of giants stood desolate.' For all Old English verse quotations I have followed the text in the Anglo-Saxon Poetic Records.

[1] 'Then the prince went and sat on a seat by the wall, pondering deeply; he looked on the work of giants, how the stone arches, set firm on pillars, supported the eternal earth-building inside' (2715b–19).

Beowulf. In *The Ruin* 2b it refers to the ruined buildings that are the subject of the poem.

> Wrætlic is þes wealstan;   wyrde gebræcon,
> burgstede burston,   brosnað enta geweorc.
> Hrofas sind gehrorene,   hreorge torras,
> hrungeat berofen,   hrim on lime,
> scearde scurbeorge   scorene, gedrorene,
> ældo undereotone.
>
> .   .   .   .
>
>   Oft þæs wag gebad,
> ræghar ond readfah,   rice æfter oþrum,
> ofstonden under stormum.[1]

In this passage *enta geweorc* could be taken in a generalized sense as being applicable to any imposing ruins, perhaps implying that the buildings mentioned must be the work of giants because all stone buildings (or, at any rate, an important class of stone buildings) were erected long ago by superhuman beings, a usage comparable to that in *Beowulf* 2717b; but the whole poem gives the phrase a particular application to Roman ruins,[2] and the use of Latin loan-words (1a, *weal-*, and 3b, *torras*) may support this. In line 7 the former inhabitants are referred to as *waldend wyrhtan* (either as one word or as two), implying that they were rulers as well as builders, which, of course, is appropriate to the Romans. Similar Roman associations are present in both examples in *Andreas*. In 1235a the reference is to stone-paved roads:

> Drogon deormodne   æfter dunscræfum,
> ymb stanhleoðo,   stærcedferþne,
> efne swa wide swa   wegas to lagon,
> enta ærgeweorc,   innan burgum,
> stræte stanfage.   Storm upp aras
> æfter ceasterhofum,   cirm unlytel
> hæðnes heriges.[3]

In this part of the poem the country of the Mermedonians, in which the scene is set, is apparently envisaged as being like a Roman province: St

---

[1] 'The stone-work of the walls is wondrous: the fates broke it, the fortified places fell apart, the work of giants crumbles; the roofs are fallen in, the towers are ruined, the barred gate is plundered; there is frost on the mortar, the defence against the weather is gaping, torn and collapsed, undermined by age ... Lichen-grey and stained red, this wall repeatedly endured one kingdom after another, still standing under storms' (1–6a and 9b–11a).

[2] For the identity of the ruins concerned see *Three Old English Elegies*, ed. R. F. Leslie (Manchester, 1961), pp. 22–8, and the works cited there.

[3] 'They dragged the bold-hearted man along the hill-passages [?], the strong-souled hero round the hillocks of stones, right as far as the roads extended, the ancient works of giants, the stone-adorned streets within the city. A storm arose among the courtyards of the town, a great outcry of the heathen host' (1232–8a).

Andrew, on arrival there, sleeps near a *ceastre* (828a) by a military road (831b, *herestræte*), and in the above passage the same Latin-based words recur (1236a, *stræte*, and 1237a, *ceaster-*). The poet may have thought in historical terms of St Andrew evangelizing the Roman empire, or he may have thought in terms of his own environment, seeing St Andrew as a Christian missionary in a pagan country, like St Augustine among the Anglo-Saxons, and describing the land of the Mermedonians in terms of England of the missionary period, with the Roman roads and other buildings that must have been so conspicuous there. Here, then, as in *The Ruin, enta geweorc* is applied to structures that are referred to partly by Latin-derived words, and may be thought of as having some kind of Roman associations. In 1495a the phrase is used of the prison in which St Andrew is confined by the Mermedonians; it refers specifically to *stapulas*, which are subsequently (1498a and 1523a) said to be of stone:

> He be wealle geseah   wundrum fæste
> under sælwage   sweras unlytle,
> stapulas standan,   storme bedrifene,
> eald enta geweorc.[1]

The prison has previously been named by a Latin loan-word (1460a, *carcerne*), and, of course, there are the same kind of Roman associations in the Mermedonian setting here as in 1235a. In the final example, the *Cotton Maxims* 2a, *enta geweorc* is applied to *ceastra* with stone walls:

> Cyning sceal rice healdan.   Ceastra beoð feorran gesyne,
> orðanc enta geweorc,   þa þe on þysse eorðan syndon,
> wrætlic weallstana geweorc.   Wind byð on lyfte swiftust,
> þunar byð þragum hludast.[2]

Here the context is minimal, but *wrætlic weallstana geweorc* is to be compared with *The Ruin* 1a. The use of the Latin loan-word, *ceastra*, in conjunction with the phrase found in *The Ruin*, again supports some degree of Roman reference.

All four of these examples of *enta geweorc* in *The Ruin, Andreas* and the *Cotton Maxims* refer to stone structures of great size, and evidently of great antiquity, and the same characteristics appear in the ruins of *The Wanderer*. Moreover, all four passages in *The Ruin, Andreas* and *Maxims* associate with the phrase imagery that is also to be found in *The Wanderer*: *The Ruin* 4b, *hrim on lime*, corresponds to *The Wanderer* 77a, *hrime behrorene*; and references to wind or storm are common to all five: *The Wanderer* 76a, *winde biwaune*, and

---

[1] 'He saw by the wall mighty pillars, wondrously firm, along the wall of the hall, columns standing, beaten by storms, the ancient work of giants' (1492–5a).

[2] 'A king must hold his kingdom. The towns that are on this earth are visible from afar, the skilful work of giants, the stone-work of the walls is a wondrous construction. The wind is swiftest in the air; thunder, when it occurs, is the loudest noise' (1–4a).

101b, *stormas cynssað*; *The Ruin* 11a, *under stormum* (and perhaps 5a, *scur-*); *Andreas* 1236b, *Storm upp aras*, and 1494b, *storme bedrifene*; and *Maxims* 3b, *Wind byð on lyfte swiftust*. In *The Ruin* the storms are a poetic image representing the process of change with the passage of time, and the same applies to *Andreas* 1494b (in each case the structures have endured what time and the natural forces of destruction could do against them); in *Andreas* 1236b, however, the storm is purely metaphorical, meaning 'tumult, uproar', the metaphor being explained by *cirm*, 'shout, outcry', in the next line. Finally, and most remarkable of all, in the *Maxims* we have a string of apparently disjointed gnomic sayings with no necessary or logical connection between one maxim and the next; but so strong is the association between the work of giants and wind or storm imagery that one maxim clearly determines the next, just as in *Andreas* 1236b the metaphor of *storm* for 'uproar' is determined by *enta ærgeweorc* in the preceding line. These passages thus show a complex of related themes in association with the phrase *enta geweorc*. First, the ancient stone buildings to which the phrase refers are a symbol of durability (like the house built on rock in the biblical parable), as in *The Wanderer* 76b and 97–8, *The Ruin* 9–10 and *Andreas* 1492–5, the theme of durability being embodied in the verbs *stondan* and *gebad*. Secondly, when in ruins, they demonstrate the opposite principle of mutability and transience, as in *The Wanderer* 78a and *The Ruin* 1–6, the theme being expressed in words like *woriað, gebræcon, burston* and *brosnað*. Imagery of wind and storm emphasizes on the one hand the capacity of ancient buildings to survive these forces (as in *The Wanderer* 76, *The Ruin* 11 and *Andreas* 1494), and on the other the failure of ruined buildings to serve their primary function of giving shelter from the weather.

The possibility of a Roman connotation in this imagery of ancient stone buildings, evidently thought of as the work of a technologically superior past, is important. In *The Ruin* it is indisputable and in *Andreas* it is arguable, and the pervasive presence of Latin loan-words is strikingly relevant (*The Ruin*: *weal-* and *torras*; *Andreas*: *Stræte, ceaster-* and *wealle*, with *carcerne* shortly before; *Maxims*: *ceastra* and *weall-*; and *The Wanderer* 76b, 80a, 88a and 98a: *weal-*). If *The Wanderer* is taken as containing, among other things, the meditations of an Anglo-Saxon poet pondering on the Roman ruins of his own country, a further dimension is added to the poem. To see this specific local occasion in its imagery enhances our response to it, just as Shakespeare's line 'Bare ruin'd choirs, where late the sweet birds sang' gains in impact if we relate it to the writer's situation in an England that must still have been richly scattered with monastic remains some sixty years after the dissolution of the monasteries. In each case a poet writing on the transience of life finds an appropriate image in the visible fact that the mighty buildings of a former time fall into ruin and decay; in Shakespeare's case, of course, the relation between theme and image is indirect, since the ruined choirs are a metaphor for leafless trees, which are in turn an image of the passing of time and life; in *The Wanderer* the relationship is direct, but is enriched by the way in which the walls both fall victim to time and show some capacity to withstand it.

The instances of *enta geweorc* in *Beowulf*, we can now see, stand somewhat apart from the others, and this distinction may contain a hint of the origin and evolution of the phrase. Possibly in *enta geweorc* as the work of smiths we have an older Germanic concept of the same type as the Norse myths of dwarfs, while in *enta geweorc* as the work of builders in stone we have a specifically English development influenced by the cultural remoteness of the Anglo-Saxons from the Roman remains in the English landscape (as opposed, for example, to the situation on the continent, where the Franks evidently thought of themselves as the inheritors and continuers of Roman civilization). *Beowulf* 2717b, with its apparent reference to the stone-work inside an ancient burial-mound, would then mark an intermediate stage in which the stone structure containing the treasure is ascribed to the same superhuman beings as had made the treasure.

The traditional craftsmen of Germanic myth, particularly on the evidence of Icelandic sources, were, of course, dwarfs, while giants (OE *eotenas*, ON *jǫtnar*) were the embodiment of an anti-human savagery, perhaps ultimately representing the destructive forces of nature. An exception to this generalization, however, appears in the Norse myth of the building of the walls of Ásgarðr, which represents a giant as a builder of mighty stone walls.[1] Also pertinent is a statement made by Saxo Grammaticus in the Preface to his *Danish History*, asserting that Denmark was formerly inhabited by giants, as may be seen from the large stone structures that they have left behind (Saxo is referring to prehistoric cromlechs and dolmens, still known in modern Danish as *jættestuer*, 'giant-rooms'; cf. *Beowulf* 2715–19, where *enta geweorc* is applied to the barrow inhabited by the dragon).[2] Saxo further speculates as to whether such giants could have existed after the flood, implying that no antediluvian structures could be expected to have survived the universal deluge. These two references, however, do not carry much weight as both are in relatively late texts, and the presence of Roman connotations in the passages discussed above may suggest the possibility of a source in classical tradition instead. Certainly giants as the builders of ancient stone ruins of vast size are

[1] See Snorri Sturluson, *Prose Edda, Gylfaginning,* ch. 42. The wall was made of large rough stones: 'en of nætr dró hann til grjót a hestinum, en þat þótt ásunum mikit undr, hversu stór bjǫrg sá hestr dró' ('and by night he got the horse to pull stones, and it seemed a great marvel to the gods what huge rocks that horse pulled'); and the builder is referred to as *smiðr*, 'a smith', and later as *jǫtunn*, 'a giant', and *bergrisi,* 'a mountain-giant'.

[2] See *Saxonis Gesta Danorum,* ed. Olrik and Ræder (Copenhagen, 1931), p. 9 (Praefatio, ch. 3, 1–9); I am indebted to my colleague, Mr R. Bailey, for this reference.

attested in one aspect of the Greek myths of the Cyclopes. The Cyclopes were of three kinds, or, at any rate, three kinds of myth are associated with them: first, they were the forgers of thunder and lightning and were the smiths of Hephaistos (something like the Norse dwarfs); secondly, they were the savage man-eaters described in Homer's version of the tale of Polyphemus and Odysseus (something like the Germanic *eotenas-jǫtnar*); and thirdly, they were the mythical builders to whom ancient stone walls were ascribed.[1] Pausanias, in his *Description of Greece*, repeatedly refers to Mycenæan ruins, particularly those of Tiryns, as κυκλώπων ἔργον, 'the work of Cyclopes'.[2] The Greek usage seems never to have become common, however, in classical or patristic Latin: there is an example in Seneca, and Pliny makes a tentative reference to Cyclopes as bronzesmiths and as the builders of towers,[3] but I am not aware of any such references among Latin writers who might have transmitted the myth (or the phrase 'work of Cyclopes/giants') to Anglo-Saxon England.

Whether the tradition of giants as ancient builders derived from the Mediterranean world or from Germanic folk-lore (or even from the former through the latter), the word *ent* does not seem to have been widely current in colloquial speech, since it failed to survive beyond the Old English period (in contrast to *eoten*, which survived for many centuries). The rapid extinction of *ent* in Middle English, even as a poetic archaism, seems to be indicated by Lawman's account of King Arthur's tower. Geoffrey of Monmouth has 'secessit Arturus cum eis in turrim giganteam',[4] which Wace translates 'A toz li rois a soi mandez / En une soe tor perrine / Que l'an clamoit Tor Gigantine.'[5] In Lawman's version this becomes

> wenden into ane huse, þe wes biclused faste,
> an ald stanene weorc, stiðe men hit wurhten.[6]

[1] See Pauly, *Realenzyklopädie der classischen Altertumswissenschaft* (1921) xi, col. 2328, and W. H. Roscher, *Lexikon der griechischen und römischen Mythologie* (Hildesheim, 1965) ii. 1, col. 1676ff., *s.v. Kyklopen.*

[2] E.g. *Description of Greece* ii (Corinth).xvi.5 (Loeb Classical Library (London, 1918–35), i, 330), referring to the Lion Gate of Mycenae; ii.xxv.8 (Loeb i, 382) and vii (Achaia).xxv.6 (Loeb iii, 322), referring to Mycenaean Tiryns; in viii (Arcadia).xxix.2 (Loeb iv, 48) the Cyclopes are classified together with the race of giants (as also later in Isidore, *Etymologiae,* xi.iii.12–16).

[3] Seneca, *Hercules Furens* 997, and Pliny, *Natural History* vii. 195–7; in modern English (as in other European languages) the word 'cyclopean' has been used to refer to ancient stone buildings (see OED, *s.v. cyclopean* 2), presumably beginning as a learned reference back to Pausanias or other Greek writers.

[4] Geoffrey of Monmouth, *Historia Regum Britanniae,* ix. 15, ed. A. Griscom (London, 1929), p. 461; Geoffrey's account of Stonehenge as the work of giants (viii. 10–12) is of interest here, especially his peculiar story that the stones were used in connection with medicinal baths; it almost looks as if he were confusing an account of Stonehenge as the work of giants with a tradition of Roman baths as the work of giants (cf. *The Ruin* 38–41 and the ensuing fragmentary lines).

[5] 'The king summoned them all to himself in a stone tower of his that was called the Gigantic Tower' (*Le Roman de Brut de Wace* 10729–30; ed. I. Arnold (Paris, 1938–40) ii, 561; I have followed the same editor's later text in *La Partie Arthurienne du Roman de Brut* (Paris, 1962), p. 96).

[6] *Layamon's Brut* 24885–6; ed. Madden (London, 1847) ii, 623; I have followed the text of *Selections*

Although Lawman uses the phrase *an ald stanene weorc* as a counterpart of *turrim/tor*, the word *ent* is strikingly absent, the implications of *gigantine* being represented by *stiðe men*, 'mighty men', a remarkable choice in a poem that frequently shows knowledge of Old English poetic language. The complex of associations remains but the traditional phrase has been partly forgotten.

However much the reference to *enta geweorc* in *The Wanderer* has in common with the other occurrences of this phrase in Old English poetry, it is distinguished from the others by the statement that the work of giants was overthrown by God. This has led to another interpretation of this passage. It has been proposed by Mr J. Burrow that *The Wanderer* 85–7 contains a reference to some specific event in the past: the ruins we see around us now (75–7) are an earnest that our own civilization will likewise collapse (78–84), 'just as once the Creator of men laid waste this earth, until . . . the old works of giants stood desolate' (85–7).[1] Taking *eardgeard* as 'world, earth', Burrow proposes that there is a reference to the flood and the consequent destruction of the work of antediluvian giants, and he cites instances of this legend in medieval writings. He does not mention, however, a passage in *Beowulf* that seems relevant in that it shows an Old English poet referring to the destruction of giants in the flood: 'syðþan flod ofsloh / gifen geotende giganta cyn'.[2] In its context, however, this passage gives an interesting pointer in another direction, for the story of the overthrow of giants by the flood is said to be depicted (or described – for the purpose of this discussion it does not matter which) on the sword that has been described in lines 1679–81 as *enta geweorc*. That is to say, the *entas* who made the sword engraved on its hilt the story of the *gigantas* who were overthrown by the flood. At first sight, it looks as if the *Beowulf* poet may be making a distinction between *gigantas* (antediluvian giants destroyed in the flood) and *entas* (post-diluvian craftsmen), but this inference is hardly justifiable: such a distinction is not general in Old English, nor even in *Beowulf*, where the words *ent, gigant* and *eoten* are used rather loosely with reference to ancient craftsmen.[3] The passage does, however, serve to remind us that

from Laȝamon's Brut, ed. G. L. Brook (Oxford, 1963), p. 103 (line 3569). Lawman refers to Stonehenge (see above, p. 259, n. 4) as *eotinde ring* (Madden 17275; Brook, *Selections* 908).

[1] J. Burrow, *N&Q* 210 (1965), 166–8.

[2] '. . . when the flood, a pouring deluge, slew the race of giants' (1689b–90).

[3] The sword from Grendel's lair is referred to as *enta ærgeweorc* (1679a), but also as *giganta geweorc* (1562b) and *ealdsweord eotenisc* (1558a); the latter phrase is applied to other swords in 2616a and 2979a, appearing in the latter line together with *entiscne helm*. In general the *eotenas* are savage giants and the *entas* ancient craftsmen, and either may be referred to as *gigantas*. Perhaps the *entas* were thought of as a special kind of *eoten*, so that while *eoten(isc)* might be used as a variant of *ent(isc)*, the reverse was not always possible. The classical associations of *ent* are also suggested by the fact that in two places where the Latin text of Orosius refers to Hercules (I.xv.7 and III.xix.2) the Old English version has *Ercol se (þone) ent*. In neither case does the word *ent* have any counterpart in the Latin text, and it presumably constitutes a commentary explaining that Hercules was an ancient

there are several references in other Old English writings to post-diluvian *entas*, namely, the race of giants who were believed to have made a great building after the flood until their work was frustrated by God; these references occur in various versions of the story of the Tower of Babel.

Stories of the Tower of Babel as the work of giants had apparently arisen out of a conflation of three biblical passages: (*a*) 'Gigantes autem erant super terram in diebus illis' (Genesis VI.4); (*b*) '... quasi Nemrod robustus venator (Septuagint, γίγας) coram Domino. Fuit principium regni ejus Babylon' (Genesis X.8–10); and (*c*) the familiar story of the Tower of Babel (without any reference to giants) in Genesis XI.1–9. From a conflation of these texts, perhaps influenced by the Greek myth of the giants who attempted to reach the home of the gods by piling Pelion on Ossa (as subsequently related, for example, in Ovid, *Metamorphoses* 1.151–62), and depending on the identification of Babel and Babylon, there had developed the legend that Nimrod was a giant and king of Babylon who, with the help of his fellow giants, tried to build a tower to reach up to heaven, until God intervened and put an end to their work by confusing their language. This is the form the legend has, for example, in Augustine, *De Civitate Dei*, XVI.4 and 11, and, substantially, in Isidore's *Etymologiae*, XV.i.4 (with further references in VII.vi.22 and XIV.iii.12), and it was in this form that it was repeated by numerous writers, including the Anglo-Saxon Alcuin in his *Interrogationes Sigewulfi*.[1]

There are many references to these biblical texts or to this legend in Old English: Ælfric has no fewer than five, in all of which the builders of the Tower of Babel are referred to as *entas*, the word he uses to translate *gigantes* in Genesis VI.4.[2] It is in earlier texts, however, that the most pertinent references are to be found, for two of the vernacular writings associated with Alfred's court

hero of superhuman stature; see *King Alfred's Orosius*, ed. H. Sweet, Early English Text Society o.s. 79 (London, 1883), p. 46, line 30, and p. 132, line 11. The etymology of *ent* is unknown, and the cognate OHG *enzo* does not illuminate its semantic history.

[1] Nos. 148–9; Migne, Patrologia Latina 100, col. 533.

[2] *The Old English Heptateuch*, ed. S. J. Crawford, EETS 160 (London, 1921), p. 99. The other references are: *De Vetere et Novo Testamento*, lines 1179–80 (*ibid.* p. 70); Ælfric's translation of Alcuin's *Interrogationes Sigewulfi*, ed. G. E. MacLean, *Anglia* 7 (1884), 40 (line 379); the homily 'In Die Sancto Pentecosten', *The Homilies of the Anglo-Saxon Church: the First Part, containing the Sermones Catholici, or Homilies of Ælfric*, ed. B. Thorpe (London, 1844–6) I, 318; and the homily 'De Falsis Diis', *The Homilies of Ælfric: a Supplementary Collection*, ed. J. C. Pope, EETS 259–60 (London, 1967–8), p. 680 (lines 74–5). This last homily was adapted by Wulfstan, retaining the reference to giants; see *The Homilies of Wulfstan*, ed. D. Bethurum (Oxford, 1957), p. 221. As noted by Professor Pope, Ælfric's 'De Falsis Diis' was translated into Old Norse, but the translation of the passage in question is closer to the bible, the Old Norse making no mention either of Nimrod or of giants, and referring to the builders of the Tower of Babel simply as 'þeim monnum hinum miclum er forðum varo' ('those mighty men of former times'); see *Hauksbók*, ed. Finnur Jónsson, Kongelige Nordiske Oldskriftselskab (Copenhagen, 1892–6), p. 157, lines 23–31. Another text in the same manuscript (*ibid*, p. 153, lines 29–33) states that Nimrod the giant and other giants ('Nemroð risi oc aðrer risar') built a town with a tower in it, the town being called Babel, later Babylon.

deal with God's destruction of the work of giants, and are therefore closer to *The Wanderer* 85–7. In King Alfred's Boethius the biblical story of the Tower of Babel is compared with the Greek myth of the giants' attack on the gods, and develops a form in which it is alleged that God not only put an end to the work on the tower but also overthrew the giants and cast down their tower; and in the Old English Orosius Babel as the work of giants is identified with the Babylon of the Jewish exile and becomes associated with the imagery of destruction and desolation that is so prominent in the biblical accounts of the fall of that city. In both these texts the themes most relevant to *The Wanderer* appear more clearly in the Old English versions than in the Latin originals.

The Latin text of Boethius has a very brief reference to the classical myth: '"Accepisti," inquit, "in fabulis lacessentes caelum gigantes; sed illos quoque, uti condignum fuit, benigna fortitudo disposuit."' To this the Munich Commentary adds the note 'loquitor secundum fidem gentilium vel veritatem tangit, quando divisio linguarum facta est'.[1] This suggestion of a reference to both pagan myth and the bible is taken up and considerably expanded by Alfred in his translation:

Hwæt, ic wat þæt ðu geherdest oft reccan on ealdum leasum spellum þætte Iob Saturnes sunu sceolde bion se hehsta god ofer ealle oðre godu, ond he sceolde bion þæs heofenes sunu, ond sceolde ricsian on heofenum; ond sceolden gigantes bion eorðan suna, ond ða sceolden ricsian ofer eorþan; ond þa sceolden hi bion swelce hi wæren geswysterna bearn, forðæmþe he sceolde beon heofenes sunu, ond hi eorðan. Ond þa sceolde þæm gigantum ofþincan þæt he hæfde hiera rice; woldon þa tobrecan þone heofon under him; þa sceolde he sendan þunras ond ligeta ond windas, ond toweorpan eall hira geweorc mid, ond hi selfe ofslean.

Ðyllica leasunga hi worhton, ond meahton eaðe seggan soðspell, gif him þa leasunga næren swetran, ond þeah swiðe gelic ðisum. Hi meahton seggan hwylc dysig Nefrod se gigant worhte ... Se Nefrod het wyrcan ænne tor on ðæm felda ðe Nensar hatte, ond on ðære þiode ðe Deira hatte, swiðe neah þære byrig þe mon nu hæt Babilonia ... Ac hit gebyrede, swa hit cynn was, þæt se godcunda wald hi tostencte ær hi hit fullwyrcan mosten, ond towearp ðone tor, ond hiora monigne ofslog.[2]

---

[1] Boethius, *De Consolatione Philosophiae,* ed. Stewart and Rand, Loeb Classical Library (London, 1918), p. 290: 'You have heard in myths, she said, about the giants attacking heaven, but, as was proper, benevolent strength put them down too' (III, pr. 12). For the Munich Commentary see K. Otten, *König Alfreds Boethius* (Tübingen, 1964), p. 129: 'here he refers either to pagan myth or to the historical truth of the division of languages' (my translations). The comparison of the biblical story with the Greek myth is also made by Bede in his commentary on Genesis; see Bede, *Libri quattuor in Principium Genesis,* ed. C. W. Jones, Corpus Christianorum Series Latina 188A, 100.

[2] 'Now I know you have often heard related in false old stories that Jove, Saturn's son, was supposed to be the chief god over all other gods, and to be the son of Heaven and to rule in heaven; and the giants were supposed to be the sons of Earth and to rule over earth, so they were like the children of a brother and sister, because he was supposed to be the son of Heaven and they of Earth. And

Especially striking here is the way in which the theme of storms and winds, Jupiter's weapons against the giants of pagan myth, is mentioned in close association with the legend of Nimrod and Babel, and the violence of the Greek myth becomes transferred to the quasi-biblical story, so that the giants of Babel are said to be slain and their work cast down. Another aspect of the translator's method appears incidentally in his representation of the conflict as a dynastic struggle between cousins, presumably accommodating the myth to a heroic pattern.

The identification of Babel and Babylon, which is the key to the relevant passage in the Old English Orosius, has a long history, reaching back into pre-Christian Hebrew tradition, and is common among patristic writers; its currency in Anglo-Saxon England is attested in the writings of Bede and Alcuin. In his commentary on Genesis, under chapter XI.1–9 (the account of the Tower of Babel), Bede writes at length on Babylon and its glory, 'superbam hujus mundi gloriam', explaining that Nimrod was its founder – 'quia civitatis illius et turris superbissimae Nemrod auctor extiterit' – and identifying Nimrod's Babel with the Babylon of Semiramis and Nebuchadnezzar; he continues with references to the fall of Babylon, quoting not only Daniel IV.30 ('Nonne haec est Babylon magna ...') but also Revelation XVIII.2 ('Cecidit Babylon magna ...'), and concludes by contrasting the names of Babylon and Jerusalem as conventionally interpreted (*confusio* and *visio pacis* respectively), the one symbolizing the mutability of earthly glory, the other the peace of eternity.[1] Alcuin's *Interrogationes Sigewulfi* considers the more restricted question as to whether Babel and Babylon are the same, and concludes that the Tower of Babel was the citadel of the city of Babylon.[2] In the passage just quoted from Alfred's Boethius it is claimed only that the Tower of Babel was very near Babylon. Nevertheless, Alfred names the site not only in accordance with the account in Genesis, *Nensar* being a garbled version of the Vulgate's *Sennar* (Authorized Version, *Shinar*; see Genesis XI.2), but also in relation to later accounts of the historical Babylon, with *Deira* as a strikingly Anglicized form of the biblical *Dura*, the place where Nebuchadnezzar set up an idolatrous image (see Daniel III.1). Thus in one word he relates Nimrod's

then it was supposed to have occurred to the giants that Jove had their kingdom, and they wanted to burst open heaven under him; so he sent thunder and lightning and winds to cast down all their work, and to kill the giants themselves. They made up false tales like this, but they could easily have told the truth if these lies had not been more attractive to them; and yet the truth was very like these lies. They could have told how stupidly Nimrod the giant behaved ... This Nimrod ordered a tower to be built on the plain called Nensar among the people called Deira, very close to the town we now call Babylon ... But it came about, as was natural, that the divine power overthrew them before they could complete it, and cast down the tower, and killed many of them' (*King Alfred's Boethius,* ed. W. J. Sedgfield (Oxford, 1899; repr. Darmstadt, 1968), pp. 98–9).

[1] Bede, *In Princ. Gen.,* ed. Jones, pp. 144–5, 156–7 and 162; also PL 91, cols. 117–18 and 126–9.
[2] No. CXLIX (omitted from Ælfric's Old English translation).

Babel both to the Babylon of the Old Testament prophetical books and (if this is not merely a scribal error) to contemporary England, since the name *Deira* would inevitably call to mind what had formerly been the southern kingdom of Northumbria, an area rich in remains of the past, both Roman and Northumbrian, and in Alfred's day an area of pagan Scandinavian settlement.

The identification of Babel and Babylon, Nimrod's tower and the city of Nebuchadnezzar and Belshazzar, becomes a potent source of emotive imagery: on the one hand, the work of giants overthrown, and on the other, the desolation of earthly glory – especially as expounded in Isaiah XIII.19–22 and, at greater length, in Jeremiah L and LI, and repeated with eschatalogical significance in Revelation XVII and XVIII (also briefly in Revelation XVI.18–21, where Babylon is said to receive the wrath of God in the form of thunder-storms and hail). It is against this background that we should see the following extract from the Old English Orosius:

Swa ungeliefedlic is ænigum menn þæt to gesecgenne, hu ænig mon mehte swelce burg gewyrcan swelce sio wæs [i.e. Babylon], oðþe eft abrecan. Membrað se ent angan ærest timbran Babylonia, ond Ninus se cyning æfter him; ond Semiramis his cwen hie geendade æfter him on middeweardum hiere rice. Seo burg wæs getimbred an fildum lande ond on swiþe emnum, ond heo wæs swiþe fæger an to locianne; ond 5
heo is swiþe ryhte feowerscyte; ond þæs wealles micelness ond fæstness is ungeliefedlic to secgenne; þæt is, þæt he is L elna brad, ond II hund elna heah, ond his ymbgong is hundseofontig mila ond seofeða dæl anre mile, ond he is geworht of tigelan ond of eorðtyrewan; ond ymbutan þone weall is se mæsta dic, on þæm is iernende se ungefoglecesta stream; ond wiðutan þæm dice is geworht twegea elna heah weall, 10
ond bufan ðæm maran wealle ofer ealne þone ymbgong ¸he is¸ mid stænenum wighusum beworht. Seo ilce burg Babylonia, seo ðe mæst wæs ond ærest ealra burga, seo is nu læst ond westast. Nu seo burg swelc is, þe ær wæs ealra weorca fæstast ond wunderlecast ond mærast, gelice ond heo wære to bisene asteald eallum middangearde, ond eac swelce heo self sprecende sie to eallum moncynne ond cweþe: 'Nu ic þuss 15
gehroren eam ond aweggewiten; hwæt, ge magan on me ongietan ond oncnawan þæt ge nanuht mid eow nabbað fæstes ne stronges þætte þurhwunigean mæge.'[1]

[1] 'It is unbelievable for anyone who is told of it how any man could construct such a town as Babylon was, or how it could afterwards be destroyed. Nimrod the giant first began to build Babylon, and King Ninus after him, and Semiramis his queen finished it after him towards the middle of her reign. That city was built on level and very even land, and it was very beautiful to behold; it is perfectly square, and the size and strength of the wall is unbelievable to hear of, for it is fifty ells thick, 200 ells high and its circumference is seventy-and-one-seventh miles; it is made of tiles and bitumen. Outside the wall is an enormous ditch in which the most immense river runs; beyond the ditch is a wall two ells high, and on top of the bigger wall stone turrets are built throughout the whole circuit. This same city of Babylon, which was the first and greatest of cities, is now the smallest and most desolate. The city, which was the most firm-set, marvellous and famous of all works, is now like a warning set up for the whole world, even as if it were itself able to speak and were to say to all mankind, "Thus I am now fallen and departed away: lo, you can look on me and recognize that you have nothing among you that is firm and strong and able to endure"' (*King Alfred's Orosius*, ed. Sweet, pp. 74–5; I have followed the text in *Sweet's Anglo-Saxon Reader*, rev. D. White-

The context of this passage makes it clear that the fall of Babylon is the work of Cyrus the Mede and that there is no reference here to God's destruction of the Tower of Babel; but the origin of the city in the work of an *ent* is explicitly stated. In the first part of the extract the translator follows the Latin fairly closely, but in the account of the walls of Babylon he translates more freely; *stænenum wighusum* is his addition, perhaps reflecting the Anglo-Saxon literary preoccupation with specifically stone structures with reference to the work of giants and to the theme of ruin. Moreover, Orosius's brief sentence on the fall of Babylon is transformed: 'et tamen magna illa Babylon, illa prima post reparationem humani generis condita, nunc paene etiam minima mora uicta subuersa est'[1] is expanded into a long independent digression (lines 12–17 above) on mutability and ruin, including the striking prosopopoeia (15–17) in which the fallen city laments the transience of earthly life, holding itself up as an exemplum. Prosopopoeia is of course a classical rhetorical device, but it figures prominently in Old English, most obviously in *The Dream of the Rood*, but also in numerous riddles and in inscriptions like that on the Alfred Jewel.

The passages from the Old English translations of Boethius and Orosius both contain original material that casts some light on the functioning of the Anglo-Saxon literary imagination, and they share a common interest in Babylon as the work of giants and its subsequent destruction in accordance with divine purpose. In the Boethius interpolation the emphasis is on God's destruction of the work of giants, with associated imagery of winds and storms; in the Orosius passage it is on the contrast between the glory of Babylon, especially as manifest in its walls, and its subsequent desolation.[2]

The full extent of the association between the Babylonian theme of these prose texts and the Roman connotations of the ruins in *The Wanderer* becomes clear when it is remembered that the comparison of Rome to Babylon (to

---

lock (Oxford, 1967), pp. 27–8). Latin quotations are from *Pauli Orosii Historiarum adversum Paganos Libri VII*, ed. C. Zangmeister (Leipzig, 1889), pp. 42–3. Orosius returns to the comparison of Babylon and Rome in VII.ii; the corresponding portion of the Old English translation in Sweet's edition is on p. 252.

[1] '... and yet that great Babylon, the first city built after the renewing of the human race [i.e. after the flood] is now after a very short time conquered, captured and overthrown'.

[2] Orosius's fascination with the size of the walls of Babylon is shared by other writers, e.g. Solinus, *Collectanea Rerum Memorabilium*, ch. 56 (ed. Mommsen (Berlin, 1895), p. 205) and Isidore, *Chronicon* 9 (PL, 83, col. 1022). In the foregoing sketch of Latin and English versions of the story of Nimrod and Babel it has not been relevant to quote the reference in *Solomon and Saturn* since this is too obscure to add anything to the other references, but it is appropriate to acknowledge my debt to R. J. Menner's studies of the legend in his edition of *The Poetical Dialogues of Solomon and Saturn*, Mod. Lang. Assoc. Monograph 13 (New York, 1941), 61 and 122–3, and in *JEGP* 37 (1938), 332–54, which have been the basis of all subsequent writings on this theme. Since the completion of the present article there has appeared N. Peltola, 'Grendel's Descent from Cain Reconsidered', *NM* 73 (1972), 284–91, in which it is suggested that references in *Beowulf* to weapons and armour as the work of giants may derive from the apocryphal Book of Enoch, and ultimately from Genesis IV.22.

become a commonplace of post-reformation protestant polemics) had already been developed in the early church, where the condemnation of Babylon, drunken with the blood of saints and martyrs, in Revelation XVII and XVIII was naturally taken to apply to the pagan Rome of the early persecutions. This is stated clearly, for example, by Tertullian in his *Answer to the Jews*: 'Sic et Babylon (*Apocalypsis* XVII.5) apud Joannem nostrum, Romanae urbis figura est, proinde et magnae, et regno superbae, et sanctorum debellatricis.'[1] The idea that Rome was a second Babylon also appears in Augustine's *De Civitate Dei*, XVIII, especially chapter 22 ('. . . condita est ciuitas Roma uelut altera Babylon'), where it is alleged that Rome was founded at the time when Babylon fell. Augustine's comparison was probably prompted by the fall of Rome to Alaric the Goth in 410, but it was left to Orosius to elaborate a series of parallels between Babylon and Rome in book II of his *Historiae adversum Paganos*, where it forms the context of the passage discussed above. Orosius, seeking to refute the pagan charge that Rome fell to the Goths because it had turned Christian, compares the histories of the two cities: Babylon and Rome are like father and son (II.i); the fall of Babylon to the Medes coincided with the founding of Rome, both towns took sixty-four years to build, and Medean Babylon fell to the Persians at the same time as Rome was freed from Tarquin (II.ii); Babylon lasted 1,160 years until sacked by the Medes, Rome lasted 1,160 years until sacked by the Visigoths (II.iii); then follows the passage quoted above: Babylon, once great, has now fallen and become a desolation; the Roman state is now in decline, but this is due not to the attacks of enemies but to old age. Of outstanding interest is the fact that Orosius's reference to the structure of the Roman state ('Romanae reipublicae moles') is changed by the Old English translator into a reference to the walls of Rome ('hiere weallas for ealdunge brosnien'). For Orosius the survival of the Roman state was a matter of importance, but the Anglo-Saxon author was more interested in the fact that with the passage of time the strongest walls crumble, in spite of whatever shield Christianity may provide for the political or social structure: for him, as for Sir Thomas Browne, 'diuturnity is a dream, and folly of expectation'.

This, then, is part of the intellectual background of the poet of *The Wanderer*, and, writing on the pervasive principle of mutability and transience in earthly life, he follows an association of ideas that he had become familiar with as part of his Christian education. In the Roman ruins around him in England, mighty at once in their endurance and in their downfall, he saw the essential nature of the legendary ruins of the city of Babylon, the work of giants destroyed by God, and the supreme exemplum of mutability and transience and the vanity of

[1] Tertullian, *Adversus Judaeos* (PL 2, col. 620); trans. *The Ante-Nicene Fathers,* ed. Roberts and Donaldson (repr. 1957) III, 162: 'So again Babylon, in our own John (Revelation XVII), is a figure of the city of Rome, as being equally great and proud of her sway and triumphant over the saints.'

worldly glory. Something not very different from the sequence of images in *The Wanderer* appears in Alcuin's Latin poem on the sack of Lindisfarne.[1] This begins with the themes of man as an exile from paradise and of the mutability of earthly life (1–16); next follows a series of contrasting images demonstrating how good gives way to bad (17, day to night; 18, spring to winter, and 21–2, fine weather to storms) and asserting the general principle of earthly mutability and ruin (25–8); then it is recalled how great cities and empires have passed away: 31–2, Babylon; 33–4, Persia; 35–6, Alexander; and 37–40, Rome. The remainder of the poem (200 lines) is not relevant here, except in so far as it demonstrates the common Anglo-Saxon tendency to see in particular events the outworking of a general principle, so that the occasion becomes exemplary, and an English ruin may inherit generalized aspects of ruin from Rome and Babylon. The interest of Alcuin's poem for us is that it shares themes and images with *The Wanderer* (exile and transience; night, winter, storms and ruin) and that it explicitly associates these with Babylon and Rome. Alcuin's poem thus reflects a literary background of ideas and images that was doubtless shared by the poet of *The Wanderer*, but the associations that God's destruction of the work of giants held for the vernacular poet can be understood more fully in the light of the passages quoted from the Old English translations of Boethius and Orosius. *The Wanderer* may be the work of a man brought up on the great texts of the Alfredian educational revival.

Another factor arising from the foregoing discussion is that the Old English prose texts concerned with Nimrod and Babylon not only share an obvious set of themes with *The Wanderer* and the other Old English poems concerned with the work of giants; in some degree there is also a common vocabulary, an important part of which is of Latin origin, i.e. *weal, ceastre, stræt* and *tor*, beside the native words *wag, burh, weg* and *stypel*. Frequently combined with this material is imagery of stone structures and of storm and wind, showing how association of ideas and lexical collocation tend to go hand in hand in Old English literary composition, most obviously in verse, but also to some extent in prose too. A striking example in verse is afforded by the verb *yōde* (*The Wanderer* 85a) in a passage referring to the work of giants. *Yōan* is a fairly rare word in extant Old English verse, and it is remarkable that one of the few other occurrences is in *Beowulf* 420b–1a, 'þær ic fife geband / yōde eotena cyn', while in *Genesis A* 1268–80 (a paraphrase of Genesis VI.1–7) the same verb, with the prefix *a-*, is used within twelve lines of a reference to giants: 'gigant-mæcgas, gode unleofe . . . eall aæōan þæt on eorōan wæs'. There is of course no

---

[1] Alcuin, *De Clade Lindisfarnensis Monasterii*, ed. Dümmler, Monumenta Germaniae Historica, Poetae Latini Aevi Carolini I, 229.

logical connection between giants and *yðan*; the association is an arbitrary feature of poetic style.¹

Finally, it remains to consider how far other images in the final section of *The Wanderer* may have been influenced by biblical accounts of Babylon. There are two important Old Testament passages on the desolation of Babylon: first, the brief summary in Isaiah XIII.19–22 – glorious Babylon will be overthrown, it will never be inhabited by men, but will become instead the resort of wild beasts and monsters ('Sed requiescent ibi bestiae, et replebuntur domus eorum draconibus', XIII.21) – and secondly, the more extended account in Jeremiah L–LI, in which three images are made prominent by repetition: ruined buildings, houses inhabited by monsters, particularly *dracones*, and destruction from the north. The images of broken walls and ruined buildings (especially Jeremiah L.15 and LI.58) find an obvious parallel in *The Wanderer*, but the other two images may have contributed something too.

The theme of dwellings abandoned by men and given over to *dracones* may have influenced the poet's choice of imagery in *The Wanderer* 97–8, a notoriously problematic passage:

> Stondeð nu on laste   leofre duguþe
> weal wundrum heah,   wyrmlicum fah.²

Here, as in the biblical accounts of Babylon, we have the vanished company of men (97; cf. Isaiah XIII.20 and Jeremiah L.30) and the abandoned wall (98a, 'wondrously high', like the walls described by Orosius), but paintings of dragons replace the living creatures of the bible (Isaiah XIII.21 and Jeremiah LI.37). The reason for this change, or the reason for mentioning a decorative motif at all, remains thoroughly obscure, but at least we have some indication as to why the poet thought it appropriate to mention the *wyrm* in connection with the theme of desolation.³ The theme of destruction from the north

¹ Other collocations resembling those in the passages discussed above are in *Andreas* 827–43a; *ceastre – herestræte – burhwealle – stan – torras – windige weallas*; and *Andreas* 1575b–80: *stormas – stanhleoðu – carcern – stræt*.

² 'In place of the beloved band of warriors there now stands a wall, wondrously high, painted with the figures of dragons [*or* serpents]'; for previous discussions of these lines see *The Wanderer*, ed. R. F. Leslie (Manchester, 1966), pp. 86–7, and ed. T. P. Dunning and A. J. Bliss (London, 1969), p. 74; and for detailed comment on the implications of *fah* see G. V. Smithers in *Studies in Language and Literature in Honour of Margaret Schlauch*, ed. M. Brahmer *et al.* (Warsaw, 1966), p. 417. OE *wyrm* had a wide semantic range, including 'dragon', the creature that haunts desolate places, whether the ruins of Babylon or an ancient burial-mound, and 'worm', the creature that devours bodies in the grave (as in *The Rhyming Poem* 75 and *Soul and Body II* 67–9, 106–7 and 111–21); this obviously allows for a good deal of flexibility in the use of *wyrm* as a poetic image.

³ The problem of *The Wanderer* 98b is intractable, but one should note that *wyrm* collocates more frequently with *fah*, 'guilty, hostile', than with *fah*, 'painted, stained': while the latter collocation is represented only by *wyrmfah* (*Beowulf* 1698a), the former occurs in *fah wyrm* (*Genesis A* 899a) and *fagum wyrme* (904b), *weorm blædum fah* (*Andreas* 769b) and *wyrm yrre cwom ... fyrwylmum fah* (*Beowulf* 2669–71a); cf. also BT *Supplement, s.v. fagwyrm*, 'basilisk'. This

provides a less striking parallel because for the English poet the north is a source of natural disaster, whereas for the prophets it is the source of a destructive people, but the account of the affliction of Babylon by hail in Revelation XVI.21 may well have influenced *The Wanderer* 104b–5: 'norþan onsendeð / hreo hæglfare hæleþum on andan'. It is possible that the poet's handling of imagery of serpents and the north represents a blending of Christian tradition and native poetic motifs ultimately of pagan origin. At any rate, both images appear together in the Edda, a point of some interest in view of the frequently noted correspondence between *The Wanderer* 108–9 and *Hávamál*, stanzas 76–7; references to the north and to walls with serpents are combined in *Vǫluspá*, stanza 38:

> Sal sá hon standa   sólo fiarri,
> Nástrǫndo a,   norðr horfa dyrr;
> fello eitdropar   inn um lióra,
> sá er undinn salr   orma hryggiom.[1]

This account may itself have been influenced by Christian traditions of the kind exemplified in *Christ and Satan* 134–6, but from passages like these (together with *The Wanderer* 97–105) one receives the impression of a widely diffused traditional imagery, appearing both in learned writings and in popular tradition, both in Christian and in pagan contexts, for which there may not be any one source. The educated Anglo-Saxon poet writing on Christian themes might have been encouraged to use the conventions of native poetry for a variety of reasons, not least because the inherited imagery of the native tradition had certain resemblances to the imported imagery of the Christian tradition. So it could come about that one particular image might acquire a varying degree of Christian associations in different poems, as is evidently the case with *enta geweorc* (which, roughly speaking, has no Christian associations in *Beowulf*, some in *The Ruin* and *Andreas*, and more in *The Wanderer*). In *The Wanderer* 73–105 the sequence of images results from the handling of the material of a Christian education in the language of a received Anglo-Saxon poetic tradition, but in a fascinating way theme and language interact on each other, the traditional language reshaping the Christian theme, and Christian associations enriching the language of poetry.

does not lead to any improved interpretation of *The Wanderer* 98b, and there is likely to be some textual corruption here.

[1] 'She saw a hall standing far from the sun on Corpse-strand; the doors face north; poison drops fell in through the roof-vent; that hall is entwined with the backs of serpents' (*Edda*, ed. G. Neckel (Heidelberg, 1962), p. 9). Snorri Sturluson, *Prose Edda, Gylfaginning*, ch. 52, interprets these stanzas as implying that the walls are woven (like wicker-work) with serpents, which blow their venom into the hall: this does not quite agree with the reference to *lióra* in *Vǫluspá*.

The influence of Christian doctrine and exegesis on Old English poetry: an estimate of the current state of scholarship

PHILIP B. ROLLINSON

Although it is a commonplace of history that Anglo-Saxon England was receptive to Christianity and to Christian-Latin culture and that English churchmen such as Aldhelm, Bede and Alcuin made an important contribution to that culture, it is only in recent years that scholars have explored and emphasized the importance of Christian tradition to the understanding of Old English poetry, especially those poems without explicit Christian content. Increased investigation of Old English prose, which is largely Christian, and the well-known work on *Beowulf* by Frederick Klaeber, Marie Padgett Hamilton, Dorothy Whitelock and others,[1] seems to have redirected 'the search for Anglo-Saxon paganism'[2] into a search – sometimes opposed[3] – for reflections of Christianity in Anglo-Saxon poetry. While in some quarters this critical and scholarly attention has been confined to the influence of Christian doctrine, ritual and interpretation of the bible, in others it has taken into account the broader cultural influences of the church, especially its transmission of the literature and learning of pagan antiquity.[4]

---

[1] See Fr. Klaeber's introduction to his 3rd ed. of *Beowulf and the Fight at Finnsburg* (Boston, 1950), pp. xlviii-li; Marie Padgett Hamilton, 'The Religious Principle in *Beowulf*', *PMLA* 61 (1946), 309-30; and Dorothy Whitelock, *The Audience of Beowulf* (Oxford, 1951).

[2] Described in E. G. Stanley's essay of this title published in nine parts, *N&Q* n.s. 11 (1964), 204-9, 242-50, 282-7, 324-31 and 455-63 and 12 (1965), 9-17, 203-7, 285-93 and 322-7.

[3] Two recent examples are Charles Moorman, 'The Essential Paganism of *Beowulf*', *MLQ* 28 (1967), 3-18 and John Halverson, 'The World of *Beowulf*', *ELH* 36 (1969), 593-608. Kenneth Sisam's opposition is noteworthy in that he suggests that the poet is relatively indifferent to matters of religion, Christian or pagan (*The Structure of Beowulf* (Oxford, 1965), pp. 72-9, esp. 78).

[4] René L. M. Derolez sceptically surveys many of the important areas of potential influence in 'Anglo-Saxon Literature: Attic or Asiatic? Old English Poetry and its Latin Background', *English Studies Today* 2nd ser., ed. G. A. Bonnard (Berne, 1961), pp. 93-105. More recently Jackson J. Campbell examines rhetorical and literary studies in the schools and the importance of classical rhetoric to Old English poetry in 'Knowledge of Rhetorical Figures in Anglo-Saxon England', *JEGP* 66 (1967), 1-20, and 'Learned Rhetoric in Old English Poetry', *MP* 63 (1966), 189-201. B. K. Martin discusses some echoes of classical Latin topoi in 'Aspects of Winter in Latin and Old English Poetry', *JEGP* 68 (1969), 375-90. I attempt to evaluate some poems in the Old English canon in terms of generic expectations established by classical and late classical authorities

On the whole the critical interest in matters of faith and doctrine has borne excellent fruit. As with Middle English and continental literatures, the most obvious result has been to generate considerable controversy over the degree of Christian potential and, in particular, of allegorical intention in certain poems, which, superficially at least, appear to be neither allegorical nor even especially Christian. Less controversial, but quite as significant, have been the better understanding and appreciation of Old English poems which are unquestionably allegorical or which obviously proceed from Christian interests. In general, as one would expect, a comprehensive knowledge of Christian thought and of the elements of Christian culture has proved to be important for the proper understanding of a number of poems. I propose to consider here the present state of opinion concerning the nature and extent of the influence which Christian doctrine and exegesis had on Old English poetry. My purpose is to survey, as to both method and value, the various ways in which this question has been explored in the last fifteen years or so. Necessarily selective, my method is to outline typical kinds of approach, identified by examples which seem to me particularly cogent, and to describe the directions each has taken.

One of the simplest but certainly most useful ways in which commonplaces of Christian exegesis have been applied to Old English poetry is as an aid to the explication of certain literal elements which are puzzling or ambiguous to the modern understanding. A notable example is Fred C. Robinson's investigation of the mysterious African woman present at the celebration of the Israelites after their crossing of the Red Sea in the Old English *Exodus*.[1] Using patristic commentaries (and Josephus), Robinson demonstrates that this woman is probably Moses's Ethiopian wife mentioned in Numbers XII.1. Although not referred to as Ethiopian or African in the Vulgate Exodus, she was identified in commentaries as Moses's Madianite wife to whom reference is made in Exodus, although not in conjunction with the crossing of the Red Sea. The commentators associate her prominently with Moses, as the Vulgate does not. She becomes an important type of the gentile church, and it is this typological importance which, as Robinson shows, very probably explains her presence in the Old English *Exodus*, not as a type but as Moses's literal African wife. Attacking a somewhat larger problem, John F. Vickrey relies on patristic sources to establish the probable content, nature and highly ironic implications of Eve's vision in *Genesis B*.[2] He significantly advances the argument that the Old English poet is much more aware of and dependent on

on grammar and rhetoric, 'Some Kinds of Meaning in Old English Poetry', *Annuale Mediaevale* 11 (1970), 5–21. This list is obviously not exhaustive.

[1] 'Notes on the Old English *Exodus*', *Anglia* 80 (1962), 373–8.
[2] 'The Vision of Eve in *Genesis B*', *Speculum* 44 (1969), 86–102.

traditional Christian views than has generally been thought. The originality of the poet's handling of the story of the fall is in no way lessened: it is simply that when Eve's vision is recognized as very like the traditional Christian visualization of God's judgement the poet's originality is understood within a more orthodox context. In a recent note Richard L. Hoffman similarly clarifies *The Judgement Day II* by investigating the commonplace patristic elaborations of the motif of penitential weeping which are echoed, and sometimes literally translated, by the Old English poet.[1]

Christian tradition has also been shown to be an important factor in the critical evaluation of some Old English poems. For example, Catharine A. Regan attempts not only to describe but also to evaluate the Old English *Vainglory* in terms of 'the patristic psychology of sin'.[2] As a result, she is able to show that the opening lines probably bear an intrinsic relationship to the rest of the poem.[3] If her conclusion that patristic psychology will not make a good poem out of an inferior one[4] accords with previous critical estimates, she makes an important point in demonstrating that this opinion must take into account what the poet is attempting and what materials are involved in his attempt. A similar approach informs the recent perceptions of Roger Lass and Robert B. Burlin of an underlying unity among the poems in the Old English *Advent*.[5] Lass bases his argument on an awareness of a liturgical way of thinking about time, history and Christ's first coming, while Burlin more comprehensively focuses on the methodology and interpretative results of typological exegesis as the keys to the poems' unity. One may question their conclusions about *how* the Christian thought is relevant to the poems' artistry, but not that it is relevant.

It is important, of course, to recognize that exegetical methods of interpretation may be relevant to different poems in different ways and indeed may not be relevant to some poems at all. We do well to heed E. Talbot Donaldson's warning against the mechanical and arbitrary application of patristic interpretative methodology to all imaginative literature, regardless of its literal tenor and tone and of customary rhetorical or generic expectations.[6] Critical discretion, grounded in a proper respect for the text, must govern the process of relating an Old English poem to its Christian background, whatever that relationship may be; and this is as true of a poem that is overtly religious

---

[1] 'The Theme of *Judgment Day II*', *ELN* 6 (1969), 161–4.
[2] 'Patristic Psychology in the Old English *Vainglory*', *Traditio* 26 (1970), 324–35.
[3] *Ibid.* p. 327.   [4] *Ibid.* pp. 334–5.
[5] Roger Lass, 'Poem as Sacrament: Transcendence of Time in the *Advent Sequence* from the Exeter Book', *Annuale Mediaevale* 7 (1966), 3–15 and Robert B. Burlin, *The Old English 'Advent': a Typological Commentary*, Yale Stud. in Eng. 168 (New Haven, 1968).
[6] 'Patristic Exegesis in the Criticism of Medieval Literature', *Critical Approaches to Medieval Literature: Selected Papers from the English Institute, 1958–1959*, ed. Dorothy Bethurum (New York, 1960), pp. 1–26, esp. 1–5.

as of any other. Recent work on *The Dream of the Rood* and the Old English *Phoenix* is particularly noteworthy in this respect. With regard to the first, Rosemary Woolf's essay 'Doctrinal Influences on *The Dream of the Rood*'[1] not only describes the fundamental Christian framework of the poem but also sensitively evaluates the poet's contribution and achievement within that framework. More recently John V. Fleming has convincingly interpreted *The Dream of the Rood* in the slightly more restricted terms of western asceticism.[2] To be sure there are other areas of interest in this very fine poem, but Woolf and Fleming have so obviously articulated a basic context in which the poem and the poet's originality are to be understood that their conclusions cannot be ignored. Understandably several more recent studies reflect in various ways the importance of their materials and conclusions.[3]

With regard to *The Phoenix*, a close examination of Lactantius's *De Ave Phoenice*, informed by a comprehensive acquaintance with scriptural exegesis, leads J. E. Cross to conclude, convincingly, that the Old English poem is not a two-part one awkwardly balancing a paraphrase of Lactantius against a moralization of the Latin poem but rather a homogeneous creation of the poet which simply relies heavily on Lactantius for factual information about the bird.[4] Cross suggests that the Old English poem is sequentially structured on, and hence is a poetic exercise in, the four levels of scriptural interpretation. The poet, he asserts, elaborates on his description of the historical, literal bird in terms of three (very broad and general) categories of Christian significance.[5] Independently of Cross, but in agreement about the poem's integrity, Joanne Spencer Kantrowitz demonstrates convincingly in 'The Anglo-Saxon *Phoenix* and Tradition'[6] that the Old English poet has modified and remade Lactantius

---

[1] *MÆ* 27 (1958), 137–53.

[2] '*The Dream of the Rood* and Anglo-Saxon Monasticism', *Traditio* 22 (1966), 43–72. Fleming appropriately observes that 'the monastic vocation is, after all, merely the Christian vocation *par excellence*' (pp. 60–1). He does insist, however, on the essentially ascetic, non-secular point of view in the poem.

[3] See for example Robert B. Burlin, 'The Ruthwell Cross, *The Dream of the Rood* and the Vita Contemplativa', *SP* 65 (1968), 23–43 and John Canuteson, 'The Crucifixion and the Second Coming in *The Dream of the Rood*', *MP* 66 (1969), 293–7. Canuteson justly modifies one of Miss Woolf's interpretative inferences (p. 296). Faith H. Patten uses Miss Woolf's essay as a point of departure in 'Structure and Meaning in *The Dream of the Rood*', *ESts* 49 (1968), 385–401, esp. 388–9. *The Dream of the Rood* has, of course, been extensively commented on. Complementing Miss Woolf's essay is one by J. A. Burrow, 'An Approach to *The Dream of the Rood*', *Neophilologus* 43 (1959), 123–33. Burrow sheds an interesting and significant light on the poem by comparing its technique to that of later medieval versions of the same theme. For a current bibliography of criticism of the poem see *The Dream of the Rood*, ed. Michael Swanton (Manchester, 1970), pp. 82–7.

[4] 'The Conception of the Old English *Phoenix*', *Old English Poetry: Fifteen Essays*, ed. Robert P. Creed (Providence, R. I., 1967), pp. 129–52.

[5] See esp. *ibid.* pp. 135–6 and 140–5.

[6] *PQ* 43 (1964), 1–13. Mrs Kantrowitz's article should be read in conjunction with N. F. Blake's introduction and notes (esp. that on the image of the seed, p. 74) to his edition of *The Phoenix* (Manchester, 1964) and his essay, 'Some Problems of Interpretation and Translation in the Old

in terms of a remarkably complex interweaving of traditional Christian symbols, not all of which are subsequently interpreted. Focusing on the Old English poet's version of the bird's rebirth, Mrs Kantrowitz shows that the superficially odd association of images of an apple, silkworm, eagle and seed grain with the phoenix makes good sense, because all these images had accrued traditional Christian symbolic meanings relating to rebirth and resurrection.

Methodologically this article has a significance extending beyond *The Phoenix* because it solves one of the basic problems in the use of traditional Christian symbolic analogies as tools of interpretation. This problem, to which Morton W. Bloomfield has called attention,[1] is that frequently the same word or image will have received from different authorities a wide variety of often contradictory allegorical or symbolic meanings. Mrs Kantrowitz finds, for example, that several interpretations of a worm were probably available to the Old English poet.[2] Since the poet indicates in the second half of his poem that he wishes the details of the bird which he has elaborated in the first half to be understood basically in terms of resurrection, Mrs Kantrowitz reasonably infers that the worm is a silkworm which, contrary to some other symbolic worms, had been construed as a symbol of Christ's and man's resurrection. 'The modern problem of interpretation', she summarizes, 'then becomes one of rebuilding the poet's range of reference, rejecting those details which seem irrelevant in the sources of allegory available to us, and accepting those multiple aspects which seem truly pertinent.'[3] Since the author of *The Phoenix* has explicitly indicated the general domain of symbolic reference, 'our part', as she says, 'is to understand the details'.[4]

Greater problems and controversy arise concerning those poems which, unlike *The Phoenix*, do not indicate a general frame of allegorical or symbolic reference or even, so it seems, any intended allegorical or symbolic meanings at all. Some recent critics appear to feel that if Old English poems allude to images or details to which Christian tradition had assigned symbolic meanings it can be assumed that not just the images but also their Christian meanings are implied without any explicit indication being required that such meanings are intended.

English *Phoenix*', *Anglia* 80 (1962), 50–62. Cross appropriately affirms the reality of the bird ('The Conception of the Old English *Phoenix*', p. 138) in the face of Blake's unnecessary exaggeration that to the poet the bird is only a symbol and nothing more ('Some Problems', p. 50). At the same time Mrs Kantrowitz's essay proves conclusively a number of Cross's assertions (e.g. that it was not necessary for the Old English poet to interpret every symbol and that the literal details of the historical bird intentionally anticipate their symbolic implications; see 'The Conception', pp. 140 and 136–7) and answers some other questions raised by Cross and O. F. Emerson (see 'The Conception', pp. 133–6).

[1] 'Symbolism in Medieval Literature' (1958), repr. Morton W. Bloomfield, *Essays and Explorations: Studies in Ideas, Language, and Literature* (Cambridge, Mass., 1970), pp. 88, n. 13, and 94–5.
[2] 'The Anglo-Saxon *Phoenix* and Tradition', pp. 5–9.   [3] *Ibid.* p. 13.   [4] *Ibid.*

A prominent method of this kind of criticism is to focus on images more or less in dissociation from the literal contexts in which they appear. Lewis E. Nicholson's *An Anthology of Beowulf Criticism* includes two essays, one by Allen Cabaniss and another by M. B. McNamee, S.J., which suggest the broad outlines of *Beowulf* as a Christian allegory.[1] Their argument is based on similarities of detail which relate Beowulf to Christ, Grendel and the dragon to Satan, and Grendel's mere to hell and the baptismal font. Nicholson himself develops this argument much more extensively.[2] His interpretation of the symbolic meaning of the funeral of Scyld Sceafing nicely illustrates the questions and interpretative problems of construing symbolic meanings which spring not from the text of a work itself but rather from a tradition of symbolic images with which the author is assumed to be familiar. Nicholson asserts that there is 'in the funeral rites of Scyld Sceafing an elaborate and impressive *figura* of Christian baptism' because 'the pagan ceremony of ship burial described here bears a striking resemblance to the sacramental typology of baptism developed by the patristic writers'.[3] Contextually the resemblance is somewhat less than striking, for Nicholson simply extrapolates the images of a ship (implicitly wooden), a mast, ice, a voyage, the sea and death in this passage of *Beowulf* (26–52): these images, he says, are intended to allude to other ships, masts, ice, voyages and deaths which were traditionally construed to have specific Christian implications. That the literal circumstances of Noah's ark and of various other ships of the church (e.g. the apostles' boat on the Sea of Galilee) differ rather dramatically from those of Scyld's funeral ship does not seem to matter.

Nicholson transmutes the paganism of Scyld's funeral into Christian-baptismal truths not because the poet says he sees this funeral as a *figura* of baptism but because, according to Nicholson, we can assume that as a Christian he ought to have so understood and intended his audience to understand the funeral.[4] Although Nicholson's impressive documentation demonstrates that a ship passing over stormy seas to a destination was a commonplace Christian metaphor or symbol for the course of the individual Christian's life on earth or for the church's historical progress through the last age over the stormy

---

[1] *An Anthology of Beowulf Criticism*, ed. Lewis E. Nicholson (Indiana, 1963). Cabaniss's essay, '*Beowulf* and the Liturgy' (pp. 223–32), first appeared in 1955 and is the more cautious of the two; McNamee's '*Beowulf* – an Allegory of Salvation?' (pp. 331–52) first appeared in 1960.

[2] 'The Literal Meaning and Symbolic Structure of *Beowulf*', *Classica et Mediaevalia* 25 (1964), 151–201.

[3] *Ibid.* p. 185.

[4] Nicholson (*ibid.*, p. 186) attributes to Scyld's retainers the pessimistic questioning about the destination of his corpse, but the text indicates that it is the poet's view: the description of the funeral (26–50a) is, understandably, in the past tense (citations from *Beowulf* are to Klaeber's 3rd ed.), but when the poet remarks that no one can know who took Scyld, he shifts to the present tense of narrator and audience (50b–2). The comment has an appropriate tone of wonder and mystery but dubiously reflects any Christian assurance.

waters of sin (and heresy) to the safe harbour of heaven and/or the New Jerusalem, it is one thing to recognize that Noah's ark traditionally symbolized the church and quite another to show that the *Beowulf* poet probably intended the funeral ship of Scyld to remind his audience of the ark or of any other such ship. Potentially every ship may be a ship of the church, every mast a cross, every ocean sin and death, every voyage the Christian journey in time and history and all ice paganism; but surely F. G. Cassidy is correct in urging caution and restraint in the modern perception of images which may allude to Christian implications in *Beowulf*.[1] Nicholson argues that the audience of *Beowulf* would have expected to perceive Christian implications in the poem because its fictional setting is recognizably pre-Christian and indeed pre-flood and hence that the text is parallel to Old Testament writings and is to be construed like the bible.[2] Although such a conception is not intrinsically unlikely, for, as is well known, the fathers habitually incorporated what they knew of secular-pagan history and myth (by euhemerization) into the chronology of Old Testament events, the evidence of such an intention in the poem itself is less than conclusive.

Charles Donahue similarly argues from Irish precedent that the *Beowulf* poet conceived of his pagan ancestors as noble monotheists under the pre-Christian natural law which governed men before the written Mosaic law, although in historical chronology these pagan ancestors may actually have lived after Christ.[3] Donahue's interpretative approach to *Beowulf*, however, is rather different from Nicholson's, although like him he perceives Christian implications. Donahue postulates a poetic method of allusion to abstract patterns in the presumably intentional correspondence of the hero Beowulf to certain Old Testament figures, a correspondence based not on similarity of image or concrete detail but on similarity of a typical kind of action. Abraham and Job are said to be models on which the deeds of Beowulf are patterned:

The first part of the poem deals with the moment where the hero arrives at a faith and hope, a trust, in God like that of Abraham. In the second part, the account of the

---

[1] 'A Symbolic Word-Group in *Beowulf*', *Medieval Literature and Folklore Studies: Essays in Honor of Francis Lee Utley*, ed. Jerome Mandel and Bruce A. Rosenberg (New Brunswick, N.J., 1970), pp. 33–4. Interestingly enough Cassidy's word of caution concludes his own suggestion, in the manner of Nicholson, that reference to the sun in *Beowulf* alludes to Christ (pp. 28–33).

[2] 'The Literal Meaning', pp. 152–66. Nicholson credits Margaret Goldsmith with reviving the idea that the narrative is intentionally cast in a historically pre-Christian setting (p. 152).

[3] '*Beowulf* and Christian Tradition: a Reconsideration from a Celtic Stance', *Traditio* 21 (1965), 55–116, esp. 58–74. Donahue thus avoids the problem Nicholson mentions ('The Literal Meaning', p. 152) of possible actual historical allusions to events of the fifth and sixth centuries. Morton W. Bloomfield discusses this problem briefly and suggests a setting under the natural law in 'Patristics and Old English Literature: Notes on Some Poems', *Comparative Lit.* 14 (1962), 39–41. Larry D. Benson shows that even without Irish Christianity and Pelagianism there is ample warrant for the poet's presentation of pagan heroes as virtuous and admirable, 'The Pagan Coloring of *Beowulf*' *Old English Poetry*, ed. Creed, pp. 202–6.

hero's death, the paradigm shifts to Job as the hero, though tempted to despair, persists in hope despite the fact that God is withdrawing His gifts. At the same time he attains to a charity such as that described by St John and hence, like the other moral heroes under the natural law, Job for example ... he becomes a *figura* of Christ.[1]

Although, Donahue argues, the problems which the dragon presents to the Geatish hero are quite different from Job's loss of wealth and family and his physical affliction, the responses of the two heroes are similar, and since Abraham and Job through their faith, hope and trust prefigure Christ, so does Beowulf.[2]

Donahue suggests that the *Beowulf* poet has presented a typological diptych, Beowulf being in one panel and Christ in the other.[3] He recognizes that the second panel will exist only in the imagination of educated Christian auditors, but he feels that the text of the poem, the first panel, sufficiently implies the second. Actually Donahue has described a triptych:[4] between the panels of Beowulf and Christ should be a panel with Abraham and Job. One wonders, though, why the poet neglected to mention these two patriarchs if they were intended to be such important paradigms and whether an audience, however Christian, would tend to perceive similarities between Beowulf and them in the absence of a large number of specific similarities of detail. Donahue naturally emphasizes those details in the poem which could be construed as indicating that Beowulf has faith, hope and trust in God. But these details are so pitifully few that if we compare the book of Job with its laments and heated dialogues to *Beowulf*, the two poems appear to be rhetorical inversions of one another (assuming, that is, that the latter is about hope and trust in God). Since there is so much else in *Beowulf*, consideration should probably be given to Kenneth Sisam's rather reasonable supposition that 'the matters to which the poet gave most space or emphasis are those which he thought it most important to convey'.[5]

From a number of related suggestions about Christian allegory and symbolism in Old English heroic verse,[6] Margaret Goldsmith's study stands out

---

[1] '*Beowulf* and Christian Tradition', pp. 86–110. My quotation is from p. 85.
[2] *Ibid.* pp. 110–16.   [3] See esp. *ibid.* p. 116.   [4] *Ibid.* pp. 86–116.
[5] *The Structure of Beowulf*, p. 60.
[6] A recent reading of *Beowulf* as Christian allegory without patristic notation is by Gregory Ziegelmaier, 'God and Nature in the *Beowulf* Poem', *ABR* 20 (1969), 250–8. T. M. Pearce notes the Christian implications of a 'southern sun' in 'Beowulf and the Southern Sun (*Beowulf*, lines 603–6)', *Amer. Notes and Queries* 4 (1966), 67–8. Thomas D. Hill similarly investigates the Christian implications of heat and cold in 'The Tropological Context of Heat and Cold Imagery in Anglo-Saxon Poetry', *NM* 69 (1968), 522–32. See also Hill's 'Two Notes on Patristic Allusion in *Andreas*', *Anglia* 84 (1966), 156–62 (with suggestions for *Beowulf*, pp. 160 and 162) and his '"Byrht Word" and "Hælendes Heafod": Cristological Allusion in the Old English *Christ and Satan*', *ELN* 8 (1970), 6–9. A similar perception of allusive Christian implication is by Paul Beekman Taylor,

as the one that grapples most extensively with the question of how *Beowulf* can be a Christian allegory, assuming that that is what it ought to be.[1] Mrs Goldsmith is convinced from the start, as a reviewer notes,[2] that *Beowulf* is a Christian allegory, but her demonstration, attempting to cope with problems which for the most part were outlined by Marie Padgett Hamilton,[3] is not altogether successful. She has some difficulty, for example, with the problem of Grendel's relationship to Cain *vis-à-vis* Heorot and Hrothgar, a problem slightly more acute than Marie Hamilton indicated.[4] In Genesis, as everyone knows, after being cursed by God, Cain goes out to build the first city, the archetypal city of men from which the tower of Babel, Sodom and Babylon proceed. Cain is not exiled from the world; he is the founder of it and of worldliness. Abel through innocent sacrifice is the spiritual hero of the City of God.[5] In *Beowulf*, of course, Grendel is an outcast from the world and the society of men, and it is Hrothgar who builds a mighty hall from an impulse embarrassingly like that behind the construction of the tower of Babel.[6] However, the *scop's* song of creation (89b–98) obviously suggests an enthusiastic and positive relationship between the construction of Heorot and God's creation of the universe, thereby, if not endorsing Heorot, praising it ironically. Mrs Goldsmith's solution to this problem is to suggest that Grendel is an allegorical externalization of the worldly, fleshly spirit of Heorot (exemplified by Unferth and the anticipated blood-feuding which will ultimately destroy the hall of Danish civilization).[7] Thus the Cain in Hrothgar and the Danes poetically breeds the

'*Heofon Riece Swealg*: a Sign of Beowulf's State of Grace', *PQ* 42 (1963), 257–9. Elsewhere Taylor argues that the Christian allegory of *Beowulf* is simply part of a larger inclusive pattern of myth, 'Heorot, Earth, and Asgard: Christian Poetry and Pagan Myth', *Tennessee Stud. in Lit.* 11 (1966), 119–30. Of related interest is the suggestion by Morton W. Bloomfield that the characterization of Unferth may have been influenced by the allegorical personifications of Prudentius's *Psychomachia*, '*Beowulf* and Christian Allegory: an Interpretation of Unferth', *Traditio* 7 (1949–51), 410–15. John Gardner attempts to construe *Beowulf* in more or less the same way as that in which Fulgentius interprets Vergil's *Aeneid*, 'Fulgentius's *Expositio Vergiliana Continentia* and the Plan of *Beowulf*: Another Approach to the Poem's Style and Structure', *Papers on Lang. and Lit.* 6 (1970), 227–62.

N. F. Blake's interpretation of Byrhtnoth as a saintly hero of the faith, 'The Battle of Maldon', *Neophilologus* 49 (1965), 332–45, is opposed by the contemporary essay of J. E. Cross, 'Oswald and Byrhtnoth: a Christian Saint and a Hero who is Christian', *ESts* 46 (1965), 93–109. For further resolutions of this question see Michael J. Swanton, 'The Battle of Maldon: a Literary Caveat', *JEGP* 67 (1968), 441–50, and George Clark, 'The Battle of Maldon: a Heroic Poem', *Speculum* 43 (1968), 52–71.

1 *The Mode and Meaning of 'Beowulf'* (London, 1970). This study, as Mrs Goldsmith observes (pp. vii–viii), is the culmination of a number of years of enquiry which produced several articles along the way.

2 Kemp Malone, *Speculum* 46 (1971), 369–71.

3 'The Religious Principle in *Beowulf*'. Nicholson reprints this essay in his *Anthology of Beowulf Criticism*, pp. 105–35.

4 'The Religious Principle', pp. 314–22.

5 See Augustine's *De Civitate Dei*, xv.ii, iv, v–viii and xvii.   6 See esp. 67b–70.

7 *The Mode and Meaning of 'Beowulf'*, esp. pp. 112 and 248.

literal Grendel who literally takes over Heorot. This shifts the problem to Beowulf, since, if he is an externalization of the Abel in Hrothgar, it is he who ought to be killed by Grendel. If he is not related to the spiritual heroism of Abel, then what is his allegorical relationship to Grendel, Hrothgar and the Danes? The same kind of problem occurs in Mrs Goldsmith's reading of the third episode.[1] The dragon becomes an externalization of Beowulf's own sinful nature, yet it is a real-fictional dragon,[2] and most interestingly the literal Beowulf, fighting a literal dragon, becomes an abstracted externalization of himself fighting his own sinful nature. As with the intrusion of Beowulf into the relationship of Hrothgar and Grendel, how Wiglaf fits into the rhetorical ontology of this fiction remains ambiguous. On the other hand, Mrs Goldsmith's hypothesis reminds one a little of later medieval dream allegories in which some externalized version of the dreamer himself appears in the dream narrative.

Although *Beowulf* continues to prove somewhat intractable material in the hands of modern Christian allegorists,[3] it has been demonstrated with more probability that allegory based on allusion to patristic analogies may indeed exist in other Old English poems which lack the kind of symbolic framework provided by *The Phoenix*. Examination of *The Seafarer* by G. V. Smithers, P. L. Henry and Daniel G. Calder is particularly interesting.[4] *The Seafarer*, of course, contains several literal remarks about spiritual and eternal rewards which transcend the difficulty and futility of earthly life[5] and the conclusion certainly seems to anticipate a Christian heaven. To this less-than-conclusive indication of some allegorical intent Smithers adds a formidable accumulation

---

[1] *Ibid.* pp. 230–44.

[2] This suggestion is, of course, not new for the dragon in *Beowulf* or for other dragons in literature and art. See, for example, Arthur E. DuBois, 'The Dragon in Beowulf', *PMLA* 72 (1957), 819–22. What is new is the extent to which Mrs Goldsmith attempts comprehensively to analyse the aesthetic workings of such internal/external relationships in *Beowulf*.

[3] Opposition to the allegorists has not been lacking. Some recent examples are Robert D. Stevick, 'Christian Elements and the Genesis of *Beowulf*', *MP* 61 (1963), 79–89; John Halverson, '*Beowulf* and the Pitfalls of Piety', *Univ. of Toronto Quarterly* 35 (1965–6), 260–78; and William Whallon, *Formula, Character, and Context: Studies in Homeric, Old English, and Old Testament Poetry* (Washington, D.C., 1969), pp. 117–38.

[4] G. V. Smithers, 'The Meaning of *The Seafarer* and *The Wanderer*', *MÆ* 26 (1957), 137–53 and 28 (1959), 1–22. Smithers's interpretation seems to work better for *The Seafarer* than for *The Wanderer*. Some reasons why are implicit in James L. Rosier's discussion, 'The Literal-Figurative Identity of *The Wanderer*', *PMLA* 79 (1964), 366–9 and in Daniel G. Calder's 'Setting and Mode in *The Seafarer* and *The Wanderer*', *NM* 72 (1971), 264–75. P. L. Henry examines and interprets in great detail all the images of *The Seafarer* in terms of their traditional symbolic implications in *The Early English and Celtic Lyric* (London, 1966), pp. 133–60. Stanley B. Greenfield cogently discusses the probabilities of literal versus Christian-allegorical readings of these two poems in 'The Old English Elegies', *Continuations and Beginnings: Studies in Old English Literature,* ed. E. G. Stanley (London, 1966), pp. 152–60.

[5] Esp. 64b–7 and 77–80a. Citations from Old English poems other than *Beowulf* are from The Anglo-Saxon Poetic Records, ed. George Philip Krapp and Elliott Van Kirk Dobbie (London and New York, 1931–53).

of evidence intended to suggest that the poem is developed around the Christian metaphor of life as a stormy voyage over the waves of sin and death. There is a striking correspondence of images. Moreover the rhetorical structure itself and the sequence of topoi in the Old English poem correspond to the structure and sequence of topoi in a number of homilies and Latin poems, familiar to or written by Anglo-Saxons, which elaborate images of seafaring in terms of the Christian *peregrinatio*. Smithers even finds several specific verbal parallels. He is perhaps most persuasive, though, where he points out that the paratactic conjunction of certain locutions in *The Seafarer*, which have a riddling quality in their literal construction, make good sense as images associated with the Christian *peregrinatio*.[1] Henry argues that the collocation of all the images in *The Seafarer* is best explained as being consistently and obliquely informed by religious symbolism, as does Daniel G. Calder, who attempts to show that the modulation of the images in the poem should be understood in terms of the poet's gradual realization of the validity and rightness of the Christian *peregrinatio*.

Using the same approach, R. E. Kaske interprets Riddle 60 and *The Husband's Message* as an elaborate, unified allegory based on allusion to images which had been traditionally assigned Christian meanings.[2] In the face of the extremely corrupt state of the text of *The Husband's Message* and of other plausible solutions to Riddle 60, for example those suggested recently by Roy F. Leslie and F. H. Whitman,[3] the evidence for traditional Christian symbolic identifications, which Kaske investigates with customary thoroughness, is not as convincing as it is in the case of *The Seafarer*. Perhaps no interpretation of these two passages in the Exeter Book, or for that matter *The Wife's Lament*, for which Kaske suggests a similar approach,[4] will ever be conclusive.

Since the indispensable element in the hypothetical poetry of allusion is that Old English poems imitate or reproduce certain images which had been invested with symbolic or allegorical implications in Christian tradition, Old English poetic versions of Old Testament stories are significant: if there is still some question as to whether the images in *The Seafarer* are meant to imply the kind of Christian seafaring which takes place in Noah's ark or the apostles' boat on the Sea of Galilee, the Moses and Pharaoh in the Old English *Exodus* are unquestionably the Moses and Pharaoh of the bible. Since the crossing of the Red Sea (Exodus xiv–xv.21) had been prominently allegorized in Christian

---

[1] See Smithers, *MÆ* 28 (1959), 7, and lines 48–52, where details of the delights of spring are joined with those of longing for the sea.
[2] 'A Poem of the Cross in the Exeter Book: *Riddle 60* and *The Husband's Message*', *Traditio* 23 (1967), 41–71. For a statement of Kaske's method see esp. 41 and 51–2.
[3] Roy F. Leslie, 'The Integrity of Riddle 60', *JEGP* 67 (1968), 451–7, and F. H. Whitman, 'Riddle 60 and its Source', *PQ* 50 (1971), 108–15. See also the introduction to Leslie's edition of *Three Old English Elegies: The Wife's Lament, The Husband's Message, The Ruin* (Manchester, 1961), pp. 12–22.
[4] 'A Poem of the Cross', p. 71, n. 81.

tradition, Bernard F. Huppé and J. E. Cross and S. I. Tucker conclude that the Old English poet has intended to convey not simply a lengthy heroic version of the event but also, or, rather, its traditional Christian implications,[1] in spite of the fact that the text itself nowhere indicates any explicit interest in such matters.

It is reasonable enough to assume that the author of the Old English *Exodus* and his audience were Christians familiar with the exegetical, homiletic and sacramental texts which relate Aaron's rod to Christ, Pharaoh to Satan, the Egyptian host to sins and the waters of the Red Sea to the baptismal font. That an author could have discussed the crossing of the Red Sea in terms of baptism, however, does not mean that he has had to, because, if that were so, we would have to assume that in the medieval Christian mind Moses, Pharaoh, Aaron's rod, the waters of the Red Sea and so forth were, like dead metaphors, meaningless except in terms of their Christian identifications. On the contrary, as Charles Donahue has observed,[2] most patristic commentary reflects Augustine's well-known insistence that historical facts and their analogous Christian significances are equally substantial and important:[3] Pharaoh was allegorized as Satan precisely because he was Pharaoh; Aaron's rod could be construed as Christ precisely because it was a rod belonging to Aaron; the Egyptian host was never just the Christian sins, for if it had been, there would have been no point in drawing an analogy between it and sins. The purpose of Christian exegesis was not simply to multiply a religious vocabulary but to reveal living analogies which were endorsed and passed on by tradition because both parts stayed alive and were meaningful as analogies.

Israelites and Egyptians therefore imply themselves,[4] and allusion to them

---

[1] Bernard F. Huppé, *Doctrine and Poetry: Augustine's Influence on Old English Poetry* (Albany, N.Y., 1959), pp. 217–23; and J. E. Cross and S. I. Tucker, 'Allegorical Tradition and the Old English *Exodus*', *Neophilologus* 44 (1960), 122–7. Huppé similarly construes the Old Testament events retold in *Genesis A* (pp. 131–216), as does Robert P. Creed, 'The Art of the Singer: Three Old English Tellings of the Offering of Isaac', *Old English Poetry*, ed. Creed, pp. 69–92. In the same fashion Jackson J. Campbell glosses *Judith* ('Schematic Technique in *Judith*', *ELH* 38 (1971), 155–72). The interpretive problem is, of course, the same for all Old English poetic versions of Old Testament stories. Cross takes numerous exceptions to Huppé's method in his review of *Doctrine and Poetry*, *JEGP* 59 (1960), 561–4, but see the explanation in his monograph, *Latin Themes in Old English Poetry* (Bristol, 1962), pp. 9–10. Cross and Tucker feel that the Old English *Exodus* gives sufficient hints of its intention to imply Christian allegorical significances. For a discussion of the early suggestion by Bright (1912) that liturgical texts are the source of the *Exodus* and hence determine its allegorical implications, see *The Old English Exodus*, ed. Edward Burroughs Irving Jr, Yale Stud. in Eng. 122 (New Haven, 1953), 14–16.

[2] 'Patristic Exegesis in the Criticism of Medieval Literature', *Critical Approaches,* ed. Bethurum, pp. 61–82.

[3] *De Civitate Dei*, xv.xxvii.

[4] So concludes E. G. Stanley in an excellent survey of verbal potentiality and problems of meaning, including problems of symbolism and allegory, 'Old English Poetic Diction and the Interpretation of *The Wanderer, The Seafarer* and *The Penitent's Prayer*', *Anglia* 73 (1955), 414–47, esp. (on poetic versions of Old Testament stories) 418. One of the best summaries of the poet's approach in the

or retelling of a story about them will not of its own accord imply their traditionally endorsed analogous relationship to Christians and sins or their relationship to any other analogy that traditionally had been, or potentially could be, suggested. The hints Cross and Tucker perceive that the poet has recognized the mystical significance of the crossing of the Red Sea are a dubious substitute for an explicit indication on his part that he intends to imply that significance in the *Exodus*. By casting the episode in the traditional garb of Germanic heroism the poet seems rather to have intended to present Moses, Pharaoh and the others as viable characters (fictionally and/or realistically) with whom the Anglo-Saxons could relate. By so doing he would have made the homiletic and sacramental texts which analogized Israelites and Christians, Egyptians and sins far more meaningful than they would have been without a Germanic context to vivify Israelites as Israelites, Pharaoh as Pharaoh and so on.

Similarly the author of *Beowulf* may have been a devout Christian, extremely knowledgeable in exegetical matters. His reminder that Cain killed Abel (108b) neither indicates that he did not know Christian interpretations of Abel, as is sometimes suggested, nor indicates that he associates those interpretations with Grendel in any way. This detail and the others from the story in Genesis which he mentions simply indicate those aspects of Cain as Cain which are pertinent to Grendel. Although Donahue may well be correct in asserting that the dying Beowulf would have suggested Calvary to some Anglo-Saxons, the poet is not thereby relieved of an obligation to show that he wishes to actualize that possibility in his text. On the other hand, there are genuine textual grounds for believing that the author of *The Seafarer* has indeed chosen his images because of their relationship to traditional comments on the Christian *peregrinatio*.

The recent scholarly and critical interest in the allegorical potentialities of Old English poetry seems to indicate that there are at least two ways in which Christian poets may allude to allegorical implications. The first is by establishing a specific framework of Christian analogies which will determine and limit the potential Christian significance of other images alluded to but not interpreted. The second is by implanting a riddling inadequacy, inconsistency or impossibility in the literal text which impels the reader to seek a meaningful interpretation from traditional Christian symbolism. Although many medieval poems combine the two methods,[1] there is no theoretical reason why a poet

---

Old English *Exodus* is by Irving, *The Old English Exodus*, pp. 34–5. He observes of the poet: 'While he was doubtless familiar with the conventional allegorization of Old Testament narrative, he seems to have been less interested in ingenious abstract interpretations than in the stories themselves. This is not to say that he was not cognizant of the total symbolic effect of the exodus story; but he was concerned with dramatizing it as a whole rather than in parts.'

[1] Stephen Manning analyses varying emphases in Middle English lyrics on explicit indication of

could not rely simply on the interspersion of such riddling, literally inadequate comments to indicate that Christian allegorical analogies are being implied not just by the literally inadequate statements but by the whole text. The critic has to decide how prominent structurally or quantitatively such interspersions are within an otherwise literally satisfactory text and to estimate how probable are Christian allegorical explanations of these interspersions as against other possible implications. A methodological spectrum of poetic composition suggests itself, ranging from extensive and explicit indication of an allegorical framework (as in *The Phoenix*) to a riddling collocation of images which makes sense only in terms of Christian analogical implications.

It would be extremely helpful if we had an encyclopaedic collection of important patristic interpretations of images and historical figures from the bible, especially if it were to include notation of the sources of particular interpretations, thus representing an enormous improvement over the *Glossa ordinaria* and the indices of Migne's *Patrologiae*. It also seems to me that the time is ripe for a substantive work taking account of all the poems in the Old English canon and studying their various potentialities of allusion to traditional Christian allegorical and typological interpretations. The considerable work already done on certain poems and the truly impressive amount of historical, archaeological, iconographic, linguistic and literary work of the last twenty years or so give reasonable hope that such a study could establish the working limits of Christian allegory and allegorical allusion in Old English poetry.

allegorical intent in combination with lines and phrases which are literally puzzling or absurd (*Wisdom and Number: Toward a Critical Appraisal of the Middle English Religious Lyric* (Lincoln, Nebraska, 1962), esp. pp. 90–137). One poem Manning discusses (pp. 111–12) is most instructive (*Religious Lyrics of the XVth Century*, ed. Carlton Brown (Oxford, 1939) no. 112). Line 23 reads: 'The pasche lambe, þat on þe croce did clym.' Since ordinary lambs do not climb crosses, the reader is forced to seek an answer to this riddling statement. In a Christian context there is only one answer: Christ who died on the cross, the Lamb of God. However, this lyric relies heavily on explicit indication of an allegorical framework: (1) it is entitled 'Off þe Resurrectioun of crist'; (2) it explicitly refers to God, the Virgin Mary and angels; and (3) the preceding line (22), 'The saikles lorde, þat slane was for þi slycht', provides a parallel explication of and preparation for line 23.

Allegorical, typological or neither? Three short papers on the allegorical approach to *Beowulf* and a discussion

The papers and discussion printed here were the substance of the English 1 (Old English) meeting of the Modern Language Association of America's annual convention in Chicago on 27 December 1971. Professor Stanley B. Greenfield (University of Oregon) organized and chaired the meeting. He and Professor Peter Clemoes have edited the proceedings, but modification has been kept to a minimum. The postscript is part of a letter sent to the chairman after the meeting.

PAPER I

William Whallon (Michigan State University)

Dante's letter to Cangrande uses the word allegorical to denote all those higher senses which may accompany the literal sense. One of them is the moral, another the allegorical, and a third the anagogical. Allegorical includes allegorical! Our key term is both generic and specific. It is like the zoological name *rattus*: the common grey rat is *Rattus norvegicus*, the common brown rat is *Rattus rattus*. So I shall say at once that for me 'the allegorical interpretation of *Beowulf*' – the subject of this panel – is the use of Christian writings to claim that the poem means more than it seems to. Many scholars nowadays are urging the relevance of the patrology: my intention here is to give an example of how their method may be impugned. I have decided to mark her visit by speaking against a minor item in *The Mode and Meaning of 'Beowulf'* (London, 1970) by Mrs Goldsmith. Mr Donahue and I were on a panel once before and should now perhaps let bygones be bygones.

The allusions in *Beowulf* to the giants – from Cain 'all monsters awoke: eotens and elves and orcs, giants too which warred with god (or God)' (111–13, cf. 1689–90) – seem partly biblical and partly non-biblical. The giants may be biblical, but their warring with god (or God) is non-biblical. Where did the poet get this non-biblical idea? He may not have gotten it anywhere; he may simply have made it up. But my impression is that he surely did get it somewhere. And I see two possibilities: the native tradition and the classical tradition. They are separated by the first sound-shift, but may in myth be sometimes the same, exactly as Tiw, Jove and Zeus are the same.

The first possibility needs only a few words. The *Vǫlospá* belongs to the same culture of alliterating half-lines as *Beowulf*. So at least some of the legends in the *Vǫlospá* are likely to have been known to the *Beowulf* poet and the people for whom he composed. When the Old Norse poem tells about the war between the giants and the gods, I gather that the legend was known to the Anglo-Saxons, and that it is wholly heathen, non-biblical, pre-Christian, Germanic. The legend may even be pre-Germanic, or common to all the Indo-European nations.

The second possibility is more complex, more interesting. Mrs Goldsmith (*Mode and Meaning*, p. 107) identifies as an ancient legend 'about the giants begotten by the sons of Cain' a passage from the ecclesiastical historian Eusebius: they lived like savages, 'giving themselves every one to all kinds of evildoing, so as to corrupt each other sometimes, to kill each other sometimes, to eat human flesh sometimes, and to venture upon battles with God (or the gods) and upon those battles with giants which are celebrated everywhere, and to conceive of fortifying the earth against heaven, and in the madness of a dislocated mind to prepare war against the God of all things himself'. Now actually this passage does not speak 'about the giants begotten by the sons of Cain', for it concerns (almost) *all* the descendants of Adam, and nowhere suggests that the giants were begotten by them. What the passage does suggest is that, having fought battles with the gods (or God) and battles with giants, *theomachias* and *gigantomachias*, the wicked men behaved, in fortifying the earth against heaven, as if they were themselves giants: the author was evidently allowing his mind to wander. Yet for our purposes Eusebius does balance the *Vǫlospá* rather evenly. Neither mentions Cain, neither blames the giants upon the loins of mankind; but both do seem to tell about the giants' warring with the gods (or God). There is only one more question to ask, and its answer will decide the contest.

Where did Eusebius get the idea? The Migne patrology (PG 20, col. 63), in a footnote, mentions Vergil's *Georgics* (1.281), the giants 'tried three times to place Ossa on Pelion'. But where did Vergil get the idea, and why should a Greek scholar like Eusebius have been reading verse in Latin? Well, both Vergil and Eusebius got the idea from the *Odyssey* (XI.315–16), the giants 'wanted to place Ossa upon Olympus, and Pelion of the shaking leaves upon Ossa, so that heaven might be scaled'. And now that we have found the idea in Homer as well as in the *Edda*, must we not assume with greater confidence than we had before that it was pre-Germanic, or common to all the Indo-European nations? In my opinion we must assume this, *whether or not* we believe that a priest among the Anglo-Saxons thought Eusebius gave him the freedom to enliven the books of Moses with the fables of Odysseus.

The one alternative is this. The legend about the war between the giants and the gods was Germanic. It was combined with the biblical story about Cain and the biblical verse about the giants in the earth (Genesis VI.4) by the *Beowulf* poet or – though I cannot credit the notion – by his teacher of religion, someone like Aldhelm. If by the poet, the combination was a natural and spontaneous one; if by the teacher, it was an artificial or contrived one, serving to make the sacred tradition seem familiar. Eusebius is not relevant at all.

The other alternative is this. The legend about the war between the giants and the gods was Homeric. It was combined with the biblical story about Cain and the biblical verse about the giants in the earth, by the poet's teacher of religion, someone like Aldhelm, who followed an obscure, muddled, heretical item in the patrology. The poet readily accepted the combination since in part it happened to agree with a Germanic legend he already knew. And Eusebius is relevant for having remembered the *Odyssey* when thinking of the giants in the bible, and for having led some cleric in England to perpetuate such mischief.

Today I prefer the former; and if tomorrow I prefer the latter I will still acknowledge only that the poet may have heard a Genesis episode contaminated with a classical version of an ancient Indo-European myth he believed in beforehand. Mrs Goldsmith is to be admired for her originality in bringing Eusebius to our notice, but neither here nor elsewhere do I see that the patrology explains the moral sense of *Beowulf*, and my vote on the allegorical interpretation of the poem continues to be *non credo*.

Margaret Goldsmith (University of Bristol)

The stories in *Beowulf* incorporate mainly secular values, but these are tested and weighed against Christian ideals evoked through irony, contrastive allusion and outright statement. Though the basic conception of the poem is I believe figural (in the widest sense of the term), I discern in the treatment of Beowulf's monster-fights what I can only call a moral-allegorical strain, indicated by specific reference to the soul. The word allegory therefore appears to me the best available to cover the non-literal aspects of *Beowulf*, but it must be understood that I use it in the broad sense that it anciently had. Among modern writers, G. N. Leech (*A Linguistic Guide to English Poetry* (London, 1969)) offers a description of allegory as 'a multiple symbol' which will serve my purpose. He also observes that an allegory 'partakes of the ambivalence and indeterminacy we have noted in ordinary symbolism. It may contain within itself no overt linguistic indication of its underlying significance, being thus completely cut loose from the anchorage of literal interpretation' (p. 163). Our problem, very obviously, is to detect and recognize and follow other kinds of indication. Allegory is open-ended, especially when the match of correspondences between one domain of understanding and another is not close. On the question of choice between literal and figurative readings, Leech is again helpful: 'Sometimes convention is the operative factor, and sometimes context. The "mental set" of the reader is also important' (p. 162). In the case of *Beowulf*, our views about the appropriate conventions and the *mental set* of the hearers are in dispute. We might perhaps begin with a look at Leech's third factor, *context*. The immediate context of the disputed passages will no doubt ask for attention, but first I should like to consider the wider context of the corpus of Anglo-Saxon poetry.

Several of the poems in the corpus would be classified as allegory by some critics, including myself, and differently by others. Examples are *The Sea-farer, The Husband's Message, Exodus* and *The Rhyming Poem*. Our disagreement is partly a question of definition of the term, and it is also partly a question of *mental set* in the critic. But there is another factor too: a question of historical imagination. Though the symbols used in these poems are sometimes natural and immediately significant to us (e.g. the stormy seas), quite often they take their significance from a cultural and religious life not generally familiar today, but accessible through other literature (e.g. the gift-seat, the green rod of Moses, the dragon's jaws). The poems which were written down and preserved are likely to have a Christian bias, and it is not really surprising that a number of pieces which contain no overt indication of an underlying significance can be shown to contain a *situational analogy* to the imagined state of the soul in its invisible world. I would emphasize that we *can* read and enter into such poems *without* much regard for the non-literal meanings, because the human predicaments or the stories appeal to us whether or not we can share the Christian poet's double vision, but if we read them literally, we may find some lines mystifying and the organization of the whole poem ill-proportioned or strange. This kind of poetry evidently owes its origin to an extension of figural thinking from moral and allegorical interpretation of the Old Testament. Of the examples I have mentioned, I should like to say a brief word about *Exodus* – a poem usually thought to be rather close to *Beowulf* in diction and attitudes.

Because we know that *Exodus* is an Old Testament story we are prepared for the possibility of allegory. No plain directive is given or required. The Old English poem is organized round the climactic event of the crossing of the Red Sea, which was a very familiar *situational analogue* of the human soul's crossing into a new life on becoming Christian. The poem appears to be for laymen: it is certainly 'about' the exemplary war-leader Moses and his victory over Pharaoh's army. But the audience is evidently expected to pick up the prophetic symbolism of the *grene tacn* (281a), the rod of living wood, which saves the Israelites and destroys the Egyptians. A few scattered hints of this sort are all that we have to prepare us for the cryptic ending of the poem. The spiritual analogy I have spoken of, the purifying of the soul as it becomes a member of the church, is unmistakably indicated when we reinstate the African woman in line 580 (cf. *Anglia* 80 (1962), 373–8). There are several texts in the Old Testament to be drawn on by a homilist who wishes to speak about Christ's love for the sinful soul, some concerning a dark woman – 'black but comely'. One of these relates to Moses as *figura Christi*: he married an Ethiopian woman. To the exegetes, she is a type of the individual soul, or of the church, the spouse of Christ. How better, then, could the Anglo-Saxon poet indicate the universal spiritual significance of his subject than by describing the African woman adorning herself after the victory that freed God's people from bondage? Yet recent editors of *Exodus* have agreed to do away with her, because they have not recognized that the poem is governed by this underlying theme and *not* by the historical progress of Moses and his army.

I now turn to *Beowulf*. The frame of reference is not so clear as in the case of *Exodus*, but we have a stepping-off point in the allusive mention of Cain, the Flood and the giants' battle with God, together with the one or two Christian-Latin loan-words which even William Whallon admits as testimony to some Christian teaching in the poet's neighbourhood. Hrothgar's long admonitory speech to Beowulf contains metaphorical references to assaults upon the soul which we should unhesitatingly read as Christianly homiletic if we came upon them elsewhere. We can try to do away with them by arguing that they don't mean what they normally would mean and that they are an interpolation anyway. Or we can take this speech as a directive to think about the battle for the soul in what follows Beowulf's successes as king. In the light of these signs of Christian belief, it is surely reasonable to work from the hypothesis that mention of God, devilry and hell in the Heorot story implies that poet and audience had been brought up as Christians, and were able to respond as readily to cryptic religious symbolism as to dark allusion in the secular tales.

The characters in the stories belong to a pre-Christian period, and the poet credits them with only an innate understanding of the creator and his moral law and judgement. So Christian observance does not come into the poem at all. But the central theme of the continuing battle between the good and evil powers, clearly pointed to by the mention of Cain's progeny and the design on the giant sword-hilt, was at the heart of the church's teaching in our period.

This is enough to justify our looking for a Christian theme or themes in the organization of the entire poem. When we realize that the dragon was then a powerful Christian symbol for the devil as tempter and as destroyer, the ultimate enemy of God and man, we do not need to ask why the poet gives no explanation of the origins of Beowulf's last adversary. The place of the dragon at the climax of Beowulf's story is as fitting and right as the place of the enigmatic African woman at the end of *Exodus*. Yet it is quite evident that Beowulf's dragon with his fifty-foot carcass is not *literally* the devil. If he *symbolizes* the devil we must seriously ask whether he is part of a symbolic action, i.e. an allegory.

Once we have entertained this idea, we can see that the apparently dual nature of the Grendel kin, who appear as giant humans and as demons, and the dual nature of their lair, as haunted mere and as hell, bear out the supposition that Beowulf's monster-fights are imagined on some level other than the simply historical. I believe we are justified in saying that their mode is figural. As *physical creatures*, Beowulf's great opponents are members of the races cursed by God in the Book of Genesis, the offspring of the serpent and of the outcast Cain. J. Halverson has recently said ('The World of *Beowulf*', ELH 36 (1969), 593–608) that they 'embody the primitive anxieties' – 'fear of the dead and the fear of being eaten'. He is so nearly right, but Grendel is not 'the dead': he has a corpse, and a heathen soul of his own. The 'primitive anxieties' are certainly embodied there, but these anxieties had already been focused for a Christian poet in images (as in the *Life of St Antony*) of the clutching giant devil and of the fire-breathing jaws of the ancient dragon *alias* Leviathan. It follows that the man Beowulf confronting these figural adversaries enlarges into a figure of mankind.

Now we can ask the crucial question: 'What has Beowulf to do with Christ?' Doctrine then current about the nature of man emphasized the primary belief that mankind was regenerated through the incarnation of God. The old Adam, fallen and harassed by Satan, had been reborn with an access of divine strength to oppose his enemy. The turning-point in the contest between the evil powers and the good was the descent of the divine man to do battle in the abyss of hell, a battle ritually re-enacted at every baptism. If we think of this pattern of redemptive history we can see in the repeated rescue of the old man by the young hero and in the decisive battle in the depths a shadowy counterpart to the sacred story. But the tale in the foreground naturally claims more of our attention.

Beowulf as a type of mankind patterns in his last days with the Old Adam. It was in fact the very curious progress of the dragon-fight that first drew me into serious study of the poem. The secular analogues have nothing like this near-failure on the hero's part, with the decisive blow struck by another hand.

Remembering Hrothgar's admonition, I judge Beowulf's trust in his single strength arrogant and misplaced and the value he puts on the treasure wrong-headed. I find myself being led into the moral allegory of a single soul, enacted against that panorama of redemptive history. At this stage the murmurs of incredulity arise. Where on earth could an Anglo-Saxon poet find a model for so large and complex a vision of man? Charles Donahue hit upon the answer twenty years ago, but, plunging into the Irish mists, he has turned away from the full implications of his comparison with Job.

Gregory's enormous moral commentary on the Book of Job has always, I suspect, been something of a Christmas pie – from which other teachers in their several corners could pull out the plums. But I have wondered why he, and his disciples in the early centuries after the conversion, had such special interest in Job. I was slow to see that Gregory's book provided an answer to the secularist and the Pelagian alike. The Book of Job asserts that only he who has a voice and an arm like God, who can master the great Leviathan, dare say 'my own right arm can save me'. This is doctrine hard to take, then and now. Gregory remarks 'And yet some men, scorning the help of God, are confident that they can save themselves by their own valour' (PL 76, col. 643). As he interprets the story, the man Job, putting his trust in God, came triumphantly through Satan's trials, in a series of spiritual battles. But then he was humbled and made to acknowledge his creaturely dependence by means of a revelation of God's infinitely greater power – a revelation which for Gregory includes something a modern might well not see at all: a description of the presently invisible enemy of every man, Leviathan, breathing fire and smoke, the very dragon of hell (Job XL and XLI, expounded PL 76, cols. 682 ff.). But there is more to it than this: the questions put to Job about his power over Leviathan were understood, together with several other passages in the book, as prophetic images of the coming defeat of the great enemy by God the redeemer. The acts ascribed to the redeemer include the mastering of the seas, the breaking of the raised arm (Job XXXVIII.15; cf. PL 76, cols. 486–7), the descent into the abyss of waters (PL 76, cols. 489–90) and the subjugation of Leviathan. Can I bring you to agree with me that more than coincidence is at work when the *Beowulf* poet speaks of the dragon's false hope with a phrase 'him seo wen geleah' (2323b) strikingly like the 'spes ejus frustrabitur eum' used about Leviathan in Job (XL.28)? Here we have it – a model for what I have traced in *Beowulf*: the god-fearing 'historical' man passing victoriously through his trials, *contrasted* with, first, the creator who governs the elements and the seasons and, next, in a series of cryptic *situational analogues*, with the redeemer who descends into the waters to quell the adversary.

There is one more strand to fit in. Hrothgar's admonition foresees a possible assault on the hero by the slayer whose insidious suggestions break through the soul's defences (1741b–7). I now ask you to consider whether or not Beowulf's meeting with the dragon is an allegory of that temptation and its repulse. First some doctrines from the homilists. The devil as dragon is often the tempter – *draco per insidias*. (As such he may be contrasted with the open adversary who walks about 'seeking whom he may devour'.) Augustine says plainly 'Draco eiecit Adam de Paradiso' (*Tract. in Ioh. Evang.*, CCSL 36, 100). Adam's fall is not expressly referred to in *Beowulf*, but I would call your attention to the traditional image of original sin as the serpent-dragon's death-bearing venomous bite (*mors a morsu*; see, e.g. a sermon by Caesarius of Arles 'On the brazen serpent and the rod of Moses', CCSL, 103, 462). This links with the better-known image of damnation as entering the dragon's mouth. Gregory elaborates on the idea of entering and yet escaping from those jaws when he discusses Leviathan (PL 76, col. 686). In the light of all this, I see Beowulf, the man of the Old Law, enticed by the dragon's treasure to pit his single strength against mankind's inveterate enemy. He is not devoured by the dragon, but the jaws close in his proud neck and he dies of the spreading poison, leaving his people a legacy of wretchedness. Our poet does not deny his hero's greatness, but as in the Book of Job the man's short-lived struggle with Satan is set in its little place in the conflict between the creator and the powers of darkness.

PAPER 3

Charles Donahue (Fordham University)

Of the considerable literature bearing on our topic, my distinguished co-panelist's *The Mode and Meaning of Beowulf* is indubitably the most important work. It is marked, in general, by careful scholarship and full of interesting suggestions. I have personally learned much from the book, and yet I find myself wholly unconvinced by its principal theses: (1) that the mode of *Beowulf* is allegorical and (2) that its ultimate meaning consists in a warning to sons of Adam who arrogantly trust in their own strength rather than in God and are immoderately devoted to wordly treasure; like Beowulf, they will in the end fight a losing battle with Satan and face at best an uncertain eternity. My purpose here is to point out two reasons why I am unable to assent to Dr Goldsmith's theses. One is based on a minor and often neglected doctrine of Augustine; the other, on the *historia secundum litteram* as presented by the text of *Beowulf*.

Dr Goldsmith approaches the text of the poem equipped with a set of convictions based in history. One of these convictions is that an English cleric of around 700 (she suggests *c.* 650–793 as the era of composition; *Mode and*

Meaning, pp. 17–19), well schooled in Augustine and Gregory the Great, would be very likely to compose a poem concealing under a surface of heroic story a wholesome Christian allegory. In my opinion that is a most improbable hypothesis. Among the many considerations telling against it is the fact that Augustine expressly forbids Christian teachers to imitate the cryptic allegories and other obscurities of scripture. Such devices (he taught) used by writers inspired by the Holy Spirit are doubtless appropriate in the texts where they occur, but their use should remain the prerogative of the inspired canonical writers. The canon has been long closed, and later Christian teachers (*posteriores*) should use the clear style approved by classical rhetorical schools. Here is what Augustine writes (*De Doct. Christ.* iv.viii.22):

> Although from writings of theirs (the canonical authors) which are easily understandable we take some models of style, we must by no means think that we ought to imitate them where they have spoken with a useful and salutary obscurity ... To be sure, canonical authors spoke thus so that those who came later (*posteriores*), understanding them correctly and explaining them, might find another grace in the church of God, not on the same level as theirs, to be sure, but consequent upon it. Those who expound canonical authors, therefore, ought not to express themselves in such a way as to give the impression that they are putting themselves forward as of like authority to be expounded in turn, but in all their words, they should strive, in the first place and most earnestly, to be understood.

It has been objected that Augustine's remarks were intended to apply only to preachers and exegetes, not to poets. I find it incredible that Augustine intended to grant to poets a privilege he denied to theologians because he regarded it as reserved to inspired canonical authors. In any case, nowhere in Augustine or, to my knowledge, in any of the early medieval Augustinians, has there been found a text suggesting that Christian poets ought to compose heroic poems that are cryptically religious.

Since there is no substantial evidence in history for an *a priori* assumption that *Beowulf* contains a hidden allegorical meaning, the case for allegory must be defended by an appeal to the literal text of the poem. There is now a long tradition of interpretation of the literal text, and there is, I believe, considerable agreement about what the literal text implies about the poet and states about the main theme of his poem. The poet, whatever else he may have been, cleric or lay, a serious Christian or a nominal one, or even a pagan, was a master of the English form of Germanic heroic verse and one learned in Germanic heroic story. His main theme is a celebration of the moral grandeur of Germanic ideals in times long ago, long before the gospel was preached in the north. That is a secular theme and the poem, according to the letter, is a secular poem. Many notable students of the poem, for example Klaeber, Chambers,

Wrenn, Malone, Tolkien, have been convinced that the poet was a serious and perhaps learned Christian. His serious Christianity, however, does not affect essentially the secularity of his theme. He is celebrating heroic virtue, not teaching Christian doctrine. Indeed, Tolkien suggests that the poet's Christianity actually heightened his awareness of the secular character of his theme, leading him to insist on the hopelessness and darkness of the world of his characters. Even those who knew of the existence of God were without any hope of a transcendent beatitude. The darkness of the background was planned to enhance the audience's appreciation of the heroic secular virtues that shone as a light in that darkness. In any case, it is clear in the literal text that the morality of the poet's pre-Christian Germania is a secular morality. It consists of a Germanic code concerned principally with the right relations between *dryhten* and *gedryht* with obligations of generosity on the one hand, courage and loyalty even to death on the other. The sanctions of this code are secular. Good repute (*dom*) says Beowulf, is the best thing a dead warrior can have. Hrothgar also speaks of eternal fame and seems to agree with the *Hávamál* that it is only fame that is eternal. Beowulf has some vague notions about a survival of consciousness (not necessarily an eternal survival) after death. No character in the poem has any glimmering of the Christian hope for an eternal and transcendent beatitude.

Hrothgar's sermon can easily be interpreted in accordance with the secular convictions of the inhabitants of the poem. Hrothgar advises his adopted son to profit by the lesson in the two *exempla* about which the sermon is structured, Heremod and the unnamed ruler. Beowulf is told that when he becomes a *dryhten* he should be a munificent distributer of rings and mild to his people. He should avoid overweening thoughts (*oferhyda*), which tell him that he can dispense with the loyalty of his people, and turn to *ece rædas*, counsels which will assure him an eternity of fame based on their loyal remembrance of his generosity.

Pre-Christian theists in the poem know about evil spirits, and Hrothgar attributes the avarice of the unnamed ruler in his second exemplum to the suggestion of a mortal enemy (*bana*), an evil spirit (*werga gast*). Dr Goldsmith, who devotes an entire chapter to the sermon, marshals all her patristic forces and sends them into the poem at this point. The *bana* with his arrow and his bad advice, becomes an excuse for introducing the entire satanology of Gregory the Great, and with Gregory's satanology comes his uncompromisingly otherworldly ethic based on his deep faith in a transcendent beatitude, and a severe interpretation of Augustine's doctrine of the two cities.

Consequently, the sermon of the pre-Christian theist Hrothgar is interpreted as a lesson in Gregorian morality. Hrothgar is warning Beowulf, in the second *exemplum*, of that arrogance (*oferhygd*) which may lead a prosperous and powerful man to trust in his own strength and forget his dependence on God. Relaxed by that arrogance, the unnamed ruler of the second *exemplum* became an easy target for the shafts of Satan. He is assailed by avarice (the love of worldly treasures for themselves); his insatiable cravings only increase as death approaches, and his soul is lost. Hrothgar implores Beowulf to guard himself against such an assault of Satan and make a better choice, namely *ece rædas*, counsels, presumably that will lead to eternal beatitude. Only when thus interpreted, we are told 'does (Hrothgar's) sermon hold together and fit the story of Beowulf' (*Mode and Meaning*, p. 206).

On the contrary, I would say that when Hrothgar's sermon is so interpreted and the secular poem thus loaded with an alien otherworldly morality, all rapport with the literal text and its celebration of secular heroic virtue has been lost. My view is perhaps supported by Dr Goldsmith's next move. She seems to invent a new end for the story of Beowulf and suggests that the warning of Hrothgar turned out to be prophetic. In his old age Beowulf did indeed become forgetful of God and guilty of an arrogant self-sufficiency. He fought a losing battle against Satanic temptation and died 'a deluded old man', 'blinded by arrogance and a desire for the treasure' (*Comparative Lit.* 14 (1962), 87).

Such a story of Beowulf fits the allegorical interpretation of the dragon fight well enough, but it cannot be justified by any substantial evidence from the literal text of the poem. On the other hand, there are many passages in the literal text that tell against it. I have some seven passages in mind, but I confine myself to one, which I believe to be decisive. It is the touching speech that the dying hero makes when he sees the treasure. Dr Goldsmith quotes three half-lines (2799–800a) from this speech (out of context) in support of her contention that at the end of his life, Beowulf was so greedy for gold that he paid with his life for the treasure. I shall translate from the beginning of the speech through the three half lines that follow Dr Goldsmith's quotation (2794–801). In the two cases where we differ, I give Dr Goldsmith's version of the meaning of the lines, not mine. The old king, revived by Wiglaf's water and seeing the gold, speaks: 'I say thanks to the Lord of all . . . for these treasures I see here before me, because I have been permitted (*moste* not *meahte*) to win such for my people before my death.' Here are the sinful half-lines: 'Now I have sold my old life for a hoard of treasures.' The following three half-lines are interpreted in the traditional fashion – with which I disagree: 'Do you [Wiglaf] henceforth take care of the needs of the people. I am unable to stay here longer.' The lines, even so taken, indicate that at the end of his life, Beowulf was humbly grateful to God for permitting him to win the hoard for the people. It had cost him his life, but his mind turned back to the needs of the people, as his command to Wiglaf shows.

How could the poet have told us more clearly that at the end of his life,

Beowulf was humble and not arrogant towards God, concerned with the needs of his people, not with treasure for its own sake? Such is the *historia secundum litteram* communicated by the plain text, and it must not be changed to accord with an allegorical interpretation, for an allegorical interpretation loses all power to convince when the imagination of the critic is not controlled by the literal text. Indeed, Augustine teaches that, even when one is interpreting inspired writings, 'nothing is derived from enigmatic allegories that is not most clearly stated elsewhere in the plain text' (*De Doct. Christ.* ii.vi.8).

DISCUSSION

Theodore Silverstein (*University of Chicago*): I'm beginning to feel old. About eight years ago we did a programme exactly like this in MLA, and the positions seemed to be about the same (*Laughter*). They say history repeats itself, so perhaps we ought to allegorize that one. I don't want to take off from where the last speaker ended, though on the whole, temperamentally, I can go his way. But I'm troubled by the very loose use of the term *allegory*. There are at least five different systems which are implied. Professor Whallon began with a reference to the letter to Cangrande, and pointed out that Dante was referring to the so-called fourfold interpretation; and when Dante gets through, he has taken one of them, the allegorical allegorical, the *rat rat*, as a model and said that everything else is in there, but he's writing in order to make people improve their lives so that they might expect a better fate in the future; therefore it's all on human action, therefore it's part of ethics and morality. This is moral allegory. And stories of all kinds have been used, as we know, from ancient times for the sake of moral allegory. As a matter of fact, Dr Goldsmith talks about its being used in a broad sense, quoting Leech, on its being open-ended. If you happen to be a *symboliste* of the C. S. Lewis persuasion, you would call that symbolism. And it's very different from a system of allegory which is precise and usually direct and intended – and according to the *symbolistes* somehow unpoetic and limited. We have also the difference between inherited traditional metaphor of the sort that you find in the *Psychomachia* and a system of this sort deriving from the interpretation of scripture. Now which of these systems is intended? If the argument is that all *histoire*, because of the attitude of the listeners (attitudes of mind), will have other meanings, the fact is anybody writing anything will suggest such meanings. *Coriolanus* during World War II was put on in Paris, and the Parisians thought it was a great thumbing of the nose against the occupying Germans. It's possible to do that. In the end the question is, when you read a piece, what warrant you have to assume that the author might have witten it allegorically, and what evidence there is in the literal text that you *must* so read it. The *littera* is indeed sacred and you cannot rewrite or reread it if it cannot take the allegory. Now, one thing that's perfectly plain in *Beowulf* is that it begins with a long prologue and that that prologue states some of the themes *Beowulf* includes. Must we read that allegorically before we ever get to the Christian references? This is a statement by a poet of what he intends to do – poets do this frequently. That there are Christian references in the poem no one can deny. Many, many years ago I pointed out, for example, that in the descent of Beowulf to fight with Grendel's dam there are descriptions very much like the Christian vision of St Paul, which was known in this period. And the Anglo-Saxons knew a great many apocryphal works. It's abundantly plain, if you read Father Shook's account of *Guthlac A* for example, that they used some of the apocryphal themes that you find in *Brendan* and so on. Now, this is full of Christian references – it's written in a Christian time. So is Shakespeare. But is that allegory? On finding such obvious things as good and evil – *The Man of Law's Tale*, you remember – good and evil, dragons and people and so on, do we have an allegorical system or do we have a moral system operating in a literal poem in which you recognize the good guys and the bad guys and people in the audience take sides? I want to hear what the difference is between allegory and literal dramatic accounts in which there are moral themes and moral preoccupations.

Goldsmith: Well, I did say we should start with our definition of the term. I think by a very strict definition of allegory the interpretation I have given would not be called allegorical. In Anglo-Saxon poetry generally I find a spectrum of fiction from, at one extreme, a poem like *The Phoenix*, in which you can see a very close correspondence, to, at the other extreme, poems in which you can hardly say whether they are or are not allegory, such as *The Wife's Lament* and *The Wanderer*. I think there is this spectrum and that it is difficult to theorize about it, and for this very reason I wouldn't work from theory, but empirically from what the poems seem to say in their own organizations.

Kenneth Lundgren (graduate student, University of Wisconsin): I'd like to put in a good word for typology. It seems to me that that's the only way we're going to end the inconclusive combat between romantic Germanism and Christian moralism. I think there is so much evidence for a typological reading of *Beowulf* that you have to be just tremendously benighted not to see it (*Laughter*). Professor Donahue, you seem to be adumbrating a typological view in your article . . .

Donahue (interrupting): Most emphatically that is what I was adumbrating, but not an allegorical point of view. I do not regard that as allegorical.

Lundgren: O.K. Let me just put in the evidence for one typological reading and then I'll let someone else talk. The word *þrowian* is used five times altogether in the poem: it is used once for the suffering that Grendel undergoes when his head is cut off posthumously, and once for Heremod's suffering; but it is used three times for Beowulf's sufferings at the fiery onslaught of the dragon. Now elsewhere in Old English the word *þrowian* is virtually a technical term for the passion of Christ. I submit that that is what it suggests here: that Beowulf's suffering at the onslaught of the dragon is like Christ's suffering on the cross.

Donahue: If we are going to talk about typology in regard to *Beowulf*, we have to seize what I think is the core of the typological point of view. It's not a literary matter: it is a way of looking at history – accepting that history itself is meaningful and that what goes before adumbrates what comes afterwards. It is all divinely inspired in that sense, so that, for example, a very important passage from the tractate on the Mass in the Stowe Missal, which I quoted in my *Beowulf* article (*Traditio* 21 (1965)), is not allegorical when it says that under the natural law Christ was known in his members. All it means is that before Christ came there were good men living under the natural law, and that by knowing their goodness men were able to understand what Christ would mean once he had appeared. If history makes sense and is progressive, then there's something to be said for typology.

Sr Jane Marie Luecke (Oklahoma State University): This is really a question, although there is an implied attitude in it: isn't it possible that the term *allegory*, like so many others, simply changed meaning, and what we have before, for example, *Everyman*, is something different? In St Paul's letters to the Corinthians about the spirit of the letter we have something broader (D. W. Robertson, I think, has written something to this effect); and this is what Augustine, it seems to me, is talking about – that there is a hidden meaning in things; and I understand this to be as broad as what we today call symbolism. So we're really talking about multiple levels of symbolism, aren't we, not about allegory as it came to be understood after *Everyman* and Spenser and so on, and as we now understand the term.

Philip Rollinson (University of South Carolina): It seems to me, Professor Donahue, that your text from Augustine refutes your own point of view, and I agree with Dr Goldsmith: I think you've missed it in your book and I think you're right, Dr Goldsmith, when you commented that Donahue is doing the same thing you are and wondered why he wasn't willing to call it allegory, because you are. Now, Professor Donahue, you stated that Augustine says, 'O.K. Preachers and teachers are not to hide things, to conceal things the way scriptures do.' But typology is hidden too. Moses didn't know that he was a type of the church (*Laughter*)! When Abraham took little Isaac up there in the hills, he didn't realize that that was figuring Christ! In your article of 1965, Professor Donahue, you suggested that the typology in *Beowulf* is one in which we have a literal text and then have to imagine the other side of the diptych. But you really imagine a triptych, because you say, 'Here's Beowulf in the eighth century. This guy has got faith, hope and trust in God.' And then you say, 'Aha! Abraham and Job – they had faith, hope and trust too. They're types of Christ; therefore I have a type of Christ here in Beowulf!' Now I think that's preposterous (*Laughter*). And I'll tell you why (*Laughter*). I read the Old English *Phoenix*, and I read Prudentius and Juvencus and about fifty other Latin Anglo-Saxon poets and French Latin poets, and they do exactly what Augustine says: they reveal, and they put the parts together. Professor Silverstein's question is very pertinent: can I mention a ship, can I mention a seafarer, can I mention a dragon, can I mention all kinds of images and details that were interpreted by analogy Christologically or mystically – can I just allude to an image like that and have my audience know, 'a seafarer – yes, the Christian *peregrinatio*'? Is that possible? If, Professor Donahue, you point out that Augustine says by implication that poets should not write that way – and I think that's right – the empirical evidence too is that medieval poets *don't* write that way. Because when Prudentius wants to say that Marcion is Cain, he *says* Marcion is Cain. He put them together. But both you and Dr Goldsmith are saying we have a poet who says A but means B.

Goldsmith: Well, first I'd like to say that when I used the word *figural* I chose it as a less strictly theological word than *typological*. The *sensus spiritualis* of the theologians is strictly inapplicable to *Beowulf*; however, I believe that an Anglo-Saxon could be brought up to think of the meaning of life in terms of multiple levels of understanding, and would in consequence be quite likely to interpret any historical situation with this multiple view. The inspiration of *Beowulf* may well have been secular in its beginnings; if you were to ask me what kind of occasion might cause a man to embark on such a poem, I would ask you to think how you might say to a king 'You are great and well-loved, but you are not immortal and you are not God.' On a secular level the poem says something like this, and perhaps the poet began to compose with such a purpose, but if he did begin so, he went on to disclose that human life is something different from what the heroic poets describe. He wrote about fraternal enmities and conflicts within society, and realized that these conflicts arise from conflicts within individuals and have to do with the relationship between God and the created world – and so, I suggest, he found himself writing about what it means to be creaturely and mortal.

Donahue: I think there's one important difference between Dr Goldsmith's method and the one we derive from a genuinely figurative treatment: Dr

Goldsmith, it seems to me, seriously disturbs the literal text in interpreting the later moral history of the hero. In other words, I can find no evidence in the literal text that Beowulf did deteriorate. The only ground for that is in an allegorical reading. Now, from a typological point of view, you ask what is the history, and whatever further you suggest about typological overtones, they do not affect the text at all. For example, if you think Beowulf suggested Christ to some of the hearers – a permissible assumption, I think: it may have been an intention of the poet – your notion of what goes on in the poem is not affected one iota because that notion rests on the literal text alone.

Rollinson: But you defy probability in doing this. Think of Job and Beowulf! It seems to me that there's a lot closer relationship between the dragon and the devil, as Dr Goldsmith suggests, than there is between Job and this hero.

Donahue: I never . . .

Rollinson: You don't defy the literal text, and you're right. But you don't work toward probability – that is, the intention of the literal text – either. It seems to me you just throw it to the winds. You say, 'Yup, there's a type, there's a picture.'

Donahue: But the hero, in his situation, found out he was mortal and vulnerable, which is what Job found out, and he went on trusting in God, regardless, which is what Job did.

Rollinson: Then does everybody who is mortal and vulnerable equal a type of Christ?

Donahue: In a very large sense, yes.

Bruce Beatie (Cleveland State University): When you talk about a type of Christ, isn't it fair to ask, 'Of what was Christ, in fact?' The narrative of the life of Christ that we have is literature too, and it is modelled upon narratives that go far back. In terms of the kinds of parallels which have been cited in this discussion, it would be fair to treat the life of Christ in our narrative as a type too. Let me put it another way: should the New Testament be treated as a type of Christ because the same narrative pattern recurs in *Beowulf*? We are dealing in ideas that are so general that either you do everything with them or you do nothing at all. They are fundamentally human situations. What is accomplished by making this kind of incredibly broad statement?

Donahue: Let me refer first to Professor Rollinson's last objection. Who will not accept that everyone is in a way a type of Christ? I think everyone is – that is, everyone suffers to a certain extent, everyone dies; but that is a meaningless way, I suppose, for the construction of a literary and imaginative work. On the other hand, what the writer of the tract on the Mass in the Stowe Missal certainly meant was that those people are in a special sense types of Christ who in their own moral excellence show forth new kinds, higher modalities, of moral beings, because they are bringing mankind a few steps along the way that will eventually lead to Christ. Now I think the *Beowulf* poet was consciously portraying his hero as that kind of man.

Rollinson: Why?

Donahue: Because I can say that there are certain connections that suggest that, and because I think the poet was writing in a tradition very different from that of St Augustine – a tradition which stressed typology a great deal more and which was based, unlike Augustinianism, on a basically optimistic view of human history as man's progress under God through natural law, the Mosaic Law and finally Christianity.

POSTSCRIPT

Geoffrey Moore (graduate student, University of Washington): To my mind the format of the debate, particularly one as lively as this, has led to a polarization false to the critical methods at stake, and false to the poem. Professor Donahue says the poem is history while Dr Goldsmith says it is allegory. But Professor Donahue's 'history' takes its force from 'typology' and Dr Goldsmith's 'allegory' from 'situational analogue', two terms distinguishable, if at all, only by a subtle analysis sympathetic to each, something which the spirit of debate does not encourage. Similarly, Professor Donahue insists that the poem is pagan at root, Dr Goldsmith that it is Christian. But it is just because Christian patristic values are so close to Germanic heroic values that Dr Goldsmith can read Hrothgar's speech allegorically while Professor Donahue can deny Christian elements in it. Again, the problem with the debate format is that it implies we must choose. I suspect instead that part of the greatness of Anglo-Saxon poetry is that it deliberately manipulates words, like *ofermod* and *oferhygd*, which participate centrally in both Christian and Germanic values but with different moral valences, in order to demand that we bring both systems to the poem, not one or the other.

In the case of Beowulf's fight with the dragon, while I would not want to deny that it has archetypal force independent of the Christian tradition, I would interpret details such as the small band of onlookers, the original loosing of the dragon due to the crime of another man, as well as the fact that Christ's battle with Satan as dragon has a central place in Christian iconography, as clear indications that the poet is here deliberately creating a 'situational analogue' to the Christian tradition. I would conclude from this that the poet asks us to measure Beowulf against Christ, to perceive that Germanic heroism, despite its great spirit, beauty, and natural dignity, cannot transcend the last test, cannot vanquish evil in the world, and that it must therefore yield to Christian faith. What I would emphatically not conclude, however, is that this comparison is in any way intended to denigrate Beowulf's character. The greatness of Christ is that he supersedes a great hero. To withdraw our respect from Beowulf in any way, emotionally or intellectually, is to destroy the central sustaining tension of the poem. Such would be the case if Hrothgar's speech to Beowulf were indeed allegorical. I find, with Professor Donahue, no need to read it as such. The parallels to Christian thought might arise from a natural overlap of value systems, and there are no allegorical signposts in the imagery. What irony there is when this passage is read from a Christian perspective is more gentle than judgmental.

Finally, I do not think we need accept Professor Donahue's suggestion that Augustine's strictures are a serious barrier to reading allegory in Anglo-Saxon poetry. Christian culture subsequently supported a great tradition of allegorical poetry, and this tradition had, after all, to begin somewhere. Furthermore, it seems natural that it should begin when men are trying to reconcile the complex emotions aroused by rival cultures; thoughts and feelings uneasily co-existing might well manifest themselves in a multi-level literary form.

Bibliography for 1972

MARTIN BIDDLE, ALAN BROWN, T. J. BROWN,
PETER A. CLAYTON and PETER HUNTER BLAIR

This bibliography is meant to include all books, articles and significant reviews published in any branch of Anglo-Saxon studies during 1972. It excludes reprints unless they contain new material. It will be continued annually. Addenda to the bibliography for 1971 are included at the appropriate places; one that concerns a book or article is preceded by an asterisk and specifies the year of publication. A.B. has been mainly responsible for sections 2, 3 and 4, T.J.B. for section 5, P.H.B. for section 6, P.A.C. for section 7 and M.B. for section 8. Peter Clemoes has been coordinating editor.

The following abbreviations are used where relevant (not only in the bibliography but also throughout the volume):

AB	*Analecta Bollandiana*
ABR	*American Benedictine Review*
AHR	*American Historical Review*
AntJ	*Antiquaries Journal*
ArchJ	*Archaeological Journal*
ASE	*Anglo-Saxon England*
ASNSL	*Archiv für das Studium der neueren Sprachen und Literaturen*
BGDSL	*Beiträge zur Geschichte der deutschen Sprache und Literatur*
BNJ	*British Numismatic Journal*
BROB	*Berichten van de Rijksdienst voor het Oudheidkundig Bodemonderzoek*
CA	*Current Archaeology*
CCM	*Cahiers de Civilisation Médiévale*
CHR	*Catholic History Review*
DUJ	*Durham University Journal*
E&S	*Essays and Studies by Members of the English Association*
EC	*Essays in Criticism*
EconHR	*Economic History Review*
EEMF	Early English Manuscripts in Facsimile
EHR	*English Historical Review*
ELN	*English Language Notes*
EStn	*Englische Studien*
ESts	*English Studies*
IAF	*Issledovanija po Anglijskoj Filologii*
IF	*Indogermanische Forschungen*
JBAA	*Journal of the British Archaeological Association*

JEGP	*Journal of English and Germanic Philology*
JEH	*Journal of Ecclesiastical History*
JL	*Janua Linguarum*
JTS	*Journal of Theological Studies*
MA	*Medieval Archaeology*
MÆ	*Medium Ævum*
MLN	*Modern Language Notes*
MLQ	*Modern Language Quarterly*
MLR	*Modern Language Review*
MP	*Modern Philology*
MS	*Mediaeval Studies*
N&Q	*Notes and Queries*
NC	*Numismatic Chronicle*
NM	*Neuphilologische Mitteilungen*
PMLA	*Publications of the Modern Language Association of America*
PQ	*Philological Quarterly*
RB	*Revue Bénédictine*
RES	*Review of English Studies*
SAP	*Studia Anglica Posnaniensia*
SBVS	*Saga-Book of the Viking Society for Northern Research*
SN	*Studia Neophilologica*
SP	*Studies in Philology*
TLS	*Times Literary Supplement*
TPS	*Transactions of the Philological Society*
TRHS	*Transactions of the Royal Historical Society*
YES	*Yearbook of English Studies*
ZAA	*Zeitschrift für Anglistik und Amerikanistik*
ZDA	*Zeitschrift für deutsches Altertum und deutsche Literatur*
ZVS	*Zeitschrift für vergleichende Sprachforschung*

1. GENERAL AND MISCELLANEOUS

Barley, N., 'Anglo-Saxon Magico-Medicine', *Jnl of the Anthropological Soc. of Oxford* 3, 67–77

Bridier, Yvonne, 'La Fonction Sociale du *Horn* chez les Anglo-Saxons', *Études Anglaises* 25, 74–7

Brown, Alan, 'Old English Bibliography 1971', *OE Newsletter* 5.2, 5–23+15a

Brown, T. J., and D. H. Turner, 'Francis Wormald 1904–72', *Bull. of the Inst. of Hist. Research* 45, 1–6

*Cameron, Kenneth, 'Professor Dorothy Whitelock', *Onoma* 16 (1971), 106–8

Clemoes, Peter, *et al.*, ed., *ASE* 1, 'Preface' (ix–xi) and 'Bibliography for 1971' (309–32)

Collins, Rowland L., Robert S. Cox, Robert T. Farrell, Milton McC. Gatch, Oliver J. H. Grosz, Matthew Marino and Joseph B. Trahern, 'The Year's Work in

Old English Studies 1970', *OE Newsletter* 5.1, 21–63 [Charles R. Carlton, 'YWOES 1968, Linguistic', pp. 57–63]

'The Year's Work in Old English Studies 1971', *OE Newsletter* 6.1, 7–41

*Denecke, Ludwig, *Jacob Grimm und sein Bruder Wilhelm* (Stuttgart, 1971)

Fell, Christine, 'The Icelandic Saga of Edward the Confessor: the Hagiographic Sources', *ASE* 1, 247–58

*Gibby, C. W., 'Bertram Colgrave: an Obituary', *Trans. of the Architectural and Archaeol. Soc. of Durham and Northumberland* n.s. 2 (1971), 109–12

Henderson, George, *Early Medieval*, Style and Civilization (Harmondsworth)

Johnson, James D., 'Byrhtnoth and the Battle of Maldon', *OE Newsletter* 5.1, 1 [a poem]

Kahrl, Stanley J., ed., *OE Newsletter*, 5.1 and 2 and 6.1

Macrae-Gibson, O. D., 'Old English Teaching Methods: an Experiment', *OE Newsletter* 5.1, 7–20

Mustanoja, Tauno F., list of publications of, *Studies presented to Tauno F. Mustanoja on the Occasion of his Sixtieth Birthday* (*NM* 73.1 and 2), preliminary pages

Newton, Robert R., *Medieval Chronicles and the Rotation of the Earth* (Baltimore) [Bede (esp. pp. 117–23) and *ASC*]

Nordenfalk, Carl, 'Francis Wormald', *Burlington Mag.* 124, 245

Pyles, Thomas, 'Kemp Malone', *Language* 48, 499–505

Robinson, Fred C., 'Old English Research in Progress, 1971–1972', *NM* 73, 690–704

Sanderson, Stewart F., 'Dr Wilfrid Bonser', *Folklore* 83, 68–9

Silkin, John, 'The Poetry of Geoffrey Hill', *Iowa Rev.* 3, 108–28

*Skovgaard-Petersen, Inge, 'Vikingerne i den nyere forskning (oversigt)', *Historisk Tidsskrift* (Copenhagen) 5 (1971), 651–721

Thundyil, Zacharias P., *Covenant in Anglo-Saxon Thought: the Influence of the Bible, Church Fathers and Germanic Tradition on Anglo-Saxon Laws, History, and the Poems 'The Battle of Maldon' and 'Guthlac'* (Madras)

*Wilson, R. M., 'English Language' and 'Old English Literature', *The Year's Work in Eng. Stud.* 50 (1971) [1969], 35–82

Wilson, R. M., 'English Language' and 'Old English Literature', *The Year's Work in Eng. Stud.* 51 [1970], 30–77

2. OLD ENGLISH LANGUAGE

*Arngart, O., 'Two Cheshire Place-Names: 1. Offerton, 2. Taxal', *SN* 43 (1971), 430–4

*Bähr, Dieter, 'Altenglisch *ísig* (*Beowulf*, Zeile 33)', *ZAA* 19 (1971), 409–12

*Bammesberger, Alfred, 'Zu altenglisch *-faerae* in Bedas Sterbespruch', *ZVS* 85 (1971), 276–9

Bammesberger, Alfred, 'Zur Vorgeschichte von westsächsisch *-síene/-sȳne* und anglisch *gesēne*', *Anglia* 90, 427–36

'Altenglisch *hligan*', *Münchener Studien zur Sprachwissenschaft* 30, 5–7

Beck, Heinrich, 'Sprachliche Argumente zum Problem des Runenaufkommens', *ZDA* 101, 1–13

Brown, Alan, 'Heifer', *Neophilologus* 56, 79–85 [*heahfore* and *healstan*]

Campbell, Alistair, *Enlarged Addenda and Corrigenda to the Supplement, by T. Northcote Toller, to 'An Anglo-Saxon Dictionary', Based on the Manuscript Collections of Joseph Bosworth* (Oxford) [issued separately or as part of the *Supplement*]

Carlton, Charles R., see under Collins, Rowland L., sect. 1

Cassidy, Frederic G., 'Old English *gārsecg* – an Eke-Name?', *Names* 20, 95–100

*Cassidy, Frederic G., and Richard N. Ringler, ed., *Bright's Old English Grammar and Reader*, 3rd ed. (New York, 1971)

Cercignani, Fausto, 'Indo-European *ē* in Germanic', *ZVS* 86, 104–10

Cox, Robert S., see under Collins, Rowland L., sect. 1

Cruz, J. M. de la, 'The Latin Influence on the Germanic Development of the English Phrasal Verb', *Eng. Philol. Stud.* 13, 1–42

Derolez, René, 'A New Psalter Fragment with OE Glosses', *ESts* 53, 401–8

Dodgson, J. McN., *The Place-Names of Cheshire, Part IV, The Place-Names of Broxton Hundred and Wirral Hundred*, English Place-Name Society 47 (Cambridge)

Duckert, Audrey R., '*Erce* and Other Possibly Keltic Elements in the Old English Charm for Unfruitful Land', *Names* 20, 83–90

Elliott, Constance O., and Alan S. C. Ross, 'Aldrediana XXIV: the Linguistic Peculiarities of the Gloss to St John's Gospel', *Eng. Philol. Stud.* 12, 49–72

Els, T. J. M. van, see sect. 5

Enkvist, Nils Erik, 'Old English Adverbial *þā* – an Action Marker?', *NM* 73, 90–6

Erdmann, Peter H., *Tiefenphonologische Lautgeschichte der englischen Vokale*, Athenäum-Skripten Linguistik 4 (Frankfurt)

'Suffixal *j* in Germanic', *Language* 48, 407–15

Gelling, Margaret, *The Place-Names of Berkshire, Part I*, English Place-Name Society 49 (Cambridge)

'The Place-Names of the Isle of Man', *Jnl of the Manx Museum* 7, 168–75

Gneuss, Helmut, 'The Origin of Standard Old English and Æthelwold's School at Winchester', *ASE* 1, 63–83

Götz, Dieter, *Studien zu den verdunkelten Komposita im Englischen*, Erlanger Beiträge zur Sprach- und Kunstwissenschaft 40 (Nuremberg)

Goldman, Stephen H., see sect. 3c

Heller, L. G., 'Runic Writing: Germanic or Indo-European?', *Papers on Lang. and Lit.* 8, 89–92

Janzén, Assar, see sect. 6

Joly, André, 'La Négation Dite "Explétive" en Vieil Anglais et dans d'autres Langues Indo-Européennes', *Études Anglaises* 25, 30–44

Jones, Charles, *An Introduction to Middle English* (New York)

Kirk, Sarah J., 'A Distribution Pattern: -*ingas* in Kent', *Jnl of the Eng. Place-Name Soc.* 4, 37–59

*Koziol, Herbert, *Invokationen, Segenswünsche, Bitten und Aufforderungen im ältern englischen Schrifttum*, Sitzungsberichte der Österreichischen Akademie der Wissenschaften 277.1 (Vienna, 1971)

Kuhn, Hans, 'Das römische Kriegswesen im germanischen Wortschatz', *ZDA* 101, 13–53

Kuhn, Sherman M., see sect. 3*c*

Lindheim, Bogislav von, 'Das Suffix *-bære* im Altenglischen', *ASNSL* 208, 310–20

Macrae-Gibson, O. D., see sect. 1

Malsch, Derry L., 'Lexical Redundancy and Historical Alternation of Tenseness in English Vowels', *Glossa* 6, 74–82

Marckwardt, Albert H., and James L. Rosier, *Old English: Language and Literature* (New York)

Marino, Matthew, see under Collins, Rowland L., sect. 1

Markey, T. L., 'West Germanic *he/er – hiu/siu* and English "she" ', *JEGP* 71, 390–405

Meritt, Herbert Dean, 'Conceivable Clues to Twelve Old English Words', *ASE* 1, 193–205

Migačev, V. A., 'Germanskij dental'nyj preterit i ego morfonologičeskij status [The Germanic Dental Preterite and its Morphophonemic Role]', *Voprosy Jazvkoznanija* 4, 80–9

*Mindt, Dieter, *Der Wortschatz der Lambeth Homilies: das Adjektiv*, Braunschweiger anglistische Arbeiten 2 (1971)

Myrkin, V. Ja., 'Germanskoe *izwez* (ètjud iz sravnitel'noj grammatiki germanskix jazykov)', *Filologičeskie Nauki* 3, 114–17

Nevanlinna, Saara, 'On the Origin of the Middle English Adverbs *bedene* and *albedene*', *NM* 73, 245–7

*Nielsen, Karl Martin, see sect. 8*i*

Nummenmaa, Liisa, 'The Quasi-Pronominal *so* in Corroborative and Additive Sentences in EME', *NM* 73, 675–82

Olszewska, Teresa, 'Szyk wyrazów w zdaniu a formy fleksyjne słów jako wyznaczniki funkcji syntactycznych w języke staroangielskim [Word-Order and Word Inflections as Signals of Syntactic Function in Old English]', *Annales Universitatis Mariae-Curie-Skłodowska* (Lublin), sectio F, 24, 311–24

*O'Neil, W. A., 'Explaining Vowel Gradation in Old English', *General Ling.* 10 (1971), 149–63

*Peeters, Christian, '*e*₁ in Gothic, Old English, and Old High German: a Phonological Study', *Linguistics* 72 (1971), 26–30

'Zur Entwicklung von *χw* im Germanischen', *ZVS* 85 (1971), 273–5

Peeters, Christian, 'On "how" in Germanic', *Studia Linguistica* 26, 116–19

Penzl, Herbert, 'Old Germanic Languages', *Linguistics in Western Europe*, ed. Einar Haugen and Werner Winter, Current Trends in Linguistics (The Hague), 9.2, 1232–81 [Old English, 1254–62]

*Plotkin, V. Ja., 'Dynamika systemy konsonantnyx fonematičnyx opozycij v istorij anglijs'koï movy [The Dynamics of the System of Consonantal Phonemic Oppositions in the History of English; with Summary]', *Inozemna Filolohija* 25 (1971), 13–18

Plotkin, V. Y. (V. Ja.), *The Dynamics of the English Phonological System*, JL, series practica 155 (The Hague)

Prins, A. A., *A History of English Phonemes from Indo-European to Present-Day English* (Leiden)

*Reszkiewicz, Alfred, *Synchronic Essentials of Old English: West-Saxon* (Warsaw, 1971)

'The Elimination of the Front Rounded and Back Unrounded Short Vowel Phonemes from Medieval English: a Reinterpretation', *Kwartalnik Neofilologiczny* 18 (1971), 279–95

Richards, Michael D., 'Ablaut Alternations in Resonant Stems of Old English Strong Verbs', *Glossa* 6, 83–8

*Rogers, H. L., 'Rhymes in the Epilogue to *Elene*: a Reconsideration', *Leeds Stud. in Eng.* 5 (1971), 47–52

*Ross, Alan S. C., 'Aldrediana XXIII: Notes on the Accidence of the Durham Ritual', *Leeds Stud. in Eng.* 5 (1971), 53–68

Ross, Alan S. C., 'Notes on Some Further Words in the Anglo-Saxon Gloss to the Durham Ritual' [Aldrediana IIB], *NM* 73, 372–80

*Samuels, M. L., 'Kent and the Low Countries: some Linguistic Evidence', *Edinburgh Studies in English and Scots*, ed. A. J. Aitken, Angus McIntosh and Hermann Pálsson (London, 1971), pp. 3–19

Stracke, J. Richard, ed., *The Laud Herbal Glossary* (Amsterdam)

Szemerenyi, O., 'A New Leaf of the Gothic Bible', *Language* 48, 1–10 [includes a note on *færðu*]

*Tinkler, John Douglas, *Vocabulary and Syntax of the Old English Version in the Paris Psalter: a Critical Commentary*, JL, series practica 67 (The Hague, 1971)

Tomovski, Dušan, 'Die nichtindoeuropäischen Vokale in den germanischen Ablautsreihen', *Wissenschaftliche Zeitschrift der Universität Halle*, Gesellschafts- und sprachwissenschaftliche Reihe 21, 101–9

Traugott, Elizabeth Closs, *A History of English Syntax* (New York)

*Voyles, Joseph B., 'The Problem of West Germanic', *Folia Linguistica* 5 (1971), 117–50

Wagner, Hans, 'Beiträge in Erinnerung an Julius Pokorny: 9. Zur Etymologie von gotisch *handus* "hand" ', *Zeitschrift für celtische Philologie* 32, 76–7

*Wilson, R. M., see sect. 1

Wilson, R. M., see sect. 1

*Windekens, A. J. van, 'L'Origine de got. *wēpn*, v. isl. *vápn*, etc. "arme": Solution d'un Vieux Problème', *Studia Linguistica* 25 (1971), 125–8

Zadorožnyj, B., 'Decjat' rokiv vyvčennja pytan' ystorycnoï fonologiï', *Inozemna Filolohija* 25, 164–7 [upon Ja. B. Krupatkin's work]

3. OLD ENGLISH LITERATURE

a. General

Bolton, W. F., 'Boethius, Alfred, and *Deor* Again', *MP* 69, 222–7

*Cassidy, Frederic G., and Richard N. Ringler, see sect. 2

Cross, J. E., 'The Literate Anglo-Saxon – On Sources and Disseminations', *Proc. of the Brit. Acad.* 58, and separately

Duncan, Edgar Hill, 'Short Fiction in Medieval English: a Survey', *Stud. in Short Fiction* 9, 1–28

Gillespie, George T., *A Catalogue of Persons Named in Germanic Heroic Literature, 700–1600, including Named Animals and Objects and Ethnic Names* (Oxford)

Grosz, Oliver J. H., see under Collins, Rowland L., sect. 1

*Hofmann, Dietrich, 'Vers und Prosa in der mündlich gepflegten mittelalterlichen Erzählkunst der germanischen Länder', *Frühmittelalterliche Studien* 5 (1971), 134–75

Koziol, Herbert, *Häufung von Substantiven gleicher Bildungsweise im englischen Schrifttum*, Sitzungsberichte der Österreichischen Akademie der Wissenschaften 278.1 (Vienna)

Marckwardt, Albert H., and James L. Rosier, see sect. 2

*Standop, Ewald, and Edgar Mertner, *Englische Literaturgeschichte*, 2nd ed. (Heidelberg, 1971)

Utley, Francis Lee, 'Dialogues, Debates and Catechisms', *A Manual of the Writings in Middle English, 1050–1500*, ed. Albert E. Hartung (New Haven) III, 669–745 and 829–902

*Wilson, R. M., see sect. 1

Wilson, R. M., see sect. 1

b. Poetry

i. General

*Bliss, A. J., 'Single Half-Lines in Old English Poetry', *N&Q* 18 (1971), 442–9

Bliss, A. J., 'The Origin and Structure of the Old English Hypermetric Line', *N&Q* 19, 242–8

Cable, Thomas, 'Metrical Simplicity and Sievers' Five Types', *SP* 69, 280–8

Crane, John Kenny, 'Simplifying the Complex and Complexifying the Simple: the Two Routes of Approach to Old English Literature', *College Eng.* 33, 830–9 [review article on Margaret Goldsmith, *The Mode and Meaning of Beowulf*; Bernard F. Huppé, *The Web of Words*; and Neil D. Isaacs, *Structural Principles in Old English Poetry*]

Gardner, Thomas, 'The Application of the Term "Kenning"', *Neophilologus* 56, 464–8

Greenfield, Stanley B., *The Interpretation of Old English Poems* (London and Boston)

Hieatt, Constance B., 'Prosodic Analysis of Old English Poetry: a Suggested Working Approach with Sample Applications', *Revue de l'Université d'Ottawa* 42, 72–82

Lee, Alvin A., *The Guest-Hall of Eden: Four Essays on the Design of Old English Poetry* (New Haven)
Levine, Robert, 'Ingeld and Christ: a Medieval Problem', *Viator* 2, 105–28
Pichaske, David R., ed., *Beowulf to Beatles: Approaches to Poetry* (Riverside, N. J.)
Shippey, T. A., *Old English Verse* (London)

ii. *'Beowulf'*

Anderson, Earl R., 'A Submerged Metaphor in the Scyld Episode', *YES* 2, 1–4
Areskoug, Malte, 'De nordiska folknamnen hos Jordanes', *Fornvännen* 1972, 1–15
*Bähr, Dieter, see sect. 2
Bandy, Stephen C., '*Beowulf:* the Defense of Heorot', *Neophilologus* 56, 86–92
Calder, Daniel G., 'Setting and Ethos: the Pattern of Measure and Limit in *Beowulf*', *SP* 69, 21–37
Farrell, R. T., '*Beowulf*', *Swedes and Geats*, *SBVS* 18, 225–86, and separately
Fast, Lawrence E., 'Hygelac: a Centripetal Force in *Beowulf*', *Annuale Medievale* 12, 90–9
Jones, Gwyn, *Kings, Beasts and Heroes* (London)
Kahrl, Stanley J., 'Feuds in *Beowulf*: a Tragic Necessity?', *MP* 69, 189–98
Knipp, Christopher, '*Beowulf* 2210b–2323: Repetition in the Description of the Dragon's Hoard', *NM* 73, 775–85
Malone, Kemp, 'Beowulf the Headstrong', *ASE* 1, 139–45
Morgan, Gerald, 'The Treachery of Hrothulf', *ESts* 53, 23–39
Nickel, Gerhard, 'Problems of *Beowulf*-Research with Special Reference to Editorial Questions', *NM* 73, 261–8
Peltola, Niilo, 'Grendel's Descent from Cain Reconsidered', *NM* 73, 284–91
*Puhvel, Martin, 'The Swimming Prowess of Beowulf', *Folklore* 82 (1971), 276–80
Sanborn, John Newell, 'A Possible Anglo-Saxon Poetic Framework: an Alternative to an Emendation', *MP* 70, 46–8
Schrader, Richard J., 'Beowulf's Obsequies and the Roman Epic', *Comparative Lit.* 24, 237–59
Storms, G., 'Grendel the Terrible', *NM* 73, 427–36
Tripp, Raymond P., Jr, 'Language, Archaic Symbolism and the Poetic Structure of *Beowulf*', *Hiroshima Stud. in Eng. Lang. and Lit.* 19, 1–21

iii. *Other poems*

*Anderson, Earl R., 'Mary's Role as *Eiron* in *Christ I*', *JEGP* 70 (1971), 230–40
*Bammesberger, Alfred, see sect. 2
Barley, Nigel, 'A Structural Approach to the Proverb and Maxim with Special Reference to the Anglo-Saxon Corpus', *Proverbium* 20, 737–50
Barlow, Frank, *et al.*, see sect. 6 [pp. 17–31, Kathleen M. Dexter, 'The Exeter Book']
*Beeton, D. R., 'The Anglo-Saxon *Exodus*', *Eng. Stud. in Africa* 14 (1971), 1–12
Berkhout, Carl T., 'Some Notes on the Old English *Almsgiving*', *ELN* 10, 81–5
*Bessai, Frank, 'The Two Worlds of The Seafarer', *Peregrinatio* 1 (1971), 1–8

Breuer, Rolf, and Rainer Schwörling, ed., *Altenglische Lyrik, Englisch und deutsch*, Universal-Bibliothek 7995–7 (Stuttgart)

Calder, Daniel G., 'The Vision of Paradise: a Symbolic Reading of the Old English *Phoenix*', *ASE* 1, 167–81

'Strife, Revelation, and Conversion: the Thematic Structure of *Elene*', *ESts* 53, 201–10

'Theme and Strategy in *Guthlac B*', *Papers on Lang. and Lit.* 8, 227–42

Campbell, Jackson J., 'Cynewulf's Multiple Revelations', *Medievalia et Humanistica* 3, 257–77

*Chickering, Howell D., Jr, 'The Literary Magic of *Wið Færstice*', *Viator* 2 (1971), 83–104

Doubleday, James F., '*The Ruin*: Structure and Theme', *JEGP* 71, 369–81

Duckert, Audrey R., see sect. 2

Farrell, R. T., 'Some Remarks on the Exeter Book *Azarias*', *MÆ* 41, 1–8

Fehér, Mátyás J., 'A *Waltharius manu fortis*, Hösköltemény avar voratkozásai', *Magyar Történelmi Szemle* 11, 41–66

Finnegan, Robert Emmett, '*Christ and Satan*, 63–64', *Explicator* 31, no. 10 [no paging]

Frank, Roberta, 'Some Uses of Paronomasia in Old English Scriptural Verse', *Speculum* 47, 207–26

Fry, Donald K., 'Type-Scene Composition in *Judith*', *Annuale Medievale* 12, 100–19

Gober, Wallace G., '*Andreas*, lines 360–362', *NM* 73, 672–4

Grant, R. J. S., 'A Note on *The Seasons for Fasting*', *RES* 23, 302–4

Greenfield, Stanley B., '*Folces Hyrde, Finnsburh* 46b: Kenning and Context', *NM* 73, 97–102

Gruber, Loren, 'The Wanderer and Arcite: Isolation and the Continuity of the English Elegiac Mode', *Four Papers for Micho Masui*, ed. Raymond P. Tripp, Jr (Denver), pp. 1–10

*Hakutani, Yoshinobu, 'Unity and Structure in Cynewulf's *Christ*', *Hiroshima Stud. in Eng. Lang. and Lit.* 18 (1971), 1–11

Hamilton, David, 'The Diet and Digestion of Allegory in *Andreas*', *ASE* 1, 147–58

Hill, Thomas D., 'Cosmic Stasis and the Birth of Christ: the Old English *Descent into Hell*, lines 99–106', *JEGP* 71, 382–9

'Satan's Fiery Speech: *Christ and Satan* 78–9', *N&Q* 19, 2–4

'Notes on the Imagery and Structure of the Old English *Christ I*', *N&Q* 19, 84–9

'The Old World, the Levelling of the Earth, and the Burning of the Sea: Three Eschatological Images in the Old English *Christ III*', *N&Q* 19, 323–5

Irving, Edward B., Jr, 'New Notes on the Old English *Exodus*', *Anglia* 90, 289–324

Johnson, Lee Ann, 'The Narrative Structure of *The Wife's Lament*', *ESts* 52, 497–501

Kirkland, James W., and Charles E. Modlin, 'The Art of *Azarias*', *MÆ* 41, 9–15

Kossick, S. G., 'The Old English *Deor*', *UNISA Eng. Stud.* 10, 3–6

Kuhn, Hans, see sect. 2

Lee, N. A., 'The Unity of *The Dream of the Rood*', *Neophilologus* 56, 469–86

*Lendinara, Patrizia, 'I *Versi Gnomici* anglosassoni', *Annali, Sezione Germanica* (Naples) 14 (1971), 117–38 [summary, p. 611]

Markland, Murray F., 'Deor: þæs ofereode þisses swa mæg', *Amer. Notes and Queries* 11, 35–6

Mitchell, Bruce, 'The Narrator of *The Wife's Lament*', NM 73, 222–34

Ohlgren, Thomas H., 'The Illustrations of the Cædmonian Genesis: Literary Criticism through Art', *Medievalia et Humanistica* 3, 199–212

'Visual Language in the Old English Cædmonian Genesis', *Visible Lang.*, summer, 253–76

see sect. 5

Osborn, Marijane, 'The Grammar of the Inscription on the Franks Casket, Right Side', *NM* 73, 663–71

Parkes, M. B., see sect. 5

Porru, Giulia Mazzuoli, *Maldon e Brunanburh* (Pisa)

Raffel, Burton, 'Scholars, Scholarship, and the Old English *Deor*', *Notre Dame Eng. Jnl* 8, 3–10

*Rogers, H. L., see sect. 2

Schneider, Karl, 'Dichterisch getarnte Begriffsrunen in der ae. Spruchdichtung (*Maxims I* und *Maxims II*)', *Annali, Sezione Germanica* (Naples) 15, 89–126

Schwab, Ute, *Caedmon* (Messina)

Die Sternrune im Wessobrunner Gebet: Beobachtungen zur Lokalisierung des clm 22053, zu BM Arundel 393 und zu Rune Poem v. 86–89 (Amsterdam)

'*Ær—æfter*, Das Memento Mori Beda's als christliche Kontrafaktur: eine philologische Interpretation', in *Studi di Letteratura Religiosa Tedesca in Memoria di Sergio Lupi* (Florence)

Susuki, Shigetake, ed., *Old English Poetry: Religious Poetry* (Tokyo)

Swann, Brian, 'Anglo-Saxon Riddles', *Antæus* 7, 12–17

Taylor, Paul Beekman, 'Charms of *Wynn* and Fetters of *Wyrd* in *The Wanderer*', *NM* 73, 448–55

Thundyil, Zacharias P., see sect. 1

*Tinkler, John Douglas, see sect. 2

Trahern, Joseph B., see under Collins, Rowland L., sect. 1

Tripp, Raymond P., Jr, 'The Narrator as Revenant: a Reconsideration of Three Old English Elegies', *Papers on Lang. and Lit.* 8, 339–61

Vickrey, John F., '*Exodus* and the Treasure of Pharaoh', *ASE* 1, 159–65

'*Exodus* and the Battle in the Sea', *Traditio* 28, 119–40

c. Prose

Bately, Janet M., 'The Relationship between Geographical Information in the Old English Orosius and Latin Texts Other than Orosius', *ASE* 1, 45–62

Bolton, W. F., 'The Alfredian Boethius in Ælfric's *Lives of Saints*, I', *N&Q* 19, 406–7

Bullough, D. A., see sect. 6

Cox, R. S., 'The Old English Dicts of Cato', *Anglia* 90, 1–42

Cross, J. E., '*De Ordine Creaturarum Liber* in Old English Prose', *Anglia* 90, 132–40 [Martyrology; homily in MS Bodley 343]

Dumville, David N., see sect. 4

Erickson, Jon L., 'The Readings of Folios 77 and 86 of the Vercelli Codex', *Manuscripta* 16, 14–23

Fowler, Roger, ed., *Wulfstan's Canons of Edgar*, Early English Text Society 266 (London)

Gatch, Milton McC., see under Collins, Rowland L., sect. 1

Gneuss, Helmut, see sect. 2

Goldman, Stephen H., 'The Old English Vercelli Homilies: Rhetoric and Transformational Analysis', *Jnl of Eng. Ling.* 6, 20–7

Hart, Cyril, 'Byrhtferth and his Manual', *MÆ* 41, 95–109

Hurt, James, *Ælfric*, Twayne's English Authors 131 (New York)

*Kniezsa, Veronika, 'Az Óangol Krónika [On the Old English Chronicle]', *Fillológiai Közlöny* 17 (1971), 1–15

Kuhn, Sherman M., 'The Authorship of the Old English Bede Revisited', *NM* 73, 172–80

'Cursus in Old English: Rhetorical Ornament or Linguistic Phenomenon?', *Speculum* 47, 188–206

*Mindt, Dieter, see sect. 2

Newton, Robert R., see sect. 1

Reynolds, R. E., see sect. 4

Robinson, Fred C., 'The Devil's Account of the Next World: an Anecdote from Old English Homiletic Literature', *NM* 73, 362–71

Soell, Werner J., 'São Cristóvão na Literatura Anglo-Saxônica', *Estudos* (Pôrto Alegre, Rio Grande do Sul) 32, 42–5

Szarmach, Paul E., 'Three Versions of the Jonah Story: an Investigation of Narrative Technique in Old English Homilies', *ASE* 1, 183–92

Szepessy, Géza, 'A "nagyszombati Vinland térkép" ', *Magyar Történelmi Szemle* 3, 73–81 [much use of the Old English Orosius]

*Tinkler, John Douglas, see sect. 2

Vriend, Hubert Jan de, *The Old English Medicina de Quadrupedibus*, diss. Groningen (Tilburg)

4. ANGLO-LATIN, LITURGY AND OTHER LATIN ECCLESIASTICAL TEXTS

*Alföldi-Rosenbaum, Elisabeth, 'The Finger Calculus in Antiquity and in the Middle Ages: Studies on Roman Game Counters', *Frühmittelalterliche Studien* 5 (1971), 1–9 [Bede]

*Bailey, Terence, *The Processions of Sarum and the Western Church*, Pontifical Institute of Mediaeval Studies, Studies and Texts 21 (Toronto, 1971)

*Bischoff, Bernhard, 'Die Überlieferung der technischen Literatur', *Artigianato e tecnica nella società dell'alto medioevo occidentale*, Settimane di studio del Centro italiano di studi sull'alto medioevo 18 (Spoleto, 1971), 1, 267–96

Bolton, W. F., 'Epistola Cuthberti De Obitu Bedae: a Caveat', *Medievalia et Humanistica* n.s. 1, 127–39

Bullough, D. A., see sect. 6

Derolez, René, see sect. 2

Dumville, David N., 'Liturgical Drama and Panegyric Responsory from the Eighth Century? A Re-examination of the Origin and Contents of the Ninth-Century Section of the Book of Cerne', *JTS* 23, 374–406

Els, T. J. M. van, see sect. 5

*Fischer, Bonifatius, 'Bedae de Titulis Psalmorum Liber', *Festschrift Bernhard Bischoff zu seinem 65. Geburtstag*, ed. Johanne Autenrieth and Franz Brunhölzl (Stuttgart, 1971), pp. 90–110

Hart, Cyril, see sect. 3*c*

Jones, Charles W., 'Some Introductory Remarks on Bede's Commentary on Genesis', *Sacris Erudiri* 19, 115–98

Ker, N. R., see sect. 5

Kerlouégan, F., 'Une Mode Stylistique dans la Prose Latine des Pays Celtiques', *Études Celtiques* 13, 275–97 [some references to Aldhelm]

*Kirby, D. P., 'Asser and his Life of King Alfred', *Studia Celtica* 6 (1971), 12–35

Lapidge, Michael, 'Three Latin Poems from Æthelwold's School at Winchester', *ASE* 1, 85–137

Masi, Michael, see sect. 5

Newton, Robert R., see sect. 1

*Ponton, Georges, 'Saint Joseph d'après l'Oeuvre de Bède le Vénérable', *Cahiers de Joséphologie* 19 (1971), 196–219

Reynolds, R. E., 'The *De Officiis VII Graduum*: its Origin and Early Medieval Development', *MS* 34, 113–51 [refers to use of the *Hibernensis* recension in OE manuscripts and by Ælfric]

Schindel, Ulrich, 'Die Quellen von Bedas Figurenlehre', *Classica et Mediaevalia* 29, 169–86

West, Philip J., 'Liturgical Style and Structure in Bede's Homily for the Easter Vigil', *ABR* 23, 1–8

'Liturgical Style and Structure in Bede's Christmas Homilies', *ABR* 23, 424–38

Whitbread, L., 'Bede's Verses on Doomsday: a Supplementary Note', *PQ* 51, 485–6

Winterbottom, Michael, ed., *Three Lives of English Saints* (Toronto) [Ælfric, *Vita Æthelwoldi*; Wulfstan, *Vita Æthelwoldi*; and Abbo, *Vita Eadmundi*]

*Wormald, Francis, 'The Liturgical Calendar of Glastonbury Abbey', *Festschrift Bernhard Bischoff zu seinem 65. Geburtstag*, ed. Johanne Autenrieth and Franz Brunhölzl (Stuttgart, 1971), pp. 325–45

Zolbrod, Paul G., 'Past and Future: Searching for a New Metaphor', *Cithara* 11, 3–15 [Bede]

5. PALAEOGRAPHY, DIPLOMATIC AND ILLUMINATION

*Alcock, N. W., 'The Clystwicon Charter (Clyst St Mary)', *Devonshire Assoc. Report and Trans.* 103 (1971), 25–33

Brown, T. J., 'Northumbria and the Book of Kells', *ASE* 1, 219–46 [with an appendix by C. D. Verey]

Dickins, Bruce, 'The Making of the Parker Library', *Trans. of the Cambridge Bibliographical Soc.* 6, 19–34

*Dodwell, C. Reginald, 'Techniques of Manuscript Painting in Anglo-Saxon Manuscripts', *Artigianato e tecnica nella società dell'alto medioevo occidentale*, Settimane di studio del Centro italiano di studi sull'alto medioevo 18 (Spoleto, 1971), II, 643–62

Els, T. J. M. van, *The Kassel Manuscript of Bede's 'Historia Ecclesiastica Gentis Anglorum' and its Old English Material* (Assen)

Erickson, Jon L., see sect. 3c

Guy, J. A., 'A Lost Manuscript of Solinus: Five Fragments from Bury St Edmunds in the Library of Clare College, Cambridge', *Trans. of the Cambridge Bibliographical Soc.* 6, 65–7

*Hart, Cyril, *The Early Charters of Essex*, 2nd rev. ed. (Leicester, 1971)

Hart, Cyril, 'Danelaw Charters and the Glastonbury Scriptorium', *Downside Rev.* 90, 125–32

Ker, N. R., 'The English Manuscripts of the Moralia of Gregory the Great', *Kunsthistorische Forschungen Otto Paecht zu ehren*, ed. Artur Rosenauer and Gerold Weber (Salzburg), pp. 77–89

Koehler, Wilhelm, *Buchmalerei des frühen Mittelalters: Fragmente und Entwürfe aus dem Nachlass*, ed. Ernst Kitzinger and Florentine Mütherich (Munich)

Lowe, E. A., *Codices Latini Antiquiores Part II, Great Britain and Ireland*, 2nd rev. ed. (Oxford)

Palaeographical Papers 1907–1965, ed. Ludwig Bieler (Oxford) [2 vols.]

Masi, Michael, 'Newberry MSS Fragments, s. vii–s. xv', *Med. Stud.* 34, 99–112

Ohlgren, Thomas H., 'Five New Drawings in the *MS Junius 11*: their Iconography and Thematic Significance', *Speculum* 47, 227–33
see sect. 3b iii

Parkes, M. B., 'The Manuscript of the Leiden Riddle', *ASE* 1, 207–17

*Petrucci, Armando, 'L'onciale romana: origini, sviluppo e diffusione . . . (sec. VI–IX)', *Studi Medievali* 3rd ser. 12 (1971), 75–132

Thomson, R. M., 'The Library of Bury St Edmunds Abbey in the Eleventh and Twelfth Centuries', *Speculum* 47, 617–45

Werner, Martin, 'The Madonna and Child Miniature in the Book of Kells, Parts I and II', *Art Bull.* 54, 1–23 and 129–39

6. HISTORY

*Alcock, Leslie, *Arthur's Britain: History and Archaeology AD 367–634* (London, 1971)

*Alcock, N. W., see sect. 5

*Arngart, O., see sect. 2

Austin, David, and David Hill, 'The Boundaries of Itchell and Crondall', *Proc.*

of the Hampshire Field Club and Archaeol. Soc. 27, 63–4 [text of P. H. Sawyer, *Anglo-Saxon Charters* (London, 1968), no. 1559]

Bailey, Keith, 'Saxon Settlements South of the Thames', *London Archaeologist* 1, 328–9

Barber, Richard, *The Figure of Arthur* (London) [Arthur seen as a *northern* Celtic figure]

Barlow, Frank, *et al.*, *Leofric of Exeter* (Exeter)

*Beeler, John, *Warfare in Feudal Europe, 730–1200* (Ithaca, 1971)

Biddle, Martin, 'The Winton Domesday: Two Surveys of an Early Capital', *Die Stadt in der europäischen Geshichte. Festschrift Edith Ennen*, ed. Werner Besch *et al.* (Bonn), pp. 36–43

Bonney, Desmond, see sect. 8*a*

Branigan, Keith, 'The End of Roman West', *Trans. of the Bristol and Gloucestershire Archaeol. Soc.*, 91, 117–28

Bruce-Mitford, Rupert, see sect. 8*d*

Bullough, D. A., 'The Educational Tradition in England from Alfred to Ælfric: Teaching *Utriusque Linguae*', *La scuola nell'occidente latino dell'alto medioevo*, Settimane di studio del Centro italiano di studi sull'alto medioevo 19 (Spoleto), 453–94

Bu'Lock, J. D., *Pre-Conquest Cheshire* (Chester)

Campbell, Miles W., 'Note sur les Déplacements de Tostig Godwinson en 1066', *Annales de Normandie* 22, 3–9

'Earl Godwin of Wessex and Edward the Confessor's Promise of the Throne to William of Normandy', *Traditio* 28, 141–58

Charles-Edwards, T. M., 'Kinship, Status and the Origins of the Hide', *Past and Present* 56, 3–33

Chibnall, Marjorie, ed. and transl., *The Ecclesiastical History of Orderic Vitalis* III: *Books V and VI* (Oxford)

Cutler, Kenneth E., 'The Godwinist Hostages: the Case for 1051', *Annuale Medievale* 12, 70–7

Dickinson, Tania M., see sect. 8*b*

Dodgson, J. McN., see sect. 2

Dumville, David N., see sect. 4

*Fell, Christine E., *Edward, King and Martyr* (Leeds, 1971)

Finberg, H. P. R., ed., *The Agrarian History of England and Wales* I. ii: AD 43–1042 (Cambridge) [pp. 1–227, S. Applebaum, 'Roman Britain'; 279–382, Glanville R. J. Jones, 'Post-Roman Wales'; and 383–525, H. P. R. Finberg, 'Anglo-Saxon England to 1042']

Gelling, Margaret, see sect. 2 (twice)

Gould, Jim, 'The Medieval Burgesses of Tamworth; their Liberties, Courts and Markets', *Trans. of the South Staffordshire Archaeol. and Nat. Hist. Soc.* 13, 17–42 [with some discussion of the pre-Conquest situation regarding both the town and the county boundaries]

*Harrison, Kenneth, 'The Reign of King Ecgfrith of Northumbria', *Yorkshire Archaeol. Jnl* 43 (1971), 79–84

*Hart, Cyril, see sect. 5

Hart, Cyril, see sects. 3*c* and 5

Haselgrove, Dennis, 'Early Fulham—a Rejoinder', *London Archaeologist* 2, 18–21 [see below, Whitehouse, Keith]

Hogg, A. H. A., 'Cerdic and the Cloven Way Again', *Antiquity* 46, 222–3

*Hooper, M. D., *et al.*, see sect. 8*c*

Huws, Daniel, 'Gildas Prisei', *Cylchgrawn Llyfrgell Genedlaethol Cymru* 17, 314–20

Janzén, Assar, 'The Viking Colonization of England in the Light of Place-Names', *Names* 20, 1–25

*Kirby, D. P., see sect. 4

Kirk, Sarah J., see sect. 2

*Kniezsa, Veronika, see sect. 3*c*

Knowles, David, C. N. L. Brooke and Vera C. M. London, ed., *The Heads of Religious Houses: England and Wales 940–1216* (Cambridge)

*Knowles, David, and R. Neville Hadcock, *Medieval Religious Houses: England and Wales*, 2nd rev. ed. (London, 1971) [appendix I (pp. 463–87): 'Religious Houses Existing at Periods before 1066']

*Lamb, John W., *The Archbishopric of Canterbury from its Foundation to the Norman Conquest* (London, 1971)

Mayr-Harting, Henry, *The Coming of Christianity to Anglo-Saxon England* (London)

McGovern, John F., 'The Hide and Related Land-Tenure Concepts in Anglo-Saxon England, AD 700–1100', *Traditio* 28, 101–18

Morton, Catherine, and Hope Muntz, ed., *The 'Carmen de Hastingae Proelio' of Guy, Bishop of Amiens* (Oxford)

*Norman, A. V. B., *The Medieval Soldier* (New York, 1971) [ch. IV, pp. 66–98, 'The Saxons']

O'Donovan, Mary Anne, 'An Interim Revision of Episcopal Dates for the Province of Canterbury, 850–950: Part I', *ASE* 1, 23–44

Pohl, Frederick J., *The Viking Settlements of North America* (New York)

Radford, C. A. Ralegh, 'Christian Origins in Britain', *MA* 15, 1–12

Radley, Jeffrey, see sect. 8*b*

Rahtz, Philip, and Peter Fowler, see sect. 8*a*

Rogers, Alan, 'Parish Boundaries and Urban History', *JBAA* 3rd ser. 35, 46–64

*Skovgaard-Petersen, Inge, see sect. 1

Soell, Werner J., 'Um reformador autêntico—São Dunstano', *Estudos* (Pôrto Alegre, Rio Grande do Sul) 32, 78–84

Symons, Thomas, 'St Dunstan in the "Oswald" Tradition', *Downside Rev.* 90, 119–24

Thundyil, Zacharias P., see sect. 1

*Vollrath-Reichelt, Hanna, *Königsgedanke und Königtum bei den Angelsachsen bis zur Mitte des 9. Jahrhunderts*, Kölner historische Abhandlungen 19 (Cologne and Vienna, 1971)

Ward, John H., 'Vortigern and the End of Roman Britain', *Britannia* 3, 277–89

*Welldon Finn, R., *The Norman Conquest and its Effects on the Economy, 1066–1086* (London and Hamden, 1971)

317

Whitehouse, Keith, 'Early Fulham', *London Archaeologist* 1, 344–7 [see above, Haselgrove, Dennis]

Whitelock, Dorothy, 'The Pre-Viking Age Church in East Anglia', *ASE* 1, 1–22

Winterbottom, Michael, see sect. 4

7. NUMISMATICS

[Aston Rowant hoard] 'Anglo-Saxon Peasant's Hoard in Wood', *Numismatic Circular* 80, 5

 'Anglo-Saxon Treasure Trove', *Seaby's Coin and Medal Bull.* 1972, 227 [175 sceattas from Grove Wood, Aston Rowant, *c.* 730]

Blunt, C. E., 'The Crowned Bust Coinage of Edmund 939–946', *BNJ* 40, 17–21

*Blunt, C. E., F. Elmore Jones and R. P. Mack, *Collection of Ancient British, Romano-British and English Coins Formed by Mrs Emery May Norweb of Cleveland, Ohio, USA. Part I: Ancient British, Romano-British, Anglo-Saxon and Post-Conquest Coins to 1180*, Sylloge of Coins of the British Isles 16 (London, 1971)

Dolley, Michael, 'Some Danish Evidence for the Commencement of Imitation of Imitation in the Hiberno-Norse Series', *Numismatic Circular* 80, 358

 'The Newest Find with Anglo-Saxon Coins from Gotland', *Numismatic Circular* 80, 450 [includes twenty-nine of Æthelred and Cnut, and six Scandinavian imitations of Æthelred II Long Cross pennies; concealed *c.* 1020]

 'The Location of the pre-Ælfredian mint(s) of Wessex', *Proc. of the Hampshire Field Club and Archaeol. Soc.* 27, 57–61

 'Some New Light on the Early Twelfth-Century Coinage of Dublin', *Seaby's Coin and Medal Bull.* 1972, 404–6

Dolley, Michael, and Jacques Yvon, 'A Group of Tenth-Century Coins Found at Mont-Saint-Michel', *BNJ* 40, 1–16 [includes two silver pennies of Athelstan (924–39), one of Olaf Sihtricson of York (941–4), a denier of Duke William Longsword of Normandy (932–42) and two imitative coins of *c.* 940; all illustrated]

Galster, Georg, *The Royal Collection of Coins and Medals, National Museum, Copenhagen. Part IV: Anglo-Saxon Coins from Harold I and Anglo-Norman Coins*, Sylloge of Coins of the British Isles 18 (London)

Grinsell, L. V., *The Bristol Mint: an Historical Outline* (Bristol)

*Gunstone, A. J. H., *Ancient British, Anglo-Saxon and Norman Coins in Midlands Museums*, Sylloge of Coins of the British Isles 17 (London, 1971)

Hall, E. T., and D. M. Metcalf, ed., *Methods of Chemical and Metallurgical Investigation of Ancient Coinage*, R. Numismatic Soc. Special Publ. 8 (London) [includes five papers important for Sutton Hoo: J. P. C. Kent, 'Gold Standards of the Merovingian Coinage, AD 580–700', pp. 69–74; W. A. Oddy and M. J. Hughes, 'The Specific Gravity Method for the Analysis of Gold Coins', 75–87; R. F. Coleman and A. Wilson, 'Activation Analysis of Merovingian Gold Coins', 88–92, and 'Analysis of the Sutton Hoo Gold Coins', 96–9; and R. Bruce-Mitford, 'The Dating of the Sutton Hoo Coins', 108–9. Also: W. A.

Oddy, 'The Analysis of Four Hoards of Merovingian Gold Coins', 111–25 [Crondall, Escharen, Nietap and Velsen]; and H. McKerrell and R. B. K. Stevenson, 'Some Analyses of Anglo-Saxon and Associated Oriental Silver Coinage', 195–209]

Kuhlicke, F. W., 'The Bedford Mint', *Bedfordshire Mag.* 13, 167–71

Lyon, Stewart, 'A "Last Small Cross" Die-Link between Warwick and London', *Numismatic Circular* 80, 2

  'The Implications of the Aethelred/Sihtric Watchet Die Link', *Seaby's Coin and Medal Bull.* 1972, 176–8

Meates, G. W., see sect. 8*e*

Metcalf, D. M., 'A Coin of Offa from Deddington Castle, Oxon.', *BNJ* 40, 171–2

Pagan, H. E., 'Mr Emery's Mint', *BNJ* 40, 139–70 [concerns the early-nineteenth-century coin forgeries of Edward Emery. Twenty Anglo-Saxon pieces from Egbert to Harold II are listed and seven illustrated]

Schweizer, F., and A. M. Friedman, 'Comparison of Methods of Analysis of Silver and Gold in Silver Coins', *Archaeometry* 14, 103–7 (includes an English silver penny of *c.* 870 and another of *c.* 1063]

Seaby, W. A., 'The Present Location of Hiberno-Norse Coins Illustrated by W. O'Sullivan in his *Earliest Irish Coinage*', *Seaby's Coin and Medal Bull*, 1972, 269–71

*Sotheby and Co., *Catalogue of the Bolton Percy (1967) Hoard of Stycas of the Kings of Northumbria and Archbishops of York . . .*, introduction by H. E. Pagan [sale on 23 June 1971]

8. ARCHAEOLOGY

a. General

Addyman, P. V., 'The Anglo-Saxon House: a New Review', *ASE* 1, 273–307

*Alcock, Leslie, see sect. 6

[Anon.] 'Archaeological Notes 1970–1', *Oxoniensia* 36, 110–12 [includes Anglo-Saxon grave groups]

  'Excavation and Fieldwork in Wiltshire, 1970', *Wiltshire Archaeol. and Nat. Hist. Mag.* 66, 188–91 [includes notes about an Anglo-Saxon cemetery at Pewsey and excavations on the late Saxon defences of Wilton]

Bonney, Desmond, 'Early Boundaries in Wessex', *Archaeology and the Landscape*, ed. P. J. Fowler (London), pp. 168–86

Brothwell, Don, 'Palaeodemography and Earlier British Populations', *World Archaeology* 4, 75–87 [includes a consideration of 'Dark Age', Saxon and medieval populations]

*Capelle, Torsten, and Hayo Vierck, 'Modeln der Merowinger- und Wikingerzeit', *Frühmittelalterliche Studien* 5 (1971), 42–100

Council for British Archaeology, *Archaeological Bibliography for Great Britain and Ireland 1970* [contains a full bibliography covering national and local periodicals and dealing with all periods]

  Archaeological Site Index to Radiocarbon Dates for Great Britain and Ireland (1971) and

First List of Addenda (1972) [Sect. 7c lists dates for English post-Roman and Saxon sites]

British Archaeological Abstracts 5 [covers material published 1 July 1971–30 June 1972]

Council for British Archaeology, Group 9, *Newsletter* 3 [contains summaries of work during 1972, including Anglo-Saxon discoveries]

Council for British Archaeology, Groups 12 and 13, *Archaeol. Rev.* 6 [surveys work done in 1971, including (sect. 7) early medieval *c.* 450–1000]

Council for British Archaeology, Scottish Regional Group, *Discovery and Excavation in Scotland 1972* [summaries of all archaeological work and bibliography for 1972, listing material also of Anglo-Saxon interest]

Dyer, James, 'Earthworks of the Danelaw Frontier', *Archaeology and the Landscape*, ed. P. J. Fowler (London), pp. 222–36

Farrell, Robert T., see under Collins, Rowland L., sect. 1

Green, H. Stephen, 'Wansdyke, Excavations 1966 to 1970', *Wiltshire Archaeol. and Nat. Hist. Mag.* 66, 129–46

Hall, D. N., and J. B. Hutchings, 'The Distribution of Archaeological Sites between the Nene and the Ouse Valleys', *Bedfordshire Archaeol. Jnl* 7, 1–16 [includes Anglo-Saxon sites]

Heighway, Carolyn M., ed., *The Erosion of History: Archaeology and Planning in Towns* (Council for British Archaeology, London) [lists all places of possible urban status in Anglo-Saxon England]

Kennett, David H., 'Bedfordshire Archaeology, 1971–2', *Bedfordshire Archaeol. Jnl* 7, 89–97 [includes Anglo-Saxon discoveries at All Saints' Church, Kempston]

*Medieval Village Research Group, *Report* 19 (1971) [contains annual summary of work done, reviews, lists and bibliographies; covers Anglo-Saxon discoveries on village sites, including accounts of church excavations, e.g. in this number the Saxon phases of Wharram Percy church]

Moorhouse, Stephen, 'The Yorkshire Archaeological Register: 1971', *Yorkshire Archaeol. Jnl* 44, 217–29 [includes Anglo-Saxon discoveries]

Owles, Elizabeth, 'Archaeology in Suffolk, 1971', *Proc. of the Suffolk Inst. of Archaeology* 32, 205–14 [includes Anglo-Saxon finds, mainly of pagan period]

Rahtz, Philip, and Peter Fowler, 'Somerset AD 400–700', *Archaeology and the Landscape*, ed. P. J. Fowler (London), pp. 187–221

Rutland, R. A., and Jillian A. Greenaway, 'Archaeological Notes from Reading Museum', *Berkshire Archaeol. Jnl* 65, 58 and 60 [Anglo-Saxon spearheads and axe found]

*Skovgaard-Petersen, Inge, see sect. 1

Wilson, D. M., 'Medieval Britain in 1970: I. Pre-Conquest', *MA* 15, 124–37 [survey of archaeological work]

*Wilson, D. R., 'Roman Britain in 1970', *Britannia* 2 (1971), 243–88 [includes references to Anglo-Saxon discoveries on Roman sites]

Wilson, D. R., 'Roman Britain in 1971', *Britannia* 3, 299–351 [includes references to Anglo-Saxon discoveries on Roman sites]

b. Towns and other major settlements

Alcock, Leslie, '*By South Cadbury is that Camelot . . .*' *Excavations at Cadbury Castle 1966–70*, New Aspects of Antiquity (London)
'Excavations at Cadbury–Camelot, 1966–70', *Antiquity* 46, 29–38
Biddle, Martin, 'Excavations at Winchester, 1970', *AntJ* 52, 93–131 [includes fifth-century finds and late Saxon domestic and ecclesiastical structures] see sect. 6
Brassington, M., 'First Century Roman Occupation at Strutt's Park, Derby', *Derbyshire Archaeol. Jnl* 90, 22–30 [includes [fig. 1] site plan of Derby showing position of Saxon town]
[Buckland, Paul, and Malcolm Dolby] 'Doncaster', *CA* 33, 273–7
Carter, Alan, 'Some Problems of Research in Historic Towns', *Museums Jnl* 72, 89–92
'The Norwich Survey: Excavations in Norwich, 1971, an Interim Report', *Norfolk Archaeology* 35, 410–16
Cunliffe, Barry, 'Excavations at Portchester Castle, Hants, 1969–71', *AntJ* 52, 70–82 [includes structures and finds of fifth to eleventh centuries]
[Cunliffe, Barry] 'Portchester', *CA* 30, 189–94
Dawson, Graham, 'The Saxon London Bridge', *London Archaeologist* 1, 330–2
Dickinson, Tania M., 'New Perspectives on Dorchester-on-Thames: Theories and Facts', Council for British Archaeology, Group 9, *Newsletter* 3, 5–6
Dolley, Michael, see sect. 7
Fowler, P. J., K. S. Gardner and P. A. Rahtz, 'Excavations at Cadbury–Congresbury, Somerset, 1971', *Proc. of the Somerset Archaeol. and Nat. Hist. Soc.* 115, 51–2 [fifth–sixth-century site]
Haslam, Jeremy, 'Medieval Streets in London', *London Archaeologist* 2, 3–7 [touches on problems of the Anglo-Saxon street system]
Hassall, T. G., *Oxford: the City Beneath your Feet. Archaeological Excavations in the City of Oxford, 1967–72* (Oxford)
'Excavations at Oxford 1970: Third Interim Report', *Oxoniensia* 36, 1–14
'Excavations at 44–46 Cornmarket Street, Oxford, 1970', *Oxoniensia* 36, 15–33
'Excavations in Merton College, Oxford, 1970', *Oxoniensia* 36, 34–48 [discusses the problem of the Saxon defences of Oxford]
Heighway, Carolyn M., ed., see sect. 8*a*
Hurst, Henry, 'Excavations at Gloucester, 1968–1971: First Interim Report', *AntJ* 52, 24–69 [includes post-Roman and late Saxon discoveries and suggests possible late Saxon origin for medieval street system]
Morton, Catherine, and Hope Muntz, ed., see sect. 6
Ó Ríordáin, Breandán, 'Excavations at High Street and Winetavern Street, Dublin', *MA* 15, 73–85 [includes much Viking material]
Radley, Jeffrey, 'Economic Aspects of Anglo-Danish York', *MA* 15, 37–57
'Excavations in the Defences of the City of York: an Early Medieval Stone Tower and the Successive Earth Ramparts', *Yorkshire Archaeol. Jnl* 44, 38–64 [with a suppl. note by R. M. Butler]

Rahtz, Philip, 'Castle Dore—a Reappraisal of the Post-Roman Structures', *Cornish Archaeology* 10, 49–54

Rahtz, Philip, and Ken Sheridan, 'Fifth Report of Excavations at Tamworth, Staffs., 1971—a Saxon Water-Mill in Bolebridge Street. An Interim Note', *Trans. of the South Staffordshire Archaeol. and Hist. Soc.* 13, 9–16

*Ramm, H. G., 'The End of Roman York', *Soldier and Civilian in Roman Yorkshire*, ed. R. M. Butler (Leicester, 1971), pp. 179–99

Shoesmith, Ron, 'Hereford', *CA* 33, 256–8

*Turner, Hilary L., *Town Defences in England and Wales: an Architectural and Documentary Study, AD 900–1500* (London, 1971)

Wade-Martins, Peter, 'Excavations at North Elmham', *Norfolk Archaeology* 35, 416–28

Wenham, Peter, 'Excavations in Low Petergate, York, 1957–8', *Yorkshire Archaeol. Jnl* 44, 65–113 [includes Saxo-Norman levels and structures]

c. Rural settlements, agriculture and the countryside

Barker, Philip, and James Lawson, 'A Pre-Norman Field-System at Hen Domen, Montgomery', *MA* 15, 58–72

Brodribb, A. C., A. R. Hands and D. R. Walker, *Excavations at Shakenoak Farm, near Wilcote, Oxfordshire. Part III: Site F* (privately ptd, Oxford) [mostly dealing with late Roman and Anglo-Saxon discoveries]

*Hooper, M. D., *et al.*, *Hedges and Local History* (National Council of Social Service, London, 1971) [Dating hedges by counting botanical species in 30-yard lengths shows that a ten-species hedge dates from *c.* 650–1000]

*Medieval Village Research Group, see sect. 8*a*

Rodwell, Warwick, 'Rivenhall', *CA* 30, 184–5

St Joseph, J. K., 'Air Reconnaissance: Recent Results, 27', *Antiquity* 46, 149–50 [discoveries of *grübenhäuser*]

d. Pagan cemeteries and Sutton Hoo

Bruce-Mitford, Rupert, *The Sutton Hoo Ship-Burial: a Handbook*, 2nd rev. ed. (London)

'The Sutton Hoo Helmet: a New Reconstruction', *Brit. Museum Quarterly* 36, 120–30

Burchard, Alan, see sect. 8*h*

Farrell, R. T., see sect. 3*bii*

Hall, E. T., and D. M. Metcalf, ed., see sect. 7

Kennett, David H., 'Seventh-Century Finds from Astwick', *Bedfordshire Archaeol. Jnl* 7, 45–51

see sect. 8*j*

Pocock, Michael, see sect. 8*h*

Sherlock, D. A., 'Saul, Paul and the Silver Spoons from Sutton Hoo', *Speculum* 47, 91–5

e. Churches, monastic sites and Christian cemeteries

*Brown, P. D. C., 'The Church at Richborough', *Britannia* 2 (1971), 225–31

Gem, R. D. H., 'Wootton Wawen Church [Warwicks]', *ArchJ* 128, 225–7

Gibb, J. H. P., 'An Interim Report of Excavations Carried Out at the West End of Sherborne Abbey in 1964 and 1965', *Proc. of the Dorset Nat. Hist. and Archaeol. Soc.* 93, 197–210

Gilbert, Edward, 'Deerhurst and Armorica', *Trans. of the Bristol and Gloucestershire Archaeol. Soc.* 91, 129–49

Godman, Colin, 'King Weston Hill, Bristol: its Prehistoric Camps and Inhumation Cemetery', *Proc. of the Univ. of Bristol Spelaeological Soc.* 13, 41–8 [the cemetery perhaps of the period 400–700]

Kennett, David H., see sect. 8*a*

*Krüger, Karl Heinrich, *Königsgrabkirchen der Franken, Angelsachsen und Langobarden bis zur Mitte des 8. Jahrhunderts: ein historischer Katalog*, Münstersche Mittelalterschriften 4 (Munich, 1971)

Meates, G. W., 'Stone-next-Faversham', *Archaeologia Cantiana* 86, 244–5 [further excavations, following work reported in *AntJ* 49, 273–94, and find of sceatta with *ETHILIRAED* in runes]

*Medieval Village Research Group, see sect. 8*a*

Radford, C. A. Ralegh, see sect. 6

Rahtz, P. A., 'Deerhurst Church: Interim Note on 1971 Excavation', *Trans. of the Bristol and Gloucestershire Archaeol. Soc.* 90, 129–35

Renn, D. F., 'Some Early Island Churches', *Proc. of the Isle of Wight Nat. Hist. and Archaeol. Soc.* 6, 266–70

Smith, Terence Paul, 'The Church of St Peter, Canterbury', *Archaeologia Cantiana* 86, 99–108 [earliest work claimed as Saxo-Norman, *c.* 1075–1115]

Taylor, H. M., 'Structural Criticism: a Plea for More Systematic Study of Anglo-Saxon Buildings', *ASE* 1, 259–72

f. Ships and seafaring

Binns, A. L., 'Sun Navigation in the Viking Age, and the Canterbury Portable Sundial', *Acta Archaeologia* 42, 23–34

Fenwick, Valerie H., 'The Graveney Boat. A Pre-Conquest Discovery in Kent', *International Jnl of Nautical Archaeology and Underwater Exploration* 1, 119–29

Oddy, W. A., 'Packing and Transporting the Graveney Boat', *International Jnl of Nautical Archaeology and Underwater Exploration* 1, 175–7

Oddy, W. A., and P. G. van Geersdaele, 'The Recovery of the Graveney Boat', *Stud. in Conservation* 17, 30–8

g. Sculpture on bone, stone and wood

Bailey, Richard N., 'Another Lyre', *Antiquity* 46, 145–6 [on a ninth-century cross-shaft at Masham, N. Riding, Yorkshire]

Blindheim, Martin, ed., *Sigurds Saga i middelalderens billedkunst: utstilling i Universitetets Oldsaksamling 1972–1973* (Oslo)

Green, Barbara, 'An Anglo-Saxon Bone Plaque from Larling, Norfolk', *AntJ* 51, 321–3

Hare, Michael J., 'An Anglo-Saxon Grave-Cover at Cardington Church', *Bedfordshire Archaeol. Jnl* 7, 83–5

Lang, J. T., 'Illustrative Carving of the Viking Period at Sockburn-on-Tees', *Archaeologia Aeliana* 4th ser. 50, 235–48

'The Castledermot Hogback', *Jnl of the R. Soc. of Antiquaries of Ireland* 101, 154–8

*Schmidt, H., 'Vikingernes husformede gravsten', *Nationalmuseets Arbejdsmark* 1970, 13–28

h. Metal-work and other minor objects

Bailey, Richard, 'A Carpenter's Axe from the College Valley', *Archaeologia Aeliana* 4th ser. 50, 277–80 [only datable at best to eighth–fourteenth centuries, but article briefly reviews pre-Conquest examples]
    see sect. 8g

Binns, A. L., see sect. 8f

Bruce-Mitford, Rupert, see sect. 8d

Burchard, Alan, 'An Anglo-Saxon Brooch from Grafton', *Wiltshire Archaeol. and Nat. Hist. Mag.* 66, 178–9

*Clarke, Joan R., and David A. Hinton, *The Alfred and Minster Lovel Jewels* (Oxford, 1971)

Cowen, J. D., 'The Southwark Knife Reconsidered', *AntJ* 51, 281–6 [regarded as east Baltic work of *c*. 1100–1300]

Lasko, Peter, *Ars Sacra 800–1200* (London)

Leeds, E. T., and Michael Pocock, 'A Survey of the Anglo-Saxon Cruciform Brooches of the Florid Type', *MA* 15, 13–36

*Nielsen, Karl Martin, see sect. 8i

Pocock, Michael, 'A Drawing by William Stukeley of Early Anglo-Saxon Brooches Discovered at Holkham, Norfolk', *AntJ* 52, 188–91

Sherlock, D. A., see sect. 8d

Williams, James, 'Tynron Doon, Dumfriesshire: a History of the Site with Notes on the Finds 1924–67', *Trans. of the Dumfriesshire and Galloway Nat. Hist. and Ant. Soc.* 48, 106–20 [includes fragments of a late-seventh- or eighth-century gold bracteate(?)]

i. Inscriptions

Beck, Heinrich, see sect. 2

Heller, L. G., see sect. 2

*Nielsen, Karl Martin, 'Rasmus Rask om de aeldre runer', *Aarbøger for Nordisk Oldkyndighed og Historie* 1971, 120–45 [with an excurs 'De engelske ringe']

j. Pottery and glass

Harden, D. B., 'Ancient Glass, III: Post-Roman', *ArchJ* 128, 78–117

Hinton, David A., 'Medieval Pottery from Swinbrook, Oxon.', *Oxoniensia* 36, 107–10 [a late Saxon-twelfth-century group]

Kennett, David H., 'An Urn from Moggerhanger and Panel Style at Kempston', *Bedfordshire Archaeol. Jnl* 7, 39–44

9. REVIEWS

Aitken, A. J., Angus McIntosh and Hermann Pálsson, ed., *Edinburgh Studies in English and Scots* (London, 1971): G. W. S. Barrow, *Scottish Hist. Rev.* 51, 200–2; Henry Hargreaves, *RES* 23, 320–1; M. H. Short, *YES* 2, 228–9; E. G. Stanley, *N&Q* 19, 305–7; B. Strang, *Jnl of Ling.* 8, 346–7

Alexander, J. J. G., *Norman Illumination at Mont St Michel 966–1100* (New York, 1970): H. B. Graham, *Manuscripta* 16, 50–2

Alexander, Michael, *The Earliest English Poems* (Berkeley and Los Angeles, 1970): J. M. Kirk, *ELN* 9, 196–9; E. G. Stanley, *N&Q* 19, 282–3

Bailey, Terence, *The Processions of Sarum and the Western Church* (Toronto, 1971): Massey H. Shepherd, Jr, *Church Hist.* 41, 259

Barlow, Frank, *Edward the Confessor* (London and Berkeley and Los Angeles, 1970): *TLS* 20 October, p. 1255; Michael Altschul, *Speculum* 47, 508–9

Barlow, Frank, *et al.*, *Leofric of Exeter* (Exeter, 1972): H. P. R. Finberg, *Devon and Cornwall Notes and Queries* 32, 187

Bech, Gunnar, *Das germanische reduplizierte Präteritum* (Copenhagen, 1969): Rolf Hiersche, *Kratylos* 15, 81–9

Beeler, John, *Warfare in Feudal Europe, 730–1200* (Ithaca, 1971): M. R. Powicke, *AHR* 77, 1424–5

Beresford, Maurice, and John G. Hurst, ed., *Deserted Medieval Villages* (London, 1971): Lloyd R. Laing, *Scottish Hist. Rev.* 51, 202–4; Lionel M. Munby, *The Local Historian* 10, 150–1; Philip Rahtz, *ArchJ* 128, 281–3; M. W. Thompson, *MA* 15, 180–2

Berger, Rainer, ed., *Scientific Methods in Medieval Archaeology* (London and Berkeley and Los Angeles, 1970): R. F. Tylecote, *AHR* 77, 492–3

Bessinger, Jess B., Jr, and Stanley J. Kahrl, ed., *Essential Articles for the Study of Old English Poetry* (Hamden, 1968): Heinz Bergner, *Anglia* 90, 208

Bessinger, Jess B., Jr, and Philip H. Smith, Jr, *A Concordance to Beowulf* (Ithaca, 1969): Paul M. Clogan, *Computers and the Humanities* 6, 233–4; Dieter Wolff, *Anglia* 89, 508–13

Binchy, D. A., *Celtic and Anglo-Saxon Kingship* (Oxford, 1970): K. H. Schmidt, *Studia Celtica* 6, 206–8; Hans Wagner, *Zeitschrift für celtische Philologie* 32, 285–8

Bishop, T. A. M., *English Caroline Minuscule* (Oxford, 1971): *TLS* 7 January, p. 20; P.-M. Bogaert, *RB* 82, 156–7; Emmanuel Poulle, *Bibliothèque de l'École des Chartes* 130, 257–9

Bloomfield, M. W., ed., *Harvard English Studies* 1 (Cambridge, Mass., 1970): Franz K. Schneider, *Thought* 47, 121–3

Bolgar, R. R., ed., *Classical Influences on European Culture AD 500–1500* (Cambridge, 1971): Salvatore D'Elia, *Athenaeum* 50, 230–6; Oswyn Murray, *N&Q* 19, 109–11

Bolton, W. F., *A History of Anglo-Latin Literature 597–1066* I: 597–740 (Princeton, 1967): Dieter Schaller, *Anglia* 90, 204–7

Brown, T. J. *et al.*, ed., *The Durham Ritual*, EEMF 16 (Copenhagen, 1969): N. R. Ker, *EHR* 87, 106; G. Storms, *ESts* 53, 351–2

Brown, William H., Jr, *A Syntax of King Alfred's 'Pastoral Care'* (The Hague, 1970): André Crépin, *Études Anglaises* 25, 78–80; Elizabeth Closs Traugott, *Language* 48, 182–4

Bruce-Mitford, Rupert, *The Sutton Hoo Ship-Burial: a Handbook*, 2nd ed. (London, 1972): Brian Hope-Taylor, *Antiquity* 46, 240–1

Burlin, Robert B., *The Old English 'Advent': a Typological Commentary* (New Haven and London, 1968): Fred C. Robinson, *Anglia* 90, 516–18

Cameron, A., R. Frank, and J. Leyerle, *Computers and Old English Concordances* (Toronto, 1970): Patrizia Lendinara, *Annali, Sezione Germanica* (Naples) 15, 189–92

Campbell, Alistair, ed., *Aethelwulf, 'De Abbatibus'* (Oxford, 1967): Dieter Schaller, *Anglia* 89, 506–8

Carlton, Charles, *A Descriptive Syntax of the Old English Charters* (The Hague, 1970): André Crépin, *Études Anglaises* 25, 78–80; Patrizia Lendinara, *Annali, Sezione Germanica* (Naples) 15, 191–3; Ursula Oomen, *Anglia* 90, 524–5

Carnicelli, Thomas A., ed., *King Alfred's Version of St Augustine's Soliloquies* (Cambridge, Mass., 1969): Klaus R. Grinda, *Anglia* 90, 519–24

Carson, R. A. G., ed., *Mints, Dies and Currency: Essays Dedicated to the Memory of Albert Baldwin* (London, 1971): Philip Grierson, *ArchJ* 128, 259–60; S. E. R[igold], *BNJ* 40, 176–8; C. H. V. Sutherland, *NC* 7th ser. 12, 349–50

Chaney, William A., *The Cult of Kingship in Anglo-Saxon England* (Manchester, 1970): Robert Brentano, *Speculum* 47, 754–5; André Crépin, *Revue de l'Histoire des Religions* 181, 195–8; R. Folz, *Revue d'Histoire et de Philosophie Religieuses* 52, 226–7; Bernard Guenée, *Revue Historique* 247, 469–71; Robert W. Hanning, *Germanic Rev.* 47, 141–3; Peter Hunter Blair, *DUJ* 64, 64–5; R. M. Wilson, *English* 108, 97

Chibnall, Marjorie, ed. and transl., *The Ecclesiastical History of Orderic Vitalis* II (Oxford, 1969): Jacques Boussard, *CCM* 14, 366–7

Clark, Cecily, ed., *The Peterborough Chronicle 1070–1154*, 2nd ed. (Oxford, 1970): Pierre Botineau, *Bibliothèque de l'École des Chartes* 129, 164–5; R. H. C. Davis, *EHR* 87, 393–4; Richard Drögereit, *Historische Zeitschrift* 214, 230–1

Clarke, Joan R., and David A. Hinton, *The Alfred and Minster Lovel Jewels* (Oxford, 1971): David Parsons, *ArchJ* 128, 280; Leslie Webster, *JBAA* 3rd ser. 35, 78

Clemoes, Peter, *Rhythm and Cosmic Order in Old English Christian Literature* (Cambridge, 1970): Heinz Bergner, *Anglia* 90, 512–13; T. A. Shippey, *YES* 2, 231–2

Clemoes, Peter and Kathleen Hughes, ed., *England before the Conquest: Studies in Primary Sources presented to Dorothy Whitelock* (Cambridge, 1971): TLS 3 March, p. 243; Frank Barlow, *Theology* 75, 263–5; G. L. Brook, *JEH* 23, 349–50; H. E. Hallam, *AUMLA* 38, 218–20; C. Warren Hollister, *AHR* 77, 1428–9; Richard W. Pfaff, *Church Hist.* 41, 404–5; C. E. Wright, *Antiquity* 46, 245–6

Colgrave, Bertram, and R. A. B. Mynors, ed., *Bede's Ecclesiastical History of the English People* (Oxford, 1969): Michael Masi, *Cithara* 11, 87–90

Davidson, H. R. Ellis, *Scandinavian Mythology* (London, 1970): D. A. Bullough, *History* 57, 256–7

Denecke, Ludwig, *Jacob Grimm und sein Bruder Wilhelm* (Stuttgart, 1971): Erich Kunze, *NM* 73, 727–8; Ruth Michaelis-Jena, *Folklore* 83, 76–7

Dick, Ernst S., *Ae. 'dryht' und seine Sippe* (Münster, 1965): Emil Ploss, *ZDA Anzeiger* 83, 121–3

Dodgson, J. McN., *The Place-Names of Cheshire* I and II (Cambridge, 1970): O. Arngart, *SN* 43, 571–8

The Place-Names of Cheshire III and IV (Cambridge, 1971 and 1972): Margaret Gelling, *N&Q* 19, 268–9; Kelsie B. Harder, *Names* 20, 68–70

Dunning, T. P., and A. J. Bliss, ed., *The Wanderer* (London, 1969): Klaus R. Grinda, *Anglia* 90, 216–20

Faiss, Klaus, *'Gnade' bei Cynewulf und seiner Schule* (Tübingen, 1967): Marianne Latendorf, *Anglia* 89, 513–16

Farmer, D. H., ed., *The Rule of St Benedict: Oxford, Bodleian Library, Hatton 48*, EEMF 15 (Copenhagen, 1968): G. Storms, *ESts* 53, 153–4; C. E. Wright, *MÆ* 41, 132–5

Fell, Christine E., *Edward, King and Martyr* (Leeds, 1971): Alistair Campbell, *N&Q* 19, 270–1

Finkenstaedt, Thomas, Ernst Leisi and Dieter Wolff, *A Chronological English Dictionary* (Heidelberg, 1970): René Derolez, *ESts* 53, 144–50; Klaus Hansen, *ZAA* 20, 74–6; Susie I. Tucker, *YES* 2, 226–7

Fisher, E. A., *The Saxon Churches of Sussex* (Newton Abbot, 1970): H. M. Taylor, *AntJ* 51, 355–6

Foote, Peter, and David M. Wilson, *The Viking Achievement* (London, 1970): D. A. Bullough, *History* 57, 256–7; R. H. C. Davis, *EHR* 87, 391–2; Helen S. Maclean, *ArchJ* 128, 280–1; O. Olsen, *AntJ* 51, 353–4; R. I. Page, *MÆ* 41, 89–94

Fowler, P. J., K. S. Gardner and P. A. Rahtz, *Cadbury Congresbury, Somerset 1968: an Introductory Report* (Bristol, 1970): H. N. Savory, *Antiquity* 46, 160–1

Fry, Donald K., *'Beowulf' and 'The Fight at Finnsburh': a Bibliography* (Charlottesville, 1969): Donald C. Baker, *ELN* 10, 127–8; Klaus Dieter Matussek, *Anglia* 90, 213–16; L. Whitbread, *ESts* 53, 249–50

Galster, Georg, *The Royal Collection of Coins and Medals, National Museum, Copenhagen. Part III: Anglo-Saxon Coins, Cnut*, Sylloge of Coins of the British Isles (London, 1970): J. D. Brady, *Speculum* 47, 125–6; H. R. Loyn, *EHR* 87, 155–6; S. E. Rigold, *MA* 15, 187–8

Gardner, Faith F., *An Analysis of Syntactic Patterns of Old English* (The Hague, 1971): Bruce Mitchell, *RES* 23, 461–3

Gatch, Milton McC., *Loyalties and Traditions: Man and his World in Old English Literature* (New York, 1971): André Crépin, *Études Anglaises* 24, 518; E. G. S[tanley], *N&Q* 79, 83

Geipel, John, *The Viking Legacy* (Newton Abbot, 1971): Gillian Fellows Jensen, *Danske Studier* 1972, 126–9; R. M. Wilson, *English* 108, 97

Gelling, Margaret, *The Place-Names of Berkshire* 1 (Cambridge, 1972): *TLS* 29 December, p. 1591

Gneuss, Helmut, *Hymnar und Hymnen im englischen Mittelalter* (Tübingen, 1968): Rossell Hope Robbins, *Speculum* 47, 759–61; Celia Sisam, *Anglia* 89, 523–6

Godfrey, John, *The English Parish 600–1300* (London, 1969): André Crépin, *Revue de l'Histoire des Religions* 180, 107–8

Goldsmith, Margaret E., *The Mode and Meaning of 'Beowulf'* (London, 1970): A. J. Bliss, *N&Q* 19, 111–13; John Kenny Crane, see sect. *3bi*; Joseph B. Trahern, Jr, *Anglia* 90, 513–16; L. Whitbread, *ESts* 53, 548–51

Gradon, Pamela, *Form and Style in Early English Literature* (London, 1971): J. D. A. Ogilvy, *ELN* 10, 140–1; R. M. Wilson, *English* 21, 23

Greenfield, Stanley B., *The Interpretation of Old English Poems* (London and Boston, 1972): *TLS* 24 November, p. 1439

Grinsell, L. V., *The Bristol Mint: an Historical Outline* (Bristol, 1972): J. Durrell, *Bristol Archaeol. Research Group Bull.* 4.6, 172–3

Gunstone, A. J. H., *Ancient British, Anglo-Saxon and Norman Coins in Midlands Museums*, Sylloge of Coins of the British Isles (London, 1971): S. E. Rigold, *MA* 15, 187–8; V. J. S[mart], *BNJ* 40, 176

Hamer, Richard, ed. and transl., *A Choice of Anglo-Saxon Verse* (London, 1970): T. A. Shippey, *YES* 2, 231

Hanning, Robert W., *The Vision of History in Early Britain* (New York, 1966): Karl Heinz Göller, *Anglia* 90, 200–4

Hart, Cyril, *The Early Charters of Essex*, 2nd ed. (Leicester, 1971): John Booker, *The Local Historian* 10, 102–3; P. Verbraken, *RB* 82, 339

Hauck, Karl, *et al.*, *Goldbrakteaten aus Sievern* (Munich, 1970): Otto Höfler, *ZDA* 101, 161–86; Roswitha Wisniewski, *Beiträge zur Namenforschung* 7, 218–22

Henderson, George, *Early Medieval*, Style and Civilization (Harmondsworth, 1972): *TLS* 18 August, p. 966.

Henry, P. L., *The Early English and Celtic Lyric* (London, 1966): Hans Wagner, *Zeitschrift für celtische Philologie* 32, 289–90

Herold, Curtis Paul, *The Morphology of King Alfred's Translation of the Orosius* (The Hague, 1968): Janet M. Bately, *Anglia* 89, 516–23; André Crépin, *Études Anglaises* 25, 78–80

[Hoops, Johannes] *Reallexikon der germanischen Altertumskunde*, 2nd ed. 1. 1 and 2 (Berlin, 1968 and 1970): R. Moosbrugger-Leu, *Schweizerische Zeitschrift für Geschichte* 20, 164–5 and 22, 182; M. W. Thompson, *MA* 15, 195

Hunter Blair, Peter, *The World of Bede* (London and New York, 1970): J. Campbell, *History* 57, 255–6; W. H. C. Frend, *Classical Rev.* 22, 286–7; Charles W. Jones, *Speculum* 47, 285–8; R. D. Ware, *AHR* 77, 124

Huppé, Bernard F., *The Web of Words* (Albany, 1970): John Kenny Crane, see sect. *3bi*; J. E. Cross, *MÆ* 41, 47–9; P. W. Rogers, *Queen's Quarterly* 79, 270–1; Earl G. Schreiber, *JEGP* 71, 106–9

Irving, Edward B., Jr, *A Reading of 'Beowulf'* (New Haven, 1968): Alvin A. Lee, *Med. Scandinavia* 4, 169–73; Gerhard Nickel, *Anglia* 90, 381–2

Isaacs, Neil D., *Structural Principles in Old English Poetry* (Knoxville, 1968): John Kenny Crane, see sect. 3*bi*

Jones, Charles, *An Introduction to Middle English* (New York, 1972): Eugene J. Crook, *JEGP* 71, 439–41

Jones, Gwyn, *A History of the Vikings* (London, 1968): R. I. Page, *MÆ* 41, 89–94

Kastovsky, Dieter, *Old English Deverbal Substantives Derived by means of a Zero Morpheme* (Tübingen, 1968): Marek Gawełko, *Kwartalnik Neofilologiczny* 19, 354–5

Kiesel, Georges, *Der Heilige Willibrord im Zeugnis der bildenden Kunst* (Luxemburg, 1969): A. Linage Conde, *Studia Monastica* 13, 205–6

Kivimaa, Kirsti, *'Þe' and 'þat' as Clause Connectives in Early Middle English with Especial Consideration of the Emergence of the Pleonastic 'þat'* (Helsinki, 1966): Uwe Carls, *ZAA* 20, 203–4

Klein, Ernest, *A Comprehensive Etymological Dictionary of the English Language* (Amsterdam, 1966–7): Gero Bauer, *Kratylos* 15, 93–7

Knowles, David, C. N. L. Brooke and Vera C. M. London, ed., *The Heads of Religious Houses: England and Wales 940–1216* (Cambridge, 1972): *TLS* 28 July, p. 897; Rhys W. Hays, *Church Hist.* 41, 537; R. H. Hilton, *EconHR* 2nd ser. 25, 698–9

Knowles, David, and R. Neville Hadcock, *Medieval Religious Houses: England and Wales*, 2nd ed. (London, 1971): Frederick Hockey, *JEH* 23, 276–7

Koskenniemi, Inna, *Repetitive Word Pairs in Old and Early Middle English Prose* (Turku, 1968): Fred C. Robinson, *Anglia* 90, 166–8

Koziol, Herbert, *Grundzüge der Geschichte der englischen Sprache* (Darmstadt, 1967): Horst Weinstock, *Anglia* 90, 163–5

Invokationen, Segenswünsche, Bitten und Aufforderungen im älteren englischen Schrifttum (Vienna, 1971): R. W. Zandvoort, *ESts* 53, 188

Kristensson, Gillis, *Studies on Middle English Topographical Terms* (Lund, 1970): Kenneth Cameron, *MÆ* 41, 161–4; Klaus Dietz, *Beiträge zur Namenforschung* 7, 194–7; Margaret Gelling, *YES* 2, 232–3

Krüger, Karl Heinrich, *Königsgrabkirchen der Franken, Angelsachsen und Langobarden bis zur Mitte des 8. Jahrhunderts: ein historischer Katalog* (Munich, 1971): Immo Eberl, *Schweizerische Zeitschrift für Geschichte* 22, 145–7

Kühlwein, Wolfgang, *Die Verwendung der Feindseligkeitsbezeichnungen in der altenglischen Dichtersprache* (Neumünster, 1967): Klaus Hansen, *ZAA* 19, 417–19

Modell einer operationellen lexikologischen Analyse: altenglisch 'Blut' (Heidelberg, 1968): Hanspeter Schelp, *ZDA Anzeiger* 83, 123–7

Kuhn, Hans, *Kleine Schriften* II (Berlin, 1971): Werner Schröder, *BGDSL* 94, 226–34

Kuryłowicz, Jerzy, *Die sprachlichen Grundlagen der altgermanischen Metrik* (Innsbruck, 1970): A. J. Bliss, *Anglia* 90, 510–12

Lamb, John W., *The Archbishopric of Canterbury from its Foundation to the Norman Conquest* (London, 1971): John Godfrey, *JEH* 23, 350–1

Lee, Alvin A., *The Guest-Hall of Eden: Four Essays on the Design of Old English Poetry* (New Haven, 1972): David Williams, *Queen's Quarterly* 79, 415–16; R. M. Wilson, *English* 21, 106

Mandel, Jerome, and Bruce A. Rosenberg, ed., *Medieval Literature and Folklore*

Studies: Essays in Honor of Francis Lee Utley (New Brunswick, N.J., 1970): R. M. Wilson, *YES* 2, 233–4; Charles G. Zug, III, *Jnl of Amer. Folklore* 85, 278–9

Marsh, Henry, *Dark Age Britain: some Sources of History* (Newton Abbot, 1970): James S. Beddie, *Speculum* 47, 133–4; Ronald D. Ware, *AHR* 77, 1427–8

Mayr-Harting, Henry, *The Coming of Christianity to Anglo-Saxon England* (London, 1972): *TLS* 22 September, p. 1121

McKisack, May, *Medieval History in the Tudor Age* (Oxford, 1971): Kurt Kluxen, *Historische Zeitschrift* 214, 755–7

McLaughlin, John C., *Aspects of the History of English* (New York, 1970): C. J. E. Ball, *Jnl of Ling.* 8, 340–2; Charles Carlton, *General Ling.* 11, 119–23

Meaney, Audrey L., and Sonia Chadwick Hawkes, *Two Anglo-Saxon Cemeteries at Winnall, Winchester, Hampshire* (London, 1970): B. N. Eagles, *Wiltshire Archaeol. and Nat. Hist. Mag.* 66, 205; V. I. Evison, *AntJ* 51, 352–3

Meid, Wolfgang, *Das germanische Präteritum* (Innsbruck, 1971): Elmar Seebold, *Kratylos* 15, 169–72

Mellinkoff, Ruth, *The Horned Moses in Medieval Art and Thought* (Berkeley and Los Angeles, 1970): Florence McCulloch, *Speculum* 47, 134–6

Michaelis-Jena, Ruth, *The Brothers Grimm* (London, 1970): A. J. Dekker, *Volkskunde* 73, 87–8

Moeller-Schina, Ute, *Deutsche Lehnprägungen aus dem Englischen von der althochdeutschen Zeit bis 1700* (Tübingen, 1969): Marek Gawełko, *Kwartalnik Neofilologiczny* 19, 242–5

Moore, D., ed., *The Irish Sea Province in Archaeology and History* (Cardiff, 1970): A.H.A. Hogg, *Welsh Hist. Rev.* 6, 96–7

Morton, Catherine, and Hope Muntz, ed., *The 'Carmen de Hastingae Proelio' of Guy, Bishop of Amiens* (Oxford, 1972): *TLS* 4 August, p. 912

Munske, Horst Haider, *Das Suffix '*-inga/-unga' in den germanischen Sprachen* (Marburg, 1964): Marek Gawełko, *Kwartalnik Neofilologiczny* 18, 322–6

Myres, J. N. L., *Anglo-Saxon Pottery and the Settlement of England* (Oxford, 1969): Albert Genrich, *Germania* 50, 333–6

'The Angles, the Saxons and the Jutes', *Proc. of the Brit. Acad.* 56 (1971): Eric Fletcher, *JBAA* 3rd ser. 35, 78–9; P. J. Tester, *Archaeologia Cantiana* 86, 255–6

Newton, Robert R., *Medieval Chronicles and the Rotation of the Earth* (Baltimore, 1972): *TLS* 22 September, p. 1124

Okasha, Elisabeth, *Hand-List of Anglo-Saxon Non-Runic Inscriptions* (Cambridge, 1971): T. J. Brown, *JBAA* 3rd ser. 35, 86–7; Rosemary Cramp, *Archaeologia Aeliana* 4th ser. 50, 300–1; Philip Rahtz, *History* 57, 412–13; D. Slay, *DUJ* 64, 255–7; M. J. Swanton, *ArchJ* 128, 278–9

Page, R. I., *Life in Anglo-Saxon England* (London, 1970): R. M. Wilson, *English* 108, 96–7

Patrologiae Cursus Completus: Series Latina, Supplementum I–IV (Paris, 1958–71): L. Bieler, *Scriptorium* 26, 76–9

Peeters, C. J. A. C., *De liturgische dispositie van het vroegchristelijk kerkgebouw* (Assen, 1969): C. A. R. Radford, *Ant* 51, 354–5

Peppard, Murray B., *Paths through the Forest: a Biography of the Brothers Grimm* (New York, 1971): Lore Segal, *Denver Quarterly* 7, 100–6

Peters, Edward, *The Shadow King: 'Rex Inutilis' in Medieval Law and Literature, 751–1327* (New Haven, 1970): Fredric Cheyette, *AHR* 77, 759–60; Basil Cottle, *JEGP* 71, 111–12; Ralph G. Giesey, *Speculum* 47, 791–3; Walter Ullmann, *Catholic Hist. Rev.* 58, 264–6

Peters, Robert A., *A Linguistic History of English* (Boston, 1968): Thomas Gardner, *Anglia* 89, 480–2; V. J. Plotkin, *Linguistics* 84, 85–9

Pilch, Herbert, *Altenglische Grammatik* and *Altenglischer Lehrgang* (Munich, 1970): Klaus Hansen, *ZAA* 19, 413–16; Jiří Nosek, *Philologica Pragensia* 15, 40–2; A. R. Tellier, *Études Anglaises* 25, 81; Wolfgang Viereck, *Jnl of Eng. Ling.* 6, 71–3; Rüdiger Zimmermann, *Kratylos* 15, 191–7

Pillsbury, Paul W., *Descriptive Analysis of Discourse in Late West Saxon Texts* (The Hague, 1967): André Crépin, *Études Anglaises* 25, 78–80

Ploss, Emil Ernst, ed., *Waltharius und Walthersage: eine Dokumentation der Forschung* (Hildesheim, 1969): Cola Minis, *Zeitschrift für deutsche Philologie* 91, 440–3

Plotkin, V. Ja., *Dinamika anglijskoj fonologičeskoj sistemy* (Novosibirsk, 1967): M. Padura, *Inozemna Filolohija* 25, 155–8

Pope, John C., ed., *Homilies of Ælfric: a Supplementary Collection* (Early English Text Society, 1967–8): J. D. Pheifer, *Hermathena* 113, 70–4

Prins, A. A., *A History of English Phonemes* (Leiden, 1972): E. H. Flint, *AUMLA* 38, 269–70

Rissanen, Matti, *The Uses of 'One' in Old and Early Middle English* (Helsinki, 1967): G. Bauer, *ESts* 52, 543–5; Broder Carstensen, *Anglia* 89, 492–4

Robinson, Fred C., *Old English Literature: a Select Bibliography* (Toronto, 1970): Peter Grenzel, *ZAA* 20, 305–6; Patrizia Lendinara, *Annali, Sezione Germanica* (Naples) 14, 600

Rosier, James L., ed., *Philological Essays . . . in Honour of Herbert Dean Meritt* (The Hague, 1970): Patrizia Lendinara, *Annali, Sezione Germanica* (Naples) 15, 203–8

Sawyer, P. H., *The Age of the Vikings*, 2nd ed. (London, 1971): Per Sveaas Andersen, *Historisk Tidsskrift* (Oslo) 3, 337–40

Schirmer, Walter F., *Geschichte der englischen und amerikanischen Literatur von den Anfängen bis zur Gegenwart*, 5th ed. (Tübingen, 1968): Stanisław Helsztyński, *Kwartalnik Neofilologiczny* 18, 313–14

Schmitt, Ludwig Erich, ed., *Kurzer Grundriss der germanischen Philologie bis 1500* (Berlin, 1970 and 1971): Gerhild Geil, *Kratylos* 15, 70–6; T. L. Markey, *Speculum* 47, 799–803; Wilhelm W. Seeger, *Monatshefte* 64, 187–8

Schwab, Ute, ed., *Waldere: Testo e Commento* (Messina, 1967): Dieter Schaller, *Deutsches Archiv für Erforschung des Mittelalters* 27, 230–1

See, Klaus von, *Germanische Verskunst* (Stuttgart, 1967): J. van Dam, *Leuvense Bijdragen* 61, 72; Heiko Uecker, *Zeitschrift für deutsche Philologie* 91, 410–11

Seebold, Elmar, *Vergleichendes und etymologisches Wörterbuch der germanischen starken Verben* (The Hague, 1970): Hans Schmeja, *Kratylos* 15, 76–81

Shannon, Ann, *A Descriptive Syntax of the Parker Manuscript of the Anglo-Saxon*

Chronicle from 734 to 891 (The Hague, 1964): André Crépin, *Études Anglaises* 25, 78–80

Shippey, T. A., *Old English Verse* (London, 1972): *TLS* 1 September, p. 1020

Siebs, Benno Eide, *Die Personennamen der Germanen* (Niederwalluf, 1970): Pierre Hessmann, *Germanistik* 13, 31

Sjölin, Bo, *Einführung in das Friesische* (Stuttgart, 1969): E. G. A. Galama, *Neophilologus* 56, 377–8; M. O'C. Walshe, *German Life and Letters* 25, 18

Smith, A. H., *The Place-Names of Westmorland* (Cambridge, 1967): Karl Inge Sandred, *SN* 44, 200–4

Southern, R. W., *Medieval Humanism and Other Studies* (Oxford, 1970): Joachim Ehlers, *Historische Zeitschrift* 214, 632–3; Francis Oakley, *AHR* 77, 1423–4

Sperk, Claus, ed., *Medieval English Saints' Legends* (Tübingen, 1970): T. P. Dunning, *SN* 44, 188; Manfred Görlach, *Anglia* 90, 507–10; Patrizia Lendinara, *Annali, Sezione Germanica* (Naples) 14, 601–2

Stenton, F. M., *Anglo-Saxon England*, 3rd ed. (Oxford, 1971): *TLS* 20 October, pp. 1255–6; Fredy Gröbli-Schaub, *Schweizerische Zeitschrift für Geschichte* 22, 380–1; H. E. Pagan, *NC* 7th ser. 12, 335–7

Preparatory to Anglo-Saxon England, ed. Doris Mary Stenton (Oxford, 1970): Peter Hunter Blair, *EHR* 87, 392; H. E. Pagan, *NC* 7th ser. 12, 335–7

Strang, Barbara M. H., *A History of English* (London, 1970): Avril Bruten, *RES* 23, 62–3; Veronika Kniezsa, *Acta Linguistica Academiae Scientiarum Hungaricae* 22, 240–2; John C. McLaughlin, *Jnl of Ling.* 8, 301–6; Rupert E. Palmer, Jr, *Language* 48, 941–7; K. C. Phillipps, *ESts* 53, 184–8; Alarik Rynell, *SN* 44, 180–8; A. R. Tellier, *Études Anglaises* 25, 432–3

Swanton, Michael, ed., *The Dream of the Rood* (Manchester, 1970): George Clark, *Speculum* 47, 551–5; Herbert Pilch, *Anglia* 90, 518–19; Barbara C. Raw, *MÆ* 41, 135–7

Thirsk, Joan, ed., *Land, Church, and People: Essays presented to Professor H. P. R. Finberg* (supplement to *Agricultural Hist. Rev.* 18, 1970): J. L. Bolton, *N&Q* 19, 163–4; R. H. Hilton, *Midland Hist.* 1.2, 48–50

Thomas, Charles, *Britain and Ireland in Early Christian Times, AD 400–800* (London and New York, 1971): Elizabeth Fowler, *Cornish Archaeology* 10, 92

The Early Christian Archaeology of North Britain (Oxford, 1971): Rosemary Cramp, *Antiquity* 46, 250–1; W. H. C. Frend, *AntJ* 52, 221–2 and *Scottish Hist. Rev.* 51, 198–200; R. P. C. Hanson, *JTS* 23, 501–3; Rosalind Hill, *JEH* 23, 348–9; J. C. Mann, *Archaeologia Aeliana* 4th ser. 50, 298–300

Turner, Hilary L., *Town Defences in England and Wales: an Architectural and Documentary Study, AD 900–1500* (London, 1971): M. W. Barley, *AntJ* 52, 222–3; John Beeler, *Speculum* 47, 814–16; R. Allen Brown, *Antiquity* 46, 252–3; A. Z. Freeman, *AHR* 77, 1105–6; D. F. Renn, *JBAA* 3rd ser. 35, 95–6; M. W. Thompson, *MA* 15, 188–90

Visser, F. Th., *An Historical Syntax of the English Language* II and III.1 (Leiden, 1966 and 1969): Simeon Potter, *YES* 1, 200–2

Vollrath-Reichelt, Hanna, *Königsgedanke und Königtum bei den Angelsachsen bis zur*

Mitte des 9. Jahrhunderts (Cologne and Vienna, 1971): *TLS* 20 October, pp. 1255–6

Wagner, Karl Heinz, *Generative Grammatical Studies in the Old English Language* (Heidelberg, 1969): Herbert E. Brekle, *Foundations of Lang.* 8, 449–55; Dieter Kastovsky, *Anglia* 89, 482–92; Elizabeth Closs Traugott, *Jnl of Ling.* 8, 297–301

Wallace-Hadrill, J. M., *Early Germanic Kingship in England and on the Continent* (Oxford, 1971): *TLS* 20 October, pp. 1255–6; Ludwig Bieler, *EHR* 87, 816–19; James A. Brundage, *Church Hist.* 41, 114; H. R. Loyn, *History* 57, 254–5; Janet L. Nelson, *JEH* 23, 271–2

Watts, Ann Chalmers, *The Lyre and the Harp* (New Haven, 1969): Gisela Figge, *Anglia* 90, 211–13

Weber, Gerd Wolfgang, '*Wyrd*': *Studien zum Schicksalsbegriff der altenglischen und altnordischen Literatur* (Bad Homburg vor der Höhe, 1969): Hartmut Beckers, *Zeitschrift für deutsche Philologie* 91, 413–14; Maria Grimaldi, *Annali, Sezione Germanica* (Naples) 14, 592–4; Edith Marold, *Germanistik* 13, 311

Welldon Finn, R., *The Norman Conquest and its Effects on the Economy, 1066–1086* (London, 1971): John Beeler, *Speculum* 47, 308–11; Barbara Dodwell, *History* 57, 113–14; H. R. Loyn, *EHR* 87, 819–21; Edward Miller, *EconHR* 2nd ser. 25, 155; Franklin J. Pegues, *AHR* 77, 497–8

Whallon, William, *Formula, Character, and Context* (Washington, D.C., and Cambridge, Mass., 1969): Kenneth R. Brooks, *MÆ* 41, 50–1; Gisela Figge, *Anglia* 90, 208–11; H. L. Rogers, *ESts* 53, 455–6

Whitelock, Dorothy, ed., *Sweet's Anglo-Saxon Reader* (Oxford, 1967): C. A. Ladd, *N&Q* 19, 140–1

Wilson, R. M., *The Lost Literature of Medieval England*, 2nd ed. (London, 1970, paperback 1972): Heinz Bergner, *Anglia* 90, 506–7; E. G. Stanley, *N&Q* 19, 282

Wright, David H., ed., *The Vespasian Psalter*, EEMF 14 (Copenhagen, 1967): E. Manning, *Scriptorium* 25, 240–1

Zupko, Ronald Edward, *A Dictionary of English Weights and Measures from Anglo-Saxon Times to the Nineteenth Centuy* (Madison, Wis., 1968): Jon B. Eklund, *Isis* 60, 242